The Political Economy of Media

The Political Economy of Media
Enduring Issues, Emerging Dilemmas

Robert W. McChesney

MONTHLY REVIEW PRESS
New York

Monthly Review Press
New York Copyright © 2008
All rights reserved

Library of Congress Cataloging-in-Publication Data
Available from the publisher

ISBN 978-1-58367-161-0 paperback
ISBN 978-1-58367-162-7 hardback

Design: Terry J. Allen

MONTHLY REVIEW FOUNDATION
146 West 29th Street – Suite 6W
New York, NY 10001

http://www.monthlyreview.org

Contents

Preface

This book is the companion volume for my 2007 New Press book, *Communication Revolution: Critical Junctures and the Future of Media.* In that book I made the argument that communication revolutions occur during critical junctures, and the policies implemented during those critical junctures largely determine the shape of the communication system for generations. I maintained that today we are in the midst of arguably the most important communication revolution in centuries, that we are seeing a dramatic increase in popular participation in media policymaking as a result, and that it is imperative that communication scholars embrace this historical moment in their research and teaching. I laid out an agenda of the sort of research issues that require extensive attention and debate. In this volume I present much of my own research along these lines, with the aim of pushing the debate forward.

This book brings together what I regard as the best elements of much of my research in the political economy of media over the past two decades. It is not meant to be representative. Several essays on the state of media studies have not been included, because they do not fall in the parameters of the volume. The chapters are divided into three main sections: 1) research specifically addressing journalism; 2) critical studies in the political economic tradition; and 3) essays on politics and the burgeoning media reform movement.

This book includes an introduction and twenty-three chapters, most of which were published as articles in journals or as book chapters in anthologies. Some of the articles are based on research that would eventually be used in subsequent books I wrote, though generally in versions different from what appears herein. Most of the selections have never been seen in book form in any manner and I suspect are largely unknown. Three of the chapters were written specifically for this volume, and one of the chapters was a memo that had been commissioned but had never before been shared with the public. Other chapters appeared in such obscure journals or anthologies that they are all but unknown even to my closest friends and colleagues. Hence a good half of the book is in effect original.

Many of the remaining pieces were first published in *Monthly Review*, the non-obscure socialist journal founded by Paul Sweezy and Leo Huberman in 1949. I had the honor of serving as co-editor of *Monthly Review* with Sweezy, Harry Magdoff, and John Bellamy Foster from 2000 to 2004, though I began writing for *Monthly Review* in 1989.

In the notes for each chapter I indicate where the piece was originally published. Several of the pieces were co-authored and I indicate the name of the various co-authors at the end of the chapter, too. These collaborators include John Nichols, Ben Scott, John Bellamy Foster, Harry Magdoff, Paul Sweezy, and Dan Schiller. I thank each of them for allowing me to use our collaborative work in this book.

At the beginning of each of the three sections I provide a short overview of the pieces in the section, and describe the context in which they were originally written.

A few of these chapters date from the 1980s, and the balance are split between the 1990s and the 2000s. Some were meant for academic readers and others for a more popular audience. My editor, Brett Clark, and I have edited the chapters for consistency and to update points where appropriate, but otherwise the pieces appear exactly as first published. The greatest amount of work Brett did was to edit out as much repetition as possible, because I tend to return to a number of familiar themes in my articles. There still is probably a bit more repetition than one would find in a monograph. My assumption is that whereas some readers may devour the book from beginning to end—and, by the way, I love you—many readers will be as likely to read only a handful of chapters, or read the chapters out of order, so I cannot assume they will know the context provided in earlier chapters.

Regarding acknowledgments, I am in a bit of a pickle. Nearly all of the chapters herein received critical readings, advice, and assistance from many scholars over the past quarter-century. In total, I suspect, the number approaches well over one hundred people. I rely to a large extent upon the criticism of my friends and colleagues to tighten and improve my work. Those dear friends and colleagues have been thanked when those pieces first appeared, or in books where the research would appear in different forms. Because it is impossible for me to recall everyone who helped on any of the chapters in this book, I will not attempt to list names for fear I might leave many deserving people off the list. I will simply make a blanket thank you to the community of scholars and activists who have educated me.

Five people deserve mention specifically for this book. Barbara Wilson, my boss at the University of Illinois, jumps through hoops to make it possible for scholars to have the time and resources to do their work. There is no better university in the United States to do critical communication research. John Nichols, my frequent co-author and political co-conspirator, always has my back and cares about my well-being like a brother. Most of the essays on journalism have an analysis distilled from long conversations between us. John Bellamy Foster, my dear friend and comrade now for thirty-five years, has supported this project from the beginning. Now that it is done we can dive into our long-overdue book on communication and monopoly capital. Brett Clark, a gifted young sociologist at North Carolina State University, took time from his busy schedule to give the entire manuscript a hard editing, the equal of any I have experienced in my career. Without him, this book would not exist. Inger Stole, whose research on advertising, public relations, and the consumer movement has opened up new worlds to me, provided constant feedback on the ideas herein, and helped me sharpen my focus on point after point. I suspect she is unaware of how much I depend upon her.

I dedicate this book to Ed Herman, Noam Chomsky, Ben Bagdikian, and the late Herb Schiller. They are not merely brilliant scholars, they are great people. They opened their arms to me when I was just getting started, and their insights, collegiality, guidance, warmth, and occasional criticism provided the cornerstones upon which most of the essays in this book were written.

Urbana, Illinois
March 2008

Introduction

This book presents research and critical analysis in the tradition known as the political economy of media, also known as the political economy of communication. (Though for the most part I will use the term "political economy of media" in this book, I regard both terms as synonymous and have used them widely in my work over the years.) In *Communication Revolution: Critical Junctures and the Future of Media*, the 2007 book that is the companion volume to this one, I laid out my assessment of the field of political economy of media, its history, its domain, its relationship to other branches of communication research, its relationship with popular politics, and the pressing research issues before it. In this book I provide examples of my own research in this tradition, in twenty-three essays written in the quarter-century from 1984 to 2008.

To understand the purpose of political economy of communication is simple. Every year thousands of media scholars conduct research on different aspects of media and communication. Many of them study the content of the programs or the effects media have upon people. Some study how audiences use media. A growing number look at technology and how that changes the media experience. Nearly all of this research assumes a certain type of media system and that the nature of this system is inviolable. It also assumes a certain type of economic structure as being a given and inalterable. In this work, although formally neutral, the "givens" of commercial media and capitalist economics generally move seamlessly from the "inalterable given" to the "benevolent and not worth questioning" category. They are not subject to critical examination, and scholars who do are sometimes regarded with skepticism if not suspicion.

The political economy of media is the field of people in this latter camp. Political economists of media do not believe the existing media system is natural or inevitable or impervious to change. They believe the media system is the result of policies made in the public's name but often without the public's informed consent. They believe the nature of the media systems established by these policies goes a long way toward explaining the content produced by these media systems. Political economists of media believe that assessing policies, structures, and institutions cannot answer all of the important questions surrounding media, but they believe their contributions are indispensable to the comprehensive study of media.

Political economists of media assume the media system is an important factor in understanding how societies function, but they do not assume it is the only or most important variable. In many cases the work of political economists of media demonstrates how media affect other, more deep-seated tendencies in society, such as racism, sexism, militarism, and depoliticization. The significance of media varies depending upon what is being considered. In general, though, the importance of media and media systems has grown over the past two centuries.

How political economy of media proceeds is somewhat more complicated. It is a field that endeavors to connect how media and communication systems and content are shaped by ownership, market structures, commercial support, technologies, labor practices, and government policies. The political economy of media then links the media and communications systems to how both economic and political systems work, and social power is exercised, in society. Specifically, in the United States and much of the world, what role do media and communication play in how capitalist economies function, and how do both media and capitalism together and separately influence the exercise of political power? The central question for media political economists is whether, on balance, the media system serves to promote or undermine democratic institutions and practices. Are media a force for social justice or for oligarchy? And equipped with that knowledge, what are the options for citizens to address the situation? Ultimately, the political economy of media is a critical exercise, committed to enhancing democracy. It has emerged and blossomed during periods of relatively intense popular political activism, initially in the 1930s and 1940s, and then decisively in the 1960s and 1970s.

The political economy of media is often associated with the political Left, because of its critical stance toward the market, and because some of its most prominent figures were and are socialists. For many of the major figures in the field, changing the media system goes part and parcel with changing the broader economic system to produce a more humane and equitable society. But the "project" of political economy of media, to the extent it can be defined, grows directly out of mainstream liberal democratic political theory. Nor is this purely theoretical: the condition upon which the entire U.S. constitutional system rests is that there must be a viable and healthy press system for self-government to succeed. Hence the mission statement for the political economy of media is clear: what structures and policies generate the media institutions, practices, and system most conducive to viable self-government?

Along these lines, it is worth restating a point I developed in *Communication Revolution*: Two factors that Thomas Jefferson and James Madison highlighted as among the greatest threats to the survival of democracy and constitutional rule in the United States were class inequality and militarism. From these two phenomena would grow corruption, secrecy, oligarchy, and a loss of liberty. To both Jefferson and Madison among the most crucial tasks of a free press were to undermine inequality by giving the poor and propertyless access to information, and also to monitor militarism on behalf of the public and prevent rulers of a rich land from following their inevitable imperial ambitions. Accordingly, political economists of media in the United States have had a particularly keen interest in the relationship of media systems and content to issues of inequality and militarism.

It is striking that inequality and militarism, the two concerns Jefferson and Madison had about the survival of the republic and the two issues that required a free press to monitor and keep in check, are arguably the central threats to self-government today. As we will see in the first section of the book, the press system has failed to fulfill the mandate provided by these two very wise men more than two hundred years ago. This may be the greatest failure of our press system today, reinforcing the greatest failures of our broader political economy.

The field of political economy of media has grown dramatically since the 1960s, for reasons that in the "Information Age" approach being self-evident.

Few people doubt the importance of media, of journalism, of entertainment culture, of communication in general for shaping the world we live in. Moreover, media are a central part of the capitalist political economy, the center of the marketing system, and a source of tremendous profit in their own right. Media do not explain everything, but understanding media is indispensable to grasping the way power works in contemporary societies. It is worth repeating that political economy of media does not come close to explaining everything about media, not by a long stretch, but what it does do is essential for scholarly analysis to be comprehensive and accurate.

This book endeavors to provide arguments and research surrounding the enduring issues that define political economy of media past, present, and future. The enduring issues include:

- the nature of journalism and its relationship to democratic practices; how media firms and markets operate
- understanding propaganda, from governments, commercial interests, and private parties
- commercial media and the depoliticization of society
- the relationship of media to racial, gender, and economic inequality
- the relationship of media to U.S. foreign policy and militarism
- the specific role of advertising in shaping media markets and content
- the communication policymaking process
- telecommunication policies and regulations
- the relationship of communication to global and contemporary capitalism
- the nature of commercialism and its impact upon culture
- public broadcasting, and the establishment of alternative media institutions and systems
- the relationship of technology to media, and to politics and society
- the relationship of media to popular social movements

This book addresses some of these enduring issues, the ones I have studied, and draws from research on those areas I have not researched myself. I hope the essays herein contribute to providing a framework for studying all of them.

Yet despite the rise of the political economy of media to some prominence in recent decades, the field has struggled with an identity crisis in the past generation, due primarily to the emergence of neoliberalism, and to the Internet. This book chronicles these new developments, what I term the emerging dilemmas, and how they necessitate some rethinking and reformulation of the field's tenets. In many respects it is the challenge of neoliberalism and the digital communication revolution that has shaped my research through much of my career. It defines most of the essays in this book.

The emerging dilemmas center on the changes in the global economy and the digital communication revolution, which are closely related. These developments undermine, or at least alter, traditional formulations of scholars in the political economy of media tradition. On the one hand is the question of the relationship of the nation-state to the economy and the communication system in an era when both operate increasingly along transnational lines, and where communication is increasingly central to the global economy. On the other hand, revolutionary digital communication technologies are in the process of blasting open the media system in a manner that is highly unusual, if not unprecedented. Much of the traditional thinking about communication—who says what to whom with what effect—has to be recalibrated.

Neoliberalism, put crudely, refers to the doctrine that profits should rule as much of social life as possible, and anything that gets in the way of profit making is suspect, if not condemned. Business good. Governments bad. Big business very good. Big government very bad. Taxes on the rich, bad. Social spending aimed at the poor and working class, even worse. Take care of number one, and everyone fend for yourself. There is no such thing as "society," only individuals in fierce competition with one another, and their immediate families, the only permissible freeloaders. (In fact, family freeloading is the occupation of choice for those of great wealth. No ruthless market for those who can afford to opt out. Nice work, if you can get it.) Extreme and growing inequality is not only acceptable, it is the carrot necessary to give the wealthy incentive to get even richer so they will invest and spur growth, and it is the stick necessary for the poor to be willing to work harder and be more productive. Markets are infallible, the unquestionably superior way to regulate human existence and the basis for all other freedoms. Human interference through governments or labor unions, no matter how well intentioned, will only make matters worse in the long run, because it will lead away from a pure market solution. In a free society the state should only enhance and extend the power of the market; it should never interfere with the pursuit of profit except in the rarest of cases, like child pornography or hard drugs. Property *über alles*. Put this way, neoliberalism is simply capitalism with the gloves off.

Neoliberalism became ascendant in the 1980s and is associated with Reagan and Thatcher. It seemed to be cemented with the overthrow of communist regimes by the early 1990s and the notion that we had reached the "end of history." There Is No Alternative, as Margaret Thatcher famously intoned. In this environment the political economy of media was thrown for a loop. What was its purpose, if all societies were best run by the market? What was the point of studying and criticizing commercial media, if that was the only plausible system, and the system toward which all nations were rapidly and inexorably moving?

Neoliberalism was the guiding principle behind capitalist globalization, the notion that free markets could bring prosperity and peace to the world if established on a global basis with minimal national government interference. In such a context, the traditional emphasis of political economy of media upon national policymaking seemed antiquated, if not reactionary. The best possible media system for nations and the world was one that let media corporations charge across the world seeking to maximize profit while ostensibly "giving the people what they want." There was no need for people to study the political economy of media unless it was to cheerlead this process.

Neoliberalism was always an ideological argument to justify shifting power to the wealthy and away from the poor; it was never an accurate description of what was taking place in the economy. Contrary to neoliberal dogma, governments were not shrinking; they were simply working assiduously to assist capital and providing far fewer services for everyone else, especially the poor and working class.[1] The prison system was growing as schools were in decline. This was especially true in the realm of media, where the entire system was based upon government-granted monopoly privileges and extraordinary direct and indirect subsides. There was hardly a free-market media system where the governments intervened after the free market created the system.

The end of the 1990s exposed the bankruptcy and contradictions of neoliberalism. The anti-globalization movement combined with the widespread rejection of neoliberal policies in democratic elections across the planet, most dramatically in Latin America, demolished the aura of "the end of history." It is now far better understood that capitalism in general and media systems in particular rely as much as ever upon the state playing a very large role. Neoliberalism was not an effort to eliminate the state; rather it was an effort to have the state work purely in the interests of capital or large media corporations. Armed with this insight, the political economy of media has been rejuvenated. Accordingly, there has been a massive increase in popular activism to shape media policies in the United States and worldwide over the past decade. In this book I address this emerging media activism as it has risen. For citizens, activists, and media scholars it is one of the striking developments of our times.

Perhaps the greatest damage done by neoliberalism, not only to the political economy of media but to critical scholarship and democratic activism in general, was its attempt to destroy the long-standing human desire that social change for the better—that would transcend the status quo of really existing capitalism—was possible, not to mention desirable. If people act like it is impossible to replace capitalism with something better, they all but guarantee it will be impossible to replace capitalism with something better. Demoralization and depoliticization are the necessary conditions for a "healthy" neoliberal society. That is why just to stand for elementary democratic practices and principles marks one as a radical.

With the demise of neoliberalism, scholars and activists are beginning to revisit the idea of imagining a more humane and democratic social order, one where profits for the few are no longer the highest social priority, but there is still a very long way to go, especially in the United States. Combined with the elimination of the old communist model as the alleged "alternative" to contemporary capitalism, humanity is now beginning a process of experimentation in democratic social structures that has not been witnessed for generations, especially in Latin America. The importance of this work cannot be exaggerated. There is a crucial role for political economists of media in this process, as communication systems are at the heart of both developing economies and political systems. It is where much of our work in the coming generation will be directed.

Another emerging dilemma for the political economy of media has been the digital communication revolution, exemplified by the Internet and wireless communication systems. These technologies are in the process of blast-

ing open the media system in a manner that is highly unusual, if not unprecedented. Much of the traditional thinking about communication—who says
what to whom with what effect—has to be recalculated in an era in which
communication and information are dramatically more accessible than ever
before, and in which time and space have collapsed. These technologies, too,
are central to the emergence of the global world order.

In the early 1990s, combined with the neoliberal tidal wave, the digital
communication revolution was presented as technologically perfecting the
case for free markets in media. Now that anyone could launch a Web site and
anyone could have access to anyone's Web site, there was a truly democratic
and competitive media system. The old media conglomerates were soon to
collapse; they were merely "rearranging deckchairs on the Titanic," with
their mergers and machinations. They could not survive the competition
wrought by the iceberg of the Internet. In this context, the government needed to eliminate subsidies to public broadcasting and rules that limited media
ownership, and simply get out of the way of media "entrepreneurs," to use
the swashbuckling term used for what were sometimes nothing more than
speculators and corporate slumlords. It was this spirit that led to the privatization of telecommunication systems across the world and to the infamous
U.S. Telecommunications Act of 1996.

There is no doubt that the digital revolution has radically transformed
media, communication, and society. Our media environment today is dramatically different from that of four decades ago, and one suspects it will
again be unrecognizable four decades from now. But what has also become
clear is that the neoliberal claims surrounding the Internet—the hype about
the Internet as a magical technology—have collapsed. Most important, the
notion that the Internet ends any role for government policies or regulations
in directing the communication system, that the Internet demands a "libertarian" model where free markets rule and governments play no role, has
proven to be false. It has ideological value for entrenched commercial interests wishing to have favorable rules, or to enhance their power, but it has no
relationship to the truth.

The media system in the United States has always been the beneficiary of
tremendous subsidies, going back to the enormous printing and postal subsidies of the early republic. Today the largest media firms receive extraordinary
subsidies ranging from monopoly licenses to TV and radio frequencies,

monopoly cable TV and satellite TV systems, copyright, and much more. The Internet is affected by both these policies and subsidies, and much like how the United States has been affected by the institution of slavery long after 1863, they will have a long-lasting influence. The dominant Internet service providers are a handful of telephone and cable companies, businesses whose success was predicated not on serving the public in a free market competition but upon receiving lucrative monopoly licenses from the government. These firms' "comparative advantage" comes in their unparalleled ability to buy off politicians and regulators; in the market they are generally disliked by consumers, and they give used car dealers a good name. These firms wish to translate their government-granted market power to the Internet era. This is what much of the battle over the principle of Network Neutrality addresses. It is, in effect, an effort by the telephone and cable TV companies to use their immense power over politicians to privatize the Internet and to have control over which Web sites users can access quickly and easily.

Likewise, policies such as copyright, advertising regulation, and media ownership rules directly shape the digital communication realm. The idea that the technology would automatically introduce viable competition has proven to be false. Policies do matter. And market economics do matter. Indeed, to a certain extent it seems the Internet encourages the monopolistic impulse in capitalism as much as the competitive one. In industry after industry—e.g., Amazon and Google—the network effects combine with market economics to point more toward monopoly.

Even if the Internet is kept open and even if broadband becomes inexpensive and ubiquitous—both huge policy battles for the coming generation—that will not address all of the core issues on the horizon. In particular, there are three overriding concerns that only become more pronounced in the digital era. First, there is the matter of the successful provision of journalism, which is currently in a deep and prolonged crisis as corporate cutbacks and erosion of standards are the order of the day. Corporate media apologists say not to worry, now that everyone is blogging we have all the journalism we can handle and then some. Digital technology will eventually solve the problem the pundits tell us; in the meantime just let the media conglomerates buy up all the media they can, lay off reporters to become "efficient," and rake in monopolistic profits so they can expand the economy and create jobs. You know the drill.

In fact, there is no endgame on the visible horizon that suggests the Internet will magically provide the journalism a self-governing people require. What is necessary are multiple newsrooms of well-paid experienced journalists with institutional support when they offend the powerful, which good journalism invariably does. The Internet offers great hopes for citizen involvement in journalism, and can transform journalism for the better, but it does not solve this fundamental political economic issue of resource allocation and institution building. That is a policy matter, and generating effective policies for the establishment of viable news media is a central dilemma our times. It has always been an issue, but with the twin blades of neoliberalism and the Internet it is approaching crisis stage.

Second, even in a digital nirvana with open, super-high-speed networks and ubiquitous inexpensive access, it will not derail the hyper-commercialism that permeates an increasing number of our institutions and indeed far too much of our social life. If anything, the Internet may prove to be the ultimate enabler of Madison Avenue and corporate America in its quest to enter our minds and empty our pocketbooks. If we learn nothing else from the political economy of media it is that commercialism comes at a very high price and with massive "externalities." Derailing hyper-commercialism, creating vibrant noncommercial zones, and protecting privacy is a mission critical in the coming era. It will not happen without organized citizens demanding explicit policies to that effect. There is a necessary role for political economists of media in helping to craft them.

Third, as much as the Internet and digital revolution empowers people, it also ensnares them and makes them susceptible to surveillance. We sacrifice something to get the gains. Only now are people recognizing the extent to which governments, often with sympathetic communication corporations assisting them, can intervene in digital communication systems to monitor our behavior, and the prospect is chilling. It is imperative that we devise policies to make governance accountable while preventing government intrusions into our privacy. We have to make the digital revolution serve our interests.

This leads directly to the ultimate and most important work of the political economy of media: understanding and navigating the central relationship of communication to the broader economy and political system. In the United States it is the ante to admission to legitimate debate, even in most academic debates, to accept that though a profit-driven economy may well have its flaws, it is the only possible course of action for a free people. Any prospective alternative entails invariably a decided turn for the worse. The Soviet example was such a nightmare that even to consider the idea that humanity might benefit from an alternative to capitalism is to open the door to a dystopia of murder, intolerance, and barbarism. Hence it is a subject not to be raised in polite company, or even considered, except to congratulate ourselves for dismissing it categorically.

Regrettably this closed-mindedness is proving a significant barrier to our getting a better understanding of how capitalism actually works and affects us and our institutions, and what more humane and just alternatives might be. As much as pledging love for markets is standard procedure in the United States, the system itself has significant flaws, some of which may prove catastrophic and unavoidable unless the system is dramatically reformed. I do not know exactly how reformable capitalism is, or what exactly superior alternatives would look like. What I do know is that getting answers to both these questions requires research, experimentation, and an open mind. If we do not think along these lines it will be ever more difficult to find humane and effective solutions to the deep social problems before us. And in view of the centrality of communication to both the economy and politics, political economists of media find themselves at the heart of this process.

SECTION I:
JOURNALISM

The five chapters in Section I were written between 2001 and 2008, and reflect the dominant concerns in my research over the past decade. For years I taught journalism in my classes at the University of Wisconsin and then at the University of Illinois, but I rarely addressed journalism directly in my research. I was strongly influenced by Herman, Chomsky, and Bagdikian, but also by numerous other scholars including Herbert Gans and Christopher Lasch as well as the accounts of working journalists, past and present. I have tried to develop the political economic critique of journalism in several ways. I wanted to exhume the very rich but mostly overlooked radical tradition of news criticism in U.S. history, and also put the emergence of professional journalism in historical and political-economic context. A good part of my research has been to demonstrate and explain the flaws in the existing mainstream journalism and to debunk the "liberal media" argument. I also have endeavored to understand and anticipate the great crisis of journalism of our times, which will be a defining issue for our field and for society until it is resolved. The purpose of this research is to assist us as we attempt to establish a media system that we can rationally expect to generate the journalism we need to engage in self-government. Because these chapters are chronologically closest together, there is somewhat more overlap than in other sections and a bit more coherence between the chapters. Some thought this topic should be a book on its own, though I think this material is stronger in a larger context. I hope these chapters demonstrate what is at stake in Section III.

1

The Problem of Journalism

Democratic theory generally posits that society needs a journalism that is a rigorous watchdog of those in power and who want to be in power, can ferret out truth from lies, and can present a wide range of informed positions on the important issues of the day. Each medium need not do all of these things, but the media system as a whole should make this caliber of journalism readily available to the citizenry. How a society can construct a media system that will generate something approximating democratic journalism is a fundamental problem for a free society, as powerful interests tend to wish to dominate the flow of information.

In this chapter I attempt to provide a political-economic framework for explaining why contemporary U.S. journalism is such a failure on all three of the above counts. I first look at the rise of professional journalism roughly a hundred years ago, and some of the problems for democracy inherent in the manner in which it developed in the United States. I then assess the two-pronged attack on the autonomy of professional journalism that has taken place over the past generation. In the second section I discuss the commercial attack on professional journalism, and in the third section I assess the conservative critique of the "liberal" media. In combination, I argue, these three factors explain the pathetic state of U.S. journalism in the early twenty-first century. The implications of my argument are that a commitment to anything remotely resembling bona fide democracy requires a vastly superior journalism, and we can only realistically expect such a journalism if there are sweeping changes in media policies and structures to make such a journalism a rational expectation.

I aspire to demonstrate the importance of political-economic analysis in journalism studies. It is commonly thought that the political economic critique of U.S. journalism is centered on looking at how large media corporations, media concentration, and advertisers corrupt the public service of journalism, undermine its professionalism, and keep it from being serious and nonpartisan, if not objective. Some critics of the political-economic approach argue that the critique is therefore of limited value, because it has a tendency to overplay its hand, and downplay the importance of professional values in journalism. These charges are misguided. On the one hand, the notion of professional journalism is a relatively recent phenomenon, and one with an important history. It did not fall from the sky and land in the newsroom of the *New York Times*. On the other hand, it is a political-economic critique that best explains the rise and nature of professional journalism as it has come into practice in the United States. Political economy is not the *only* analysis that explains professionalism, but it is indispensable to any analysis.[1] At any rate, the bottom line is clear: grasping the origins and nature of professional journalism is the necessary starting point for any critique of contemporary journalism, political economic or otherwise, that is worth its salt.

The Rise of Professional Journalism

The notion that journalism should be politically neutral, nonpartisan, professional, even "objective," did not emerge until the twentieth century. During the first two or three generations of the Republic such notions for the press would have been nonsensical, even unthinkable. The point of journalism was to persuade as well as inform, and the press tended to be highly partisan. The free press clause in the First Amendment to the constitution was seen as a means to protect dissident political viewpoints, as most newspapers were closely linked to political parties. It was understood that if the government could outlaw or circumscribe newspapers, it could effectively eliminate the ability of opposition parties or movements to mobilize popular support.

It would kill democracy. What few Americans know is that the government actively subsidized the press through printing well into the nineteenth century, and postal subsidies to this day. A partisan press system has much to offer a democratic society as long as there are numerous well-subsidized media providing a broad range of opinions.[2]

During the nineteenth century, the logic of newspaper publishing changed from being primarily political to being primarily commercial. The press system remained explicitly partisan, but it increasingly became an engine of great profits as costs plummeted, population increased, and advertising — which emerged as a key source of revenues—mushroomed. During the Civil War, President Lincoln faced press criticism—from some newspapers in the Northern states—that would make the treatment of Lyndon Johnson during Vietnam, Richard Nixon during Watergate or Bill Clinton during his impeachment seem like a day at the beach.[3] A major city like St. Louis, for example, had at least ten daily newspapers for much of the middle- to late-nineteenth century. Each newspaper tended to represent the politics of the owner and if someone was dissatisfied with the existing choices, it was not impossible to launch a new newspaper. By contemporary standards, it was a fairly competitive market.

But it was only a matter of time before there would be a conflict between the commercial economics of the press and its explicitly partisan politics. It became a growing problem during the Gilded Age. Following the logic of accumulation, the commercial press system became less competitive and ever more clearly the domain of wealthy individuals, who usually had the political views associated with their class. Commercialism also fostered corruption, as newspapers turned to sensationalism and outright lying to generate sales.[4] Throughout this era, socialists, feminists, abolitionists, trade unionists, and radicals *writ large* tended to regard the mainstream commercial press as the mouthpiece of their enemies, and established their own media to advance their interests. Consider, for example, the United States in the early 1900s. Members and supporters of the Socialist Party of Eugene V. Debs published some 325 English and foreign language daily, weekly, and monthly newspapers and magazines. Most of these were privately owned or were the publications of one of the 5,000 Socialist Party locals. They reached a total of more than two million subscribers.[5] *Appeal to Reason*, the socialist newspaper based in Kansas, alone had a readership of nearly a million.[6]

From the Gilded Age through the Progressive Era, an institutional sea change transpired in U.S. media not unlike the one taking place in the broader political economy. The dominant newspaper industry became increasingly concentrated into fewer chains and the majority of communities only had one or two dailies. The economics of advertising-supported newspapers erected barriers to entry that made it virtually impossible for small, independent newspapers to succeed, despite the protection of the constitution for a "free press." The dissident press, too, found media market economics treacherous, and lost much of its circulation and influence throughout the first third of the twentieth century, far in excess of the decline in interest in "dissident" politics. (How much the collapse of the independent press contributed to the demise of popular politics is a matter of no small importance in media studies.)

At the beginning of the twentieth century these developments led to a crisis for U.S. journalism. It was one thing to posit that a commercial media system worked for democracy when there were numerous newspapers in a community, when barriers to entry were relatively low, and when immigrant and dissident media proliferated widely, as was the case for much of the nineteenth century. For newspapers to be partisan at that time was no big problem because there were alternative viewpoints present. But it was quite another thing to make such a claim by the early twentieth century when many communities only had one or two newspapers, usually owned by chains or very wealthy and powerful individuals. Everywhere concentration was on the rise, and almost nowhere were new dailies being launched successfully to enter existing markets. For journalism to remain partisan in this context, for it to advocate the interests of the owners and the advertisers who subsidized it, would cast severe doubt on the credibility of the journalism. Likewise, sensationalism was less of a problem when there were several other newspapers in the community to counter it.

During the Progressive Era, criticism of the capitalist press reached fever pitch in the United States and was a major theme of muckrakers and progressive social critics, to an extent never equaled subsequently.[7] Leading reformers, like Robert LaFollette of Wisconsin, argued that the commercial press was destroying democracy in its rabid service to the wealthy. As Henry Adams put it, "The press is the hired agent of a moneyed system, set up for no other reason than to tell lies where the interests are concerned." Criticism extended across the political spectrum; in the 1912 presidential race all three challengers to President Taft—Debs, Roosevelt, and Wilson—criticized the capitalist bias of the press. In 1919 Upton Sinclair published his opus, *The Brass Check*, which provided the first great systematic critique of the limitations of capitalist journalism for a democratic society. Sinclair's book was filled with example after example of explicit lying and distortion of the labor movement and socialist politics by the mainstream press.[8] In short, it was widely thought that journalism was explicit class propaganda in a war with only one side armed. The parallel critique of the press argued that greedy publishers encouraged a fraudulent sensationalistic journalism that played very loose with the truth to generate sales. In combination, the widespread acceptance of these beliefs was very dangerous for the business of newspaper publishing, as many potential readers would find newspapers incredible, propagandistic, and unconvincing.

It was in the cauldron of controversy, during the Progressive Era, that the notion of professional journalism came of age. Savvy publishers understood that they needed to have their journalism appear neutral and unbiased, notions entirely foreign to the journalism of the Republic's first century, or their businesses would be far less profitable. They would sacrifice their explicit political power to lock in their economic position. Publishers pushed for the establishment of formal "schools of journalism" to train a cadre of professional editors and reporters. None of these schools existed in 1900; by 1920, all the major schools such as Columbia, Northwestern, Missouri, and Indiana were in full swing. The revolutionary and unprecedented notion of a separation of the editorial operations from the commercial affairs—termed the separation of church and state—became the professed model. The argument went that trained editors and reporters were granted autonomy by the owners to make the editorial decisions, and these decisions were based on their professional judgment, not the politics of the owners and the advertisers or their commercial interests to maximize profit. As trained professionals, journalists would learn to sublimate their own values as well. Readers could trust what they read and not worry about who owned the newspaper or that there was a monopoly or duopoly in their community.[9] Indeed, if everyone followed professional standards, press concentration would become a moot issue. Who needed more than one or two newspapers if every paper basically would end up running the same professionally driven content? Owners could sell their neutral monopoly newspapers to everyone in the community and rake in the profits.

It took decades for the professional system to be adopted by all the major journalistic media. And during the 1930s and 1940s, prominent journalists like George Seldes and Haywood Broun struggled for a vision of professional journalism that was ruthlessly independent of corporate and commercial influence, a vision that collapsed with the smashing of popular politics following the Second World War. The first half of the twentieth century is replete with owners like the *Chicago Tribune*'s Colonel McCormick, who used their newspapers to advocate their fiercely partisan (and, almost always, far-right) views. When the Nazis came to power, for example, the *Tribune*'s European correspondent defected to the Germans so he could do pro-Nazi shortwave radio broadcasts to the United States.[10] But by midcentury even laggards like the *Tribune* had been brought into line. In the famed Tribune Building in Chicago, urban legend has it that editorial workers and the business side of the paper were instructed to use separate elevators, so the editorial integrity of the newspaper would not be sullied. What is important to remember is that professional journalism looked awfully good compared to what it immediately replaced. The emphasis on nonpartisanship and factual accuracy, the discrediting of sensationalism, who could oppose that? It has been and is roundly hailed as the solution to the problem of journalism.

Over time it has become clear that there was one problem with the theory of professional journalism, an insurmountable one at that. The claim that it was possible to provide neutral and objective news was suspect, if not entirely bogus. Decision making is an inescapable part of the journalism process, and some values have to be promoted when deciding why one story rates front-page treatment while another is ignored.[11] This does not mean that some journalism cannot be more nonpartisan or more accurate than others; it certainly does not mean that nonpartisan and accurate journalism should not have a prominent role to play in a democratic society. It only means that journalism cannot actually be neutral or objective, and unless one acknowledges that, it is impossible to detect the values at play that determine what becomes news, and what does not. The way journalism evolved in the United States was to incorporate certain key values into the professional code; there was nothing naturally objective or professional about those values. In core respects they responded to the commercial and political needs of the own-

ers, although they were never framed in such a manner. To the extent journalists believe that by following professional codes they are neutral and fair—
or, at least, they need not entertain the question of bias—they are incapable
of recognizing and addressing this inherent limitation of the craft. Scholars
have identified three deep-seated biases that are built into the professional
code that journalists follow, and that have decidedly political and ideological
implications.[12] These biases remain in place to this day; indeed, they are
stronger than ever.

First, to remove the controversy connected with the selection of stories,
professional journalism regards anything done by official sources, e.g., government officials and prominent public figures, as the basis for legitimate
news. In the partisan era of journalism, newspapers would stand behind
story selection as representing their values, what they thought was important. Such an attitude was anathema in professional times. Relying on
sources as the basis for legitimate news helped solve that problem. Then, if
chastised by readers for covering a particular story, an editor could say, "Hey,
don't blame us, the governor (or any other official source) said it and we
merely reported it." It also has the important added benefit of making the
news fairly easy and inexpensive to cover—merely put reporters where official sources congregate and let them report what they say. This is a crucial
factor in explaining why coverage of the U.S. presidency has grown dramatically during the twentieth century: there are reporters assigned to the White
House and they file stories regularly, regardless of what is taking place. In the
late nineteenth century, coverage of the president occupied maybe 2 or 3 percent of the "news hole" in U.S. newspapers. By the middle-to-late twentieth
century, the president dominated 10 to 25 percent of the news, depending
upon the scope of the survey.

The limitations of this reliance upon official sources are self-evident. It
gives those in political office (and, to a lesser extent, business) considerable
power to set the news agenda by what they speak about and, just as important, what they keep quiet about. When a journalist dares to raise an issue
that no official source is talking about, he or she is accused of being unprofessional, and attempting to introduce his or her own biases into the news.
Shrewd politicians and powerful figures learn how to use journalistic conventions to their advantage.[13] Journalists find themselves where they cannot
antagonize their sources too much, or they might get cut off and become inef-

fectual. Political journalism has often degenerated to simply reporting what someone in one party says, and then getting a reply from someone on the other side of the aisle, or who takes a dissenting position within the community of official sources. All in all, the reliance on official sources gives the news a very conventional and mainstream feel, and does not necessarily lead to a rigorous examination of the major issues.

As the old saying goes, the media do not necessarily tell you what to think, but they tell you what to think about, and how to think about it. If one wants to know why a story is getting covered, and why it is getting covered the way it is, looking at sources will turn up an awfully good answer a high percentage of the time. It is not just about whether a story will be covered at all, but, rather, how much attention a story will get and the tone of the coverage. In view of the fact that legitimate sources tend to be restricted to political and economic elites, this bias sometimes makes journalists appear to be stenographers to those in power—exactly what one would expect in an authoritarian society with little or no formal press freedom.

Many working journalists recoil at these statements. Their response would be that professional reliance on official sources is justifiable as "democratic" because the official sources are elected or accountable to people who are elected by the citizenry. This is not a dictatorship. The reporter's job is to report what people in power say and let the reader/viewer decide who is telling the truth. The problem with this rationale for stenography is that it forgets a critical assumption of free press theory: even leaders determined by election need a rigorous monitoring, the range of which cannot be determined solely by their elected opposition. Otherwise the citizenry has no way out of the status quo, no capacity to criticize the political culture as a whole. If this watchdog function grows lax, corruption invariably grows, and the electoral system decays.

In addition to this reliance on official sources, experts are also crucial to explaining and debating policy, especially in complex stories. As with sources, experts are drawn almost entirely from the establishment. Studies on the use of news sources and experts invariably point to the strong mainstream bias built into the news. An analysis of national TV broadcast news for 2001, for example, found that the sources and experts used were overwhelmingly white, male, Republican, and wealthy. The emphasis upon Republicans can be explained mostly by the Republican administration. The news covers people in power. They also have seemingly accepted business domination of the political economy as legitimate. There were 955 representatives of corporations on the newscasts as opposed to thirty-one representatives of labor.[14]

A second flaw in journalism is that it tends to avoid contextualization like the plague. This was the great strength of partisan journalism: it attempted to take every important issue and place it in a larger political ideology, to make sense of it. But under professional standards, to provide meaningful context and background for stories, if done properly, will tend to commit the journalist to a definite position and enmesh the journalist (and medium) in the controversy professionalism is determined to avoid. Coverage tends to be a barrage of facts and official statements. What little contextualization professional journalism does provide tends to conform to official source consensus premises. The way to assure that news selection not be perceived as ideologically driven is to have a news hook or a news peg to justify a news story. If something happens, it is news. This meant that crucial social issues like racism or environmental degradation fell through the cracks of journalism unless there was some event—like a demonstration or the release of an official report—to justify coverage, or unless official sources wanted to make it a story so they could talk about it repeatedly. For those outside power to generate a news hook was and is often extraordinarily difficult. The 1968 report of the Kerner Commission on Civil Disorders, for example, specifically cited the poor coverage and lack of contextualization by journalism of civil rights issues over the years as strongly contributing to the climate that led to the riots of the 1960s.[15]

Both of these factors helped to stimulate the birth and rapid rise of the public relations (PR) industry, the purpose of which was to surreptitiously take advantage of these two aspects of professional journalism. It is not an accident that the PR industry emerged on the heels of professional journalism. By providing slick press releases, paid-for "experts," ostensibly neutral-sounding but bogus citizens groups, and canned news events, crafty PR agents have been able to shape the news to suit the interests of their mostly corporate clientele. Powerful corporate interests that have a distinct concern about government regulation spend a fortune to see that their version of science gets a wide play in the news . . . as objective truth.[16] Media owners welcome PR, as it provides, in effect, a subsidy for them by providing them with filler at no cost. Surveys show that PR accounts for anywhere from 40 to 70

percent of what appears as news. Because PR is only successful if it is surreptitious, the identity of the major players and knowledge of their most successful campaigns is unknown to the general public. During the 1990s the PR
industry underwent a major consolidation, and today the three largest advertising agency companies, which now offer full-service corporate communication to their clients, own eight of the ten largest U.S. PR firms.[17]

The combined effect of these two biases and the prominence of spin is to
produce a grand yet distressing paradox: journalism, which, in theory,
should inspire political involvement, tends to strip politics of meaning and
promote broad depoliticization. It is arguably better at generating ignorance
and apathy than informed and passionately engaged citizens.[18] Politics
becomes antiseptic and drained of passion, of connection to the lives people
lead. At its worst, it feeds a cynicism about the value and integrity of public
life.[19] So it is that on some of those stories that receive the most coverage, like
the Middle East or the Clinton health-care proposal in the early 1990s,
Americans tend to be almost as ignorant as on those subjects that receive far
less coverage.[20] The journalism is more likely to produce confusion than
understanding and informed action. This creates a major dilemma for journalism over time. It is well understood that democracy needs journalism;
viable self-government in our times is unthinkable without it. What is less well
perceived is that journalism requires democracy. Unless there is a citizenry
that depends upon journalism, that takes it seriously, that is politically
engaged, journalism can lose its bearings and have far less incentive to do the
hard work that generates the best possible work. The political system
becomes less responsive and corruption grows. Thus we can restate the
paradox of professional journalism as follows: journalism in any meaningful
sense cannot survive without a viable democracy. This implies journalism
must become aggressively and explicitly critical of the anti-democratic status
quo, it must embrace once again the old adage of "afflicting the comfortable
and comforting the afflicted." In short, the logic suggests that to remain democratic, to continue to exist, journalism must become . . . unprofessional.

The third bias of professional journalism is more subtle but arguably the
most important: far from being politically neutral, within the constraints of
the first two biases, it smuggles in values conducive to the commercial aims
of the owners and advertisers as well as the political aims of the owning
class. Ben Bagdikian refers to this as the "dig here, not there" phenome-

non.[21] So it is that crime stories and stories about royal families and celebrities become legitimate news. (These are inexpensive to cover and they never antagonize people in power.) So it is that the affairs of government are subjected to much closer scrutiny than the affairs of big business. And of government activities, those that serve the poor (e.g., welfare) get much more critical attention than those that serve primarily the interests of the wealthy (e.g., the CIA and other institutions of the national security state), which are more or less off-limits. This focus on government malfeasance and neglect of corporate misdeeds plays directly into the hands of those who wish to give more power and privileges to corporations, and undermine the ability of government to regulate in the public interest. As Ed Baker observes, professional practices, along with libel laws, "favor exposing governmental rather than private (corporate) wrongdoing."[22] This, too, plays into the promotion of cynicism about public life. The corporate scandals of 2002 finally forced certain corporate excesses into the news, but what was immediately striking was how all the criminal activity had taken place for years without a shred of news-media interest. The genius of professionalism in journalism is that it tends to make journalists oblivious to the compromises with authority they routinely make.

Establishing if there actually *is* a pro-corporate bias in the news is not an easy task, and has been a source of more than a little controversy over the years. Although studies show the topic of corporate power is virtually unmentioned in U.S. political journalism, it is highly controversial to accuse journalism of a pro-corporate bias.[23] In the 1990s, for the first time, what amounts to a controlled experiment shed new light on the debate. Charles Lewis was an award-winning journalist who left network television to form the Center for Public Integrity (CPI) in the early 1990s. Receiving funding from foundations, Lewis assembled a large team of investigative journalists, and had them do several detailed investigative reports each year. The purpose was to release the reports to the news media and hope for coverage and follow-up investigative work. Lewis notes that when his group releases exposés of government malfeasance, they tend to receive extensive coverage and follow-up. The CPI broke the story, for example, about President Clinton's "leasing" the Lincoln Bedroom in the White House to major campaign contributors. When the CPI issues a report on corporate malfeasance, in contrast, Lewis says the press conference is virtually empty and there is almost no coverage or follow-up. What makes this striking is that the exact same journalists do these reports.[24] Were Lewis unprincipled, he would logically discontinue doing corporate exposés.[25]

Imagine if the president or the director of the FBI ordered news media not to issue any critical examinations of corporate power or class inequality in the United States. It would be considered a grotesque violation of democratic freedoms and a direct challenge to the viability of the Republic. It would constitute a much greater threat to democracy than Watergate; one would probably have to return to the Civil War and slavery to find a comparable threat to the union. The American Civil Liberties Union (ACLU) would go ballistic. Yet, when the private sector control of journalism, through professional practices, generates virtually the exact same outcome, it goes unmentioned and unrecognized in political culture. It is a non-issue.

Although the professional code incorporates these three general biases, it is also malleable; it is not fixed in stone. Over the years it has been influenced by factors such as the rise of radio and television, or new communication technologies.[26] It is also true that the organized activities of the mass of people can have the ability to influence the shape of journalism. In moments of resurgence for social movements, professional journalism can improve the quantity and quality of coverage. Certainly there was a notable shift in coverage of issues surrounding African Americans and women from the 1950s to the 1970s, reflecting the emergence of the civil rights and feminist movements. It works in the other direction, too. In the 1940s, for example, when the U.S. labor movement was at its zenith, full-time labor editors and reporters abounded on U.S. daily newspapers. There were several hundred of them. Even ferociously anti-labor newspapers, like the *Chicago Tribune*, covered the labor beat. The 1937 Flint sit-down strike that launched the United Autoworkers and the trade union movement was a major news story across the nation. By the 1980s, however, labor had fallen off the map and there were no more than a couple of dozen labor beat reporters remaining on U.S. dailies. The story was simply no longer covered. Hence the 1989 Pittstown sit-down strike—the largest since Flint—was virtually unreported in the U.S. media, and its lessons unknown. As the labor movement declined, coverage of labor was dropped. People still work, poverty among workers is growing, workplace conflicts are as important as ever, but this is no longer as newsworthy as it was when organized labor was more powerful.[27]

The most important source of altering the professional code comes from the owners. Their constant drumbeat for profit, their concern with minimizing costs and enhancing revenues, invariably influences the manner in which news is collected and reported. We turn to this subject below.

Professional journalism hit its high-water mark in the United States from the 1950s into the 1970s. During this era, journalists had relative autonomy to pursue stories and considerable resources to use to pursue their craft. There was a strong emphasis upon factual accuracy, which is all to the good. The best journalism of the professional era came (and still comes) when there were debates among official sources or when an issue was irrelevant to elite concerns. In these cases, professional journalism could be sparkling. Likewise, during this golden age of professional journalism, the political culture, official sources, especially though not exclusively in the Democratic Party, were considerably more liberal than they would be by the 1980s. Along with the increase in social activism overall, this opened up opportunities for journalists to take risks and cover stories that would be much more difficult as the entire political class became increasingly enthralled with the market. So someone like Ralph Nader routinely received extensive and fairly sympathetic press coverage for his consumer campaigns during the 1960s and early 1970s. The consumer and environmental legislation he is responsible for pushing into law during this period is little short of astounding by contemporary standards. By the 1990s he had basically been scripted out of the political culture and journalism, leading him to enter electoral politics to express his frustration with the status quo.

But one should not exaggerate the quality of journalism or the amount of autonomy journalists had from the interests of owners, even in this "golden age." Even at the height of the golden age there was an underground press predicated upon the problems in contemporary journalism, and hard-edged criticism of the flaws of existing journalism abounded. In every community there was a virtual Sicilian code of silence for the local commercial media, for example, regarding the treatment of the area's wealthiest and most powerful individuals and corporations. Media owners wanted their friends and business pals to get nothing but kid-glove treatment in their media and so it was, except for the most egregious and boneheaded maneuver. Likewise, newspapers, even prestigious ones like the *Los Angeles Times*, used their power to aid the economic projects of the newspaper's owners.[28] And pressure to shape editorial coverage to serve the needs of major advertisers was a recurring problem.

If the system of professional journalism has had deep-seated biases built into its code that have deadened it as a democratic force, that does not mean that there have not been many good, and some great, journalists who nevertheless have done brilliant work. Decade after decade newsrooms have produced outstanding journalists whose contributions to building a democratic and just society have been immeasurable.[29] In recent times, one thinks of the work of the *Philadelphia Inquirer*'s Donald Bartlett and James Steele.[30] Some of the most impressive work often has come in the form of books, ranging from those of Rachel Carson and Robert Caro to Studs Terkel and Betty Friedan. The list is really quite long. To some extent, this reflects the ability of books to convey detailed reports, but it also highlights how many great journalists had to leave the routine of standard newsroom journalism in order to do the stories they deemed important. Their work points out what can be done but generally is not being done. Along these lines, it is worth noting that many of the twentieth-century's finest journalists—Ben Bagdikian, George Seldes, A.J. Liebling, I.F. Stone, David Halberstam, Bill Moyers, and William Greider—have been among its foremost press critics. In short, the great work has been done not because of the system as much as in spite of it. As discussed below, the degree of difficulty for committed journalists has only increased in the past two decades.

The Commercialization of Journalism

Professional journalism emerged not to the opposition of most media owners, but to the contrary, with their active sponsorship. There was a struggle between owners and progressive journalists to determine the contours of professional journalism in its first generation or two, but by the mid-twentieth century it had settled for the most part into its current form. It made sense for media owners to grant some autonomy to journalists because it gave their product more credibility and worked to enhance their commercial prospects. The autonomy it granted journalists was always relative and the manner in which the professional code evolved put significant limitations on the capacity of professional journalism to serve as a democratic force.

Moreover, the professional journalism "deal" was never made in a formal contract, and news workers' unions never were powerful enough to wrestle control over journalism (and budgets) from media owners in their contract negotiations. By the 1980s the "deal" made less and less sense for media owners. Relaxation of media ownership regulations along with general market pressures led to wave after wave of media deal making, with the largest firms that owned news media much larger relative to the balance of the corporate community than their predecessors had been. These firms, often media conglomerates, which paid vast sums to purchase news media wanted and needed to generate significant returns to pay down debt and satisfy investors; to these firms the idea that they should provide some degree of autonomy to their news divisions became increasingly nonsensical, except for their PR pronouncements. After all, the workers in the other properties of their media empires were not granted such autonomy; they were expected to deliver directly and immediately to the firm's bottom-line success.

In this context, journalism increasingly became subjected to an explicit commercial regimentation; the protection from commercial pressure provided by professionalism was undermined. Though this is the primary factor and the overarching factor to explain recent developments in journalism, it is not the sole factor. The rise of commercial news media enabled by new technologies—in particular round-the-clock TV news channels and the Internet—have increased the need for ongoing attention-getting stories, with less emphasis on their significance of the story by traditional standards.[31] Libel court rulings and government secrecy laws and regulations have made it much more difficult and cost prohibitive to do investigative work on corporations and government affairs. One of the ironies of neoliberalism—as manifested in the Bush-Cheney variant—is that its contempt for government (and much professed love for the wisdom of private citizens) does not extend to encouraging the citizenry to have much of a clue of what the government is doing in its name.[32] Likewise, as journalism becomes more explicitly directed by market concerns, the overall depoliticization of society will hardly encourage the development of political coverage. And finally, the conservative campaign against the "liberal media" has produced a chilling effect on journalism's willingness to ask tough questions of many of those in power. In combination, over the past two decades this has led to a sustained attack on the professional ideal, a sea change in journalism, and a crisis in the field greater than any other period with the possible exception of the late Gilded Age and the Progressive Era.

The commercial attack on the professional autonomy of journalism has been widely chronicled and assumes many forms.[33] I highlight the main trends, and some of the more striking implications for democracy. For starters, the trend has been toward a cutback in the resources allocated to journalism. By the 1990s, if not earlier, commercial news media were "forced to embrace the financial discipline required by parent companies that no longer looked at news as a golden child and free spending spirit even when it refused to be bound by life's practicalities."[34] A 2002 Project for Excellence in Journalism survey of U.S. journalists found them "a grumpy lot," due largely to budget cuts, lower salaries, no raises, and job insecurity.[35] There was a virtual newsroom uprising at the *Wall Street Journal* in December 2002, for example, when parent company Dow Jones announced sweeping cuts in the number of senior journalists while the firm's executive ranks were untouched.[36] The media firms argue that such cutbacks are necessary to remain competitive, but many journalists claim that giant firms use their market power to strip down resources for news to make a short-term profit grab. In 2001 the publisher of the *San Jose Mercury-News*, Jay Harris, resigned his position to protest what he regarded as the entirely unnecessary editorial cutbacks at his paper, mandated by parent company Knight-Ridder. As Harris put it, his newspaper, like most others, was raking in enormous profits. The cutbacks were unjustifiable.[37]

Lowballing editorial budgets has proven extremely profitable, at least in the short term. The great commercial success story of U.S. journalism has been the Fox News Channel, which has cut costs to the bone by basically replacing more expensive conventional journalism with celebrity pontificators.[38] Using this formula, Fox News was able to generate roughly equivalent profits to CNN by 1999–2000, while spending far less than CNN to do so.[39] The operating profit at News Corporation's U.S. cable channels, which includes the Fox News Network, more than tripled from the third quarter of 2001 to the third quarter of 2002.[40] The rise of media conglomerates has made it far easier for firms to spread their editorial budgets across several different media, so that a key trend has been to have the same journalist report for a media firm's newspaper, Web site, TV station, and radio station, or some combination of the above.[41] The Internet only accelerates this process. This provides much of the incentive for firms to become large conglomerates, as it gives them tremendous cost savings compared to those firms that do not have a similar arsenal of media properties.[42] Indeed, even separate firms are partnering (especially where regulations prohibit them from merging) to spread the editorial budgets across several media.[43] When ABC News and CNN were negotiating a merger in 2002, one observer deemed it "an unholy alliance that could only make sense to cost-cutters."[44] One Wall Street analyst thought the merger would lead to cost savings (including labor costs) of $100 million to $200 million.[45] As Av Westin, the six-time Emmy Award-winning CBS journalist put it in 2001: "To expect that any corporate manager will reinvest savings in better news programming is, I fear, a delusion."[46]

The effects of this budget-cutting mania on journalism arguably have been entirely negative. It has meant a relaxation or alteration, sometimes severe, of professional news standards. Professional standards have not collapsed entirely. There remains a ruthless requirement that journalists not invent sources or consciously lie in their journalism. And journalists exposed for blatantly violating these norms will usually be fired and have to move on to new professions.[47] But the nature of what gets covered and how it gets covered, the meat and potatoes of journalism, have changed, all for the worse. Factual accuracy and honesty are all well and good, but it is not the be all and end all of journalism if the story in question concerns a celebrity's trial or a donkey getting a shampoo. The broader question is how the decline in resources and the pressure to generate profits pushes factually accurate journalism to concentrate upon some stories over others. To paraphrase Trudy Lieberman, you can't report what you don't pursue.[48]

And it is here that the attack on professional standards is striking. Fewer reporters means it is easier for public relations executives to get their client's messages into the news unadulterated by journalism. As two executives for Edelman Public Relations exulted in 2000, as a result of media consolidation and conglomeration, there are fewer reporters and resources, and, therefore, "an increased likelihood that press releases will be used word-for-word, in part if not in whole."[49] International coverage has been a victim of corporate cost cuts. Likewise, investigative journalism—original research into public issues, not merely reporting on what people in power are talking about, once considered the hallmark of feisty "Fourth Estate" journalism in a free society—

is now on the endangered species list. It costs far more to do hard investigations than it does to do official source stenography, and requires skilled experienced journalists. It is much more lucrative to have less-experienced journalists fill the news hole with the proclamations and debates of those in
power and stories that are easier to cover. Investigative journalism is also suspect in the new world order because the media firm has little incentive to
produce a journalism that might enmesh it in conflict with some powerful
business or governmental institutions. A five-year study of investigative journalism on TV news completed in 2002 determined that investigative journalism has all but disappeared on the nation's commercial airwaves. Much of
what was passed off as original investigative work—put at 1 percent of TV
news programming—included stories such as "women illegally injecting sil-
icone at parties."[50] As Charles Lewis points out, a good portion of what
appears as investigative work on network TV news is actually the reporting
of leaks or government reports where reporters are spoon-fed by sources.[51]
And even then, as Greg Palast observes, the reporter often just presents it as
someone else making the charge, no actual journalistic inquiry into the truth
of the matter takes place.[52]

The combination of increasing need to rely upon PR and a declining
commitment to investigative journalism plays directly into the hands of powerful commercial interests, especially in environmental and public health stories where scientific expertise is necessary to explain public issues. (That is,
if the stories are even covered.) It is here, as Sheldon Rampton and John
Stauber demonstrate, that corporations have been able to generously provide
the media with their self-interested version of science and undermine public
understanding of the issues.[53]

Indeed, in the current environment, it is decreasingly the case that the
reporter will bother to investigate to find out who is telling the truth if there
is a factual dispute among official sources. The professional reliance upon
official sources as the basis for news—always a problem—has been reduced
to the absurd. To investigate factual disputes among official sources would
take time and cast the pall of bias over the journalist, depending upon whom
the findings favored. When, for example, in 2002 Democrats criticized
Halliburton for not paying taxes under Dick Cheney's leadership, the press
ran the charges and a response from Halliburton denying the charges. No
journalist, in the professional mainstream press at least, appeared to attempt

to investigate to determine who was telling the truth.[54] This environment becomes a scoundrel's paradise, as one can lie with virtual impunity; it becomes the function of one's opponents, not journalists, to establish the truth, and one's opponents can always be dismissed as partisan. It also means that journalists are far more comfortable putting political debate in terms of strategies and spin, rather than digging and locating the actual facts in the matter and letting the chips fall where they may. So it was that much of the press coverage of the political response to the corporate scandals of 2002—to which I return below—dwelled upon how the parties hoped to spin the issue to their advantage.[55] (Need it be pointed out that this obsession with how politicians spin—to the point that journalists sometimes chastise politicians who fail to spin them effectively, rather than with getting at the truth—breeds a certain contempt for public life.[56]) Av Westin chronicled the deterioration of professional journalism practices in detail in his handbook for TV journalists, and their implications:

> As a result, the audience has become accustomed to shoddy reporting to the point that the average viewer does not necessarily expect quality journalism and probably could not discern the difference between a well-produced story and a below-average one. The sad truth is that because the mass audience cannot perceive the difference, management is reluctant to spend more money to improve the product.[57]

Another area where professional standards have relaxed is with regard to commercialism. Journalists have long faced pressure to shape stories to suit advertisers and owners, and much of the professional code has attempted to prevent this, or at least to minimize this. But corporate management increasingly grinds away at their news divisions to play ball with the commercial needs of the parent firms. Over time it has been successful, and those who survive in the new world order of corporate journalism tend to internalize the necessary values. One survey conducted by the trade publication *Electronic Media* in 2001 found that the vast majority of TV station executives found their news departments "cooperative" in shaping the news to assist in "nontraditional revenue development," in which the news department cooperates with major advertisers to co-promote events and uses advertisers as experts in stories.[58] The Pew Research Center survey of 300 journalists released in

2000 found that nearly one-half of journalists acknowledged sometimes consciously engaging in self-censorship to serve the commercial interests of their firm or advertisers, and only one-quarter of them stated this never happened to their knowledge.[59]

This commercial penetration of professional journalism assumes two direct forms. First, commercial interests directly penetrate the news, corrupting its integrity. This process has been well chronicled.[60] To some extent it entails savvy corporate marketers, who produce slick video features to be played on TV newscasts as news stories, but also include a plug for the firm's product.[61] It also includes when the traditional "news hole" increasingly permits commercial messages, such as selling obituaries, running advertisements on the front page, or putting commercial overlays over editorial content, be it in print or broadcast.[62] More ominously, the practice of permitting advertisers to influence the news and how it is covered has become more common. This has been especially true in areas of health care and medicine, where the commercial corruption of reporting has become, pun intended, epidemic.[63] In 2002 an editor of the *New York Post* went so far as to inform publicists that a good way to get coverage in her paper was for someone to buy an advertisement.[64]

Along these lines, the traditional professional prohibition against journalists accepting bribes to write stories in a particular manner is under attack. In an increasingly commercialized journalism "market," where profit maximization is the firm's explicit defining objective, journalists figure they might as well get theirs too. So it has developed that journalists have become "pitchmen" for products.[65] PBS and CBS correspondent Charlie Rose, for example, was master of ceremonies for Coca-Cola's annual shareholders meeting in 2002.[66] This is strongly encouraged by the tendency to market newscasters as "celebrities" and "brands" as a relatively inexpensive way for media firms to increase ratings, sales, and profits from their news assets.[67] In 2002, for but one small example, a New York TV weatherman agreed to go out on televised dates, which would be critiqued on air by his colleagues the next day.[68] Accordingly, the prohibition against journalists accepting direct commercial bribes remains, but it is less impressive with all the indirect commercial influences taking place. And the downside of being more explicitly commercial in journalistic practices is not as ominous as it once was. When an ABC medical journalist was suspended for a week for endorsing Tylenol in a radio commercial in 2002, she left ABC to accept a lucrative position at Johnson & Johnson, Tylenol's parent company.[69] In another case, a Baltimore health reporter, who had been fired by a Baltimore TV station because of her "blundering efforts to make money from the medical institutions she had been covering" was able to parlay her ties into a weekly TV health news program that was described by one Baltimore journalist as "an alarming parade of commercial tie- ins."[70] Like the professional commitment to factual accuracy, the professional prohibition against explicit commercial bribery remains standing, but appears increasingly to be beside the point.

The second form that commercial penetration of journalism assumes is also a traditional problem for commercial journalism that professionalism was meant to eliminate: journalists using their privileges to report favorably on their owner's commercial ventures or investments. In an era where journalism is increasingly produced by large media conglomerates with vast nonjournalistic holdings, and where the barrier between editorial and commercial is withering, the problem has returned to the fore with a vengeance. The major TV networks have used their news programs to promote their other media fare in news stories, such as when ABC News promoted Disney's 2001 film *Pearl Harbor* or played up the fictitious town of Push, Nevada, which was the name of a short-lived prime-time series.[71] ABC News also seemingly killed stories that cast negative light on parent company Disney's other holdings, including a report on pedophiles being employed at a Disney theme park.[72] NBC News featured more than twice the amount of news coverage of the 2002 Winter Olympics than did *ABC World News Tonight*, and nearly seven times more coverage than *CBS Evening News*. Is it any surprise that NBC paid for the rights to broadcast the Winter Olympics?[73] CBS was not to be outdone. In 2000 its news programming did frequent "reports" on its "reality" program *Survivor*, and loaned out a journalist to do a weekly interview program to discuss developments on another "reality" show, *Big Brother*.[74] In 2001 AOL Time Warner's CNN Headline News channel acknowledged that it was plugging other AOL Time Warner products and channels in its news headlines; the practice was a logical outcome of the corporate commitment to "synergy."[75] "The drive to achieve synergy," journalist Ken Auletta stated in 2002, "is often journalism's poison."[76]

The corporate/commercial pressure on news often takes place indirectly, and is therefore less likely to be recognized as such by journalists or the public. The flip side of the reluctance to spend money on investigative or international coverage, and the reluctance to antagonize powerful sources, is an increased emphasis on largely trivial stories that give the appearance of controversy and conflict but rarely have anything to do with any significant public issue. Study after study reveals a general decline in the amount of "hard news" relative to fluff.[77] Some argued that in the aftermath of the 9/11 terrorist attack, U.S. news media had seen the light and returned to their "historic mission," but such fantasies were short-lived.[78] A central preoccupation of the news has become the activities of celebrities, especially with regard to their personal lives.[79] So it was that during 2001 and 2002 the news was dominated with stories about Winona Ryder's shoplifting trial, Robert Blake's murder arrest, and Gary Condit's affair.[80] A politician stands a far greater chance to become the object of news media scrutiny if she or he is rumored to have not paid ten parking tickets or if they failed to pay a bar bill than if they used their power to quietly funnel billions of public dollars to powerful special interests. The justification for this caliber of journalism is that these stories are popular and therefore profitable, and commercial news needs to "give the people what they want," but to a certain extent, leaving aside the question of whether journalism should be determined by marketing polls, this is circular logic.[81] The motor force behind this journalism is as much supply as demand. It is cheaper and easier to cover than "hard" news, and never enmeshes the media firm in a controversy with anyone in power, while providing an illusion of controversy to the public. Over time whatever taste the public has for this type of fare is only encouraged through extensive exposure. Had a similar commitment to the more expensive and risky exposés of government and corporate corruption been made, one suspects a public taste might have been developed for those stories as well. But that is not an option the people are given.

Celebrities and trivial personal indiscretion are not all that commercial journalism favors. Likewise, stories that emphasize violence meet the commercial criteria as well. The news, especially television news, is awash in stories about traffic and airplane accidents, fires, and murders.[82] The Washington serial sniper story of October 2002 was a textbook example of this phenomenon. It generated high ratings and took no great skill or expense to cover. It received round-the-clock coverage, yet the news media had little to report, so much of the "news" was idle speculation, bland repetition, or hashing over rumors. As Ted Koppel put it, the media were "going nuts" over what he termed a "dreadful but relatively minor threat" in the bigger scheme of things.[83] It was, by and large, a waste of time, but a commercially lucrative waste of time.

Another crucial way in which the commercialization of journalism covertly alters the news is by constantly pushing journalism to be directed to the lucrative markets desired by media owners and big ticket advertisers. Given the constant pressure for profit, this concern with generating news content that will attract the most lucrative target audience has grown to an obsession.[84] The days when journalism was a public service directed at the entire population—obviously never entirely accurate—are long gone. Today much of journalism is increasingly directed at the middle class and the upper class while the working class and the poor have been written off altogether.[85] Coverage of labor issues has plummeted, for example, in the past generation and barely exists any longer in the news media.[86] Part of any explanation for the relatively nonexistent and distorted treatment of African Americans and Latinos in the news owes to their not being especially attractive economically to advertisers.[87] Ben Bagdikian captured this class bias well:

> If the Dow Jones Industrial Average dropped steadily for twenty years it would be Front Page and leading broadcast news day after day until the government took action. That 32 million of our population have their housing, food, and clothing "index" drop steadily for more than 30 years is worth only an occasional feature story about an individual or statistical fragments in the back pages of our most influential news organizations.[88]

Along these lines, a survey released by the Catholic Campaign for Human Development in 2003 showed that most Americans had no idea that nearly 33 million of their compatriots lived in fairly dire poverty; most of them thought the total was between one and five million.[89] The flip side to the marginalization of the poor and working class from the news has been the elevation of business to center stage. If labor reporting went from being a standard position on nearly all major news media two or three generations ago to being extinct by 2003, business reporting skyrocketed, to the point where business news and general news seemingly converged. Although the majority of Americans have little direct interest in the stock market—and it is far from the most pressing immediate economic issue in their lives—the operating assumption in the news media became that all Americans are active stock traders with a passionate concern about equity and bond markets. Schools of journalism have responded to this development, and chairs in business journalism have mushroomed across college campuses. "Business journalism is hot," a Columbia University J-School official noted. "Journalists see it as a career track."[90]

Regrettably, the turn to business journalism has not meant that the affairs of corporations and investors have been subjected to hard, critical scrutiny in terms of how they affect public life. It has not even meant necessarily that there has been increased scrutiny of business behavior to protect investors and consumers.[91] To the contrary, business journalism is, as one observer put it, "teeming with reverence for the accumulation of wealth."[92] To some extent this is due to the rah-rah capitalism ethos that marinates the corporate media as much as corporate America, but it is also due to the pressures highlighted above: reliance upon business sources and marginalizing critical sources, use of corporate PR as the basis for news, and fear of antagonizing corporate advertisers.[93] The corruption of business reporting was such, with puff pieces extolling the virtues of this or that company, that in 2002 the New York Stock Exchange was pressing for regulations that would require journalists to disclose the financial interests of the stock market analysts they used in their news stories.[94] By 2002 mainstream media critics concurred that business journalism, rather than monitoring the excesses of the business expansion of the 1990s, actually played a strong part in magnifying them and "inflating the bubble."[95] As one journalist put it, "The bubble was filled with hot air from hyperventilating journalists."[96] Yet few journalists ever questioned the turn away from labor and toward business. It was incorporated into the professional code and most journalists internalized it as proper and beyond reproach. Even today after the massive corporate scandals of 2001–2, the central role of business news and the virtual absence of news concerning the working class and poor is taken for granted by professional journalists. It is not seen as "self-censorship" to shape the news in such a manner. That is the genius of professionalism as a form of regulation.

It is with regard to the corporate scandals of 2001 and 2002 that all of these core problems for contemporary journalism come together: low-ball budgets, deification of official sources, lack of investigative work, enhanced attention to the editorial concerns of advertisers, emphasis on the trivial, the glorification of business, and the exile of the poor and working class. The results were one of the darkest and most depressing episodes in the recent history of U.S. journalism and its nearly thorough abrogation of its role as a watchdog over power as a feisty Fourth Estate. The news coverage played a large, perhaps even decisive, role in the collapse of anything remotely close to a democratic resolution to this crisis.

The crisis emerged when Enron filed for bankruptcy in 2001, followed by WorldCom's $107 billion free fall and bankruptcy in 2002.[97] Arthur Andersen, Global Crossing, and a host of other firms followed in the wake.[98] What was striking about these historically unprecedented corporate collapses was not simply that they were fraught with fraud and corruption, with workers, taxpayers, and investors bilked out of billions and billions of dollars. After all, that might be considered capitalism as usual, if you can get away with it, and many did and do. What was most striking about these scandals, as two journalists put it, was that "the fraud occurred in the most heavily regulated and monitored area of corporate activity."[99] Enron was described by Charles Lewis, the journalist responsible for much of the investigation into its activities, as "a company inordinately dependent on government favors."[100] Much of the fraud perpetrated by Enron, WorldCom, Global Crossing, and the others was the result of their being able to have politicians push through highly dubious "deregulation" schemes that opened the door to billion-dollar rip-offs that would have been impossible otherwise.[101] Along these lines, firms like Enron and Arthur Andersen were among the largest political contributors to political candidates in the nation; although the majority of money went to Republicans, Democrats had a solid place at the trough.[102] Global Crossing "tossed more money around town than Enron," observed *Business Week*, and, if anything, it spread its largesse more toward Democrats than Republicans as it sought government support for its activities.[103] In short, this was not a business scandal, this was a political scandal of the highest magnitude. It went directly at the issue of corruption in governance and the broader political economy that is built into the system and that takes place across the government, most notably at its very highest levels.

In this context, let us consider the nature of the news coverage of corporate scandals. Most striking, despite the vast resources devoted to busi-

ness journalism in the 1990s, the media missed the developing story *in
toto*. It failed in its role as an early alarm system for social problems.[104] It is
worth noting that by the mid-1990s the alternative press was beginning to
report on evidence of Enron's chicanery, and Ralph Nader and his cohorts
were aggressively pointing to the highly dubious nature of Enron's and
WorldCom's activities, among others, but this was resolutely ignored by
the mainstream.[105] Indeed, as the *New York Times* later conceded, when
WorldCom CEO Bernard Ebbers spoke to the National Press Club in
2000, as the Ponzi scheme WorldCom had been using to grow was unraveling, the assembled journalists gave him a loud round of applause and the
mood was "celebratory."[106] Enron was named by *Fortune* magazine as
"America's Most Innovative Company" every single year from 1995 to
2000.[107] A data search of mainstream news (and business news) coverage
for the word "Enron" prior to 2001 finds "little but praise for its market
innovations."[108] It subsequently became known that these firms had courted the media with the same vigilance and skill they courted politicians.
Both the *New York Times* and Viacom had major business ventures with
Enron, for example, and Enron paid several prominent journalists amounts
ranging from $50,000 to $100,000 to "consult" for them.[109] Enron played
all the angles; it was an original underwriter for a major PBS six-part series
on globalization that eventually aired in 2002, with Enron's name removed
from the list of funders.[110]

The financial collapse of these firms by 2001 and 2002, along with the
transparent use of fraudulent and illegal techniques to bilk people out of billions finally made this a news story, a very big news story. Moreover, there
were grounds to think this would be a political scandal of the highest magnitude, arguably on a par with or exceeding Watergate. For starters, President
George W. Bush, Vice President Cheney, as well as their administration had
extremely close relations with Enron and its executives. Enron CEO
Kenneth Lay and his fellow Enron executives had also been major contributors to George W. Bush's political career.[111] At a 1997 party for then Enron
CEO Rich Kinder, at which Enron executives joked about using bogus
accounting tricks to make "a kazillion dollars" and attended by then-Texas
governor George W. Bush, former president George H. W. Bush told Kinder:
"You have been fantastic to the Bush family. I don't think anybody did more
than you did to support [my son] George."[112] The payoff for Enron of having

George W. Bush enter the White House was immediate: its executives played a prominent role in helping Vice President Cheney develop an energy policy in 2001, and the Bush administration helped reduce Enron's culpability (and that of many other corporations) for the California energy scandal in the newly deregulated market in 2001.[113]

One would have imagined the Democrats would have had a field day with this issue. After all, the comparatively trivial Whitewater scandal generated a special prosecutor who had more than five years and a large staff and budget to have open season on any aspect of President Clinton's conduct, though no crimes concerning Whitewater were ever established. And had the Democrats gone to war on this issue, journalists would have had ample "official source" input to warrant massive coverage of the corporate scandals as a political crisis of the highest magnitude. But Democrats did not pursue this route, for any number of reasons, but one in particular stands out: the Democrats, too, were culpable. They, too, had presided over the deregulation fiascos and they, too, had corporate blood money filling their campaign coffers.[114] If this story was pursued, there was no telling where it would stop. Consequently, the Democrats, led by longtime deregulation proponent Senator Joseph Lieberman of Connecticut, shared the Republicans' desire to downplay the political aspects of the crisis and convert it into a business scandal, where a few rogue CEOs stepped out of line and needed the long arm of the law to corral them so investors could sleep in peace again.[115] Accordingly, with no official sources pushing this as a political scandal, journalists easily converted it into a business story. Some of the reporting in the business and trade press was first rate, but the crucial link between corporate crime and political corruption all but disappeared. Accordingly, the story then became decidedly less important and was relegated to the business pages, to be replaced by whatever the official sources wished to talk about, like the prospective war on Iraq. This inability to provide criticism of the system as a whole—even when it is well deserved—is an inherent flaw of professional journalism.

But the petering out of the press coverage of the corporate scandals of 2001 and 2002 went beyond the traditional limitations of professional journalism. It also reflected the core problem of entrusting the news to large, profit-motivated, and self-interested business organizations. The CEO of the New York Times Company put it well in 2002:

Historically, the press's ability to act as a check on the actions of government has been helped by the fact that the two institutions are constitutionally separated, organizationally and financially. The press does not depend on government officials either for its standing or its resources. But it has a much more intricate relationship with big business. Today's news media are themselves frequently a part of large, often global corporations dependent on advertising revenue that, increasingly, comes from other large corporations. As public companies themselves, the news media are under the same kind of pressure to create "shareholder value," by reducing costs and increasing earnings, as are other public companies. And they face numerous conflicts of interest as they grow larger and more diversified.[116]

In short, the corporate news media have a vested interest in the corporate system. The largest media firms are members in good standing in the corporate community and closely linked through business relations, shared investors, interlocking directors, and shared political values with each other. This pushes the corporate news media, as Tom Shales puts it, to "paint as rosy a picture of the economy as possible."[117] This encouraged the press coverage of the corporate political scandals of 2001 and 2002 to revert to a "crisis management mode," where the structural and institutional determinants of the corruption are unexamined and unexposed.[118] By golly, the system works.

There is yet one further layer to this story that is necessary for a full understanding of the news coverage of the corporate scandals of 2001 and 2002, and that concerns the conduct of the media corporations themselves. These firms are hardly innocent bystanders perched on the moral high ground as they report upon the Enrons and Global Crossings of the world. Their CEOs, like the executives at Enron, have seen their salaries shoot off the charts while earnings stagnate and layoffs abound.[119] Their CEOs, too, made killings selling off vastly overpriced stock when they knew their firm was a clunker but the media were still reporting on it as if it was an up and comer.[120] Media firms, too, à la WorldCom and Enron, traditionally employed questionable accounting practices that inflated profit expectations and fleeced workers.[121] Moreover, a stunning number of major media corporations and executives were under investigation for criminal activities by 2002, including Disney CEO Michael Eisner, Rupert Murdoch's News Corporation, Charter Communications, and Vivendi Universal.[122] In keeping with the notion that the closer an industry is to being explicitly regulated, the higher the likelihood of extreme corruption, media firms are a natural hotspot for flim-flam. In 2002 five former executives at the bankrupt Adelphi Communications (a regulated cable TV company) were arrested and charged with "orchestrating one of the largest frauds to take place at a U.S. public company."[123] The media company on the top of the corporate crime blotter was none other than AOL Time Warner, which faced a series of lawsuits and criminal investigations from the Securities and Exchange Commission and the Department of Justice. It was charged with heavily distorting its books, including inflating its advertising revenues one time by nearly $200 million.[124] Some of AOL Time Warner's dubious deals that were under investigation by the SEC included complex transactions with the discredited Qwest Communications and WorldCom.[125] Media firms historically have been reluctant to cover their own misdeeds in their news media, and they could hardly be enthusiastic about a no-holds-barred journalism that would get to the bottom of the corporate crime issue and let the chips fall where they may.[126]

In combination, then, the press coverage of the corporate crime scandal of 2001 and 2002 helped it go from being a potential hurricane to a mild evening rain. "Looking back on 2002," a public interest group observed, "it is hard to avoid the conclusion that the big corporations won. Confronted with a crisis of epic proportions, they emerged with bloodied noses and sullied reputations, but little more."[127] In the summer of 2002, when the crisis was at its peak, both Bush and Cheney gave speeches railing against corporate misconduct, while at the same time aggressively fundraising from corporations and wealthy individuals for campaign contributions.[128] But even before then, in the spring, the business press acknowledged the storm had passed, and corporate reform would be, at most, modest.[129] It was left to syndicated columnist Molly Ivins into put the matter in perspective. In a column outlining the chummy connection between the relevant members of Congress responsible for overseeing the investigation of corporate fraud with the very industries most likely to have engaged in crime, Ivins concluded: "They've already called off the reform effort; it's over. Corporate muscle showed up and shut it down. . . . Bottom line: It's all going to happen again. We learned zip from our entire financial collapse. Our political system is too bought-off to respond intelligently."[130] The economist Mark Weisbrot cap-

tured the irony of the situation: "Our Congress and the executive branch
have become so corrupted by our system of legalized bribery—political campaign contributions—that they cannot even enact positive reforms that are
desired by most of the business class."[131]

So far I have discussed the direct and indirect commercial pressures
upon journalism and their almost entirely negative impact. There is also a
broader political-economic pressure, one that is magnified by the increasingly explicit commandment to market news to target audiences. In a largely
depoliticized society, there may be little effective demand for political journalism. Depoliticization is built into the broader political culture of the
United States, and it has grown arguably over the decades; the media tend to
encourage the process but they are not primarily responsible for it. As I mentioned above, it is often noted that democracy requires journalism; what is
less frequently emphasized is that journalism requires democracy. Unless
there is strong political culture there will be little demand for excellent journalism. And if, as will tend to accompany a depoliticized society, the political system is corrupt and removed from popular influence, journalists have
less incentive to produce hard-hitting exposés, because they know nothing
tangible in the form of political reform will result. So what has emerged in the
United States is that a significant number of outstanding investigative reports
are done, but there is far less follow-up by other journalists to push the story
along, especially if no one in power is excited by the story. The stories fall like
stones to the bottom on the ocean; there is no echo effect.

This dilemma leads to a fork in the road for the corporations that direct the
U.S. news media. Do they attempt to battle the tide, provide hard-hitting and
powerful political journalism even if it costs more and may not have a great deal
of immediate market demand, in the hope of generating a strong market for the
news down the road?[132] This is made ever more difficult because professional
journalism has a tendency to avoid controversy and passion so much that it is
not well suited to rousing the citizenry. What is passed off as serious news is
often the dreadfully dull reporting of debates or pronouncements among people in power.[133] Or do they acknowledge politicization, especially among the
commercially crucial 18–34 age group, and tailor the news to make it more
entertaining and engaging to that target audience? Do they, in other words, opt
for what Susan Douglas calls the "narcissism bias," meaning news that accepts
and therefore encourages political withdrawal by emphasizing trivia and

"lifestyle" reporting?[134] The news media have opted for this latter route as it makes far more commercial sense in the short term, but it also undermines the *raison d'être* of journalism.[135] If people want light entertainment and unchallenging tidbits for their journalism, it makes far more sense to watch a comedy program than the news, and many Americans do exactly that. One 2000 study showed that more than one-third of Americans under thirty regard comedy shows like Jay Leno's *Tonight Show* as their primary source for news.[136] Accordingly, a significant trend that has emerged in recent years is for local commercial television stations to discontinue their news programming.[137] After watering down and dumbing down TV news to the point it is a standing joke, while making a killing with inexpensive and inane fare, stations eventually find they have a shrinking audience so they close down the store. They have stripped the public airwaves for parts, so to speak.

One measure of the deep and severe crisis afflicting U.S. journalism is to consider the morale and assessment of working editors and journalists. For decades journalists were highly sensitive to outside criticism of their profession, and proud of their role in society. Bookstores teemed with volumes penned by journalists telling of their impressive accomplishments. No more. In what is almost a sea change in temperament, the morale of journalists has gone into a tailspin as a result of the commercial assault on the news. Prominent journalists and media figures like John Hockenberry, David Halberstam, PBS president Pat Mitchell, and Walter Cronkite decry the current situation, with Cronkite going so far as to question whether democracy can "even survive."[138] Rank-and-file reporters compile volumes on the decline of journalism, replete with case study after case study.[139] Even Leonard Downie Jr. and Robert G. Kaiser, the current national editor and associate editor of the *Washington Post*, in their 2002 *The News About the News: American Journalism in Peril* make a devastating critique of the bankruptcy of U.S. journalism, significantly due to commercial pressures, that would have been unthinkable two decades earlier.[140] Study after study, scientific or anecdotal, confirm this trend in chilling detail. Harvard's Howard Gardner and two other scholars published a long-term study of journalists in 2001, finding that journalists are "overwhelmed" by the commercial pressures on their craft, and find contemporary journalism a "nightmare." They despair because they are not "allowed to pursue the mission that inspired them to enter the field."[141] The *Columbia Journalism Review* published the results of a survey of TV news directors that concluded that, due overwhelmingly to commercial factors, "pessimism rules in TV newsrooms."[142] Linda Foley, the president of the journalists union, the Newspaper Guild, reports that the number one concern of her members, far more than wages and job security, is the decline of their craft becasue of commercial pressures.[143]

Contemporary U.S. journalism still has its defenders, of course, though they are fewer in ranks and they appear to have less swagger.[144] The defense ultimately falls back upon the position that this is the media system we have, it is the best possible system for our society, so anything it generates has got to be good. And insofar as the news media raise these concerns about the commercialization of journalism before the public—something done very, very rarely—it tends to start and finish with the assumption of the inviolability of the *status quo*, hence handcuffing critical analysis. Increasingly, in academia and on the margins, however, sober voices are beginning to think (and write and speak) what was once unthinkable: Is the corporate, commercial regulation of journalism compatible with a democratic society? Jay Harris, former publisher of the *San Jose Mercury News*, argues that the media are "so essential to our national democracy" that they should not "be managed primarily according to the demands of the market or the dictates of a handful of large shareholders."[145] James Carey of the Columbia Journalism School, arguably the most influential U.S. journalism scholar of the past generation, concluded a 2002 essay on the state of the news with the somber assessment that "the reform of journalism will only occur when news organizations are disengaged from the global entertainment and information industries that increasingly contain them." As Carey added, "Alas the press may have to rely upon a democratic state to create the conditions necessary for a democratic press to flourish and for journalists to be restored to their proper role as orchestrators of the conversation of a democratic culture."[146] The political economic analysis of the media may well be entering its moment in the sun.

But Wait, Don't the Media Have a Liberal Bias?

Absent so far in this discussion of journalism has been an assessment of the proposition that the U.S. news media have a liberal, even left-wing, political bias. The reason I have neglected this argument thus far is that this particular critique is not an institutional or political economic critique; indeed, political-economic analysis highlights the severe shortcomings of this claim. But the claim that the news media have a liberal political bias is so widespread that it has come to play a crucial ideological role in the functioning of the news media system. In 2001 and 2002 no less than *three* books purporting to demonstrate and elaborate upon the media's liberal bias rested high atop the bestseller list.[147] It has become, in effect, the official opposition to the media status quo, and is so regarded by a large number of Americans. Even more important, the right-wing campaign against the "liberal media" has influenced media content, pushing journalists to be less critical of rightwing politics in their never-ending (and never successful) quest to establish their lack of bias against the political right. For these reasons the conservative criticism of the "liberal media" merits our attention.

The very idea of a "liberal" bias in the news media is a very American proposition; in Britain and Canada, for example, there is nothing remotely close to it in magnitude. To some extent that is a measure of just how successfully the notion of professional journalism was ingrained during the twentieth century in the United States, with the organizing principle that democratic journalism should be, could be, and must be politically impartial.[148] Once the notion of professional journalism became dominant, the importance of the views and conduct of working journalists assumed greater importance relative to the broader institutional determinants of journalism. Mainstream media analysis is mostly concerned with commercial and government encroachment on journalistic autonomy, and with journalists receiving proper professional training. The conservative critique is a variant of the mainstream analysis and is concerned with how journalists would abuse their newfound power to distort the news to serve their own political agendas. This, too, was and is considered a violation of the professional code. Such criticism would have been nonsensical prior to the professional era, when journalism explicitly represented the values of the owners, who tended to have the politics of the owning class, to be conservative. The conservative critique is based then on four propositions: (1) the decisive power over the news lies with the journalists, and owners and advertisers are irrelevant or relatively powerless; (2) journalists are political liberals; (3) journalists use their power to advance liberal politics; and (4) objective journalism would almost certainly present the world exactly as seen by contemporary U.S. conservatives. For this argument to hold, the first three conditions must be met. For this argument to hold, and for one to maintain a commitment to professional journalism as it is presently understood, the fourth condition must also be met.

The first point is intellectually indefensible and is enough to call the entire conservative critique of the liberal news media into question. No credible scholarly analysis of journalism posits that journalists have the decisive power to determine what is and is not news and how it should be covered. In commercial media, the owners hire and fire and they determine the budgets and the overarching aims of the enterprise. As Robert Parry puts it, "in reality, most journalists have about as much say over what is presented by newspapers and TV news programs as factory workers and foremen have over what a factory produces."[149] Successful journalists, and certainly those who rise to the top of the profession, tend to internalize the values of those who own and control the enterprise. Sophisticated scholarly analysis examines how these commercial pressures shape what become the professional values that guide journalists.[150] In fact, conservatives tacitly acknowledge the transparently ideological basis of the claim that journalists have all the power over the news. The real problem is not that journalists have all the power over the news, or even most of the power, it is that they have *any* power to be autonomous from owners and advertisers, whom conservatives generally regard as having the proper political worldview, so their influence is not a problem. (Some conservative media critics like Brent Bozell attempt to argue that media corporations have a left-wing political bias, but the evidence used to support these claims is so preposterous most conservatives avoid the topic altogether.)[151] Newt Gingrich, with typical candor and a lack of PR rhetoric, laid bare the logic behind the conservative critique: what needs to be done is to eliminate journalistic autonomy, and return the politics of journalism to the politics of media owners.[152] This also helps to explain why U.S. conservatives tend to be obsessed with pushing public broadcasting to operate by commercial principles; they know that the market will very effectively push the content to more politically acceptable outcomes, without any need for direct censorship.[153]

The second proposition—that journalists are liberals—has the most evidence to support it. Surveys show that journalists tend to vote Democratic in a greater proportion than the general population. In one famous survey of how Washington correspondents voted in the 1992 presidential election, something like 90 percent voted for Bill Clinton. To some conservative critics, that settles the matter. But the first point undermines the importance of how journalists vote, or what their particular political beliefs might be. What if owners and managers have most of the power, both directly and through the internalization of their political and commercial values in the professional code? Surveys show that media owners and editorial executives vote overwhelmingly Republican. An *Editor & Publisher* survey—published November 2—found that in 2000 newspaper publishers favored George W. Bush over Al Gore by a 3-to-1 margin, while newspaper editors and publishers together favored Bush by a 2-to-1 margin. In addition, why should a vote for Al Gore or Bill Clinton be perceived as a reflection of liberal politics? On many or most policies they are moderate to conservative Democrats, very comfortable with the status quo of the U.S. political economy.

What this begs for, then, is an analysis of what, exactly, a liberal is.[154] To listen to the shock troops of conservative media critics, support for Gore or Clinton is virtually indistinguishable from being an anarcho-syndicalist or a Marxist-Leninist. One right-wing pundit echoed this sentiment when he called the editors of the *Philadelphia Inquirer* "die-hard old school socialists."[155] But this is absurd. The actual record of the U.S. news media is to pay very little attention to what might be called the political left, and by this we mean not only socialists and radicals but also what would be called mild social democrats by international standards. What attention the Left actually gets tends to be unsympathetic, if not explicitly negative. Foreign journalists write about how U.S. left-wing social critics who are prominent and respected public figures abroad are virtually non-persons in the U.S. news media.[156] To the extent there is a basis for the claim, conservatives are able to render synonymous Clinton-Democrats and radical leftists because of their main criteria for what a liberal is. It is based upon what are called social issues, such as a commitment to gay rights, women's rights, abortion rights, civil liberties, and affirmative action. And indeed, on these issues a notable percentage of journalists tend to have positions similar to many of those to their left.

The Achilles heel for this conservative critique of journalist liberalism, and therefore entirely absent from their pronouncements, however, is a consideration of journalists' views on issues of the economy and regulation. Here, unlike with social issues, surveys show that journalists hold positions that tend to be more pro-business and conservative than the bulk of the population. Indeed, by looking at questions surrounding class and economic matters, the (suspect) argument that journalists' personal biases and political opinions determine the news would lead in a very different direction than conservative media critics suggest. Over the past two generations, journalism, especially at the larger and more prominent news media, has evolved from being a blue-collar job to becoming a desirable occupation of the well-educated upper-middle class. Urban legend has it that when the news of the stock market crash came over the ticker to the *Boston Globe* newsroom in 1929, the journalists all arose to give Black Monday a standing ovation. The rich were finally getting their comeuppance! When the news of the stock market crash reached the *Globe* newsroom in 1987, in contrast, journalists were all frantically on the telephone to their brokers. As recently as 1971 just over one-half of U.S. newspaper journalists had college degrees; by 2002 nearly 90 percent did. The median salary for a journalist at one of the forty largest-circulation newspapers in the United States in 2002 was nearly double the median income for all U.S. workers.[157] Journalists at the dominant media are unlikely to have any idea what it means to go without health insurance, to be unable to locate affordable housing, to have their children in underfunded and dilapidated schools, to have relatives in prison or the front lines of the military, to face the threat of severe poverty. They live in a very different world from most Americans. They may be "liberal" on certain issues, but on the core issues of political economy, they are hardly to the left of the U.S. population, and they tend to be quite comfortable with the corporate status quo. To the extent their background and values determine the news, it is unlikely to expect journalists to be sympathetic to traditional liberal, not to mention left-wing, policies and regulations.

As for the third proposition, that journalists use their power to advance liberal politics, the evidence is far from convincing. One of the core points of the professional code is to prevent journalists from pushing their own politics into the news, and many journalists are proud to note that though they are liberal, their coverage tends to bend the stick the other way, to prevent the charge that they have a liberal bias and are unprofessional. As one news producer stated, "The main bias of journalists is the bias not to look like they favor liberals."[158] "One of the biggest career threats for journalists," a veteran Washington reporter wrote in 2002, "is to be accused of 'liberal bias' for digging up stories that put conservatives in a bad light."[159] Moreover, research shows that though many journalists may have liberal politics on social issues, few of them are political junkies. Often they are cynical and depoliticized, much like the general public. If they are obsessed with advancing a political agenda, they tend to become columnists or leave the profession, as the professional constraints are too great. At its best, though rarely, the conservative critique has emphasized not the aggressive liberalism of individual reporters—for which there is little evidence—but rather how liberal political values are inscribed into the professional code.[160] This is where the conservative critique has a political-economic basis. Hence any journalist who receives professional training, regardless of personal political inclinations, is trained to adopt liberal politics and regard them as neutral and nonpartisan. But, to the extent this argument holds, this is a liberalism that is fully comfortable with the status quo; it is the left wing of elite opinion; it is not radical. (And as elite opinion has moved to the right, the liberalism of the professional code has diminished.) To the extent professional autonomy collapses so too does the importance of the liberal bias built into the professional code.

As for the final proposition, that truly objective journalism would invariably see the world exactly the way Rush Limbaugh sees it, this points to the ideological nature of the exercise. Despite the attention paid to the news, there has never been an instance of conservatives criticizing journalism for being too soft on a right-wing politician or unfair to liberals or the left. It is a one-way street. Conservatives would respond that this is what all media criticism is about—whining that your side is getting treated unfairly. In 1992 Rich Bond, then the chair of the Republican Party, acknowledged that the point of bashing the liberal media was to "work the refs" like a basketball coach does, with the goal that "maybe the ref will cut you a little slack on the next one."[161] And some journalists come to dismiss examinations of journalistic bias as exercises in opportunism that simply come with the territory. They can say, "Hey, we are being shot at from both sides, so we must be doing it right." The problem with that response is that it absolves the media of actually addressing the specific charges; since they balance each other they can be dismissed categorically. As one wag has pointed out, even the Nazi media had a few fanatical critics who thought it was insufficiently anti-Semitic or anti-Communist, at least in the 1930s.

Since it was therefore getting "shot at from both sides," does that mean the Nazi press was doing it right? Political economy, like all scholarship, attempts to provide a coherent and intellectually consistent explanation of journalism that can withstand critical interrogation. The conservative critique of the liberal news media is an intellectual failure, riddled with contradictions and inaccuracy.

So why is the conservative critique of the liberal news media such a significant force in U.S. political and media culture? To some extent this is because the conservative critique of the liberal media has tremendous emotional power, fitting into a broader story of the conservative masses battling the establishment liberal media elite. In this world, spun by the likes of Ann Coulter and Sean Hannity, conservatives do righteous battle against the alliance of Clinton, Castro, Bin Laden, drug users, gays, rappers, feminists, teachers' unions, vegetarians, and journalists who hold power over the world. As one conservative activist put it, the battle over media is a "David and Goliath struggle."[162] At its strongest, and most credible, the conservative critique taps into the elitism inherent to professionalism and to liberalism, though this populism turns to mush once the issue of class is introduced. Some conservative media criticism backs away from fire breathing, and attempts to present a more tempered critique, even criticizing the rampant commercialization of journalism. Bernard Goldberg's *Bias*, for example, was criticized for its shoddy use of evidence, but aspects of the critique having little to do with the "David versus Goliath" mythology rang true, and made the book credible.[163] As Steve Rendall of the left-liberal media watch group Fairness & Accuracy in Reporting (FAIR) put it, "Big chunks of the book actually point to FAIR's point of view."[164]

The main reason for the prominence of the conservative critique of the liberal news media has little or nothing to do with the intellectual quality of the arguments. It is the result of hardcore political organizing to produce that result. The conservative movement against liberal journalism was launched in earnest in the 1970s. Pro-business foundations were aghast at what they saw as the anti-business sentiment prevalent among Americans, especially middle-class youth, usually a core constituency for support. Mainstream journalism, which in reporting the activities of official sources was giving people like Ralph Nader sympathetic exposure, was seen as a prime culprit. At that point the pro-business "neoliberal" political right began to devote enormous resources to criticizing and changing the news media.[165] Around one-half of all the expenditures of the twelve largest conservative foundations have been devoted to the task of moving the news rightward. This has entailed funding the training of conservative and business journalists at universities, creating conservative media to provide a training ground, establishing conservative think tanks to flood journalism with pro-business official sources, and incessantly jawboning any coverage whatsoever that is critical of conservative interests as being reflective of "liberal" bias.[166] The pro-business Right understood that changing media was a crucial part of bringing right-wing ideas into prominence, and politicians into power. "You get huge leverage for your dollars," a conservative philanthropist noted when he discussed the turn to ideological work.[167] There is a well-organized, well-financed, and active hardcore conservative coterie working to push the news media to the right. As a *Washington Post* White House correspondent put it, "The liberal equivalent of this conservative coterie does not exist."[168]

The success of the right-wing campaign in popularizing the view that the news media have a liberal bias has been accomplished to some extent by constant repetition without any significant countervailing position. Crucial to the promotion of the idea that the news media are liberal have been, ironically enough, the so-called liberal media. One study of press coverage between 1992 and 2002 finds that references to the liberal bias of the news media outnumber those to a conservative bias by a factor of more than 17 to 1.[169] It is trumpeted far and wide by the media, such that the conservative critique is well known to millions of Americans as the *only* dissident criticism of the media. The conservative critique is in some respects the "official opposition" of professional journalism, because in a sense journalists have to be seen as "liberals" for the system to have credibility. Were journalists seen as cravenly bowing before wealth and privilege, it would undermine the credibility of the enterprise as an autonomous democratic force. After all, that is a significant part of what led to the rise of professional journalism in the first place. The conservative criticism is also rather flattering to journalists; it says to them: you have all the power and the problem is you use that power to advance the interests of the poor and minorities (or government bureaucrats and liberal elitists) rather than the interests of corporations and the military (or middle America). A political economic critique, which suggests that journalists have much less power and that they are largely the unwitting pawns of forces that make them the agents of the status quo, is much less flattering and almost nowhere to be found.

Of even greater significance, this right-wing campaign has been successful in actually making the news media more sympathetic to right-wing politicians and pro-corporate policies. The move of journalism to the right has been aided by three other factors. First, the right wing of the Republican Party, typified by Reagan and now Bush, has gained considerable political power while the Democratic Party has become significantly more pro-business in its outlook. This means that editors and journalists following the professional code are simply going to have much greater exposure through official sources to neoliberal and conservative political positions. The body of liberal official sources that existed in the 1960s and 1970s is relatively smaller and far less influential. Second, as we discussed above, the basis for the conservative critique of the liberal media—the autonomy of journalists from owners, the separation of church and state—has diminished over the past twenty years. There is less protection to keep journalists independent, implicitly and explicitly, of the politics of the owners. Yet the conservative critique lives on, as prominent as ever. To the extent it does is an indication of how much the critique is an ideological exercise in harassing the media to provide more pro-neoliberal coverage, rather than a genuine attempt to make sense of how and why journalism is produced the way it is. Third, conservatives move comfortably in the corridors of the corporate media. This is precisely what one would expect. Journalists who praise corporations and commercialism will be held in higher regard (and given more slack) by owners and advertisers than journalists who are routinely critical of them. Much is made of Rupert Murdoch's Fox News Channel, which seemingly operates as an adjunct of the Republican Party, but the point holds across the board.[170] Several progressive radio hosts, for example, have had their programs cancelled although they had satisfactory ratings and commercial success, because the content of their shows did not sit well with the station owners and managers.[171]

In sum, the conservative campaign against the liberal media has meshed comfortably with the commercial and political aspirations of media corporations. The upshot is that by the early years of the twenty-first century the conservatives have won. The *Washington Post*'s E. J. Dionne Jr. termed this a "genuine triumph for conservatives." "The drumbeat of conservative press criticism has been so steady, the establishment press has internalized it."[172] By 2001, CNN's chief Walter Isaacson was soliciting conservatives to see how he could make the network more palatable to them. In their quieter moments conservatives acknowledge the victory, though they will insist that the victory is justified.[173] But the general pattern is that conservative pundits dominate in the commercial news media with the incessant refrain that the media are dominated by liberals. The news media diet of the average American is drawn from a menu tilted heavily to the Right. Talk radio, which plays a prominent role in communities across the nation, "tends to run the gamut from conservative to . . . very conservative," as one reporter puts it.[174] By 2003, a Gallup poll showed that 22 percent of Americans considered talk radio to be their primary source for news, double the figure from 1998.[175] TV news runs from pro-business centrist to rabidly pro-business Right, and most newspaper journalism is no better. All told, the average American cannot help but be exposed to a noticeable double standard that has emerged in the coverage of mainstream politicians and politics.

Looking at the different manner in which the press has portrayed and pursued the political careers of Bill Clinton and George W. Bush reveals the scope of the conservative victory. A Nexis search reveals that there were 13,641 stories about Clinton avoiding the military draft and a mere forty-nine stories about Bush having his powerful father use influence to get him put at the head of the line to get into the National Guard.[176] Bill Clinton's small-time Whitewater affair justified a massive seven-year, $70 million open-ended special investigation of his business and personal life that never established any criminal business activity, but eventually did produce the Lewinsky allegations. Rick Kaplan, former head of CNN, acknowledged that he instructed CNN to provide the Lewinsky story with massive attention, despite his belief that it was overblown, because he knew he would face withering criticism for a liberal bias if he did not do so.[177] George W. Bush, in contrast, had a remarkably dubious business career in which he made a fortune flouting security laws, tapping public funds, and using his father's connections to protect his backside, but the news media barely sniffed at the story and it received no special prosecutor.[178] One doubts the head of CNN goes to sleep at night in fear of being accused of being too soft on Bush's business dealings. Or imagine, for one second, what the response of Rush Limbaugh, the Fox News Channel, talk radio, and soon thereafter the entirety of political journalism, would have been if more than a year after the 9/11 attack a president such as Al Gore had not yet captured Osama bin Laden? The list goes on and on. As Robert Kuttner observed in 2003, "What if there were a failed administration and nobody noticed?"[179] It may help to explain why polls have shown that throughout much of his presidency Bush received fairly high approval ratings from voters, but when queried on specific issues they tend to disagree with him.

The conservative campaign against the liberal media is hardly the dominant factor in understanding news media behavior. It works in combination with the broader limitations of professional journalism as well as the commercial attack upon journalism. Conservative ideology and commercialized, depoliticized journalism have meshed very well, and it is this combination that defines the present moment.

2

A Century of Radical Media Criticism
in the United States

Conventional wisdom about the history of U.S. journalism chronicles the rise of a sanctified forum for democratic deliberation, a catalyst for the revolutionary experiment in self-government. Cultural lore imagines the Founding Fathers ordaining America's newspapers as the truest public servants. A fair and balanced press system then went on to hound politicians, expose corruption, and inform the people down through the generations, perfecting its trade. This narrative has been a staple of our civics classes for generations—and for good reason. It is in the United States, and the United States alone, that press freedom is the centerpiece of the entire political project. It is the shining star of a democratic political economy that we project as central to our global domination.

So sacred is this sublime historical portrait that the bottom-line principle that our free press is the envy of the world is not even subject to critical analysis; it is an article of faith if one believes in the United States, in freedom, in democracy. The hallowed U.S. tradition of a free press was not built in a day, it was enshrined over decades of dutiful service. Contemporary critics are routinely dismissed as disgruntled politicos totally disconnected from mainstream U.S culture and press history.

Of course, the conventional wisdom could hardly be further from the truth. The moral and analytical tradition of critical media scholarship not only exists, it is expansive and damning in its portrait of the cracks in the democratic foundation of the U.S. system of commercial journalism.[1] For over a century, a wide variety of media critics have consistently portrayed the serious antidemocratic tendencies of a commercial system of mass media. The critique dates from the origins of the modern media and lays out a steadily more convincing argument as the decades pass, prognoses are confirmed, and the contradictions of commodified, centralized sources of public information worsen and rot the core of U.S. political culture. Today's most notable radical media critics—such as Bagdikian, Herman, Chomsky, Baker, and myself—are not voices in the wilderness.[2] They are a part of an aggressive critique in U.S. journalism history, and they are arguably the vanguard of a new wave of critical commentary taking place right now in the United States. Far from being renegade scholars, their research has set the standard by which contemporary academic work in the field is judged.

Even defenders of the faith now admit that U.S. journalism is in the midst of a full-blown crisis, and an expanding group of writers are looking for answers. The symptoms of the crisis—a decline in hard news, a lack of investigative and process stories, staff cuts, concentrating ownership structures, closure of independent papers, more advertising, trends toward info-tainment, and bias in the name of balance—have become widely recognized as they continue to fester. Our bookstores and talk shows are awash with media critics from across the political spectrum. The deeper roots of why all this is happening—the near total replacement of public service priorities by commercial imperatives—have begun to appear. At a time when Bill Moyers, William Safire, John McCain, and Jon Stewart are all addressing similar problems in the media, they become increasingly hard to ignore.

Public interest groups have begun to speak out and to organize their members to raise awareness and agitate for reform. For example, Fairness & Accuracy in Reporting, founded in the late 1980s, has become a center of sophisticated media criticism. Consumer and citizen advocacy groups like Consumers Union, Consumers Federation of America, Media Access Project, Center for Digital Democracy, and Common Cause are waging the media battle on Capitol Hill. Moreover, activist groups have been energized across the country to organize and agitate for a better media system—Free Press, Prometheus Radio Project, Media Channel, Reclaim the Media, and Media Tank, just to name a few.

Tellingly, this critical movement also includes many journalists. A 2004 poll of media workers indicated that 83 percent felt that a decline in quality due to commercial pressure was the most serious problem facing the American newsroom.[3] It is a cancer that plagues not only the news and views we see in the paper every morning but the lives of working editors and reporters. The Newspaper Guild has been an ardent critic of the commercial media for many years, giving voice to the dissatisfaction of the rank-and-file reporters. With them stand Leonard Downie Jr. and Robert Kaiser, both senior editors at the *Washington Post*, who offered up a scathing critique of contemporary journalism in their recent book, *The News About the News: American Journalism in Peril*.[4] It chronicles a downward spiral in the industry. Downie and Kaiser's critique is not a shot in the dark. It is the latest broadside in a volley of insider whistle-blowing. It is a story carried in some form nearly every week by progressive opinion magazines such as *The Nation*, *The Progressive*, and *The American Prospect*, as well as trade publications like the *Columbia Journalism Review*.

But there is more, much more; the surge of activity we have witnessed in the last few years is the tip of the iceberg. The richness of this radical critique of the commercial system of news production by scholars, activists, and journalists is not a recent phenomenon at all. The historical record of similar critiques has a depth that is unmatched by any equivalent analytical theme in media history. This is a body of work that stands on a central and recurrent argument—that commercial journalism in the United States has been at best a mixed blessing and at worst a complete failure for democracy. It has taken advantage of its power to advance the specific political and economic agendas of media owners and advertisers while depoliticizing or misinforming the citizenry. It has abdicated its responsibilities to democratic self-government in the pursuit of greater revenues and higher returns for investors. These disastrous trends are, at root, not a function of editors and reporters, who indeed often struggle mightily to resist these forces. Rather, the commercial system in which they operate demands compromises with an anti-public agenda.

These are radical criticisms precisely because they see the source of the problem not in the incompetence or selfish nature of individuals, but rather in the industrial structures and the logic of commerce that make such journalism their necessary product. The core argument defines the structure of a privately controlled, for-profit media system as fundamentally at odds with democratic social goals. Market power is based on the idea of reducing competition, streamlining production, leveraging preexisting advantages, and selling for the maximum price what may be produced for the minimum cost. Free-market governance of the media system tends to produce fewer and fewer voices over time as competition is eliminated to increase profits. Diversity gives way to homogenization as each competitor races to the bottom to find the least costly, most saleable stories. Meanwhile, the few industrial players large enough to survive this kind of competition find themselves ideally situated to lever up their influence to advance a political agenda. The circumstances of oligopoly markets trading in public information and debate naturally lead down the path toward lower quality, less diversity, and hollow integrity in the news. The market is simply a poor mechanism for arbitrating democratic deliberation and comprehensively reporting public affairs.

This radical tradition of U.S. journalism criticism has roots that reach back to the origins of the modern commercial media system in the late nineteenth century, though this is not widely realized or understood. Indeed, it is one of the great problems of contemporary media studies that this recurrent theme in journalism history has been all but forgotten for decades. Only now is it beginning to surface again. The sheer magnitude of the quantity of criticism is astonishing.

But our argument here reaches much further than simply highlighting the existence of a rich tradition of radical press criticism. We also argue that this rich tradition, rather than being a marginal or fringe phenomenon in opposition to the dominant mainstream perspective, can make a legitimate claim to being *the* mainstream tradition of thought about a free press in the United States. Its rival—the celebration of the unwavering integrity of the U.S. commercial media system—is not really a critical tradition so much as a set of assumptions that has migrated into conventional wisdom. But as common as this image has become, we should ask ourselves at what point in modern times this rosy picture has *not* been called into serious question by the conditions of social life in the United States. We should ask ourselves at what point in the last century a large chunk of the American people have not felt themselves badly underrepresented by the press. We should ask ourselves when the gatekeeper of democratic public debate was not legitimately criticized as the arbiter of commercial rather than civic values. The fact is that there has *never* been such a time. The critique has been ever present, assuming ferocious proportions every few decades when systemic abuses reached the critical mass of intolerable corruption.

If there is such a historical wealth of radical press criticism in the United States, how and why has it been ignored to the extent that it is? To no small degree, this reflects the success of the commercial media system; in a concrete sense the system works sufficiently well to satisfy a significant portion of the population. But the public's complacency is not a coincidental by-product. It is imperative for the largest media firms to propagate the notion that the U.S. media system is a "natural" development, and that they are the worthy and appropriate overlords of the press. Control over the media system is a highly sensitive issue, much like control over the economy, and those who benefit from the status quo prefer that it be a topic left unexplored. You might say that economics produces a hollow form of journalism, and that politics sustains it for its own ends. James Carey eloquently summarizes this kind of media system:

> It is a journalism of fact without regard to understanding through which the public is immobilized and demobilized and merely ratifies the judgments of experts delivered from on high. It is, above all, a journalism that justifies itself in the public's name but in which the public plays no role, except as an audience; it is a receptacle to be informed by experts and an excuse for the practice of publicity.[5]

Journalism today has much more in common with the elites it supposedly regulates than with the public on whose behalf it supposedly speaks. In this climate, opposition is difficult to mount. But radical media criticism has never been criticism for criticism's sake. It is a structural critique with the intent of changing the system so there will be better journalism. It ebbs and flows, tending to grow in periods of broad social turmoil, when all the leading institutions are subject to popular interrogation. And it is when there is a sense that the criticism might actually lead to a change in the media system for the better that the quantity and quality of radical media criticism positively blossoms.

The history of modern U.S. press criticism begins at the pivotal moment in the late-nineteenth century when U.S. journalism gradually switched from being primarily a political press system to being a full-fledged commercial press system. As the nineteenth century advanced, the press system began to take on the commercial aspects that would come to dominate it. Newspapers had remained explicitly partisan throughout the middle section of the century. But as production costs declined, capacity rose, and advertising revenues picked up, publishers began to increase in size and circulation. The number of papers available in any given city began a slow and steady drop as ad dollars flowed to the largest players. Debate waned as partisanship was blunted to attract a larger and more diverse readership. Competition began to erode and near-monopoly profits rolled in, sustaining a conglomeration of chain newspaper companies.

In short, commercialism trumped partisanship as the central modus operandi. However, we should think of this not as a substitution but rather as a reversal of priorities. Mass-circulation newspapers were engineered for economic reasons, but the consequences were political, that is, mass media altered the way power operated in society. By industrializing the production of ideas and concentrating the marketplace of their distribution, a small group of elites came into possession of the reins of public discourse and with them the ability to shape the political fortunes of the nation. The relationship between economic gain and political control determined the basic nature of modern journalism and has oscillated around the media system ever since. Over time, these two forces have begun to blend together, gaining momentum and power through the decades with the advance of technology and the further consolidation of the marketplace.

Just as they are today, the political and economic interests of elites were naturally conservative and deeply intertwined. Publishers depended on retailers to advertise; retailers depended on manufacturers to produce; and everyone depended on the financiers to float the upper echelon of economic development. The politicians often came from these ranks and served this class with quite explicit design. They presided over the status quo and had no intention of allowing that favorable situation to change. Newspapers became a powerful device for social control and public manipulation.

During the Progressive Era, these conditions provoked a bitter backlash. These were the first modern press critics. Their circumstances, their arguments, and their fury are so similar to today's debate over the mass media that we could literally interchange the words of early twentieth-century and early twenty-first century critiques. This is not history repeating itself. This is a systemic social problem that has gotten progressively worse over time. This history prefigures both our contemporary crisis and the voices calling for change.

Critics, using the fierce language of class conflict, argued that most large newspapers were conservative and carried the biases of wealth and privilege. The press was outspoken against all forms of transformative social change. By and large, publishers opposed labor, civil rights, social democracy, and any effort to redistribute wealth to help the disadvantaged. In political coverage, mainstream parties received reasonable treatment, but radical ideas were shunned and excoriated. The parameters of political debate acceptable to owners were the limits within which journalists could write. There were, of course, exceptions—notable among them were the famous muckrakers. However, these crusading journalists were more radical in critique than they were in solution. The handful of muckrakers who did harbor revolutionary fervor, notably Upton Sinclair and Charles Edward Russell, were quickly banished from the mainstream media shortly after their most famous works were published. The quality reporting of Tarbell, Steffens, and Baker were the exceptions to the general rules of big-business journalism in the Progressive Era.

The other economic consequence of big-business publishing in the Progressive Era was yellow journalism. Sensationalism was the hallmark of the low-price metro dailies. Then as now, disaster, crime, sex, scandal, and celebrity sold well. Higher circulation meant higher ad rates and higher profits. More and more papers joined the tabloid game, and it became a race to the bottom as each tried to outdo the other to grab more readers. Fabrication and the exclusion of serious news to make room for scandal became routine. This pattern was profitable, but it was also politically useful. The more distracted and out of touch the polity became with the core concerns of governance, the less likely it became that they would attentively and aggressively oppose the policies of the elites. Sensationalism thus combined with suppression, omission, and thinly veiled political advocacy to produce a commercial media system with a strong conservative political bias that also effectively depoliticized the citizenry. This was the first great crisis of commercial journalism. Yet the power of the press lords appeared overwhelming. Will Irwin, writing in 1911, commented: "The American press has more influence than it ever had in any other time, in any other country. No other extra-judicial form, except religion, is half so powerful."[6]

The social spectrum, dissident books, and articles spoke of a "crisis in journalism." Conservatives shunned what they considered the immorality propagated by tabloid newspapers and the dilution of proper social norms through exposure to indecent publications. Progressives exposed the economic connections between the business community, the publishers, and corrupt politicians. Journalists denounced the dominance of the profit motive and conservative politics over editorial integrity. Academics like sociologist Edward Ross pointed out the deep contradictions between commercialism and democracy in the press. Upton Sinclair, in his 1920 retrospective on press criticism in the Progressive Era, *The Brass Check,* covered all of these issues and called for a total transformation of the commercial system. It was common knowledge that the press was anti-labor, anti-reform, and pro-business. Sinclair commented: "One could take a map of America and a paint-brush, and make large smudges of color, representing journalistic ownership of whole districts, sometimes of whole states, by special interests."[7] Public trust in the free press receded to a state of outright skepticism of almost anything written in the newspapers.

The savviest publishers realized that journalism needed to have the trappings of neutrality and balance in order to regain its sullied credibility. The idea born to quell this crisis was professionalism, a means to bring a degree of objectivity to the news columns. Journalists should be professionals, autonomous from the business office and the politics of owners. They should be trusted by the public to faithfully serve the goals of truth and fairness. These were the new codes of the newsroom. It was a dramatic departure from the rules of nineteenth-century partisan journalism and a concession to the critics of twentieth-century commercial journalism. All of the nation's major schools of journalism were consequently founded in the Progressive Era. With the formal declaration that a wall stood between the interests of the publisher (both commercial and political) and the integrity of the news columns, the press hoped to reenter the public's good graces.

It was a false compromise from the beginning. Sinclair was particularly derisive of the veil of professionalism dropped over business as usual. He explained that "professional" journalists must always be ready to adapt their opinions to the "pocket-book of a new owner."[8] Another well-known journalist, John Swinton, concluded: "Our talents, our possibilities and our lives are all the property of other men. We are intellectual prostitutes."[9] For any working journalist, the idea that the newsroom, notorious for poor working conditions and scandal-mongering, would suddenly become an institution of responsibility and esteem, stretched the imagination. Nonetheless, the idea of professionalism had serious staying power.

Professionalism, the residual filters of wartime propaganda, and relative economic prosperity all came together in the 1920s to close down the most strident press criticism of the Progressive Era. The decade saw a reconfiguration of the news media system in which professionalism began to take root in a new distribution of papers that opted either for muted sensationalism or sophisticated reporting targeted to elite readers.

Meanwhile, the life of the "professional" reporter turned out not to carry the standard of living promised by a higher class of occupation. Even as publishers earned higher and higher profits, journalists were held in the role of low-paid public servants. The ethos of the reporter as watchdog, whistle-blower, and representative of the public blended with an ascetic obligation to work long hours for relatively low wages. These conditions were paradoxically treated at the institutional level as badges of honor. In most cases, the unionized print shop men earned more than the "white-collar" editorial employees. Despite the similarities with the working class in terms of standard of living, the publishers encouraged reporters to hold themselves up as though they stood beside lawyers and doctors in the social hierarchy. This disparity between title and working conditions put enormous pressure on the fragile compromise of professionalism. How autonomous were newsrooms laboring under tyrannical working conditions?

Consequently, the main challenge to the practice of commercial journalism in the 1930s came from within the profession. The early years of the Depression saw the life of the journalist change from bad to worse. Many reporters were laid off. Almost everyone who remained on the job endured a substantial pay cut, often down to the threshold of subsistence wages. Reporting on the New Deal and national recovery took on a far more visceral importance to journalists. In the 1920s, they could look at politically motivated editorial decisions and stories forced on them by the business office with an attitude of nose-holding cynicism. They were seldom personally affected. In the 1930s, the destructive attacks orchestrated in the majority of daily newspapers across the country on the Roosevelt administration and the labor movement struck a sharply antagonistic chord.

Meanwhile, another great crisis in public confidence shook the newspaper business. William Allen White, renowned liberal editor of the *Emporia Gazette*, addressed the issue of crisis in his presidential address to the American Society of Newspaper Editors. He began by praising the U.S. press as an institution with high standards, great integrity, and laudable public service accomplishments. Then he proceeded to the real issue at hand: "Yet we must not ignore the bald fact that in the last decade a considerable section of the American press, and in particular the American daily newspaper press, has been the object of bitter criticism in a wide section of American public opinion."[10] A liberal government was openly at odds with a conservative press. Many journalists on the inside told tales of suppression, distortion, intentional misrepresentation, and the intimidation of any reporter who felt inclined to challenge these editorial policies. Desperate to hold their jobs, they did not resist.

The turmoil of the 1930s brought the publishers' abuses of the free press as a commercial vehicle and a narrow ideological platform under uncomfortable scrutiny. Many looked at the disparity of the 1932 and 1936 elections— near overwhelming rejection of FDR by the press and yet resounding victories at the polls—as a sure sign that the public's right to a free press had been badly neglected. Given the awakening class politics of the moment, the underprivileged sectors of the public took little time to notice that they were the ones underreported, misrepresented, and ardently opposed by their erstwhile First Amendment trustees. How could the lion's share of the public's press be anti-labor, anti-New Deal, and anti-FDR in direct contradiction to the vast majority of Americans?

Among the most vocal critics were famous journalists such as Ferdinand Lundberg, George Seldes, and Oswald Garrison Villard. These were joined by the preeminent journalism scholar of his day, A. M. Lee, and FDR's secretary of the interior, Harold Ickes. Systemic critique coming from inside the industry arguing on behalf of the people might well have had the power to overturn the system for the better. It was undeniably a mainstream critique in ways it had never been before and has never been since. FDR himself got into the act in a letter to Joseph Pulitzer Jr.: "I have always been firmly persuaded," he wrote, "that our newspapers cannot be edited in the interests of the general public, from the counting room."[11]

In 1933, a group of journalists took an unexpected and unprecedented leap into the fray by founding the American Newspaper Guild. In the early years, when the stakes were highest and the odds were longest, the leaders of the Guild, notably syndicated columnist Heywood Broun, quickly saw that the first steps for the fledgling union had to be big ones. The Cleveland branch released this telling statement in late August of 1933:

> Squeezed between the pressures of advertisers and stockholders, between exorbitant tolls of syndicates and press services, and the unionized requirements of the mechanical trades, newspaper editorial employees have from the industry's infancy been the most notoriously exploited of all producer groups in this country which require similar standards of intelligence, skill and industry. . . . It is now time that local room staffs start living and working for something more than the byline and a pat-on-the-back.[12]

Broun and his fellow Guildsmen denounced the compromise of professionalism as bankrupt and put forward the union as a solution promising true autonomy and public service. The need for the Guild and the resistance it met were represented as evidence that the free press was in tatters. In 1935, reporter Isabelle Keating reflected that journalists were coming around to the truth that "the romantic legend of the newspaper reporter's freedom is smashed now, smashed to bits. The truth is that this freedom has been a sham, a patent fraud for years. Only recently has the reporter awakened to the truth, and the American Newspaper Guild, the newswriters' union, is evidence of the fact."[13] By June 1941, the Guild had over 17,000 members, 100 contracts covering 127 daily and Sunday newspapers, and ten contracts with wire services. The Guild represented 48 percent of eligible journalists nationwide, with branches in over 80 percent of large metropolitan areas.[14] The newsmen were at the forefront of the social movement of industrial unionization. They were the men and women who saw that it was their labor that marked the nexus of democratic public debate and political-economic power.

This crucial revolt of journalists, unique to the 1930s, shook up the very idea of journalism for the last time in the twentieth century. Much like in the Progressive Era, ideology and war intervened to abruptly halt this rapidly

changing social reality in the United States. An anti-Communist purge left
the unions weakened, and the propaganda effort of the Second World War
infected every arena of public media. The war changed everything. Fierce
structural press criticism retreated into a tamer call for industry self-regulation as the only viable solution to media flaws.

Perhaps no document better captures the emerging pattern of strong critiques with weak solutions than the Hutchins Commission report on the
freedom of the press. In some of the most straightforward and intellectually
sophisticated analysis of the press system ever performed, a handful of the
leading intellectuals in the country laid out an honest portrayal of the problems with the U.S press. But the solutions they offered were ineffectual and
largely dependent upon the good faith of publishers, as if simply identifying
the problems would be enough to reverse them. In many ways, the blueprint
of quality journalism, its difficulties and its possibilities, served as a reinvig-
oration of professionalism—a new code of ethics for journalists. The norms
of objectivity, neutrality, and balance had taken a beating in the 1930s and
been knocked loose from the foundations laid at the close of the Progressive
Era. The late 1940s set them back in place with a degree of solemnity that
masked the toothless reform of the policy prescriptions.

The new ethos of professionalism papered over serious structural degradation in the media system. Between 1909 and 1940, the proportion of
newspapers to population in the United States declined by half. The number
of one-paper towns tripled. By 1940, fourteen publishers controlled a third
of all national newspaper circulation. Between 1930 and 1944, the industry
experienced a net loss of two hundred papers, leaving 40 percent of national
circulation in non-competitive markets.[15] Morris Ernst, legal counsel for the
Newspaper Guild in the 1930s, reflected in 1945:

> The pipelines of thought to the minds of the nation are being contracted and
> squeezed. About thirty men realistically dominate the conduits of thought
> through the ether, the printing presses, and the silver screen. Without wide
> diversity of thought, freedom of speech and press become idle bits of a worn-
> out shibboleth. The cartelization of the mind of America is well on the way.[16]

Nonetheless, the elevated critique of commercial journalism sunk out of
the mainstream. The generations that followed the war experienced the

"American century," an era of unprecedented economic growth and global dominance. These decades are often seen as the high watermark for professional journalism in the United States. The Watergate scandal, where the *Washington Post* launched a wave of reporting that led to the resignation of President Richard Nixon, is the capstone of this era. But we should not exaggerate the independence of the journalism, nor its quality. Commercial pressures still existed. And with its reliance on official sources as the basis for news stories, journalism had a very establishment cast. This was painfully apparent during the Vietnam War, when the news media parroted the range of official debate in Washington for years, despite substantial evidence that they were being fed lies and half-truths.

The postwar generation provided some of the most insightful press criticism of the century. This was the era of C. Wright Mills, I. F. Stone, A J. Liebling, and a young Ben Bagdikian. It was also the era of press reviews, publications formed by journalists to review the mainstream press out of their concern that the journalism being produced was deeply flawed. The same problems evident in the first half-century still infected the media system. However, the strength of the embrace that patriotism and nationalism held the image of U.S. journalism made it that much more difficult to believe that the emperor wore no clothes.

The third great wave of radical press criticism began haltingly in the late 1970s, blossomed during the 1980s, and exploded by the end of the 1990s. In the ashes of the New Left's defeat, many activists began to look for explanations for why they could not generate more popular support for their politics, and, more broadly, why so many people were misinformed and depoliticized. For some feminists, antiwar activists, and progressives, any viable answer had to address the media system and the role it played in American life. Todd Gitlin's *The Whole World Is Watching* is the classic work in this genre.[17] Through the Reagan era, people began to recognize the explicit frames that guided news coverage, the power of the establishment to control facts and marginalize dissent, and the filters of propaganda through which news traveled before consumption by the polity. Citizens needed to learn how to "decode" the news media and understand the structural basis for its flaws, if for nothing more than intellectual self-defense. Much of the work of Edward S. Herman and Noam Chomsky, including their 1988 masterpiece, *Manufacturing Consent: The Political Economy of the News Media*, articulates this reality.

In perhaps the most striking development of the last generation, the media industries themselves underwent significant structural transformation. On the one hand, within each sector—for example, newspapers, magazines, book publishers, cable TV companies, music companies—there was a wave of consolidation leaving fewer and fewer massive firms with more and more market share. Despite the explosion in the raw numbers of media channels, the degree of ownership concentration had never been higher. Such consolidated markets made it all but impossible for start-up firms to have a chance to compete successfully. This is why independent production has more or less ceased to exist in mainstream media outlets. Ben Bagdikian, in the six editions of *The Media Monopoly* (first published in 1983, with the latest updated version appearing in 2004 as *The New Media Monopoly*), has chronicled this crisis.

Throughout the 1990s, journalists from across the media system started speaking out against the corporate control of the press and the failure of quality public interest reporting to survive the pressure of the bottom line. Paradoxically, as the media giants proceed to launch new media channels in print, broadcast media, and on the Internet, the diversity of viewpoints available for public attention seems to decline. Multiplicity has been confused with diversity in the digital age, and critics are beginning to realize the colossal implications of this mistake. Fewer companies and fewer journalists are covering fewer stories with fewer resources. Reporters are stretched thin and increasingly rely on the shortest path to an "objective" story, regurgitating official press releases from both sides of any given issue—thus producing "balance" but not always truth or even analysis.[18] The same stories are then distributed over an ever-expanding number of media channels. It is a dream scenario for the business office. It is a nightmare for journalists and the reading public.

It is small wonder that the critique of the system is broadening. But these developments alone are insufficient to characterize this era as a great moment in radical media criticism. For such a moment truly to exist, there has to be a sense that the criticism can lead to a structural change in the system, to political activity. The politicization of media issues in the United States may well have crystallized in 2003 with the massive and unprecedented public campaign to overturn the Federal Communication Commission's relaxation of media ownership rules. Long considered a regulatory agency "captured" by the industries it regulated, the Commission reckoned on the standard amount of public participation—that is to say none—when it undertook to remove limits on concentrated media ownership.

The Commission was met with an incredible backlash from the public, the Congress, and eventually the courts, which overturned a ruling in June of 2004—not least because of the climate of public opinion. We will not go into detail on the background and nature of the 2003 fight over the FCC's relaxation of the media ownership rules, given that I covered this information in "The Problem with the Media."[19] The critical fact here is public participation. Over 2 million Americans registered their opposition to relaxing media ownership rules during 2003. They caught the FCC and Congress entirely by surprise. Members of Congress said the issue received more public feedback than any other issue they faced except for the war on Iraq. Organizations ranging from Common Cause to the National Rifle Association stated that this issue struck a chord with their membership like few others. Poll after poll showed that the vast majority of Americans opposed what the FCC did, and that the more people knew about the issue, the more they opposed relaxing media-ownership rules.

For the first time in generations, radical press criticism of commercial media was connecting with political activism and resonating in the broader political culture. FCC Commissioner Michael J. Copps wrote in his dissenting opinion to the FCC's deregulatory ruling that the debate over media ownership in 2003 had awoken a "sleeping giant" in the U.S. public. The demand for a better, more diverse, more representative media system resonated across the political spectrum. Copps concluded profoundly: "The media concentration debate will never be the same. This Commission faces a far more informed and involved citizenry. The obscurity of this issue that many have relied upon in the past, where only a few dozen inside-the-Beltway lobbyists understood this issue, is gone forever."[20] It remains to be seen whether this will be the foundation of a much more broad and sustained movement for media reform or whether it was a one-shot deal, but by any account, what happened in 2003 was extraordinary.

To conclude, the rediscovery of radical media critics in the United States is important for today's debates precisely because of its absence from historical understanding. In broad terms, the existence of a widespread rejection of commercial journalism at its inception and throughout its development shifts the burden of proof in contemporary debates. The status quo can no longer stand on the assumption of immaculate conception and a birthright of established authority. Not only was the merger of commerce and the democratic public sphere challenged at the turn of the century, it was flatly opposed. The arguments of the opposition have persisted, strengthened, and been proven accurate decade after decade. Seen in this light, the debate over the legitimacy of the commercial press demands an equal obligation from critics and proponents alike to make a persuasive case for historical validity. Rhetorically, it is no longer a criticism of a heretofore unchallenged system entrenched in the foundation of liberal democracy, but rather the most recent manifestation of a longstanding, ongoing debate about what that foundation was and should be. Studying the structural press criticism across numerous eras amounts to locating the indisputable common denominators of the current crisis. It is a tool for greater understanding, stronger critique, and a robust movement for that elusive goal: change.

3

Upton Sinclair and the Contradictions of Capitalist Journalism

Beginning in the 1980s, there was a significant increase in awareness of the deep flaws of mainstream journalism among those on the U.S. Left. Writers such as Todd Gitlin, Herbert Schiller, Gaye Tuchman, Ben Bagdikian, and Michael Parenti, each in his or her own way, drew attention to the incompatibility between a corporate-run news media and an ostensibly democratic society. The work of Edward S. Herman and Noam Chomsky, in particular, introduced an entire generation of progressives to a critical position regarding mainstream journalism. As the title of their masterful *Manufacturing Consent* indicated, the capitalist news media are far more about generating support for elite policies than they are about empowering people to make informed political decisions.

What is not so well known across the Left, not to mention elsewhere, is that this radical criticism of the limitations of a capitalist-sponsored journalism is not a recent phenomenon. It dates back to the birth of both modern monopoly capitalism and modern commercial media, roughly one hundred years ago. Radical criticism of the press was an integral component of the many large social movements of the Progressive Era, which sought to resist the effects of accelerating capitalist development. It was a time of striking similarity to the present, mirroring in particular the corruption of democracy by political and economic elites whose control over the media strangles

public awareness, debate, and activism. However, unlike today, radical criticism of capitalist journalism was a dominant theme on the Left during the
Progressive Era, particularly in the socialist, anarchist, and progressive press.
This was the Golden Age of radical press criticism, and Upton Sinclair was
at its epicenter.

Upton Sinclair is best remembered for his novel *The Jungle*, the 1906
muckraking exposé of labor and sanitary conditions in the Chicago stockyards. The book catapulted the then-twenty-seven-year-old author into
international prominence, and Sinclair remained a highly acclaimed and
widely read author until his death in 1968. What has been forgotten is that
although he wrote ninety-two books and twenty-nine pamphlets, for much of
Sinclair's career he was known as a "two-book author." The other book,
besides *The Jungle*, was *The Brass Check*, which he published himself in
1919. In *The Brass Check*, Sinclair made a systematic and damning critique
of the severe limitations of the "free press" in the United States. "The thesis
of this book," he wrote, is "that American Journalism is a class institution
serving the rich and spurning the poor."[1] If *The Jungle* was notorious for its
aggressive assaults on capitalist industry, *The Brass Check* pulled even fewer
punches. The title is a reference to the chit issued to patrons of urban broth-
els at the time. Sinclair drew an analogy between journalists and prostitutes,
both beholden to the agenda, ideology, and policies of the monied elites that
owned and controlled the press. It was an integral part of his broader critique
of the corruption of U.S. politics and the appalling nature of capitalism:
"Politics, Journalism, and Big Business work hand in hand for the hood-
winking of the public and the plundering of labor."[2]

With the ostensible voice of the public in the hands of the editors and
news writers of the capitalist press, Sinclair saw that he and the movements
for social justice could never expect a fair deal. The very public opinion the
socialists sought to mobilize against the social order was wielded not by the
democratic polity but by the elites who ruled them. So long as this situation
continued, there could be no justice. The press was the key to every political
issue in isolation and essential to the success of the larger movement as a
whole. By the time Sinclair sat down in 1919 to write *The Brass Check*, he
did so knowing that this book was of far greater significance than any he had
written before. In the text of the book itself, he called it "the most important
and most dangerous book I have ever written."[3]

Yet though *The Jungle* remains a staple of American literature, *The Brass Check* has been all but forgotten. This is the case despite its groundbreaking critique of the structural basis of U.S. journalism, arguably the first such systematic critique ever made. Anticipating much of the best in more recent structural media criticism, Sinclair explained the class bias built into journalism in a four-part systemic model emphasizing the importance of owners, advertisers, public relations, and the web of economic interests tied into the media system and invested in its control of public opinion. Integrating the critique of the press into the larger history of Progressive Era activism, Sinclair pointed to the centrality of the media in all of the problems of social injustice which attended the rise of modern capitalism.

Yet, those historians who bother to mention *The Brass Check* dismiss it as ephemeral, explaining that the problems it depicts have been solved. As John Ahouse, Sinclair's bibliographer put it, the criticism made by Sinclair in "*The Brass Check* played an important part by provoking and broadening a debate that eventually led to greater objectivity in the American press."[4] Sinclair, the curmudgeonly muckraker, helped clean up the newsrooms much like he helped clean up the stockyards. We can all move on to some other more pressing social issue.

Many of the concerns Sinclair had about commercial journalism did not disappear with the rise of professionalism and "objectivity"—a development he witnessed and regarded with disdain as a sham solution. Moreover, as commercial pressures on the integrity of U.S. journalism have intensified over the past two decades, much of Sinclair's critique now appears startlingly accurate. What then explains the erasure of *The Brass Check*, not to mention the entire radical tradition it crystallizes, from public consciousness, or even from the reading lists of contemporary media scholars, both mainstream and critical?

In our view, the explanation is that in this book Sinclair analyzes a central and powerful institution in the United States—the commercial press—and offers an unambiguously radical critique. The fact that attacking the press system was considerably more sensitive, difficult, and controversial than criticizing meatpackers or robber barons was quickly and immediately apparent to Sinclair.

From the outset, *The Brass Check* faced an opposition unlike any other book he published. For starters, each of the first two hundred pages contained the potential for a libel suit. He could not even find a commercial book publisher willing to tackle the project, so he self-published the book, something he did on only a few other occasions in his career. And the book was hardly lacking in commercial promise. Sinclair organized ten printings of *The Brass Check* in its first decade and sold over 150,000 copies. He did not even copyright the book, hoping to maximize his readership, but also knowing that no one was likely to reprint it and join him in the hot seat. Indeed, at one point, he had difficulties securing sufficient paper from recalcitrant vendors to reprint the book.[5]

Nor did the hostility of the established media powers end there. Most newspapers refused to review the book, and those few that did were almost always unsympathetic. Many newspapers, like the *New York Times*, even refused to run paid advertisements for the book. Critics loosely charged that Sinclair had been sloppy with his facts in *The Brass Check*, and the book did not stand up to close scrutiny. Sinclair, a fanatic for factual accuracy, directly challenged any of those he criticized in *The Brass Check* to sue him for criminal libel—often in the footnotes of later editions of the book—if they could prove a single word in the text was false. No suits were ever forthcoming. Indeed, in 1921, the Associated Press announced it was appointing a commission to review, collect evidence, and denounce the charges Sinclair made about the AP in *The Brass Check*. The project was quietly abandoned without any report, formal or informal, being issued.[6]

In our view it was this smear campaign, more than anything else, which led to the virtual disappearance of *The Brass Check* by the middle of the century. Sinclair was effectively powerless to reply in the mainstream media, so unanswered charges and innuendos assumed the aura of truth. Sinclair moved on to other pressing matters. His media criticism was always part of a broader commitment to social justice, and in the 1920s and 1930s there were numerous causes to engage his attention.

That it was Upton Sinclair who spearheaded the attack on the capitalist press was no small matter. During much of the first two-thirds of the twentieth century, Sinclair was a public figure of the highest magnitude, something of no small accomplishment for an avowed socialist. H. L. Mencken asserted that Sinclair was, "by far" the most widely translated American author abroad. In 1941, George Bernard Shaw told Sinclair, "When people ask me what has happened in my lifetime, I do not refer them to the newspaper files or to the authorities, but to your novels." As Greg Mitchell puts it, "No American writer converted more young people to socialism."[7]

But he was also much more than a writer. Sinclair was directly involved in social experiments like group-living cooperatives, and he had a keen interest in health food. Most important, he ran for public office on several occasions, usually as a socialist. He was never effectively a party politician tied to specific ideologues or doctrines—but he was never far from the action. His greatest success came in 1934 when he ran as the Democratic candidate for governor of California on his End Poverty in California (EPIC) platform. In the words of the *New York Times*, it was "the first serious movement against the profit system in the United States." As Greg Mitchell has brilliantly chronicled, Sinclair was defeated after an extraordinary war of sophisticated propaganda conducted by the state's wealthy elite, including the leading Hollywood moguls and the news media.[8] The brass check, indeed!

As talented as Sinclair was, and as remarkable as his career was, he is best understood not as some exceptional genius, but rather as representative of broad developments in the United States in the first half of the twentieth century. This was especially true of the media criticism Sinclair provided in *The Brass Check*. The crisis of the press Sinclair wrote about was commonly discussed all across American society during the Progressive Era. The basis for the crisis was fairly clear. Traditionally, newspapers in the United States had been highly partisan. The views represented in the pages were those of the owner; the editor and publisher were indeed one. A major city might have ten to twenty daily newspapers, or more, each representing a distinct political viewpoint. No single paper dominated the market, and if someone was dissatisfied with the existing range of viewpoints, it was not impossible to launch a new newspaper. The market was relatively competitive.

All of that changed by the end of the nineteenth century as newspaper markets became vastly less competitive. The largest newspaper magnates—Pulitzer, Hearst, Scripps—had constructed "chains" of newspapers across the country that often accounted for one of the two newspapers in a given market if it did not hold an outright monopoly. Moreover, what economists call "barriers to entry" made it much more difficult for new entrepreneurs to found competitors. Advertising became the largest source of revenues; it rose from relative insignificance in the mid-nineteenth century to accounting for some two-thirds of newspaper income by the beginning of the twentieth century. This greatly enhanced the concentration process. Advertisers tended to flock to the paper or papers that offered the most readers at the lowest "cost per thousand." This tended to drive marginal papers out of business, strengthening the monopolies of wealthy owners or chains in all but the largest cities. Despite the immense profitability of daily newspapers in the United States throughout the twentieth century, no more than a few upstart newspapers have successfully entered established markets since 1920. This is a classic indicator of monopoly, or, at least, oligopoly. Newspaper publishing was a big business.

This concentration in newspaper markets, along with the rise of advertising, was the foundation for the crisis of journalism in the Progressive Era. It was one thing to have stridently partisan journalism when there were numerous papers in a community offering a range of viewpoints, and it was not that difficult to launch a new one. It was quite another matter to have stridently partisan journalism when there were only one or two newspapers, and they clearly represented the politics of their owners, which were usually decidedly conservative. Journalism in such a context has the scent not unlike that of official propaganda in an authoritarian society where there are formal restrictions on press freedom. This was the context that Sinclair was addressing.

Conventional accounts of the crisis of journalism in the Progressive Era, including the most frequently cited history by Frank Luther Mott and the most thorough study by Marion Marzolf, have tended to emphasize the increase in sensational fare—or what was termed "yellow journalism"—as profit-hungry publishers published whatever was necessary to attract the mass readership that would win over advertisers.[9] The hallowed obligation of the democratic press to accurately report public affairs was brushed aside by a wave of new gimmicky features, trumpeting the lies of elite interests who used their papers to manipulate national politics. Progressives encamped with Senator Robert La Follette of Wisconsin frequently flayed the commercial press in the pages of *La Follette's Magazine*, warning of the perversion of democratic processes through the manufacture of public opinion.

Universities organized conferences to address the problems of degraded public information, manipulation of prejudice, and the agenda setting by the web of vested interests behind the commercial press system. Editors and journalists within the system expressed their own concerns, advocating the endowment of a noncommercial press, the creation of fairness and accuracy bureaus, and the restriction of advertising revenues. Between 1900 and 1920, hundreds upon hundreds of critical articles were printed in the popular press, from socialist newspapers to mass circulation magazines.

At the root of this almost universal opposition were some very simple concerns. "If the country is governed by public opinion, and public opinion is largely governed by the newspapers," Harvard professor Hugo Munsterberg wrote in 1911, "is it not essential to understand who governs the newspapers?" The power of the press was axiomatic. "The American press has more influence than it ever had in any other time, in any other country," Will Irwin wrote in 1911. "No other extrajudicial form except religion, is half so powerful." Charles Edward Russell expressed the sentiments of many, when he wrote in *La Follette's* in 1910, "If the people of the entire United States could be informed every day of exactly what happens at Washington and the reason for it, the peculiar stranglehold that the corporations have upon national legislation would last no longer than the next election."[10]

If the conventional accounts saw the problem with journalism as commercialism out of control, with everyone the loser, the radical press critics saw it in stark class terms. "A subservient press and a free government cannot abide under the same roof," Max Sherover wrote in a socialist political pamphlet. And the subservience was to big business. Liberal editor Hamilton Holt, though a far cry politically from socialism, quoted a journalist off the record to make a very similar point: "The business of a New York journalist is to distort the truth, to lie outright, to pervert, to vilify, to fawn at the foot of Mammon, and to sell his country and his race for his daily bread. We are the tools and vassals of rich men behind the scenes." La Follette was a constant critic of the press system. In a speech to a convention of magazine publishers in Philadelphia, in February 1912, he warned of the dangerous forces at work in the press: "The control comes through the community of interests, that interdependence of investments and credits which ties the publishers up to the banks, the advertisers, the special interests."[11]

Although the radical criticism was laced with anger at editors and reporters who failed to tell the truth, this was never a conspiracy theory. The premise was never that the problem was bad people; to the contrary, the problem was that it was a bad system that forced good and bad people to do bad things. The central logic of capitalist news production corrupted its democratic purpose to the very core. "It cannot be denied," one socialist wrote, "that the financing of large-scale newspapers and magazine enterprises depends, with but few exceptions, on the good will of the business community. And this goodwill cannot be had without serving the interest of the business community." One editor of the *Boston Common* argued: "It is not accident nor the special depravity of publishers but the cold logic of commercial necessity which brings into being the fact that in most of the great battles against special privilege the big newspapers are found openly or stealthily lined up on the side of privilege." Industry proposals for internal reform smacked of futility. Professor Edward Ross of the University of Wisconsin advocated the notion of an endowed press with these sentiments: "To urge the editor, under the thumb of the advertiser or of the owner, to be more independent, is to invite him to remove himself from his profession. As for the capitalist-owner, to exhort him to run his newspaper in the interest of truth and progress is about as reasonable as to exhort the mill-owner to work his property for the public good instead of for his private benefit."[12]

In this radical press criticism, advertising was regarded as a particularly negative force and the primary instrument of corruption. "When the news-columns and editorial page are a mere incident in the profitable sale of mercantile publicity, it is strictly 'businesslike' to let the big advertisers censor both," Professor Ross wrote in 1910. La Follette termed advertising "a subtle new peril," and he informed journalists that it would "in time seek to gag you." "It is the big advertiser," William Salisbury, a prominent journalist, concluded, "who is the gold-sceptered king of American journalism—the king who can do no wrong."[13]

Sinclair, too, more than any previous press critic, zeroed in on advertising and its ignominious implications for a free press. "Everywhere in the world of Journalism, high and low, you see this power of the advertiser," he writes. "This system of publicity in return for advertising is a fundamentally dishonest one, but it is inseparable from the business of publishing news for profit, and the legitimate and the illegitimate shade into one another so gradually that it would be hard for an honest editor to know where to draw the line."[14] Moreover, to Sinclair, the political biases of advertisers made it vastly more difficult for socialist pro-labor publications to survive in the marketplace. "For some strange reason," he noted of a magazine that generated a large circulation but still could not generate enough revenue to break even, "the packers of hams and bacon, the manufacturers of automobiles and ready-made clothing, of toilet perfumeries and fancy cigarettes, would not pay money to a Socialist magazine!"[15]

Sinclair's genius in *The Brass Check* is, in part, to sift through much of this entire body of criticism and distill it into a coherent monograph. Combined with his own extensive experience as a journalist and political activist, it makes for a heady brew. There is, for example, the rudimentary basis of a sophisticated critique of the use of propaganda by powerful forces to subvert democracy: "Journalism is one of the devices whereby industrial autocracy keeps its control over political democracy; it is the day-by-day, between-elections propaganda, whereby the minds of the people are kept in a state of acquiescence, so that when the crisis of an election comes, they go to the polls and cast their ballots for either one of the two parties of their exploiters."[16] "You will miss the point of this book," Sinclair writes later, "if you fail to get clear the perversion of news and the betrayal of public opinion is no haphazard and accidental thing; for twenty-five years . . . it has been a thing deliberately planned and systematically carried out, a science and a technique. High-priced experts devote their lives to it, they sit in counsel with the masters of industry, and report on the public minds, and determine precisely how this shall be presented, and how this shall be suppressed."[17]

The scope of the opposition is testament to the depth of the crisis in the press. The Progressive Era was awash in progressive, independent media. Members and supporters of the Socialist Party alone published some 325 English and foreign language daily, weekly, and monthly newspapers and magazines. Most of these were privately owned or were the publications of one of the five thousand Socialist Party locals. They reached a total of more than two million subscribers. *Appeal to Reason*, the legendary socialist weekly in which Sinclair had his own page, had a readership of more than 750,000. But the monopolistic, advertising-supported media marketplace elevated the degree of difficulty for the alternative press such that it was virtually impossible to become "mainstream." Sinclair had contempt for the idea that radicals should content themselves with financially insolvent media on the margins, dismissing that notion as a clear indication that "bourgeois thought is bankrupt."[18]

For Sinclair, it is the treatment of movements for social justice that is the real measure of journalism in his era, and it is here that he found the treatment of labor, socialists, and feminists so unsympathetic and hostile, that it became an enormous barrier to the peaceful exercise of democracy. "Journalism follows this simple and elemental rule," he writes, "if strikers are violent, they get on the wires, while if strikers are not violent, they stay off the wires; by which simple device it is brought about that nine-tenths of the telegraphic news you read about strikes is news of violence, and so in your brain channels is irrevocably graven the idea-association: Strikes—violence! Violence—strikes!"[19]

The point of *The Brass Check* is not merely to criticize commercial journalism, but to explain the reasons so the system may be changed. "The thing I am interested in saying is: The Prostitution of journalism is due to such and such factors, and may be remedied by such and such changes."[20] Although a socialist, Sinclair was loathe to have a government monopoly over newspapers or journalism. He presents a range of solutions in *The Brass Check*, including several that would work within the system. He called, for example, for powerful independent unions of journalists. "In every newspaper-office in America the same struggle between the business-office and the news-department is going on all the time."[21] "One purpose of this book," he concluded, "is to advocate a union of newspaper workers, so that they may make their demands as an organization, and not as helpless individuals."[22] He also urged organized labor to establish well-funded independent newspapers. For several years after the publication of *The Brass Check*, Sinclair collected money pledges to launch "an honest weekly newspaper entitled the *National News*, serving no party or cause, but giving the facts to the people."[23] Sinclair abandoned the newspaper idea when it became a drain on his time; he preferred to write books.

Sinclair is to be commended for his willingness to offer plans for reform in addition to providing a critique of the status quo. That his solutions did not measure up to his critique is another example of the supreme difficulties that have faced radical media critics. "The American people thoroughly despise and hate their newspapers," Sinclair observed, "yet they seem to have no idea what to do about it, and take it for granted that they must go on reading falsehoods for the balance of their days."[24] The commercial news media were an especially strong adversary, with their domination over the dissemination of ideas and their influence over politicians. Those politicians that dared attack the press barons, like Robert M. La Follette, earned powerful enemies who would then work to undermine their political careers and agendas.[25] Whatever success media reform would enjoy at the time of *The Brass Check* would depend largely on the success of the socialists and the La Follette branch of the progressive movement. When those movements were crushed, by the 1920s, the prospects for media reform, dim to begin with, disappeared with but a handful of exceptions.[26]

It is ironic that observers at the time argued that the rise of professionalism effectively resolved Sinclair's main criticism of the news media. Though the notion of professional journalism was introduced in the Progressive Era, it resolved very little at the time—hardly surprising since it has never served as more than a rhetorical stand-in for its supposed accomplishments despite becoming internalized as a rule by the mid-twentieth century. Even if it could be credibly developed, the revolutionary idea that the political views of the news media would not automatically reflect those of the owner began as just that, an idea. The much ballyhooed construction of the "Chinese Wall" that would separate the business office from the editorial office would take time to reinforce. The trained professionals who would refuse the biases of the ownership and sublimate their own partisanship had yet to be trained to do so. Moreover, it was a major obstacle to the legitimacy of the practice that this was an informal agreement, made by the owners because it legitimated their product in the face of more concentrated ownership and was therefore very good business. Nonetheless, for most establishment observers, professionalism in the Progressive Era was the perfect solution, and it worked.

But Sinclair was anything but a mainstream observer, and enough of a socialist to think any solution that left the power in the hands of the owning class was invariably flawed. He believed that, ultimately, those who own, hire, fire, and set budgets determine the values of the medium. Quoting Will Irwin, he noted that the "subordinates" drift "inevitably toward the point of view held by their master."[27] "A professional journalist," he concludes, "may be defined as a man who holds himself ready at a day's notice to adjust his opinions to the pocket-book of a new owner."[28] There were plenty of disillusioned journalists floating around to confirm the sentiment. Professionalism lowered the menace of commercial journalism just below the threshold of public outrage and held it there with a combination of mild internal reform and stunningly comprehensive public relations to compensate for the ever-present reality of business as usual. Will Irwin captured this duality vividly: "Publicly, the controlled newspaper assumes to exercise its ancient office of tribune of the people. Privately, it serves wealth. Publicly, so that it may keep its subscribers, it pretends to favor progress; privately that it may guard its owners sources of revenue and social position, it suppresses and denatures the news which would assist that process. The system is dishonest to its marrow."[29]

In the decades since *The Brass Check* was first published, professionalism in journalism has become far more sophisticated. It has provided a measure of autonomy for journalists from commercial pressures, and it has placed a premium upon factual accuracy. That is all to the good. But professional journalism's basic claims of fairness and social neutrality have come under sustained criticism, and there is ample evidence to justify Sinclair's skepticism. To be blunt, the newly minted code for professional journalists had, as media critic Ben Bagdikian points out, several distinct biases written into it that reflected the commercial and political needs of the owners.

The bogus neutrality of professional journalism is evident in the manner in which it tends to cover anti-capitalist social movements. In professional journalism, business is assumed to be the natural steward of society, while labor is seen as a less benevolent force and Left politics generally are held in suspicion. A cartoon from the late 1940s in the *CIO News* captured progressive sentiment toward this trend in the news media. It showed the cigar-smoking fat boss caricature manipulating two levers connected to a skull cap fitted over the head of a person identified as the American public. One lever is for radio, the other for newspapers. The message being pumped into the head is "business is good, labor is bad."

During the past thirty years, it has gotten even more difficult for progressives to receive satisfactory press coverage in the mainstream media. This is due primarily to the tightening corporate ownership over the news media that has resulted from government deregulation of broadcasting and lax enforcement of antitrust statutes. Over the past twenty-five years, the U.S. media system has been consolidated in the hands of a small number of colossal conglomerates. To give some sense of proportion, in 2000 AOL purchased Time Warner in the biggest media deal ever, valued at around $160 billion. That was 470 times greater than the value of the largest media deal in history that had been recorded by 1979. The nine or ten largest media conglomerates almost all rank among the three hundred largest firms in the world; in 1970 there were only a couple of media firms on that list.

These media conglomerates often pay a premium price for TV networks or newspaper chains, so they have huge incentive to apply the same commercial logic to their newsrooms that they apply to their other divisions. Why should they grant editors carte blanche when their other managers are held to a strict accounting of all their moves? The logical result has been a reduction in resources for journalism, a decline in costly and controversial investigative reporting, and a softening up of journalistic standards to permit less expensive and more commercially attractive journalism. First in line for the corporate guillotine was international reporting, which costs a great deal of money and adds little to the bottom line. Labor coverage has fallen off the map, and more lucrative "business journalism"—pitched to the top quarter of the population, if that—has become so widespread that it has effectively merged with general news. This tendency for business journalism to become the defining modality for journalism generally effectively established and celebrated the triumph of "market forces" as the beneficent guiding light of American democracy and public affairs—a boldly ideological move couched in the trappings of disinterested reportage.

In short, the media owners have increasingly abandoned the professional "deal" because it no longer makes economic sense. One measure of the attack on the autonomy of the newsroom can be found in the plummeting morale of working journalists. Well into the 1980s, journalists were among the staunchest and most sensitive defenders of the media status quo. They enjoyed their privileges and were convinced that they used them for the betterment of society. During the last fifteen years, in what amounts to a sea change, journalists have grown despondent over the collapse of their autonomy. The Pew Center surveys of journalists showed a marked increase in demoralization over the course of the 1990s. The editor of the *Chicago Tribune*, James Squires, left his job, arguing that he had witnessed the "death of journalism" due to the "corporate takeover" of the news.[30]

So the twenty-first century finds us in a position not entirely unlike the one found by Sinclair and his compatriots eighty-plus years ago. The media are exceptionally concentrated, the journalism is of dubious integrity, journalists are demoralized, and the political system is awash in corruption. Upton Sinclair's *The Brass Check* is not only the capstone of the first great generation of modern press criticism, but is also the first thoroughgoing critique of the modern era of capitalist journalism, an era in which we most certainly remain. The political crisis of capitalist journalism remains an unavoidable and central facet in understanding our current predicament, and there is no reason to think the problem will go away of its own volition. Any democratic reckoning will have to come to terms with the core problems that capitalist control over journalism and media pose for a free and self-governing society.

4

Telling the Truth at the Moment of Truth: U.S. News Media and the Invasion and Occupation of Iraq

A popular Government, without popular information or the means of acquiring it, is but a prologue to a farce or a tragedy; or, perhaps, both. Knowledge will forever govern ignorance; and a people who mean to be their own governors must arm themselves with the power knowledge gives.
—James Madison[1]

The notion of a free press, of an institution that monitors those in power and those who wish to be in power, that ferrets out truth from lies, that draws public attention to the pressing issues of our times, is a cornerstone of liberal democratic theory. In practice, even in liberal democratic capitalist societies, press systems have never accomplished these laudable goals, though certain press systems, usually through progressive activism and reforms, have come much closer than others. The primary internal impediments to a viable free press have been private ownership of the media, and the drive to maximize profit, often through selling advertising. The primary external barriers are the difficulty of promoting a participatory democratic political culture in a class-divided society, as well as the constant pressure, direct and indirect, that elites put on the press to have it support elite aims. Radical press criticism, beginning most notably in the work of Marx, has never rejected Madison's notion of a free press.[2] To the contrary, the gist of radical press criticism has emphasized the irreconcilable nature of the free press ideal with a capitalist society.

The greatest test of a press system is how it empowers citizens to monitor the government's war-making powers. War is the most serious use of state power, organized sanctioned violence; how well it is under citizen review and control is not only a litmus test for the media but for society as a whole. Those in power, those who benefit from war and empire, see the press as arguably the most important front for war, because it is there that consent is manufactured, and dissent is marginalized. For a press system, a war is its moment of truth.

With regard to the United States, it would be difficult to exaggerate how deeply concerned the founders were with limiting the war-making power of the government, of keeping the president in particular under strict control by Congress. The founders were no friends of egalitarianism or democracy— but they were resolutely opposed to tyranny. All of them learned from Montesquieu that history from Greece and Rome to modern times had repeatedly demonstrated that a state's existence as a self-governing republic was incompatible with becoming a militaristic empire defined by secrecy and hierarchy. And they understood that a viable free press was the only mechanism that could provide citizens with the precious commodity most frequently denied them by their governors: the information necessary to control those with the power to send the nation's children to their deaths on distant killing fields.

It is the press that is singularly responsible, therefore, for the maintenance of civilian control over the military, and the prevention of empire run amok. When the U.S. Supreme Court considered the meaning of freedom of the press in the Pentagon Papers case in 1971, Justice Potter Stewart wrote: "In the absence of governmental checks and balances present in other areas of our national life, the only effective restraint upon executive policy and power in the areas of national defense and international affairs may lie in an enlightened citizenry—in an informed and critical public opinion which alone can here protect the values of democratic government." Such great words and sentiments notwithstanding, the track record of the U.S. media over the past century in relation to U.S. overseas wars, and the broader role of the United States in the world, has been dreadful. Time and time again the system has spread lies and half-truths and crushed dissent, which more often than not proved to be justified by the facts. In the United States, honest reflection is always done with hindsight, premised on the notion that we have learned from the past and that these problems in the media have been eliminated. After putting this pattern in historical perspective, this essay analyzes the U.S. media coverage of the invasion and occupation of Iraq in 2003–5. As we shall see, in this moment of truth for a free press, the truth was almost nowhere to be found.

Manufacturing Consent for War

Beginning with the 1898 Spanish-American War, the United States has engaged in scores of foreign military operations and several major wars involving the deployment of U.S. troops. In nearly all of these major wars—the Spanish-American War, the First World War, the Second World War, Korea, Vietnam, the Central America proxy wars of the 1980s, and the first Gulf War—a clear pattern emerged: the U.S. president wished to pursue war while the American people had severe reservations. In nearly every case the White House ran a propaganda campaign to generate public support for going to war, a campaign that bent the truth in line with the view that the ends (war) justified the means (lies). This is not to say that all of these wars by definition were improper. A powerful case, for example, can be made for U.S. participation in the Second World War. But even in that case, President Roosevelt was concerned that the American people would not fall in line no matter how strong the evidence. So, as the saying goes, he "lied" us into war.

The news media were placed in a recurring dilemma in each of these wars. The administration was pursuing aggressive propaganda campaigns to whip up popular support for war, and a key battleground was winning favorable press coverage. The news media in each case were presented with the dilemma of either challenging the administration's pro-war line, demanding hard evidence for claims, digging deep to see that the full story was put before the American people, or going along more or less with the pro-war line. In principle, credible journalism should hold the nation's rulers to the same evidentiary standards it holds the enemies of the nation's rulers. We take no pleasure in reporting that the news media in nearly every case opted

for Plan B. In the case of Vietnam, where the Pentagon Papers and the taped
sessions in President Johnson's office document the shameless duplicity of
the government, the willingness of the news media to parrot administration
lies was a thorough abrogation of the requirements of a free press, with disastrous consequences for millions of lives. At journalism schools, these
episodes are considered embarrassing moments in the history of U.S. journalism, and not dwelt upon in the curricula. What is dwelt upon is the
reporting that challenged official fiction years after the lies were told and the
lives were lost.

The explanation of why the news media fail to get the fundamental facts
before the American people concerning the decision of whether to go to
war, be it in 1917, 1941, 1950, 1964, or 2003, are deep-seated. One could
argue that the patriotic impulse is such that any journalism will have the
strong tendency to "root for the home team," as some have put it. But this
analysis begs the question of why the patriotic impulse exists in different
forms at different times, why some in society express it more fervently than
others, how the patriotic impulse is enforced, how it manifests itself through
media institutions and professional practices, and how we explain the
exceptions. In short, the patriotic impulse explanation leads to far more
questions than answers.

To explain the woeful coverage of U.S. wars requires a look at the broad
crisis in journalism I have analyzed at length elsewhere.[3] By the early twentieth century and thereafter, major news media were large commercial organizations and therefore tended to be conservative institutions. Those who
owned and managed these firms tended to be comfortable with the worldview of those atop the social structure, because that is where they also
resided, and were supportive of government policies that were understood to
advance those interests. Moreover, most media owners did not want to be
accused of being unpatriotic or treasonous. The system had done well by
them. From a structural or sociological perspective, one would not expect
that commercial news media organizations would pose a critical challenge to
a strong pro-war campaign.

But what about the editors and working journalists who composed and
edited the news? Some of them proudly hailed from the working class.
Certainly they had no similar allegiance to the policy imperatives of the elite.
To the extent that they had a certain autonomy from the implicit and explicit

institutional prerogatives of the owners, the nature of press coverage was far less certain. Here we might even expect some stubborn interrogation of the powers-that-be. Regrettably, that has only rarely been the case. The primary problem has been the emergence of what is called "professional journalism," which coincided with the emergence of the United States as a global military power. All of the limitations of the version of professional journalism that solidified its hold on newsrooms in the United States by the 1940s—reliance on official sources, fear of context, and the unstated "dig here, not there" mandate—worked in combination to make professional journalism a lapdog more than a watchdog as the drums of war beat louder.

The factor most scholarship emphasizes in this regard is professional journalism's reliance upon official sources. If people in power are debating an issue, journalists have some wiggle room to root around and explore it. If people in power agree on an issue, presuppose it, or do not seriously debate it, it is almost impossible for a journalist to raise it without being accused of partisanship and pushing an ideological agenda. So it is rarely done, and when it is done it is dismissed as bad journalism.

The ability of official sources to determine the range of legitimate debate is a regrettable tendency for most political stories, but it is nothing short of a disaster for the coverage of the U.S. role in the world. Here ordinary citizens rely to an even greater extent upon the media than they do for domestic politics, where their daily experience can provide some corrective to skewed press coverage. Moreover, there is typically a greater consensus among "official sources" on the U.S.'s benign role in the world than there is on any other issue, except, perhaps, the greatness of U.S.-style capitalism as the only legitimate way to organize an economy.

There are two fundamental presuppositions—actually, articles of faith—that guide U.S. foreign policy. They are accepted by "official sources" in both political parties, and they are almost never questioned in major U.S. news media. The first presupposition is the notion that the United States is a benevolent force in the world and that whatever it does, by definition, is ultimately about making the world a more just and democratic place. This is a pleasing assumption, and it puts a necessary fig leaf over what may be less altruistic aims. This presupposition also makes it possible for there to be almost no debate or discussion of the actual role of the United States in the world. Many Americans accept the official story that the United States is a benevolent giant, attacked on all sides by powerful evil-doers. That the United States accounts for almost half of all military spending in the world; that U.S. military spending dwarfs the second largest military power by a factor of eight; that the United States has hundreds of foreign military bases in literally scores of nations—all of this is largely unmentioned and unknown to Americans. It is simply assumed away. And that leaves most Americans largely clueless about how the United States is perceived in the rest of the world.

The second article of faith that is generally unquestioned by the American media is the notion that the United States, and the United States alone, has a "007" right to invade any country it wishes. The United States also reserves the right to "deputize" an ally to conduct an invasion if it so desires, otherwise other nations are not permitted to engage in the invasion business. This presents a small problem for the political elite and for the news media. After all, the UN Charter and a number of other treaties signed by the United States prohibit the invasion of one nation by another unless it is under armed attack. Moreover, the U.S. Constitution characterizes treaties as the highest law of the land, so that if the United States violates international law, it arguably warrants presidential impeachment. To top it off, in popular discourse the United States proudly promotes itself as favoring the rule of law, and a main argument against all of its adversaries is invariably that they ignore treaties they have signed. That is sometimes used as a rationale for a U.S. invasion.

This is not to say that there is not highly competent and quality reporting on U.S. foreign policy, only that it tends to stay within the parameters of what official sources consider legitimate. The truly great reporting, from people like I. F. Stone and Seymour Hersh, went boldly outside these parameters. (Some of the best reporting on the U.S. role in the world, not surprisingly, comes from American reporters working outside the United States, where reliance upon U.S. official sources as the basis for legitimate news and opinion plays a much more limited role.)

In combination, the limitations of professional journalism, the influence of owners, the linkages of media institutions to the power structure of society, and the internalized elite presuppositions, have led to what can only be characterized as a palpable double standard in coverage of the U.S. role in the world. None have demonstrated this more convincingly than Edward S. Herman and Noam Chomsky in *Manufacturing Consent.*[4] Stories that support the aims of U.S. policymakers get lavish and sympathetic treatment; stories of similar or greater factual veracity and importance that undermine U.S. policy goals get brief and unfavorable mention. As Howard Friel and Richard Falk have demonstrated in their research, the U.S. news media, including the most respected newspapers like the *New York Times*, turn a blind eye to U.S. violations of core international law, while having no qualms about playing up the violations of adversaries. It would be nearly impossible for the coverage to be more unprincipled.[5]

The Contemporary Crisis in Journalism

The problems with U.S. media coverage described above were evident from the 1960s into the 1980s, the so-called golden age of professional journalism. Press coverage exhibited severe flaws even when the newsrooms were relatively flush with resources and had as much autonomy as they ever would. The main developments in journalism over the past two decades that have eroded professional journalism—corporate consolidation and organized right-wing attacks on the "liberal media"—have only made the situation worse.

The corporate downsizing and cutback epidemic has been especially hard on international coverage. The sharp reduction in the number of foreign correspondents working for U.S. news media has been a familiar story over the past two decades. These are positions that cost a lot of money, and to the managers in charge they don't seem to generate any black ink on their corporate balance sheets. Moreover, managers argue that people don't seem to care if there is less international coverage, or if what passes for international coverage has less to do with politics and more to do with easy-to-report natural disasters and plane crashes. So from the corporate worldview, axing these positions is a no-brainer.

The resulting problem with not having many foreign correspondents who have a familiarity with the language, history, and customs of the regions they are covering has become painfully clear over the past fifteen years. When conflicts break out in the Balkans, Africa, South Asia, or elsewhere, U.S. news media have few if any reporters on the ground to provide context for the story. This means that there is less capacity for journalists to provide a counterbalance to whatever official story Washington puts forward. At its worst, foreign reporting becomes celebrity journalists and anchors being air-dropped into a crisis area and shepherded around by representatives of the U.S. government. This is not a recipe for independent journalism.

The right-wing critique of the "liberal" media has not helped matters either. Antiwar criticism of a Democratic war-maker from the right, though rare, is kosher if framed in hyper-nationalist terms. Thus Sean Hannity attacked Clinton's Kosovo war in terms he later characterized as treasonous when they were used by others about President Bush's Iraq war. A constant theme of the right-wing critique of the "liberal" news media is that journalists are insufficiently patriotic; this translates into journalists being extra-sensitive to prove their nationalist credentials. Again, this is not conducive to critical analyses of foreign wars.

The combined effect of commercial and conservative attacks on professional journalism is to undermine the formal adherence to a neutral and nonpartisan position. This does not mean mainstream media can become explicitly partisan to the left; that is more unthinkable than ever. Nor does it mean that most news media have dropped their formal commitment to political neutrality. It means that there are a growing number of media that push a partisan pro-Republican political agenda, often under a thin veneer of being "fair and balanced." So the Fox News Channel, Sinclair Broadcasting, the *New York Post*, the *Washington Times*, the editorial page of the *Wall Street Journal*, and most of talk radio all serve as standard-bearers for the Republican right. They aggressively promote right-wing policies and bash Democrats who get in the way. In coverage of Republican wars this translates into aggressive pro-war posturing and wholesale rabid condemnation of antiwar criticism as unpatriotic or treasonous. Because the rest of the news media tend to be timid by comparison, this right-wing phalanx sets the tone for coverage to an extent that is out of proportion to its size. And the rest of the press becomes even more hesitant to contradict the government line.

All of this came together in the coverage of the terrorist attacks of September 11, 2001, and the subsequent invasion and occupation of Afghanistan. Despite the massive amount of attention the news media devoted to the topic—it was arguably the biggest U.S. news story in a half-century—coverage was heavily propagandistic. Elementary questions about the administration's performance in failing to prevent the attack were not pursued. Hard looks at the relationship of the Bush administration, the U.S. government, Al Qaeda, and other Mideast governments were all but nonexistent. Even to broach the question of why the terrorists attacked the United States—as if there might be a rational explanation beyond the idea that these were madmen who hated us "because of our freedoms"—was dismissed as implicitly condoning the attack and mass murder.

Guided by the Bush administration and "official sources," within hours of the 9/11 attacks, these terrorist acts had been converted from vicious crimes against humanity, from criminal acts of terror, to acts of war. The War on Terror entailed a push for a broad militarization of society and, immediately, for the invasion and bombing of Afghanistan, a nation that did not attack the United States on 9/11.

The truth about 9/11 is still largely unknown. But what pieces have emerged, mostly in the margins, and with all too little pressure from mainstream media, suggest that much of what was presented as received wisdom in the months following the 9/11 attacks was incorrect, if not nonsense. The testimony of Richard Clarke as well as the report of the 9/11 Commission both highlight the negligence of the administration in failing to stop the terrorist attack or in addressing it properly afterward. One can only imagine what mainstream media, egged on by Fox News, the *Wall Street Journal* editorial page, talk radio, and the *New York Post*, would have done to a President Gore or a President Clinton in a similar situation. In the immediate aftermath of the 9/11 attacks, courtesy of a hyperventilating press, President Bush was reborn as a cross between Abraham Lincoln and Winston Churchill.

The press was eating out of the Bush administration's bowl. If media truly constituted the most important front in modern war, the stars were in alignment for a bold invasion that had been atop the wishlist of the main Bush foreign policy advisors for years, but was once thought too politically controversial to accomplish: the invasion of Iraq.

Buildup to the Invasion of Iraq

It was in this environment that the United States was able to launch an invasion and occupation of Iraq on entirely bogus grounds. The three major justifications offered explicitly and implicitly by the Bush administration to generate public support for the war were: (1) that Iraq illegally possessed weapons of mass destruction and was poised to use them on the United States in the immediate future; (2) that Iraq had been somehow connected to the attacks on 9/11, so pursuing Saddam Hussein was a rational next step in the campaign against bin Laden; and (3) Iraq was the leading terrorist state, 9/11 notwithstanding, so the War on Terror had to go through Baghdad.

The second and third claims were unsubstantiated on their face, and borderline preposterous. The Bush administration was careful about making these claims in any official setting, but utterly shameless about turning to these claims to win support on the home front. The legal case the United States made for a "preemptive" invasion of Iraq was the issue of Iraq's possession of weapons of mass destruction capable of being used against the United States. This case was made with considerable fanfare, both for domestic audiences and to generate global support, but there was significant evidence undermining its credibility. As is now established beyond any and all doubt: there were no weapons of mass destruction in Iraq, the Bush administration pushed its claims with little concern for evidence, and the news media participated in this fraud to an appalling extent. (The May 2005 disclosure of the pre-invasion British intelligence Downing Street memo that provided damning evidence about how the United States was cooking intelligence to justify the invasion of Iraq—the "smoking gun memo"—was the final nail in a well-shut coffin.) This episode has been diagnosed in detail, and is now considered one of the darkest moments in the entire history of U.S. journalism.

Omitted, too, in the coverage was the inescapable fact that the U.S. invasion of Iraq violated international law.

The media institutions themselves were hawkish. The *Columbia Journalism Review* subsequently reviewed the editorial pages of the six top dailies that influence public opinion—including the *New York Times*, the *Washington Post*, the *Wall Street Journal*, and *USA Today*—and determined that all of them failed to hold the Bush administration to an adequate standard of proof. *Editor & Publisher* determined that of the top fifty daily newspapers in the nation, not a single one was strongly "antiwar" on its editorial page.

The reliance upon official sources to frame the debate and set the agenda is mostly responsible for the disgraceful press coverage of Bush administration lies. As Jonathan Mermin put it in a brilliant essay in *World Policy Journal*, conventional journalism means "journalists continue to be incapable of focusing on an issue for perspective on U.S. foreign policy that has not been first identified or articulated in official Washington debate." Here it is important to note that most Democratic leaders did not assume an antiwar position, so there was little countervailing framing coming from officialdom. Mermin scoffs at the idea that elite consensus justifies journalists regurgitating the government position uncritically: "The absence of opposition to a Republican military intervention among Democratic politicians is not persuasive evidence that the policy is sound, or even that presumptively informed and thoughtful people believe it sound." What it adds up to, in clear contradiction to the spirit and intent of the First Amendment, is "if the government isn't talking about it, we don't report it."[6]

A comprehensive analysis of the sources used on TV news in the weeks leading up to the U.S. invasion—when a significant percentage of the U.S. population was opposed to an invasion—showed that 3 percent of the U.S. sources employed were antiwar, and over 70 percent were decidedly pro-war. A Fairness & Accuracy in Reporting (FAIR) survey of nightly news coverage on NBC, ABC, CBS, PBS, CNN, and Fox during the first three weeks after the invasion found that pro-war U.S. sources outnumbered antiwar sources by 25 to 1. Moreover, the on-air experts that TV news relied upon were generally "establishment" figures and so by definition uncritical.[7]

Press coverage reached its nadir immediately preceding the invasion. In February 2003 Colin Powell went before the United Nations to make the definitive case for invading Iraq. Powell provided little verifiable evidence for his extravagant claims. Six months later, Associated Press correspondent Charles J. Hanley fact-checked Powell's speech, and "utterly demolished" it, as *Editor & Publisher* put it.[8] Regrettably the best journalism all too often tends to be in postmortems, when the political consequences are minuscule. At the time of Powell's speech, when the fate of peace hung in the balance and when independent experts were puncturing most of his claims, the news media regurgitated Powell's points and praised them for their veracity in a manner that could not have been exceeded by Stalin's stooges. Gilbert Cranberg, formerly of the *Des Moines Register*, has compiled a comprehensive study of the press coverage of Powell's speech. Among the terms used by the leading U.S. papers to describe the merits of Powell's case: "a massive array of evidence"; "a sober, factual case"; "an overwhelming case"; "a smoking fusillade . . . a persuasive case for anyone who is still persuadable";

"an ironclad case . . . incontrovertible evidence"; "an accumulation of painstak-ingly gathered and analyzed evidence"; "succinct and damning evidence . . . the case is closed."[9]

In past wars like Vietnam, apologists for gullible press coverage could argue that the news media had no way of knowing that the Johnson adminis-tration was lying to them, and that the Gulf of Tonkin incident was a ruse. Such was not the case with Iraq. At every step of the way there was an impressive amount of material in the international press and on the Internet that contradicted the Bush administration's line. For example, consider the powerful and immediate rebuttal to Powell's UN speech by Glen Rangwala of Cambridge University.[10] It was all but ignored. Former Marine and Republican weapons inspector Scott Ritter—who spent years on the ground in Iraq—carefully repudiated all of the Bush administration claims.[11] As a result he was subject to a character assassination campaign that made it eas-ier for a news medium to turn to celebrities like country music singer Lee Greenwood, action movie star Chuck Norris, or ex-football player Mike Ditka as if they were credible experts. A journalist did not have to be I. F. Stone to see that there was something fishy about the official story; all she had to do was keep her eyes open and her critical faculties working.

Moreover, unlike Vietnam, the invasion of Iraq was met by a massive anti-war movement in the United States *before* any bullets were expended. Hundreds of thousands of Americans took to the streets in February 2003 to protest the planned invasion of Iraq. Following the familiar pattern for dissi-dent opinion, press coverage was minimal and dismissive.

Managing the Home Front During War

Perhaps the most striking development in press coverage of the invasion and war was the policy of "embedding" journalists with military units, so they could see firsthand how the war was developing. Proponents of the policy argued it would protect journalists from enemy fire and make it possible for them to get stories that would be otherwise unattainable.

Embedded reporting in combination with full-throttle jingoism on U.S. television news made it difficult for journalists to do critical work. "I think the press was muzzled, and I think the press was self-muzzled," stated CNN's

Christiane Amanpour, arguably the most respected foreign correspondent on U.S. television, a few months later. "I'm sorry to say, but certainly television and, perhaps, to a certain extent, my station was intimidated by the administration and its foot soldiers at Fox News. And it did, in fact, put a climate of fear and self-censorship, in my view, in terms of the kind of broadcast work we did."[12]

The problems continued after the formal defeat of Saddam Hussein's army during the liberation that immediately became an occupation. The U.S. news media were caught entirely by surprise. Indeed, the term "occupation" had never been used prior to the invasion. Mermin quotes PBS's Jim Lehrer, who defended this omission: "The word occupation . . . was never mentioned in the run-up to the war. It was liberation. This was [talked about in Washington as] a war of liberation, not a war of occupation. So as a consequence, those of us in journalism never even looked at the issue of occupation."[13]

At the same time, it was imperative for the Bush administration that the best possible spin be put on the war, that it be regarded at home as a success, especially with an election coming up. The one great advantage the Bush administration had was that it could use its power to heavily promote stories that painted the picture it wanted to be seen, and by remaining quiet it could pour water on those stories it did not wish to see developed. When information continued to emerge discrediting the Bush administration's rationale for the war, and the nature of the "liberation," like the "Downing Street memo" of British intelligence, the White House sealed its lips, Democrats meekly obliged, and reporters had little to work with. As a result journalistic mountains were converted into molehills.

Conversely, stories like the toppling of the Saddam Hussein statue in Baghdad, President Bush dressing up in flight-suit drag and appearing below a giant "Mission Accomplished" banner, the "rescue" of Jessica Lynch, as well as the capture of Saddam Hussein and the Iraqi election of early 2005, all got lavish attention at the time such attention was needed. Each of these was held up as a critical juncture, the moment the tide was turning and the Bush administration's policies were being proven "right." But, in each instance, the passage of only a few days or weeks would reveal that the tide had not turned—and that the administration's approach remained as ill-fated as ever.

Consider the prison torture scandal at Abu Ghraib prison. Award-winning Associated Press reporter Charles Hanley broke a story on U.S. torture of Iraqi prisoners in fall 2003, but, as Mermin notes, it "was ignored by the major American newspapers." Hanley explained to Mermin that his "was not an officially sanctioned story that begins with a handout from an official source," noting at the same time the "very strong prejudice toward investing U.S. official statements with credibility while disregarding statements from almost any other source."[14] Hanley's story featured Iraqis recounting their personal experience at Abu Ghraib. It did not provoke a Bush photo-op in a warden's costume in front of Abu Ghraib, or a steady stream of official press releases drawing attention to it. When it finally was broken with photographic evidence by Hersh and CBS News in the United States, the story received plentiful coverage. But it was a classic case in which the line of investigation stopped at low levels, and exonerated those in charge of the overall policy. Without any push from official sources the story faded away. Indeed, it went unmentioned during the 2004 presidential campaign debates.

One year after the Abu Ghraib story broke, Seymour Hersh reflected on the whitewash of extensive and persistent U.S. war crimes, which he among others has documented, and the role the U.S. media played. "It's a dreary pattern," Hersh wrote. "The reports and subsequent Senate proceedings are sometimes criticized on editorial pages. There are calls for a truly independent investigation by the Senate or the House. Then, as months pass with no official action, the issue withers away, until the next set of revelations revives it." There were ten official military inquiries into Abu Ghraib, but they "are all asking the wrong questions. . . . The question that never gets adequately answered is this: what did the president do after being told about Abu Ghraib?"[15]

A major area of tension between the Bush administration's wish to paint the rosiest possible picture and the responsibility of reporters to present a more accurate picture of what is transpiring in Iraq is the reporting of the war's toll in human lives. The U.S. government wishes to minimize the public's awareness of the human cost of the war, both to the Iraqis and to U.S. soldiers. Wary of Vietnam-like images, the Bush administration fought to keep this information strictly out of public view. Iraqi casualties were not recorded, and reporters have been unable to get to the places where most of these casualties occur. As a result, Michael Massing notes, journalists have been "exceedingly cautious" in making estimates.[16] While few U.S. journalists had any interest in this subject, the respected British medical journal *The Lancet* published a study by Johns Hopkins University scholars who estimated the Iraqi civilian death toll at 100,000 in October 2004, before the second siege of Falluja, with a majority of the deaths due to U.S. military actions.[17] The report caused a tempest for a day or two, as it exceeded the figures accepted by U.S. news media by a factor of seven or eight. But the issue died quickly enough, as no U.S. official source wished to dwell on this topic. This lack of interest in keeping an accurate accounting of Iraqi civilian deaths tends to undermine the official claim that this war is motivated by a great concern for the welfare of the Iraqi people.

Media Moment of Truth

Although U.S. journalism, especially in coverage of wars, tends to run in packs, it is not monolithic. Even at its worst there is usually an exception that proves the rule. In addition, among the ranks of journalists are many highly principled and courageous reporters, who entered the profession not to serve as a conduit for those in power, but to shine a light on those in power on behalf of the citizenry. As the dissonance grew between the official story offered by the White House and largely regurgitated in the media, and the actual horror story on the ground in Iraq, many journalists took a hard look at media performance and the state of the profession. By the end of 2003 the *Columbia Journalism Review*, *Editor & Publisher*, and other leading industry publications or journalism reviews—not to mention the first-rate work done by groups like FAIR and publications like the *New York Review of Books* and *The Nation*—had presented probing criticisms of media coverage of the war.

In early 2004 the *New York Times* made the unprecedented gesture of offering a mea culpa for its flawed coverage of the weapons of mass destruction controversy, while the *Washington Post* allowed its media reporter, Howard Kurtz, to write an extended critique of its coverage.[18] Each newspaper implicitly acknowledged its role in leading the nation to war on bogus grounds, yet neither explicitly took responsibility. The confessions were halting and unenthusiastic, but, in a field where admissions of fundamental error are about as welcome as getting root canal surgery without a painkiller, they sent a powerful shot over the bow of journalism nationwide. This occurred on the heels of Howard Dean's rise to the top of the Democratic field, running on an essentially antiwar platform, and when observers were beginning to use words such as "quagmire" to describe the U.S. occupation of Iraq. The apologias were the tip of the journalistic iceberg. Many journalists were appalled by the war, humiliated by the poor performance of the news media, and frustrated by the Bush administration's deception. Some critics predicted that the working press would get a wake-up call from the scandalous coverage of the Iraq war and turn its anger on Bush in advance of the November election. If there was going to be room for more independent and critical coverage of the U.S. war on Iraq, in early 2004 conditions in newsrooms were as ripe as they ever would be.

Alas, it would not come to pass. The impulse for media self-criticism is quickly tempered by the deeply ingrained institutional realization that it is not healthy to encourage the public to keep the hood up any longer than necessary so they can inspect the engine. Few other major media took the bait and pursued the issue of how the media were complicit in sponsoring a devastating and illegitimate war. It was difficult to avoid Danny Schechter's conclusion that the mainstream press made minimum concessions on its Iraq coverage as a form of damage control. It had no interest in laying out the whole truth.[19]

The *New York Times* certainly wanted to get the incident in its rearview mirror as quickly as possible. The *Times* quietly removed Judith Miller (the reporter whose uncritical and whole-hog reliance on extremely dubious sources in 2003 gave tremendous legitimacy to the Bush administration's lies about Iraq possessing weapons of mass destruction) from her beat, but she was not formally censured. Miller herself was unapologetic. "My job isn't to assess the government's information and be an independent intelligence analyst myself," she is quoted by Mermin as saying. "My job is to tell readers of the *New York Times* what the government thought about Iraq's arsenal."[20]

The way journalists adapted to the coverage of the occupation of Iraq was not to tell the truth and let the chips fall where they might. As one Baghdad correspondent for a large U.S. newspaper told Massing in October 2004, "The situation in Iraq was a catastrophe," a view shared "almost unanimously" by his colleagues. A widely circulated email that September by Farnaz Fassihi, a Baghdad correspondent for the *Wall Street Journal*, was a devastating critique of the U.S. war, "a foreign policy failure that will haunt the United States for decades to come." Fassihi concluded: "The genie of terrorism, chaos and mayhem has been unleashed onto this country as a result of American mistakes and it can't be put back into the bottle." Massing notes that other U.S. correspondents in Baghdad were startled at the attention Fassihi's email received. "Everyone was marveling and asking what we were doing wrong if that information came as a surprise to the American public," one of them told Massing.[21]

Such a candid view of conditions in Iraq was regarded by the evolving conventions of professional journalism as partisan, unprofessional, and not objective—regardless of whether or not it was true—because it was a thorough repudiation of the Bush administration's position. It was not *balanced*, "balance" being defined not by the evidence but by accommodation to powerful interests. This point cannot be overemphasized: the balance editors employed had nothing to do with the evidence, and everything to do with keeping the Bush administration and the political Right off their backs. "Every story from Iraq is by definition an assessment as to whether things are going well or badly," a U.S. newspaper correspondent in Baghdad told Massing. "Editors are hypersensitive about not wanting to appear to be coming down on one side or the other."[22] (There is little evidence that appearing too pro-administration on the war caused many editors to shudder in fear.) Once Fassihi's email was spread across the Internet, the *Wall Street Journal* received pressure to remove her from the beat because she could no longer be regarded as "objective." Fassihi was immediately sent on a vacation until after the November U.S. election, though the *Journal* stated that this had nothing to do with her email.

Edward Wasserman reflected upon this conundrum in the *Miami Herald*: "I can only imagine the current mind-set of supervising editors: If we give prominence to this story of carnage in Iraq, will we be accused of anti-administration bias? And—here it gets interesting—will we therefore owe our readers an offsetting story, perhaps an inspirational tale of Marines teaching young Iraqis how to play softball?" So by following the obsession with balance, the news reports presented a confusing and skewed picture of the reality on the ground in Iraq. And it meant that the logical hard questions that would emerge from tough-minded reporting—like what on earth accounts for this mess?—got lost in the contradictory and incoherent picture provided by "balanced" reporting.[23] "Balance" did mean that a number of quality reports could get through, especially in the print media. In the months before the November election, there were several first-rate examinations in the mainstream press of the failures of the U.S. occupation. But the TV news coverage was far more pro-war, generally dismissing or ignoring facts that got in the way, with Fox News the exemplar, though far from alone in its patriotic charge.

It did not help matters that John Kerry and leading Democrats did not oppose the war per se—only how it was being executed. Kerry was no antiwar candidate, and the war, amazingly enough, was not a defining issue in the 2004 campaign. This meant there was no "official" antiwar source to embrace what critical reporting there was, draw voter attention to it, and encourage journalists to do more of the same. Not surprisingly, public opinion surveys indicated that in the fall of 2004 a significant percentage of Americans—and most Bush voters—still believed Iraq possessed weapons of mass destruction and that Saddam Hussein was shown to have been a major supporter of Al Qaeda, and hence lurked behind the 9/11 attacks. In view of how much media coverage was devoted to these issues, a more thorough repudiation of the press could barely be imagined. (What would people have thought of the U.S. media system if in 1944 a survey had found that a majority of Americans thought China was responsible for the attack on Pearl Harbor?)

Democracy Invariably Ascendant

Because the core articles of faith remain inviolable in U.S. journalism and politics, U.S. media coverage of U.S. foreign wars inexorably slides into providing a view compatible with those atop society. Despite the thorough invalidation of every official reason provided by the Bush administration to invade and occupy Iraq, journalists made almost no effort to locate more plausible explanations for such a major war. It would not have taken long for an inquiring reporter to find serious experts able to discuss the following factors: the imperial drive encouraged by the existence of a massive military-industrial complex; the geopolitical and economic advantages of having permanent military bases and a client regime/friendly ally in the heart of the Middle East; the domestic political advantages for a president to have the populace whipped into wartime fervor; the security needs of Israel, a close ally of the United States; and, of course, oil. Such explanations can be found in elite journals, in the business press, in intelligence reports, and in academic studies. Such an approach is applied in popular analyses of the motives of any other nation throughout history, but such inquiry was and is off-limits in U.S. politics and in U.S. mainstream journalism. To leading U.S. politicians and journalists, the United States is a benevolent nation, always working with the ultimate objective of promoting democracy.

When the United States finally convened an election in Iraq on January 30, 2005, it was trumpeted with a massive PR blitz by Washington, and the media obediently responded. The election was regarded as a wondrous democratic moment and viewed without criticism in the news media. Finally, the war was won! And, finally, too, the real reason why the United States had invaded and occupied Iraq could be declared: to bring democracy to the entire Middle East—and, of course, to liberate the women! This explanation was embraced across the political spectrum, as it tapped into the core presuppositions about the U.S. role in the world. But empirical support for the democratic claim also evaporated as the situation in Iraq grew even more grim for the U.S. forces and the elected government by mid-2005.[24]

As the United States celebrated the triumph of freedom and democracy, elementary questions went unasked. On what grounds should the U.S. claim to be concerned with democracy be taken seriously? Is the United States a purely philanthropic power that has no military or economic designs? Why did U.S. occupation authorities in Iraq work so hard to delay elections? If the U.S. favors democratic rule, why ignore the fact that most Iraqis voted for parties calling for an early or even immediate end to the U.S. occupation? Is it legitimate to invade a nation to install democracy? If it is legitimate, is every non-democracy in need of an invasion, or just some? Which ones? Is Iraq just the first nation on a list of those that should be invaded? What about Iran? What about Pakistan? Or Saudi Arabia? Or Kuwait? And who makes the decision about which country to invade, and who does the invading? If the United States can do it to Iraq, can India do it to Pakistan? Can Russia invade Uzbekistan? Can Venezuela invade Colombia? These are the kinds of questions that must be answered if the invasion of Iraq is to be justified in terms of "democracy." Otherwise it is just the law of the jungle, with all talk about democracy so much bunkum.

In the U.S. media system, these questions almost never get asked; the subject never gets sustained attention.

The problems besetting U.S. journalism are deep-seated and will not go away unless there is structural change in the media system, such that truthful reporting on affairs of state can be a rational expectation. This requires immediate political organizing to change the policies upon which the media system is based, and it requires making media reform part and parcel of broader movements for peace and social justice. In the end, media reform and social justice will rise or fall together. We need a press system that tells the truth.

5

How to Think About Journalism:
Looking Backward, Going Forward

"The condition of American journalism in the first decade of the twenty-first century can be expressed in a single unhappy word: crisis."[1] So began a 2007 report made by a scholar ensconced in the heart of mainstream academia. Such a comment would have been far less plausible in the political mainstream only a decade earlier, and its rapid evolution to becoming the new conventional wisdom among both academics and much of the news media is a little short of breathtaking. For the past quarter-century this argument was made primarily by critical analysts of the U.S. news media, especially those from the political economy of media tradition. In the 1980s and well into the 1990s it was subject to categorical dismissal by many journalists and journalism professors, if not outright ridicule. No longer do critical scholars need to present piles of evidence to make even mild criticism of the status quo. Today it is those who wish to defend the commercial system as doing a superior job at generating quality journalism that must provide the hard evidence. Only a handful of true believers, often those wed materially to the system, make much of an effort to do so.

In this chapter, to conclude my discussion of journalism I wish to address the contours of the now roundly accepted crisis in journalism, and suggest how we may most fruitfully consider it. There is an opportunity before us to reinvigorate journalism and, with that, democratic governance in the United

States. But we need to correctly understand the source of the problem to pre-
scribe the solutions. There are many prospective solutions before us, but
some may turn out to be of limited value for journalism and, of singular
importance, for democracy. Or, to put it in more stark terms, and to make
clear what is at stake: without viable journalism we not only make democracy
unthinkable, we open the door to a tyranny beyond most of our imaginations.[2] I argue herein that the political economy of media is uniquely positioned to provide the insights necessary for constructive action.

The place to start is by understanding what we mean by viable journalism for a democracy, what the crisis of journalism entails, and what caused it.
What exactly does a democratic journalism entail? I believe it must provide
a rigorous accounting of people who are in power and people who wish to be
in power, in both the government and corporate sector. It must have a plausible method to separate truth from lies, or at least prevent liars from getting
away scot-free. And it must provide a wide range of informed opinions on the
most important issues of our times; not only the issues of the day, but the
major issues that loom on the horizon. These issues cannot be determined
primarily by what people in power are talking about. Journalism must provide our early warning system. It is not necessary that all news media provide
all these services; that would be impractical. It is necessary that the media
system as a whole make such journalism a realistic expectation for the citizenry. Indeed, the measure of a free press is how well a system meets these
criteria. Understood in this manner, journalism requires resources, institutions, legal protection, and people who work at it full-time to be successful.
It may benefit from more than that, but these conditions are indispensable.

And understood this way, our current news media earn a low grade, even
using a curve.

What does the crisis of journalism entail? The corruption of journalism,
the decline of investigative reporting, the degeneration of political reporting
and international journalism, the absurd horse race coverage of campaigns,
the collapse of local journalism, the increasing prevalence of celebrity and
scandal are now acknowledged by all but the owners of large media firms
and their hired guns. *Washington Post* editors Len Downie and Robert
Kaiser wrote a critique of journalism in 2002 that was nothing short of devastating in its evaluation of how commercial pressures are destroying the
profession.[3] The 2006 "Report from the Project for Excellence in

Journalism" observes, "At many old-media companies, though not all, the decades-long battle at the top between idealists and accountants is now over. The idealists have lost." The same report gave an accounting of the state of journalism worth citing at length:

> Most local radio stations, our content study this year finds, offer virtually nothing in the way of reporters in the field. On local TV news, fewer and fewer stories feature correspondents, and the range of topics that get full treatment is narrowing even more to crime and accidents, plus weather, traffic and sports. On the Web, the Internet-only sites that have tried to produce original content (among them Slate and Salon) have struggled financially, while those thriving financially rely almost entirely on the work of others. Among blogs, there is little of what journalists would call reporting (our study this year finds reporting in just 5% of postings). Even in bigger newsrooms, journalists report that specialization is eroding as more reporters are recast into generalists.
>
> In some cities, the numbers alone tell the story. There are roughly half as many reporters covering metropolitan Philadelphia, for instance, as in 1980. The number of newspaper reporters there has fallen from 500 to 220. The pattern at the suburban papers around the city has been similar, though not as extreme. The local TV stations, with the exception of Fox, have cut back on traditional news coverage. The five AM radio stations that used to cover news have been reduced to two.
>
> As recently as 1990, the *Philadelphia Inquirer* had 46 reporters covering the city. Today it has 24.[4]

In February 2007, the *Washington Post* published an article on the state of international coverage in the U.S. news media by veteran foreign correspondent Pamela Constable. She wrote:

> Instead of stepping up coverage of international affairs, American newspapers and television networks are steadily cutting back. The [*Boston*] *Globe*, which stunned the journalism world last month by announcing that it would shut down its last three foreign bureaus, is the most recent example.
>
> Between 2002 and 2006, the number of foreign-based newspaper correspondents shrank from 188 to 141 (excluding the *Wall Street Journal*, which publishes Asian and European editions). The *Baltimore Sun*, which had cor-

respondents from Mexico to Beijing when I went to work there in 1978, now has none. *Newsday*, which once had half a dozen foreign bureaus, is about to shut down its last one, in Pakistan. Only four U.S. papers—the *Journal*, the *Los Angeles Times*, the *New York Times* and the *Washington Post*—still keep a stable of foreign correspondents.

Although more than 80 percent of the public obtains most of its foreign and national news from TV, the major networks are also closing down foreign bureaus, concentrating their resources on a few big stories such as Iraq.

In the 1980s, American TV networks each maintained about 15 foreign bureaus; today they have six or fewer. ABC has shut down its offices in Moscow, Paris and Tokyo; NBC closed bureaus in Beijing, Cairo and Johannesburg. Aside from a one-person ABC bureau in Nairobi, there are no network bureaus left at all in Africa, India or South America—regions that are home to more than 2 billion people.[5]

Working journalists routinely state that few outside the newsroom truly grasp how completely commercialism has gutted journalism over the past two decades. Linda Foley, the head of the Newspaper Guild, the union for print journalists, states that the number one concern of her members, by far, is how commercial pressure is destroying their craft. In December 2006 working journalists across the nation held a national day of protest to draw attention to the corporate demolition of journalism.[6] In the 1980s journalists tended to be the strongest defenders of the status quo. That is ancient history.

So thorough is the recognition that the existing corporate system is destroying journalism, that the acclaimed scholar Michael Schudson—who has been a singular critic of political economists who made structural criticism of U.S. news media, and who for years has argued that things are not so bad with the press—is concerned about Wall Street's negative impact on journalism. He wrote in 2007: "While all media matter, some matter more than others, and for the sake of democracy, print still counts most, especially print that devotes resources to gathering news. Network TV matters, cable TV matters, but when it comes to original investigation and reporting, newspapers are overwhelmingly the most important media. Wall Street, whose collective devotion to an informed citizenry is nil, seems determined to eviscerate newspapers."[7]

As I chronicled in chapter 4, in 2002 and 2003 the news media largely abrogated their duty by uncritically publishing administration lies and exaggerations that were instrumental in taking this nation to an unnecessary, illegal, and disastrous war.[8] So indefensible was the press coverage that both the *New York Times* and *Washington Post* issued apologies. In 2007, the former *Des Moines Register* editorial page editor Gilbert Cranberg took an arguably unprecedented step of demanding a formal public inquiry into the failure of the news media in reporting the buildup to the Iraq invasion.[9] I could go on and on and discuss Britney Spears and the other salacious idiocies that have become more prevalent in the news, particularly broadcast news, but we are long past the point where one needs to pile on to make this point.

Allow me to put what I have just described in somewhat different terms, to highlight how the conventional thinking of scholars and journalists has been so inadequate to address the current situation. Imagine if the federal government had issued an edict demanding that there be a sharp reduction in international journalism, or that local newsrooms be closed or their staffs and budgets slashed. Imagine if the president had issued an order that news media concentrate upon celebrities and trivia, rather than rigorously investigate and pursue lawbreaking in the White House, or critically evaluate the case the White House was making for invading another nation. Had that occurred, there would have been an outcry that would have made Watergate look like a day at the beach. Newsrooms would have exploded with rebellion. It would have been second only to the Civil War as a threat to the Republic. Professors of journalism and communication would have gone on hunger strikes; hell, entire universities would have shut down in protest. Yet, when quasi-monopolistic commercial interests effectively do pretty much the same thing, with a wink and a nod from the politicians in power, and leave our society as impoverished culturally as if it had been the result of a government fiat, it passes with barely minor protest in most newsrooms and in journalism and communication programs. That is in the process of changing . . . I hope.

One might inquire why it took so long for journalists and mainstream scholars to recognize these trends and ponder their significance. To no small extent that is a testament to the power of the professional journalism ideology. This canon removes the media system from critical analysis and places the emphasis on how well individual journalists execute their professional duties. (Hence the obsession with "liberal bias" of individual journalists, rather than the commercial and political biases of the system.) This was one of the great benefits of professional journalism to monopolistic newspaper owners, who wanted a framework for understanding journalism that removed them from the picture and made their role a given, mandated by the Constitution and the sages on Mount Rushmore rather than a variable that was of fundamental significance, should be debated, and could be changed. So the core problems in the structure were ignored, and because most working journalists are principled and competent, and because much good work is done even when the system is in crisis, many were oblivious to the overarching trends. But no longer.

The real concern is what accounts for the present crisis. In much of conventional parlance, the crisis is due primarily to the Internet providing competition to the dominant commercial news media and draining resources from the traditional journalism. This has led to an economic downturn for broadcast news and, especially, for daily newspapers, the guts of news procurement in the United States. As the Internet takes away advertisers and readers, daily newspapers lay off journalists, board up newsrooms, and prepare to join the horse and buggy in the annals of U.S. history. And the marketplace has provided no economic alternative to generate the resources for journalism as we know it online so society loses. The market has spoken, for now at least. Technology killed the goose that laid the golden egg. To add insult to injury, in the minds of some professional journalists, for all the blather about "new media" and their empowering effect, on balance the Internet has hastened the degradation and commercialization of news values across the board.[10]

The solution, to listen to the media corporations, is to permit existing media companies to merge and combine and become effective monopolies at the local level. Governments should, in effect, ratchet up their inducements, privileges, and direct and indirect subsidies to the media giants so they will have the resources to provide us with the journalism we need.[11] And we need not worry about monopoly because the Internet is providing a forum for everyone else.

The strength of this argument is that it has an element of evidence to support it. Newspaper revenues and profits are falling as its readership has flattened and is skewing older, much older. Moreover, at present, it is nowhere near profitable to transition from ink and paper to digital production and online distribution for newspapers. One study concluded "that a newspaper needs to attract two or three dozen online readers to make up for—in terms of advertising revenue—the loss of a single hard-copy reader."[12] But to stop the analysis here is misleading. Newspapers remain profitable on their operating expenses. They may not be raking in the monopolistic profits that made the balance of the business community envious for much of the twentieth century, but very few are shuttering their doors. And newspapers may well find a way to remain viable in the digital era.[13] The matter is less clear with regard to broadcast news media, which have gone even further in abandoning journalism. But the merger of broadcast news with Internet operations is advancing as well.

The weakness of "the Internet has killed the economic basis for journalism" argument is that the crisis in journalism emerged long before the Internet. In the 1980s and certainly by the 1990s news media were cutting back on reporters and resources. They were doing so when they were flush with money, because it was the profitable thing to do in the short term, and in the long run we will all be dead. News media were discouraging hard-hitting and expensive investigative reporting and softening their standards on trivial but commercially friendly news stories about celebrities and the like. By the early 1990s, in fact, a small but vocal group of prominent journalists were already declaring the "death of journalism." In their view, from their experiences, the corporations that dominated the U.S. news media—and that had become fewer in number due to considerable consolidation—were running it into the ground as they sought ever greater profits.[14] The corporate mind-set had little respect for the autonomy of professional journalism and was inclined to seeing the news converted into an immediately profitable undertaking first and foremost.

By then, too, before the World Wide Web the marked decline in youth newspaper readership was evident. Some, like Ben Bagdikian, argued that if the news media stopped doing actual news and started doing "infotainment" and "lifestyle" reporting to allegedly draw these young readers/viewers into the fold it would ultimately fail. Hollywood would easily trump the news media in providing young people with entertainment; once the news media stopped doing original and important journalism they would have a difficult time attracting new and younger readers and viewers. And if young people were not in the practice of being regular readers or viewers of conventional news, it would be much harder to draw them in as they grew older with their media patterns well established.[15]

Put this way, the policy solution offered by the industry and its advocates—to permit increased media concentration so the handful of media giants remains flush with profits—is a non-starter. The media giants were scrapping resources to journalism when they were swimming in profits, because there was even more money to be made by gutting the newsroom. Good journalism costs money so it is always tempting to water down the fare. Why on earth should anyone believe they are not going to continue to gut newsrooms when their profits are even harder to come by? Indeed the one clear outcome of permitting firms to establish ownership of newspapers, cable channels, and broadcast stations in the same community—media company towns, if you will—is that they will eliminate competing newsrooms and have one newsroom serve all outlets. With far less competition that invariably leads to a nonchalant approach to the news and no great punishment for a continued reduction in resources for journalism over time. The sad truth is that the media firms determined long ago that doing journalism was bad for the bottom line, and that conviction is more strongly held than ever, if one looks at these firms' actions rather than listen to their rhetoric. To the extent that Bagdikian and others made a plausible argument about the long-term wisdom of spending more on journalism in the short term, the response of the media corporations seems to have been to let some other chump test out that theory. If it works, they will join in the party. In the meantime, they will cash in their chips.

There is even a larger problem with the conventional wisdom that the crisis in journalism is due to the Internet: it rests on the assumption that all was fine with the world of U.S. news media in the not-too-distant past. Such an assumption, as I have demonstrated in this book, is bogus. Part of the problem is the misunderstanding about the origins and nature of professional journalism. The conventional explanation for the emergence of professional journalism had relied upon technology—for example, the telegraph and Associated Press making it necessary to have neutral content acceptable to a broad range of papers—or how it was in the economic interest of monopolistic publishers eager to serve the public-at-large to publish nonpartisan journalism so as not to alienate part of the market. Although these were important factors, what tended to be missing was a crucial component: the immense public dissatisfaction with the sensationalistic and decidedly conservative journalism of the times. New research, including extensive work by Ben Scott, highlighted just how significant a factor this public controversy was in pushing the emergence of professional journalism. In addition, there was a concurrent intense struggle between newspaper publishers and journalists to define professional journalism and gain control over the newsroom.[16] This struggle boiled over in the 1930s and 1940s with the organization of the Newspaper Guild. I will not keep you in suspense: the journalists lost.

Understood this way, professional journalism, which emerged over the course of the first half of the twentieth century, was far from perfect. The type of professional journalism that emerged was one more conducive to the needs of media owners than to journalists or citizens. Professional journalism's capacity to keep implicit commercial values out of the news was always nebulous, as the power to hire and fire and set budgets always resided with the owners. It allowed a certain measure of autonomy and independence for journalists from commercial and political pressures—and it certainly looked to be an improvement over what it replaced—and it has a commitment to factual accuracy that is admirable and perhaps its greatest legacy. Professional journalism's core problem, and by no means its only problem, is that it devolved to rely heavily upon "official sources" as the basis of legitimate news. Official sources get to determine what professional journalists could be factually accurate about in the first place. It gets worse. When elites were in general agreement, as was often the case concerning fundamental economic and foreign policies, professional journalism spoon-fed the conventional wisdom, which was often dead wrong, and offered little protection for the citizenry. But from the Gulf of Tonkin to Operation Iraqi Freedom our finest professional journalists did spoon-feed the misleading propaganda accurately.

This reliance upon official sources has always made professional journalism especially susceptible to well-funded corporate public relations, which could mask its self-interest behind a billion-dollar fig leaf of credentialed expertise. This problem only increases as newsrooms have fewer and fewer journalists to interrogate the PR claims. So it was that between 1995 and 2005 nary a single one of the nearly 1,000 refereed academic research journal articles on climate change disputed the notion that something fundamental, dangerous and influenced by humans was taking place. Yet our news media sources representing the interests of oil companies and other major polluters provided a significant official opposition to the notion that global warming was a problem or that pollution had anything to do with it. How significant? Over one-half of the 3,543 news articles in the popular press between 1991 and 2005 expressed doubt as to the existence and/or cause of global warming. The public would rationally assume this was an issue very much under debate by scientists and the best policy would be to do nothing until it was sorted out. This data is often presented as *prima facie* evidence of the power of corporate public relations laid bare. It is that, but it is even more a statement on weaknesses built into professional journalism as it developed in the United States.[17]

There are some who suggest—argue may be too strong a word for this position—that concerns about the decline of conventional journalism are greatly exaggerated because people learn about politics and the world around them through many other means than the news media. In particular, entertainment media such as *The Onion* and the Jon Stewart, Stephen Colbert, and Bill Maher comedy shows are increasingly where young people learn about the world.[18] Ben Barber has noted that one antidote to the commercialization of society (and toothless journalism) may come from Hollywood films, which in his view have demonstrated surprising and impressive social awareness in recent years.[19] Popular music, too, often addresses social and political issues. Maybe we don't need the news after all, or its importance has been exaggerated?

The problem with this reasoning is that the social commentary of comedians, filmmakers, and musicians is predicated upon a certain baseline understanding of the world that is provided by journalism. Jay Leno once commented that he has had to "dumb down" his political humor considerably and he now sets up his jokes with elementary background information: e.g., "You know Democrat Harry Reid is the Senate Majority Leader. . . ." Much of Stewart's and Colbert's humor is that by avoiding the increasingly counterproductive practices of mainstream journalism they can get directly to the truth of the matter, a truth largely obscured in the news, hence highlighting the asininity of much of what passes for contemporary political journalism.

No better example of this comes with the buildup to the U.S. invasion of Iraq in 2003. In January 2008 a comprehensive study by the nonpartisan Center for Public Integrity determined that there were fully 935 lies—with several hundred coming from President Bush and Vice President Cheney—told to the American people to generate popular support for a war in Iraq. These were not "gray area" statements, as the CPI's detailed database makes clear.[20] Nor were they oversights or merely clumsy missteps. As the report concludes, the lies "were part of an orchestrated campaign that effectively galvanized public opinion and, in the process, led the nation to war under decidedly false pretenses."[21] In mainstream professional journalism this has all been filed away in the dark memory hole, to the extent it is even acknowledged. When the same people who lied us into Iraq present fantastic and unsubstantiated claims about how swimmingly the Iraq War is going and about why the United States may well need to invade or destabilize a number of other nations, the respected professional journalists takes these claims quite seriously and at face value. Those who call the administration and its publicists liars are accused of making "solidarity-seeking buzz phrases," and certainly not of sufficient rectitude to report the news in a professional manner.[22]

Comedians need not suspend judgment and regurgitate what those in power say. They can simply tell the truth and let the chips fall where they may. Sometimes merely repeating what the president or a pro-administration pundit says verbatim can produce waves of laughter because of its absurdity. But, again, this is not necessarily reason for celebration, and it certainly does not solve the media problem in the United States. Ralph Nader once commented that the finest political satire and humor he ever saw was in the old Soviet Union. The humor was so biting and embraced because the official news media were so deplorable. Few, if any, would argue the people of the Soviet Union had a plausible political information system for a free society. Although it is well and good that, unlike in the old USSR, social critics are not imprisoned or working underground and are treated respectfully as long as they are entertainers and comedians, it would be far better if the same viewpoints were not dismissed as outside the range of legitimate debate, even lunacy, as soon as we entered the world of journalism.

So if having viable journalism is mandatory for a self-governing society, the current crisis is at the very center of what type of world we will be living in for the coming generations. And here, as with the disastrous invasion and occupation of Iraq, the place to look for answers is not with the people who created the problem or ignored the smoke signals and pooh-poohed the critics until the status quo was up in flames. Instead, the prudent course would be to look at the critics whose analysis best explains the current crisis of journalism and whose analysis has been on the mark the longest. In short, this is where we need look to the political economy of media.

Recall that in the 1960s and 1970s, professional journalism was riding high in the United States. Our news media were seen as effective at keeping our leaders in check and allowing citizens to have the power to govern their own lives. Bookstores were filled with tomes by heroic journalists discussing the great work they had done vanquishing the powerful and protecting the Republic. There was clear dissent to this generated by the New Left and the social movements of the 1960s, but surprisingly little compared to the uproar surrounding media in the 1930s or the Progressive Era or today. In the late 1970s, the field of sociology produced four notable books that dissected professional journalism, by Mark Fishman, Gaye Tuchman, Herbert Gans, and Todd Gitlin.[23] This outstanding research dramatically advanced the hard process of examining U.S. journalism critically. But it tended to accept the dominant institutional arrangements as a given. The institutions were unassailable, and the work tended to concentrate upon newsroom organization, professional practices, and the implications for content.

Soon thereafter, Ben Bagdikian's *The Media Monopoly*, published in 1983, and Herman and Chomsky's *Manufacturing Consent*, published in 1988, advanced this critique to draw in the political economic framework of analysis.[24] These two books fundamentally changed the way the news media were regarded, not only in the political economy of communication subfield and among activists in the United States, but eventually to a much broader public.[25] Bagdikian's work is often cited for quantifying the extent of concentrated media ownership in the United States, but it did far more than that. It also began the crucial process of linking up the development of professional journalism to the manner in which the newspaper industry was restructured in the early part of the twentieth century. It demonstrated the cozy relationship between media corporations and politicians, putting the lie to the idea of a feisty Fourth Estate. And Bagdikian pointed to an immediate future where journalism would get considerably worse, and the best aspects of professionalism would get demolished by corporate pressures.

Manufacturing Consent connected the step of linking up a structural explanation of news media content with an argument about how news tended to serve elite interests in the United States and was often significantly pro-pagandistic and antidemocratic. The work highlighted the important role media play in politics in general, and for popular and progressive political movements specifically. This work, and the research it inspired, demolished the notion that professionalism in journalism was neutral, objective, or dem-ocratic. It also illustrated the way commercial imperatives shaped the news directly and indirectly, through influencing how the professional code emerged.

It is arguable that nowhere has the power of political economy of media been more evident than in its critique of journalism. Many of the main insights are now roundly accepted, though often without acknowledging the political implications. It has provided the foundation for understanding the present crisis in journalism and therefore it may provide keen insights into the solutions. The starting point for a political economic analysis is that structure matters. Institutions matter. They matter a great deal. The impor-tance of structures, of institutions for shaping journalism and media content directly and indirectly is well understood when looking at other nations; it is only recently that American exceptionalism in this regard has begun to erode. It is not that owners and advertisers and managers need to directly interfere with or censor editors and journalists; it is more the case that orga-nizational structures transmit values that are internalized by those who suc-cessfully rise to the top.

This point was made clear to me back in the 1980s when I was told about the visit of a group of Soviet journalists to the University of Washington in Seattle. Apparently some U.S. journalism professors criticized the Soviet journalists to their faces for not being professional or objective, for even being stooges for the Communist Party and the state. The Soviet journalists, who came from the elite media like *Pravda*, *Tass*, and *Izvestia*, recoiled at this criticism. They were independent professional journalists, they explained. That their values and news judgment may have coincided with the needs of the party and the state was simply a convergence of responsible and educated minds. No KGB agents held AK-47s to their heads as they went about their work. No state censors harassed them. (Perhaps the journalists said this just to satisfy the KGB agents in their midst, but they convinced their skeptical American hosts of their sincerity.) No one told them what to write. They were every bit as free as American journalists, maybe more so because they had no profit-starved owners or advertisers to pester them. In a manner they were correct. The Soviet journalists who rose to the highest echelons had so internalized the dominant values of the Soviet system that they needed no direct intimidation to comply. Indeed, such pressure would have been destabilizing and only acceptable during a crisis.

Those Soviet journalists who did not internalize the necessary values fell by the wayside. And periodically there would be examples like Vladimir Danchev who would make clear how intelligent and responsible it was not to make waves in a Soviet newsroom. Danchev was the accomplished Radio Moscow announcer who in 1983 termed the Soviet forces in Afghanistan as "occupants," and "invaders," and stated the Afghan forces opposing the USSR were "defending the country's territory."[26] Danchev disappeared from his job and it was later acknowledged he was dispatched to a mental hospital in Uzbekistan for "psychiatric treatment." Because Danchev's father was a high-ranking party official, he was rehabilitated and allowed to return to work many months later at a lower position, with less autonomy.[27] I suspect it only took one incident like that every few years to communicate the proper values to those remaining in the Soviet news media who wished to succeed.[28]

I am loathe to compare Soviet media to the commercial news media system in the United States because there are so many important differences, and the U.S. system is vastly more open and free than the long-gone Communist system, but on this matter there are clear and noteworthy parallels.[29] U.S. journalists have internalized the values of their profession and those values have biases built into them. The professional code has eroded but values—political and commercial—are still communicated to journalists. And those that rise to the top of the corporate news media in the United States today tend to be those who internalize them and regard them as appropriate. When they see an iconic editor the stature of Bill Kovach leave the *Atlanta Constitution* and *Atlanta News* because, in part, he had the temerity to suggest great journalism is willing to critically investigate the most powerful businesses in Georgia against the wishes of the papers' owners, smart journalists accept that there are some stones best left unturned. When they see an accomplished investigative journalist like Gary Webb driven from the profession for having the audacity to investigate the CIA, smart journalists learn that this is a topic best left to others, unless they are clearly encouraged or supported by someone inside the intelligence establishment. I could go on and on, and I have in my earlier work.[30]

Those journalists whose antennae fail, or who do not internalize the dominant institutional values, do not end up in psychiatric hospitals in the U.S. version of Uzbekistan; they end up working beats other than politics, or they end up at the bottom of the journalism food chain, maybe as freelancers, or they look for work teaching journalism at a college or university, or they go into some other line of work.[31] But the starting point everywhere is to understand that the institutional and structural context is the main determinant. It does not answer all questions surrounding journalism, but even those it cannot answer it can provide necessary and useful context. This is where political economy of media has proven to be so valuable during this crisis.

From political economy of media research there are a handful of propositions to guide understanding, scholarship, and action. I discuss these in great detail in chapter 3 of *Communication Revolution*, so for our purposes I will summarize them in brief forthwith.

First, media systems are not *natural* or *inevitable;* they are the result of explicit policies and subsidies. The types of media systems societies end up with are strongly influenced by the political economy of the nation, but it is not a mechanistic or vulgar relationship. That commercial media is not a "default" system is clear from liberal democratic political theory: free people opt for the institution of private property because they regard it as the best way to advance their values. Likewise, a free people opt for commercial media because they determine it is the best way to promote the type of press system they deem desirable. And, of course, in democratic theory a free people may decide to have a noncapitalist economy, and likewise they may decide to have a noncommercial media system.

But, to be clear, the two matters are distinct in theory and in practice. Even in capitalist societies, it is not a given that the entirety of the media or communication system will be run for profit. Capitalist societies, including the United States, have had elements, sometimes significant, of their communication systems operating outside the marketplace during their history. When telegraphy came along, or radio broadcasting nearly a century later, the United States was certainly a capitalist nation, but there were debates about whether these emerging industries should be conducted by private profit-maximizing concerns, even by people who favored capitalism other-wise. Even today, professional journalism, perhaps the defining characteris-tic of our free press in our media textbooks, is explicitly a public service that does not, at its best, follow the commercial logic of the companies that house it. A core principle of professional journalism is to provide a safehouse for public service in the swamp of commercialism.

In short, media systems are created, even if the playing field is sloped at an ever greater angle toward dominant commercial interests.

Second, the First Amendment is not a piece of protectionist legislation meant to grant special privileges to investors in the communication sector to be exempt from government regulation.[32] It does not lock us into the status quo and render all structural media reforms unconstitutional. The oft-stated "libertarian" or neoliberal position—the idea that the Constitution requires that capitalists be the natural rulers of all media, to do as they please without government interference, regardless of the nature of the content they pro-vide—is dubious, if not bogus. The "libertarian" position holds that almost any regulation of media is unconstitutional. Media companies have consis-tently argued that it violates the First Amendment to, among other things, limit how many broadcast stations or cable companies a corporation can buy. Their argument rests on the assumption that media companies are just like individuals and that a good democracy must treat them like individuals.

C. Edwin Baker has done trailblazing research on the relationship of free-dom of the press and freedom of speech. Baker concludes that court inter-pretations of the Constitution clearly see the press as a necessary institution distinct from people exercising free speech rights, and also as distinct from other commercial enterprises.[33] But in academic discourse the question is usually framed as: "Does the press get special privileges individuals do not have?"[34] It is not usually framed as: "Can the media be saddled with extra obligations that individuals do not have?" or "Can the people enact policies to create a press that meets its constitutionally understood functions better than the existing press is doing?" Baker's theory, although supported by the evidence, is outside the mainstream of constitutional law at present, and the implications have not been addressed by the Supreme Court, but it could become important in the years to come. Baker has argued persuasively that the First Amendment permits the government to play an active role in creat-ing media and structuring the media system.[35]

During the founding period, when freedom of the press was being discussed, often by Jefferson and Madison, there was no sense they regarded the press as an inherently market-driven institution, where the right to make profit was sacrosanct.[36] Accordingly, Jefferson and Madison were obsessed with subsidizing the distribution of newspapers through the post office and supporting newspapers through printing subsidies as well.[37] An institution this important is not something you roll the dice of the commercial marketplace on and hope you get lucky. They understood the press in a pre-capitalist, if not noncapitalist, sense—and primarily as a political institution.[38] Nor did Madison or Jefferson have a romanticized notion of journalism. Jefferson's correspondence from his years as president is filled with screeds against the press of his day as an agent of destruction.[39] Such press pushed him not to censorship, but to policies to promote a better press.[40]

Moreover, when the Supreme Court has actually pondered what freedom of the press means under the First Amendment, it has not endorsed the neoliberal model of maximum profits equal maximum public service.[41] In some of the most important cases, the opinions suggest that freedom of the press is not an individual right to do as one pleases to make money. To the contrary, freedom of the press is in the Constitution to make self-government possible. The extraordinary majority opinions in the 1945 *Associated Press v. United States*,[42] and the 1971 Pentagon Papers (*New York Times v. United States*) case,[43] make that clear.[44] The spirit in several of these opinions is that the state has not only the right but the *duty* to see that a viable press system exists, for if such a media system does not exist the entire constitutional project will fail. If the existing press system is failing, it is imperative that the state create a system that will meet the constitutionally mandated requirements. At any rate, these opinions hardly suggest that the First Amendment is meant to provide a constitutional blank check to corporate media to do as they please, regardless of the implications for self-government.

At the same time, this is nothing if not a complex matter. The problem of establishing a press system, providing direct and indirect subsidies, yet preventing censorship and state domination defies a simple solution. And there may be no ideal solution, only a range of solutions where some are better than others.

Third, the U.S. media system is largely profit-driven, but it is not a free market system. The media and communication systems in the United States have been the recipients of enormous direct and indirect subsidies, arguably as great as or greater than any other industry in our economy. When communication firms claim they work in free markets, it should provoke more howls than a Jerry Lewis film festival in France. All commercial enterprises benefit by government spending, and hence get indirect subsidies (roads, public health, public schools, etc.). But the subsidies provided to media and communication firms go far beyond that. One need only start with the value of the monopoly licenses that are given for free to commercial radio and TV stations or to spectrum for satellite television, or monopoly cable TV and telephone franchises. The best estimate of FCC staffers of the market value of the publicly owned spectrum today—which is given to commercial broadcasters at no charge—is around $500 billion.[45] When one considers all the wealth created on the backs of the free gift of spectrum to broadcasters since the 1920s, all the empires built upon it, the total transfer is certainly well into the hundreds of billions of dollars. Nor are the public gifts to broadcasters, cable companies, and telephone companies the only subsidies, as I chronicle in *Communication Revolution*.

The term "government subsidies" tends to be held in disrepute in the United States, unlike "business investment," which is sacred, so let me be clear about this. I think subsidies can be good, and I think that in principle they are necessary. Subsidies are costs that are supposed to have benefits. It is in our interest that the extent and role of subsidies in our media system be recognized and appreciated. Copyright, for example, is a necessary evil, a "tax on knowledge," as the Founders understood it in the Constitution. It is necessary to give authors an incentive to write books, for creative people to generate content. The benefit of the massive printing and postal subsidies in the first few generations of the Republic, for example, was the establishment of an extraordinary press system and, with that, arguably the most advanced political democracy in the world. Our Founders regarded subsidies, in effect, as the price of civilization, or at least a viable republic. Many of our major communication revolutions, from the telegraph and radio to satellite communication and the Internet, were spawned as a result of massive government subsidies.

Even if one wanted a truly "free-market" media system, without direct or indirect subsidies, it would be awfully difficult, if not impossible, to construct. And, ironically, to implement and maintain anything remotely close to a truly competitive market would require extensive government coordination, probably far beyond what currently exists.[46] It would never happen naturally. But the last thing the dominant commercial interests want is their subsidies removed; as far as I can tell, the "free-market" think tanks are dedicated to promoting corporate domination in concentrated markets of the heavily subsidized communication system, rather than ending the heavily subsidized communication system. One need only look at how the self-proclaimed pro-free-market editorial page of the *Wall Street Journal* carries water for AT&T and the big government-created telephone and cable powerhouses to see how the notion of free markets in the realm of media and telecommunication is mostly a rhetorical ploy to protect entrenched monopolistic power.[47]

This argument over subsidies leads directly to the fourth proposition: the central importance of the policymaking process in structuring a media system. The question is not whether we will have subsidies and policies, but rather, what will the subsidies and policies be, what institutions will they support, and what values will they encourage and promote? When we talk about media, what most of us are concerned with, ultimately, is the content the media system produces and the effect that has upon our lives. But the content is shaped to a significant extent by the institutional structures of media systems, which is why political economists devote so much time to studying that issue. And the institutional structures are determined by policies and subsidies, which are in turn determined by the policymaking process. So that takes us to the nucleus of the media atom.[48]

The policymaking process in the United States has grown increasingly undemocratic as media and communication have become ever more lucrative industries. The policies and subsidies are made in the public's name but without the public's informed consent. That is pretty much how communication policymaking has been conducted in the United States. Monopoly broadcast licenses, copyright extensions, and tax subsidies are doled out all the time, but the public has no idea what is going on. Extremely powerful lobbyists battle it out with each other to get cushy deals from the FCC, whose members and top staffers almost inevitably move to private industry to cash in after their stint in "public service."

Above all else, the FCC has been dedicated to making the dominant firms bigger and more profitable. Congress, too, is under the thumb of big money.

The one thing the big firms all agree upon is that it is their system and the public has no role to play in the policymaking process. And because the news media almost never cover this story in the general news, hardly anyone outside of the industry—until recently—has any idea what is going on. If anything, they are fed a plateful of free-market hokum, extolling an industry that "gives the people what they want."

The empirical evidence is devastating: in the first six months of 2006 alone, communication and technology firms spent $172 million on lobbying in Washington, more than any other sector or group.[49] How serious is this lobbying army? Representative Edward Markey of Massachusetts states that the largest communication firms each have a lobbyist assigned to *each* member of Congress on the relevant committees.[50] In January 2007, AT&T convened a meeting of its Capitol Hill lobbying army. A standing-room-only audience attended in a conference room described as "the size of a stadium."[51] These firms also spend commanding amounts in candidate contributions and for public relations. When these firms do engage with the public on pressing policy matters, it is often in the form of phony "Astroturf" front groups—that is, the "fake grass roots."[52] Combine this with the extraordinarily high percentage of FCC members and top FCC officials (as well as members of Congress and congressional aides on the relevant committees) who leave the agency through the "golden revolving door" and go on to lucrative careers working for the firms and industries they were once theoretically regulating in the public interest.[53]

The fairy tale of free markets protects the corporate media system from the public review it deserves. I recall an exchange I had with Jack Fuller, a top executive of the Tribune Company, at a 2002 University of Illinois conference on the future of family-owned newspapers. Fuller, the president of Tribune's publishing subsidiary, was presented as the thinking person's media boss because he has written some books. Fuller thundered to the audience about how offensive he found it that he even had to travel to Washington and countenance the right of the government to have any say whatsoever over the affairs of his company. He said he found that to be a dire attack on the First Amendment. I asked Fuller about the many extremely valuable monopoly radio and TV licenses the Tribune Company accepted from the government at no charge, and how that affected him as he was working up his anger over government meddling in the affairs of Tribune.

Fuller paused and explained that the Tribune Company had no interest in broadcasting, but had been asked by the government to take the valuable monopoly licenses. We were left to assume nobody else wanted the opportunity to have a multimillion-dollar industry handed to them at no charge, and the Tribune Company was just being a good Samaritan, helping out a government in distress.

In fact, Fuller had it exactly wrong. Back in the 1920s, the Tribune Company sent its top lawyer, Louis Caldwell, to Washington to work for the government's newly created Federal Radio Commission, specifically to allocate the radio stations to commercial interests. At the time, Caldwell argued that the government needed to have draconian power over selecting who was allowed to have a monopoly radio broadcasting license and, conversely, who was not. Caldwell argued that determining the rulers of the airwaves was a government job of such magnitude that it could not be trusted to as democratic a body as Congress, which might be unduly influenced by people without sufficient expertise to make the right call. This expertise was to be found, apparently, exclusively in the hands of engineers and lawyers working for the commercial broadcasting industry. Coincidentally, as a result of Caldwell's labor, the Tribune Company's WGN was awarded at no charge one of the handful of clear channel signals, worth, even then, countless millions of dollars. Once the commercial system was in place and the lucrative monopoly licenses had been doled out in complete secrecy, Caldwell did a 180-degree turn and argued that any regulation of commercial broadcasting violated the First Amendment.[54] Jack Fuller was carrying on in Caldwell's tradition.

As the Fuller encounter demonstrates, the propositions of the political economy of media undercut the positions of communication corporations and their advocates by shining a light on the two great and indefensible blind spots upon which their arguments for the status quo are based. The first blind spot was the "immaculate conception" notion of the U.S. media system, the idea that corporations "naturally" assumed control because it was the American way. It requires the "immaculate conception" for industry and its defenders to shift seamlessly into a righteous lather about transgressions of the state. I recall being invited to the Milt Rosenberg program on (Tribune-owned) WGN radio in 1999 to discuss my book *Rich Media, Poor Democracy*. To provide the home team perspective, Rosenberg also invited an editor from the *Chicago Tribune* to join us. Both the editor and Rosenberg conceded that some of my criticism of the media system was accurate, but waxed on about the evils of government censorship and how WGN had a First Amendment right to operate as it pleased. When I was asked to respond, I merely asked why WGN had been granted the monopoly license in the first place. Why not the Chicago Federation of Labor or some other commercial enterprise? Why did we assume that WGN was the rightful steward of that frequency? Initially flummoxed, both the editor and Rosenberg conceded the point and quickly moved on to another topic.[55]

The second blind spot is the extent of public subsidies. Communication firms and their advocates love to wave the flag of free market economics; acknowledging the extent of their massive public subsidies blows up the free market argument. What was striking to me during my research was that the four main "free market" think tanks in Washington—the Cato Institute, Heritage Foundation, American Enterprise Institute, and Progress and Freedom Foundation—which often weigh in on behalf of communication corporations and against government "interference" with free markets, did no discernible research on the extent of subsidies.[56] When the state funnels tens of billions of dollars in subsidies to the firms that often bankroll these think tanks, it is not worth noting; if pressed, they confess it is troubling and move on to another topic. But when the government asks for anything in return for those subsidies, it is like the Sword of Damocles is being held over the very survival of freedom in our land.

Once the importance of the policymaking process is understood and the corruption of the process is grasped, our understanding of communication changes dramatically. Consider the term "deregulation," which is used frequently by journalists and scholars to describe when big media firms look to see media ownership rules relaxed or eliminated. If we had a free-market media system, this use of the term would be accurate, in the sense that market forces would play a larger role than the state in setting the terms of competition. But in telephony, broadcasting, cable, or satellite communication, the term is pure propaganda. It is meant to imply a competitive market outcome, when as often as not this "deregulation" leads to far less market competition.

So political economy of media not only explains the crisis of journalism, it explains how we get the institutions that produce the crisis in journalism.

Accordingly, it points the way forward: structural change, through policy reform. We have to create a system that makes it rational to produce great journalism, and the clear lesson we have is that the really existing market-place will not do the job. It has failed. As our friends in public relations like to say, we have to go in a different direction.

The prospect of engaging in policy reform and structural change is a difficult pill to swallow for many journalists and citizens, weaned on the notion that we have a press system entirely independent of the government, and that any government involvement puts us dangerously close to a slippery slope to tyranny. Even recognizing the failures of the marketplace and the cornerstone role of government policies and subsidies in building our press system, for many observers the notion of recognizing the state's role remains anathema, and there is an almost palpable desperation to find an alternative that avoids politics. This is understandable, but a frank recognition of the government role should also make possible a careful consideration of enlightened government policies. It is simply untenable and serves only to protect entrenched corporate interests to presuppose that there are two and only two alternatives for the American people: either a corporate status quo that guts journalism or *1984*. There are innumerable other models for a press system, many arguably superior to what exists, if we only open up our minds and expand our horizons, and look to our own history.

There is more than a little irony to hear proponents of the status quo raise concerns about the dangers of state interference and censorship in our media system if measures are taken for constructive structural change. The same media corporations that raise these concerns often acquiesce to government policy—especially on military matters, where dissidence is most important. It was striking that public and community broadcasters in the United States—who receive direct government subsidies in addition to indirect subsidies through their monopoly broadcast licenses—showed more criticism of the U.S. government during the invasion and occupation of Iraq (though at times, not much) than the "independent" commercial news media.[57] Moreover, these same firms that are so obsessed with government intrusion on the press demonstrate little concern about the expanded police state activities of the government or, of direct pertinence, of increased government secrecy. This is true for their actual news coverage and with their lobbying arsenals in Washington. For every lobbying dollar these firms spend to battle for open government, I suspect countless hundreds of thousands, or millions, or tens of millions, are spent to promote corporate rights to hold an ever larger number of government monopoly licenses and to generally promote their profitability above all else. The relationship may be impossible to compute mathematically because in most cases the former number is likely to be zero.

Not that the concern with state censorship is illegitimate. Quite the contrary. Direct state censorship is unacceptable. It is imperative to have policies that protect the integrity of freedom of speech and promote a climate that is welcoming to dissent. What political economy recognizes is that the policies, and the structures they foster, implicitly encourage certain values and discourage others, encourage certain types of content, and discourage alternatives. Enlightened policymaking recognizes that and seeks to create a range of structures that can provide for the information needs of the people, and that allows for as much openness, freedom, and diversity as possible. That is freedom of the press.

This does not mean that reforms that do not directly challenge the commercial system are meaningless, merely that they are insufficient on their own to get the job done. Nearly all of the seemingly nonstructural solutions to the crisis in journalism are worth pursuing and have some value.

It would be outstanding, for example, if our schools and universities did a better job of educating budding journalists. At the same time, this approach is of limited value. What good is it to educate journalists in public-service values if there are few paying jobs for them or if they end up covering celebrity scandals or regurgitating press releases and providing stenography to power? It would also help if our schools and colleges educated students in general to appreciate the role and importance of news, and how media operate. This is often termed media literacy. This would create better content and market demand for that content. Likewise, it would be helpful if student media were expanded at universities and high schools across the nation, rather than being cut back. Research demonstrates the key role student media play in fostering an appreciation for journalism and freedom of the press.[58]

It would also be helpful if entrepreneurs could find ways to use the new communication technologies to find a lucrative market for quality popular journalism. But so far this has not happened, and even if it does the effect of

the Internet on commercial journalism, as noted earlier, has been to accentuate the flaws in contemporary journalism as much as to erase them.[59] The
clear lesson of U.S. history is that we need to have a sector producing journalism walled off from corporate and commercial pressures. It would help
matters if philanthropists and foundations began to devote significant portions of their portfolios to increasing the amount and quality of news and
public information. But that has not happened yet, and if it did there would
remain knotty problems about where these funds would go and how these
news media would be managed.

Note, too, that though these approaches may not be especially "structural,"
all of these approaches are determined by public policies, by politics, to
varying degrees. Journalism education and media literacy require resources,
often public resources. Indeed, media literacy probably necessitates a public
campaign to win over school boards. Getting viable student media in high
schools and colleges is very much a public policy issue, and a crucial one for
media reform at that. Making it possible for new entrepreneurs to enter the
journalism field is greatly aided by government anti-monopoly regulation,
and by tax and credit rules that lower barriers to entry. Government advertising and postal rates can also play a significant role, too, in easing the way for
new media players to enter markets. Likewise, it will require policy assistance
to make it possible for philanthropies or nonprofit organizations to play a
larger role. These organizations exist and have their range of operations
determined by public policy. In fact, all of these seemingly "inside the system" efforts to rejuvenate journalism depend upon an aroused citizenry and
public policy activism. They are elements of the media reform movement.

Nowhere is the importance of policy more striking than with the Internet
and the digital revolution, and it is here that people often regard the Internet
as some sort of magical technology unaffected by policy. As noted before,
media chieftains argue that ownership restrictions are irrelevant today
because the Internet has blasted open the system, generating millions of new
media. They are not the only ones. Critics of corporate media and capitalism
sometimes join the chorus, stating that citizens can do whatever they want
online, as long as they get their act together. Technology has slain the corporate media system, and the future is very much up for grabs. The blogosphere is democracy's tidal wave to overwhelm the commercial news media
status quo. The King Is Dead. Long Live the King.

Wouldn't our lives be easy if this were true? The argument is fatally flawed: the openness of the Internet is due to policy as well as technology. Telecommunications companies and cable companies have the power to censor the Internet and work hand-in-hand with the governments that grant them monopoly license to do exactly that. We see that in nations like China where major U.S. firms work with the Chinese authorities to create a tightly controlled Web and digital communication world.[60] But it is also true in the United States, where the largest telecommunication companies worked closely with the Bush administration to illegally spy on U.S. citizens. In 2008, as these words were written, the Senate was enmeshed in an intense fight between Democrats and the Bush administration, which was obsessed with getting "retroactive immunity" for the telecommunication companies for their illegal spying written into the extension of the Foreign Intelligence Surveillance Act.[61]

This matter deserves more treatment, because for all the understandable hype about how the Internet and digital communication liberate people and revolutionize our lives, they also come at a price, the elimination of privacy as we have known it and allowing the government and corporate interests to know a great deal more about us, generally surreptitiously. The threat of state harassment is greater today than at any time in our history. For many Americans this may seem like an abstract threat, or a concern only to those engaged in crime or terrorism. Far more apparent is how marketers and commercial interests are extending and deepening their penetration of our lives through cyberspace. Back in the early 1930s, James Rorty called advertising "our master's voice," referring to corporations and the power they held in U.S. society.[62] In his view advertising provided a pervasive propaganda for capitalism and for corporate domination of society. To the extent that this is true, Rorty lived in a noncommercial socialist republic in the 1930s compared to what Americans experience today.[63] These intrusions can be limited, but technology will not do the job for us. To protect privacy and freedom requires explicit policies, and a government committed to the rule of law. Unless we take proactive steps, we may come to regret the day the computer was invented.

There are additional policy issues that must be resolved successfully for the Internet to even begin to fulfill its promise for society, and for journalism. For starters, if the Internet is to provide the foundation for free speech and a free press, it has to be ubiquitous, high speed, and inexpensive.

Our goal should be to have broadband access as a civil right for all Americans, at a nominal direct fee, much like access to water. This is not simply for political and cultural reasons, but for economic reasons as well. Already the decline of broadband speeds and the broadband penetration rate in the United States compared to European and Asian rivals is a factor undermining economic innovation and growth. A 2007 article in *Information Week* put the U.S. situation in context: "The United States currently ranks twelfth in broadband adoption rates, significantly down from its ranking of fourth in 2001, according to the Organization for Economic Co-operation and Development, a thirty-nation group committed to the development of democratic governments and market economies. The International Telecommunications Union lists the United States as twenty-first worldwide for broadband penetration rate in 2005. Point Topic shows the United States in twentieth place by number of households with broadband access and nineteenth by individual broadband access. Those ranks have been falling, not rising, in recent quarters."[64]

What accounts for the U.S. decline? The first place to look is the stranglehold of the telephone and cable giants over broadband, due to their government-granted monopoly franchises granted in the pre-Internet era. These firms have no great desire to offer a service to poor people or difficult-to-reach rural areas, and they certainly have no interest in a ubiquitous service. It is far better to have a dirt lane to scare consumers into paying more to get faster service. And because broadband is an effective duopoly in the United States there is little market pressure to generate the speeds and lower costs that other nations are achieving. That would require enlightened regulation and planning in the public interest, something the battalions of lobbyists these firms employ are commissioned to prevent.

The relationship of the telecommunication and cable giants to the progressive development of the Internet is not in doubt: it is almost nonexistent. As Representative Edward Markey, Democrat of Massachusetts and chair of the subcommittee that oversees the Internet and telecommunication matters, put it in a 2007 speech, "AT&T was offered, in 1966, the opportunity to build the Internet. They were offered the contract to build it. But they turned it down. Now let me ask you this: what has AT&T done since then to develop the Internet? The answer is: nothing. What has Verizon done to help invent the World Wide Web? Nothing. What did they do in order to invent the browser? Nothing. These companies did virtually nothing to develop any-thing that has to do with what we now know as the Internet today." [65]

What the telephone and cable companies are singularly distinguished in is lobbying; their entire business models have been built on wooing politi-cians and regulators for monopoly licenses and sweetheart regulations much more than serving consumers. It is the basis of their existence.[66] They hope to parlay their world-class lobbying muscle into carving out a digital gold mine at this critical juncture. The boldest effort, and where the most impor-tant fight lays, is over their efforts to effectively privatize the Internet. The telephone and cable companies want the right to control which Web sites and services you can have access to, and which you cannot. If the AT&Ts and Verizons and Comcasts of the world are able to pull this off, all bets are off for the radical potential of the digital revolution.

This struggle to keep the Internet open, to prevent the telephone and cable giants from controlling which Web sites get favored treatment is the battle to preserve Network Neutrality. The huge cable and phone companies are champing at the bit to set up a "fast track" on the Internet for their favored sites or those sites that give them a cut of the action. Web sites that refuse to pay a premium would get the slow lane, and probably oblivion. The cable and telephone companies claim they need to have this monopoly power to generate sufficient profits to build out the broadband network, but the evidence for this claim is nonexistent. Jeff Chester states: "Cable and tele-phone subscribers have paid for a super-fast broadband network several times over. Network Neutrality will do absolutely nothing in terms of dent-ing returns or slowing down deployment. Look, the reason that the cable and phone companies oppose Network Neutrality is they're desperate to extend their monopoly business model from multichannel video to the broadband world."[67] As an appalled Markey put it in 2007, "And now they say they have a right to put up the toll roads, showing up as though they should own it all."[68] While describing what the phone and cable companies are trying to do, Columbia University law professor Tim Wu explained: "You know, com-panies can do two things, they can either offer more value, or they can try and extract cash from companies because they're in a position to threaten them. The first helps the economy, the second is just extortion. It's the Tony Soprano system, you know, it's like a protection racket, and it's not an eco-nomically productive activity."[69] The stakes are so high that much of the balance of the business community, not to mention everyone else in society, is in favor of Network Neutrality, to the extent they know it is an issue at all.[70]

The next great battleground for Net Neutrality is going to be cell phones and wireless communication. "We are about to open a new front in the Net Neutrality wars: wireless," writes Michael Calabrese of the New America Foundation. "Cellular phone and data today is a nightmare image of what the Internet would be like without Net Neutrality—and, as the world goes wireless, it may be the way of the future, unless we push back."[71] Tim Wu and Milton Mueller have launched research into this area, but much more needs to be done.[72] In many ways this is the signal free speech battle of the digital era.[73]

The future of a free press is dependent upon ubiquitous, inexpensive, and super-fast Internet access as well as Network Neutrality. In 2008, for example, the *Capital Times* of Madison, Wisconsin, became the first U.S. daily newspaper to convert its operations to primarily digital production and distribution—it went from ink and paper to bits. It could do so because of an agreement with the other daily newspaper in Madison that allowed the *Capital Times* a revenue base to cover what would be obvious losses for the immediate future as it entered the digital world.[74] It did this despite concerns that many of its older and poorer readers would lose access to the paper, and recognizing the uncertainty that Net Neutrality would be maintained so the phone and cable companies would not demand a ransom for the newspaper to have access to the public. For the Internet to develop as the viable basis for a free press, ending the digital divide and stopping of corporate privatization of the Internet (and the broader realm of digital communication) are mandatory.

That being said, although necessary, protecting online privacy, establishing a ubiquitous and high-speed Internet, and maintaining Net Neutrality will not solve the crisis of journalism. Among the most important lessons we have learned in the past decade has been that doing good media, even in the digital era, requires resources and institutional support. The Internet does many things, but it does not wave a magic wand over media bank accounts. I recall a conversation I had with a prominent, retired television journalist in 2004. He told me with great enthusiasm that with the Internet all of his journalistic needs were met: he could find all the reporting he needed from around the world on his computer. He went on and on about how he now read the great newspapers of the world online every morning. He compared his blissful situation with the Dark Ages: B.I. (Before Internet), when access to such a range of news media would have been pretty much impossible, even for world leaders and corporate CEOs. I asked this retired journalist what the Internet informed him about doings in Schenectady, New York. He looked at me quizzically, thinking I must be from Schenectady and probably feeling some measure of sympathy for me. But, as I explained, my point was that the Internet made existing journalism available, but it was not creating lots of new journalism, and by that I mean research and reporting, not just commenting on someone else's research and reporting. And, I told him, it was not clear how existing journalism would segue to the Internet and maintain its revenue base while commercial pressures were lowering the resources going to journalism overall. In community after community, like Schenectady, there was precious little journalism, and *Le Monde* was assigning no correspondents to cover the Schenectady School Board meeting. He conceded the point.

This is not to deny the potential of the blogosphere, social networks, and citizen journalists. No matter what happens, their emergence is radically changing journalism, and often for the better.[75] Even beyond the notion of citizen journalists, the digital revolution is opening up the potential of access to information that still boggles the mind, even as we approach the end of the second decade of the World Wide Web. The ability of people to collaborate and work together to share and expand knowledge—exemplified by wikis— is revolutionary, in the literal meaning of the word.[76] But the need for paid journalists who work full-time, have resources, generate expertise, and have institutional support to protect them from governmental or corporate harassment remains as strong as ever. And having competing newsrooms of such journalists is just as important. Citizen journalism and social information networks will flower in a marriage with enhanced professional journalism, not as a replacement for it.

So we cannot sit by and expect the Internet or the marketplace to solve the crisis. In fact, the crisis is so severe, and the stakes are so high, even if we could win the policy fights for more journalism education, more media literacy, more student media, more local commercial media, more foundation support, digital privacy, and ubiquitous, inexpensive, super-fast Internet access with Net Neutrality, that would be helpful but insufficient to accomplish the task at hand. There is no magic policy bullet to solve the problem, no single policy to pursue to correct the situation. There are three layers of policy solutions, moving from those just mentioned to the more radical. And, as we will see, even those are insufficient, or, perhaps better put, cannot be won without a broader movement for social reform.

The second layer of policies are those that more aggressively shape the news media system and are legitimate within the range of policy debates in the United States. These include antitrust and communication laws to promote diverse media ownership as well as using postal subsidies to encourage a broad range of publications. The single most valuable of these may be the tradition of establishing nonprofit and noncommercial broadcast media, specifically public and community broadcasting, and public access television channels. In other nations public and community broadcasters have been a stalwart of quality independent journalism, and buffers against commercial degeneration.

We can now see that the obituary for public broadcasting was premature. In the 1990s it was widely assumed that the plethora of digital channels rendered publicly subsidized media moot because there would be an array of commercial options for every conceivable need. Now it is clear that not only is that not the case, but in fact there are core media needs that commercialism can never fulfill. Accordingly, we have to rethink public media in a revolutionary manner, and with digital technologies we have the tools to do so. It can be a pluralistic and heterogeneous sector with a variety of structures and missions. Noncommercial and nonprofit public media remain strikingly popular in those nations where the institutions have been well established, and even in the United States, where public broadcasting has been at most a marginal institution, it has shown surprising resiliency. (Britain spends more than fifty times more per capita in public funds on the BBC than the United States does on NPR and PBS.) It is true that the *broadcasting* in "public broadcasting" may soon be obsolete, but the *public* will not. We are now in a period when we have to reimagine the forms and structures of nonprofit and noncommercial media, developing a palette of policy options to study, debate, and consider. And the vision must be broad, going far beyond what has been done in the past—and beyond journalism to broader cultural production as well. Moreover, if this work is not done and done successfully, there is every reason to believe that U.S. public broadcasting, specifically public television, will continue to decline, if not disintegrate.[77]

There are two areas where public and community broadcasters cum media can play a central role: first, in the provision of local journalism. The commercial broadcasting system has degraded, if not abandoned, this aspect of its operations. If our public and community broadcasters had BBC-type funding, which would translate into some $20 billion annually, there could be multiple competing public newsrooms, with different organization structures, in scores of communities. That may provide a competitive spur to the commercial news media to get back in the game, especially as they see there is an interest in the material. Yes, I know, people will say $20 billion is a lot of money, and will require massive tax hikes to be justified and nobody will be willing to go for that. But spending that sort of money is small potatoes and hardly subject to debate when Wall Street howls about a crisis or when there is a Third World country to invade on the other side of the globe. No one asks where the money is going to come from then; apparently it is a matter of small concern. It is all a matter of priorities. And even with far less than $20 billion, public and community media could do wonders for the currently decimated local news media landscape.

Second, one concern generally underdiscussed is how the Internet allows Americans to construct a personalized media world where they share common experiences with fewer and fewer of the fellow citizens. As Cass Sunstein argues, this "Daily Me" that people construct on their Web makes them share far less with each other than in the past, especially with people they might disagree with on matters of politics or culture. This may be a form of "freedom" for the individual, but it exacts what may be a very high social cost. What follows is a "group polarization," as people grow less informed, less respectful, and more distrustful of people outside their own group. There is a withering of the experiences that provide the bonds that make us understand that we are all in this together. Sunstein concludes that this produces a "real problem for democracy."[78] In addition, this "group polarization" is strongly egged on by the desire or need of marketers to split Americans up into bite-sized demographic groups so it is easier to sell them things. As Sunstein's analysis implies, journalism is at the center of what Americans need to share if we are going to have a viable republic. The evidence is in: commercial journalism is comfortable serving the demographic groups that are most profitable for the owners and desirable to advertisers, and disregarding less lucrative parts of the population.[79] It is public broadcasting cum media that is best positioned to provide the basis for a common shared journalism to which all Americans can relate. Public and community media cannot do this by themselves, nor should they, but they can provide a necessary and valuable foundation.

Even if we win great victories on this second layer of policy measures, I do not think it would be sufficient. I think we need to go to a third and more radical layer, and begin to rethink the structures and organizations of news media in a fundamental way. We need to acknowledge the limitations of the options available in the first two layers of policies, and expand and enhance our options. We need to consider policies to encourage local ownership, employee ownership, and/or community ownership of daily newspapers, knowing that newspapers will be largely digital within a generation, and hence indistinguishable with other media forms. What we are talking about is the social production of journalism. We need to seek guidance from the experiences of other nations and from our own history. As noted above, what is striking when one studies the real history of freedom of the press in the United States is that the Founders did not regard the First Amendment as authorizing media to be a source of profits above all else. Jefferson and Madison, in particular, promoted a series of extraordinary subsidies—in particular, printing and postal—to spawn a far more vibrant print culture than would have existed had the matter been left to the market. They understood self-government would be impossible without a vibrant press, and the government had a duty to assure such a free press existed. We need to go back to their spirit and attack the problem with an open mind.

In short, it is imperative that we conduct research on alternative policies and structures that can generate journalism and quality media content. The process has begun. More than a decade ago, Dean Baker was arguing for a $100 tax credit that a taxpayer could donate to any nonprofit news medium of her choice. This would spawn a potentially multibillion-dollar subsidy for the nonprofit media sector with no government role in selecting the recipients of the money. The idea seemed fanciful then; today it is enlightened. Already, people like Orville Schell, former dean of the University of California—Berkeley School of Journalism, and Geneva Overholser, former editor of the *Des Moines Register* and now professor at the University of Missouri School of Journalism, are putting their minds to this project.[80] Charles Lewis, the legendary founder of the Center for Public Integrity, makes a powerful case for a substantial nonprofit sector to be responsible for journalism.[81] The *Columbia Journalism Review*, the flagship for professional journalism, devotes sympathetic features to the issue of establishing policies and government subsidies that might better produce journalism than the commercial system.[82] This would have been unthinkable a decade ago. What was once considered "radical" is now fair game for some of the more established members of the journalistic profession.[83] We know we are in uncharted waters when, in 2006, the heir to the Chandler newspaper fortune acknowledges the failure of the system that made him fabulously wealthy and calls for community ownership of newspapers.[84]

So this is how the political economy of media diagnoses the crisis of journalism, and how it points the way forward. At this point an occasional response is, understandably, "Wait a second, what about the audience, the public? Are they not responsible for this mess? If they really had an interest in the type of journalism you propose as necessary for self-government, wouldn't commercial media be certain to give it to them?" The logic is powerful. The traditional rejoinder from journalists is that journalism is not supposed to be determined by market values, but that it has an innate social duty regardless of how much public interest there might be in the material. Political economists like to point out that the public's lack of interest in conventional news may be due to the fact that conventional news is so fruitless. It is the supply-side factors—far lower costs and lack of controversy with powerful political and commercial interests—that pushed the news to celebrity and scandals and natural disasters and regurgitating political spin, not public demand. But once exposed to a steady diet of crap the public has not been able to develop a taste for great journalism, and the market provides less of it as a result. It is understandable people would lose interest in journalism; so there is a downward spiral. Sometimes, flustered, I have barked out that this approach of assigning responsibility for the deplorable state of journalism to the public is tantamount to "blaming the victim." Clearly, I argued, we need to look at the system.

But this response, by journalists or by political economists, and, in occasional fits, by me, is insufficient and inadequate. The criticism con-

cerning the audience is correct at a fundamental level, and if political economy of media stops its analysis of journalism at this point its value is understandably questioned. If ours were a politicized society, where people were
engaged with politics as a matter of fundamental importance, even life and
death, the sort of drivel that passes for journalism today would be impossible, even in a commercial system. The cause of depoliticization runs deeper
than the news media. Our lousy journalism may reinforce depoliticization,
but it does not cause it. There is something more profound here. By this
logic, changing media alone would not ipso facto produce a highly politically engaged democracy. In fact, media reform in isolation from other
reforms, if such a prospect were even plausible, probably could only be
partially successful.

Far from being a repudiation of political economy of media, this criticism
completes the political economy of media and its analysis of journalism.
There are two sides to the political economy of media coin. On one side, the
side upon which this chapter has concentrated, we examine the firms, owners, labor practices, market structures, policies, occupational codes, and subsidies that in combination provide the context for the production of journalism and media. The other side of the political economy coin looks at how
journalism as a whole, the media system as a whole, interacts with broad
social and economic relations in society. Does the media system tend to challenge or reinforce broader trends within society? It is here that we find the
source of depoliticization, and this is a staple insight of political economy
and critical theory, drawing from C. Wright Mills, Herbert Marcuse, and C.
P. Macpherson among others.[85] In short, in a society with significant social
and economic inequality, depoliticization is encouraged by those who are
atop the social structure, especially in democratic societies. Looked at from
the perspective of those at the bottom, the further down the social pecking
order one goes, depoliticization is a more rational response by a person
because it is a frank acknowledgement of how much power an individual
actually has. Why waste time learning about a political world you have no
influence over? It is only a form of self-torture.[86]

The political economy of media has always been about the task of
enhancing participatory democracy; media and communication systems are
a means to an end, with the end being social justice and human happiness.
We need satisfactory journalism and media systems to have a just and sus-

tainable society. We study media so closely, because in a democratic society journalism is the primary means through which the mass of people may effectively equip themselves to effectively participate. It is a central political battlefield. But media are far from the only variable, as important as they are.

Understood in this manner, political economy of media offers two additional observations about how to think about journalism. The first goes to journalists and those who aspire to be journalists. It is written, often and accurately, that democracy requires journalism. It is not an exaggeration that our entire constitutional system is predicated on there being an informed and engaged citizenry, and the press system is charged with the task of making that possible. That is the point of the most eloquent opinions on freedom of the press by Hugo Black and Potter Stewart. But the converse is every bit as true and even more important: journalism needs democracy. Journalism is not agnostic about whether a society is fascist or authoritarian or democratic. Its survival as a credible entity depends upon their being democracy. If a society is formally democratic, with rampant inequality and vast demoralization and depoliticization, journalism as defined at the outset of this chapter will be especially contentious and difficult to conduct, and the news will tend to gravitate toward propaganda. Journalism is committed to ending information inequality and therefore has a stake in seeing the lessening of social inequality. Journalism requires a society committed to openness, the rule of law, and justice to prosper. Journalism opposes corruption and secrecy and attacks on civil liberties and therefore has a stake in lessening militarism, as Madison and Lincoln both understood militarism: a powerful force that unchecked leads inevitably to corruption, inequality, secrecy, attacks on civil liberties, and the end of the Republic.[87]

Some of our greatest journalists, from George Seldes and Haywood Broun and I. F. Stone to Bill Moyers and Amy Goodman and Charles Lewis, have understood the importance of democracy for journalism. This did not make them less professional, less concerned with fairness or factual accuracy. This did not make them treat one political party with kid gloves and another party with a guillotine. It did not justify a double standard. It only gave them a much stronger sense of mission and of what is at stake. They saw and see journalism as representing the interests of all those outside of power, those without a voice, those who desperately need journalism to effectively govern their lives in a contest with those who own and dominate the country and see journalism often as a nuisance, and who are none too excited about the prospect of an informed population.

The second observation applies to journalists and everyone else. The battle to reform media and to establish the basis for the journalism a free society requires cannot be fought in isolation. It is necessarily part of closely related political movements to make our electoral system, voting systems, and political campaigns more fair and open. It is part of broader social and political movements for justice, to democratize the institutions of our society and draw people into the heart of public life. It is only in the context of people coming together to struggle for social change that depoliticization is vanquished and victory becomes plausible, even inevitable. Media reform is necessary to make such democratic politics possible and such democratic politics must enjoy a measure of success for media reform to make any genuine advances. Journalism depends upon media reform; media reform and broader movements for social justice rise and fall together.

SECTION II:
CRITICAL STUDIES

The nine chapters in Section II cover a broad range of topics and were written between 1987 and 2003. What unites studies of sports, the emergence of commercial broadcasting in the United States, philanthropic foundations and media policy making, public broadcasting, the First Amendment, advertising and hyper-commercialism, neoliberalism, the new economy, and global communication is my critical approach and my political economic framework. Many of these chapters address the enduring themes of the political economy of media tradition. A few of these chapters would appear in different versions in my books, but most were stand-alone pieces. To the extent these chapters provide valuable insights, it is a testament to my field as much as it is to me. Several of the issues touched on here return in Section III, where the critique metastasizes into essays on media politics and social change.

6

The Battle for the U.S. Airwaves, 1928–1935

Much mass communications research assumes that the character of the U.S. media system—private, operated for profit, subsidized by advertising revenues—is innate. Some scholars believe the best possible system has been adopted; others, perhaps less positive, assume the system is entrenched and immune to challenge. Such presuppositions are troubling. By treating the institutional and social relations of mass communication as given, normal, and implicitly neutral if not socially beneficial, scholars are prevented from addressing vital political and intellectual issues facing late twentieth-century communications.[1]

This chapter debunks the central myth that the modern corporate, commercial mass media system in the United States is the "natural" system and that it was adopted, if not enthusiastically, at least with minimal qualms. Because questions of how the media are owned, structured, and operated are distinctly political issues in virtually all other nations, this situation presumably represents a classic case of American exceptionalism. But history reveals that the United States was not exceptional. True, the social and political implications of the print media's for-profit, advertising-supported foundations have not been subject to legislative debate. In broadcasting, however, the right and need for the government, if not the public, to establish a coherent policy and even to establish the basis of the industry was by and large accepted from the outset.

This chapter will examine the opposition to the network-dominated, advertising-subsidized U.S. broadcasting system that emerged between 1928 and 1935. This opposition insisted that network, for-profit, commercial broadcasting was inimical to the communication requirements of a democratic society and attempted to generate popular support for a variety of measures that would substantively recast U.S. broadcasting. Curiously, this chapter of U.S. broadcasting history has been largely ignored in the otherwise extensive scholarship on the development of U.S. broadcasting, which has concentrated on the period preceding 1928.[2] This article attempts to shed light on a too-long overlooked period in communications history and, in doing so, to challenge some of the received wisdom of mass communications researchers in general and communications historians in particular.

U.S. broadcasting in the mid-1920s was far different from the system that would be entrenched only a few years later. Several hundred nonprofit broadcasters had commenced operations in the first half of the decade, the majority affiliated with colleges and universities, and well over two hundred of these (approximately two-fifths of all stations) remained on the air in 1925.[3] Although still largely overlooked in mass communications literature, these nonprofit broadcasters are now recognized as the true pioneers of U.S. broadcasting, who were, as one of the leading radio engineers of the period observed, "at the start of things distinctly on the ground floor."[4] As for the ostensibly for-profit broadcasters, they were hardly professional broadcasters in the modern sense of the term. The majority were owned and operated by newspapers, department stores, power companies, and other private concerns, and their *raison d'être* was to generate favorable publicity for the owner's primary enterprise.[5] Indeed, as late as 1929, few if any private broadcasters were thought to be earning profits from the business of broadcasting, and there was little sense, in public discourse at least, that they ever would.[6]

The National Broadcasting Company (NBC), established in 1926, and the Columbia Broadcasting System (CBS), established in 1927, did not have much of an impact until after the passage of the Radio Act of 1927. Throughout the late 1920s, NBC presented itself not as a traditional for-profit corporation but as a public service corporation that would sell advertising only as necessary to subsidize high-quality noncommercial fare.[7] And commercial advertising, the other pillar of the emerging status quo, did not begin its stampede to the ether in earnest until 1928.[8] As has been amply documented in the major studies of the period, commercial advertising was very controversial and more than a little unpopular throughout the 1920s.[9] Few contemporary observers foresaw the role that NBC, CBS, and commercial advertising would assume in short order. Indeed, in all public discourse on the matter prior to 1927, there was general agreement that nonprofit broadcasting should play a significant and perhaps even a dominant role in the U.S. system and that commercial advertising's potential contributions to the field should be regarded with great skepticism.[10]

Hence there is little reason, on the surface, to regard the passage of the Radio Act of 1927 as some sort of mandate for network-dominated, advertising-supported broadcasting, as that system barely existed at the time and absolutely no one was discussing the issue in those terms. Moreover, the Act was hurriedly passed in February after a federal judge had ruled the Department of Commerce's licensing of stations unconstitutional in 1926. With any effort at regulation discontinued, the ether had become a mass of chaos; two hundred new broadcasters immediately commenced operations, the total wattage increased by nearly 75 percent, and few stations respected the frequencies occupied by other broadcasters.[11] The committee deliberations and floor debate concerning the Radio Act of 1927 were what one might expect of emergency legislation; there was almost no discussion of what the legislation would mean for the type of broadcast system to be created.[12]

The Radio Act of 1927 established the Federal Radio Commission (FRC) for one year to allocate broadcast licenses and bring order to the airwaves by reducing the total number of stations. The law gave the FRC only one directive in its allocation determinations: to favor those station applicants that best served the "public interest, convenience or necessity." The primary reason that even these criteria were put in the statute was to ensure the bill's constitutionality; otherwise, the bill's sponsors argued that it was essential to give the FRC complete latitude to operate as it saw fit.[13] The commercial broadcasters were vocal in their support of having the FRC, rather than Congress, determine licensing criteria.[14]

Budgetary problems and the death of two key members prevented the FRC from taking any significant actions to reduce the number of stations in its first year.[15] Congress renewed the FRC in 1928 for a year and then in 1929 indefinitely. There was no sense during this period that the Radio Act of 1927 and the FRC were anything more than temporary measures. The topic of broadcast regulation was before Congress at every session until the passage of the Communications Act of 1934, when the matter would be disposed of, seemingly, for all time.

At the congressional committee hearings on whether to extend the FRC in early 1928 and again in early 1929, FRC members were questioned about the unchecked and stunningly rapid emergence of network broadcasting over the previous two years as well as the noticeable decrease in the number of non-profit broadcasters. "The great feeling about radio in this country," commented Senator C. C. Dill, Democrat of Washington and one of the authors of the Radio Act of 1927, "is that it will be monopolized by the few wealthy inter-ests."[16] FRC members were repeatedly admonished to protect the nonprofit broadcasters and prevent all the choice frequencies from falling into the hands of NBC or CBS.[17] In addition, in 1928 Congress passed the Davis Amendment, which required the FRC to reallocate the entire spectrum in order to provide more stations to the underrepresented southern and western regions of the nation.[18]

Three of the five FRC members were appointed to an "allocating commit-tee." One member, Harold Lafount, had served as a director for several radio manufacturing firms in his native Utah and was a proponent of the capitalist development of the ether. "What has education contributed to radio?" Lafount asked in 1931. "Not one thing. What has commercialism con-tributed? Everything—the lifeblood of the industry."[19] The other two commit-tee members were a McGraw-Hill utility trade publication editor who was on loan to the FRC for a year and a broadcaster who would leave the FRC to become an executive at CBS in 1929.[20]

THE FRC CRYSTALLIZED THE DOMINANT TRENDS within broadcasting over the previous two years and made no effort to counteract them. The allocat-ing committee held a number of meetings with radio engineers and repre-sentatives of the networks and the commercial broadcasters' trade associa-tion, the National Association of Broadcasters (NAB), as they determined their plan. These conferences and sessions were barely publicized, and the nonprofit broadcasters and concerned nonbroadcasters did not have an opportunity to present their opinions. Given the background of the FRC members, the manner in which they operated, and the sources they employed, the result of their deliberations is not surprising.[21]

In August 1928, the FRC announced its reallocation plan under General Order 40. Forty of the ninety available channels were set aside to be 50,000-watt clear channels that would have only one occupant nationally. The other fifty channels would house the remaining 600 or so broadcasters who could operate simultaneously on the same channel at much lower power levels; broadcasters in the same region would share a frequency by using it at different times of day. Anyone could challenge existing broadcasters for their frequency assignments at the end of their three-month terms. In general, the FRC had competing applicants share the contested frequency, with the station deemed most worthy allocated the majority of the hours. In the long run, the station accorded the fewest hours on a shared channel often found it very difficult to stay on the air. This direct head-to-head competition for the scarce broadcast channels created great antipathy between the contending applicants, particularly, as was often the case, when commercial broadcasters successfully challenged nonprofit broadcasters.[22] In any case, without the FRC actually having to turn down many license renewal applications, there were 100 fewer stations on the air by the autumn of 1929.[23]

With General Order 40, all stations, except for a handful of network-affiliated clear channel stations that had been established by the FRC the previous year, were assigned to new frequencies and new power levels.[24] The networks were the big winnners. In 1927 NBC had twenty-eight affiliates and CBS sixteen, for a combined 6.4 percent of the broadcast stations; within four years they together accounted for 30 percent of the stations. And this alone vastly understates their new role, as all but three of the forty clear channel stations were owned by or affiliated with one of the two networks. Indeed, when the number of hours broadcast and the level of power are considered, NBC and CBS accounted for nearly 70 percent of U.S. broadcasting by 1931.[25] By 1935, only four of the sixty-two stations that broadcast at 5,000 or more watts did not have a network affiliation.[26] Moreover, commercial advertising, which barely existed on a national level prior to 1928, grew by leaps and bounds to an annual total of 172 million by 1934.[27] One commentator noted in 1930 regarding the emerging status quo that "nothing in American history has paralleled this mushroom growth."[28] This point has also become a staple insight among broadcast historians.[29]

The other side of the coin, however, was reflected in the equally dramatic decline in nonprofit and noncommercial broadcasting. Nonprofit broadcasters found themselves in a vicious cycle. The FRC, noting the nonprofit broadcast-ers' lack of financial and technological prowess, lowered their hours and power (to the advantage of well-capitalized private broadcasters) and thus made it that much more difficult for them to generate the funds to become successful. "Now the Federal Radio Commission has come along and taken away all of the hours that are worth anything and has left us with hours that are absolutely no good for commercial programs or for educational programs," wrote the despondent director of the soon-to-be-extinct University of Arkansas station. "The Commission may boast that it has never cut an educational station off the air. It merely cuts off our head, our arms, and our legs, and then allows us to die a natural death."[30] The number of stations affiliated with colleges and universi-ties declined from ninety-five in 1927 to less than half that number by 1930, while the total number of nonprofit broadcasters declined from some 200 in 1927 to less than a third of that in 1934. Moreover, almost all of these stations operated with low power on shared frequencies. By 1934, nonprofit broad-casting accounted for only 2 percent of total U.S. broadcast time.[31]

In defending the reallocation in its *Third Annual Report*, the FRC equated capitalist broadcasters with "general public service" broadcasters, because their quest for profit would motivate them to provide whatever programming the market desired. In contrast, those stations that did not operate for profit and that did not derive their revenues from the sale of advertising were termed "propaganda" stations, more interested in spreading their particular viewpoint than in satisfying audience needs. Hence the FRC argued that it had to favor the capitalist broadcasters, since there were not enough stations to satisfy all the "propaganda" groups; these groups would have to learn to work through the auspices of the commercial broadcasters. Moreover, the FRC's emphasis upon the need for the highest-quality technical equipment tended to work to the advantage of the capitalist broadcasters.[32]

AS THE CONTOURS OF MODERN U.S. BROADCASTING fell into place with aston-ishing speed, a coherent and unrepentant opposition to the emerging capital-ist domination of the airwaves developed for the first time. "The battle was begun in earnest," noted one of the leading groups that arose to oppose the status quo, "in the summer of 1928 soon after the enactment of the Commission's General Order 40."[33] The primary opposition came from the ranks of the displaced and harassed nonprofit broadcasters, particularly those affiliated with colleges and universities. Many educators felt their stations were being left "unprotected" by the FRC as they were "attacked constantly by commercial broadcasters."[34]

In 1929 and 1930, educational broadcasters repeatedly protested to the U.S. Office of Education and the FRC that they were "being driven off the air at a rate that threatened their complete extinction."[35] In 1929, at the urging of the National Education Association (NEA), Secretary of the Interior Ray Lyman Wilbur authorized a group of educators and commercial broadcasters to study how to promote educational broadcasting, but the group split predictably along institutional lines, with the network representatives claiming that since they were more than willing to accommodate the needs of educators, independent educational stations were unnecessary. The final report of the Wilbur Committee, issued in early 1930, presented both sides of the matter but refused to recommend reserving a fixed number of channels for educational broadcasting. It recommended, instead, that the educators learn to cooperate with the commercial broadcasters.[36] The commercial broadcasters were delighted and thought the report settled the matter; the educators thought the report simply ignored the crisis of survival in which they were enmeshed.

Finally, in the summer of 1930, after repeated demands by educators, U.S. Commissioner of Education William John Cooper called a conference of educational and nonprofit broadcasters to organize a plan of attack before Congress for "new radio legislation" that would protect nonprofit broadcasters before the "commercial stations will have practically monopolized the channels open for radio broadcasting."[37] The October meeting in Chicago led to the creation of the National Committee on Education by Radio (NCER), which would comprise representatives of nine leading national education organizations.[38] Although this would be a nongovernmental body, Cooper arranged for the NCER to receive a five-year $200,000 grant from the Payne Fund, and he appointed Joy Elmer Morgan, editor of the NEA *Journal,* as the NCER's director. The NCER was established for the purpose of having Congress reserve 15 percent of the channels for educational use, assisting the educational stations in their seemingly endless hearings before the FRC, and conducting research to enhance education by radio.[39]

For the next five years the NCER would lead a relentless fight to arrest the commercial domination of the ether. The NCER had a full-time staff of at least three people, and it published a monthly newsletter, *Education by Radio*, with a controlled circulation that reached 11,000 by 1934. To the NCER, it was axiomatic that cooperation between educators and commercial broadcasters was "not possible." "That practice has been tried for nearly a decade and has proved unworkable," Morgan stated in 1931. "It is no longer open to discussion." Although the educational community was not unanimous or necessarily vociferous in its support of the NCER, the majority of educational organizations formally supported the NCER legislative agenda. And, at times, some educational groups—like the National Congress of Parents and Teachers, which resolved for the complete nationalization and decommercialization of broadcasting in 1932—called for much more radical reform of broadcasting than that proposed by the NCER.[40]

It would be inaccurate, however, to characterize the NCER as a trade organization trying to make the best possible deal for itself. Morgan, a midwestern populist who had cut his teeth in the public utilities movement of the progressive era, brought to the broadcast struggle a missionary's zeal for reform and a very broad and deeply political definition of education and educational broadcasting.[41] "As a result of radio broadcasting," he informed one audience in 1931:

> there will probably develop during the twentieth century either chaos or a world-order of civilization. Whether it shall be one or the other will depend largely upon whether broadcasting be used as a tool of education or as an instrument of selfish greed. So far, our American radio interests have thrown their major influence on the side of greed. . . . There has never been in the entire history of the United States an example of mismanagement and lack of vision so colossal and far-reaching in its consequences as our turning of the radio channels almost exclusively into commercial hands.[42]
>
> "I believe we are dealing here," Morgan told the national convention of the National University Extension Association in 1932, "with one of the most crucial issues that was ever presented to civilization at any time in its entire history."[43]

IN ADDITION TO THE NCER, participants in the fight for broadcast reform included other nonprofit broadcasters, members of the newspaper industry, and civic groups. The two most active nonprofit broadcasters were the Chicago Federation of Labor (CFL), whose WCFL was the only labor station in the nation, and the Paulist Fathers religious order of New York, which operated WLWL, the only Catholic station in the northeast United States. Both stations had begun in the mid-1920s with tremendous public service aspirations; by the end of the decade they were both struggling for survival as the FRC assigned most of their hours to affiliates of NBC and CBS, respectively. In the early 1930s both WCFL and WLWL, after continued frustration before the FRC, would lead efforts to enact reform legislation.[44]

Although the American Federation of Labor (AFL) hierarchy resisted the idea of establishing a national nonprofit labor radio channel throughout the 1920s, the more militant CFL, responding to membership pressure, regarded a labor station as essential since, as one union local observed, the commercial stations were generally "used by the enemies of organized labor for the spreading of anti-union propaganda."[45] Indeed, throughout the late 1920s and early 1930s, opposition to private, commercial broadcasting was nearly uniform in the resolutions of various labor unions and federations across the nation—except for the AFL executive council.[46]

The director of WCFL, Edward Nockels, also represented the AFL on broadcast legislation on Capitol Hill in the early 1930s. After General Order 40, Nockels stated that "all of the 90 channels for radio broadcasting" had been "given to capital and its friends and not even one channel to the millions that toil."[47] Nockels brought the same sense of mission to the battle for broadcast reform as the NCER's Morgan. "With the exception of the right to organize," Nockels enthused in 1930, "there is no goal more important of attainment to the American labor movement than one radio wavelength with a nation-wide network over which it can broadcast Labor's message to all citizens of our country. This is the modern phase of the right of free speech." Nockels concluded that "whoever controls radio broadcasting in the future will eventually control the nation."[48]

In addition to displaced nonprofit broadcasters, some elements of the newspaper industry agitated for restrictions on the commercialization of the ether, which they regarded as a prime reason for the economic woes of the print media in the depths of the Great Depression. In both Britain and Canada, for example, the daily newspapers played major roles in encouraging the noncommercial development of their national broadcasting systems.[49] And in the United States in the early 1930s, major newspaper trade unions frequently resolved for the complete or near-complete nationalization and decommercialization of broadcasting on explicitly selfish grounds.[50] Among the newspaper publishers, there was considerable hostility to the increasing use of the ether as an advertising medium, especially in the late 1920s and at the beginning of the 1930s.[51] The American Newspaper Publishers Association (ANPA) even formed a radio committee in the 1920s to address the threat to newspaper publishing brought about by the development of commercial broadcasting. The most active daily newspaper publisher in the fight to reform broadcasting was H. O. Davis, owner of California's *Ventura Free Press*, who published two books critical of the status quo, promoted reform ideas before the ANPA, and even hired a full-time lobbyist to work on behalf of broadcast reform throughout the early 1930s.[52]

Davis's efforts notwithstanding, an alarmed commercial broadcasting industry was able to defuse any threat to their control in short order; indeed, by 1932 or 1933 Davis had been effectively marginalized, and the major newspapers had become allies of the commercial broadcasters in their efforts to thwart the opposition movement. The commercial broadcasters approached the newspaper industry on two levels. First, they emphasized that government restrictions on commercial broadcasting could easily be extended to newspapers. As an NBC vice president told the San Francisco Advertising Club in 1932, he and William Randolph Hearst had discussed the reform efforts and had agreed that "any threat to commercial advertising on the radio is a threat to all forms of advertising."[53]

Second, the commercial broadcasters strongly encouraged newspapers to either purchase their own stations or affiliate with local stations. By late 1931, 139 radio stations had newspaper owners or affiliations, and another 100 stations would be added to this fold in the next twelve months.[54] The networks were especially aggressive in their efforts to establish newspaper affiliations; thirty-five of the ninety CBS network stations had newspaper owners or affiliations by 1932. "We only know here that newspaper-owned stations have increased their revenues through network broadcasting," CBS president William S. Paley commented, citing instances of newspapers tripling their broadcast advertising revenues in a single year. "Nor are these examples exceptions."[55] This strategy paid off quickly. In 1932 the chairman of the ANPA's radio committee quit in disgust, noting that the newspapers that owned radio stations were stonewalling all of his efforts to develop a coherent broadcast anticommercialist platform for the organization.[56] "So long as a goodly array of journalists are close corporate allies of radio," the trade publication *Broadcasting* assured its readers, the broadcasting industry need "pay no heed to the tempest in the teapot that certain press interests have been trying to create."[57]

The opposition to the status quo was also joined by many civic groups with no particular material stake in the outcome of the fight. The most important of these was the American Civil Liberties Union (ACLU). Prior to 1932, the ACLU had stayed out of the legislative efforts to recast U.S. broadcasting, not regarding it as a free expression issue. However, by early 1933 the ACLU had become overwhelmed with criticism of U.S. broadcasting for its censorship of radical and nonmainstream opinions and for its unwillingness to air controversial public affairs broadcasting: "Censorship at the stations by the managers is constantly exercised in a most unenlightened fashion," ACLU director Roger Baldwin observed in a 1933 memo:

> . . . all this with an eye to protecting the status quo. Only a comparatively few small stations voice critical or radical views, and these are in constant danger of either going out of business or being closed up. Protests by the Civil Liberties Union when the larger stations censor programs have resulted in no relief. The Federal Radio Commission pays no attention to such complaints.[58]

Shortly thereafter the ACLU established its Radio Committee to deal with "the restrictions on broadcasting inherent in the American system."[59] The Radio Committee was advised to study the "whole matter" of broadcasting and develop a "practical plan" to reform the system and better meet the free expression requirements of a democratic society.[60] For the balance of the decade the ACLU would be active in the battle for broadcast reform.

The ACLU's response to network commercial broadcasting mirrored that of the U.S. intelligentsia in general. The NCER's Morgan was not far from the truth when he stated in 1933 that it was impossible to find *any* intellectual in favor of the status quo, unless that intellectual was receiving money or air time from a commercial broadcaster.[61] Given the economic and political crisis embracing the world during this period, broadcasting was not foremost on the minds of U.S. intellectuals. Nonetheless, more than a few, including such prominent figures as John Dewey, Walter Hale Hamilton, Alexander Meiklejohn, Charles A. Beard, Norman Thomas, Jane Addams, Upton

Sinclair, Frederick Lewis Allen, E. P. Herring, Bruce Bliven, and H. L. Mencken, published articles and gave speeches arguing on behalf of major reform.[62] Others, like William Orton of Amherst College, Jerome Davis of the Yale Divinity School, social critic James Rorty, and pioneer radio scientist Lee DeForest, published and spoke actively on behalf of the opposition movement, often coordinating their activities with the NCER, the ACLU, and other opposition groups.[63]

THREE THEMES UNDERSCORED VIRTUALLY all criticism of the status quo by the various elements of the opposition movement. First, the opposition movement argued that the airwaves should be regarded as a public resource and broadcasting as a public utility. By this reasoning, turning broadcasting over to a relative handful of private broadcasters who sought to satisfy selfish goals was a scandalous misuse of a public resource. Moreover, the FRC had established the existing system entirely outside of public view; even Congress seemed largely oblivious to what had taken place. Hence, the public had yet to exercise its right and duty to determine broadcast policy.

Second, and perhaps most crucially, the opposition movement argued that a network-dominated, for-profit, advertising-supported broadcast system would invariably shade its programming to defend the status quo and would never give fair play to unpopular or radical opinions. The entire opposition movement was propelled by a profound desire to create a broadcasting system that would better promote its vision of a democratic political culture.

Third, the reformers criticized the nature of broadcast advertising and the limitations of advertising-subsidized programming, particularly in regard to the lack of cultural, educational, and public affairs programming that the system seemed capable of profitably generating. Some of this criticism had a distinctly elitist tone.[64]

Moreover, the opposition movement was insistent in its belief that increased regulation of the existing system could not produce the desired social results. At best, noted the NCER's Morgan, "this kind of arrangement would result in perpetual warfare"—a warfare that the opposition movement must lose.[65] As one naval captain who was amenable to a government-owned communications system on national security grounds noted in 1933, the "large companies" would invariably triumph in any regulatory scheme that left the ownership and support mechanisms of the industry unaltered. "With clever executives and high-priced lawyers, the Government administrators have little chance in the long run to resist such pressure, due to the ever-changing personnel in the Government, regardless of the unquestioned faith-fulness of the employees."[66] Few among the opposition movement were will-ing to concede the "unquestioned faithfulness" of FRC members and employees, many of whom went on to lucrative careers with the networks, with the NAB, or as commercial broadcasting attorneys.[67] One trade publi-cation even commented in 1934 that Washington had become a "happy hunting ground" for "former members of the FRC legal staff" as they par-layed their government experience into lucrative retainers from commercial broadcasting interests.[68]

Armed with this critique and perspective, the opposition movement advocated any number of plans to re-create U.S. broadcasting, but three in particular received the most attention in the early 1930s. One plan was to have the government set aside a fixed percentage of channels—generally either 15 or 25 percent—for the exclusive use of nonprofit broadcasters. The second plan was to have Congress authorize an extensive and independent study of broadcasting with the aim of providing for an entirely new broadcast system. This plan was based on what had transpired in Britain and, particu-larly, Canada, which in 1932 announced—to no small extent due to its dis-taste for what it saw taking place to the south—the establishment of a non-profit and noncommercial broadcasting system.[69] To the opposition move-ment, it was axiomatic that any independent study of broadcasting would resolve to alter the status quo. The third plan was to have the government establish a series of local, regional, and national nonprofit and noncommer-cial stations that would be subsidized through taxes and operated by a con-gressionally approved board of directors of prominent citizens. This plan also was inspired by the experiences in Britain and Canada and, indeed, in most of the world. The government stations would supplement, not replace, the existing commercial networks.

Indeed, with the exception of one or two isolated comments, none of the elements of the opposition movement advocated the complete nationalization and decommercialization of broadcasting. All the plans pointedly created what the opposition movement regarded as a dual system. "And out of the competition between them," one reformer told Congress in 1934 as he out-lined his plan for a series of government stations, "there would unquestionably issue a much higher program standard and far less discrimination against vast sections of the public who are now essentially excluded from genuine enjoyment of radio."[70] The NCER characterized Australia, which had one commercial network and one noncommercial network, as a "listener's utopia."[71] Interestingly, with but one exception, throughout the early 1930s no proponent of the status quo took seriously the opposition movement's proposals for a mixed system; all efforts to create space for nonprofit and non-commercial broadcasting were approached as if they were specific efforts to eliminate for-profit, commercial broadcasting in its entirety.[72]

One basic and overriding problem plagued the opposition movement throughout its existence: how to subsidize high-quality nonprofit broadcasting. Clearly, the existing system of nonprofit stations with dilapidated facilities, restricted hours, and low power, attempting to rely upon donations from listeners, handouts from philanthropists, and grants from nonprofit groups, had proven unsatisfactory, particularly as the economy was grinding to a halt. To many members of the opposition movement the answer was obvious: have the government subsidize nonprofit broadcasting by establishing a series of government stations (à la Britain) to be bankrolled by annual license set fees. "A charge of $1.00 per set would provide America ten times the funds which we would need for a generous program of broadcasting," the NCER's Morgan informed a convention of educators in 1932.[73] This was a touchy subject in U.S. politics, however. Some elements of the opposition movement, like the ACLU, were more than a little skeptical of granting the government a larger role in communications. Even those that did not share the ACLU's innate skepticism toward the state, like the NCER, began lobbying for a state-subsidized system only years after most of their leaders, including Morgan, had gone on record in its favor.[74] "A government-controlled radio system," two members of the opposition movement noted in 1931, "whether or not hypothetically desirable, is highly impracticable, almost impossible."[75]

The only real alternative to having the government play a larger role was using advertising to subsidize nonprofit broadcasting. This idea was anathema to the NCER, the ACLU, and much of the opposition movement, which regarded advertising as every bit as bad as network domination. But nonprofit stations like WCFL and WLWL repeatedly defended their right to sell advertising to subsidize their operations.[76] This became the basis of the fundamental tactical split in the opposition movement. The NCER, the ACLU, and the *Ventura Free*

Press, among others, dropped the fixed-percentage idea to promote a government study or a government network. WCFL and WLWL, in contrast, were not especially interested in schemes that did not address the specific plight of their stations. Hence, they showed little enthusiasm for the government plans or for any program that might restrict their sale of advertising.

IN ADDITION TO THE OPPOSITION MOVEMENT being divided over tactics, it faced at least three other major barriers. First, the radio lobby—NBC, CBS, and the NAB—had quickly emerged "as one of the most effective trade associations in the United States" and one of the most powerful lobbies in Washington.[77] Its control of the airwaves gave the radio lobby greater than customary leverage over publicity-conscious politicians—a point lost on neither the commercial broadcasters nor the opposition movement.[78]

In addition, the commercial broadcasters spared no expense in the early 1930s in a public relations campaign to establish the status quo as the only innately "American" and only innately "democratic" method for organizing broadcasting services.[79] With their abundant resources, the radio lobby was able to overwhelm the underfunded communications of the angered opposition movement.[80] Finally, each network established an "advisory council" of prominent citizens to offer advice on public affairs programming and to reassure the public that the network would be responsible and socially neutral in its broadcasting. Although even the most cursory examination of these advisory groups indicates that they had little effect on network operations, they were heavily emphasized by the commercial broadcasters before Congress and the public.[81] As one NBC internal memo observed regarding the network's advisory council, "a great deal of weight will be put to it in the public mind."[82]

Second, given the clear contrast between the political strength and financial wherewithal of the radio lobby and that of the opposition movement, the reformers obviously needed extensive (and preferably sympathetic) print coverage. Unfortunately, what little coverage the press offered was strongly oriented toward presenting the position of the commercial broadcasters. This delighted the radio lobby, which provided the press with a continual stream of press releases.[83] It angered and puzzled the opposition movement, for the most part, which could not understand why their cause seemed to be getting short shrift.[84] In any case, this proved to be a formidable obstacle for the reformers.

Third, the legal community, with few exceptions, rallied to the defense of the status quo.[85] The American Bar Association (ABA) established a Standing Committee on Communications in the late 1920s with "the duty of studying and making recommendations on proposed radio legislation."[86] This ABA committee was chaired by Louis G. Caldwell, who had been the FRC's first General Counsel during the implementation of General Order 40 and had emerged as one of the leading commercial broadcasting attorneys in the nation.[87] The ABA committee, staffed almost entirely by commercial broadcasting attorneys, turned out annual reports ranging from forty to one hundred pages that argued in no uncertain terms that any reform of the status quo would be disastrous. Although these reports were never voted upon by the ABA, they were relied upon by Congress and presented to Congress and the public as the expert, neutral opinion of the U.S. legal community. The opposition movement was appalled by this apparent conflict of interest but had little success in challenging the ABA committee's legitimacy.[88]

Curiously, from 1928 to 1933 the ABA committee, like the commercial broadcasting industry, was opposed to any congressional involvement with broadcast policy and favored granting the FRC unconditional power to act as it pleased. "The radio administration within a nation," Caldwell wrote in 1930, "must have a life and death power over the radio conduct of its subjects such as it neither has nor desires over their conduct in other matters." Caldwell argued that "such matters cannot safely be prescribed by statute" and were "unsuited for decision by a legislative body."[89] As for the seeming threat to free expression implicit in granting the FRC arbitrary power to license broadcasters, the legal community was not particularly concerned. "If all this be censorship," the ABA committee reported in 1929, "it seems unavoidable and in the best interests of the listening public."[90]

The campaign to restructure U.S. broadcasting experienced three distinct phases over the period 1930–1935. The first stage, from 1930 until President Herbert Hoover left office in the spring of 1933, was clearly the high water-mark for popular discontent with U.S. broadcasting, far surpassing anything that would develop subsequently. Public distaste for commercial broadcast fare was being repeatedly communicated to members of Congress. "Many members on both sides of the Capitol are aroused by local conditions," *Broadcasting* informed its readers, and they "have heard protests from constituents" regarding the nature of the U.S. system.[91] WCFL's Edward Nockels

estimated that 70 percent of the Senate and 80 percent of the House supported legislation to set aside channels for nonprofit broadcasters, and there is little evidence to contradict his assessment.[92]

Nevertheless, reform legislation failed to get through Congress during this
period, for two reasons. First, this was the trough of the Great Depression,
and the preponderance of congressional activity was dedicated to legislation
for economic recovery. "Were it not for the disturbing economic situation,"
Broadcasting observed in 1931, "Congress might blunder into the political
radio morass camouflaged by these lobbying factions."[93] Second, though
there was considerable support for reform among the rank-and-file members
of Congress, relevant committee leaders were nearly unanimously opposed.
"We have been lucky," modestly observed NAB president Harry Shaw in a
speech to the NAB Board of Directors on the legislative situation in 1932.
"We have been content to leave the protection of this industry to a few of our
friends in certain places."[94] "If it were not for a little group of reactionary leaders in both branches of Congress," an incensed Nockels observed in 1931,
reform "legislation would have been passed by this time."[95] And, indeed,
when the Senate passed a rider to a bill in 1931 that would have established a
national, nonprofit labor network, the congressional leaders were able to have
the bill tabled at the end of the session.[96]

The most important congressional leader in this regard was Senator Dill,
who by the early 1930s had established himself, in the words of *Broadcasting*,
as "unquestionably . . . the most influential voice in federal radio control of
any figure in public life."[97] As ACLU counsel Morris Ernst stated emphatically
in 1931, "There is no use in drafting material which will not be acceptable to
him."[98] Behind a veneer of progressive rhetoric, Dill repeatedly stonewalled
all efforts to get reform legislation through his Senate Committee on Interstate
Commerce. In January 1932 he and another senator, responding to the public outcry for broadcast reform, had the Senate pass a measure authorizing the
FRC to study the opposition movement's criticisms.[99] The FRC report
released that summer, *Commercial Radio Advertising*, was based largely on
the uncritical acceptance of the responses of commercial broadcasters to a
short questionnaire. Predictably, it praised the status quo and dismissed the
opposition movement's concerns as without merit.[100] The commercial broadcasters were elated, while the opposition movement labeled the report "not a
fact-finding document but a defense of the present radio system."[101] The FRC

report successfully defused the momentum for reform and left the opposition movement soberly regarding its prospects. By 1933, the ACLU and the NCER would agree that Senator Dill was a "weak sister" who would provide no assistance to the opposition movement.[102]

The second stage of the campaign, which lasted from March 1933 until the Communications Act of 1934 was signed into law in June of that year, was the decisive period when Congress finally enacted permanent broadcasting legislation. The opposition movement was initially quite encouraged by the change in administrations and hoped that President Roosevelt would assist their cause. Indeed, many key members of the New Deal were outspoken critics of commercial broadcasting and advocates of sweeping reform.[103] Moreover, one of Roosevelt's closest political and personal friends, ambassador to Mexico Josephus Daniels, was an unabashed proponent of completely nationalized broadcasting. "There is no more reason why other communications industries should be privately owned than the mails," he wrote the president in one of numerous letters on the subject.[104] Nevertheless, Roosevelt chose not to take a public position on the broadcast debate, while his aides worked behind the scenes to assist the commercial broadcasters with their legislative agenda (see below). Clearly Roosevelt was in no mood to take on an uphill fight against a powerful and entrenched communications industry, particularly when he enjoyed less than perfect relations with the nation's largely Republican newspaper industry. As even Daniels advised him, he had more important battles to fight.[105]

By 1933 the broadcasting industry had largely stabilized after the shake-up following General Order 40. The commercial broadcasters determined that the time was ripe for permanent broadcasting legislation that would eliminate the annual forum on Capitol Hill for "attacks by unfriendly groups" and "speed up the movement toward a more thoroughly stabilized broadcasting industry."[106] They sought, ideally, to have the Radio Act of 1927 reenacted verbatim and to have a body similar to the FRC established permanently; indeed, the commercial broadcasters were the only group uniform in its praise of this otherwise most controversial body.[107] Yet the industry had no desire for Congress to debate or discuss how best to organize the U.S. broadcasting system, let alone have any public discussion of the issues involved.[108] Avoiding such discussion would have been impossible in earlier sessions of Congress, but the commercial broadcasters were confident of their support among the key figures in Washington, most notably Senator Dill and the president.

In the fall of 1933 President Roosevelt had Secretary of Commerce Daniel Roper appoint a committee of government department representatives to prepare recommendations for the "construction of needed legislation" in the area of communications.[109] This Roper Committee operated in secrecy, took no outside testimony, and recommended in January 1934 that the status quo be maintained but that all communications regulation be housed under one administrative agency.[110] This was precisely what the commercial broadcasters had desired.[111] Although the Roper Committee did not even discuss broadcasting in its deliberations, the subject nevertheless was included in the report's final recommendations. (This point was brought to the president's attention by a member of the Roper Committee who filed a "minority report" to indicate his displeasure with the lack of attention broadcasting had received.)[112]

At the request of Secretary Roper, in January 1934, President Roosevelt authorized Roper to establish an independent Federal Committee to Study Radio Broadcasting (FCSRB) under the Office of Education, which would take up the structural and regulatory issues that the Roper Committee had neglected.[113] The opposition movement was elated; for once it would have a forum to present its case. The commercial broadcasters and Senator Dill, however, were confounded. They informed the president in no uncertain terms that such a study was unnecessary, due to the 1932 FRC study, and that it would not be used in the drafting of legislation, as was its ostensible purpose.[114] The president quietly canceled the FCSRB in late February. The NCER was informed that "this matter, for the time being, will be entirely handled by the Congress."[115]

Dill and his counterpart in the House, Representative Sam Rayburn, Democrat of Texas, now sought to rush the proposed legislation through committee hearings and have it brought to the floors of the House and Senate for a vote as quickly as possible.[116] Their bills essentially reenacted the Radio Act of 1927 and established a new Federal Communications Commission (FCC) to regulate all the communications industries; in short, with minor qualifications, these bills were precisely what the commercial broadcasters had desired. Dill hoped to stem any potential opposition to the proposed legislation by having his bill authorize the new FCC to thoroughly study communications and report any suggestions for reform legislation the following year. "If we leave out the controversial matters," Dill stated, "the bill can be passed at this session."[117] Indeed, Dill announced that he would not permit broadcasting to be discussed during the upcoming committee hearings on the legislation, since the unresolved broadcasting issues would now be taken up by the new FCC.[118] The commercial broadcasters crowed their approval of this tactic; they had long felt more secure with their fate in the hands of regulators rather than elected officials.[119]

Although some elements of the opposition movement had become demoralized and had given up any hope for immediate attention from Congress, the Paulist Fathers' John B. Harney submitted an amendment to the Dill communications bill during the committee hearings that would have required the new FCC to set aside fully 25 percent of the channels for nonprofit broadcasters. The committee voted against the Harney proposal, but Senators Robert Wagner, Democrat of New York, and Henry Hatfield, Republican of West Virginia, agreed to introduce the amendment on the Senate floor. Father Harney and the Paulists engaged in a whirlwind campaign to generate support for the measure, particularly from Catholic organizations and parishes around the nation. Within a few weeks the Paulists had over 60,000 signatures on petitions supporting the measure and had the active support of Edward Nockels and much of the labor movement.[120] In April the trade publication *Variety* reported that the now-termed Wagner-Hatfield amendment stood "better than a 50-50 chance of being adopted."[121]

The radio lobby attacked the Wagner-Hatfield amendment in late April and early May as if, as an NAB representative later explained, its passage "obviously would have destroyed the whole structure of broadcasting in America."[122] Both the White House and the FRC lobbied members of Congress against the legislation.[123]

After it became apparent that Father Harney would have his amendment introduced in the Senate, Senator Dill installed a clause in his communications bill, section 307(c), that would require the new FCC to hold hearings concerning the idea of reserving 25 percent of the channels for nonprofit broadcasters and then report to Congress with their recommendations the following year. This was enough to convince wayward senators that the Wagner-Hatfield amendment was not necessary.[124] The amendment was defeated on the Senate floor on May 15 by a vote of 42-23. Immediately thereafter, the Senate approved Dill's communications bill with section 307(c) by a voice vote. In the House, which had stricter rules, Representative Rayburn was able to keep the Harney amendment from getting to the floor for a vote or even being discussed in the floor debate. After the House passed the Rayburn communications bill in early June, the bills went to conference, where the differences were ironed out; Dill telephoned Henry Bellows, the NAB's chief lobbyist, and informed him, "We have been very generous to you fellows." Bellows would later comment: "When we read it, we found that every major point we had asked for was there."[125]

President Roosevelt signed the Communications Act of 1934 into law on June 18. The bill was lost in the media coverage of the stack of New Deal bills that had been passed at the end of the congressional session. When it was covered, it was characterized as a "New Deal in Radio Law" that was aimed at "curbing monopoly control in radio" and that boldly harnessed antagonistic private power and forced it to act in the public interest. Neither the Roosevelt administration nor Senator Dill did anything to discourage this patently bogus interpretation.[126]

WITH THE PASSAGE OF THE COMMUNICATIONS ACT OF 1934, Congress effectively removed itself from substantive broadcast policy issues for the balance of the century, ushering in the third stage. The only "legitimate" opportunity remaining for the opposition movement to present its case was in the October 1934 FCC hearings mandated by section 307(c), which required the FCC to evaluate the Wagner-Hatfield fixed percentage concept. The outcome of the hearings was never in doubt; most elements of the opposition movement regarded them as a "setup for the broadcasters," and, indeed, two of the three FCC members who would be at the hearing announced to the NAB convention in September that there was no way they would alter the status quo, regardless of what transpired at the upcoming hearings.[127] In January 1935, the FCC formally issued its report to Congress: there was no need to alter the status quo, and efforts should be made to assist disenfranchised nonprofit groups in utilizing commercial broadcasting facilities.[128] In effect, this was the cooperation thesis advanced by the Wilbur Committee in 1930 and rejected at the time on its face. The opposition movement had, at best, delayed the full stabilization of the airwaves from 1929 or 1930 to 1935.

Ironically, precisely as the window for reform was being slammed shut, the NCER formally proposed the creation of a federal chain of noncommercial stations.[129] The proposal was ignored, and the opposition movement quickly unraveled. The Paulist station WLWL sold its license to Arde Bulova in 1937 and went out of business. Labor station WCFL abandoned its efforts for membership contribution support and became an advertising-supported NBC affiliate by the mid-1930s; despite its labor pedigree, it became largely indistinguishable from the capitalist broadcasters. The NCER attempted to improve relations between educators and commercial broadcasters and the FCC but finally closed down in 1941. The ACLU Radio Committee remained active with a somewhat radical broadcast legislative platform well into the second half of the decade, when it finally discontinued these efforts in view of their complete lack of success.[130] By the end of the decade the ACLU had finally accepted the legitimacy of the industry's capitalist and commercial basis, as much for pragmatic reasons as for any philosophical change of heart, and it began to resume its traditional concern with government censorship. The broadcast system was now deemed fundamentally sound rather than fundamentally flawed.

In the second half of the decade, as the industry became economically and politically consolidated, the commercial broadcasters strove for ideological closure. In this campaign they triumphantly located commercial broadcasting next to the newspaper industry as an icon of American freedom and culture and, with considerable historical revisionism if not outright fabrication, removed it from critical contemplation. The opposition movement was correspondingly written out of the dominant perspective on the development of U.S. broadcasting, and the conflict of the early 1930s was erased from the historical memory. "Our American system of broadcasting," Radio Corporation of America president David Sarnoff informed a nationwide audience over NBC in 1938:

> . . . is what it is because it operates in the American democracy. It is a free system because this is a free country. It is privately owned because private ownership is one of our national doctrines. It is privately supported, through commercial sponsorship of a portion of its program hours, and at no cost to the listener, because ours is a free economic system. No special laws had to be passed to bring these things about. They were already implicit in the American system, ready and waiting for broadcasting when it came.[131]

The implications of this logic were not always left unspoken. "He who attacks the fundamentals of the American system" of broadcasting, CBS president Paley informed an audience in 1937, "attacks democracy itself."[132]

Also quickly forgotten was the position of the legal community and the commercial broadcasting industry in favor of arbitrary and unchecked commission regulation of broadcasting prior to 1934. Now that the industry was entrenched and beyond political challenge, any further regulation was determined to have more negative than positive possibilities for the industry. Suitably, Louis Caldwell led the campaign, beginning in late 1934, to recognize existing property rights in the ether and eliminate government licensing and regulation of broadcasting, all in the name of the First Amendment. Caldwell compared the Communications Act of 1934 to "the ordinances of the Star Chamber" and argued that with the legal recognition of the government's right to regulate broadcasting, "the clock of liberty has been set back three hundred years."[133] The campaign for deregulation was unsuccessful, but the resulting system by the late 1930s acknowledged the government's right to regulate broadcasting only after the marketplace and industry self-regulation had proven abject failures. In effect, there developed a de facto privatization of the airwaves and, with that, what broadcast historian Philip Rosen has termed the "myth of regulation."[134]

By the end of the decade, and thereafter, the notion that the American people had a right to determine whatever broadcast system they deemed superior for society was effectively dead. In 1945 Paul Lazarsfeld would observe that the American people seemed to approve of the private and commercial basis of the industry. "People have little information on the subject," he noted, "they have obviously given it little thought."[135]

THE U.S. SYSTEM OF BROADCASTING emerged not as the result of a consensus but rather as a result of conflict in which there were clear winners and losers. Because much of U.S. broadcasting history has underemphasized this opposition, it has had the earmarks of a history written by the victors. Even the otherwise outstanding critical scholarship, with its emphasis on the period preceding 1928, seemingly has accepted the notion that the American people went along willy-nilly with the establishment of the status quo.

It is true that the opposition movement was unable to generate popular momentum for its cause. Certainly, the might of the commercial broadcasters made any alternative system highly problematic. Nonetheless, it is an error to argue that the system was thoroughly consolidated by the mid-1920s or to assume that Americans were ignorant of, apathetic toward, or even enthusiastic about commercial broadcasting. The commercial broadcasters and their allies did everything within their (substantial) power to monopolize the process of making broadcast policy throughout the period in question. And, in this sense, there has never really been a legitimate public debate over the issues the opposition movement attempted to raise.

Moreover, it is a debate that is still worth having. The concentration in the 1990s of not only broadcasting but all mass media in the hands of some two-dozen enormous corporations would wrinkle the brows of Joy Elmer Morgan and Edward Nockels.[136] Advertising has continued its seemingly unshakable course, in the words of Stuart Ewen, into "every nook and cranny" of American, and, indeed, international life.[137] The concerns of the 1930s opposition regarding the limitations of the modern media system for the exercise of a democratic political culture have moved front and center in the contemporary critiques of U.S. political culture.[138] Now, more than ever it would seem, researchers must be willing to analyze what is arguably the root cause of the problem rather than concentrate solely on marginal effects. As this article has endeavored to show, there is an important legacy for this approach and a rich American tradition of no-holds-barred communications analysis. With the recognition of this tradition, adherence to time-worn but unproven presuppositions may seem less tenable.

7

The Payne Fund and Radio Broadcasting, 1928–1935

The Payne Fund took an interest in the educational potential of radio broadcasting from its very beginning. In 1926 then-president H. M. Clymer visited the British Broadcasting Corporation (BBC) to inspect its educational program. He returned to the United States convinced that the "B.B.C. points the way" for Americans.[1] Immediately thereafter the Payne Fund hired Armstrong Perry, a freelance journalist who had followed broadcasting closely since 1921, to serve as its full-time radio counsel. In addition the Payne Fund provided annual funding of $10,000 to Dr. W. W. Charters at Ohio State University to conduct research in radio education. The Payne Fund was instrumental in assisting Charters form the Institute for Education in Radio (IER) in 1930. The IER held annual conferences in Columbus and published its proceedings. Eventually the IER incorporated television into its activities; the rechristened Institute for Education in Radio and Television remained active and prominent for decades.[2]

Had the Payne Fund's interest in radio broadcasting been limited to Charters's research and the IER, its contribution would be fairly unremarkable, at least in comparison with its other activities at the time. As it developed, however, the Payne Fund quickly found that, in pursuing its aim of promoting the educational usage of radio, it was thrust into the center of the political debate over how the United States might best organize its broadcasting system. As Perry wrote to Clymer, the "Payne Fund happened to be organized at a critical moment" in the development of U.S. broadcasting.[3] Thus, despite its reticence to become associated with political controversy, the Payne Fund spent some $300,000 in the early 1930s to subsidize two campaigns to reform U.S. broadcasting. These campaigns, the National Committee on Education by Radio (NCER) and the *Ventura Free Press* radio campaign, argued that a network-dominated, advertising-supported broadcasting system is inimical to the communication needs of a democratic society. They attempted to rouse congressional and public support for legislation that would create a significant nonprofit and noncommercial broadcasting sector, while many of their officers were sympathetic to the out-and-out nationalization of broadcasting. In this battle, the Payne Fund and the campaigns it supported were in direct conflict with the two networks that had come to dominate U.S. broadcasting in short order—the national Broadcasting Company (NBC) and the Columbia Broadcasting System (CBS).

In this chapter I chronicle the Payne Fund activities to reform U.S. broadcasting. Although the movement for broadcast reform failed, it left an important legacy for future generations of media critics. In many respects, the broadcast reform movement generated the first wave of sophisticated U.S. media criticism, anticipating much of the best contemporary criticism.[4] Moreover, to the extent that the Payne Fund was responsible for launching, funding, and, at times, even directing much of his reform activity, the Fund played an important role in the development of U.S. communications policy. In short, with its campaign to reconstruct U.S. broadcasting, the Payne Fund went far outside the traditional activities associated with foundations and left a deep imprint on U.S. communications and political history.

The Founding of the NCER

U.S. radio broadcasting was about to undergo a dramatic transformation as the Payne Fund made its first forays into the field. Before 1927, broadcasting had been a haphazard, albeit bustling, industry. Most of the six hundred or so stations were operated either by nonprofit groups, especially colleges and universities, or by business concerns such as newspapers, car dealerships, and public utilities to shed favorable publicity on the owner's primary enterprise. The industry was uniformly unprofitable, which is not surprising since there was almost no direct advertising over the air until the last two or three years of the decade. The passage of the Radio Act of 1927, which created the Federal Radio Commission (FRC) to bring order to the airwaves, brought some stability to the industry, although the regulation it authorized was only temporary. Legislation to establish a permanent basis for communications regulation would be before Congress at every session until the passage of the Communications Act of 1934, which remains the law to this day. With scarcely any congressional or public oversight, the pro-commercial broadcasting FRC instituted a general reallocation in 1928 that effectively assigned all the stations to new frequencies and provided them with new lower allowances. For all intents and purposes, this largely unpublicized reallocation determined the shape of AM radio for the remainder of the century.[5]

NBC and CBS were the big winners. Whereas they barely existed in 1927, by 1931 their affiliated stations accounted for nearly 70 percent of U.S. wattage. By 1935 only four of the sixty-two stations that broadcast at 5,000 watts or more did not have a network affiliation; fully 97 percent of total nighttime broadcasting, when the smaller stations were off the air, was controlled by NBC or CBS.[6] Moreover, advertising rushed to the air in landslide proportions between 1928 and 1933, despite the economic expression. From virtual nonexistence in 1927, radio advertising expenditures rose to more than $100 million in 1929. Over 80 percent of these expenditures went to 20 percent of the stations, all network owned or affiliated.[7] As one commentator noted in 1930, "Nothing in American history has paralleled this mushroom growth." This has since become a standard observation of U.S. broadcasting history.[8]

In 1927 and 1928 the goal of the Payne Fund was to assist in creating a "school of the air," whereby educational programs for both children and adults would be broadcast by educators over the commercial stations. The Payne Fund had no qualms about working through the auspices of two networks; however, it was insistent that all educational programming be determined by professional educators without commercial interference. Both NBC and CBS informed Perry in 1928 that they would be willing to provide the necessary airtime and facilities "without charge" for a national school of the air "supervised by educational authorities."[9] Perry spent much of 1928 attempting to find a philanthropist or educational group willing to subsidize a school of the air, without success. "I see no evidence," he concluded in 1929, "that any educational organization will do so on a national basis."[10] By spring of 1929 Perry and Clymer were convinced that the prospects for educational broadcasting were dismal and that "schools will be flooded" with "radio programs prepared for advertising purposes rather than educational value." Using contacts in the National Education Association (NEA), they convinced Secretary of the Interior Ray Lyman Wilbur, whose department housed the Office of Education, to convene a meeting in May 1929 to address the crisis in educational broadcasting. The Payne Fund provided $5,000 to pay for the meeting and any subsequent activities.[11]

The May 24 meeting led to the formation of the Advisory Committee on Education by Radio, soon dubbed the "Wilbur Committee," to study the crisis in educational broadcasting and report back to Wilbur with recommendations. The Payne Fund helped subsidize the expenses of the committee, and it assigned Perry to work for the group until it filed its report. Perry spent the balance of 1929 traveling across the United States interviewing broadcasters and educators to determine possible solutions. In the course of his investigation, he became radicalized. He concluded that the commitment of NBC and CBS to provide free airtime and facilities was evaporating because the networks were able to sell their time to advertisers. There was the stark possibility, he concluded, that "all the time available on stations covering any considerable territory will be sold for advertising purposes."[12] In addition, Perry finally located a group of educators who seemed to grasp the importance of radio for education: the college and university broadcasters. These stations had been decimated by the FRC's reallocation of 1928 and their inability to raise sufficient funds. The number of college stations had fallen from more than a hundred in 1925 to half that figure by 1929.[13] Perry became convinced that the only hope for education on radio was to protect these stations and, moreover, to create a viable nonprofit and noncommercial sector in U.S. broadcasting.

Perry's influence on the Wilbur Committee was unmistakable. The report of the fact-finding subcommittee concluded that "it is clear that the basic purposes of the two groups [broadcasters and educators] are widely divergent" and that the commercial broadcasters seemed intent upon occupying all the frequencies. "Apparently, the only thing that could prevent this would be an early and united effort on the part of broadcasters to have radio channels permanently reserved for the use of educational stations." The NBC and CBS representatives on the Wilbur Committee filed "minority reports" to protest the alleged unwillingness of the networks to provide airtime for educational broadcasts.[14] When the final report was submitted to Wilbur in February 1930, it elected not to antagonize the commercial broadcasters, accepting at face value their declarations, of interest in educational broadcasting. To the delight of NBC and CBS, the report merely recommended that the Office of Education establish a section to coordinate educational broadcasting and to "attempt to prevent conflicts between various broadcasting interests."[15]

This was not a thorough defeat, however, for the proponents of independent educational stations. Wilbur immediately authorized the creation of the new radio section, but since there could be no funding for another year, the Payne Fund "lent" Perry to Commissioner of Education William John Cooper to oversee the new office. Cooper instructed Perry to take charge of all radio correspondence and to keep him "up to date on radio." "This places me in a very satisfactory position," Perry wrote to Ella Phillips Crandall, secretary of the Payne Fund. "It apparently means that we can go right on with the investigations that the Payne Fund would like to make independently if they were not made under the auspices of the Office of Education."[16] Perry used his position to convince both Wilbur and Cooper that the existing situation was unsatisfactory and that the FRC was uninterested in protecting educational stations. His argument was buttressed by the collapse of twenty-three more college stations in the first seven months of 1930.[17] By the end of the summer, Cooper accepted Perry's contention that educators needed to organize in order to have protective legislation passed by Congress. Perry also used his position in the Office of Education to mobilize virtually unanimous support by national educational organizations for broadcast reform.

The most important battle for Perry came with the officers of the Payne Fund, who until that point had revealed no desire to engage in a political battle with the commercial broadcasters. Crandall wrote Perry that the Payne Fund did not wish to encourage "prolonged and obstinate opposition among educators to safe and sane co-operation with commercial companies."[18] Perry repeatedly wrote to Crandall on the need to directly challenge in Washington, D.C., the domination of broadcasting by the networks if there was to be any hope for adequate educational or cultural fare. Eventually Crandall and Frances Payne Bolton, president of the Payne Fund, accepted Perry's position. Crandall wrote Perry in July 1930 that there was "no opposition within the Executive Committee of the Fund" to the direction his work was taking and she urged him to formally "lay out a new plan of action more valuable than the original project." Crandall acknowledged that the Payne Fund's primary mission now was "to see facilities and time reserved for educational purposes free from all other considerations" and that the campaign would "be a direct blow against the monopolistic intentions and efforts of the commercial broadcasters."[19] In September Perry was informed that the Payne Fund had set aside $200,000 for a five-year grant to support an educator activist group. To no avail, the networks and the Radio Corporation of America (RCA), NBC's parent company, attempted furtively to undercut Perry's credibility with Wilbur, Cooper, and Bolton.[20]

After meeting with Bolton and, Crandall, Perry convinced Cooper to convene a meeting of educators to form a group to lobby for broadcast reform. Perry prepared the list of invitees and the meeting was called for Chicago so as to be closer to the Midwest's land-grant universities that housed the largest educational stations.[21] In Cooper's opening address to the October 13 meeting, he stated that the conference was called to address "the fear that before education knows what it wants to do commercial stations will have practically monopolized the channels open for radio broadcasting."[22] Unlike the Wilbur Committee, this group made no pretense of trying to work with the commercial broadcasters; that strategy was presupposed as bankrupt. By the end of the one-day conference, the NCER had been established. It would be an umbrella organization of nine leading national education organizations, including the NEA.[23] The Chicago conference also resolved that the first order of business for the new NCER would be to lobby Congress for legislation that would set aside 15 percent of the channels for educational use. Joy Elmer Morgan, the editor of the *NEA Journal*, was appointed by Cooper to chair the NCER; thereafter, Cooper had nothing formal to do with the group, stating that it would be inappropriate for a government official to work with a group chartered to lobby Congress on a specific issue. No great thought had gone into determining the 15 percent proposal; as Morgan noted, it was merely "an emergency and not a final measure."[24]

Throughout November and December, the Payne Fund negotiated with Morgan and educators to determine the nature of the relationship between the Fund and the NCER. Given the Payne Fund's distaste for publicity, it had little interest in playing more than a secondary role in the operations of the new group. As Crandall put it, the Fund wanted to avoid "the untenable position of undertaking to do for educators what educators are now prepared to do for themselves."[25] The Payne Fund Executive Committee formally approved the five-year $200,000 grant to the NCER on January 20, 1931. Over the next few years, Bolton and Crandall would meet with Morgan once or twice each year to discuss the general status of the group. Bolton was very sensitive about appearing intrusive; in 1932 she would "emphatically" disavow to Morgan "the least intention or desire to influence the policies of your Committee when our judgments may be at variance." Nevertheless, Bolton added that "we are not like other groups, we of the Payne Fund. We are keenly interested in every possible angle of the activities which we sponsor and we like to be known for our ideas as well as our money."[26] Over the years as the Payne Fund became increasingly dissatisfied with the performance of the NCER, it was tempted to play a somewhat larger role, a temptation it mostly resisted.

At the outset, at least, the Payne Fund regarded the establishment of the NCER as the culmination of its work in radio, "the fulfillment of the Payne Fund's objectives and efforts over a period of approximately three and one-half years," as one memo put it. One educator noted to the Fund that its funding of the NCER "will go down as one of the milestones of educational achievement."[27] Perry could not help but see the irony in the Payne Fund's turn to supporting a group like the NCER from its original desire to work with the commercial networks. As he wrote to an executive at CBS in March 1931:

> I certainly am aware that your company holds a very vigorous opinion against the setting aside of certain channels for educational broadcasting. The opinion has helped to turn hundreds of thousands of dollars of philanthropic money, which was appropriated for the purpose of developing public interest in your educational programs and those of other companies into other channels where it is developing a nationwide reaction against commercial broadcasting.[28]

The NCER: Personnel, Programs, and Problems

The NCER was chartered so that each of the nine member organizations would appoint a representative to it, all of whom would attend quarterly meetings to determine basic policy decisions. Joy Elmer Morgan, the NEA representative, was formally elected the NCER's chair. He maintained his paid position at the NEA throughout his tenure. The full-time staff throughout the early

1930s was composed of Tracy Tyler and Armstrong Perry, although Perry's salary was paid for independently by the Payne Fund. Tyler, who earned a Ph.D. in education at Columbia University in 1931, ran the office and edited the NCER's four-page newsletter, *Education by Radio*. Tyler also coordinated the distribution of educational programs among the college stations, and he directed the research activities of the NCER, which the Payne Fund insisted should be a component of its program. *Education by Radio* was the NCER's most visible project; with a controlled circulation that reached more than 10,000 by 1934, this twice-monthly publication consisted mostly of reprints of speeches and articles from other publications, plus brief news items. Morgan characterized *Education by Radio* as necessary to counteract the "misinformation" that "has been spread so deliberately by selfish and greedy interests that even public officials have found it difficult to get the facts."[29]

Perry left his position at the Office of Education to join the NCER early in 1931. His primary function was to serve as director of the NCER's Service Bureau, the purpose of which was to represent educational stations in hearings before the FRC. Since station licenses were valid for only three months, and since commercial stations increasingly attempted to usurp the channels held by educators as the profit potential of the airwaves became apparent, this was a vital service. "Ever since the new broadcast structure was put in effect in the fall of 1928," the director of the University of Illinois station wrote to a member of Congress in 1930, "we wasted practically all of the money that our university has put into our broadcasting efforts" defending ourselves before the FRC, so that "it has been impossible for the people of the state . . . to benefit from the educational features which we have attempted to give them."[30] At Perry's insistence, the NCER hired Horace Lohnes as the Service Bureau's counsel to represent college stations at no cost in FRC hearings. Perry and Lohnes had their work cut out for them; between February 1, 1932, and September 26, 1934, there were 1,426 applications by commercial interests before the FRC for the use of frequencies at least partially occupied by educational broadcasters. The Service Bureau was credited with helping to stabilize the number of university stations by the end of 1932.[31]

Perry remained active on several other fronts as well. He was the NCER's official expert on international broadcasting, traveling abroad, studying other systems, and representing the NCER at international radio conferences in

1932 and 1933. Perry also served as the liaison between the NCER headquarters in Washington and the Payne Fund offices in New York City. He filed periodic confidential reports to Crandall regarding the NCER. Although candid, Perry's memos rarely engaged in political infighting. Because the NCER was largely the product of his labors, he wanted to see it succeed and to be held in high regard by Crandall and Bolton.

Between 1931 and 1934, Tyler, Perry and Morgan made hundreds of speeches and wrote scores of articles promoting the cause of broadcast reform. It was Morgan, however, more than anyone else, who gave the NCER Its public identity. Strongly influenced by the Midwest's populist tradition, Morgan had been active in the public utilities movement during the Progressive Era.[32] In his capacity with the NEA he had become convinced that it was absurd to think that commercial broadcasters would provide adequate educational programming. "That practice has been tried for nearly a decade and has proved unworkable," Morgan stated in 1931. "It is no longer open to discussion."[33] Nor was education merely a matter of classroom pedagogy to Morgan. "When we talk about education's rights on the air, we are not talking about the needs and wishes of some special group. We are talking about the needs of the people themselves."[34]

Morgan regarded the fight for broadcast reform as central to the general battle for political democracy. He cast the struggle in almost apocalyptic terms:

> As a result of radio broadcasting, there will probably develop during the twentieth century either chaos or a world-order of civilization. Whether it shall be one or the other will depend largely upon whether broadcasting be used as a tool of education or as an instrument of selfish greed. So far, our American radio interests have thrown their major influence on the side of greed. . . . There has never been in the entire history of the United States an example of mismanagement and lack of vision so colossal and far-reaching in its consequences as our turning of the radio channels almost exclusively into commercial hands.[35]

"I believe we are dealing here," Morgan informed a meeting of educators in 1932, "with one of the most crucial issues that was ever presented t civilization at any time in its entire history." In the depths of the Depression, Morgan wrote that the United States cannot "solve any of it major political problems without first solving the radio problem."[36]

Given this type of rhetoric and the NCER's formal positions, relations between the group and the commercial broadcasters were hostile from the outset. Tyler summed up the feelings of all associated with the NCER when he stated that "the commercial broadcasters . . . are doing all they can to wreck the educational stations." The commercial broadcasters' trade organization, the National Association of Broadcasters (NAB), formally resolved against the 15 percent measure at its November 1930 convention, even before the measure had been introduced in Congress.[37] The commercial trade publication *Broadcasting* constantly disparaged the NCER in its pages, characterizing the group as "misguided pedagogues" with "silly demands." Morgan, in particular, was loathed. *Broadcasting* dismissed him as "coming from the ranks of primary school men," who "had to be fighting something all the time" with an "unreasoning sort of crusading."[38]

A primary problem the NCER faced, and, indeed, never overcame, was its inability to unite all the national educational organizations and major educators in the cause of broadcast reform. At a formal level, they were mostly successful in this regard. Virtually every major national educational group did officially support the aims of the NCER during this period. Some non-NCER organizations were even more radical. For example, the National Congress of Parents and Teachers (NCPT) passed resolutions calling for the complete nationalization of broadcasting. Moreover, a 1933 NCER survey of 631 college administrators found that only 4.4 percent expressed themselves as "being satisfied with the system of radio now in use."[39] Nonetheless, these figures and endorsements overstate the degree of support that broadcast reform had among educators. Even a director of the NCER-member Association of College and University Broadcasting Stations confided his distaste for the NCER's approach since it would precipitate a long and bitter fight and alienate the friendship of the commercial stations. In his mind, "We can get more by being friendly to the big commercial broadcasters."[40]

The educators' inability to unite was apparent even among those radio projects subsidized by the Payne Fund. Perry, Morgan, and Tyler were mostly contemptuous of Charters and the IER, regarding them as unwilling to risk antagonizing the commercial networks and the NAB.[41] "At each of the past institutes we have had only one side presented and we have heard only of the 'wonderful showmanship' of the big station broadcasts," wrote one frustrated NCER activist about the annual IER conference in 1931:

I would like to have the merits of the average commercial programs and the big chain programs discussed by some persons who do not assume it to be axiomatic that these programs are the acme of perfection and superior in every way to anything that ever existed before or that can ever be produced again in the future.[42]

The antagonism between Charters and the NCER came to a head just weeks after the NCER was launched, when the Payne Fund sought to have the Ohio State radio research and the NCER research conducted jointly. The Fund regarded this "coalition" as "greatly desired," going so far as offering to double the research budget for both programs if they agreed to the marriage.[43] The union never came about, mostly due to NCER resistance. As one memo critical of Charters stated, his research bureau "must stop doing those things which are a part of the commercial set-up and which the commercial people will gladly pay for themselves."[44] The two sides had minimal contact thereafter.

In addition to whatever natural suspicion of the NCER program among educators existed, two other factors played a large role in keeping the NCER from guiding a united front into battle on Capitol Hill. First, the commercial broadcasters did not sit idly by as the NCER challenged the legitimacy of their control of the airwaves. As Morgan put it, the radio lobby sought to "interpenetrate and paralyze all the groups working for radio reform."[45] "Every one of the educational organizations connected with his [Morgan's] Committee is being besieged by the radio trust outfit," one Payne Fund memo stated in 1932, "and Brother Morgan knows it well." The primary means the networks employed to divide the educators was to offer some of them free air-time. Morgan finally called an emergency meeting with Crandall to discuss, with little effect, the "attempts of the radio interests to interpenetrate their organization." Ironically, the commercial broadcasters enjoyed their greatest success with Morgan's own NEA, which developed a regular program of broadcasting over NBC under NEA official Florence Male. As Perry noted, this left Morgan "constantly in a somewhat ridiculous position, not being supported by his own organization."[46]

Second, the NCER was not the only national organization dedicated to education by radio. In 1930, working closely with NBC executives, the Carnegie Corporation established the National Advisory Council on Radio in Education

(NACRE). Directed by Columbia University adult educator Levering Tyson, the NACRE took an explicitly sympathetic stance toward commercial broadcasting, regarding it as entrenched and beyond challenge, and dismissing reform efforts as "fruitless and unwarranted."[47] The NACRE's function was to provide educational programs to be broadcast over CBS and NBC, though the connection with the latter network was so strong that the NACRE was considered NBC's de facto educational branch.[48] Although the NACRE had little formal support among national educational organizations, it included many prominent educators and public figures on its board of directors, including Robert M. Hutchins, president of the University of Chicago, Elihu Root, Charles Evans Hughes and Walter Dill Scott, president of Northwestern University. Tyson was effusive in his praise of commercial broadcasting in his public statements and equally critical of the reformers, especially the NCER. The NCER, he noted, was "a belligerent and propagandistic organization" that had "attempted in every way to throw sand in our machinery."[49]

Tyson was no shill for the NBC or CBS, however; he acknowledged that they "are not interested" in the NACRE "from any educational motive."[50] Tyson realized that his leverage over the networks was the threat of reform. "Broadcasting's position in this country is not overly secure," Tyson wrote to one NBC executive in 1932 to convince NBC not to cancel a NACRE series when NBC had sold the scheduled time to advertisers. "I have no hesitation in stating to you that many influential members of the Council were supporters of the theory of government broadcasting until the success of our programs convinced them that the American system is and can be workable." Thus Tyson warned that if the NACRE series was canceled, "it will be perfectly apparent to these individuals that American radio will always be relegated to the pure commercial, and that all the public service for which the medium itself gave such promise is mere bunk."[51] Tyson won this particular skirmish, but it portended the fate of noncommercial cultural fare over the networks as advertisers were increasingly willing to pay for all the desirable time slots.

The CER detested the NACRE, regarding it as "a smokescreen to further the efforts of radio monopolies in gobbling up broadcasting."[52] More broadly, the tension between the NCER and the NACRE reflected the conflict between the Carnegie Corporation and the Payne Fund over which organization, and which approach, would direct education by radio. Bolton agreed to support the founding of the NCER only after her inquiries determined that the NACRE's approach "is not particularly popular with the educators of this country."[53] Both sides realized that, by launching the NCER, the Payne Fund was effectively repudiating the NACRE' cooperative stance toward the networks. "If Payne Fund money was not available," Tyson observed, "this whole agitation would die from lack of nourishment." Accordingly, Tyson worked assiduously between 1931 and 1935 to "shut off this source of Payne Fund money," by attempting "the possibility of bringing Mrs. Bolton into our camp."[54] Bolton politely resisted all these overtures. Crandall, however, had no patience or sympathy for Tyson or the NACRE whatsoever. "Tyson's pandering to the commercial interests" is blatant, she wrote to Bolton in 1932, "and his intellectual dishonesty toward the educational cause "is clear."[55]

In any case, the existence of the NACRE gave the strong impression of an educational community divided, even confused, with regard to broadcasting. With a lavish budget, the NACRE was far more visible than the NCER, and, with its rhetoric extolling education by radio, difference between the two groups were sometimes difficult to glean, even to those active in educational radio. As the radio committee of the NCER-member National University Extension Association noted, the two groups "presumably represent the same faction, and yet the two are quite far apart in so far as any cooperation is concerned."[56] Broadcasting historian Erik Barnouw has noted that among the public and educators there existed a "glorious confusion" about what each of the groups stood for. Even some of the scholarship on this period has failed to differentiate between the two groups.[57]

The Ventura Free Press Radio Campaign

The Fund's sponsorship of broadcast reform did not end with the NCER. In 1931 it launched an eighteen-month radio campaign, costing some $50,000, under the auspices of the *Ventura Free Press*, a small daily newspaper in Ventura, California, just north of Los Angeles. The campaign had a three-pronged mission: (1) to mobilize newspaper opposition to commercial broadcasting, concentrating on the American Newspaper Publishers Association (ANPA), the trade organization of the newspaper industry; (2) to attempt to encourage extensive and sympathetic coverage of the broadcast reform fight in the nation's newspapers; and (3) to lobby on Capitol Hill far the passage of broadcast reform legislation. With the Payne Fund's commitment to the bold *Ventura Free Press* radio campaign, the Fund's blossoming apposition to commercial broadcasting had reached full flower. In short, it wanted to marshal more resources to the cause it had almost stumbled upon in its desire to promote the educational application of radio.

The campaign was the brainchild of H. O. Davis, a wealthy retired magazine and movie studio executive who had come to the Payne Fund's attention in 1930 with a plan to launch a monthly magazine for young working-class women. Although Davis's plan never got off the ground, he impressed Bolton and Crandall enough to get himself elected to the Payne Fund Board of Directors in July 1930.[58] Davis quickly realized that the radio project was becoming a consuming passion for Bolton and Crandall, "the most impressive example" of what the Payne Fund could accomplish, as Crandall explained to him.[59] Davis then put together his radio proposal. It called for the campaign to be directed out of the offices of the *Free Press*, a newspaper he had recently purchased, to give it legitimacy among newspaper publishers and editors. The Payne Fund not only approved Davis's plan, but also donated to Davis the services of S. Howard Evans, who had come to the Fund to serve as an assistant to the president in 1930. A "Bull Moose" Republican, Evans was held in the highest regard by Bolton and Crandall. His task for the *Ventura Free Press* campaign was to "handle the political side of the radio fight," in Washington and with the ANPA.[60] Davis then hired two veteran journalists, Walter Woehlke and Harold Carew, to direct the publicity side of the operations from Southern California.

The Payne fund made the grant to Davis under the one condition that the Fund's involvement be kept strictly confidential. This was non-negotiable, the Fund insisted, because it would be highly embarrassing for Bolton's husband, U.S. Representative Chester Bolton, Republican of Ohio, if it were public knowledge that his wife's organization was funding such a controversy-laden enterprise. The secret was kept rigorously; Representative Bolton and the NCER, aside from Perry, were unaware of the Payne Fund role in the *Ventura Free Press* radio campaign. Evans moved out of the Payne Fund offices and worked out of his home on Long Island for the next two years; he was now officially the special editorial representative of the *Ventura Free Press*, although he remained on the Payne Fund payroll.[61]

The *Free Press* campaign was launched with much fanfare in July 1931. "The objective of the campaign, as I understand it," Woehlke wrote, "is the complete overthrow of the present system."[62] Davis's first general mailing to publishers was unequivocal. The campaign was a "national attack on the radio combine" with the goal of the "removal of advertising from the air," along with the elimination of the "exploitation" of radio for "private profit."[63]

Two problems plagued the campaign from the outset, particularly as it attempted to gain the endorsement of the ANPA, which Davis logically thought would be highly sympathetic due to its fear of radio advertising. First, many publishers were suspicious of Davis's motives, thinking "that anyone endeavoring to solve the radio problem without asking them to cough up must have some ulterior motive." Similarly, publishers could not understand how any West Coast newspaper, let alone the *Ventura Free Press*, "could afford an eastern representative."[64] Davis pleaded with Bolton and Crandall to let him tell the truth about the Payne Fund's involvement, but they budged only to the extent that they would let Davis confide to a few select publishers that Evans was a Payne Fund employee. This was far from satisfactory.[65] Second, many newspaper publishers insisted that the *Ventura Free Press* provide an acceptable alternative before they would support a campaign to smash the existing system. Although Evans and Davis both considered fully nationalized broadcasting as "distinctly preferable to a private monopoly," they realized that such a proposal would never fly among the conservative publishers, or even the public at large. Despite much effort, Davis never could determine a suitable reform model that could satisfy the publishers.[66]

The *Ventura Free Press* efforts collapsed in 1932 when major newspapers with network radio affiliations were able to overwhelm the reform movement. Then, in December 1933, with the Biltmore agreement that ended a nine-month press-radio "war" over how competitive broadcast news was becoming to the press, the ANPA committed itself to opposing broadcast reform legislation in Congress in return for the networks and the NAB agreeing to limit sharply their broadcasting of news.[67]

The *Ventura Free Press* campaign was not much more successful in its attempt to generate favorable press coverage of the reform movement. This was recognized as essential for the reformers if they were to penetrate the public support necessary to force Congress to confront an entrenched and profitable industry. The *Free Press* campaign certainly did its part; it sent out

monthly newsletters, called "anti-commercialism radio bulletins," to some
two thousand publishers as well as providing a free new service on broadcast
reform to some five hundred newspapers. Consequently, the *Ventura Free
Press* dubbed itself the "most widely quoted newspaper west of the
Rockies."[68] The commercial broadcasters were well aware of the *Free Press*
publicity; *Broadcasting* termed it "probably the most vicious campaign ever
leveled against American radio."[69]

Nevertheless, the *Free Press* campaign barely made a ripple in the public
consciousness. NBC's sizable press department alone easily overwhelmed the
Free Press output.[70] Moreover, radio news was rarely covered in the news sections; it was generally the province of a distinct radio section that provided
daily program listings and notes about the programs. Radio editors, in particular, quickly developed a shamelessly dependent relationship to the networks, which provided them with the material they used to fill their pages. In
1931, for example, a survey of a hundred leading radio editors found that they
overwhelmingly favored the "American plan of private enterprise in broadcasting."[71] Perhaps the extent to which the press downplayed or ignored the
reform movement is revealed by the lack of criticism the generally sensitive
broadcasters made regarding the press coverage.

In both of these areas and even more so in its congressional lobbying the
Free Press campaign was handicapped by its inability to develop a satisfactory
working relationship with the NCER. Certainly the secret basis of the Payne
Fund's role did not help matters. Davis insisted that Crandall see to it that the
NCER "openly endorse the *Free Press* campaign and aggressively work with
it."[72] Crandall tried to comply, bringing Davis, Evans, and Morgan together
for a meeting in June 1931. The meeting failed to accomplish its mission. As
Crandall noted, "It soon became evident . . . that there was no possibility of a
meeting of the minds." Morgan insisted that reform was a long-term project in
which each of the groups should be allowed to pursue separate courses, while
Davis and Evans argued that "an immediate emergency program" was the
only hope for defeating the commercial broadcasters.[73] Thereafter, the *Free
Press* campaign personnel continually disparaged the NCER in their internal
correspondence and in their memos to the Payne Fund, characterizing the
educators as politically incompetent. "The whole educational crowd,"
Woehlke wrote to Evans after the NCER's Tyler had failed to mail him a
report as he had promised, "is a bunch of theorists with no idea of how to run

a publicity campaign. Tell them to jump off the North end of a ferry boat going South."[74]

Although the Payne Fund never intervened in this conflict between its two broadcast reform projects, Bolton's sympathies seemed to lie with the *Free Press*. Bolton informed Davis that the *Free Press* campaign "gives such evidence of activity that I am breathless."[75] She followed the campaign with a singular devotion, in contrast to her more distant stance toward the NCER, reading copies of all the considerable correspondence exchanged between Crandall and Evans and Woehlke and clipping all the *Ventura Free Press* editorials for a scrapbook. Bolton probably did not clip anything else from the *Free Press*, however. In her enthusiasm for Woehlke's and Carew's editorials, she requested that the entire newspaper be mailed to her. Bolton was "quite shocked at the character of the paper itself," regarding it as "a sensational sheet" with a "quite unnecessary emphasis on crime."[76] Therefore, Bolton could probably see why major newspaper publishers had difficulty taking the *Free Press* seriously as a selfless national advocate of public-service broadcasting.

The Broadcast Reform Movement: Critique, Proposals, and Problems

Had the Payne Fund not subsidized the NCER and the *Ventura Free Press* radio campaign, there still would have been a broadcast reform movement in the early 1930s. Organized labor, progressive religious groups, the American Civil Liberties Union (ACLU), and a few other groups actively lobbied in Washington for reform legislation.[77] Nonetheless, the Payne Fund bankrolled the efforts to mobilize the educators and the newspapers, and, along with labor, these were the constituencies that most concerned the commercial broadcasters. Moreover, the Payne Fund's grants to the NCER and the *Free Press* radio campaign dwarfed all the other reform group budgets. In this sense, it is clear that the broadcast reform movement would have been but a shadow of what it was had the Payne Fund not taken part. In addition to the organized reform efforts, the cause of broadcast reform received the nearly unconditional support of the U.S. intelligentsia.[78]

Nor was discontent with commercial broadcasting limited to activists and intellectuals in the early 1930s. The initial public response to commercialized broadcasting was far more negative than it would be subsequently; radio advertising in particular was generally detested as an unwelcome intrusion into people's homes. As the *Free Press*'s Woehlke noted upon joining the radio campaign, "I know that dissatisfaction with the present broadcasting system and its results is well nigh universal. Out of one hundred persons you will not find more than five who are satisfied; of the other 95%, more than one-half are ready to support any kind of movement for a drastic change."[79] This assessment was accepted to various degrees by the industry, the FRC and radio editors as well. "Radio broadcasting," *Business Week* informed its readers in 1932, "is threatened with a revolt of the listeners. . . . Newspaper radio editors report more and more letters of protest against irritating sales ballyhoo." One pro-status quo radio editor even cautioned that "due to too much advertising and too much mediocre program material," public sympathies were moving toward "Government control."[80]

In short, especially in 1931 and 1932, the broadcast reformers regarded themselves as the legitimate representatives of the vast majority of Americans; there was no sense of their being an elite attempting to force their own agenda onto a popularly embraced commercial system. In this context, the task for the reform movement was to convert this dissatisfaction into support for structural reform.

Although from a fairly wide range of backgrounds, these broadcast reformers along with the NCER and the *Free Press* radio campaign were in general agreement in their criticism of commercial broadcasting. If the Payne Fund had initially become involved in broadcast reform due to its concern about education, those affiliated with the NCER and *Free Press* campaign soon adopted a broad-based critique of the status quo in which the limited role of education was but one brick, perhaps a cornerstone, in a larger edifice.

Three themes dominated the reform movement's critique of commercial broadcasting. First, all the reformers emphasized that the system was flawed on grounds of free expression: it would be inherently biased against broadcasting programming that was critical of big business and the status quo. Morgan argued that "genuine freedom of thought" over U.S. radio was impossible: "The very points at which facts are most needed if people are to govern themselves wisely are the points at which freedom of speech is most certain to be denied."[81] When combined with an appreciation of the enormous role radio was playing in U.S. politics and culture, the reformers' concern reached fever pitch. As Davis put it, "This inevitable monopoly constitutes the great-est danger American democracy has ever been exposed to."[82]

Second, the reform movement was uniformly critical of the influence of advertising over programming. Most commercial programs were regarded as trivial and inane, and it was seen as inevitable that advertisers would down-play educational, cultural, or controversial fare to favor inexpensive, unoriginal entertainment programs. One NCER member stated that "it is unavoidable that a commercial concern catering to the public will present a service as low in standards as the public will tolerate and will produce the most profit." "In order to get large audiences," Morgan observed, "they cultivate the lower appeals." It would be difficult to exaggerate the NCER's contempt for radio advertising. On another occasion, Morgan noted that "commercialized broad-casting as it is now regulated in America may threaten the very life of civiliza-tion by subjecting the human mind to all sorts of new pressures and selfish exploitations."[83]

Third, the reformers regarded the commercial system as the product of a mostly secretive process in which the public and even Congress had played almost no role. This was grossly offensive to the reformers' democratic sensi-bilities. "So the question really is," Perry noted, "do we want to submit to the regulation of radio by the people whom we elect to rule over us, or do we want to leave our radio channels in the hands of private concerns and private indi-viduals who wish to use these public radio channels for their own profit?"[84] In total, this was explicitly radical criticism. To the reformers, the experience of the FRC had made it clear that it was absurd to think that a government agency could possibly make private broadcasters act in the public interest. It is a "fact that the radio channels belong to the people," stated an NCER organizer, "and should not be placed in the hands of private capital."[85]

Given this critique, it should be no surprise that most reformers were hearty in their praise of the BBC, which was a noncommercial, nonprofit cor-poration with a monopoly over British broadcasting. Morgan, like Evans and Davis, had gone on record as regarding the BBC model as the best option for the United States.[86] To Perry, the BBC provided the "ideal" example of a "broadcasting service maintained primarily for the benefit of all radio listen-ers" and was the solution to "the whole world problem of broadcasting."[87] The NCER even tried to get the BBC to formally endorse its activities, but the BBC demurred, informing Perry that "it does not wish to meddle in American affairs.[88] These sentiments notwithstanding, the reform movement never advocated the complete nationalization and de-commercialization of U.S. broadcasting. For the NCER and the *Free Press* this was due mostly to the belief that it would be impossible to accomplish such a measure politically, since the public would not support it. Others, like the ACLU, were concerned that the government would play too large a role in the nation's communications system.

This left the reform movement in a conundrum. As Woehlke acknowledged, the reformers could never expect public support unless they could indicate "a new road leading to better things."[89] Given the economic depression and the decision of the major foundations either to support the status quo or to remain out of broadcasting, the question of how to fund nonprofit broadcasting if not by the government hung like a noose around the reformers' necks. As Perry acknowledged to Crandall upon the founding of the NCER with its mandate to lobby for 15 percent of the channels, "Our problem still is unsolved: the finding of financial support for college and university stations."[90] For that reason alone, the 15 percent scheme was almost dead in the water before it reached Congress. The reform movement never did agree on a uniform alternative and then coalesce to work on its behalf. In Washington, this meant that the reform groups generally worked in isolation. After a few months on Capitol Hill, a frustrated Evans wrote to Woehlke, "Every son-of-a-gun and his brother has a definite idea about the way it should be handled."[91] To some extent, this inability to unite also revealed the lack of political savvy of many of the reformers, who, though well intentioned, seemed clueless about how to win a fierce political struggle.

Nor were these the only problems that plagued the reform movement. If its critique of the status quo on the grounds of a pro-big business bias might generate mass support in a decade of intense labor activism, the reform movement's critique of advertising at times harbored a profound elitism, which dismissed entertainment programming categorically and could only repel mass support. "Even the so-called entertainment aspects of the programs are such that no civilized person can listen to them without nausea," one critic wrote. "This is often the result of a deliberate policy on the part of the advertiser, who finds that people of low intelligence respond most readily to his commercial appeal, and therefore baited his trap with material intentionally designed to reach those that are not quite bright." Another reformer confessed that his "ideal broadcasting station" would make no "hypocritical pretense" of attempting "to present something for everyone." Rather, all the programming would "be aimed at and above a frankly upper-middle class" audience.[92]

The NCER and the *Ventura Free Press* radio campaign tended to eschew this tendency to blame the audience for commercial fare in the early 1930s, although these sentiments were not entirely absent from their correspondence. They argued instead that commercial fare was intended to please advertisers, not listeners. As the system became entrenched however, the educators gradually accepted the notion that the commercial broadcasters "gave the people what they want," whereas the educational stations were chartered for a higher calling, for which there was an admittedly limited audience.

Moreover, the *Ventura Free Press's* efforts notwithstanding, the reformers were ineffectual in their attempts to communicate their existence, let alone their position on broadcast reform, to the bulk of the populace through the mass media. Most Americans, no matter how dissatisfied with radio advertising and programming, probably had no idea that there was a movement afoot to address these concerns in Congress, or that it was the public's right to do so.[93]

These problems paled, however, in contrast to the largest barrier that impeded the progress of the reform movement: the strength of the radio lobby of NBC, CBS, RCA, and the NAB, which the NCER soon realized was "one of the most powerful here in Washington."[94] Besides having the sort of political leverage that traditionally accompanies great wealth in U.S. politics, the radio lobby had two other advantages. First, it was well positioned to publicize its own version of U.S. broadcasting, one in which it was an innately American and democratic system that responded directly to listener desires through the marketplace.[95] Second, through their policy of providing free airtime to any member of Congress who desired it, CBS and NBC did much to undercut any budding insurgency. Moreover, it was the network lobbyists who were responsible for scheduling members of Congress for their broadcasts. For example, between January 1931 and October 1933, U.S. senators made 298 free appearances over NBC.[96] As Morgan put it, "The politicians are too eager to use radio to come out for reform."[97]

One first-term member of the House of Representatives, Thomas R. Amlie, Republican of Wisconsin, laid out the situation in stark terms in a confidential letter to the NCER in 1932. "I wanted to do something that would call attention to the inherent evils of our present commercialized form of broadcasting," he wrote. Amlie then described how after he sponsored legis-

lation that would have prohibited radio advertising on Sundays, the broadcasters of Wisconsin formally condemned him, the NAB attacked his bill, and
it was dropped by the pertinent House committee "without as much as a
voice of protest on the Floor of the House." Amlie attributed this to the fact
that "members of Congress are dependent upon these stations for many
favors." He concluded that "this is a factor you must overcome if you are to
get anywhere with your program."[98] Amlie's letter seemingly confirmed the
prediction of the CBS executive who confided to Perry late in 1930 that the
newly formed NCER "would fail because the political cards were stacked
against them."[99] Despite this self-confidence, however, the radio lobby would
leave nothing to chance in the early 1930s. Its fear was always that the reformers' critique would develop a significant base of support among the citizenry
before the system was fully in place and no more susceptible to political challenge than any other major U.S. industry.

The Battle on Capitol Hill

On January 8, 1931, Senator Simeon Fess, Republican of Ohio, introduced a
bill, soon dubbed the Fess Bill, calling for the FRC to reserve 15 percent of
the channels for educational institutions. Fess, the former president of
Antioch College, did so after meeting with Joy Elmer Morgan. The radio
lobby opposed the bill; indeed, before 1933 it was opposed to passage by
Congress of any radio legislation since it was quite happy with the manner in
which the FRC was stabilizing the airwaves for commercial exploitation.[100]
The broadcasters' agenda was assisted by two factors. First, the economic
depression dominated the thinking of Congress. "Were it not for the disturbing economic situation," *Broadcasting* observed, "Congress might blunder
into the political radio morass camouflaged by these lobbying factions."[101]
Second, though there was support for reform among rank-and-file members
of Congress, perhaps reflecting the degree of public antipathy to the status
quo despite the strength of the radio lobby, the ranking members of the congressional committees that handled radio legislation, especially James
Couzens, Republican of Michigan, and C. C. Dill, Democrat of Washington
State, were staunch defenders of the industry. This became most apparent
when a bill to set up a national nonprofit radio channel to be operated soley

organized labor passed the House and Senate in 1931, only to be squelched by the committee chairs in conference. "If it were not for a little group of reactionary leaders in both branches of Congress," the chief labor radio lobbyist observed, "this legislation would have been passed."[102]

The Fess Bill never made it out of committee that winter, but the NCER was convinced that its prospects were outstanding in the session of Congress that would convene in December 1931. Bolton was less certain. Using her numerous contacts on Capitol Hill, she determined that there was considerable support in Congress for the idea of broadcast reform, but most members found the Fess Bill an unacceptable alternative.[103] In the fall of 1931 Evans moved to Washington to begin actively lobbying as the representative of the *Ventura Free Press*. "Things look awfully good here," he noted after gauging the degree of hostility to commercial broadcasting on Capitol Hill, but, like Bolton, he soon realized that the Fess Bill was unpassable.[104] Moreover, he recognized that there was a pressing need to come up with a workable piece of legislation. "Mr. Average Congressman is undoubtedly dissatisfied with the present condition of radio," Evans informed Woehlke. "But I doubt if he will be likely to give up the present system for one the merits of which cannot be definitely ascertained."[105] While the NCER continued to lobby for the Fess Bill, Evans threw his support behind a measure that called for a complete congressional investigation of broadcasting, with the purpose of gathering facts for establishing a new broadcast setup.

The winter of 1931-32 was the high watermark of discontent with commercial broadcasting. It was clear to congressional defenders of the status quo that some radio legislation would almost certainly pass Congress and that the legislation would probably be harmful to industry interests. Accordingly, Couzens and Dill proposed and got passed Senate Resolution 129 in January 1932, which called for the FRC to make a thorough study of the various criticisms of broadcasting and report back to Congress by the summer. This was a devastating blow to the reformers, since the congressional leaders could now claim that no radio legislation should be considered until the FRC completed its study. Moreover, that the FRC would endorse the status quo was a foregone conclusion. It December 1931, to quell the rising tide of criticism, the FRC had released a statement commending the "American system of broadcasting" as the "best ... in the world" and asserting that no reforms were necessary.[106] Davis insisted that the *Free Press* continue to "make every possible effort to get action at this session of Congress." He told Crandall that "it would be very difficult to keep the radio matter alive through another year."[107]

Since the FRC was now conducting a study, the bill Evans had favored mandating a congressional study of radio was withdrawn. From February to April Evans pushed relentlessly on behalf of new legislation that would put sharp limits on the amount of advertising permitted over the air. Davis repeatedly implored Crandall to get the NCER to support Evans's activities. Although Perry agreed with Davis, since Fess had withdrawn his measure in January after SR 129 had passed, Morgan refused to cooperate, informing Davis that he supported only the NCPT's resolution calling for the complete nationalization and decommercialization of broadcasting. "Mr. Joy Elmer Morgan," Davis wrote to Crandall incredulously, "does not even approve the campaign he is conducting."[108] By now the NCER's lobbying had assumed an almost surreal quality. While Tyler spent the spring urging educators to support the Fess Bill, which was no longer viable, Morgan supported a measure that no one was seriously considering, all the while informing NCER members that reform legislation would almost certainly pass "during the next winter."[109] When the *Free Press* advertising limits proposal failed in April, the two branches of the Payne Fund's radio activities were leading in opposite directions. In a sober memorandum shortly thereafter, Crandall was unsparing toward the NCER as a lobbying agency, stating that it made "no effort . . . to understand the entire political situation in Congress and out of it regarding radio legislation."[110]

In June the FRC issued its response to SR 129. The report, *Commercial Radio Advertising*, was lavish in its praise of the status quo and dismissed all criticism unconditionally. The commercial broadcasters were elated, arguing that this settled the matter for all time. The reformers were distraught; Davis called the report "a joke."[111] The summer of 1932 was a somber period for the broadcast reform movement. "We expected to get several bills," Davis despondently noted to Woehlke, "and we failed to get any."[112] The only heartening development for the reformers took place in Canada, where, after years of study and public hearings, Parliament had formally resolved to establish a non-profit broadcasting system in April 1932. Indeed, the only American to testify in Ottawa that spring had been Joy Elmer Morgan, who urged the Canadians to avoid commercial broadcasting in no uncertain terms. "Until your visit," the Canadian leader of the movement for nonprofit, noncommercial broadcasting later wrote Morgan, "the committee had regarded the American situation as largely satisfactory."[113] The U.S. reformers believed that if they could get a similar study authorized by Congress to be conducted by independent citizens not affiliated with the industry, as the FRC clearly was, it could only resolve for a noncommercial system like that in Britain or Canada.

Thus, when Congress reconvened, the *Free Press* put all its effort behind legislation to establish an "investigation of the whole field of radio broadcasting." "If the federal investigation of radio fails," Evans wrote to Davis, "we are practically sunk anyway."[114] The NCER also formally announced its support for a study, after being encouraged to do so by Crandall.[115] The campaign for a radio investigation never got anywhere, however. On the one hand, *Commercial Radio Advertising* had been the result of such a study, albeit by the FRC; and that was enough to satisfy most members of Congress that another study was unnecessary. On the other hand, virtually all of the members of Congress who had worked for broadcast reform had been defeated in the 1932 elections. Whether the radio lobby was responsible for these defeats is not clear; in any case the message was probably clear to those who came to Congress in the winter of 1932–33. "In both Houses of Congress there is no one," Evans informed Woehlke after a month of lobbying, "with whom we can play ball to get ahead in radio.[116] Finally, in January 1933, Evans acknowledged defeat. "I must say that the situation has developed to a point," he wrote to the NCER, "where I am convinced that further radio agitation in Washington is futile at the present time."[117]

In this context, the Payne fund asked Evans prepare a memorandum concerning whether the fund should drop its campaign for broadcast reform and, like the NACRE, simply accept the status quo and cooperate with the commercial broadcasters. Evans acknowledged that that reform movement probably would never "successfully undermine commercial broadcasting in this country." He insisted, however, that the "fundamental structure of broadcasting" was still "absolutely unsound and that the public remained dissatisfied with "excessive commercialism." Evans concluded that the Payne Fund should stay the course, as "the whole structure needs to be reorganized."[118]

The Payne Fund accepted Evans's counsel and then made two fundamental decisions. First, it terminated the *Ventura Free Press* radio campaign. In California, Waehlke and Carew were released, while Evans, returned to work at the Payne Fund offices in New York, where he would act as a consultant on radio and other matters. With the termination of the *Free Press* radio campaign, the mood at the Payne Fund regarding its radio projects was rapidly transformed from one of enthusiasm, even euphoria, to one of despair. H. O. Davis would later inform Crandall how much he "regretted" that it had been "impossible for us to carry the campaign to a successful end."[119] Second, Crandall advised the NCER to suspend its lobbying as well and to "concentrate all their forces on creating local opinion which would later be reflected to Congress."[120]

To this end, the NCER hired a field organizer to travel across the nation, meet with educators and the public at large, make speeches and generally drum up support far broadcast reform. The field organizer, Eugene Coltrane, did so at a breakneck pace throughout 1933, until faltering health and the prospect of a job as a college president led him to resign the post early in 1934. The NCER also managed to have broadcast reform made the official college and high school debate topic for the 1933–34 academic year. The commercial broadcasters were terrified by the debate topic, since it would expose broadcast reform issues to fifteen hundred college and six thousand high school debate teams in thirty-three states. The networks and the NAB went to great expense to promote a positive view of the status quo, and they were able to defuse the situation. "We were able to comply with the objective without damage," NBC president Merlin Aylesworth informed RCA's David Sarnoff.[121] In short, without any appreciable increase in press coverage, these NCER attempts to rouse public opinion had little visible impact.

The one hope remaining far the NCER was to gain the support of Franklin D. Roosevelt, who was inaugurated as president in March 1933. "Unless the big business [sic] has somehow entrenched itself with President Roosevelt," an NCER board member noted, "the program of protecting radio for its best public purpose would fit admirably into his entire program."[122] The reformers were encouraged by the presence of several broadcast reform sympathizers in the Roosevelt administration, including Adolph A. Berle and the chairman of the Tennessee Valley Authority (TVA), Dr. Arthur Morgan, who argued that not only radio but the entire mass media should be operated on a nonprofit basis, "just as are the public schools."[123] The most outspoken advocate of reform was the ambassador to Mexico, Josephus Daniels, perhaps Roosevelt's most trusted friend in politics, who repeatedly implored the president to nationalize radio broadcasting in his correspondence from Mexico City.[124] Nonetheless, the president elected not to ally with the reformers and take on an uphill fight with the powerful commercial broadcasters. To some extent, he did not want to jeopardize his ability to take to the airwaves whenever he desired, which the broadcasters granted him, thereby bypassing the largely Republican newspaper industry.[125] Moreover, the communications industry tended to be Democratic and to support the overarching agenda of the New Deal.[126]

By this time the broadcasters were in favor of passing legislation that would establish the permanent regulation of broadcasting, thus providing a "thoroughly stabilized" industry and thereby eliminating the basis for the, annual "attacks by unfriendly groups" in Washington.[127] In February 1934 Dill introduced a bill to establish the permanent regulation of broadcasting and create a Federal Communications Commission (FCC) to replace the FRC. Otherwise the bill rephrased the Radio Act of 1927 mostly verbatim. A similar bill was introduced in the House. The Roosevelt administration and the NAB announced their support of the bills. Given these conditions, and the lack of any active reform lobbying on Capitol Hill, "all signs pointed to a quick passage," as broadcast historian Philip T. Rosen has noted.[128]

Then, most unexpectedly, Father John B. Harney, Paulist Fathers' superior general, whose station had recently lost an ongoing struggle with the FRC to gain more time on the frequency it shared with a CBS station, entered the fray. In March, Harney went to Washington and arranged to have Senators Henry Hatfield, Republican of West Virginia, and Robert Wagner, Democrat of New York, introduce an amendment that would require the new FCC to set aside 25 percent of the channels for the use of nonprofit groups. With little media coverage, Harney and the Paulists launched a whirlwind campaign among national Catholic organizations, generating more than 60,000 signatures on petition in three weeks in April.[129] The radio lobby seemingly had been caught flat-footed; whereas with labor, education, and the press it had carefully cultivated allies over the years, it was unprepared for this onslaught from the previously dormant Catholics. By the end of April, the trade publication *Variety* warned that the Wagner-Hatfield amendment stood "better than a 50-50 chance of being adopted." The NAB proclaimed that it "brings to a head the campaign against the present broadcasting setup which has been smoldering in Congress for several years."[130] To defuse the momentum for reform, Dill added a clause to his communications bill, Section 307(C), that required the new FCC to study the Wagner-Hatfield proposition and then report back to Congress with recommendations early in 1935.

While Harney received the support of organized labor in his lobbying effort, he was unable to get any help from the NCER despite repeated, at times frantic, overtures in March and April. Indeed, Tyler informed Harney that he thought Dill's Section 307(c) would be a victory for the reform movement.[131] Harney was astounded that Tyler could regard Dill as "at all in sympathy" with broadcast reform.[132] He implored Perry to bypass Tyler and take the matter up with others in the NCER. "We must not let this opportunity knock at our door in vain. A better day will hardly come in our lifetime."[133] Although Perry found some support from college broadcasters across the nation, the NCER's other Washington-based operatives, Tyler and Morgan, could not be aroused, believing that the reform cause could do even better in the coming sessions of Congress. An exasperated Perry began to express his deep reservations about the NCER leadership to Crandall, confessing his "feeling of personal responsibility" for the "exasperatingly slow progress made."[134]

In early May the radio lobby attacked the Wagner-Hatfield amendment as if "its passage obviously would have destroyed the whole structure of broadcasting in America," as the NAB's chief lobbyist put it.[135] Behind Senator Dill, the measure was defeated on the floor of the Senate 42–23 on May 15; Dill's communications bill passed on a voice vote later the same day. Dill's inclusion of Section 307(C) was the decisive factor that convinced many wavering senators that it was better to let the "experts" on the new FCC evaluate the 25 percent idea before putting it into law. The House soon passed its version of the same bill and Roosevelt signed the Communications Act of 1934 into law on June 18. "When we read it," the NAB's lobbyist later commented, "we found that every point we had asked for was there."[136] Now only one opportunity remained for the reformers to advance their cause: the FCC hearings on whether to reserve 25 percent of the channels for nonprofit institutions as mandated by Section 307(C). Harney and organized labor, the groups mostly responsible for the hearings, refused to participate, regarding them as "a pro forma affair, designed to entrench the commercial interests in their privileged position."[137] Indeed, two of the three FCC members who would conduct the October hearings informed the NAB convention in September that they would refuse to recommend any change in the status quo.[138]

Ironically, the NCER agreed to direct the side arguing on behalf of the 25 percent measure, although it informed the FCC that it "had not suggested the enactment of the specific legislation under discussion." Perry agreed with the position of the Paulists and labor on the fraudulent nature of the hearings, while Tyler and Morgan believed that the FCC hearings "would be better than no study at all."[139] The subsequent hearings were a colossal mismatch; the NCER did not even attempt to coordinate the statements of its witnesses and the educators' combined testimony consisted mostly of contradictory statements. After both sides had made their presentations, NBC's chief lobbyist informed New York headquarters that the industry case "was done to perfection" and "was simply overwhelming so far as the opposition's case was concerned."[140] Morgan thought he had a breakthrough when he and Tyler used their contacts with the TVA to have a TVA representative appear at the hearings on one of the final days and make a statement calling for the establishment of a chain of noncommercial government stations. The stunned broadcasters immediately demanded an explanation from the White House, which then forced the TVA to withdraw its statement.[141] A frustrated Morgan continued to insist that the original TVA statement was actually the New Deal position on radio, but his efforts to do so only drew him condemnation from all sides in view of the second TVA statement.

When the FCC hearings drew to a close in early November, the stark reality facing the NCER began to sink in. "It seems to me that the commercial broadcasters have got such a firm grip on the situation," one college president and longtime NCER loyalist wrote Tyler, "that it is going to be difficult for it ever to be broken up." In a confidential memorandum on the NCER to Bolton, Crandall noted that "the organization and administration of the committee from the beginning has been unsatisfactory," and she recommended that the Payne Fund let the group dissolve when its grant expired in 1935, unless the NCER had entirely new leadership.[142] The November 20 meeting of the NCER was marked by severe criticism of Morgan and his handling of the FCC hearings, with Morgan responding by shouting "insults," as Perry put it, to the assembled educators.[143] In January 1935 the FCC released its report to Congress in response to Section 307(C); to no one's surprise it recommended against the fixed-percentage proposal. When Congress reconvened that month, it showed no interest in broadcast reform legislation, regarding the matter as settled with the passage of the Communications Act and the formation of the FCC, which itself now regarded commercial broadcasting as the officially authorized system unless informed otherwise by Congress. The political battle for the control of U.S. broadcasting, including television as well as radio, as much as it ever existed, was now formally concluded.

That point was not immediately clear to the NCER. In March, under the direction of the president of the University of Wyoming, Arthur Crane, who would soon replace Morgan as NCER chairman, the NCER announced an ambitious plan to have the federal government establish a series of nonprofit, noncommercial stations to be supported by tax dollars.[144] The NCER hoped to capitalize on the lessening hostility toward government ownership as the New Deal entered its most liberal phase. Instead, the proposal did not receive a trace of recognition and was quietly dropped by the early summer. The NCER then abandoned its lobbying efforts forever.

If the economic and political consolidation of commercial broadcasting was accomplished by 1935, the ideological consolidation was completed in the remainder of the decade. With the collapse and disappearance of organized opposition, this process was quick, almost inexorable. As RCA president David Sarnoff informed a nationwide NBC audience in 1938, "Our American system of broadcasting is what it is because it operates in American democracy. It is a free system because this is a free country."[145] CBS president William S. Paley informed a group of educators in 1937 that "he who attacks the American system" of broadcasting "attacks democracy itself."[146] Only a few years earlier the same comment would have been met by derision; in 1937 it barely received notice. The system was now off-limits to fundamental attack. Not only was the capitalistic basis of U.S. broadcasting unchallenged in legitimate discourse, it was elevated to the point where such criticism was unthinkable. Commercial broadcasting would continue to receive substantial criticism in subsequent years; however, with the dominant role of the profit motive sacrosanct, critics were left arguing for making the marketplace more competitive, not eliminating it. Besides being ineffectual, this criticism left the core relations unquestioned.

The Payne Fund responded to the shifting currents, with the encouragement of the broadcasting industry. As Perry noted in 1934, "The industry fully understands that if it can get the Fund to withdraw its support commercial radio will have an almost clear field." In September 1935 two NBC executives made a presentation to Bolton to impress upon her the network's commitment to educational programming. One week later, a friend of Bolton's in the House of Representatives confidentially informed her that if she persisted in funding a group that advocated that "the present broadcasting structure be scrapped," and it might put the Payne Fund in "danger."[147] Bolton then decided to renew the NCER but under the condition that it "refrain from controversy or an attack" on the industry and that it be "restricted to educational" work. In short, the new NCER would work through the existing system. Tyler, Morgan, and Perry all resigned and the NCER offices in Washington were closed. Evans took charge of the NCER in January 1936 with a two-year $15,000 grant, working out of the Payne Fund's New York headquarters. Evans never abandoned his personal hatred for commercial broadcasting and his belief in the need for radical structural reform, describing himself in 1936 as "advocating Christianity in a world that is decidedly pagan," but he reconciled himself to the impossibility of reform and the Payne Fund's explicit mandate to the reformed NCER to work within the status quo.[148]

As Perry commented in December 1935, the capitulation of the NCER and the entrenchment of the commercial broadcasters seemingly made the NACRE the apparent winner in the battle to determine the course of educational broadcasting.[149] Ironically, however, precisely as the NCER found itself embracing the status quo, the NACRE released a major study of its relations with NBC from 1932 to 1935 that denounced cooperation between educators and commercial broadcasters as unworkable and failed.[150] Outraged, NBC, perhaps because it no longer needed the NACRE for public relations purposes, made it clear that it had no desire to reconcile the differences between the organizations. The Carnegie Corporation disbanded the NACRE the following year.

The years that followed were difficult times for educators concerned with broadcasting. They had to come to grips with their marginal situation and hope to exact concessions from the FCC and the networks with minimal leverage. In this context, the Payne Fund quietly terminated the NCER in 1941 after the resignation of Evans, who was increasingly frustrated by the group's lack of influence over policy. With the possibility of suggesting fundamental structural changes in the broadcasting setup verboten, those who wished to encourage educational or nonprofit public service radio and television found themselves in an absurd position. Their efforts could be successful or secure only to the extent that they did not interfere with the profitability, existing or potential, of the commercial broadcasters—that is, to the extent that they were ineffectual.

Conclusion

This chapter has chronicled the role the Payne Fund played in attempting to establish a public debate over how the United States might best structure its broadcasting system and, furthermore, lead the drive to establish a significant, even dominant, nonprofit and noncommercial sector. The Payne Fund was remarkable in two respects. First, the Payne Fund broadcast reform campaign indicates the extent to which the Fund was willing to challenge powerful institutions in pursuit of its principles, even against great odds. In this regard it displayed a degree of courage, a willingness to take on the powers that be that has been all too absent in the liberal major foundations of the 1930s and thereafter. To some extent this may be attributed to the period and that commercial broadcasters were not yet sacrosanct in U.S. political culture. The fact remains, however, that the Payne Fund alone recognized the fundamental importance of the ownership and control of broadcasting in a democratic society and was then willing to devote resources to bringing about radical change.

Second, whereas many other democratic nations had extensive public hearings and debates before determining the types of broadcasting systems they eventually established, in the United States these decisions were made quietly, behind closed doors; by self-interested elites, with minimal public participation. Regardless of the obvious limitations of the *Ventura Free Press* radio campaign and, in particular, the NCER, and the uphill fight they would have faced in even the best of circumstances, the fact remains that the Payne Fund is largely responsible for whatever fundamental debate there has been about the merits of a network-dominated, profit-motivated, and advertising-supported broadcasting system in the United States. Considerable scholarship suggests that any of these concerns regarding the concentration and commercialization of the media are perhaps more pressing today than ever before.[151] In addition, the advent of revolutionary communication and information technologies, along with dramatic changes in the world political economy, is forcing a global reappraisal of how societies can best organize their communication systems. The Payne Fund experience may provide a tradition to draw from as we face important questions of the relationship of communication to democracy, and the complex problems associated with generating answers to these questions, in the years to come.

8

Media Made Sport:
A History of Sports Coverage in the United States

Sport and the mass media enjoy a symbiotic relationship in U.S. society. On the one hand, the staggering popularity of sports is due, to no small extent, to the enormous amount of attention provided it by the mass media. On the other hand, the media are able to generate enormous sales in both circulation and advertising based upon their extensive treatment of sports. Media attention fans the flames of interest in sports and increased interest in sports warrants further media attention. This notion of symbiosis also provides a fruitful manner of approaching the history of the sport-mass media relationship in the United States. Virtually every surge in the popularity of sports has been accompanied by a dramatic increase in the coverage provided sports by the media. Furthermore, each surge in the coverage of sports has taken place during a period in which the mass media have sharply increased their penetration into the nooks and crannies of U.S. social life.

Yet the nature of this symbiotic relationship extends far beyond some sort or "you scratch my back and I'll scratch yours" phenomenon. The nature of the sport-mass media relationship has been distinctly shaped by the emerging contours of U.S. capitalism since the 1830s. Much of sports and virtually all of the mass media have been organized as commercial enterprises throughout this history. Many of the specific developments in the sport-mass media relationship can be fathomed only through the continual recognition that each of these institutions has been constituted of individual units first and foremost striving for economic profit in some level of competition with each other. However, sport emerges as an institution especially well suited culturally and ideologically to the emerging industrial capitalism of the century, as well as— and indeed far more so—to the mature corporate capitalist society of the twentieth century.

This chapter will review some of the critical developments in the sport- mass media relationship and the nature of sports journalism over the past 160 years. This is an ambitious goal, particularly for such a brief essay, and hence two provisos must be offered at the outset. First, some very important material must be either ignored or dealt with only in a most cursory fashion. The focus of the narrative will be to develop the notion of the symbiotic relationship as characterized above and therefore will draw upon material that best helps to illuminate this theme. Second, this chapter will make no attempt to explain the spectacular rise in the popularity of sports. This is a tremendously com- plicated issue that has rightly attracted attention from a host of disciplines. Although this chapter posits mass media coverage as a *sine qua non* to the rise of sports to its position as a cornerstone of modern U.S. culture, this is not meant to imply that media coverage alone caused the emergence of sports. Indeed, the mass media have largely capitalized upon other currents in U.S. society and used them to their own advantage.

Prior to the 1830s, the preponderance of newspapers and magazines were directed at a relatively small and well-to-do portion of U.S. society. Nonetheless, between the American Revolution and the era of Jacksonian democracy, the literacy rate gradually increased. The first three decades of the nineteenth century witnessed a sharp increase in magazine publishing, with several hundred magazines commencing operations during this period. These magazines were quite unlike those found in the periodical industry that would emerge later in the century. In a manner similar to the newspaper industry of the period, magazine publishing was not especially profitable and, indeed, most publishers linked their magazines to other professions and interests, fre- quently of a political nature. There was nothing remotely resembling a profes- sion of journalism at this time; in general the editor-publisher was the sole owner, manager, and primary author for his or her particular magazine.

The first U.S. magazine dedicated to sports made its debut in the late 1820s. Seven sports magazines appeared between then and 1835, but only two would survive more than three years. These magazines, and the U.S. reading public, were strongly influenced by the well-established sporting magazine industry of Great Britain, which had emerged by the 1790s. The dominant U.S. sports magazines of this period were John Stuart Skinner's *American Farmer* and *American Turf Register* and William Trotter Porter's *Spirit of the Times*. Sport was generally considered vulgar and disreputable among a large portion of the U.S. reading public at the time. Hence these magazines tended toward the coverage of more respectable endeavors, like horse racing, and tread gently in their treatment of sports such as boxing, which tended to appeal to the lower classes. Magazines like *Spirit of the Times* published columns of schedules and results from race courses all over the country.[1] Many of those who wrote for the sporting press did so under pseudonyms, to protect their real identities.[2]

U.S. society entered a period of dramatic social change in the 1830s and 1840s. The first great wave of industrialization swept the Northeast, and the populations of the major cities swelled with immigrants from abroad and from the countryside. There was a tremendous expansion in the size of the reading public as well as a growing interest in sports. In addition, it became clear that magazine publishing could be a very profitable enterprise. Porter's *Spirit of the Times* became the dominant sport periodical and saw its circulation expand to 100,000 by the 1850s. Porter expanded coverage to boxing, and he made a concerted effort to establish cricket as the national game in the 1840s.[3] By the 1850s Porter decided to emphasize the emerging sport of baseball as the national game, and he did much to popularize the rules and terminology of the sport. This process was accentuated by Frank Queen's *New York Clipper*, which was founded in 1853 and quickly replaced the *Spirit of the Times* as the premier sporting weekly. The *Clipper* employed Henry Chadwick, the first full-fledged U.S. sportswriter, whose efforts to popularize baseball earned him the nickname of "The Father of the Game."[4]

The 1830s and 1840s also witnessed the birth of the modern newspaper industry, which would generate profit as much from the sale of advertising space as from circulation. With decreasing printing costs and an expanding market, there emerged the "penny press," aimed at a working-class and middle-class urban readership.[5] Though coverage was modest by later standards, sport began to receive regular attention from newspapers vying for a large readership. James Gordon Bennett's *New York Herald* was in many respects the pacesetter, with its coverage of prizefighting, thoroughbred racing, and trotting matches. Bennett was one of the first exponents of "sensationalism" as a means of generating circulation, and sport fit comfortably within this rubric. Yet sport was far from acceptable as a topic for newspaper coverage: Bennett's *Herald* occasionally expressed regret at the role of sport in society but continued to cover it nonetheless. Horace Greeley's *New York Tribune* also covered major sporting events, as did Henry Raymond's very respectable *New York Times*, albeit with considerable regret. By the Civil War, major prizefights and horse races received coverage in most daily newspapers, but there was still nothing along the lines of a regular sports page or sports department. Coverage was sporadic, seasonal, and highly regional.[6]

During the middle third of the nineteenth century, sports became increasingly organized and commercialized. The Civil War introduced baseball to an entire generation of Americans, as the troops on both sides played the game when time permitted. Indeed, baseball emerged as the preeminent national team sport during this period. By 1869 the first publicly proclaimed professional baseball team was established, and an organized league of professional teams, the National League, followed shortly thereafter. A number of sportswriters, particularly Henry Chadwick, actively encouraged the creation of the professional league and helped to standardize the game's rules.[7] Chadwick and a handful of other metropolitan sportswriters were responsible for the development of box scores and the extensive statistical analysis of baseball.[8] The development of organized professional play, with standardized rules and statistics, would permit vastly expanded coverage of baseball in the future.

The sporting press of the mid-nineteenth century also performed a crucial function by actively working to legitimate sport as a cultural institution. The Puritan legacy of general hostility toward sport was greatly undermined by the developments of the nineteenth century. The newspapers of the major cities and the sport magazines became increasingly assertive by midcentury concerning the health benefits of athletics to urban dwellers. Indeed, the tone gradually shifted from a mild defense of athletics to the promotion of sport as the ideal mechanism to train men to compete in the battle of life, particularly in the unnatural urban environment.[9] By the end of the century, there would be an extensive "Muscular Christian" movement that would extol the virtues of sport for society.[10] Though the general acceptance of professional sports would take considerably longer, this was a necessary first step.

The 1880s and 1890s were another period in which there was a surge of interest in, as well as media coverage of, sports. In addition, this was a period of intense industrialization, immigration, and urbanization; in many respects this was the period of United States transformation into a modern, industrial world power. Professional baseball became entrenched as the national spectator sport and by the beginning of the twentieth century two national leagues fielded professional teams in most of the major cities of the Northeast and Midwest. Boxing moved from the saloon brawls of the 1830s and 1840s to organized bouts held in large buildings. Recreational activities such as golf and bicycling came to play a prominent role in the lives of countless middle- and upper-class Americans.

This was the period in which newspapers began the process of supplanting weekly magazines as the primary medium covering sports. Sport magazines did not suffer during this period by any means. There were forty-eight sport periodicals in the 1890s, compared to only nine in the 1860s and three in the 1840s.[11] Indeed, the *National Police Gazette*, which was transformed into a sporting magazine by Richard Kyle Fox, surged to a nationwide circulation of 150,000 by the 1880s. Some issues sold as many as 400,000 copies. With a large readership among the "masses," the *National Police Gazette* emphasized boxing and baseball and was generally regarded as the "arbiter of sports news."[12] In many respects Fox showed newspaper publishers the potential for attracting a mass readership through sport coverage.

Newspaper circulations soared to previously unimagined heights in the 1880s and 1890s as technological innovations reduced the cost of printing while the swelling cities provided an enormous market. U.S. capitalism was continuing to evolve and commercial advertising was becoming a primary competitive sales weapon for retail businesses. Newspaper publishing was becoming a big business and publishers were beginning to accrue nearly one-half of their revenues from advertising. Sports, with its proven capacity to attract readers, became a logical area of emphasis in this era of "yellow journalism," a period in which the journalistic conventions of earlier times were shredded in the competitive fight for profit. To some extent the sensationalism of the late nineteenth century was but a much larger version of the emergence of the penny press in the 1830s.

New York, Chicago, and a handful of other major cities were the forerunners in sports journalism during this period: other cities would follow suit gradually over the following generation, depending upon their level of development of sport and sport journalism. James Gordon Bennett's *Herald* continued to provide ample coverage of sport but was passed by in the 1880s by Charles Dana's *New York Sun* and Joseph Pulitzer's *New York World*. In 1883, Pulitzer established the first sport department, and prominent fights or races received front-page coverage. Most major newspapers had their own sports editors and staffs by the end of the century. In 1895, William Randolph Hearst, in the midst of his circulation war with Pulitzer, introduced the first distinct sports section in his *New York Journal*. This innovation caught on gradually in the major cities before becoming a staple item for a major daily newspaper in the 1920s.[13] And with the emergence of the telegraph, newspapers were capable of providing timely sports information from anywhere in the nation.

This was the period that witnessed the emergence of sports journalism as a distinct genre. As David Voigt has observed, baseball writers in particular "enjoyed greater literary freedom" than other newspaper writers and they tended to develop an "exaggerated, colorful descriptive style."[14] Sportswriters became celebrities in their own right. The prose was often colorful and entertaining. Newspaper publishers bid for the services of the most popular sportswriters. Indeed, the development of the newspaper sports department and the regular sports section clearly enhanced interest in sport during this period; one no longer needed to attend games or be an athlete to enjoy sports. The newspapers did everything they could to encourage this development, even going so far as to publish the rules of various games to educate the uninitiated.

The last two decades of the nineteenth century truly marked the crystallization of the modern sport-media symbiotic relationship. Professional baseball teams were becoming recognized as a source of civic pride, and newspapers found it incumbent upon themselves to support their cities' franchises. In Kansas City, for example, the *lack* of a developed sports journalism probably prevented the success of Major League Baseball there in the late nineteenth century.[15] Sportswriters such as Henry Chadwick served as advisors to the baseball owners on the most weighty of issues. When the baseball writers formed a national association in 1887 to standardize scoring and promote the game, they noted that, as for the relationship of the owners and the baseball writers: "All sides now recognize that their interests are identical. The reporters have found in the game a thing of beauty and a source of actual employment. The game has found in the reporters its best ally and most powerful supporter. Hence the good feeling all along the line."[16]

From the turn of the century until the end of the First World War, sport consolidated its position in U.S. society and increasingly became a national phenomenon. Whereas many newspapers outside of the major cities had very little coverage of sports in the 1880s and 1890s, by 1910 virtually every paper gave prominent play to major sporting events, like championship prizefights and horse races, and the World Series in baseball, which had been established in 1903. This "nationalization" of sports was greatly encouraged by improvements in transportation, communication, and social mobility. In addition, the First World War, in a manner far more extensive than the Civil War, encouraged the nationalization of sport by popularizing and promoting sport among soldiers from all regions of the nation.[17]

The 1920s was the decade in which sport assumed its modern position as a cornerstone of U.S. culture. The decade is commonly referred to as the "Golden Age of Sports" in both common and academic parlance. Noted sport historian John Rickard Betts has observed that "sport swept over the nation in the 1920s and, at times, seemed to be the most engrossing of public interests."[18] Warren Susman has written that

> it was in the '20s that the American infatuation with professional athletics began, giving a virtual coup de grâce to religion as the non-economic and non-sexual preoccupation of millions of middle-class Americans.[19]

In the 1920s sport emerged as a prime source of entertainment and communal bonding for Americans in a society that had been revolutionized over the preceding two generations.[20] This was also the decade when sports moved to its position as an indispensable section of the daily newspaper— Robert Lipsyte has argued that the Golden Age of Sports was really the Golden Age of Sportswriting.[21] In the 1920s, tendencies that had been hinted at for forty years crystallized, and the basic dynamic that propelled the sport-newspaper relationship to the present day came into play; hence that era merits a relatively close exposition.

To understand why newspapers would turn over such a substantial portion of their pages to sport, it may be helpful to turn to a broader political economic view of U.S. society. The 1920s was the decade that marked the complete establishment of oligopolistic, corporate capitalism as the political economic system of the United States. As Alfred DuPont Chandler has noted, by the end of the First World War

> ... the shakedown period following the merger movement was over. The successful mergers were established and the unsuccessful ones had failed. Modern business enterprise dominated American industries, and most of these same firms continued to dominate their industries for decades.[22]

Chandler's schema was certainly present in the newspaper industry of the 1920s.[23] As Alfred McClung Lee notes, after the First World War, "the major units in the industry have become huge, relatively stable, monopolistic ventures."[24] The total number of newspapers declined, while circulation increased by 25 percent. Major newspaper chains came to dominate the industry, and by 1933 fully forty cities with populations over 100,000 were one-newspaper towns.[25]

Another basic aspect of corporate capitalism also had a serious impact upon the newspaper industry. Advertising, which had been on the periphery of the economy in the nineteenth century, became a primary form of competition for large corporations in oligopolistic industries where explicit price warfare had become generally recognized as unhealthy.[26] Advertising accounted for only 50 percent of newspaper revenues in 1890: by 1929 the portion had risen to 75 percent.[27] The growth in advertising sales largely fueled the newspaper boom of the 1920s, and indeed it has accounted for the growth not only in the newspaper industry but in the broadcast media as well ever since. In short, profitability in newspaper publishing was now based on the capacity of the newspaper to attract a large readership that could then be "sold" to commercial advertisers.

In this context, the three dominant editorial trends of U.S. newspapers in the 1920s become understandable, and coverage of sport fit quite comfortably within each of them. First, newspapers tended to decrease their coverage of "hard news" and politics and instead emphasized escapist and sensational fare that would attract the largest possible readership.[28] Sport fit perfectly within this conception of the press. A 1930s survey revealed that fully 80 percent of all male newspaper readers read some portion of the sports page on a frequent basis.[29] One survey of circulation managers in the 1940s indicated their belief that fully 25 percent of all newspapers were sold on the basis of their sports sections.[30]

Second, newspapers tended to standardize and rationalize the editorial process to reduce costs. In an oligopolistic market, these cost reductions could be passed along almost directly to the bottom line. This led to what Villard has termed the "mass production of dailies."[31] The wire services enjoyed a period of great expansion after the First World War, as syndicated material was far less expensive than staff-generated material.[32] In addition, one survey has shown that as much as 50–60 percent of all news articles appearing in the metropolitan press of the 1920s—including the "prestige" papers—were generated by press agents for specific interests.[33]

Coverage of sport fit perfectly within this rubric. Much of the copy was generated by wire services: in the 1920s the Associated Press established a separate sports department, with a full-time staff of twelve.[34] Furthermore, sport promoters and organizations were often willing to underwrite newspapers' expenses to gain coverage; indeed, this was the standard practice in professional baseball.[35] And, finally, outright payoffs to sports editors and reporters for coverage were not uncommon, particularly with regard to boxing.[36]

Third, newspapers of the 1920s began to de-emphasize the strident political partisanship that had been expected of publishers in the nineteenth century.[37] As Silas Bent noted in 1927: "The deplorable fact is that mass production demands a product which will offend as few as possible among hundreds of thousands of readers."[38] Yet, though professing nonpartisanship on the surface, newspapers, as huge corporations supported largely through advertising from other businesses, became what John Tebbel has termed "by and large a conservative defender of the status quo."[39]

Sport was very well suited to the editorial needs of the emerging giant newspaper corporations. Sport was ideologically "safe" and did not antagonize any element of the desired readership. It did not even offend those who were put off by the sex and sensationalism of the front page. Sport also lent itself to all sorts of civic boosterism on the part of the newspaper. As sport gave cohesiveness and identity to a community, a newspaper's coverage and promotion of sport could be considered a significant contribution to its metropolis. Finally, coverage of sport never called into question the dominant social relations. It offered the spirit and excitement of conflict and struggle in a politically trivial area.

Whereas one survey showed that the average newspaper devoted .04 percent of its editorial coverage to sport in 1880 and 4.0 percent in 1900, by the 1920s the proportion of editorial space ranged from 12 to 20 percent for virtually every daily newspaper.[40] Sport historian Benjamin Rader has observed that "nothing before or since—not even the cool waves of television—created quite the same hot romance between sport and the public as the newspapers in the 1920s."[41] The typical sports section, which was commonplace by the 1920s, was filled with color and excitement. It would have been difficult *not* to be a sports fan if one read a newspaper and had the slightest inclination in that direction. Sportswriters were major figures; at best, styles ranged from the colorful verse of Grantland Rice to the literary stylishness of Paul Gallico, Damon Runyon, and Westbrook Pegler. At worst, there was a pervasive cliché-ridden mediocrity. All sportswriters tended to glorify sport heroes and present them as larger-than-life figures.[42]

As sport and sports coverage flourished in the 1920s, so did their symbiotic relationship. The close interaction between sports promoters and sportswriters was at times so corrupt that it led more than one sportswriter to quit.[43] Newspapers even became promoters themselves on occasion; Captain Joseph Medill Patterson, publisher of the *Chicago Tribune* and the New York *Daily News*, helped introduce the amateur boxing Golden Gloves competitions in both Chicago and New York. Arch Ward, sports editor of the *Chicago Tribune,* was responsible for devising both the baseball All-Star Game and the College All-Star Football Game.[44] Newspapers across the country became active in promoting participant and spectator sport activities in their communities.

Baseball, boxing, and college football were the prime beneficiaries of the sport boom in the 1920s. Major League Baseball was still the premier spectator sport and had the strongest standing relationship between management and the press. Its attendance doubled in the 1920s, and Babe Ruth of the New York Yankees became a national hero. Boxing was able to shed its reputation for sleaziness and become a national institution of sorts; heavyweight champion Jack Dempsey even had an audience with an "unusually talkative" President Coolidge. This would have been unthinkable a generation earlier.[45] No small part of boxing's surge was due to the extraordinarily skillful promotional work of Tex Rickard, who managed both Madison Square Garden's boxing cards and heavyweight champion Jack Dempsey. Rickard was especially adept at cultivating the press, and it was not uncommon for him to use payoffs to assure favorable publicity.[46]

Perhaps the most dramatic success story of the 1920s was the emergence of college football. Prior to the 1920s, college football was generally a sport played by well-to-do college boys for their fellow students, family, and alumni. In the 1920s the sport became a mass attraction; revenues for sixty-five leading football schools more than tripled during the decade. Colleges built enormous stadiums to accommodate the spectators, often with generous assistance from local businesses and alumni, and fifty-five new concrete stadiums were constructed as seating capacity nearly tripled during the decade.[47] The intense pressure to field a winning team brought scandal and corruption to this "amateur" sport. Many academics were dismayed by the emphasis on football played by students who often were little more than professionals.[48]

The controversy over the huge role of intercollegiate football dominated U.S. campuses through the 1920s. Indeed, an extensive study of the subject funded by the Carnegie Corporation placed a large part of the blame on newspapers for "distorting" the importance of football in college life. The study examined several major urban newspapers and discovered that the space allocated to college sports, mostly football, had more than tripled between 1913 and 1927.[49] Like baseball and boxing, college football lent itself especially well to newspaper coverage. There were several conferences with set schedules and championships, breeding the sort of statistics, scores, and heroics that the sporting press coveted. There was scarcely any remorse expressed by publishers or sports editors for their extensive coverage and promotion of the college game. One social critic commented that the press treated college football like a "heroic god that the American masses are supposed to worship."[50]

The 1920s was also a watershed decade for the sport-mass media relationship because of the emergence of radio broadcasting. In 1922, radio was found in only one of every 400 homes, but by 1929 one-third of U.S. homes had radios.[51] During the early and mid-1920s, sport was capitalized upon by broadcasters to promote the acceptance of this new medium.[52] Sports were not yet broadcast on a regular basis, but ad hoc networks were established for major prizefights, football games, and the World Series. When the Dempsey-Tunney championship bout was broadcast in 1927, it was estimated that it generated sales of over $90,000 worth of radio receivers in one New York department store alone.[53]

Yet as much as sport contributed to popularizing radio, radio contributed even more to the popularity of sport; it opened up new vistas for millions who had never had access to a major sporting event in the past. The emergence of broadcasting continued the nationalization of sport and helped to entrench it even more as a fundamental social institution. The dominant sports broadcaster of the 1920s was Graham McNamee, who had little understanding of sports and frequently made errors while broadcasting sports events. Nonetheless, McNamee had a soothing voice and a tremendous for the dramatic. According to *Radio Digest*, 127 fight fans dropped dead listening to McNamee's tense description of the second Tunney-Dempsey heavyweight fight.[54] McNamee was the first instance of a sports broadcaster who was a celebrity and, for career purposes, an entertainer above all else.[55]

By the early 1930s, radio broadcasting had become dominated by two major networks, the National Broadcasting Company (NBC) and the Columbia Broadcasting System (CBS), which were finding it very profitable to sell time on the network stations to advertisers. Advertisers soon began to purchase the right to broadcast major sports events. In 1934, for example, the Ford Motor Company paid $100,000 for the privilege of sponsoring the World Series on both major networks.[56] Yet many in baseball were convinced that radio broadcasting of baseball games would hurt attendance, and in 1932 the owners came very close to forbidding teams to let their games be broadcast.[57] By the 1940s this fear had subsided, and all the Major League teams had contracts with broadcasters and advertisers to broadcast all of their home games. The New York Yankees, for example, received $100,000 per year from three advertisers in the late 1930s. Most teams had their own broadcasters, who would be on the payroll of either the advertisers or, more likely, the teams themselves. This set the pattern for the "unobjective" or "homer" baseball announcing that still exists today.

Radio broadcasting of sports events reached its mature stage in the late 1940s and early 1950s. The networks broadcast all major national sports events and, furthermore, most professional baseball and major college football teams had contracts either with broadcasters or, more likely at this point in time, directly with advertisers who would then negotiate their own deals with commercial stations to broadcast the games. Most baseball teams could not sell the rights to broadcast their "away" games; rather, stations would "re-create" the games in their studios, with announcers improvising the action off the

Western Union ticker. When the courts ruled in 1955 that broadcasters had to pay teams for the right to re-create their games, the practice came to a virtual halt.[58]

Radio sports broadcasting held its own quite well in a competitive sense during the first decade of televised sport and well into the late 1950s. Although sport played a prominent role during television's early years, it did so in a manner that would not anticipate the sports-television "revolution" of the late 1960s and early 1970s. The nature of the technology made it difficult to telecast team sports effectively. Indeed, two of the leading sports on television were professional wrestling and Roller Derby. They were often broadcast during prime time, since they were ideally suited for low-budget television: a single camera could focus on one or two people at a time. Both sports consisted of staged violence, and the promoters were so eager for publicity that they frequently would not even charge stations for broadcast rights.[59] At its high point, wrestling was broadcast by over 200 stations on a weekly basis, but it was quickly relegated to the fringes of television, along with Roller Derby, as television turned to baseball and football and more expensive non-sports prime-time fare by the mid-1950s.

The one traditional U.S. sport that was permanently altered by television in the late 1940s and 1950s was boxing. Like wrestling, it was ideally suited to the technology of the period. Rader has noted that during this period "the passionate affair between television and professional fighting turned into an orgy."[60] Fight nights were commonplace on television during this period over both the networks and independent stations and some local broadcasters even staged their own fight cards. The saturation of boxing over the air led to the demise of local fight clubs, as fight fans now stayed home to watch the fights on TV: there were but fifty fight clubs in 1960, compared to 300 in 1952, and the number of professional boxers declined by more than 50 percent. Furthermore, sluggers came across on television far more effectively than finesse fighters, and promoters and producers gave brawlers the highest priority. Finally, there was an incessant need not only for fighters to fill out the television cards but for fighters with winning records who would make desirable match-ups. Since both of these criteria were impossible to fill, the result was a wave of corruption and scandal unusual even by boxing's own standards. The sport entered the 1960s a shell of its former self: the first effect of television on organized sports was a knockout punch.[61]

Both Major League Baseball and college football were apprehensive about telecasting their regular season games during the early 1950s. Both were suffering from severe attendance slumps after the Second World War, and minor league baseball, like boxing clubs, had been decimated. Many felt that television was to blame. The National Collegiate Athletic Association (NCAA) even placed severe restrictions on the ability of broadcasters to televise college football games: these restrictions began to be lifted only when colleges began to sense the amount of money that could be made.[62] Furthermore, those who managed the major networks were far from convinced that sports programming was especially profitable; it was deemed to have little appeal for affluent viewers and women.[63]

Everything began to change by the late 1950s and early 1960s. First, television came to penetrate the overwhelming majority of U.S. homes: it was now clearly a mass medium. Second, the technology for sports broadcasting radically improved with the advent of color television, videotape (with its slow-motion and instant-replay capacities), satellites, and portable cameras. Third, Congress passed the Sports Broadcasting Act of 1961, which permitted professional sports teams in a league to negotiate as one unit with broadcasters. This had previously been considered an infringement of antitrust laws. Fourth, the networks and stations began to purchase broadcast rights directly from the teams and leagues and then sold time on those telecasts to advertisers. These two developments made sports broadcasting potentially a far more lucrative operation for sports owners and broadcasters alike. But the most critical factor was simply that certain advertisers discovered that sports provided access to a very desirable market—not only for "blue-collar" products like beer and razor blades, but for big-ticket items like automobiles and business equipment.

The first sport to ride the wave of all these factors was professional football through the National Football League (NFL). In the early 1950s, pro football was a minor attraction, relative to baseball and the college game, with a fairly small but devoted following. With national exposure in the late 1950s and early 1960s, the sport, which seemed ideal for video transmission, captured the national imagination. Within a decade it became America's leading spectator sport. The commissioners Bert Bell in the late 1950s and later Pete Rozelle understood fully the importance of television to the league's success. In 1958, Bell permitted "television time-outs" to increase the amount of advertising revenue each game could generate.[64] Rozelle's function was basically to negotiate television contracts, something at which he proved rather adept. In 1962, CBS agreed to pay the NFL $4.5 million per year for broadcast rights; just two years later, as Nielsen ratings climbed by 50 percent, Rozelle negotiated a pact with CBS that called for $14 million per year.[65] Broadcast revenues had become the independent growth variable in the future of the NFL.

The tremendous success of the NFL on CBS drew the envy of entrepreneurs in major cities without NFL franchises as well as of the other major television networks, NBC and ABC. In 1960, the American Football League (AFL) was established and had a contract with ABC prior to its first kickoff. This was a major development in the sport-mass media relationship: The networks, with an eye on anticipated advertising sales, essentially created or encouraged the creation of new sports products with the hope that audiences would develop. And when new sport products were not created to satisfy advertisers, existing sport enterprises were radically altered to maximize potential broadcast rights payments.[66]

The AFL survived strictly on the basis of its ABC contract in the early 1960s. Then, in 1965, after NBC lost its bidding war with CBS for NFL rights, NBC agreed with the AFL to a rights contract worth $42 million over five years. This was an astronomical sum that nearly approached the NFL contract with CBS. The aim of NBC with this contract, quite clearly, was to provide the new league with the wherewithal to field a major-league product. In effect, the network had become a co-promoter of the AFL. The plan worked. The AFL began to sign top NFL players and the NFL, once it realized that the NBC contract guaranteed the AFL's existence, agreed to a merger. As part of the deal, NBC was permitted to telecast half of the merged league's games along with CBS.

The 1960s witnessed the first wave of the TV sports explosion. ABC, the weakest of the three networks, was the most aggressive; it launched *Wide World of Sports* in 1961. This was a weekly program that covered a variety of sports events and was another example of a network becoming essentially a sports promoter. ABC also pioneered coverage of the Olympic Games, taking them from relative anonymity to the premier sporting event that was telecast every four years. Rights payments for Summer Olympics broadcasts jumped from a then astronomical $5 million in 1968 to several hundred million dollars by the 1980s. ABC also pioneered prime-time sports on a regular basis with its highly successful *Monday Night Football* in 1970. *Monday Night Football* was predicated on the notion that prime-time success for sports depended upon making it an entertaining production first and foremost. Furthermore, ABC was at the forefront of the movement to incorporate new technologies and techniques into its sports coverage, from instant replay to slow motion. To no small extent, ABC rode its success with sports programming from third place to the top of the heap among the networks by the mid-1970s. The director of ABC's sports division, Roone Arledge, was rewarded with a promotion to head of the network's news division.[67]

During the 1960s, Major League Baseball, professional basketball, professional hockey, college football, and college basketball all enjoyed network broadcast contracts. By the 1970s, both NBC and CBS began to appreciate fully the immense profitability that sports programming offered. During the 1970s, the annual number of network hours of sports programming increased from 787 to 1,356; by 1984 the annual hours of sports programming was 1,700, double the figure for 1974. Advertisers were increasingly delirious with the sports market. A Simmons market research survey conducted in 1981 found that six times as many affluent males aged 18–49 watched pro football as watched *Dallas.* By the mid-1980s the three networks were selling over $1 billion in advertising for their sports programming, which was not much less than the gross revenues of the various professional sports leagues.[68] In addition, countless hours of sports programming were televised on a local basis. Sports broadcasters had little relation to their counterparts in the sports departments of newspapers. They were celebrities and entertainers in their own right whose presence on the air could sway ratings (and advertising revenues) significantly. Hence the leading sportscasters by the 1980s earned seven-figure incomes, and even local sportscasters frequently earned incomes in six figures.

The major professional leagues and college "amateur" sports of football and basketball all profited mightily from the advertising dollars eager to sponsor their broadcasts. By 1982 the NFL had a five-year contract with the three networks worth $2 billion. Some business analysts estimated that a few NFL teams might be able to cover their expenses before they even sold any tickets. Major League Baseball's network contract was worth $1.1 billion for six years in the 1980s, and this was for only the World Series and a handful of regular season games telecast on a national basis. Most teams made considerably more money through the sale of the rights to their regular-season games to local stations.

The networks became desperate for sports programming to occupy their weekend daytime hours. By the late 1970s a number of "trash sports" were created by the networks—for instance, celebrity tennis matches, battles of network "superstars"—but most of them failed to deliver high enough ratings. Creating sports that the public would accept as legitimate has proven to be a tricky business. Numerous professional leagues have been formed, all in hopes of emulating the AFL and cashing in on the television money. The World Football League, World Team Tennis, World Hockey League, and American Basketball Association all failed to get precious network contracts and had to disband. Lack of a TV contract simply made it impossible for a sports league to survive in any form of direct competition.[69] In the 1980s the United States Football League was established. So clearly was this an effort to seize advertising dollars through rights payments that the league's first commissioner was Chet Simmons, a career sports executive for ABC and, later, the Entertainment and Sports Network (ESPN). The USFL disbanded in 1986, after it received only a token dollar from its antitrust suit against the NFL, in which the USFL claimed that the NFL had a monopoly on network broadcast rights payments. Thus the explosion in sports revenues due to television has had several losers in addition to its winners.

More than a few analysts have looked at these casualties and predicted that sports, in general, were being overexposed on television and that eventually public sentiment would turn against them. That has yet to happen, at least in the minds of the all-important advertisers who have subsidized the boom. Not that revenues and profits have increased without upheaval; as with any industry, there have been ups and downs for specific firms and general excesses caused by speculative frenzy. Nevertheless, the general pattern has been upward. In the 1980s several cable networks have been established that have given sports coverage prominence: indeed, they rank among the few cable operations that have had any success. Specifically, ESPN was established to broadcast sports 24 hours a day. Upon its creation, one ESPN executive remarked, "We believe the appetite for sports in this country is insatiable."[70] Aimed at a smaller and more sophisticated market than that targeted by network sports coverage, ESPN has raised the level of sports broadcasting significantly.

The importance of TV has never been greater for sport. By the 1970s it had become axiomatic that successful management of professional sports leagues and franchises is based on the capacity to best exploit rights payments. To a certain extent commercial sport has been colonized by the advertising community. Sport's insatiable hunger for these advertising dollars accounts for many of the recent major developments in U.S. sport: new leagues; vast increases in "championship" events, such as college football bowl games; new forms of sport, such as indoor soccer; enormous salaries, as players attempt to capture some of the booty; changes in rules meant to increase "excitement," to appeal to the less sophisticated fan and to allow for more commercial interruptions; and lengthened schedules. Many purists feel that this commercialization has degraded and cheapened sport. In any case, the shapes of both sport *and* the mass media have been permanently changed.

It has not been television alone that has exploited sport (and vice versa) over the past thirty years. Radio, which was forced to find a new role after television replaced it as the centerpiece in living rooms, was still a superior and, for advertisers, relatively inexpensive means of transmitting games. Virtually every professional or major collegiate sports team receives some radio broadcast rights payments, including many lower-level college teams that are unable to generate large enough audiences to attract TV contracts.

Magazines, which had developed into an immensely profitable and highly concentrated industry on the basis of the emergence of national advertising, have also become an increasingly important medium for sports since the 1950s.[71] Though there was a dramatic increase in the coverage of sports in general-circulation magazines in the first half of the century, the only sports-specific magazines were those like *Ring* and the *Sporting News*, which were essentially the trade publications for boxing and baseball.[72] With the emergence of television in the 1950s, general-interest magazines began to struggle for survival, as they could no longer compete on a cost-per-thousand basis with the networks for national advertising. The magazine industry began to focus more on specific subjects that would attract readerships with distinct interests and more sharply defined demographic characteristics. These more select readerships would then impress important groups of advertisers and justify the relatively high cost of the advertising. Sports—especially the major team sports, plus golf, tennis, and Olympic sports—tended to attract the types of educated, affluent, and consumption-oriented audiences that many major advertisers fantasize about. A host of major sports publications have been launched since the 1950s. *Sports Illustrated*, which was first published by Time-Life in 1954, has been the most successful, with a circulation of several million copies per week. It is generally regarded as the best sports magazine in terms of the quality of writing and production.

Newspapers have also adjusted to the advent of television, with its implications for sports, and the two media have found that they can enjoy a very complementary relationship. The level of sports coverage remained in the 12 to 20 percent of editorial content range that had been established in the 1920s until the 1970s, when it tended to move upward for the very reasons it was so high in the first place: sports coverage was very popular, relatively inexpensive, and noncontroversial. *USA Today*, the state-of-the-art national newspaper launched by Gannett in the early 1980s, devoted fully 25 percent of its editorial space to sports. To many it seemed that sports was responsible for the preponderance of the newspaper's circulation; Frank Deford described it as "a daily *Sporting News* wrapped in color weather maps." Newspapers were also increasingly narrowing their focus to middle-class readers over less affluent inner-city and blue-collar residents who held minimal interest for major advertisers. Thus sports with a decidedly non-middle-class following—bowling, stock car racing, tractor pulls—received scant attention in the nation's sports sections.[73] Furthermore, sports with limited commercial exploitation were generally accorded minimal attention. Hence the extraordinary explosion in women's athletics over the past generation has been relatively underreported.

The nature of newspaper sports journalism changed as well. With the emergence of extensive sports telecasting, far less energy was expended recounting the story of the game, which most readers would have seen for themselves. Rather, newspapers began to provide more analysis, background information, and statistical data that other media found it difficult to provide. At sportswriting's very best, some exceptional writers like Red Smith of the *New York Times* began to combine a critical intelligence with a great love of sport. Furthermore, reporters began to center their game stories on quotes from players and coaches; the postgame trip to the locker room became standard operating procedure for the sportswriter. At its worst, this approach has produced a mindless formulated genre of reporting that essentially entails the stringing together of a series of cliché-ridden and superficial quotations.

In addition, sportswriting became more serious, particularly with the spectacular increase in sports revenues brought on by television rights payments and all the attendant changes that increase brought for the world of sport. The "real world" had invaded the sports page. Some have even attempted to extend the "adversarial" stance of the newsroom toward politicians, government officials, and criminals to the relationship between sportswriters and athletes and sports promoters. However, though this has had some impact, it contradicts the fundamental symbiotic nature of the sport-newspaper relationship. Most sports sections eagerly promote professional and commercial sports in their communities, if for no other reason than to assure employment for sportswriters.

Sports has risen to staggering and unprecedented levels of importance in U.S. society, dominating U.S. life in a manner that only a few observers have paused to recognize.[74] I have endeavored in this chapter to reveal how integral the commercial mass media have been to the development of this cultural edifice that Robert Lipsyte has aptly termed "SportsWorld."[75] Whether it can make further inroads remains to be seen; however, there is no reason to anticipate any step backward. Insofar as advertising is fundamental to modern capitalist political economy, it has outpaced the balance of the economy and many experts anticipate continued relative rapid growth. The economic foundation for the modern sport-media boom will remain intact until advertisers find some source of programming radically superior to sport. Hence every indication is that the sport-media marriage will continue to evolve in its present pattern, with all the implications that entails, for some time to come.

9

Public Broadcasting in the Age of
Communication Revolution

In 1995, U.S. conservatives attacked the federal subsidy that supports public broadcasting with great fervor. Though the grant to the Corporation for Public Broadcasting, the Public Broadcasting System (PBS), and National Public Radio (NPR) was extended, at a reduced rate, for three additional years by Congress, the handwriting was on the wall: government-subsidized broadcasting in the United States was nearing an end. I believe this is unfortunate and that it is very much in our interest to be expanding through any number of measures the nonprofit and noncommercial media sector. In what follows I will put the fight over U.S. public broadcasting in historical context. By doing so, I hope to explain the sorry state of U.S. public broadcasting. I will also link the fight over public broadcasting to broader political economic trends. The crisis of public service broadcasting—meaning nonprofit broadcasting with minimal advertising—is global in nature, so the dimensions of the U.S. struggle become more clear in a global light. The right-wing assault on U.S. public broadcasting may best be regarded as another instance of corporate attack on democratic institutions, with the important aim of limiting the ability of Americans to examine and debate the manner in which their society is actually ruled. In addition, it is part and parcel of a process whereby the market is becoming the unquestioned regulator of all aspects of social life wherever profits may be made; a process I believe to have disastrous political and moral implications.

The attack on public service broadcasting in 1995 came during an era of nearly unprecedented technological revolutions in communication and information. By all accounts, they were central to a dramatic restructuring of human societies. One need only consider the rapid development of the Internet—which is only the tip of the iceberg—to appreciate the dimensions of what lies before us. Although some proponents of the communication technologies assert that they will provide immense new competition in the marketplace of ideas, thereby rendering moot the need for publicly subsidized media, the dominant trend in journalism and communication is for the media industries increasingly to fall under oligopolistic corporate control. Ben Bagdikian is the best known chronicler of the control exerted by approximately twenty enormous corporations over global communication and almost all of U.S. journalism. That figure was significantly larger only a decade ago and many observers expect it to continue to fall.

There are many reasons to be alarmed by this oligopolistic corporate control. Every theory of democracy worth the paper it is written on recognizes that independent journalism is necessary to provide the informed participating citizenry that is the foundation of self-government. These enormous corporations often find this type of journalism controversial, expensive, and counterproductive to their political and economic interests. This is hardly a new phenomenon; it has been a major tension in profit-driven commercial journalism since its emergence in the nineteenth century. The censorship of our media and journalism is overwhelmingly the result of how it is owned and subsidized. Professional journalism is best viewed in this context. While it permits a degree of journalistic autonomy from media owners and advertisers, as well as the personal biases of journalists, media professionalism also internalizes many of the commercial values of the capitalist media and encourages journalists to be oblivious to the compromises with authority they are constantly making. In addition, the media corporations increasingly find the traditional practice of journalism unprofitable. The relative amount of resources devoted to journalism has fallen sharply in the past fifteen years. Our news media is increasingly prey to sophisticated public relations campaigns serving corporate America and commercial pressures to provide inexpensive, unthreatening schlock journalism centered on entertainers, athletes, and royal families.

Critics like Noam Chomsky and Edward Herman are on the mark when they argue that even well-subsidized U.S. corporate and commercial journalism has tended to promote elite interests and undermine the capacity for popular rule. Nonetheless, the collapse of journalism—even by mainstream standards—is startling. Traditional journalistic autonomy has become a direct casualty of the insatiable drive for profit that rules our media system and our economy. This trend stands in stark contrast to the promise of the new information and communication technologies to break down barriers and contribute to the democratization of society.

The critical question facing us is whether the new technologies can rejuvenate journalism and political democracy or whether the corporate, commercial domination of journalism and the communication industries will be able to subsume the technologies within their profit net and assure that the corporate domination of both U.S. society and the global political economy remain unquestioned and unchallenged. While I may consider this a critical question, it is not a prominent question in U.S. political culture. Here, to the contrary, the notion that the new communication technologies, as well as the entire communication industry, should be ruled by corporations seeking maximum profit is sacrosanct. Such is also the case in our news media and to a large extent our intellectual community. The notion that the commercial basis of media, journalism, and communication could have troubling implications for democracy is excluded from the range of legitimate debate. Indeed, the dominant public debate over communication policy in the United States today is whether the only vestiges of nonprofit broadcasting—PBS and NPR—should be eliminated so we may have a thoroughly market-driven system.

The corporate, commercial domination of U.S. communication was not always considered a given, or something innately benevolent, American, and democratic. When radio broadcasting first emerged in the 1920s, few thought it had any commercial potential and most regarded it more along the lines of public education. In those countries most similar to the United States—Britain, Canada, Germany, and France—broadcasting was developed as a nonprofit and noncommercial enterprise under varying forms of public control. It was called public service broadcasting. When NBC and CBS finally realized the profit potential of U.S. broadcasting and seized control in the late 1920s, they were met by ferocious public opposition to the capitalist exploitation of radio.

This broadcast reform movement, as I characterize it, argued that commercial broadcasting was inimical to the communication needs of a democratic society. The reformers argued that nonprofit and noncommercial broadcasting had to be the dominant sector of any adequate U.S. radio system. Most of these reformers were also comfortable with the state playing a significant although never monopolistic role in a more democratic broadcasting setup. Although this movement had left support, it was not a "left-wing" movement per se and it drew support from diverse groups of U.S. society, including labor, education, and religion, as well as intellectuals, civil libertarians, farmers, women, and journalists. It probably had as much support among Republicans as it did among Democrats.

All of these broadcast reformers were united in their thorough distaste for commercial broadcasting, their belief that the commercial system was structurally unsound and incapable of reform through self-regulation, government regulation, or competition, and their belief that radical structural reform was the only solution. All aspects of the reform movement stressed that if a handful of corporations dominated U.S. broadcasting and if their primary motivation was profit, it would be absurd to think it possible for broadcasting to provide the type of journalism and controversial public affairs programming for which the medium had the potential. In addition, the reformers thought it absurd and irresponsible to permit commercial values to rule broadcasting as they did so many other areas of U.S. life. The broadcast reformers lost for a number of reasons, not the least of which was the ample political clout of the broadcasting industry, which was able to dominate both politicians and the media coverage of the debate. With the passage of the Communications Act of 1934, which established the Federal Communications Commission (FCC) to regulate telecommunications and which remains the governing statute, fundamental structural questions have been off-limits in U.S. political debate. Although the opponents of commercialism were crushed, I believe they provide an important key to understanding the current nature of the debate over communication issues and the generally weak and unstable nature of U.S. public service broadcasting as it has developed.

Since 1935 all broadcast and communication policy debates have been predicated upon the notion that the needs of the private sector come first, and that these are largely compatible with the public interest. The consolidation of the status quo after 1935 was accomplished with breathtaking speed. There have been dissidents on the FCC, but they have been mostly ineffectual. When structural reform became off limits, the only legitimate manner in which to criticize U.S. broadcasting became to state that it was uncompetitive and therefore needed aggressive regulation. This was a far cry from the critique of the early 1930s reformers; they had argued that the problem was not merely a lack of competition but, more fundamentally, they argued that if a broadcast system is market-driven it will tend to serve the well-to-do and downplay programming that might empower the disenfranchised or serve any public value not defined by its profitability. In short, broadcasting had to be removed from the marketplace altogether to begin to fulfill its social promise. With the consolidation of the status quo, the broadcast reform movement quickly disintegrated and this radical tradition of communication criticism was marginalized if not forgotten. The broadcast reformers were defeated in a highly undemocratic manner, in which commercial interests did everything in their immense power to prevent public or even congressional awareness of the issue. In this sense, the matter of how best to employ the new communication technologies has never been addressed in an open forum in the United States, making the United States exceptional in that regard.

The need for such a fundamental public debate has never been more pressing. We are at a point where technological revolution is creating an upheaval in the existing communication systems and a democratic society needs much study, examination, and debate to best utilize communication, the central nervous system of any society. Yet there is not much prospect for such a debate in the foreseeable future. Why is that? If the concerns of the 1930s about corporate control and commercialism remain with us today, in fact if they are more pronounced, why has no broadcast reform movement emerged to carry the mantle of the 1930s reformers? I believe there are three factors that undermined the 1930s reformers, which have made any subsequent anticapitalist media efforts fail even to get off the ground. I argue, therefore, that those who wish to put the ownership and control of communication on the agenda need to come to terms with these three factors.

First, capitalism is off-limits as a topic of legitimate debate in U.S. political culture. This was true, for the most part, in the early 1930s and it is certainly true today, as we have reached the alleged "end of history." There are many reasons for this, but a major factor is the general strength of the business community and the weakness of labor. As a result, it has become an article of faith that the market is the superior regulator of human activity, and the class basis of capitalism is scarcely mentioned or presented as a factor exogenous to the workings of the system. This has provided a superior shield for the owners of society, including the media capitalists. Although most sociological evidence points to the nature of ownership, subsidy, and control—in short, structural or institutional factors—as the major factors that determine media performance, the topic is off-limits in the United States. Second, the corporate media from the 1930s to today have actively and successfully cultivated the notion that capitalist media are synonymous with democratic media and that democratic media are synonymous with American media. Therefore a threat to corporate rule is a threat to democracy and the U.S. Constitution. My research suggests that commercial broadcasting was one of the first industries to employ modern-day public relations techniques in a significant (even overpowering) manner. Third, the corporate media industry has unique powers that make it the envy of the corporate community. On one hand, given the media control over news and communication, few politicians wish to antagonize the owners of the media. It is quite acceptable for politicians to bash the alleged liberalism of journalism, but it is political suicide to attack corporate control of the industry. On the other hand, the corporate media control how any debate over media issues will be presented to the public. The track record of the commercial news media in this regard is unequivocal: the status quo of media power is off-limits for public examination. Moreover, when it suits corporate media interests, the news will be employed to advance the corporate media position.

This last point might provide a good entry point into the nature of the public debates concerning the information superhighway. Politicians today are even less willing to challenge the corporate control of communication than they were in the 1930s. This is the most dynamic element of the global economy, and both U.S. political parties are battling to ingratiate themselves to the corporate overlords of these new fiefdoms.

The Clinton administration was emphatic in its commitment to profit before public service in the area of information and communication policy, and it had considerable corporate support from the communication and information industries. As for the Republicans, they proudly trumpet their position that high profits are the best determinant of what is in the public interest, in communication as elsewhere. Hence, whatever "battle" raged over establishing the legal and structural framework for the new $700 billion communication system took place among capitalists over which firms and sectors would dominate. The rest of us, uninformed by the corporate news media and therefore deemed to be uninterested, had our opportunity to participate as consumers once our unelected rulers divvied up the pie for themselves. That's democracy, American style.

Not only is corporate and commercial domination of media and communication unassailable in our political culture, but it is on the offensive. Hence elements of the political right have aggressively sought to eliminate publicly subsidized broadcasting in the United States since the Nixon administration, and especially since Reagan's victory in the 1980 election. This may seem absurd in view of the marginal nature of public broadcasting in the U.S. media landscape, but to the right there are very important principles involved. The Right is correct in this, but the principles involved are not necessarily those conservatives are discussing. To understand the current attack on public broadcasting, it helps to see the system in its historical context.

The defeat of the broadcast reform movement in 1934 led to the Dark Ages of U.S. public broadcasting. If the 1930s reformers sought a system where the dominant sector was nonprofit and noncommercial, all subsequent advocates of public broadcasting had to accept that the system was established primarily to benefit the commercial broadcasters, and any public stations would have to find a niche on the margins, where they would not threaten the existing or potential profitability of commercial interests. This made public broadcasting in the United States fundamentally different from that in Britain or Canada or nearly any other nation with a comparable political economy. Whereas the BBC and the CBC regarded their mandate as providing a service to the entire nation, the U.S. public broadcasters realized that they could only survive politically by not taking listeners or viewers away from the commercial broadcasters. The function of the public or educational broadcasters, then, was to provide that programming that was unprofitable for the commercial broadcasters to produce. At the same time, however, politicians and government officials hostile to public broadcasting have also insisted that it remain within the same ideological confines as the commercial system. This encouraged U.S. public broadcasting after 1935 to emphasize elite cultural programming at the expense of generating a large following. In short, since 1935 public broadcasting in the United States has been in a no-win situation. The major function of nonprofit broadcasting in the United States from 1920 to 1960 was, in fact, to pioneer new sections of the electromagnetic spectrum when the commercial interests did not yet find them profitable.

Thus it was educational broadcasters who played an enormous role in developing AM broadcasting in the 1920s, and then FM radio and even UHF television in the 1940s and 1950s. In each case, once it became clear that money could be made, the educators were displaced and the capitalists seized the reins. Arguably, too, this looks like the fate of the Internet, which has been pioneered as a public service by the nonprofit sector, with government subsidies, until that point when capital decides to take over and relegate the pioneers to the margins. The 1930s broadcast reformers were well aware of this tendency and refused to let the FCC push them into new technologies where there would be no access to the general public. After 1935, the proponents of public broadcasting had no choice in the matter. Even with these limitations, the commercial broadcasters were wary of public broadcasting and fought it tooth and nail well into the 1960s. After many halting starts, Congress passed the Public Broadcasting Act of 1967, which led to the creation of the Corporation for Public Broadcasting, and soon thereafter PBS and NPR. The commercial broadcasters finally agreed not to oppose public broadcasting, primarily because they believed the new public system could be responsible for doing the unprofitable cultural and public affairs programming that critics were constantly lambasting them for neglecting. There was a catch, however. The initial plan to have the CPB funded by a tax on receivers, similar to the BBC method, was dropped, thus preventing public broadcasting from receiving the stable source of income necessary for planning as well as editorial autonomy. At the outset it was determined that we would have a public system, but it would be severely handicapped. In short, this was the only public system the commercial broadcasters would permit. Although U.S. public broadcasting has produced some good fare, the system has been supremely compromised by its structural basis, and it is a farce in comparison to the great public service systems of Europe. Indeed, in international discussions of public broadcasting, the term "PBS-style system" is invoked to refer to a public system that is marginal and ineffective. It is the fate that the BBC, CBC, and others wish to avoid.

The funding system is the primary culprit. The government only provides around 15 percent of the revenues, and the public stations depend on corporate donations, foundation grants, and listener/viewer contributions for the balance. In effect, this has made PBS and NPR stations commercial enterprises and it has given the large corporations that dominate their subsidies tremendous influence over content, in a manner that violates the fundamental principles of public broadcasting. It has also encouraged the tendency to appeal to an affluent audience rather than a working-class audience, since those viewers/listeners have far more disposable income to contribute. When the federal subsidy is fully eliminated, the bias toward corporate interests and an upper-income target audience will be magnified.

Moreover, although the federal grant in 1995 was only around 15 percent of the public broadcasting budget, this provided congressional right-wingers—who oppose public broadcasting in principle—with opportunities to constantly harass PBS and NPR. These conservatives will not be satisfied until public broadcasting is crushed, but they use their positions to intimidate public broadcasters into violating their professional judgment regarding programming to appease the Right and keep their meager subsidies alive. The conservatives are obsessed with seeing that nothing gets through the public system that falls outside of the ideological boundaries provided by the implicit censorship of a commercial system. (Then, of course, to the extent that the public system duplicates commercial broadcasting, it is irrelevant and unworthy of support.) And, as almost all examinations of public broadcasting reveal, this right-wing attack has had a devastating effect on PBS and NPR content, especially concerning news and public affairs. It is one of the reasons the public system has barely offered a critical alternative to the journalism and public affairs coverage found on the commercial media.

For some on the political Left who oppose commercial broadcasting in principle, the corruption of PBS to the point where its prime-time public affairs are now dominated by the political right in a thoroughly unbalanced manner has been so profound that they agree that it is proper to end the public subsidy and let the system become more explicitly commercial. To these leftists, the battle over public broadcasting is being fought among the elite and there is little to be gained regardless of the outcome for the bulk of the citizenry. Indeed, with the success of conservatives and neoliberals in dominating the programming of PBS, the logical question is why then are so many conservatives still obsessed with the elimination of U.S. public broadcasting? Republicans state that the revolutionary expansion of channels produced by the communication revolution has rendered absurd the argument for government-subsidized broadcasting. The free market can now effectively meet consumer demand and there is no justification for wasting taxpayer money to subsidize one of the competitors. The government has no business interfering with the free market. And, indeed, PBS and NPR stations will survive without a federal subsidy by becoming more explicitly commercial enterprises. Defenders of public broadcasting will emphasize that this turn to commercialism will undermine what makes public broadcasting special and important, but that is a tough argument to make stick in our political culture, despite the clear truth that the marketplace places ideological constraints upon its programming. If the same defenders accept the marketplace as such a wonderful regulator elsewhere, why not in broadcasting? This is the theme that Republicans continually hammer home.

Now let's be clear: the much pronounced principle that the government should not interfere in markets is utter nonsense. The very same people who so piously state this eagerly support several hundred billion dollars of annual military spending, a significant purpose of which is to subsidize activities that the marketplace would not support. Major U.S. industries, including aeronautics, computers, and electronics would be shadows of their present selves if they had to do without these subsidies. For example, at one point fully 85 percent of research and development in the electronics industry was paid for by the federal government, although the eventual profits accrued to private firms. The rest of the federal budget and tax code is also chock full of subsidies for corporations and the wealthy. More specifically, the entire process by which the government has licensed the publicly owned airwaves at no charge to capitalist broadcasters for the past eighty years has been a massive subsidy to a multibillion-dollar industry. In reality, the entire history of communications in the United States is one of repeated direct and indirect government subsidies to private business. The real principle implied is that the government should only subsidize the wealthy and powerful and those whose support is necessary to keep them in power to serve further the wealthy and powerful. Programs that serve the poor and working class—such as welfare, unemployment insurance, day care and health care subsidies, the minimum wage, the right to unionize, public education subsidies, public housing, public job training—are on the chopping block. This was the platform of Bill Clinton and the Democrats, albeit packaged in different rhetoric. This real principle might also explain why the conservatives are taking dead aim at public broadcasting. After all these years, the public system, with its valuable channels, appears to have some notable commercial potential. By tradition, this is the ideal time to turn them over to private interests. Along these lines, several major communication firms, including Rupert Murdoch's News Corporation, TCI, and Bell Atlantic, were rumored to be interested in taking control of the some of the more valuable public stations.

But even if there were no corporate interest in acquiring the public system, conservatives still would be attacking PBS and NPR because the Right wants to disband publicly subsidized journalism and investigative reporting. The Right is obsessed with what it regards as the liberal bias of U.S. journalism and it believes this liberal bias is most apparent on PBS and NPR. To accept the argument that U.S. journalism overall has a liberal bias requires a belief in the presupposition that editors and journalists have almost complete control over what goes into the news, and since journalists tend to be liberal, the news is liberal. In conservative analysis, the institutional factors of corporate ownership, profit motivation, and advertising support have no effect—or, better stated, no *negative* effect—on media content. When conservatives fuse this presupposition with new class theory, liberal journalism becomes a major threat to the survival of the Republic. New class theory argues that U.S. society is not dominated by the wealthy and powerful and managed primarily to satisfy their selfish aims, but rather that the interests of the rich and the working class are effectively identical and good. In new class theory, the main threat to these "good guys" comes from an alleged super-powerful "new class" of liberal intellectuals—including journalists—seeking to dominate U.S. society in an unholy alliance with government bureaucrats, college professors, non-fundamentalist ministers, welfare recipients, and illegal immigrants. There is little time to discuss this point now, but it strikes me as so much self-serving nonsense, predicated on a complete obfuscation of the class basis of U.S. society. Likewise, the notion that journalists have complete control over the news is ludicrous and indefensible.

The conservatives are right about one thing, though. Journalists do tend to be liberal, but it is a liberalism that is rigidly defined by being on the "left side" of the spectrum of elite opinion. The conservatives err in collapsing liberals and radicals into one montage of leftishness that ranges unambiguously from Hillary Clinton to Hugo Chávez; to make conservatism "populist," it is mandatory that the "alternative" to their position be the elitist corporate liberalism of the U.S. Democratic Party and the *New York Times*. There is no place for a genuine class-based, principled left position except as caricature. In truth, the real chasm in U.S. politics and media culture is between those within the range of elite opinion—the conservatives and the liberals—and those outside it, who tend to regard the world in terms of class power and are, by definition, radicals. Journalists are almost never radicals, but some genuine progressives have survived and done good work over the years by taking advantage of what journalistic autonomy has existed. This has proven ever more difficult in recent years, as elite opinion has moved rightward, bringing along with it journalistic "liberalism." Under the severe commercial constraints and corporate cutbacks facing journalists, they are hard-pressed to interject any politics that might antagonize their bosses. To the extent that journalists do determine the news, for the most part they are fighting an uphill battle with their sources and the public relations industry for control of the news. In short, the autonomy of journalism has been greatly undermined.

Now, what is interesting is that conservatives have no qualms about this whatsoever. In fact, one could argue that the entire conservative media project is predicated on crushing journalistic autonomy and having a feeble journalism that kowtows to the interests of not only media owners and advertisers, but the wealthy and powerful in general. In this context, it is no surprise that Newt Gingrich urged media owners and advertisers to crack the whip on the "socialists" in the newsroom, to see that the news conform to the owners' and the advertisers' political agenda. This explains why conservatives are so obsessed with smashing, or at least intimidating, nonprofit and noncommercial broadcasting. They realize full well that the marketplace implicitly censors journalism to keep it within a range they consider acceptable. Conservatives live in fear of a journalism not constrained by profit imperatives and commercial support. It is true that much of public broadcasting journalism and public affairs programming is indistinguishable from commercial journalism. That is why Democrats support public broadcasting and why some leftists oppose it. Nonetheless, on occasions stories slip through and programs get produced that would never clear a commercial media hurdle. This is especially true on public radio and with some of the more progressive community stations that would suffer the most without any federal grant money. And this is precisely why it is so important for those who believe in journalism, free expression, and democracy to fight on behalf of public broadcasting.

This is far more than a battle among the elite for control of media turf. The market has declared war on journalism. It is now more necessary than ever for public policy to mandate a well-funded, independent journalism and communication system, not merely in the fight for public broadcasting but in any number of creative measures to politicize our culture. Once the principle of publicly funded broadcasting is abandoned, it will be ever more difficult to reinstate it. The right-wing assault on public broadcasting is not an isolated or exceptional phenomenon. It is part and parcel of a wholesale attack on all those institutions that have some autonomy from the market and the rule of capital. Thus public libraries and public education—two institutions far more significant than public broadcasting in U.S. culture—are being primed for privatization and an effective renunciation of the democratic principles upon which they were developed. Advertising-supported schools and schooling-for-profit, notions regarded as obscene only two decades ago, are moving to the center of education policy debates. The closest case to public broadcasting is that of higher education. Here, too, the Right prattles on about leftist thought police and politically correct speech codes, when in fact the dominant trend for U.S. universities is to turn increasingly to professional education and orient research toward the market. In short, the Right wishes to eliminate the autonomy of the university and see it thoroughly integrated into the capitalist economy. The extent to which this is accomplished, as with public broadcasting or public education, is the extent to which our ability to generate a democratic and critical debate concerning our future is reduced. The reign of capital becomes more entrenched and commercial values become more "natural." The Right knows this and it is about time the rest of us realize it, too.

The political nature of the right-wing assault on public broadcasting in the United States becomes clearer when one takes a global perspective. Whereas in the United States public broadcasting has been a marginal enterprise, it has tended to be a far more significant, even dominant, component of the media landscapes in many other nations. In virtually every nation of the world, the rapid globalization of capitalism has encouraged the privatization and commercialization of formerly public broadcasting systems. On one hand, this is due to pressure by transnational firms, the major advertisers both in the United States and globally, to have a broadcast system dedicated to serving their needs first and foremost. On the other hand, this process is abetted by the global fiscal crises of nation-states, crises encouraged by both economic stagnation and the general attack on the social components of the state by global capital and the International Monetary Fund (IMF). In this context, eliminating the expensive public subsidy to broadcasting and permitting advertisers to bankroll and capitalists to direct broadcasting seems the only feasible option.

The global attack on public broadcasting also has a political edge. Be it in Germany, Scandinavia, or India, neoliberal promarket conservative forces lead the battle against public broadcasting. These are also the same forces that are doing battle to limit national autonomy and popular democracy in the face of the new world order of transnational capital. We live in a paradoxical situation where more of the world is formally democratic today, yet most people feel like the fundamental decisions in their societies are increasingly beyond their political control. The institutions necessary for self-government to be effective are being obliterated by market forces. Edward Herman has characterized this process as the "end of Democracy." Aggressive, feisty journalism is the last thing the rulers of the new world order want or need, and if journalism is left to the market, it may well be the last thing they will get. Over much of the world, international broadcast news is provided by CNN, a global network explicitly targeted to the upwardly mobile consumers of the world. In other words, CNN provides a market-driven context for journalism in which at least 80 percent of the world's population is written off as irrelevant. If this is a democratic journalism, it is the democracy of Hobbes.

In sum, while the specific fate of U.S. public broadcasting can be characterized as "small potatoes" in the big scheme of things, the principle it represents goes directly to the question of what type of society will dominate in the United States and globally for the coming generations. Will it be one in which the market and profits are sacrosanct, off-limits to informed political debate? Will it be one in which the notion of citizen will be replaced by that of consumer and where we will have a society formally based on one-dollar, one-vote rather than one-person, one-vote? Will we have a society where people are regarded primarily as fodder for corporate profitability, or will we have a society where citizens have the right to actually determine whatever economic system they regard as best for society? This was precisely how the 1930s broadcast reformers understood the long-term implications of the fight for the control of broadcasting; it remains the fundamental question before us.

I would like to conclude by returning to the more general issue of the communication revolution, since public broadcasting policy is really only a subset of that broader topic. Karl Marx wrote somewhere that the supreme contradiction of capitalism was the ever mounting tension between the increasing socialization of production and the continued private appropriation of surplus. To put it somewhat differently, the core problem is that a capitalist-controlled, profit-motivated society increasingly undermines and warps the capacity of that society to fulfill its growing special and technological potential. I believe this observation is useful in comprehending what has been and is taking place in both the United States and the world.

On one hand, technological advances mean that only a fraction of the workforce can now produce what a fully employed economy did just forty-five or fifty years ago. Yet because this is a capitalist society, this has not translated into a higher living standard, a more relaxed and pleasant quality of life, or a commitment to repairing our ecology and urban environments, although these seem like rational expectations. To the contrary, living standards have plummeted and the quality of life is disintegrating. Why? Because these new technologies are there not to serve the common good, but to produce profit. Although the contributions of the market have been immense through the centuries, increasingly our global economic system seems bent on irrational destruction in the wanton and uncontrollable pursuit of profit.

This might also provide a context for considering the revolutionary potential of the communication and information technologies that exist or loom on the horizon. The proponents of a forthcoming utopia are correct in that these technologies *do* have world-historical potential, in a manner not unlike the printing press or the Industrial Revolution. However, to the extent that these technological enthusiasts believe these technologies can override the logic and power of capital, there is little evidence to support such a view. Moreover, to the extent to which our society, or any society for that matter, fails to examine and debate alternative policies in communication, is the extent to which our democracy is incomplete.

This point was clear to the broadcast reformers of the 1930s. They understood that journalism and communication were central to democracy, and that a communication system dedicated to profit could never provide the arena for the discourse so necessary for a meaningful democracy. One could look at the 1930s reformers and say that the manner in which they were crushed merely highlights the futility of opposing capital and that it is utopian and absurd to think it possible to do more than to eke out small concessions on the margins. But when one looks at the United States and the world today, where even the social democratic and liberal measures of past generations are now considered unrealistic and are being terminated, is it not even more utopian to think the system has room for reform in any meaningful sense? I am not suggesting that immediate political revolution is the only option, merely that the only manner to exact change will be by honestly assessing the situation and doing battle with those forces that are leading the assault on democracy. At present there is a tendency to avoid the truth because the social system seems impervious to radical change and speaking the truth to those in power might jeopardize chances at wrangling concessions from them. When we stop speaking the truth to power, we soon stop speaking it to each other, and it is only a matter of time until we stop looking for it or even recognizing it.

This tendency to compromise our vision to accommodate the interests of the powerful—to censor ourselves—may well be the most dangerous and reactionary idea of them all, and one that we can and must abolish. As Noam Chomsky likes to say, "If you act like there is no possibility for change, you guarantee that there will be no change."

10

The New Theology of the First Amendment: Class Privilege Over Democracy

The First Amendment stands as the crown jewel of the U.S. Constitution. Although it often has been ignored and violated throughout U.S. history, the First Amendment is the republic's shining commitment to individual freedom of expression and to the protection of the institutional requirements for an informed electorate and a participatory democracy. Yet what exactly the First Amendment signifies and does has been the subject of considerable debate over the years. Currently or in the near future, any number of cases are and will be working their way through the court system that would seek to prohibit any government regulation of political campaign spending, broadcasting, and commercial speech (e.g., advertising or food labeling) on the grounds that such regulation would violate citizens' and corporations' First Amendment rights to free speech or free press. Each case raises quite distinct constitutional issues concerning the First Amendment, but they share the common effect of protecting the ability of the wealthy and powerful few to act in their self-interest without fear of public examination, debate, and action.

It is no surprise that the political Right and the business community approve of this extension of First Amendment protection to these activities. To the extent commercial activities are given First Amendment protection, it makes the rule of capital increasingly off-limits to political debate and government regulation. And if political campaign contributions cannot be regulated, it puts the entire political process ever more firmly under the thumbs of the wealthy. What is striking, however, is that the venerable American Civil Liberties Union (ACLU) has lined up, more often than not, as an advocate of these "extensions" of the First Amendment. Wrapped in the most flowery jargon imaginable, the ACLU promotes the notion that this interpretation of the First Amendment is the truly democratic one.

I argue in this chapter that the ACLU and progressives who might be persuaded by the ACLU's logic are making a terrible mistake, and one that cannot be justified if one maintains a commitment to political democracy. This error is part and parcel of a broader process whereby the First Amendment has become more a mechanism for protecting class privilege than for protecting and promoting freedom and democracy. In my view, progressives need to stake out a democratic interpretation of the First Amendment and do direct battle with the Orwellian implications of the ACLU's commercialized First Amendment. And, as should be clear, this is far more than an academic battle: the manner in which the First Amendment is interpreted has a direct bearing on our politics, media, and culture. That is why the political Right and business community have devoted so much attention to converting it into their own possession.

The Utopian Case for a Commercialized First Amendment

Beginning in the 1970s, the U.S. Supreme Court has rendered a number of decisions that have increasingly extended First Amendment protection to corporations and commercial activities. As for political contributions, the Supreme Court first considered whether the government could constitutionally regulate campaign contributions in 1976, in *Buckley v. Valeo*. It upheld that right on balance, but the Court also stated that individuals had a First Amendment right to contribute as much of their own money as they wished to their own political campaigns, à la Ross Perot. The ACLU is among those who want not only to maintain this aspect of *Buckley v. Valeo*, but also to grant First Amendment protection to nearly all other forms of campaign contributions. As an ACLU counsel notes, government limitations on campaign spending "would trammel the First Amendment rights of political parties and their supporters."

This claim is made despite the chilling effect that the current cash-driven electoral system has on the nature and caliber of U.S. participatory democracy. The electoral system in the United States is in severe crisis, a crisis typified by low voter turnout, a narrow range of debate where substantive issues are studiously ignored, and a degree of depoliticization that makes perfect sense for such a vapid political culture. The current system elevates people with no credentials, but vast inherited fortunes, to almost automatic political prominence—like Steve Forbes, Michael Huffington, and U.S. Senator Herb Kohl to mention just a few—while marginalizing dedicated citizens with lifetimes of public service (but who refuse large contributions on principle) like Ralph Nader. The cash-driven electoral system is not the only factor that explains the decrepit state of U.S. politics, but it is among the prime culprits. And whether or not it is the cause, it is impossible to think of any solution that leads to the revitalization of U.S. electoral politics without significant reform of campaign spending.

The ACLU's argument, in a nutshell, goes something like this: if the First Amendment is applied to any and all forms of speech, then the net result will be a flowering marketplace of ideas. As long as the government is kept away from speech, only good things will happen for democracy. And the ability to spend money on campaigns is an inexorable aspect of speech; if it is regulated then we are on a slippery slope where all other forms of speech may soon be under government regulation and censorship. After all, censorship is contagious. This is basically the same argument used to extend the First Amendment to broadcasting, advertising, and other commercial activities.

At its most eloquent, this liberal argument for extending the First Amendment to political spending and, with qualification, to many commercial activities promises the greatest possible democratic political culture. But we have massive firsthand experience to show how absurd this claim is. In the past forty years the First Amendment has been extended by the courts to cover vast areas—generally commercial—and our media and electoral systems may be the least regulated in the developed world. By the ACLU laissez-faire formulation this should be the golden age of participatory democracy. But this is arguably the low point in U.S. democratic participation. In many respects we now live in a society that is only formally democratic, as the great mass of citizens have minimal say on the great public issues of the day, and such issues are scarcely debated at all in any meaningful sense in the electoral arena. This political marketplace of ideas looks a lot more like a junkyard than a flower bed. To paraphrase a line from a Woody Allen movie, if John Stuart Mill were around today, he would never stop throwing up.

There are two flaws with the ACLU vision. First is the notion that the government is the only antidemocratic force in our society. Government can be and at times is a threat to democracy—and deserves constant vigilance—but this is not a meritocratic society otherwise. Nearly all theories of democracy from Aristotle to Madison to the present have recognized that democracy was fundamentally incompatible with pronounced social inequality. In our society, corporations and the wealthy enjoy a power every bit as immense as that enjoyed by the lords and royalty of feudal times. This class power works through means like campaign spending to assure inequality and limit democracy. Second, markets are not value-free or neutral; they not only tend to work to the advantage of those with the most money, but they also by their very nature emphasize profit over all else. A commercial marketplace of ideas may generate the maximum returns for investors, but that does not mean it will generate the highest caliber of political exchange for citizens. In fact, contemporary evidence shows it to do nothing of the kind.[1]

If income and wealth were relatively equally distributed in the United States, I would be open to an argument that equated political spending with speech.[2] But we do not live in anything remotely close to an egalitarian society. The top 1 percent of the population owns one-half of the financial wealth, while the bottom 80 percent has around 6 percent. The top 1 percent of the population receives nearly 20 percent of U.S. income while the bottom 80 percent of the population divvies up around 45 percent of U.S. income. (Note: These statistics are from the mid-1990s; in 2008 the situation is even more dire.) Letting people spend as much money as they want is simply letting people at the top buy their ways out of a genuine democracy with a level playing field. Even leaving aside the hundreds of millions spent by corporate PACs (and why should we?), something along the lines of 90 percent of all individual campaign contributions come from those with annual incomes in excess of $100,000—i.e., from only the very top few percentage points of the U.S. income distribution. Is it any surprise that government policies pushed by both major parties—each dependent upon massive gifts from those with money in order to compete—have increased the polarization of U.S. society? And is it any surprise that countless Americans—especially from the lower 80 percent—regard U.S. politics as a sick joke? Can anyone possibly think this will change as long as our elections are auctions?

But what about concerns of the slippery slope, that if the government regulates campaign contributions it will open the door to the regulation of the content of books and magazines and the infringement of other freedoms? The slippery slope principle is legitimate, but it simply does not apply willy-nilly. There is no evidence that anyone has ever had any trouble distinguishing the regulation of campaign contributions from the censorship of the press or speech. In a related area, for fifty-some years the federal government has been regulating advertising, and to my knowledge it has never led to a single case of some zealous regulator sliding down the slope to begin censoring editorial content surrounding the ads.

The Absolutist Defense

At this point ACLU liberals stop defending the extension of the First Amendment to political spending (or commercial speech) from the claim that this is a good or necessary thing for democracy that can be verified empirically, and begin to invoke so-called principle. The argument goes that speech needs no defense to be protected by the First Amendment; it is a civil right with value to the individual that simply cannot be abridged. This is sometimes characterized as the "absolutist" position, and, in the end, this principle provides the strongest case for protecting spending and perhaps even extending the First Amendment to new commercial activities. But it still does not fly, because absolutism is anything but absolute. Modern free speech absolutism and civil libertarian groups like the ACLU were born in the tumultuous first decades of the twentieth century, with strident commitments to the protection of dissident political opinion and labor activism from government harassment. Absolutism was inspired by the promise of democracy, but, after defining what speech was necessary for democracy, it was also absolutist in its rejection of any government regulation, regardless of the justification.

Hence absolutism, and arguably any theory of the First Amendment for that matter, has two components. The theory must first determine what constitutes "speech," or, put another way, what speech is protected. Then, once that determination has been made, it is protected absolutely. But even the most strident "absolutist" cannot avoid determining what speech qualifies, or what constitutes speech. Hence today the debate is over whether advertising, or food labeling, or campaign contributions are speech. I have no qualms about extending the First Amendment net to include areas that may not have any clear connection to politics, but I think principle is necessary to guide the debate. And a good start is this: if the rights to be protected by the First Amendment can only be effectively employed by a fraction of the citizenry, and their exercise of these rights gives them undue political power and undermines the ability of the balance of the citizenry to exercise the same rights and/or other constitutional rights, then it is not necessarily legitimately protected by the First Amendment.

The first great wave of twentieth-century absolutists, including people like Alexander Meiklejohn, argued that the First Amendment protected any and all political speech under any and all circumstances. But they also argued that commercial speech (like advertising) was not protected by the First Amendment, but rather by the Fifth Amendment and its "freedom to contract" clause. Indeed, Meiklejohn argued that if commercial speech were given the same weight under the First Amendment as political speech, the First Amendment would lose its integrity and soon become primarily a tool for commercial interests who had no particular interest whatsoever in politics and public life per se.[3] That is exactly what is happening today. Meiklejohnian absolutism, like all other theories of the First Amendment, presents several problems determining what exactly is protected speech, but it has the core strength of keeping its eyes on the prize: democracy.

Since campaign spending was not a particularly pressing issue in the first two-thirds of the twentieth century—due largely to the lack of paid TV political advertising—it does not get discussed much by the first generation of absolutists, people like Meiklejohn, Hugo Black, and, later, Thomas Emerson.[4] But there is every reason to assume that it would have been considered a form of speech had it ever been tested in the courts before *Buckley v. Valeo* in 1976. Commercial speech, however, was never considered fair game for First Amendment protection by the first great generation of absolutists, nor by their most principled academic heirs today. When the Supreme Court considered whether advertising should be protected by the First Amendment from government regulation—in 1942—the Supreme Court, including absolutist Black, voted 9-0 against that proposition.

The Opening to a Corporate, Commercial First Amendment

The extension of the First Amendment to cover corporate and commercial activity is a recent phenomenon, taking place over the past thirty-five or forty years. This was not due to any profound philosophical debates or discussions over the meaning of freedom and democracy. To the contrary, this "extension" of the First Amendment was basically a conservative response by the court system to the sheer commercialization of the culture and the corporate domination of society, as the market began to spread into every nook and cranny of social life. When commercialism penetrates everything, and when noncommercial public life diminishes or merges with commercialism, the capacity to distinguish between the two is compromised. This position was fueled to some extent by aggressive media, advertising, and corporate lobbies ever eager to eliminate government regulation of their activities, and always quick to invoke high-minded principle to justify their self-interest. If not on the law faculties, then at least in the popular mind these corporate interests and their think-tank ideologues have been among the leading definers of this newfangled "absolutism." And, regrettably, the ACLU has increasingly accepted this Philip Morris interpretation of the First Amendment.

But this, alone, only begins to explain this striking shift in interpretation of the First Amendment. The critical factor that accentuated the problem with maintaining a strict line between political and commercial speech was the commercialization of the press. The commercialization and corporate ownership of media have also been the primary reasons for the explosion of political campaign costs that underlies the concerns about unregulated political spending. In this way the issue of whether campaign contributors are protected from government regulation by the First Amendment is indelibly linked to the commercialization of the culture and of the First Amendment.

Although discussions of the First Amendment protection of a "free press" often simply take discussions of individual speech and apply them to the press without qualification, there are important differences. It is one thing to assure individuals the right to say whatever they please without fear of government regulation or worse. This is a right that can be enjoyed by everyone on a relatively equal basis. Anyone can find a street corner to stand on to pontificate. It is another thing to say any individual has the right to establish a free press to disseminate free speech industrially to a broader audience than could be reached by the spoken word. Here, to the extent that the effective capacity to engage in free press is quite low for a significant portion of the population, the free speech analogy weakens. Moreover, those with the capacity to engage in free press are in a position to determine who can speak to the great mass of citizens and who cannot. This accords special privileges to some citizens who can then dominate public debate.

The core issue for First Amendment theorists, then, is whether the First Amendment protects the rights of press owners absolutely, regardless of the implications for democracy, much as it protects individual speech regardless of the content of that speech. The alternative is to view the First Amendment protection of a free press as a social right to a diverse and uncensored press. In this view the right to a free press is a right enjoyed by all citizens equally, not just by press owners. Here the explanation for constitutional protection is implicitly linked to the need for a free press in order to have a functioning democracy. Otherwise there is no more need of its inclusion in the First Amendment than there would be for a guarantee of the right to establish a bread-baking business or a shoe repair service. As Meiklejohn points out, those commercial rights are explicitly covered in the Constitution by the Fifth Amendment.

Indeed, there is little dissent to the argument that the free press clause was inserted in the First Amendment to protect democracy. As the press system of that era was explicitly connected to political parties and factions, such protection was necessary to protect minority political opinion from direct harassment by the dominant political party that controlled Congress and the government. Was this a legitimate concern? Absolutely. Only a few years after the adoption of the First Amendment, the crisis surrounding the Alien and Sedition Acts emerged, in which the dominant Federalist Party attempted to use the law to muzzle the voices of Republican newspaper editors.[5]

The conflict between the antidemocratic potential of a private press system and the needs of democracy was not an important debate for much of U.S. history. During the Republic's early days, the press system was highly partisan, often subsidized by government printing contracts or partisan contributions, politically motivated, and relatively noncommercial. In this period even small political factions found it relatively easy to publish and support all shades of political organs. One need only consider the broad array of abolitionist and feminist newspapers in the first half of the nineteenth century to appreciate the capacity of the press system to accommodate a wide range of political opinion. Later, during much of the nineteenth century, the partisan press system was replaced by a highly competitive, yet still fairly political, commercial press system. In this system there was still relative ease of entry to the market, and a cursory glance at any city of moderate size would tend to find a diverse press representing nearly every segment of the population. The press systems of the Republic's first century were far from perfect, but they were also not by any means a primary barrier to political democracy.

All this began to change toward the end of the nineteenth century, when the press (and, later, media) became an important capitalist industry, following the explicit logic of the commercial marketplace. Over time the media system became vastly less competitive in the economic sense. Not only were most media industries concentrated in the hands of a small number of large firms; barriers to entry made new competitive challenges almost impossible. Hence the "ease of entry," which made the free press protection in the First Amendment a near universal right for citizens was effectively eliminated. Along these lines, virtually no new daily newspapers have been successfully launched in existing markets in the United States since the First World War, despite their immense profitability and growth. And likewise, no new major Hollywood film studios have been established in seventy years. Moreover, the logic of the marketplace has led to the conglomeration of media giants so that the largest firms, like Time Warner and Disney, have dominant holdings across nearly every major media sector.

And that's not all. The media have become increasingly dependent upon advertising revenue for support, which has distinct implications for the nature of media content. Modern advertising only emerged with the arrival of corporate capitalism in the past century, and is conducted disproportionately by the very largest corporations. In the business press, the media are often referred to in exactly the way they present themselves in their candid moments: as a branch of the advertising industry. This corporate media system has none of the intrinsic interest in politics or journalism that existed in the press of earlier times. Its commercialized news fare, if anything, tends to promote depoliticization, and all evidence suggests that its fundamental political positions, such as they are, are closely linked to political and business elites. In view of ownership and subsidy, anything else would be astonishing. To be fair, the formal right to establish free press is exercised by dissidents on the margins, but the commercial system is such that these voices have no hope to expand beyond their metaphorical house arrest.

The rise of this corporate media system augurs a moment of truth for the First Amendment and its protection of a free press. Are corporations the same as people? Do shareholders and executives at corporations—clearly driven by law and the market to maximize profit regardless of the social implications—have the unconditional right to censor media content? Should investors be granted the First Amendment right to select and censor journalists when they have no more concern for the press than they have for any other potentially profitable investment? Is it right that this capacity to censor be restricted to the very wealthiest Americans, or those they hire to explicitly represent their interests? How does one distinguish what speech is necessary for politics—and thereby absolutely protected by the First Amendment—when it seems that all speech is increasingly concerned only with commercial gain, and political democracy is not even a prerequisite for its existence? Being an absolutist for a commercial media system then appears to have precious little to do with democracy and a great deal to do with protecting a powerful industry (and the class that owns it) from the same legal potential for public accountability that other similar industries face. And if the First Amendment covers corporate media, by what logic should it not cover corporate advertisers, or food manufacturers, or commerce in general?

This conflict first emerged in the Progressive Era, when chain newspaper ownership, one-newspaper towns and advertising had converted much of the U.S. press into blatant advocates for the status quo, while the formal right to launch newspapers meant little to dissidents who could not survive commercially in a semi-monopolistic market.[6] The material response to this crisis was the introduction of "professional" and "objective" journalism, and formal university-level schools of journalism, usually at the urging of the largest newspaper publishers. By the logic of professionalism, the journalists would produce a neutral product that did not reflect the biases of the owners, the advertisers, or themselves. Hence, while the owners maintained control of the industry and First Amendment protection, they would informally recognize the need for autonomous journalism with integrity that the public could trust. How successful or viable professionalism has been as a counterbalance to corporate commercial media control has been the subject of considerable debate over the years.[7] Many observers concede that journalistic autonomy has been shrunk or eliminated under commercial pressures from corporate owners.

Some Meiklejohnians—most notably Jerome Barron—would eventually argue that a commitment to the spirit of the First Amendment required the government to intervene to assure that semi-monopolistic newspapers provide a diverse range of views.[8] But for the most part those in the Meiklejohnian tradition have shied away from this response to the antidemocratic implications of the corporate media market: the prospect of government intervention in the press is *by definition* censorship and is therefore not acceptable under any circumstances. The experience with fascist and authoritarian media systems justifiably gave everyone trepidation about government-regulated media. And when the Supreme Court heard Barron's argument in *Miami Herald v. Tornillo* in 1974, it voted 9-0 against his position. Justice William O. Douglas displayed his utter contempt for Barron's position by reading a newspaper during his argument. It is worth noting, however, that the Supreme Court did not directly state that the right of the First Amendment belonged to the owners. The government cannot regulate "the exercise of editorial control and judgment," Chief Justice Warren Burger's opinion stated. Justice Byron White's concurring opinion noted that the government cannot "insinuate itself into the editorial rooms of this nation's press."[9] Clearly, the Court accepted the traditional presupposition that there is no important distinction between owners and editors, and its concern was to protect editors, not investors. In fact, editors and journalists have no First Amendment protection unless ceded by the owners. Wallowing in the nineteenth-century mythology preferred by the corporate media lawyers and ideologues, the Supreme Court has never directly addressed what the First Amendment means for a free press in the modern corporate commercial system.

There are two other "Meiklejohnian" solutions to the crisis of democracy generated by a corporate-dominated, commercially marinated media system. The most radical is to eliminate commercial media for the most part and create a large, nonprofit, noncommercial media system accountable to the public. In the Progressive era, for example, John Dewey and others proposed that newspapers be established as nonprofit and noncommercial enterprises, supported by endowments like universities, and managed through direct public election (or election by the workers) of their officers. Even press magnate Joseph Pulitzer broached the idea of converting his newspapers into nonprofit trusts to be run like universities, but he backed down, one suspects, when his heirs got wind of the idea.

The less radical solution is to accept the existence of the corporate media giants, seek to regulate at least the broadcasters, and then tax the media giants or use public monies to establish a viable nonprofit and noncommercial media system that can service the needs of those citizens unable to own media corporations. But proposals like these have met with significant corporate opposition and concerns that they would let the government control media to an unacceptable extent, no matter how the nonprofit media system might be structured. From the Progressive Era to the present day, the corporate media giants have fanned this flame, using their immense resources to popularize the notion that a gulag-style, darkness-at-noon media system is the only possible alternative to the corporate, commercial status quo. Hence any challenge to their power was a challenge to democracy. It may well be that the various commercial media industries—from newspaper publishers to broadcasters to film studios to advertisers—have been the foremost practitioners of public relations in this century. Anything more than marginal structural media reform, it is clear, cannot be successfully implemented unless it is part of a broader political challenge to the business domination of U.S. society.

Broadcasting, on balance, offered the most hope for those who wished to see a First Amendment committed to democratic media, as the limited number of possible channels meant that there was no escaping that the government would determine who would broadcast and who would not, and the terms under which they would broadcast. All Supreme Court decisions have affirmed the right of the government to regulate broadcasting in a manner that would be unconstitutional with the print media. In broadcasting, at least, the First Amendment has formally been acknowledged to be the property of viewers and listeners as much as licensed broadcasters.

Broadcasting provided the Waterloo as such for Meiklejohnian absolutism. In the late 1920s and early 1930s, the government in effect turned over the very best slots to a handful of private commercial operations including NBC and CBS, with virtually no public or congressional debate on the matter. Sections of the U.S. population were appalled by this giveaway and the resulting commercial carpet bombing of the publicly owned airwaves. In the 1930s the ACLU, inspired by its mentor Meiklejohn and with the active encouragement of Dewey, was so alarmed by the explicit and implicit censorship in corporate and advertiser control of radio—especially against labor and the Left—that it argued that the very system of commercial broadcasting was a violation of the

First Amendment. For most of the 1930s the ACLU worked to have the government establish a nonprofit and noncommercial radio system that would foster more coverage of social issues and public affairs, greater exchange of ideas, and diversity of opinion. The ACLU only backed off from this position when it became clear that corporate power was entrenched and unchallengeable. After abandoning its commitment to structural reform, the ACLU went from being proponents of an aggressive regulation of commercial broadcasters in the public interest to being ambiguous defenders of the commercial broadcasters ability to do whatever they pleased to maximize profits without government interference.[10] Eventually many liberals connected to the ACLU and elsewhere began to concentrate on defending the First Amendment rights of commercial broadcasters to censor material as they saw fit.

Since then the ACLU and the liberal community in general have shown increased willingness to include commercial activities under the rubric of the First Amendment, even if their relationship to political democracy is weak or nonexistent. When the line between what is commercial and what is political is muddled, as it became over the course of the twentieth century, absolutists and civil libertarians have two options. One is to extend the First Amendment to include more commercial fare, and the other is to narrow the First Amendment down so that it only covers noncommercial and even nonprofit speech. The former course offends no one in power and comports to the existing social structure, hence requiring no social change. The latter course goes directly counter to the trajectory of the political economy, hence demanding an explicit commitment to sweeping institutional change in the media industries and placing one in direct conflict with dominant media and corporate power. The latter course regards the First Amendment as a fundamentally radical statement, not a fundamentally conservative one. This is the logical trajectory of Meiklejohnian absolutism, and its decline mirrors the general decline of the democratic Left in the United States.

Conclusion

As impractical as Meiklejohnian absolutism seems today, its analysis hit the bull's-eye. As Meiklejohn feared, we are losing our capacity to distinguish public life from the commercial realm, with public life suffering as a consequence. It is a primary factor in the raging depoliticization and atomization of social life. Indeed, this is a theme that resounds in some of the most penetrating social criticism, ranging from C. Wright Mills and Jurgen Habermas to Noam Chomsky and Robert Putnam. It is a crisis that the proponents of extending the First Amendment to all campaign contributions and commercial speech are incapable of addressing, so it is one they dismiss as irrelevant. As legal scholar David Kairys noted, in the nineteenth century the image of the market was used to expand the boundaries of free speech, whereas in the twentieth century the image of free speech has been used to expand the power and terrain of the market.[11]

In the hands of the wealthy, the advertisers and the corporate media, the newfangled First Amendment takes on an almost Orwellian caste. It defends the right of the wealthy few to effectively control our electoral system, thereby taking the risk out of democracy for the rich, and making a farce of it for most everyone else. These semi-monopolistic corporations that brandish the Constitution as their personal property eschew any public service obligations, and claim that public efforts to demand them violate their First Amendment rights, which in their view means their unimpeded ability to maximize profit regardless of the social consequences. Indeed, the media giants use their First Amendment protection not to battle for open information, but to battle to protect their corporate privileges and subsidies.[12]

This points to the extraordinarily unprincipled nature of the ACLU's position on the First Amendment. The tragedy of this interpretation is not that it regards government as the sole enemy of democracy. It is that it spends all its time jousting with government when regulation might possibly challenge the prerogatives of the wealthy, but steadfastly ignores the widespread activities of the government to shape the marketplace of ideas on behalf of corporate and commercial interests. Hence the fact that the federal government has turned over valuable radio and television channels to a small number of commercial firms at no charge and with virtually no public debate is not considered a violation of the First Amendment, or a matter of concern to civil libertarians. Yet this activity has put distinct limits on the range of ideas that could emanate from the resulting broadcasting system.

And the fact that the U.S. government subsidizes a top-secret national security apparatus to the tune of at least $30 billion per year—with a significant amount of its work going to the dissemination of propaganda and the harassment of political dissidents—is also not apparently a First Amendment concern. Indeed, evidence suggests that the ACLU's Washington office effectively cooperated with the CIA's efforts to censor the writings of its former employees in the 1980s.[13] In Meiklejohn's perspective, the very existence of the CIA signified that this was not a democratic society, because the rulers had a weapon of immense power unaccountable to the citizenry. The modern-day corporate-friendly absolutists, in contrast, prefer to evoke a self-righteous posture celebrating their courageous stance on behalf of freedom, all the while never saying anything that would anger anyone in power. And nowhere is that more apparent than in the case of extending First Amendment protection to all forms of political contributions.

It would be comforting to think that we could depend on the Supreme Court to do the right thing and reverse *Buckley v. Valeo* and reclaim the First Amendment for democracy, but we cannot. The Court was appointed by politicians who benefit from the status quo, and it has shown a lack of backbone on related issues. And the courts tend to be conservative institutions, generally reversing earlier decisions only when they see significant changes in social attitudes on an issue. The job for progressives and activists, then, is to raise holy hell about our corrupt electoral system and our bogus corporate media system, and make it a key target of a social movement that takes direct aim at social inequality and class privilege. We need to link up electoral reform with media reform as well, so that we can create the type of accountable non-profit and noncommercial media sector that can actually stimulate public participation. And in the process of doing so we need to pressure the ACLU to return to its roots as a force for justice and democracy, or expose it as a liberal fig leaf for plutocracy.[14] As the old saying goes, if we create pressure in the streets, we might get some results in the suites.

11

The Commercial Tidal Wave

For a long time now it has been widely understood within economics that under the capitalism of giant firms, corporations no longer compete primarily through price competition. They engage instead in what economists call "monopolistic competition." This consists chiefly of attempts to create monopoly positions for a particular brand, making it possible for corporations to charge more for the branded product while also expanding their market share. Competition is most intense in what Thorstein Veblen called the "production of salable appearances," involving advertising, frequent model changes, branding of products, and the like. Once this logic takes over in twentieth- and now twenty-first-century capitalism it is seemingly unstoppable. All human needs, relationships, and fears—the deepest recesses of the human psyche—become mere means for the expansion of the commodity universe under the force of modern marketing. With the rise to prominence of modern marketing, commercialism—the translation of human relations into commodity relations—although a phenomenon intrinsic to capitalism, has expanded exponentially.

Advertising is part of the bone marrow of corporate capitalism. Yet it does not happen on its own. It requires advertising-friendly policies and regulations to allow it to flourish. Once these conditions are established it becomes a self-propelling system. Advertising has become such a dominant source of revenue for the media industries that those media outlets that do not attract advertising find themselves at a decided disadvantage in the marketplace.

Advertising thus becomes ever more ubiquitous. One of the ironies of advertising in our times is that as commercialism increases, it makes it that much more difficult for any particular advertiser to succeed, hence pushing the advertiser to even greater efforts. Many in advertising are not necessarily excited by the push to increase commercialism—sometimes they are downright critical of the effect on culture—but feel powerless to challenge it.[1] "It's the ultimate challenge," one ad executive stated in 2000. "The greater the number of ads, the less people pay attention to them. One ad is the same as another now. People simply don't believe them anymore."[2] The declining effectiveness of individual ads, as overexposed consumers develop immunities, has become a source of real concern for marketing firms, which find themselves forced to run faster and faster just to stand still. In the words of David Lubars, a senior ad executive in the Omnicom Group, consumers "are like roaches— you spray them and spray them and they get immune after a while." The only answer is to spray them some more.

The resulting commercial tidal wave assumes many forms. On the one hand, it means that traditional commercial media are increasing the amount of advertising. Radio advertising has climbed to nearly eighteen or nineteen minutes per hour, well above the level only a decade earlier. Television has been subjected to a similar commercial marination. Until 1982, commercial broadcasters operated under a non-binding self-regulatory standard of no more than 9.5 minutes per hour of advertising during prime-time and children's programming.[3] Even with that standard commercial broadcasters were lambasted for carpet bombing the population with ads. However, today that looks like a veritable noncommercial Garden of Eden. By 2002, advertising accounted for between fourteen and seventeen minutes per hour of prime-time programming on the major networks, easily an all-time high.[4] The amount of time devoted to advertising on television during prime time grew by more than 20 percent between 1991 and 2000.[5] Popular programs like *The Drew Carey Show* had over nine minutes of advertising over a half hour.[6] And that's not the half of it. In addition to the amount of commercial time increasing, the shorter fifteen-second spot, which barely existed in the 1980s, has come to account for nearly a third of the commercial time on TV. So the total number of ads increased even more dramatically.[7] Broadcasters took advantage of new digital compression technologies to "squeeze" programs down in length to insert even more advertising.[8] The quest to commercialize the airwaves was pushing to new frontiers. Digital ads were inserted *into* baseball telecasts, visible during the game itself.[9] The UPN Network even proposed running onscreen advertisements during its programs.[10]

All of this hyper-commercialism leaves advertisers frustrated, as their particular messages are more likely to get lost in the shuffle, but their recourse invariably is to ratchet up the sales effort accordingly. It also infuriates viewers, who do whatever they can to avoid the commercial onslaught. New technologies, such as digitalized personal video recordings, make this considerably easier, much to the dismay of media executives.[11] "You're getting to the stage where television advertising in certain product sectors and to certain target groups simply becomes wallpaper," one ad executive stated in 2002, "and even if you did spend more on it, it wouldn't work."[12] The immediate solution to this problem has been a massive increase in "product placement" in entertainment programming, where the product is woven directly into the story so it is unavoidable, and its message can be smuggled in when the viewer's guard is down. Coca-Cola, for example, paid $25 million to AOL Time Warner so that, among other things, characters in the WB Network's *Young American* series would "down Cokes in each episode."[13]

Much of the impetus for the inexpensive "reality" programs has been their affinity with product placement.[14] Coca-Cola had such success as the ubiquitous product displayed on Fox's 2002 *American Icon* program, that the fee for "joint sponsors" for its subsequent reality show was set at $25 million apiece. "In so-called reality shows," one industry observer noted, "branded products have become as prominent in the plot as in the commercials."[15] Mark Burnett, the producer of *Survivor*, states that he "looked on *Survivor* as much as a marketing vehicle as a television show."[16] Advertisers' products were made part of the story line—for $12 million each in the 2001 season. NBC's 2003 reality show, *Restaurant*, was actually produced by Interpublic, the advertising agency giant, so it could give their "top clients access to product integration deals."[17] With new digital technologies, the sky is the limit for commercialism. AOL Time Warner has developed "virtual" advertising, where products are placed retroactively in reruns for popular shows like *Law & Order*.[18]

Product placement has developed to such an extent on television that by 2003 a formal independent rating service, iTVX, had been established to assess the impact and value of product placements on television programs. The iTVX service evaluates the value of product placements on the basis of how long the product is onscreen, how prominently it is displayed, and whether it is incorporated into the story line. There are ten levels to which product placements are assigned depending upon their quality, ranging from a clear product logo in the background of a scene to a Level 10, "the ultimate in product placement," when "a show's entire episode is written around the product." One classic example of a Level 10 placement was a *Seinfeld* episode where the characters ate branded candy throughout the show. According to one industry observer, the value of a Level 10 placement is "off the charts," and well in excess of traditional advertising because it is more likely to be watched and remembered.[19]

Nor is product placement limited to television. On commercial radio, broadcasters increasingly use that portion of the broadcast day not explicitly turned over to advertising, to promote material they are quietly paid to air. Product placement in motion pictures has become a standard practice and is booming, even among the most respected directors. All the studios now have top-level executives in charge of departments dedicated to giving "corporate America" what it wants, as one trade publication put it.[20] In addition to explicit payments, advertisers make deals to promote the film in their other advertising in exchange for having the product appear in the film.[21] *Advertising Age* praised Steven Spielberg's 2002 *Minority Report* that "starred" Lexus and Nokia, while numerous other marketers including Pepsi's Aquafina and Reebok had supporting roles.[22] Even Disney's Miramax Films, the vaunted "independent studio" famed for its edgy work, made a deal with Coors beer in 2002. Coors will be the only beer to appear in Miramax movies, and Coors will be, in effect, the official beer of the studio, sponsoring Miramax movie premiers and promoting Miramax films. Whenever the name Miramax is seen, the name Coors will not be far behind.[23] In 2001 the competition between Disney's *Monsters, Inc.* and AOL Time Warner's *Harry Potter and the Sorcerer's Stone* was characterized as every bit as much a competition between Pepsi and Coca-Cola, so heavily involved were they in the marketing of the two films.[24]

Outside of films marketed exclusively to kids, nothing tops British agent 007 in the product placement department. Back in the 1960s, the first few James Bond films refused any product placement because the directors thought it "unseemly." "In today's very competitive movie environment," an executive working on the 2002 Bond film, *Die Another Day*, stated, "these additional marketing monies have become a necessity."[25] *Die Another Day* was so laden with product placements that *Variety* called it an "ad-venture," while the *Financial Times* noted that James Bond has now been "licensed to sell." The film featured twenty-four major "promotional partners" that ponied up more than $120 million in promotions and advertising to support the film.[26] James Bond has become a "walking, talking, living and killing billboard."[27]

As always, the children's market, where resistance to commercialism is weakest, is the pioneer for ad creep. Threshold Digital Research Labs, a subsidiary of Threshold Entertainment, which produced the new animated film *Foodfight!*, issued a news release on April 30, 2001, declaring that the coming film attraction "incorporates thousands of products and character icons from the familiar packages of products in a grocery store." The story line of this movie-length commercial (or multi-commercial) is about how internationally branded characters battle the evil Brand X for control of the grocery store. Corporations holding brand names that star in the film include: Procter & Gamble (Mr. Clean, Mr. Pringle), Interstate Food Brands (Dolly Madison, Twinkie the Kid, Wonderbread), Pepsi/Frito Lay (Chester Cheetah), Coca Cola Company (Coke), Starkist/Heinz (Charlie the Tuna), M&M Mars (M&M's, Skittles), Uncle Ben's (Uncle Ben), and many others. (When the film was finally released in 2008, there were some changes but the plot and description from 2001 remained basically intact.)

In the adult realm, ESPN, with the help of digital ad firm Princeton Video Image, has been inserting what seem to be product billboards on the walls behind home plate in its Major League Baseball broadcasts. Fans at the games, however, cannot see them because the billboards are not there. During the coverage of the arrival of celebrities at the 2001 Grammy Awards viewers watching the event on television saw a virtual street banner and logos on an entry canopy and sidewalks. The arriving celebrities, however, saw none of these advertisements, since they were not really there, but were inserted digitally for television viewers.

Marketers are seemingly unperturbed by this increase in stealth (and sometimes not so stealth) advertising in the form of product placements. "Maybe it is a subliminal commercial message," one executive stated about film product placement in 2002, "but there are so many much more overt commercial messages, especially in America, that I don't think anybody worries about it."[28] All of this has self-evident implications for what types of films will attract product placement and what types of films will therefore be more likely to get made. David Mamet's 2000 *State and Main* had as a running gag the effort of a Hollywood producer to place a computer product in a nineteenth-century period film. And the amount of advertising preceding the showing of films at movie theaters themselves—something considered unthinkable in the United States just a generation ago—continues to escalate and become more sophisticated.[29]

Product placement and commercialism in general have spread across the media and culture. Once people get accustomed (or resigned) to having commercialism everywhere, as in movie theaters, the bottom comes out of the cup and long-standing standards fade quickly into the past. Video games aggressively incorporate products into their content. "This is the next frontier of product placement," an Intel executive stated. "You're not just watching products, you're actually using them."[30] The British author Fay Weldon was paid a handsome fee to place Bulgari jewelry prominently in her 2001 novel, aptly named *The Bulgari Connection*. The book was not especially successful and the practice met with much criticism, but the direction is clear.[31]

Essentially the same thing has been done for years in children's books, which are full of branded objects and licensed characters. In the last few years this has taken on new dimensions. Millions of books are now being sold that have snack foods as their protagonists. Parents can currently choose between books starring Cheerios, Froot Loops, M&M's, Pepperidge Farm Goldfish, Skittles, Reese's Pieces, Sun-Maid raisins, Oreo cookies, and others. In a manner similar to the toy market, publishers and authors pay licensing fees to food companies in order to use the licensed products in their books. The food companies obtain not only the licensing fees but are also able in this way to market to toddlers sitting on their parents' laps. More than 1.2 million copies of Simon and Schuster's *The Cheerios Play Book* were sold in just two years. One of Simon and Schuster's newest entries is *The Oreo Cookie Counting Book*. "It teaches children to count down from 10 cookies to 'one little Oreo . . . too tasty to resist.' "

The long-standing notion of the separation between the advertising and editorial/creative sides of media is rapidly crumbling. To some extent this is due to ad clutter, and to some extent it is due to new ad-skipping technologies, but mostly it is due to the greed of media companies desperate to attract commercial support. The clout of large advertisers has grown; approximately

80 percent of U.S. ad spending is funneled through the eight largest companies that own advertising agencies, like Omnicom or Interpublic, which gives
them considerable ability to name their tune with corporate media firms more
than willing to play ball. "The tables have turned," Wendy's marketing chief
stated in 2002. If media firms do not accommodate their wishes, "marketers
will take their ad dollars to other places. There are too many ways to reach
consumers." Accordingly, Wendy's was able to have Rosie O'Donnell tout
Wendy's salads during an episode of her talk show, and eat one of the salads
on air.[32] The list goes on and on. The USA Network held top-level "off-the-
record" meetings with advertisers in 2000 to let them tell the network what
type of programming content they wanted in order for USA to get their advertising.[33] "The networks didn't use to want us," the J. Walter Thompson executive in charge of Ford's TV account stated in 2002. "I sense a sea change. . . .
I've been amazed by people's willingness to write [Ford] into scripts. I've had
to remind them to keep it entertaining."[34] AOL Time Warner's TNT cable
channel sent out an open call to advertisers in 2000, in an effort to get products placed in all its programs wherever possible.[35] Comcast's G4 game show
TV channel offered advertisers an opportunity to have their commercial
appear as part of the programs. As a G4 executive said to advertisers, "If you
have an idea, we'll play."[36]

In a sense this is a return to broadcasting's early days, when advertisers
actually produced the programs that went on the air. And, fittingly enough,
soap operas have rapidly embraced the explicit commercialization of editorial content. In 2002, Revlon was given a prominent role in Disney-owned
ABC's *All My Children* in exchange for millions of dollars in advertising.[37] But
what is happening now goes far beyond what was done from the 1930s to the
1950s in radio and television, in both scope and intensity. It is the media firms
that are leading the push now, and they are most definitely pushing the commercial envelope. "As the competition for ad dollars intensifies," one Disney-
owned ESPN executive stated, "we are exploring alternative ways to give
advertisers added value for their time. We have to think outside the box."
ESPN has begun work on "long-form" commercials where products are integrated into entertaining segments on sport.[38] In 2002 ABC's *Monday Night
Football* featured ads with announcer John Madden that were virtually
indistinguishable from the program itself.[39] News Corporation's cable television
sports show *The Best Damn Sports Show Period* assumed by 2003 the "leading

role in blurring the boundaries between advertising and programming," when it made the mascot for its largest advertiser, Labatts beer, a recurring character on the program.[40] By 2002 commercial broadcasters were gearing up to develop "eBay-TV," whereby direct selling of products could be done in conjunction with programming.[41] The media firms claim all this commercial involvement has no influence over actual media content, but this claim fails to pass even the most basic giggle test, it is so preposterous. "Who are they kidding," the *Los Angeles Times* TV columnist wrote in 2002. "Why would companies pony up cash without expecting some input over how it is spent?"[42]

In sum, we are rapidly moving to a whole new paradigm for media and commercialism, where traditional borders are disintegrating and conventional standards are being replaced with something significantly different. It is more than the balance of power shifting between media firms and advertisers; it is about the marriage of editorial/entertainment and commercialism to such an extent that they are becoming indistinguishable. Infomercials, for example, which once were Madison Avenue's tackiest contribution to commercial culture and which generated $14 billion via TV sales in 2001, increasingly resemble standard commercial entertainment programming.[43] "Traditional advertising will not go away," an ad executive stated in 2002, but it "requires an entirely new set of creative tools."[44] "Product placement is silly and overblown," another ad executive stated. It can only work "if it's integral to the story line."[45] Accordingly, the largest advertising agencies have begun working aggressively to co-produce programming in conjunction with the largest media firms.[46] In 2003, AOL Time Warner's WB network worked with advertisers on the first program without any commercial interruptions, but with advertising messages incorporated directly into the show.[47] Produced by Michael Davies, who developed the reality show *Who Wants to Be a Millionaire*, the idea is to create "a contemporary, hip *Ed Sullivan Show*" in which singers and other entertainers will perform on a set completely dominated by a product logo, such as Pepsi, and comedy routines will be designed around particular products being sold.

Likewise, advertising agencies and corporate marketing departments are now producing their own media, in particular glossy magazines, which are often indistinguishable from traditional commercial media. Newhouse's Conde Nast publishing house launched *Lucky*, a magazine where advertising motifs dictate the design of every editorial page, and all editorial copy is linked to specific products. "Articles, in the traditional sense, are nowhere to be found."[48] This "custom publishing market" was valued at $1.5 billion in 2001 and has been growing at 10 percent per year; traditional commercial magazine publishing revenues dropped 11.7 percent in 2001. "These magazines are direct marketing vehicles, but they're more than that," one publishing executive stated in 2002. "They are also intended to have a look and a feel of a real magazine."[49]

Along similar lines, firms like Microsoft and DaimlerChrysler produced lavish film shorts (and paid for them) to be shown in theaters before feature presentations; these were meant to be regarded as entertainment with the sales pitch low-key.[50] "Eventually there will be entire channels devoted to commercials," one advertising executive predicted. "It's all just content."[51] And, indeed, the pioneer in this regard is BMW, which launched its own 24/7 channel on DirecTV in 2002. The channel features entertainment programming based around BMW automobiles. "I'm hoping it's the tip of the iceberg," an enthusiastic DirecTV executive stated.[52]

The crucial development here follows from the logic implicit in corporate advertising. It is to give brands personality, and to "brand" that personality on our brains. All of this has precious little to do with the actual attributes of the product or service being sold. As Coca-Cola's chief marketing officer put it in 2002, when people buy a can of Coke, "they are not buying a product. They are buying the idea of the branding imagery, the emotional connection—and that is all about entertainment."[53] As an executive working with Anheuser-Busch put it: "The idea is not about promoting a product specifically, but connecting with consumers on an emotional level."[54] And the commercial media are joined to marketers at the hip in these endeavors. Disney, for example, has its characters provide the basis for the General Mills line of fruit snack products and it ties Nestle's Wonderball chocolate bar to its children's films, to mention just a couple.[55]

Another key area where the merger of commercialism and content has become more and more prevalent is in recorded music, and here again the consequences are troubling. Late in 2002, for example, Pepsi and Sony Music signed a groundbreaking deal whereby Sony artists will be promoted and distributed in many places Pepsi is sold, and Pepsi will get exclusive rights to use Sony music in its global marketing campaigns. "Music is part of our DNA," a Pepsi executive stated. "Working with Sony lets us bring it to life in the marketplace. The umbrella idea is that Pepsi is bringing you music first. It reinforces Pepsi's connection and leadership in music as a marketer at the same time it allows Sony to get airplay for artists early and often."[56]

AOL Time Warner struck a deal with Toyota in 2002 that, among other things, called for a single from Phil Collins's new CD to be used during Toyota TV commercials for its Avalon sedan. "We are looking for new and innovative ways to get music out to the public," an AOL Time Warner executive explained. "Toyota is the most collaborative partner we ever had. This is real co-marketing."[57] Toyota, Chrysler, and Honda all sponsor alternative music tours, "hoping to slip in some brand messages to a jaded demographic."[58] In 2002 Chevrolet sponsored the "Come Together and Worship Tour" of evangelical Christian artists, at the same time it was the exclusive sponsor of *Rolling Stone*'s twenty-eight-page 2003 calendar insert in an issue with Eminem on the cover.[59]

The list goes on and on. "Now every record label," one Disney executive stated, "is searching for a strategic marketing person to reach out to corporate America as a way to extend marketing budgets." All of this is in contradiction to popular music's long-standing role as a rebellious and anti-authoritarian medium. And it is that anti-authoritarianism that makes music so attractive as a convincing sales vehicle to corporations.[60] One can only wonder how rebellious the music sponsored by marketers and advertising agencies can be. "You don't want it *to appear* like you are selling out," the president of a teen marketing firm explains, "There's a fine line"[61] (emphasis added).

Nowhere in popular music is this tension more dramatic than in hip-hop music. Because of the nature of the genre—lyrics are central—and the access to difficult-to-reach markets, this has become a dream come true for marketers. "Once our audience takes to a product," the editor of the hip-hop magazine *The Source* stated, "their influence is tremendous on the rest of the population."[62] Bragging about products in rap music has been a staple since the very beginning; in 1979 the Sugarhill Gang rapped about their "Lincoln Continental and sunroof Cadillac." When Run D.M.C. rapped about Adidas shoes in 1986, their promoter was able to win a breakthrough $1.5 million endorsement contract from the running shoe manufacturer. That appears quaint by today's standards. As one reporter put it: "On any given week, *Billboard*'s Hot Rap Tracks chart is filled with songs that serve as lyrical consumer reports for what are, or will be, the trendiest alcohol, automobile, and fashion brands." By the end of 2002 the hip-hop label Def Jam was negotiating a deal with Hewlett-Packard to have the computer maker's products featured in the songs of Def Jam artists in exchange for extensive play in the company's advertising campaigns.[63] Sean "P. Diddy" Combs has converted his music career into a marketing empire; his Blue Flame company "helps companies build brands that are targeted to trend-setting consumers." This is "the future of advertising and marketing in America," one observer noted, "a really good example of the avant-garde of the advanced entertainment-hype complex. They have managed to take what started out as a single product—which was music—and turn it into a lifestyle."[64] The commercial cart is pulling the hip-hop horse. "We sang 'My Adidas' because we liked them," said D.M.C. of Run D.M.C. "That's the difference. Now a lot of guys are just hoping to get that phone call."[65]

But to break commercialism down by media category, like music or film, is somewhat misleading in the era of the media conglomerate. The larger trend developing is for marketers to link with larger conglomerates and work massive product placement/advertising/promotional deals across the media firm's entire arsenal of media assets. So it was in 2002 that MasterCard negotiated a deal with Universal Studios worth over $100 million, to make MasterCard an integral part of Universal theme parks, movies, home videos, and, possibly, music. This is where the commercial value (and competitive advantage) of having a media conglomerate comes into play.[66]

Much of the media have been commercial institutions in the United States for generations, and what is described here is simply a massive and qualitative leap in a preexisting commercialism. Its flames are fanned by the privatization urged on by neoliberal policies. Concurrently, and every bit as important as what is described herein, there is an ongoing privatization and commercialization of virtually all those institutions—media and otherwise—that have been decidedly and explicitly noncommercial.[67] This includes public broadcasting, public education, art, university education, and government activities.[68] In grand irony, even "anti-establishment" institutions like independent films increasingly turn to explicit corporate sponsorship.[69] As Thomas Frank and Matt Weiland put it, we are in an age when people are channeled to "commodify your dissent," with all that suggests about the range of opinions that will be encouraged.[70] Fittingly, "cause-related marketing," where advertisers link their product to some worthy social cause to enhance their bottom line, has boomed over the past decade.[71] Indeed, advertising itself is far too narrow a concept to encompass the effects of the rampant commercialism that now confronts us. Much attention is devoted today to how marketing and public relations are effectively merging, as both swallow up and direct the entire culture.[72] In this sense the commercial tidal wave is interchangeable with a broader media torrent, or blizzard, that overwhelms our senses.[73] The culture it generates tends to be more depoliticized, garish, and vulgar than what it has replaced.[74]

Indeed, the spread of commercialism to new frontiers is so widespread as to be almost numbing. In 2002 Nike and Microsoft pasted advertising decals on the streets and subway stations of Manhattan, and the Broadway show *La Bohème* featured commercial props in its set.[75] Everything now seems fair game: buildings use digital technologies to sport "urban wall displays" that are to old-fashioned billboards what rocket ships are to the horse and buggy;[76] the tops of taxicabs, public garages, subway entrances, the walls above urinals, golf holes, even baby buggies are being festooned with advertising.[77] Advertising-packed TVs have been placed on city buses, in elevators, and in checkout lines.[78] Using a special steamroller-like machine, Dori's Beach 'n Billboard Inc. in New Jersey has imprinted the state's beaches with more than 650,000 square feet of Snapple iced tea and Skippy peanut butter ads. NBC even established a Patient Channel to bombard people with advertising in hospitals. As a correspondent for *Electronic Media* quipped, "If you're sick of TV advertising, a hospital bed might not be the best place for you."[79] In 2001 the California Horse Racing Board voted to drop bans on advertising on jockeys and horses.[80] Taking it one step further, grade-D celebrities like Tonya Harding and Danny Bonaduce were among the twenty or so public figures that began sporting temporary tattoos for advertisers.[81] Leaving no stone unturned, in 2002 a firm called Government Acquisitions LLC began selling advertising space on police cars in scores of communities.[82]

Product placement ads are even being inserted in news broadcasts by major networks. During its coverage of New Year's Eve 2000 in New York CBS blotted out real billboards for NBC and Budweiser on One Times Square, the building where the ball drops at midnight, and digitally substituted the CBS logo. This became well known only because CBS was hit with a lawsuit from OTS Signs which rents billboard space there for as much as $1 million.

As part of this process of commercial penetration two crucial and note-worthy developments have taken place. First, marketers have had to become much more sophisticated in their techniques at commanding the attention of their desired target audience. It would astonish almost any person to see the extent of the research deployed by marketers and advertising agencies to brand their imprint on consumers' brains. Focus groups, psychologists, and cultural anthropologists are *de rigueur* in marketing research.[83] Modern marketing is clearly the greatest concerted attempt at psychological manipulation in all of human history. A crucial development in the early twenty-first century has been the rise of "guerilla" marketing, that is, smuggling sales messages into particular "target audiences" by aggressively spreading "buzz" about a hip new product or using other unorthodox and surreptitious methods.[84] Alissa Quart's 2003 book *Branded* chronicles these techniques for marketing to teenagers and their implications in chilling detail.[85] "One of the tenets of teen advertising is that they don't smell the sell," a top ad executive stated in 2000. "You can do amazing things if you live where [teens] live and learn to speak to them in a voice they find appealing."[86] The ideal is to have "potential buyers" learn "about a brand from their coolest friends."[87] Or as another marketer put it, "Buzz doesn't happen by accident. This is just real-life product placement."[88] One of the most striking uses of guerilla marketing tactics is called "urban marketing," where firms like Coca-Cola send teams of hip young African-Americans with vans full of soda and hip-hop music "to the sweltering streets to engage in a block-by-block battle to win over the hearts and wallets of lower-income, mostly African-American consumers." Maze Jackson, the director of "urban marketing" for one advertising agency, says it is "more authentic" and allows the firm to zero in on "urban trendsetters." "We incorporate ourselves into the urban landscape," Jackson states.[89] In short, even personal relationships are now deployed to sell.

Second, the race to imprint the brand on the target audience increasingly turns to younger and younger people. The booming value of the global market for children's licensed products was some $132 billion in 2002. Hence the children's market has received extraordinary attention in recent years and it is here that the commercial tidal wave is most striking. In 2001, children's programming accounted for over 20 percent of all U.S. television watching.[90] In addition, children are increasingly recognized as the necessary location for building brand awareness, even for adult products. The key is to reach them before their brand decisions have been made, and before their defenses to advertising are well developed. Mike Searles, president of Kids-"R"-Us, a chain of specialty children's stores, explains that where commercial marketing to children is concerned, "all these people understand something that is very basic and very logical, that if you own this child at an early age, you can own this child for years to come." In effect, "companies are saying, 'Hey, I want to own the kid younger and younger and younger.' "

This explains why the hotel chain Embassy Suites, for example, signed a $20 million deal with Viacom's children's channel Nickelodeon. "We found in research that 95 percent of kids could name at least one hotel chain," a Nickelodeon executive enthused.[91] Traditionally noncommercial venues such as public schools and school textbooks are now loaded up with commercial messages.[92] According to Joel Babbit, former president of Channel One, which is present in schools across the nation, "The biggest selling point to advertisers" of this type of compulsory education via commercial TV is the lack of freedom it imposes in "forcing kids to watch two minutes of commercials." The virtue from an advertiser's standpoint, he explains, is that "the advertiser gets a group of kids who cannot go to the bathroom, who cannot change the station, who cannot listen to their mother yell in the background, who cannot be playing Nintendo, who cannot have their headsets on." Childhood in the United States is becoming first and foremost a commercial indoctrination from one's earliest memories, with the explicit purpose of enhancing the profitability of the marketers, not the well-being of the children.[93] In the words of Nancy Shalek, President of Shalek Advertising, which handles advertising campaigns for children's clothing, "Advertising at its best is making people feel that without their product, you're a loser. Kids are very sensitive to that. If you tell them to buy something they are resistant. But if you tell them they'll be a dork if they don't, you've got their attention. You open up emotional vulnerabilities and it's very easy to do it with kids, because they're the most emotionally vulnerable."

For a society whose politicians and citizens love to speak of their commitment to children, the actual track record points in the opposite direction. Ironically, when the Centers for Disease Control wished to address the epidemic of childhood obesity brought on to some extent by nonstop TV advertising for sugar products and junk food, it did so by purchasing TV ads.[94]

It must also be noted that this hyper-commercialization of the culture is recognized and roundly detested by the citizenry, although the topic scarcely receives a whiff of direct attention in the media or political culture. An advertising industry survey conducted in December 2002 found that a "whopping 75 percent of U.S. consumers believe advertising intrusion into content has increased over the past year," and most of them found the development very negative. The only good news for marketers was that younger people tended to be somewhat less critical of hyper-commercialism than their elders, though the antipathy was still intense, with 44 percent of people under thirty-five expressing concern about the encroachment of advertising into editorial content.[95] But with regard to hyper-commercialism, interestingly enough, the mantra of "giving the people what they want" does not apply. To the contrary, people are given a "choice" from within the range of what generates the most money for the dominant firms in oligopolistic markets. In all likelihood, as the *Los Angeles Times* TV critic noted in 2003, people then grow "indifferent to such excesses or, more likely," he concluded, they are "bludgeoned into submission by them."[96] In due time, as people select from this commercially marinated menu, they can expect to be informed by academics and the punditocracy that they are getting what they want.

Indeed, for all their lauding of choice, marketing professionals have much more manipulative and dominating designs. As one market researcher put it at the Seventh Annual Consumer Kid's Conference in Arizona in May 1995, "Imagine a child sitting in the middle of a large circle of train tracks. Tracks, like the tentacles of an octopus, radiate to the child from the outside circle of tracks. The child can be reached from every angle. This is how the [corporate] marketing world is connected to the child's world." As Gary Ruskin, head of Commercial Alert, a group founded by Ralph Nader, observes, "In our business culture, children are viewed as economic resources to be exploited, just like bauxite or timber."

Nor are children the only ones to be treated in this way. "After trying to watch the heavily hyped Winter Olympics," John Updike sardonically commented to the National Arts Club in 1984, "I have no doubt that the aesthetic marvels of our age, for intensity and lavishness of effort and subtlety of both overt and subliminal effect, are television commercials. With the fanatic care with which Irish monks once ornamented the Book of Kells, glowing images of youthful beauty and athletic prowess, of racial harmony and exalted fellowship, are herein fluidly marshaled and shuffled to persuade us that a certain beer or candy bar, or insurance company or oil-based conglomerate, is . . . the gateway to the good life."

All of this leads to deeply troubling implications for the exercise of democracy in the classical sense of the term. The democratic philosopher Alexander Meiklejohn put it well when he noted that if commercialism provides the logic for all speech, the commitment to public communication disintegrates under the obsession with material self-interest. The truth is far less important than what one can convince people to believe in to get them to serve your commercial needs.[97] What was written by Paul Baran and Paul Sweezy, in their 1964 book *Monopoly Capital*, holds true for today, and then some:

> It is sometimes argued that advertising really does little harm because no one believes it anymore anyway. We consider this view to be erroneous. The *greatest* damage done by advertising is precisely that it incessantly demonstrates the prostitution of men and women who lend their intellects, their voices, their artistic skills to purposes in which they themselves do not believe, and that it teaches [in the words of Leo Marx] "the essential meaninglessness of all creations of the mind: words, images, and ideas." The real danger from advertising is that it helps to shatter and ultimately destroy our most precious non-material possessions: the confidence in the existence of meaningful purposes of human activity and respect for the integrity of man.[98]

What such a commercial culture tends to produce—and what the avalanche of commercialism encourages—is profound cynicism and greed, both cancerous to public life. The message is constant: all our most treasured values—democracy, freedom, individuality, security, cultural diversity, equality, education, community, love, health, human development—are reduced in one way or another to commodities provided by the market. Social problems either cannot be solved or can be solved through individual material consumption. Likewise, human happiness is to be located in individual material consumption as well.

Rafts of academic books have been published in the past decade—and more are certain to come—explaining that this commercialization of life is actually very complex and nuanced and cannot be adequately described in such a categorical manner. This is true enough and any close examination must take this into account. Some go on to assert that commercial cultures hold the potential for popular sovereignty, albeit in a form we may not yet understand. But in the classical sense of the term democracy—the notion of informed self-government—our current path leads to no plausible democratic destination. As James Rorty wrote some seventy years ago, advertising represents "Our Master's Voice," that of the wealthy, and the culture it dominates will always ultimately be biased to serve the interest of the privileged few.[99]

The struggle against advertising is therefore essential if we are to overcome the pervasive alienation from all genuine human needs that currently plays such a corrosive role in our society. But in resisting this type of hyper-commercialism we should not be under any illusions. Advertising may seem at times to be an almost trivial if omnipresent aspect of our economic system. Yet, as the great mainstream economist A. C. Pigou long ago pointed out, it could only be "removed altogether" if "conditions of monopolistic competition" inherent to corporate capitalism were removed. To resist it is to resist the inner logic of capitalism itself, of which it is the pure expression.

12

Noam Chomsky and the Struggle
Against Neoliberalism

Neoliberalism is the defining political economic paradigm of our time—it refers to the policies and processes whereby a relative handful of private interests are permitted to control as much as possible of social life in order to maximize their personal profit. Associated initially with Reagan and Thatcher, neoliberalism has for the past two decades been the dominant global political economic trend adopted by political parties of the center, much of the traditional Left, and the Right. These parties and the policies they enact represent the immediate interests of extremely wealthy investors and less than one thousand large corporations.

Aside from some academics and members of the business community, the term neoliberalism is largely unknown and unused by the public at large, especially in the United States. There, to the contrary, neoliberal initiatives are characterized as free market policies that encourage private enterprise and consumer choice, reward personal responsibility and entrepreneurial initiative, and undermine the dead hand of the incompetent, bureaucratic, and parasitic government, which can never do good (even when well intentioned, which it rarely is). A generation of corporate-financed public relations efforts has given these terms and ideas a near-sacred aura. As a result, these phrases and the claims they imply rarely require empirical defense, and are invoked to rationalize anything from lowering taxes on the wealthy and scrapping environmental regulations to dismantling public education and social welfare programs. Indeed, any activity that might interfere with corporate domination of society is automatically suspect because it would impede the workings of the free market, which is advanced as the only rational, fair, and democratic allocator of goods and services. At their most eloquent, proponents of neoliberalism sound as if they are doing poor people, the environment, and everybody else a tremendous service as they enact policies on behalf of the wealthy few.

The economic consequences of these policies have been the same just about everywhere, and exactly what one would expect: a massive increase in social and economic inequality, a marked increase in severe deprivation for the poorest nations and peoples of the world, a disastrous global environment, an unstable global economy, and an unprecedented bonanza for the wealthy. Confronted with these facts, defenders of the neoliberal order claim that the spoils of the good life will invariably spread to the broad mass of the population—as long as the neoliberal policies that exacerbated these problems are not interfered with by anyone!

In the end, proponents of neoliberalism cannot and do not offer an empirical defense for the world they are making. To the contrary, they offer—no, demand—a religious faith in the infallibility of the unregulated market, drawing upon nineteenth-century theories that have little connection to the actual world. The ultimate trump card for the defenders of neoliberalism, however, is that there is no alternative. Communist societies, social democracies, and even modest social welfare states like the United States have all failed, the neoliberals proclaim, and their citizens have accepted neoliberalism as the only feasible course. It may well be imperfect, but it is the only economic system possible.

Earlier in the twentieth century some critics called fascism "capitalism with the gloves off," meaning that fascism was pure capitalism without democratic rights and organizations. In fact, we know that fascism is vastly more complex than that. Neoliberalism, however, is indeed "capitalism with the gloves off." It represents an era in which business forces are stronger and more aggressive, and face less organized opposition than ever before. In this political climate business attempts to codify their political power and enact their vision on every possible front. As a result, business is increasingly difficult to challenge, and civil society (nonmarket, noncommercial, and democratic forces) barely exists at all.

It is precisely in its oppression of nonmarket forces that we see how neoliberalism operates—not only as an economic system, but as a political and cultural system as well. Here the differences with fascism, with its contempt for formal democracy and highly mobilized social movements based upon racism and nationalism, are striking. Neoliberalism works best when there is formal electoral democracy, but when the population is diverted from the information, access, and public forums necessary for meaningful participation in decision making. As neoliberal guru Milton Friedman put it in *Capitalism and Freedom*, because profit making is the essence of democracy, any government that pursues antimarket policies is being antidemocratic, no matter how much informed popular support they might enjoy. Therefore it is best to restrict governments to the job of protecting private property and enforcing contracts, and to limit political debate to minor issues. (The real matters of resource production and distribution and social organization should be determined by market forces.)

Equipped with this perverse understanding of democracy, neoliberals like Friedman had no qualms over the military overthrow of Chile's democratically elected Allende government in 1973, because Allende was interfering with business control of Chilean society. After fifteen years of often brutal and savage dictatorship—all in the name of the democratic free market—formal democracy was restored in 1989 with a constitution that made it vastly more difficult (if not impossible) for the citizenry to challenge the business-military domination of Chilean society. That is neoliberal democracy in a nutshell: trivial debate over minor issues by parties that basically pursue the same pro-business policies regardless of formal differences and campaign debate. Democracy is permissible as long as the control of business is off-limits to popular deliberation or change; i.e., so long as it isn't democracy.

Neoliberal democracy therefore has an important and necessary by-product—a depoliticized citizenry marked by apathy and cynicism. If electoral democracy affects little of social life, it is irrational to devote much attention to it; in the United States, the spawning ground of neoliberal democracy, voter turnout in the 1998 congressional elections was a record low, with just one-third of eligible voters going to the polls. Although occasionally generating concern from those established parties like the U.S. Democratic Party that tend to attract the votes of the dispossessed, low voter turnout tends to be accepted and encouraged by the powers that be as a very good thing since nonvoters are, not surprisingly, disproportionately found among the poor and working class. Policies that quickly could increase voter interest and participation rates are stymied before ever getting into the public arena. In the United States, for example, the two main business-dominated parties, with the support of the corporate community, have refused to reform laws—some of which they put on the books—making it virtually impossible to create new political parties (that might appeal to non-business interests) and let them be effective. Although there is marked and frequently observed dissatisfaction with the Republicans and Democrats, electoral politics is one area where notions of competition and free choice have little meaning. In some respects, the caliber of debate and choice in neoliberal elections tends to be closer to that of the one-party Communist state than that of a genuine democracy.

But this barely indicates neoliberalism's pernicious implications for a civic-centered political culture. On the one hand, the social inequality generated by neoliberal policies undermines any effort to realize the legal equality necessary to make democracy credible. Large corporations have resources to influence media and overwhelm the political process, and do so accordingly. In U.S. electoral politics, for just one example, the richest one-quarter of 1 percent of Americans make 80 percent of all individual political contributions and corporations outspend labor by a margin of ten to one. Under neoliberalism this all makes sense; elections then reflect market principles, with contributions being equated with investments. As a result, it reinforces the irrelevance of electoral politics to most people and assures the maintenance of unquestioned corporate rule.

On the other hand, to be effective, democracy requires that people feel a connection to their fellow citizens, and that this connection manifests itself though a variety of nonmarket organizations and institutions. A vibrant political culture needs community groups, libraries, public schools, neighborhood organizations, cooperatives, public meeting places, voluntary associations, and trade unions to provide ways for citizens to meet, communicate, and interact with their fellow citizens. Neoliberal democracy, with its notion of the market *über alles,* takes dead aim at this sector. Instead of citizens, it produces consumers. Instead of communities, it produces shopping malls. The net result is an atomized society of disengaged individuals who feel demoralized and socially powerless.

In sum, neoliberalism is the immediate and foremost enemy of genuine participatory democracy, not just in the United States but across the planet, and will be for the foreseeable future. It is fitting that Noam Chomsky is the leading intellectual figure in the world today in the battle for democracy and against neoliberalism. In the 1960s, Chomsky was a prominent U.S. critic of the Vietnam War and, more broadly, became perhaps the most trenchant analyst of the ways U.S. foreign policy undermines democracy, quashes human rights, and promotes the interests of the wealthy few. In the 1970s, Chomsky (along with his co-author Edward S. Herman) began researching the ways the U.S. news media serve elite interests and undermine the capacity of the citizenry to actually rule their lives in a democratic fashion. Their 1988 book, *Manufacturing Consent*, remains the starting point for any serious inquiry into news media performance.

Throughout these years Chomsky, who could be characterized as an anarchist or, perhaps more accurately, a libertarian socialist, was a vocal, principled, and consistent democratic opponent and critic of Communist and Leninist political states and parties. He educated countless people, including myself, that democracy was a non-negotiable cornerstone of any post-capitalist society worth living in or fighting for. At the same time, he has demonstrated the absurdity of equating capitalism with democracy, or thinking that capitalist societies, even under the best of circumstances, will ever open access to information or decision making beyond the most narrow and controlled possibilities. I doubt any author, aside from perhaps George Orwell, has approached Chomsky in systematically skewering the hypocrisy of rulers and ideologues in both Communist and capitalist societies as they claim that theirs is the only form of true democracy available to humanity.

In the 1990s, all these strands of Chomsky's political work—from antiimperialism and critical media analysis to writings on democracy and the labor movement—have come together, culminating in work like *Profit Over People*, about democracy and the neoliberal threat. Chomsky has done much to reinvigorate an understanding of the social requirements for democracy, drawing upon the ancient Greeks as well as the leading thinkers of democratic revolutions in the seventeenth and eighteenth centuries. As he makes clear, it is impossible to be a proponent of participatory democracy and at the same time a champion of capitalism or any other class-divided society. In assessing the real historical struggles for democracy, Chomsky also reveals that neoliberalism is hardly a new thing; it is merely the current version of the battle for the wealthy few to circumscribe the political rights and civic powers of the many.

Chomsky may also be the leading critic of the mythology of the natural "free" market, that cheery hymn that is pounded into our heads about how the economy is competitive, rational, efficient, and fair. As Chomsky points out, markets are almost never competitive. Most of the economy is dominated by massive corporations with tremendous control over their markets and which therefore face precious little competition of the sort described in economics textbooks and politicians' speeches. Moreover, corporations themselves are effectively totalitarian organizations, operating along nondemocratic lines. That our economy is centered around such institutions severely compromises our ability to have a democratic society.

The mythology of the free market also submits that governments are inefficient institutions that should be limited, so as not to hurt the magic of the natural laissez-faire market. In fact, as Chomsky emphasizes, governments are central to the modern capitalist system. They lavishly subsidize corporations and work to advance corporate interests on numerous fronts. The same corporations that exult in neoliberal ideology are often hypocritical: they want and expect governments to funnel tax dollars to them, and to protect their markets from competition for them, but they want to be assured that governments will not tax them or work supportively on behalf of non-business interests, especially the poor and working class. Governments are bigger than ever, but under neoliberalism they have far less pretense to addressing non-corporate interests.

Nowhere is the centrality of governments and policymaking more apparent than in the emergence of the global market economy. What is presented by pro-business ideologues as the natural expansion of free markets across borders is quite the opposite. Globalization is the result of powerful governments, especially that of the United States, pushing trade deals and other accords down the throats of the world's people to make it easier for corporations and the wealthy to dominate the economies of nations around the world without having obligations to the peoples of those nations. Nowhere was the process more apparent than in the creation of the World Trade Organization in the early 1990s and the secret deliberations it held on behalf of the Multilateral Agreement on Investment (MAI).

Indeed, it is the inability to have honest and candid discussions and debates about neoliberalism in the United States and elsewhere that is one of its most striking features. Chomsky's critique of the neoliberal order is effectively off-limits to mainstream analysis despite its empirical strength and because of its commitment to democratic values. Here, Chomsky's analysis of the doctrinal system in capitalist democracies is useful. The corporate news media, the PR industry, the academic ideologues, and the intellectual culture writ large play the central role of providing the "necessary illusions" to make this unpalatable situation appear rational, benevolent, and necessary (if not necessarily desirable). As Chomsky hastens to point out, this is no formal conspiracy by powerful interests; it doesn't have to be. Through a variety of institutional mechanisms, signals are sent to intellectuals, pundits, and journalists, pushing toward seeing the status quo as the best of all possible worlds, and away from challenging those who benefit from that status quo. Chomsky's work is a direct call for democratic activists to remake our media system so it can be opened up to anti-corporate, anti-neoliberal perspectives and inquiry. It is also a challenge to all intellectuals, or at least those who express a commitment to democracy, to take a long, hard look in the mirror and to ask themselves in whose interests, and for what values, do they do their work.

Chomsky's description of the neoliberal/corporate hold over our economy, polity, journalism, and culture is so powerful and overwhelming that for some readers it can produce a sense of resignation. In our demoralized political times, a few may go a step further and conclude that we are enmeshed in this regressive system because, alas, humanity is simply incapable of creating a more humane, egalitarian, and democratic social order.

Chomsky's greatest contribution may well be his insistence upon the fundamental democratic inclinations of the world's peoples and the revolutionary potential implicit in those impulses. The best evidence of this possibility is the extent to which corporate forces go to prevent genuine political democracy from being established. The world's rulers understand implicitly that theirs is a system established to suit the needs of the few, not the many, and that the many therefore cannot ever be permitted to question and alter corporate rule. Even in the hobbled democracies that do exist, the corporate community works incessantly to see that important issues like the MAI are never publicly debated. And the business community spends a fortune bankrolling a PR apparatus to convince Americans that this is the best of all possible worlds. The time to worry about the possibility of social change for the better, by this logic, will be when the corporate community abandons PR and buying elections, permits a representative media, and is comfortable establishing a genuinely egalitarian participatory democracy because it no longer fears the power of the many. But there is no reason to think that day will ever come.

Neoliberalism's loudest message is that there is no alternative to the status quo and that humanity has reached its highest level. Chomsky points out that there have been several other periods designated as the "end of history" in the past. In the 1920s and 1950s, for example, U.S. elites claimed that the system was working and that mass quiescence reflected widespread satisfaction with the status quo. Events shortly thereafter highlighted the silliness of those beliefs. I suspect that as soon as democratic forces record a few tangible victories the blood will return to their veins, and talk of no possible hope for change will go the same route as all previous elite fantasies about their glorious rule being enshrined for a millennium.

The notion that no superior alternative to the status quo exists is more far-fetched today than ever, in this era when there are mind-boggling technologies for bettering the human condition. It is true that it remains unclear how we might establish a viable, free, and humane post-capitalist order—the very notion has a utopian air about it. But every advance in history, from ending slavery and establishing democracy to ending formal colonialism, has at some point had to conquer the notion that it was impossible to do because it had never been done before. As Chomsky points out, organized political activism is responsible for the degree of democracy we have today, for universal adult suffrage, for women's rights, for trade unions, for civil rights, for the freedoms we do enjoy. Even if the notion of a post-capitalist society seems unattainable, we know that human political activity can make the world we live in vastly more humane. As we get to that point, perhaps we will again be able to think in terms of building a political economy based on principles of cooperation, equality, self-government, and individual freedom.

Until then, the struggle for social change is not a hypothetical issue. The current neoliberal order has generated massive political and economic crises from East Asia to eastern Europe and Latin America. The quality of life in the developed nations of Europe, Japan, and North America is fragile and the societies are in considerable turmoil. Tremendous upheaval is in the cards for the coming years and decades. There is considerable doubt about the outcome of that upheaval, however, and little reason to think it will lead automatically to a democratic and humane resolution. That will be determined by how we, the people, organize, respond, and act.

13

The New Economy: Myth and Reality

In the last few years of the 1990s, the idea of a "New Economy" gained wide currency, almost rivaling "globalization" as a neologism that characterizes our era. Thus *The Economic Report of the President, 2001*, begins: "Over the last 8 years the American economy has transformed itself so radically that many believe we have witnessed the creation of a New Economy." This New Economy is seen, first and foremost, as consisting of those firms and economic sectors most closely associated with the revolution in digital technology and the growth of the Internet. The rapid convergence of information technologies—including computers, software, satellites, fiber optics, and the Internet—has, it is believed, fundamentally altered the economic landscape. Since the mid-1990s, these revolutionary technological developments have, it is argued, spilled over into the wider economy, generating higher productivity growth, a sustained acceleration of economic growth, lower unemployment, lower inflation, and an attenuation of the business cycle.

For many the focal point of the New Economy was the high-flying technology stocks that carried stock market speculation to new giddy heights during what came to be known as the "millennium boom." This was rationalized by business (though with growing nervousness after the sharp fall in technology stocks in the second half of 2000) as a measured response to the opportunities offered by the New Economy—and not simply a speculative bubble.

Meanwhile, a vast new wave of corporate mergers beyond anything ever seen before took place—for which the dual rationale was globalization and the rise of the New Economy.

No one was a stronger proponent of the New Economy thesis than former Federal Reserve chairman Alan Greenspan. In a speech on "Structural Change in the New Economy" delivered to the National Governors' Association on July 11, 2000, Greenspan argued that "it is the proliferation of information technology throughout the economy that makes the current period appear so different from preceding decades. . . . One result of the more-rapid pace of IT innovation has been a visible acceleration of the process that noted economist Joseph Schumpeter many years ago termed 'creative destruction'—the continuous shift in which emerging technologies push out the old." Among the advantages of the New Economy is the ability of corporations to generate a flood of information in miniseconds, allowing them to "reduce unnecessary inventory and dispense with labor and capital redundancies." In a speech on "The Revolution in Information Technology" delivered at Boston College on March 6, 2000, Greenspan claimed that "until the mid-1990s, the billions of dollars that businesses had poured into information technology seemed to leave little imprint on the overall economy." But beginning in 1995 that changed, and the spillover effects of digital technology were revolutionizing Old Economy sectors, making the New Economy a more universal phenomenon. "Computer modeling, for example, has dramatically reduced the time and cost required to design items ranging from motor vehicles to commercial airliners to skyscrapers."[1]

The New Economy has also been associated with the development of a more flexible workforce: non-unionized, highly mobile, just-in-time workers, sometimes embodying new job skills. Comparing the more highly unionized labor forces of Europe and Japan to that of the United States, Greenspan stated in July 2000: "The relatively inflexible and, hence, more costly labor markets of these economies appear to be a significant part of the explanation [of why the New Economy has been slower to develop there]. The elevated rates of return offered by the newer technologies in the United States are largely the result of a reduction in labor costs per unit of output. The rates of return on investment in the same new technologies are correspondingly less in Europe and Japan because businesses there face higher costs of displacing workers than we do."

The existence of the New Economy, in the sense of the advent of a dynamic information technology sector within the economy that has been a spur to accumulation, is not to be doubted. Clearly, it constitutes something distinct in the history of capitalism. Two other ideas associated with the New Economy are, however, more open to question. First, it is contended that the New Economy constitutes a new technological-industrial revolution, comparable to the introduction of the steam engine or the automobile in its effect on the overall economy, and that it is remaking the entire Old Economy in its image, ushering in a new era of permanently higher productivity. According to *Fortune* magazine (June 8, 1998), "The [computer] chip has already transformed our lives at least as pervasively as the internal-combustion engine or the electric motor." Second, it is often suggested that the New Economy has attenuated, if not altogether eliminated, the business cycle. Thus Thomas Petzinger Jr. observed in the *Wall Street Journal* (December 31, 1999) that "the business cycle—a creation of the Industrial Age—may well become an anachronism." In the balance of this piece, we will take a look at these two claims.

A New Industrial Revolution?

Some idea of the importance of the New Economy sector to the overall economy can be seen in the fact that although information technology only accounted for at most about 6 percent of GDP during the third quarter of 2000, about a quarter of the total economic growth since 1995 can be attributed to this sector together with telecommunications.[2] As shown in table 1, the share of information technology investment in total investment in industrial equipment and software (equal to total private non-residential fixed investment minus investment in structures) rose from less than one-third in 1980 to more than one-half in 2000.

Are we then witnessing a new Industrial Revolution, equivalent to the first Industrial Revolution, which began at the end of the eighteenth century (centered on the steam engine), or the second industrial revolution, which began at the beginning of the twentieth century (centered on the automobile and electricity)? For many purveyors of the New Economy idea, not only is this a new industrial revolution, but it is this which has suspended all economic

TABLE 1

Information Technology Investment in the U.S. Economy, 1980-2000 (billions of dollars)

Year	(1) Total Investment in Industrial Equipment and Software	(2) Investment in Information Processing Equipment and Software[a]	(3) Col. 2 ÷ Col. 1 (percent)
1980	227.0	69.6	30.7
1985	334.3	130.8	39.1
1990	427.8	176.1	41.2
1995	620.5	262.0	42.2
1999	917.4	433.0	47.2
2000[b]	1,036.9	532.1	51.3

a. Includes computers, software, and other information processing equipment.
b. Data for 2000 is preliminary incorporating "advance" estimates for the fourth quarter.
Sources: *Economic Report of the President*, 2001, Table B-18, p. 296; *Survey of Current Business*, January, February 2001, National Income and Product Accounts, Table 5.4.

laws, including the business cycle, pointing to a period of long-term, rapid growth, with no foreseeable end.

The facts, however, support none of this hype. In this connection it is useful to distinguish between the sector that produces computers and where these products are used in the business economy. Contrary to a widespread view, computers are not used equally everywhere within business. Conference board economists Robert H. McGuckin and Kevin Stiroh have provided an analysis of the eight private sectors of the economy that use computers most intensively—each with more than 4 percent of their capital in the form of computers. This includes three service sectors—trade, FIRE (finance, insurance, and real estate), and other services, and five manufacturing sectors—non-electrical machinery, electrical machinery, printing and publishing, instruments, and stone, clay, and glass. The percentage of total value added in the economy and the share of computer capital input within business accounted for by each of these industries in 1991 is shown in table 2. Most significant is that 76.6

percent of all computer input within business in 1991 occurred in trade, FIRE, and other services (which encompasses various personal services, including legal services, health care and software). Only 11.9 percent of computer input into business is accounted for by the five computer-intensive sectors in manufacturing listed in table 2, and a further 11.5 percent by twenty-seven other industries (including agriculture, mining, transportation, construction, communication, and public utilities, among others).

TABLE 2

Eight Most Intensive Computer-Using Sectors, U.S. Economy, 1991

Sector	Percentage of Total Value-Added in the Economy	Percentage of Total Computer Capital Input within Business
Manufacturing		
Non-electrical Machinery[a]	2.2	4.6
Electrical Machinery	1.9	2.5
Printing and Publishing	1.7	2.4
Instruments	1.5	1.5
Stone, Clay, and Glass	0.6	0.9
Services		
Trade	15.4	14.2
FIRE[b]	14.7	32.2
Other Services[c]	25.1	30.2

a. Computer and office equipment is one of the classifications included in the Non-Electrical Machinery sector.
b. Finance, Insurance, and Real Estate.
c. Includes business and personal services e.g. software, health care, and legal services.

Sources: Robert H. McGuckin & Kevin J. Stiroh, "Computers Can Accelerate Productivity Growth," *Issues in Science and Technology* (National Academy of Sciences), vol. XIV, no. 4 (Summer 1998), Table 1, p. 42; Kevin J. Stiroh; "Computers, Productivity, and Input Substitution," *Economic Inquiry*, vol. 36, no. 2 (April 1998), pp. 175-91.

To be sure, the structure of demand for computers shown here is partly a reflection of the enormous weight in the economy assumed by services, and particularly financial services. But a technological revolution that finds more than three-quarters of its business demand in the service industries (including finance, retail and wholesale trade, marketing, legal services, health services, entertainment, and other personal services) may be seen as falling somewhat short of an all-round "industrial revolution."[3] The service industries, rather than representing high-productivity growth in the economy, generally represent just the opposite (if productivity growth means anything in this context).[4]

Indeed, when it comes to an empirical examination of the New Economy thesis that the digital revolution since the mid-1990s has heightened productivity throughout the economy, the most that can be said is that there still is little or no hard evidence that computers have generated much progress in this area. The upturn in productivity, which accompanied the upturn in the business cycle, has naturally encouraged the view that this can be explained by the information technology revolution. But is the jump of 1.33 percentage points in average annual rate of productivity growth—which rose from 1.42 percent in 1972–1995 to 2.75 percent between fourth-quarter 1995 and fourth-quarter 1999—really a result of the productivity-enhancing effect of information technology, spilling over into the overall economy? This question has been taken up most systematically by Robert J. Gordon, professor of economics at Northwestern University. Gordon "peels the onion" of productivity growth to show a surprising explanation, very different from the received truth in the establishment and the public. Gordon looked into the various factors contributing to the leap in rates of productivity. He explains and demonstrates the effect of a variety of contributing factors such as the cyclical upturn of the economy, technological acceleration in the production of computer hardware, and technological changes in factories producing durable goods. His striking result is that the contribution computer use has made is surprisingly low. Of the 1.33 percentage-point rise in productivity growth referred to above, only 0.07, "a mere pittance," can be attributed to the use of computer technology and software outside of durable goods production. In sum, he found that the effect of digital technology on productivity was small on the whole; such advance as there was took place almost entirely in the manufacture of durable goods.[5]

It is of course widely believed that the rapid expansion of the Internet has been the device that has allowed the productivity effects of the New Economy to diffuse throughout the economy. But the facts, as Gordon's analysis of productivity has shown, do not warrant such a conclusion at present. Computers are widely available in offices, but rather than increasing the productivity of business, the opposite effect often seems to apply, as employees use their corporate Internet access to look up stock quotes related to their personal investments, to do online shopping, or to carry on email correspondence. Studies show that consumer-oriented Web sites get their highest usage not in the evenings or on weekends, but in the daytime, Monday to Friday, when people are at work. The proliferation of laptop computers, faxes, satellites, the Internet, etc., has dramatically altered the newspaper business, yet between 1987 and 1997 productivity in the newspaper industry dropped by an average annual rate of 2.3 percent.[6]

The digital revolution certainly is a technological revolution with widespread effects; the important thing from an economic standpoint, however, is that it is not epoch-making, as in the case of the steam engine, the railroad, and the automobile. It still has not produced "a radical alteration in economic geography with attendant internal migrations and the building of whole communities," each requiring or making possible the production of numerous new goods and services, on the same scale as did the steam engine, the railroad, or the automobile in the first and second industrial revolutions.[7]

The Taming of the Business Cycle?

The economic expansion that began in March 1991 has been accompanied by an explosion of stock market valuations and of corporate (and consumer) debt. As Yale economics professor Robert Schiller observed in his book *Irrational Exuberance*:

> The Dow Jones Industrial Average . . . stood at around 3,600 in early 1994. By 1999, it had passed 11,000, more than tripling in five years. . . . However, over the same period, basic economic indicators did not come close to tripling. U.S. personal income and gross domestic product rose less than 30%, and almost half of this increase was due to inflation. Corporate profits rose less than 60%, and that from a temporary recession-depressed base.[8]

The "millennium boom," Schiller goes on to observe, is the "largest stock market boom ever." Price-earning ratios (the real S&P Composite Index for stock prices divided by the ten-year moving average of real corporate earnings on the index) hit 44.3 in January 2000, the highest level ever recorded up to that time, with the closest historical parallel in September 1929 (just before the stock market crash), when the ratio hit 32.6. For Schiller and many others the dizzying inflation of share prices on the stock market has all the character-istics of a classic speculative bubble, traceable to factors that have nothing to do with "rational economic fundamentals," given the much slower relative growth of earnings.

Significantly, it was Alan Greenspan, in a speech in Washington on December 5, 1996, who coined the term "irrational exuberance" to describe this dangerous situation. Here it is worth noting that there were a number of problems facing Greenspan in his role as Federal Reserve chairman. He had to try to keep the economy flying high as long as possible, and help to engi-neer a soft landing when it was not. Both of these aspirations are of course well beyond the powers of any individual or any institution, including the Federal Reserve chairman and the Federal Reserve Board. Hence, a certain amount of "jawboning" designed to influence the markets is part of the game. Greenspan's statements were often aimed at calming down the speculating, lest the market take a major dive and upset the apple cart, while also serving to warn business that there was a very real danger. At the same time his pro-nouncements more generally were aimed at rationalizing for investors the anarchy of the market, in order to build a general sense of stability and confi-dence. Thus just months after his "irrational exuberance speech," Greenspan was extolling the virtues of the New Economy. The ballooning of stock valu-ations and the seemingly over rapid growth of the economy in general were not irrational in the main, but were in large part justified by the productivity expansion brought on by the New Economy. It was now possible to have lower unemployment without the threat of inflation—precisely because of this growth of productivity. As it is now commonly put in the economic literature, the "speed limits" of the economy had changed.

Over the course of every long boom in the history of industrial capitalism, economic interests have sought to account for continuing growth and stock market expansion by arguing that a New Era has arisen, which has tamed, or even eliminated the business cycle. Such New Era pronouncements are always rooted in some notion of changing technology and/or business organization. Prior to the 1929 stock market crash that introduced the Great Depression, it was commonly argued that a New Era had emerged with the growth of the large monopolistic capitals, which were able to manage and regulate the econ-omy more efficiently, smoothing out the economic swings and decreasing or eliminating the downswings altogether. Irving Fischer, professor of economics at Yale, and the most prestigious U.S. economist of his day, is reported to have declared, on the basis of such New Era thinking—just prior to the stock market peak in 1929 (which was closely followed by the crash)—that "stock prices have reached what looks like a permanently high plateau."[9]

Similar views are being promoted today. For example, in a July/August 1997 article titled "The End of the Business Cycle?" for *Foreign Affairs* (the leading U.S. foreign policy journal, published by the Council for Foreign Relations), Steven Weber argued that "changes in technology, ideology, employment, and finance, along with the globalization of production and consumption, have reduced the volatility of economic activity in the industrialized world. For both empirical and theoretical reasons, in advanced industrial economies the waves of the business cycle may be becoming more like ripples."

Greenspan himself, though hardly claiming that the business cycle had been eliminated, suggested, as we have seen, that the increased control of inventories resulting from the development of computerized information systems and just-in-time production had enormously reduced the forces generating recession. "Prior to the IT revolution," he argued in a speech before the Joint Economic Committee of Congress on June 14, 1999, "the paucity of timely knowledge of customers' needs and of the location of inventories and materials flows throughout complex production systems" necessitated the maintenance of "substantial programmed redundancies," including "doubling up on materials" if businesses were to function properly. In the New Economy, however, business management has been able "to remove large swaths of inventory safety stocks and worker redundancies." The advent of processes such as bar-scanning devices and satellite location of trucks has reduced delivery times. The growth of Internet Web sites has speeded up and in some cases streamlined the way business transactions are conducted.

Moreover, along with his claim that structural productivity growth had shifted upward with the advent of the New Economy, Greenspan also insisted that wages had been kept down and unit labor costs restrained by increased job insecurity of workers at any given level of unemployment, due to globalization and the creation of more flexible labor markets, which were taken as hallmarks of the New Economy. Consequently, workers threatened by "flexibility" (which has often meant the growth of nonstandard and contingent jobs, such as work through temporary help agencies) opt for job security where possible rather than rocking the boat with wage demands. In testimony before the Joint Economic Committee on March 20, 1997, Greenspan noted: "In 1991, at the bottom of the recession, a survey of workers at large firms by International Survey Research Corporation indicated that 25 percent feared being laid off. In 1996, despite the sharply lower unemployment rate and the tighter labor market, the same survey organization found that 46 percent were fearful of a job layoff."

The argument on job insecurity, which focuses on a more intense class struggle imposed from above and the increasing costs of losing a job (particularly given the rising indebtedness of the working class), gets closer to the truth in explaining why "wage inflation" did not ignite during the economic expansion, than do claims regarding structural improvements in productivity. Nevertheless this argument, like all other dominant economic perspectives, suffers from a view of the business cycle ushered in by monetarism and Reaganomics that sees inflation (especially so-called wage inflation) as the primary cause of recessions. The truth is that economic downturns have more fundamental causes related to accumulation, the buildup of overcapacity, etc., that are relatively independent of mere price movements. It is not a squeeze on profit margins, due to rising wage costs—supposedly forcing firms to raise prices—that generally accounts for the onset of economic crisis. More important is the overinvestment and overexpansion of debt that occurs whenever the forces that initially propelled the boom start to peter out. And underlying this are structural problems of overexploitation, uneven distribution of income of wealth, and lack of effective demand that are always present under capitalist conditions. Such basic truths of accumulation, which were widely acknowledged in the days of the Keynesian revolution, remain as valid today as ever—the New Economy notwithstanding.

The deceleration of real GDP growth in the fourth quarter of 2000, dropping from 2.2 percent in the third quarter to 1.1 percent in the fourth quarter, generated widespread concern within business. Most ominous was that real nonresidential fixed investment fell 0.6 percent in the fourth quarter, as opposed to a rise of 7.7 percent in the third, with investment in equipment and software declining by 3.5 percent. All of this occurred simultaneously with a dramatic drop in the NASDAQ stock index (dominated by dot-coms), followed by a general decline on the New York Stock Exchange.

Whether these events presage a full-fledged economic crisis, no one knows at this point [late February 2001]. What is significant, however, is the surprise with which this apparent turnaround was viewed even in supposedly knowledgeable quarters. Some had clearly come to believe, history notwithstanding, that periods of rapid *technological* progress were themselves guarantees against business downturns. Others had bought into the idea that the New Economy was new precisely in the New Era *extra-economic* sense of overcoming the business cycle. The point to remember, however, is that business cycles have been a regular feature of capitalism since the early part of the nineteenth century and continue to live on despite dreams about the flood of information available to corporations in miniseconds, and similar notions. None of the empirical and theoretical claims associated with the New Economy—technological revolution, rising productivity, rising profit margins, and the like—are proof against the business cycle. Indeed, cyclical downturns most often occur not in spite of but because of such developments. That is, a high rate of accumulation can itself lead to crisis. Overexpansion of capacity relative to consumer buying power is an essential feature of a capitalist economy throughout its history—in the state of competitive capitalism, in the monopoly stage, and in the current phase of accelerating globalization and new technology.

Nor is the expansion of the financial system, including the participation of more and more people in speculative markets, a guard against crisis. Financial crises, like economic crises more generally, are endemic to accumulation under capitalism. Such economic instability arises not from mismanagement, shortage of information, or lack of business and consumer confidence, but from the dynamics of class-based accumulation. The outstanding contribution made by the new technology in creating mountains of information that can spread around the world at the speed of light can contribute to a meltdown of the money markets as effectively as it contributed to its ballooning. News or hints of a break in the fragile financial network, which is based on thinly spread layers of debt, can reach the money market headquarters with a speed too fast for central banks to prevent a chain reaction on the way down.

Next to Greenspan himself, Michael Mandel, economics editor for *Business Week*, has probably done more than anyone else to propagate the current New Economy hype. Yet, instead of arguing that the New Economy is impervious to the business cycle, Mandel wrote a book, *The Coming Internet*

Depression, that points to the probability of a severe New Economy crisis, arising specifically out of what he calls the "tech cycle." The tech cycle, Mandel argues, stands for the fact that "the business cycle has been reincarnated in a different garb for the information age." The expansion phase of the tech cycle, he says, is characterized by rapid technological innovation; easy available funding for start-ups (as a result of venture capital); strong productivity growth; investment booms as companies scramble to keep up with the technology; the holding down of inflation due to productivity gains and competitive pressures; and buoyant stock markets. All of this conveys the main thrust of the New Economy idea. But Mandel says that there is also a contraction phase to the New Economy's tech cycle: technological stagnation; the drying up of venture capital; weak productivity growth; falling investment; rebounding inflation; and depleted stock markets. Insofar as the tech cycle is seen as displacing the traditional business cycle, Mandel's analysis is altogether questionable. But his claim that the various forces that sent the New Economy up can also, once these forces have been spent, lead to its turning down—and indeed account for a drastic downturn—adds an element of rationality to the New Economy hype. High tech, Mandel argues, means "high volatility."

Making things even more perilous, Mandel argues, is the extent to which the New Economy boom has been financed by debt, both corporate and household, which introduces the possibility of cascading defaults. The ratio of household debt to disposable income rose from 80 percent in 1989 to around 100 percent today.[10] The debt of non-financial corporations, meanwhile, rose by 34 percent between the beginning of 1997 and the beginning of 2000. Such extensive borrowing means more pain in the downturn of the cycle—particularly for workers who have borrowed out of necessity to compensate for stagnant real wages.

It is also worth noting that the United States benefited in the 1990s from the relative prosperity of its economy in relation to Europe and Japan. An economic resurgence in Europe and Asia, however, Mandel warns, could "trigger a financial crisis in the U.S., and perhaps even globally." The New Economy boom in the U.S. had been financed to a considerable extent by an expanding flow of money from overseas. "In 1995," he notes, "foreign money was only 8% of total U.S. investment (residential and business). By the first quarter of 2000, foreign money had risen to 26% of total investment." All of this has made the United States a net debtor on a massive scale, "with the value of its overseas liabilities exceeding the estimated value of assets overseas by more than $1 trillion at the end of 1999." It is conceivable that such conditions could lead to a devastating run on the dollar causing foreign investors to pull out their investments even more quickly than they put them in. This could generate a global financial crisis. With "a sell-off of the dollar," as economists John Eatwell and Lance Taylor wrote in *Global Finance at Risk*, "the potential disequilibria—portfolio shifts away from the U.S., bigger international obligations on its debt, and growing financial stress on the household sector—could begin to feed on one another and on the views of the markets. At that point . . . all hopes for global macro stability could disappear." The globalization of the disastrous consequences of a New Economy bust could generate a world economic meltdown.

Michael Mandel's book, following the competitive dictates of the business-press market, is subtitled *Why the High-Tech Boom Will Go Bust, Why the Crash Will Be Worse Than You Think, and How to Prosper Afterwards.* This is prognostication and hyperbole, not science. Although it is entirely rational to recognize that the New Economy thesis, even if assumed correct, has its downside, which could lead to a severe crisis, it is good to remember that much of what is taken as already proven about the New Economy is illusion. The investment boom associated with the digital economy is real. But the thesis that there has been a structural (not cyclical) elevation of productivity throughout the whole economy, and that this (rather than the class struggle and the restructuring of the labor market) accounts for relatively high employment accompanied by relatively low inflation, is extremely doubtful at best. Indeed, the commonsense economic assumption that higher productivity automatically means higher economic growth is itself questionable. Some of the fastest expansion of jobs and value-added in the U.S. economy in recent decades has been in those sectors—services, and especially financial services—that are notorious for their low productivity gains, and that are associated with the accumulation of money capital rather than the expansion of production.

Hence, the economic downturn that now appears to be upon us will most likely have much more in common with a classic business cycle, in which the central role is played by the buildup of overcapacity, than with the "tech cycle" described by Mandel. Indeed, excess capacity is appearing in industry after industry and on a global scale. As reported by Floyd Norris in the

New York Times (February 16, 2001), the global telecommunications industry—the highest of high-flying sectors of the late-'90s boom—is facing a "black hole." The enormous capital expenditures have created capacity that far outruns demand. And credit has dried up, even as vast sums are needed to complete massive projects already well under way. "Weaker companies, meanwhile, are failing. 'Piece by piece, they are starting to default up the chain,' said Charles Clough of Clough Capital, a money management firm. . . . Eventually, there will be growth to absorb the excess capacity. But that will take years, not months. The financial markets have still not fully discounted the pain to come."

There is no question that the magical new technology of the information age has dramatically changed aspects of personal and social life. It promises to do even more as time goes by. Indeed, all major technological revolutions over the course of capitalist development have contributed their share in altering the way we live. But in no case did any of these earlier technological revolutions create a new economy, or a new tech cycle, any more than has today's digital revolution. The economic laws of motion of capitalism remain in force.

We are living through an unprecedented situation marked by dramatic new developments, including not only the New Economy boom and bust, but also an unheard of polarization of wealth, rampant globalization, and the greatest merger wave in history aimed at the takeover of larger and larger sections of the world market by a relatively small number of global-monopolistic corporations. Rather than trying to predict what will happen under these rapidly changing circumstances we should be keeping our eyes on the main contradictions and tendencies that will feature prominently in any future developments, recognizing all along that this is a phenomenon of capital accumulation and crisis—and hence class struggle.

14

The Political Economy of International Communications: Foundations for the Emerging Global Debate About Media Ownership and Regulation

This chapter addresses the changing balance of public and private control over media and telecommunications in the global political economy, patterns of concentration and investment in the overall communication sector, and possibilities for improving the contribution of media and telecommunications to development in different parts of the world. I begin by discussing global media and then look at telecommunications. I conclude by making a few general proposals that would improve the possibility that media, telecommunications, and new information technologies could be more systematically used to improve the situation of disadvantaged groups and nations.

It is axiomatic in nearly all variants of social and political theory that the communication system is a cornerstone of modern societies. In political terms, the communication system may serve to enhance democracy, or to deny it, or some combination of the two. Less commented upon, although no less significant, the communication system has emerged as a central area for profit making in modern capitalist societies. A great deal of research is therefore carried out to assess the relationship of communication as a private activity to the broader and necessary social and political duties that are also to be performed by the same communication systems. This indeed is a central and recurring theme in media studies. The dual life of the communication system, at once a pivot of the emerging global economy and a key foundation of political democracy, constitutes a vital tension on the world stage. It is imperative that citizens organize to create new communication policies that will better preserve and promote democratic values.

Before doing that, it is important to debunk some of the mythology that impedes scholars from undertaking clear analysis, and prevents citizens from being effective participants in media and communication policymaking. One of these myths is the idea of the "free press," which emerged most dynamically in the United States, and now, with the rise of neoliberalism and the global media system, has increasingly become an international phenomenon. The unhelpful assumptions about relations between government and private sector in the media underlying this myth fog of the actual power relations at hand therefore inhibit the capacity to move toward establishing a more democratic and humane media system, and a more democratic and humane society. The assumptions take what is a complex and difficult problem for any society, how best to organize media and communication to protect core values, and turn it into a simplistic antagonism between the state and the media. There are several reasons for this faulty framework, but one stands out at the top of the list: the power of the dominant media and communication corporations to defend their interests and propagate a mythology to protect their privileged role in society. To do the mythology justice requires that the first part of this chapter focuses on the United States.

The Mythology of Freedom of Communications in the United States

The conventional view of the proper relationship of the government to the media, as it developed in the United States, is well known: the focus is on the free press, generated by private citizens independent of government censorship and control. Early in the history of the Republic, this meant media organized by religious organizations or political parties, even dissident parties out of power.[1] But over the course of U.S. history, the notion of a nongovernmental sector has come to mean that media and communication are, in effect, a function to be provided by profit-seeking businesses competing in the marketplace. (A broader notion of the nongovernmental sector—going well beyond the corporate-dominated, profit-driven private sector—remains in place in parts of Europe and across much of the world. To the extent the U.S. model is spreading, however, we may expect expanding pressure for the vision of the nonstate sector to be equated with the corporate sector.) According to conventional wisdom, the First Amendment to the U.S. Constitution guarantees this private freedom and as long as the government keeps its hands off the media, the flow of information and ideas will be safe. Without government intervention, a healthy media system will invariably rise from the rich soil of political freedom. Let the government intervene, no matter how well intended the intervention may seem, and alarm bells should go off in the minds of all liberal and right-thinking people. The government and the private media are by nature in conflict. To paraphrase the immortal words of Thomas Jefferson, if a society could have either media or government but not both, the sane choice for free people is media.

Even this summary account allows us to isolate some fatal shortcomings. It is not that the antagonism between the government and private media does not exist. Nor is it the very legitimate concern about state suppression of the press. To the contrary, what is inadequate and wrong about this conventional framing is the notion that the state plays little or no role in establishing the communication system, and that state-media relations naturally tend to be antagonistic, with the further implication that this antagonism leads invariably to a healthy democratic political culture.

In the United States as elsewhere, however, the state has always been a crucial and necessary player in the formation of successive communication systems. Not only did the United States Postal Service constitute the young nation's original—and highly dynamic and expansive—telecommunication infrastructure, but postal subsidies, which predate the revolution and are important to this day, likewise stimulated the rise of the newspaper and magazine industries. Other federal funding flows underwrote development of stage coach, railroad, steamship, and air transport industries in succession.[2] Government printing contracts subsidized the partisan press until the middle of the nineteenth century.[3] Libraries and public schools purchased books and created a readership for them.[4] Copyright, allowing authors limited right to monopolistic control over their output in exchange for their contributions to the public domain, was considered such an important policy that it was written into the Constitution. Without the government-sanctioned and enforced monopolies provided by copyright, the modern commercial communication system as we know it would be unthinkable.[5]

Early on, federal authorities also accorded large grants to the fledgling private telegraph systems of the United States.[6] Federal support, including funding, also helped underwrite the extension of a unified telephone network to rural areas. When broadcasting came along the government allocated monopoly rights to extraordinarily valuable spectrum. It did the same in granting monopoly rights to cable television franchises a few decades later. Although the government did not receive a penny in return for these monopoly rights, the value of this transfer of public property to private hands is placed in the hundreds of billions of dollars, if not more. Of the eight or nine massive media conglomerates that dominate the U.S. (and, increasingly, global) media system, the clear majority was built upon the super-profits and leverage generated by having a radio, television, or cable monopoly license. Once these firms wrest the valuable monopoly licenses, their public relations staff and executives—with no sense of irony—will sometimes sound the alarm bells about "government intervention" in the "free market," if some regulator discusses an unfavorable regulation.[7] In the corporate view, their privileges were won by Immaculate Conception, and should be regarded as natural and inviolable thereafter.

So the question is not whether the government plays a role in establishing communication systems, because it plays a foundational role. The question is, whose interests and what values do government communication policies encourage? When one puts the question this way, it has the effect of turning over what seemed like an unmovable rock and revealing a seamy underside of U.S. democracy. For the history of U.S. communication policy has been corrupted by powerful special interests, who repeatedly have done everything in their considerable power to prevent or deflect informed public participation. So it was in the 1920s and 1930s when a handful of private interests gained control over the airwaves and established commercial broadcasting in the United States, and so it has tended to be since.[8] Today the regulatory and policymaking process is arguably more corrupt than ever, as tens of millions of dollars have made members of Congress and regulators beholden to powerful corporate lobbies, and the overwhelming majority of the public has no clue that policies are being made in their name but without their informed consent.[9]

Very much in accord with the larger pattern of capitalist development in the United States over the past two hundred years, the communication system changed from a local and small-scale enterprise during the nation's first few generations to a concentrated site of massive profit generation by the end of the nineteenth century. Newspapers had been highly partisan institutions closely connected to the political process for the first fifty to one hundred years of the Republic's history. By the Progressive Era, newspapers, still the dominant news medium, were beginning to be held by big chain owners and an increasing number of communities came to have but a single newspaper or, perhaps, a duopoly.[10] This generated an early crisis in communications—an early expression of the tension between market practices and democratic values.

The traditional partisanship of the press, where the editorial perspective of the paper invariably reflected the perspective of the owner, would no longer work. It was one thing to have highly partisan journalism in competitive markets where a broad range of views were available and where a new newspaper could be launched without massive amounts of capital. It was quite another thing to have highly partisan journalism in monopolistic markets where barriers to entry prevented any new competition. In that environment, highly partisan journalism was suspect from a democratic perspective. It should be added that the partisanship was generally of a stridently pro-capitalist, anti-labor perspective.[11]

This was nothing short of a legitimacy crisis for capitalist media in a democratic society. There was much sentiment among progressives and socialists to radically transform the press system to make it a nonprofit institution under the control of communities.[12] The ultimate solution was far less radical: it was the emergence and consolidation, early in the twentieth century, of so-called professional journalism, which was to be nonpartisan, politically neutral, and, to its most fervent acolytes, objective. For the first time the editorial content in the news media would not automatically reflect the viewpoints of the owner (or, increasingly, the advertiser). Journalism would be produced by trained professionals who would not even let their own values cloud their judgment. There were no journalism schools in the United States in 1900; by the First World War almost all the major journalism schools had been established, almost always at the behest of powerful publishers.[13]

In the conventional wisdom, professional journalism solved the problem of monopoly capitalist control over the media for a democratic society. It did and does no such thing, however. Alongside its merits, which are trumpeted to all corners of the world, professional journalism also tends to generate a tepid journalism that reflects the range of existing elite opinion. It therefore reinforces conventional business-as-usual politics and marginalizes the new, the critical, and the radical, especially if it is threatening to entrenched economic interests. It presupposes the capitalist status quo as the natural and proper democratic ordering of social life. On the most ominous work of the state that requires the greatest democratic monitoring, engaging in war, professional journalism has proven to be mostly a stenographer to those in power. All in all, it provides little threat to the "weak" democracy that characterizes the United States today, with its tolerance for corruption combined with rampant citizen ignorance and depoliticization.[14]

In short, when one combines all of the above, the often stated idea that the private communication system has an adversarial relationship with a government hell-bent on socialism is ludicrous. Even a more temperate version of the same argument should be regarded with suspicion. Private, corporate media and governments are far better seen as partners, and both are far more adept at serving those who sit atop the social pyramid than those who are found closer to the bottom. This is a "weak" democracy by traditional standards. Indeed, the main defense of the current caliber of democracy in the United States is that it is the best one can hope for.

The Move to Neoliberalism: The U.S. System Goes Global

The United States is important in this context because it is the U.S. model of communication provision (including both media and telecommunications) that is being exported across the planet. Policy debates have been similar in many nations, except that outside the United States, public interest advocates have tended to be somewhat more successful and corporate media interests perhaps have not been as effective. The emergence of powerful systems of public broadcasting in most of the world's democracies in the twentieth century is a testament to the strength of anti-corporate citizens lobbies. As far as issues of global communication policy—telegraphy, telephony, spectrum allocation, and so forth—are concerned, these have almost always been hashed out among the elite of the nation-states, with minimal public involvement. The most powerful nations dominated successive rounds of negotiations, the United Kingdom before the First World War, and the United States after 1945.[15]

The odd ones out, so to speak, in this arrangement, have been the world's poor nations. Prior to the 1960s, most of those located in Asia and Africa were colonies and others, like the small Latin American republics, were treated like semi-colonies. Their communication systems were designed to suit the needs of the colonial masters. Following the post–Second World War wave of national independence, the so-called Third World nations organized a campaign to establish the New World Information and Communication Order (NWICO).[16] The idea, developing within the more encompassing context of a demand by these countries for a New International Economic Order, was to insist—in the United Nations Educational, Scientific, and Cultural Organization (UNESCO) and other venues—that industrialized countries provide the resources needed by poor nations to establish viable communication systems of their own, allowing them to become genuinely independent of their former colonizers. This program was far from perfect or well organized, and it met with an icy response from industrialized countries. Capping years of unrelenting effort to divert, deflect, or derail it, the United States under President Ronald Reagan (and its chief ally, the United Kingdom, under prime minister Margaret Thatcher) withdrew from UNESCO. The movement's disintegration followed, as the global political economy began to be reorganized on some new lines.[17]

In fact, the trajectory followed since the 1980s by the global political economy has run directly counter to notions like the NWICO. The age of neoliberalism, or corporate globalization, unleashed national and international policies highly supportive of business domination of all social affairs—with minimal countervailing force. The market became the font of all that was good and true in the world. Profit-seeking corporations and globe-trotting investors were the heroes of economic development. Unions, tariffs, taxes, public investment, and regulations—anything that got in the way of corporate accumulation strategies—were the evil demons on the world stage. Government was to be lean and mean, at least with regard to serving the interests of the poor or working class. With regard to the needs of the wealthy and large corporations, governments were to be sympathetic and benevolent, though this point was not to be given much attention. The idea that people could govern their lives through informed self-government and a vibrant public sphere was dismissed as overrated; after all, such political cultures invariably interfered with the market and tended therefore to be economically inefficient. Instead people were only to be trusted in the market, as buyers and sellers. Everything else was secondary.

Why has this taken place? The dramatically altered context of the 1990s—not only the continuing enlargement of the defining unit of contemporary enterprise, the transnational corporation, but also the collapse of Soviet socialism, coupled with China's embrace of the market—created new space in which to reorganize and expand the processes of capitalist globalization. The agencies of market-led development were quick to make use of these opportunities. Corporate foreign direct investment shot skyward, and a spectacular surge ensued in cross-border corporate mergers and acquisitions: the value of completed cross-border buyouts rose from less than $100 billion in 1987 to $1.14 trillion (current dollars) in 2000.[18] Under way was a reconfiguration of ownership and operations that was remaking nationally integrated markets and production systems into "a global market for goods and services and . . . an international production system, complemented by an increasingly global market for firms."[19] This transformation, still ongoing, both relies on and largely motivates a concurrent process of corporate-led transformation around communications.[20]

Few industries, indeed, have been as changed by capitalist globalization as communications. Before the 1980s and 1990s, national media systems were typified by domestically owned radio, television, and print media. There were considerable import markets for films, TV shows, music, and books, and these markets tended to be dominated by U.S.-based firms. But local commercial interests, sometimes combined with a state-affiliated broadcasting service, were both substantial and significant. Media systems were primarily national, and often possessed at least limited public-service features. Telecommunication monopolies were generally under the direct control of state ministries of posts and telecommunications, and these unitary national networks coordinated international traffic flows using standard rate-sharing formula.[21]

All of this began to change rapidly as a transnational corporate-commercial communication system began to be crafted and a new structural logic put in place. The conventional explanation of globalized communication centers

on technology suggested that radical improvements in communication technology make global media flows and global business operations feasible and
that, in general, this is all to the good. However, this is a misleading account.
Underlying new communication technology has been a political force—the
shift to neoliberal orthodoxy, which relaxed or eliminated barriers to commercial exploitation of media, foreign investment in communication systems, and
concentrated media ownership. There is nothing inherent in the technology
that requires neoliberalism; new digital communications could be used, for
example, simply to enhance public service provision if a society elects to do
so. Encased in a framework of neoliberal practice and policy, however, communications instead suddenly become subject to transnational corporate-
commercial development.

The rise of neoliberalism was complex but, where possible, carefully
orchestrated. The U.S. government, in particular, aggressively and persistent-
ly acted as if only a profit-driven media system as in the United States, with
U.S.-style professional journalism, could be considered acceptable for a free
society. As many nations came up short in that department, the government
worked to eliminate barriers so the world's people could have greater exposure if not to U.S.-based, then at least to U.S.-style commercial media. Once
the national deregulation of media took place in major countries like the
United States and the United Kingdom, it was followed by transnational
measures like the North American Free Trade Agreement (NAFTA) and the
World Trade Organization (WTO), all intent on establishing regional and
global marketplaces.[22] However, the United States selectively opened significant portions of its unrivaled domestic media market, chiefly in film, recording, and publishing, but with limited extension as well to broadcasting and
telecommunications to increasingly extensive foreign corporate investment.

Neoliberal development of the global media system has not been unop-
posed. While emerging media conglomerates pressed for policies to facilitate
their domination of markets throughout the world, strong traditions of protection for domestic media and cultural industries persisted. Countries ranging
from Norway, Denmark, and Spain to Mexico, South Africa, and the Republic
of Korea keep their small domestic film production industries alive with government subsidies. In the summer of 1998, culture ministers from twenty
countries, including Brazil, Mexico, Sweden, Italy, and Côte d'Ivoire, met in
Ottawa to discuss how they could build some ground rules to protect their

cultural fare from what they referred to as the Hollywood juggernaut. Their main recommendation was to keep culture out of the control of the WTO. A similar gathering in 1998, sponsored by UNESCO in Stockholm, recommended that culture be granted special exemptions in global trade deals. The basic trend, just the same, was clearly in the direction of opening markets ever further to corporate-commercial exploitation. If the WTO is explicitly a pro-commercial organization, the International Telecommunication Union (ITU) has only become one after a long march from its traditional commitment to public service values in telecommunications.[23]

Proponents of neoliberalism in every country argue that cultural trade barriers and regulations harm consumers, and that subsidies inhibit the ability of nations to develop their own competitive media firms. Strong commercial-media lobbies within countries often assert that they have more to gain by opening up their borders than by maintaining trade barriers. In 1998, for example, when the UK government proposed a voluntary levy on film and theater revenues (mostly Hollywood films) to benefit the UK commercial film industry, UK broadcasters, not wishing to antagonize the firms who supply their programming, lobbied against the measure until it died.

The European Commission (EC), the executive arm of the European Union (EU), also finds itself in the middle of controversy concerning media policy. On the one hand, the EC is committed to building powerful pan-European communication companies that can go toe-to-toe with the U.S.-based giants. On the other hand, it is committed to maintaining some semblance of competitive markets, so it occasionally rejects proposed media mergers as being anti-competitive.[24] The wave of commercialization of European media has put the EU in the position of condemning some of the traditional subsidies to public service broadcasters as "noncompetitive."[25] Despite some controversy, public service broadcasting, once the media centerpiece of European social democracy, was placed on the defensive, and increasingly reduced to locating a semi-commercial niche in the global system.[26] Yet, as a quasi-democratic institution, the EU is subject to some popular pressure that is unsympathetic to commercial interests. But, rather than reversing, this only qualifies the general direction.

To grasp the momentous, multifaceted changes in political-economic structure that resulted from acceptance, or at least acquiescence, to neoliberal principles, one must start with the global system, and then factor in differences at the national and local levels. This chapter first examines the media sector and then telecommunications. "What you are seeing," says Christopher Dixon, media analyst for the investment firm PaineWebber, "is the creation of a global oligopoly. It happened to the oil and automotive industries earlier this century; now it is happening to the entertainment industry." A few leading conglomerates thus dominate the larger process of reorganization, and aspire to grow still larger and more diversified to reduce risk, avoid being outflanked by rivals, and enhance profit-making opportunities. The upside is high; this is a market that some anticipate will have trillions of dollars in annual revenues within a decade.

The Global Media System

The rise of a global corporate media oligopoly has two distinct but related facets. First, it means the dominant companies—roughly one-half U.S.-based, but all with significant U.S. operations—are moving across the planet at breakneck speed. The new mantra for these dominant companies is to capitalize on the potential for growth abroad without being outflanked by competitors—in part because the U.S. market is well developed and only permits incremental expansion; in part because advertisers increasingly demand the ability to market to most-desired consumers on an integrated transnational basis; and in part because, to sell most effectively, program-sourcing and distribution too are being reconstituted as transnational operations. As Viacom chief executive officer (CEO) Sumner Redstone has put it, "Companies are focusing on those markets promising the best return, which means overseas." Frank Biondi, former chairman of Vivendi's Universal Studios, asserts that "99 percent of the success of these companies long-term is going to be successful execution offshore."

The dominant media firms increasingly present themselves as supranational entities. Bertelsmann CEO Thomas Middelhoff bristled when, in 1998, some said it was improper for a German firm to control 15 percent of both the U.S. book publishing and music markets. "We're not foreign. We're international," Middelhoff said. "I'm an American with a German passport." In 2000 Middelhoff proclaimed that Bertelsmann was no longer a German company. "We are really the most global media company."[27] Likewise, AOL Time

Warner's Gerald Levin stated, "We do not want to be viewed as an American company. We think globally."[28] And Vivendi Universal's CEO, Maurice Messier, who lives in New York as well as Paris, has rejected any hint that the company he heads is French.

Second, consolidation within and across each and every market segment is the order of the day. As local and regional media markets develop, specific companies—in many cases, new ones, built up around privatized broadcast systems or constituted around new media—began to link up rapidly with one or another of a few emergent global giants. In each industrial niche, in turn, concentration duly increased, even as new subsidiaries of huge global media conglomerates continued to form. To give a small example, the U.S. market for educational publishing was controlled by four firms in 2000, whereas it had two-dozen viable players as recently as 1980.[29]

The logic guiding media firms in all of this was clear, get very big very quickly, or get swallowed up by someone else, just as it was in many other industries. "There will be less than a handful of end-game winners," the CEO of Chase Manhattan announced in September 2000. "We want to be an end-game winner."[30] In short order, the global media market came to be dominated by nine transnational corporations (TNCs): General Electric (owner of NBC), Liberty Media, Disney, AOL Time Warner, Sony, News Corporation, Viacom, Vivendi Universal, and Bertelsmann. None of these companies existed in its present form as recently as fifteen years ago; in 2000, nearly all of them rank among the largest 200 non-financial firms in the world.[31] Of the nine, only five are truly U.S. firms, though all of them have core operations there. Between them, these nine companies own the major U.S. film studios; the U.S. television networks; 80–85 percent of the global music market; the majority of satellite broadcasting worldwide; all or part of a majority of cable broadcasting systems; a significant percentage of book publishing and commercial magazine publishing; all or part of most of the commercial cable TV channels in the United States and worldwide; a significant portion of European terrestrial television; and on and on and on.

These behemoths were created by the largest merger movement ever to hit the communication industry. "I'm a great believer that we are going to a world of vertically integrated companies where only the big survive," said Gordon Crawford, an executive of Capital Research & Management, a mutual fund that is among the largest shareholders in many of the nine firms listed above.[32]

For firms to survive, *Business Week* observes, speed is of the essence—"time is short."[33] The rapidity of the consolidation process has indeed been positively stunning. "In a world moving to five, six, seven media companies, you don't want to be in a position where you have to count on others," Peter Chernin, the president of News Corporation states. "You need to have enough market-place dominance that people are forced to deal with you." Chernin elaborates: "There are great arguments about whether content is king or distribution is king. At the end of the day, scale is king. If you can spread your costs over a large base, you can outbid your competitors for programming and other assets you want to buy."[34] By 2000, massive cross-border deals, like Pearson merging its television operations with CLT and Bertelsmann, or Vivendi purchasing Universal, were increasing in prominence.[35] Through such takeovers, in turn, large chunks of national communication industries were recast as units of transnational combines.

Chernin's firm, Rupert Murdoch's News Corporation, though it lags behind some of its rivals in revenues, may be the most aggressive global trail-blazer, but cases also could be made for several of the others. Murdoch spun off Sky Global Networks in 2000, consolidating his satellite television services that run from Asia to Europe to Latin America.[36] His Star TV dominates in Asia with thirty channels in seven languages.[37] News Corporation's television service for China, Phoenix TV, in which it has a 45 percent stake, in 2000 reached 45 million homes there and enjoyed an 80 percent increase in advertising revenues (admittedly from a small base) over the prior year.[38] And this barely begins to describe News Corporation's entire portfolio of assets: Twentieth Century Fox films, Fox TV network, HarperCollins publishers, television stations, cable TV channels, magazines, over 130 newspapers, and professional sports teams.

Consolidation within the global media system is linked strongly to reciprocal changes in the structure of world advertising. Advertising is a business expense made preponderantly by the largest firms in the economy. The commercial media system is the necessary transmission belt for business to market their wares across the world; indeed, globalization as we know it could not exist without it. A whopping three-quarters of global spending on advertising ends up in the pockets of a mere twenty media companies.[39] Spending on advertising grew by leaps and bounds in the past decade as television was opened to commercial exploitation, and was increasing at more than twice the rate of the growth of gross domestic product (GDP) before the bottom fell out of the market in 2001.[40] Five or six super-advertising agencies emerged over the same span to dominate this $400 billion global industry. The consolidation in the global advertising industry was just as pronounced as that in global media, and the two are related. "Mega-agencies are in a wonderful position to handle the business of mega-clients," one ad executive notes.[41] It is "absolutely necessary . . . for agencies to consolidate. Big is the mantra. So big it must be," another executive stated.[42]

But we must not neglect an important second tier of less than 100 firms, which are national or regional powerhouses. Between one-third and one-half of second-tier firms come from North America; most of the rest are from Western Europe and Japan. Sometimes these companies control niche markets, like business or trade publishing. Many national and regional conglomerates have been established on the backs of publishing or television empires, as in the case of Denmark's Egmont. Each of these second-tier firms is a considerable enterprise in its own right, often ranking among the 1,000 largest companies in the world and doing more than $1 billion per year in business. In the countries where they are economically significant, they characteristically exercise an important influence over domestic policymaking. The roster of second-tier media firms from North America includes Dow Jones, Gannett, Knight-Ridder, Hearst, and Advance Publications, and among those from Europe are Mediaset, Prisa, Pearson, Reuters, and Reed Elsevier. The Japanese companies, aside from Sony, remain almost exclusively domestic producers. Several others are based in less developed countries.

Although the continuing proliferation of new media has created some new opportunities for smaller firms, across the globe there has been a shakeout in national and regional media markets, with smaller units getting eaten by medium firms and medium firms being swallowed by big ones. Compared with ten to twenty years ago, a much smaller number of much larger firms now dominate the media at the national and regional levels. In the United Kingdom, for example, one of the few remaining independent book publishers, Fourth Estate, was sold to Murdoch's HarperCollins in 2000.[43] A wave of mergers has left German television advertising—the second-largest television market in the world—in the hands of Bertelsmann and the remnants of the Kirch Group.[44] Indeed, a wave of mergers has left all of European terrestrial television dominated by five companies, three of which rank in the global first tier.[45]

The situation may be most stark in New Zealand, where the newspaper industry is largely the province of the Australian-American Rupert Murdoch and
the Irishman Tony O'Reilly, who also dominates New Zealand's commercial
radio broadcasting and has major stakes in magazine publishing; Murdoch
controls pay television. In short, the rulers of New Zealand's media system
could squeeze into a closet.

Second-tier corporations, like those in the first tier, themselves perceive a
need to reach beyond national borders. "The borders are gone. We have to
grow," the chairman of Canada's CanWest Global Communications stated in
2000. "We don't intend to be one of the corpses lying beside the information
highway."[46] "We have to be Columbia or Warner Brothers one day."[47] The
CEO of Bonnier, Sweden's largest media conglomerate, says that to survive,
"we want to be the leading media company in Northern Europe."[48] Australian
media moguls, following the path blazed by Murdoch, have the mantra:
"Expand or die." As one puts it, "You really can't continue to grow as an
Australian supplier in Australia." Mediaset, the Berlusconi-owned Italian television power, is angling to expand into the rest of Europe and Latin America.
Perhaps the most striking example of second-tier globalization is Hicks,
Muse, Tate and Furst, the U.S. radio/publishing/television/billboard/movie
theater power that has been constructed almost overnight. Between 1998 and
2000 it spent over $2 billion purchasing media assets in Mexico, Argentina,
Brazil, and Venezuela.[49]

Second-tier media firms are hardly "oppositional" to the global system.
This is true as well in developing countries. Mexico's Televisa, Brazil's
Globo, Argentina's Clarin, and Venezuela's Cisneros Group, for example, are
among the world's 60 or 70 largest media corporations. These firms tend to
dominate their own national and regional media markets, which have been
experiencing rapid consolidation as well. They have extensive ties and joint
ventures with the largest media TNCs as well as with Wall Street investment
banks. In Latin America, for example, the second-tier firms work closely with
the U.S. giants who are carving up the commercial media pie among themselves. Televisa or Globo can offer News Corporation, for example, local
domination of the politicians and the impression of local control over their
joint ventures. And like second-tier media firms elsewhere, they are also establishing global operations, especially in countries that speak the same language. As a result, the second-tier media firms in the developing countries

tend to have distinctly pro-business political agendas and to support expansion of the global media market, which puts them at odds with large segments of the population in their home countries.

Together, less than 100 first- and second-tier giants control much of the world's media: book, magazine, and newspaper publishing; music recording; television production; television stations and cable channels; satellite television systems; film production; and motion picture theatres. But the system is still very much in formation. The end result of all this activity by second-tier media firms may well be the eventual creation of one or two more giants, and it almost certainly means the number of viable media players in the system will continue to plummet. Some new second-tier firms are emerging, especially in lucrative Asian markets, and there will probably be further upheaval among the ranks of the first-tier media giants. And corporations get no guarantee of success merely by going global. The point is that the new structural logic of the communication industry leaves them little choice in the matter. To anticipate a point made more fully below, some, perhaps many, will falter as they accrue too much debt or as they enter unprofitable ventures. However, we are probably closer to the end of the process of establishing a stable global media market than to the beginning. And as it takes shape, there is a distinct likelihood that the leading media firms in the world will find themselves in a very profitable position. That is what they are racing to secure.

The global media system does not conform to the axiomatic principle of competition propounded by mainstream economists. Many of the largest media firms have some of the same major shareholders, own portions of one another, or have interlocking boards of directors. When *Variety* compiled its list of the fifty largest global media firms for 1997, it observed that "merger mania" and cross-ownership had "resulted in a complex web of interrelationships" that would "make you dizzy." The global market strongly encourages corporations to establish equity joint ventures in which the media giants all own a part of an enterprise. This way, firms reduce competition and risk, and increase the chance of profitability. As the CEO of Sogecable, Spain's largest media firm and one of the twelve largest private media companies in Europe, expressed it to *Variety*, the strategy is "not to compete with international companies but to join them."

In some respects, indeed, the global media market more closely resembles a cartel than it does the competitive marketplace found in economics textbooks. In competitive markets, in theory, numerous producers work hard and are largely oblivious to each other as they sell what they produce at the market price, over which they have no control. This fairy tale, still regularly regurgitated as being an apt description of our economy, is ludicrous when applied to the global media system. The leading CEOs are all on a first-name basis and they regularly converse. Even those on unfriendly terms, like Murdoch and AOL Time Warner's Ted Turner, understand they have to work together for the "greater good." "Sometimes you have to grit your teeth and treat your enemy as your friend," the former chairman of Universal, Frank Biondi, concedes.[50] The head of Venezuela's huge Cisneros group, which is locked in combat over Latin American satellite television with News Corporation, says about Murdoch: "We're friends. We're always talking."[51] Moreover, all the first- and second-tier media firms are connected through their reliance upon a few investment banks like Morgan Stanley and Goldman Sachs that direct most of the huge media mergers. Those two banks alone put together fifty-two media and telecom deals valued at $450 billion in the first quarter of 2000, and 138 deals worth $433 billion in all of 1999.[52]

The issue of cartelized coordination versus true economic rivalry is a complicated one and in some respects the system still generates fierce corporate and market competition. But in the political realm, above all, support for deepened corporate-commercial system development is both concerted and general. This form of conscious coordination makes the media giants particularly effective political lobbyists at the national, regional, and global levels.

But what about media content? Global conglomerates can at times have a progressive impact on culture, especially when they enter countries that had been tightly controlled by corrupt, crony-controlled media systems (as in much of Latin America) or those that had significant state censorship over media (as in parts of Asia). The global commercial media system is radical in that it will respect no tradition or custom, on balance, if it stands in the way of profits. But ultimately it is politically conservative, because the media giants are significant beneficiaries of the current social structure around the world, and any upheaval in property or social relations—particularly to the extent that it reduces the power of business—is not in their interest.

The "Hollywood juggernaut," or the specter of U.S. cultural imperialism, remains a central concern in many countries for obvious reasons. Exports of U.S. films and television shows increased by 22 percent in 1999, and the list of the top 125 grossing films for 1999 is made up almost entirely of Hollywood fare.[53] When one goes country by country, even a "cultural nationalist" country like France had nine of its top 10 grossing films in 1999 produced by the Hollywood giants.[54] "Many leftist intellectuals in Paris are decrying American films, but the French people are eating them up," a Hollywood producer noted.[55] Likewise, in Italy, the replacement of single-screen theaters by multiplexes has contributed to a dramatic decline in local film box office revenues.[56] The moral of the story for many European film-makers is that you have to work in English and employ Hollywood moviemaking conventions to succeed.[57] In Latin America, channels controlled by media giants overwhelm local cable television and the de facto capital for the region is Miami.[58]

The notion that Hollywood firms are merely purveyors of U.S. culture is ever less plausible as the media system becomes increasingly concentrated, commercialized, and globalized. The global media system is better understood as one that advances corporate and commercial interests and values, and denigrates or ignores that which cannot be incorporated into its mission. There is no discernible difference in the firm's content, whether they are owned by shareholders in Japan or France or have corporate headquarters in New York or Sydney.

As the media conglomerates spread their tentacles, there is reason to believe they will encourage popular tastes to become more uniform in at least some forms of media. Based on conversations with Hollywood executives, *Variety* editor Peter Bart concluded, "The world film-going audience is fast becoming more homogeneous." Whereas action movies had once been the only surefire global fare—with comedies considerably more difficult to export—by the late 1990s, comedies like *My Best Friend's Wedding* and *The Full Monty* were doing between $160 million and $200 million in non-U.S. box-office revenues.

When audiences appear to prefer locally made fare, the global media corporations, rather than flee in despair, globalize their production. Sony has been at the forefront of this, producing films with local companies in China, France, India, and Mexico, to name but a few.[59] India's acclaimed domestic film industry—Bollywood—is also developing close ties to the global media giant.[60] This process is even more visible in the music industry. Music has always been the least capital-intensive of the electronic media and therefore the most open to experimentation and new ideas. U.S. recording artists generated 60 percent of their sales outside the United States in 1993; by 1998 that figure was down to 40 percent. Rather than fold their tents, however, the four media transnationals that dominate the world's recorded-music market are busy establishing local subsidiaries in places like Brazil, where "people are totally committed to local music," in the words of a writer for a trade publication. Sony, again, has led the way in establishing distribution deals with independent music companies from around the world.

With hypercommercialism and growing corporate control comes an implicit political bias in media content. Consumerism, class inequality, and individualism tend to be taken as natural and even benevolent, whereas political activity, civic values, and anti-market activities are marginalized. The best journalism is pitched to the business class and suited to its needs and prejudices; with a few notable exceptions, the journalism reserved for the masses tends to be the sort of drivel provided by the media giants on their U.S. television stations. In India, for example, influenced by the global media giants, "the revamped news media . . . now focus more on fashion designers and beauty queens than on the dark realities of a poor and violent country."[61] This slant is often quite subtle. Indeed, the genius of the commercial media system is the general lack of overt censorship. As George Orwell noted in his unpublished introduction to *Animal Farm*, censorship in free societies is infinitely more sophisticated and thorough than in dictatorships, because "unpopular ideas can be silenced, and inconvenient facts kept dark, without any need for an official ban."

Lacking any necessarily conspiratorial intent and acting in their own economic self-interest, media conglomerates exist simply to make money by selling light escapist entertainment. The late Emilio Azcarraga, the billionaire founder of Mexico's Televisa, reflected this position in saying that Mexico was a country with a modest, downtrodden class, which would always be downtrodden, and television had "the obligation to bring diversion to these people and remove them from their sad reality and difficult future."[62] The combination of neoliberalism and corporate media culture tends to promote a deep and profound depoliticization. One need only look at the United States to see the logical endpoint.[63] But depoliticization has its limits, as it invariably runs up against the fact that we live in a social world where politics have tremendous influence over the quality of our lives.

Finally, a word should be said about the Internet, the two-ton gorilla of global media and communications. The Internet is increasingly becoming a part of our media and telecommunication systems, and a genuine technological convergence is taking place. Accordingly, there has been a wave of mergers between traditional media and telecom firms, and each of them with Internet and computer firms. Already companies like Microsoft, AOL Time Warner, and Telefónica have become media powerhouses in their own right. It looks like the global media system is in the process of becoming a globally integrated, commercial communication system where a handful of "super-companies" will rule the roost. The notion that the Internet would "set us free" and permit anyone to communicate effectively, hence undermining the monopoly power of the media giants, has not materialized. To the extent the Internet becomes part of the commercially viable media system, it seems to be under the thumb of the usual corporate suspects. Although the Internet offers extraordinary promise in many regards, it betrays no intrinsic anti-commercial logic or principle. Paradoxically, commercially viable media content Internet sites remain few and far between—and, today, it would be difficult to find an investor willing to bankroll any additional attempts. This shift attests to a sea change in the overall economic climate.

Global Consolidation: A Two-Stage Process

The pace and extent of communication industry reorganization have been breathtaking. Yet two stages in the consolidation process should be distinguished. During the first phase, between the mid-1980s and the year 2000, mergers and acquisitions across media industry segments and across national borders were especially prolific. Complexities and obstacles, of course, were evident. Rupert Murdoch almost drove his News Corporation into bankruptcy around 1990 by buying too much too fast. In some countries, moreover, especially developed market economies such as Germany and the United States, limits continued to be placed on foreign corporate takeovers of domestic electronic media. But the process of consolidation continued, enabled and, in important ways, driven, by the high-flying stock market, which inflated the valuations of the very largest companies to astonishing levels. In the first half of 2000, reaching fever pitch, the number of merger deals in global media,

Internet, and telecommunications totaled $300 billion, triple the figure for the first six months of 1999, and exponentially higher than the figure ten years earlier.[64] The currency used for most of these transactions was the inflated stock of the acquiring company but, because takeover targets also enjoyed inflated valuations, these were unprecedentedly expensive transactions full of fat fees for helping lawyers, accountants, and investment bankers.

But then, the neoliberal reorganization of global communications shifted into a distinctly different phase, itself a direct outgrowth of the first. It was abundantly clear by 2001, following the collapse of the technology stock bubble, that transnational consolidation in the communication industry had ceased to be driven by the upward movement of share prices and the resulting euphoria of investors (and, often, executives) about virtually any proposed transaction. Henceforth, system development would be governed by different considerations. To be sure, the new framework continued to be set by the financialized capitalism that had established the mores of the casino as the core principles of the political economy. Predictably enough, with the collapse of the technology stock bubble in 2000, it would be the dog-eat-dog logic of the shakeout that dominated. Companies rendered suddenly vulnerable by nuances of what had been a generally shared past practice entered a period of multifaceted crisis.

A vital result of the buildup of would-be global communication companies over the course of the 1990s was massive corporate indebtedness. Using inflated stock to pay for equally overvalued acquisitions and selling bonds in order to outbid rivals competing for programming rights, communication companies found themselves saddled with enormous debt loads; Disney, to choose an example, in 2002 owed $11.9 billion for sports programming for its ESPN and ABC networks.[65] AOL Time Warner carried $22.8 billion in debt at the end of 2001, before it paid $7 billion to Bertelsmann to extricate from a prior partnership venture.[66] Company after company found itself reeling from obligations; some, such as Adelphia, a second-tier U.S. cable operator, apparently tried to hide them. This growing debt overhang ultimately became a source of profound instability.

Blue-chip media behemoths found themselves declaring staggering, unprecedented, write-offs; after its market value plunged from $290 billion to $135 billion, AOL Time Warner, to take the most egregious example, was set to take an "impairment charge for goodwill" of $54 billion.[67] But other giants, from Vivendi Universal to News Corporation to Liberty Media, followed down the same track.[68] Purporting that these were only an accounting convenience, the companies were actually taking gigantic financial losses, as well as admitting that future profits would not be what they had earlier forecast.

Even in developed market economies such as Germany and the United Kingdom, the turmoil that resulted was sufficient to jeopardize leading components of existing national communication systems. In the United Kingdom, the costs of obtaining soccer rights knocked the world's biggest digital terrestrial television project (ITV Digital, backed by UK broadcasters Granada and Carlton Communications) to its knees, even as NTL, the country's largest cable television system operator, reported a $15.8 billion loss and defaulted on interest payments on its even larger debt—triggering a restructuring process that seemed certain to alter the control structure of British television.[69] "Britain may soon be left with one cable television operator and British Sky Broadcasting, the satellite digital platform controlled by Rupert Murdoch," observed the *Financial Times* in 2002.[70] This debacle actually had wider repercussions, owing to the increased transnationalization of the industry. NTL had had a significant stake in one of France's biggest cable television companies, and when it defaulted the ownership of the company, Noos, came up for grabs.[71]

In Germany, meanwhile, the deeply indebted Kirch Group was compelled to enter into a restructuring that forced Leo Kirch himself out of a business he had controlled for half a century.[72] Far more important was that the resulting structural reorganization, however it turned out, was likely to push the country's media system in a more commercial direction. Possibly, the process would vest strategic control of Kirch in a foreign corporation—Rupert Murdoch, CEO of News Corporation, which indirectly controls a minority stake in one of Kirch's subsidiary companies, at one point convened a meeting with Kirch's German banking creditors in Los Angeles "to discuss its fate."[73] Such a power shift "would mark the first time foreigners have controlled a major broadcaster in the world's second-largest media market, and has many Germans fearing international media companies would introduce cut-throat competition and tabloid journalism to their TV market."[74] With a national election looming, the liquidation of Kirch threatened to become a political football, and it seemed possible that German interests would intervene to preserve national control.[75] In Argentina, where under International

Monetary Fund (IMF) tutelage much of the national economy had already been sold off to foreign owners, both cable television companies and telecom operators went into the limbo of default. The bank-led reorganization, that this prompted, hardly seemed a recipe for increasing public service and accountability.[76]

Thus powerful momentum was generated behind another round of industry consolidation, whose beneficiaries are ultimately likely to be the very largest and strongest global media companies. "Here comes another wave of media mergers," editorialized one industry enthusiast.[77] A comparable process gripped global telecommunications.

Telecommunications

The recent expansion of global access to voice telephony has been almost violent. During the 1990s, wire-line phone access shot upward, and increasing from a tiny base as recently as 1990, 1 billion mobile phones were in use by 2002. Yet, once again, change has been qualitative as well as quantitative.

Modernization of networks occurred mainly to support the expansion of transnational capitalism; but accelerated network development at the expense of prevailing policies and practices once again initially evolved within the postwar U.S. domestic market. By elevating the precepts of liberalization of commercial market entry, and rapid buildouts of specialized systems and services aimed at privileged user groups, U.S. policymakers empowered a few thousand giant corporations and their affiliated managerial and technical strata, as well as a burgeoning group of high-tech network system and service suppliers.

However, because large business users of telecommunications were mostly transnational companies, the U.S. model began to be exported by the 1970s. The political complexities of this transition were deftly managed. Responding to interventions by organizations of business users were U.S. Federal Communications Commission directives altering key ground rules for the conduct of U.S. international telecommunications.[78] Albeit with some internecine jostling, the World Bank, IMF, ITU, and other organizations enrolled in the liberalization effort. As the confidence of U.S. power groups increased, bilateral negotiations, U.S. trade law, and encompassing multilateral initiatives were all pursued. Ultimately, the institutional basis of world telecommunications was transformed.

As with the culture industry, the promise of access—in this case access to the gigantic U.S. domestic market for corporate network systems and services—functioned explicitly as a strategic weapon; as one Clinton administration trade official explained, "We boldly offered to open up our market fully, in return for concessions from others."[79] Access to the U.S. market did not come cheap.

The unremitting focus of U.S. agencies was enhanced market access for transnational corporate carriers, largely on behalf of their largest corporate customers. The then-deputy U.S. trade representative, Richard W. Fisher, elaborates: "In the end, the calculus was clear: any broad-based agreement that rapidly opened up global markets to U.S. firms clearly played to our advantages. While we were offering other countries access to a market no other country individually could match, a critical mass of market opening offers would provide opportunities that U.S. firms were uniquely positioned to exploit."[80] Fisher was referring specifically to the WTO Agreement on Basic Telecommunications, forged in 1997. This pact helped harmonize national operating frameworks, subjecting some seventy signatories to binding commitments enforced by a multilateral dispute settlement process, and thereby established more uniformly liberal market access to network equipment and services—worldwide.[81]

There really is no historical precedent for the institutional overhaul of world telecommunications on which the WTO agreement drew—and on which it builds. Between 1984 and July 1999, within a broader context of state-asset privatization, around $244 billion in state-owned systems were transferred to private ownership.[82] As a result, over half (ninety) of the 189 members of the ITU had wholly or partially privatized their existing telecommunication operators by 1999, and eighteen had done so completely. Of the remaining state-owned operators, more than thirty planned to privatize. The process itself was characteristically structured to ease market entry by transnational carriers. By early 2000, twenty-five countries had pledged to allow majority foreign-owned carriers seeking to furnish international voice service using their own wholly owned and controlled networks.[83]

Limits, of course, continued to be placed on the process of liberalization. An important one developed from the continuing role played by national governments within their domestic telecommunication industries. In many countries, including developed market economies such as Germany, France, and Japan, and poorer nations such as India and, prospectively, China, the state remained a dominant investor in a partly private dominant telecommunication operator. Elsewhere, as in Mexico, the state continued to grant various forms of preferment to national capital in telecommunications over transnational providers. Such constraints, now rendered "trade restraints" in conformity with the WTO-based regime, were closely monitored by U.S. authorities, who consistently sought to eliminate them.[84]

The fundamental goal, again, was to develop capacious and upgraded networks on a scale sufficient to underwrite transnational capitalist reorganization across the globe. Between 1990 and 2000, the volume of announced mergers and acquisitions in worldwide telecommunications totaled an estimated $1.616 trillion.[85] Cross-border takeovers constituted a significant share of this total. Just in the period between 1997 and 2000, the number of activated international private line circuits (referring to the in-house corporate and organizational telecommunication networks that employ leased circuits and other proprietary facilities on a full-time basis) increased more than tenfold, greatly outstripping the growth enjoyed by international dial-up circuits over the same interval.[86] Domestically integrated networks run by national flag carriers thus began to be superseded in scope and function by transnational systems. The result was to grant license to carriers and business users to assimilate networks as desired into a vast and growing range of business processes: payroll accounting, employment relations, inventory, sales, marketing, research and development, and so on. By revolutionizing network systems and services, large corporations acquired new freedom of maneuver in their attempts to reintegrate their operations and, collectively, the most dynamic segment of the larger market system, on a broadened, supranational basis.

Huge outlays were needed to provision digital capitalism with this central production base and control structure: transnationally organized networks, employing a lengthening list of media including wireless, telephone lines, cable television systems, fiber optics, satellites, and the software-defined means for network access, operation, and management. With the zealotry of a high-tech-oriented religious revival, through the late 1990s the financial markets seemingly answered every call for capital with a raft of network suppliers. As a bevy of entrepreneurs obtained the cheap debt financing they sought to build vast new networks, often employing Internet and related technologies, existing giants such as AT&T, WorldCom, and Sprint reacted by joining the stampede. The threat to wire-line systems evidently posed by wireless networks prompted an additional investment surge (though U.S. carriers did not become as exposed as their counterparts in western Europe, where carriers spent $100 billion on licenses to provide Internet-enabled wireless phone systems, and projected investment of another $100 billion to build such networks.[87] Rival network operators each spent billions of dollars a year to build systems with which to link office complexes throughout the world's central cities. Corporate network users based in every economic sector put out additional billions on the tangle of system hardware and software they needed to enlarge and modernize their burgeoning proprietary networks.

Network-related information technology investment by carriers and business users functioned as the pivot of the late 1990s U.S. economic boom.[88] Here, in the most highly developed core of the global market system, telecommunications in 1999 accounted for no less than 16 percent of the capital spending of Standard & Poor's 500.[89] Global expenditures on telecommunications, including both investment and service revenues, totaled trillions of dollars. But it cannot be emphasized enough that this astronomical investment outlay was chiefly financed with debt: worldwide, between 1996 and 2001, banks lent an estimated $890 billion in syndicated loans to the telecommunication industry; an additional $415 billion of debt was furnished by the bond markets; and $500 billion more was raised from private equity and stock market issues.[90]

The result was a sudden, stunning enlargement of information-carrying capacity, principally on profitable, high-density traffic routes. Most of the 39 million miles of fiber-optic cable circuitry laid in the United States over the last two decades of the twentieth century were installed between 1996 and 2000.[91] Especially, but not only, on U.S. trans-Atlantic and trans-Pacific routes, new submarine cable systems added unprecedented increments to available network capacity.[92]

Internet systems and services drew much of this investment, and in turn helped prompt a significant spatial reconfiguration. Between 1950 and 1975 or so, truly inclusive national telecommunication infrastructures had been established throughout the developed market economies.[93] By 1997–99, however, fully half of global telecommunication investment was being absorbed by "developing and transition," that is, non-OECD countries.[94] Might the less-developed nations at last "leap-frog" into an era of abundant network access? Might global channels of electronic communications finally be opened to the voices of the many? A top U.S. trade official enthused that the liberalized political economy of network systems was both magnificently benevolent and self-perpetuating: "Peer pressure by liberalizing countries has created a virtuous cycle where countries now compete for global investment by offering more attractive investment opportunities and more effective regulatory regimes."[95] Snowballing network investment would engender not only near-universal global access, but a treasure trove of informational benefits.

There is no denying that access to telecommunications has been expanded spectacularly. Despite the fascination and delight occasioned for a few years in the business press by corporate-led networking initiatives, the latter should not be romanticized: the real effects of networking the market system have been as contradictory as the political economy to which these systems themselves are hardwired. For example, the character of system development continues to be fundamentally uneven. Less capacious satellites still find heavy use by small, low-income countries, despite the fact that optical fibers offer greater efficiency and economy, because undersea cable operators lack incentive to make the giant up-front outlays needed to introduce fiber on these "thin routes." The world's coastal zones, similarly, may be connected to high-bandwidth cables but, as one market study delicately notes, "it can take much longer for terrestrial infrastructure to reach inland areas." Metropolitan-area networks (MAN), finally, may be proliferating throughout western Europe and the United States, but—the same study continues—"economically less-developed regions and countries may have a long wait before MAN build-out reaches their cities."[96] Deepening overcapacity in some markets, in other words, is matched by unremitting undersupply in others.

Moreover, global network development has revealed and, in some cases, actually created, new kinds of vulnerability. Burgeoning transnational network systems steeply accelerated the speed and volume of international financial capital flows—some implications of which became painfully evident, for example, in the Asian financial crisis of 1997–98. However, the September 11, 2001, attacks on New York's World Trade Center crippled 3.5 million private data lines for corporate customers, including some 20 percent of the data lines serving the New York Stock Exchange.[97] Newfound vulnerabilities also afflicted the auto industry and other innovators of just-in-time inventory systems when, following the attacks, cross-border trucking and air transport were delayed and disrupted.

Overall social priorities also continued to be skewed, from above, to reflect the needs of business network users and investors. As market entry policies were relaxed, specialized services aimed at corporate users were intensively cultivated, and system development conformed ever more closely to transnational corporate preferences. In the United States, as national priorities shifted from roads, airports, power plants, and bridges to telecommunication networks, these existing infrastructures deteriorated—and the hectic pace and giant scale of disruptive telecom network buildouts itself contributed to this erosion.[98] Corporate ownership and performance norms were established, and profits were made to flow disproportionately to investors rather other interests, while the existing, often very limited, social welfare character of the telecommunication industry was undercut. Characteristically, rates were "rebalanced" to favor business users (above all, those making international calls) over low-volume residential callers.[99] In what had been a heavily unionized industry, collective bargaining rights were typically withheld from employees working to build and service newly deregulated network systems; and layoffs as a by-product of competition became standard practice.[100] Quality of service, now more comprehensively tied to the ability to pay, declined for many households.[101] Cheats and scams, overbilling of calling-card users, illegally transferring long-distance accounts to new carriers, charging telephone users for services they did not order—became standard practice throughout large portions of the now-deregulated industry.[102] Finally, the "virtuous" investment cycle propelled by networks actually massively destabilized the accumulation process.

Stoked by investment bankers and beguiled by business plans that had forecast uninterrupted exponential growth of Internet traffic, telecommunication carriers took on gargantuan debt to finance their network modernization and expansion projects. In two years, British Telecom's debt ran up to 50 billion euros, Deutsche Telekom's to 60 billion euros, and France Telecom's to 64 billion euros.[103] Across the Atlantic Ocean, newly founded U.S. communication carriers alone were carrying a total of $74 billion in debt by late 2000, requiring an annual interest expense of about $7 billion;[104] and AT&T's debt reached a high of perhaps $62 billion late in 2000.[105] During 2001, all told, some $250 billion of telecommunication industry debt (mostly bonds), a share of which bore rapidly declining ratings, needed to be refinanced.[106]

Debt finance had led to an equally unparalleled buildup of network capacity. Scattered analysts began to worry that the scale of duplicative system expansion might be outpacing demand by the late 1990s, when "private-line" circuit prices were dropping sharply, with the prospect of further significant declines (European bandwidth prices, likewise already decreasing, were projected to decline by 50 percent a year for several years).[107] Prices for circuits on transoceanic fiber-optic cables experienced analogous, though uneven, declines.[108] But Wall Street analysts imperturbably forecast continued profit growth, and investment capital continued to pour into the industry. In consequence, by one account a mere 2.6 percent of U.S. long-distance network capacity was actually in use in early 2001.[109] Comparable overcapacity was apparent throughout Europe, and in transoceanic submarine cable systems, where "each new Atlantic cable adds as much bandwidth as all the previous infrastructure put together."[110]

In the last half of 2000, amid the rapid decline of technology stocks, telecommunication industry executives began to reckon with the glut that market liberalization had induced. The ensuing debacle dwarfed the near-concurrent rout of the dot-coms. And George Gilder's vaunted "telecosm," with its promise of "infinite bandwidth," now looks more like a body-strewn battlefield than a cornucopia.[111] The stock market value of the entire telecommunication sector, including operators and equipment manufacturers, fell by $3.8 trillion between its peak (of $6.3 trillion) in March 2000, and September 2001—between four and five times the combined losses on all of Asia's stock exchanges during the Asian financial crisis of the late 1990s, estimated at $813 billion.[112]

Huge financial losses began to be reported, first by big telecom equipment manufacturers such as Lucent, Nortel, and Ciena, and upstart competitive service providers such as Global Crossing, Level 3, and Metromedia Fiber. But by 2002 it was clear that even the dominant telecommunication operators were not immune to the slide. Qwest, BellSouth, and WorldCom showed growing weakness, as did the debt-saddled KPN, France Telecom, and Deutsche Telekom in Europe.[113] Japan's NTT took a $16 billion charge—the largest ever reported by a non-financial Japanese corporation—to meet the losses produced by its multibillion-dollar investments in the U.S. network industry.[114] The spiral of destabilization cast in question the very survival of blue-chip companies like AT&T.[115]

Debt reduction suddenly became the industry's overriding priority. Still deferring to investors, telecommunication industry executives now undertook a drum roll of competitive rate cutting, network investment pullbacks, employee layoffs, asset sales, business reorganizations, and bankruptcies. Telecommunication industry bonds, widely classed as sub-investment-grade ("junk") offerings, constituted as much as one-third of the entire junk bond market by 2001.[116] Job losses in the technology sector dominated by networks constituted 41 percent of the 650,000 jobs eliminated in the United States between January 1 and May 31, 2001.[117] Broadband system development in the United States slowed markedly, as even the "world powers of interactivity," as a rival executive recently called AOL Time Warner and Microsoft, together with the giant local telephone companies, pared investments in this still strategically crucial area.[118]

The ultimate costs of the industry's rivalrous network-building binge remained ominously unclear. As technology spending by business users and the carriers that sought to serve them plummeted, the newfound centrality of that investment within the global economy ensured that the decline's repercussions ramified outward.[119] Because networking provided an increasingly general platform for new cycles of capital accumulation, it was likewise notably implicated in a resurgence of economic stagnation. In mid-2001, central bankers continued to worry that, appearances to the contrary notwithstanding, the telecommunication crisis (as the *Financial Times* reported) "could still destabilize the global financial system."[120]

Revelations about accounting chicanery at major telecommunication companies did little to enhance the picture.[121] But it seems that obscure accounting innovations, deployed as a strategy for bolstering apparent revenues and profits, were engendered on a vast scale throughout the U.S.-based industry, at least. Early in 2002, it seemed all but certain that this continuing meltdown would bring about a new cycle of transnational concentration in telecommunications; when Sweden's Telia agreed to purchase Finland's Sonera in March 2002, therefore, analysts openly cast the deal as "a starting shot for consolidation."[122]

Conclusion

For much of the 1990s even those who were alarmed by the antidemocratic implications of the neoliberal globalization process tended to be resigned. The power of the capitalist profit motive was such that it could not be prevented from establishing a world system based on transnational corporations and markets, and unchecked capital flows. Likewise, the globalization of the corporate media system continued. As one Swedish journalist noted in 1997, "Unfortunately, the trends are very clear, moving in the wrong direction on virtually every score, and there is a desperate lack of public discussion of the long-term implications of current developments for democracy and accountability."[123] It was presented as unexceptionable, natural, or inexorable. And for those in power, those who benefited by the new regime, such thinking made their jobs vastly easier.

But, as we said at the outset, the truth is that there is nothing "natural" about neoliberal globalization. It requires extensive changes in government policies and an increased role for the state to encourage and protect certain types of activities. The massive and complex negotiations surrounding NAFTA and the WTO provide some idea of how unnatural and constructed the global neoliberal economy is. Or consider copyright, and what has come to be considered intellectual property. There is nothing natural about this. It is a government-granted and enforced monopoly that prevents competition. It leads to higher prices and a shrinking of the marketplace of ideas, but it serves powerful commercial interests tremendously. In the United States, the corporate media lobby has managed to distort copyright so the very notions of the public domain or fair use, so important historically, have been all but obliterated. The U.S. government leads the fight in global forums to see that the corporate-friendly standards of copyright are extended across the planet and to cyberspace. The commitment to copyright monopolies, now granted for ninety-five years to corporations, as the *sine qua non* of the global economy shows its true commitment is to existing corporate power rather than to a mythological free market. And, although government coercion and press censorship remained a problem across the planet, with recent struggles between the state and the press taking place in Russia, Hungary, and Angola, an all-too-familiar contrary tendency was for the dominant commercial media to enjoy a cozy and corrupt relationship with the dominant political forces—not least, in the power centers of metropolitan capitalism.[124]

The traditional myth of the relationship of the state to the private sector in U.S. media has become the neoliberal myth on a global scale. The myth now has become transparently a tool of propaganda. The Enron affair highlighted again how closely intertwined the U.S. government is with the largest private corporations. The widespread graft associated with neoliberal privatizations and deregulations—in telecommunications more than anywhere else—has resulted in a wave of corruption of world historical proportions. If the market is God and public service is bunk, why on earth would anyone enter government, except to feather their own nest, by any means necessary? For those at the receiving end of neoliberal globalization—the bulk of humanity—the idea that people need to accept neoliberal globalization as a given is untenable. For those committed to democracy above neoliberalism, the struggle is to require informed public participation in government policy making. Specifically, in view of the importance of media, the struggle is to democratize communication policymaking.[125]

This goal is paramount, even in the context of seemingly more virulent problems and correspondingly more urgent reforms—food, water, medicine, and education. This is because the communication system comprises the indispensable institutional basis for social deliberation—discussion, debate, and decision making—beyond elite forums. Where the communication system is controlled by centralized profit-making groups—and where, today, is it not?—the people cease to have a means of clarifying social priorities and organizing for social reform.

There are no simple solutions to the question of how best to organize media and telecommunications to promote a healthy economy and democratic values, just like there is no simple answer to how best to structure the global political economy. Moreover, it is clear that the two debates are very closely related, in view of the significance of communications to both capitalism and democracy.

But two overarching principles are central to any reform platform. First, it is imperative that the debates on these topics be widespread and held up in the light of day. They must be democratized. If we know one thing from history it is this: if self-interested parties make decisions in relative secrecy, the resulting policies will serve the interests primarily of those who made them. As the old saw goes, "If you're not at the table, you're not part of the deal." Our job, as scholars, as citizens, as democrats, is to knock down the door and draw some more chairs up to the table. And when we sit at that table we have to come educated with the most accurate understanding of what is taking place and what is possible in order to determine what we can generate.

Second, the principle of public as opposed to corporate-commercial control must be reaccredited, strengthened, and enlarged. There are several proposals that have been made to strengthen and democratize the media and telecommunication sectors. Although there are significant differences in these proposals as one moves from one country to another, they all gravitate around a handful of ideas and principles. The sector independent of corporate and commercial control must be strengthened, and it is highly desirable to have a significant part of this sector insulated from direct control by the state.

SECTION III:
POLITICS AND MEDIA REFORM

The earliest incarnation of the first chapter in the section was initially written in graduate school in 1986 and the final chapter in the section was written in 2008. Over the course of twenty-two years, these chapters deal in one manner or another with media reform politics and organizing. Perhaps more than anything, these chapters provide a clear historical record of how dramatically the movement has grown and how markedly the terrain has shifted. They complement chapters in my books *It's the Media, Stupid* (2000), *Our Media, Not Theirs* (2002), *The Problem of the Media* (2004), *Tragedy & Farce* (2005), and *Communication Revolution* (2007), where I chronicle and assess the U.S. media reform movement in considerable detail. In this section I weave in the emerging dilemmas of neoliberalism and the digital communication revolution, as they are at the heart of understanding developments in media politics. To be blunt, it is where these two emerging dilemmas collide that we see the explosion of media reform activism. This, too, could have possibly been a stand-alone book, though I think it is stronger paired with the larger media critique.

15

Off-Limits: An Inquiry Into the Lack of Debate Over the Ownership, Structure, and Control of the Media in U.S. Political Life

It has become nearly axiomatic among scholars, political activists, and, indeed, the public at large that the agencies of mass communication play a very important role in modern societies. In particular, the media are seen as being central to the functioning of a society's polity and the development of its political culture. In many nations the very issues of how the media are controlled, structured, and subsidized are inexorably linked with issues of free expression and participatory democracy. Hence debates over media policy are carried on in the political arena and can attract popular discussion. And in a period of political upheaval and rapid social change, control over the media becomes an issue of the utmost importance.

These observations notwithstanding, the United States has remained distinctly immune from this tendency. Despite having a media structure that has become largely concentrated in the hands of enormous corporations and that earn the lion's share of their revenues from the advertising expenditures of other major corporations, U.S. political culture has failed to question the suitability, let alone the legitimacy, of its media system for the development and functioning of a democratic polity.[1] This remains the case despite a considerable body of evidence which suggests that the oligopolistic, commercial basis of the U.S. media has a pronounced impact upon the nature of the messages communicated to the citizenry. Allowing for oversimplification, the modern U.S. media tend to reinforce the fundamental economic and social contours of U.S. society while ignoring, trivializing, or demonizing social movements that challenge the legitimacy of the status quo.

Accordingly, the primary, if not exclusive, style of popular media criticism in the U.S. merely presupposes the institutional basis of the media system and posits the actions of individual reporters and editors as the independent variable. This mode of analysis reaches its apogee in the works of right-wing media critics who dismiss the corporate and commercial basis of the industry as being of any explanatory value and, rather, assert that the psychological and personal attributes of professional media workers are almost exclusively responsible for any bias to be found in the modern media. With few exceptions, these right-wing critics serve to "harass" media employees in order to pressure them to follow the broad corporate interests of their owners and advertisers and the corporate community as a whole, rather than veer from them in exercising their professional obligations.[2]

Three hypotheses are presented here to explain why analysis of and debate regarding the basic institutional and structural arrangements of the media system have been and are "off-limits" in U.S. political culture and why the type of criticism mentioned above proliferates. A presupposition for this discussion is the premise that a contemporary democratic society should determine the nature of its media system, and therefore the lack of such a debate is and has been a weak spot in U.S. political culture.

Three Hypotheses for the Lack of Debate Over Fundamental Media Structure

Before proceeding to the three hypotheses that account for why basic media issues are off-limits in U.S. political culture, it is necessary to mention the most frequently offered "casual" hypothesis for this state of affairs. This is, quite simply, that Americans don't care, not simply about media policy but about any traditional political issues whatsoever. This is a very important observation and an examination of this condition is arguably the single most important issue facing U.S. social scientists in the late twentieth century. However, this observation is at best a description of a situation; it really explains nothing. Indeed, it begs a number of critical intellectual questions. Most notably, the apathy, cynicism, and ignorance that have typified U.S. politics for some time can hardly be explained as some aspect of "human nature" or the innate "American" instinct. The preponderance of international, historical, and anthropological research argues to the contrary. Hence, the "apathy" thesis is only useful if it initiates vital research and debate. When offered as the final word on this subject, or any subject for that matter, one has left the realm of explanation and entered the domain of apologetics.

The first hypothesis is that the inability to publicly debate the capitalist basis of the media is a function of the general inability to make fundamental criticism of capitalism itself in U.S. political culture. Capitalism has been off-limits as a topic of political discussion since at least the First World War and arguably as far back as the 1890s. As one historian has noted hyperbolically, "After World War I, capitalism was made a part of the Constitution."[3] In the case of the broadcasting reformers, it was probably easier to criticize capitalism in the early 1930s than at any other time since the First World War, particularly in intellectual circles, but this point is often exaggerated.[4] It was still far from legitimate in political debate to question the capitalist basis of the political economy as was evidenced by the deference to the principle of private property elicited by most members of the opposition movement.

It lies outside the scope or capacity of this discussion to explain why capitalism became off-limits for critical discussion by the second decade of the twentieth century; suffice it to say that this coincided in broad historical terms with the maturation of corporate capitalism as the reigning political economic model and, moreover, with the ascension of U.S. capitalism to its position as the dominant force in the world economy. In addition, this removal of capitalism from the range of legitimate debate corresponded to the elimination of the left as a viable factor in U.S. political life since the First World War. And this removal of capitalism from the range of legitimate debate has made it that much more difficult for a left critique of U.S. society to reemerge in subsequent years. For the most part, the Left has struggled to maintain an identity and presence on the margins of the academe, divorced from any popular base, with all the pitfalls that entails for radical social theory and analysis.

The absence of a viable left has proven to be a critical factor accounting for the lack of debate over the control and structure of the media. In much of western Europe, for example, the groups that have tended to politicize the media often have been groups that tend to take a critical stance toward capitalism such as the Labour Party in Britain and the Social Democrats in Scandinavia. These groups have tended to recognize that concentrated private control and reliance upon advertising have, in effect, meant control by members of the capitalist class, which was inimical to their notion of a socialist democracy. This comparison should not be applied categorically, however; there is also a strong tradition for media policy to become resolved less on ideological lines than simply along logistical lines, as evidenced by the French Socialist "privatization" of broadcasting in the 1980s on the belief that the state system had been dominated by Gaullist Party sympathizers. In any case, the United States has not had any broad-based left political force since the demise of the socialists after the First World War that would, by definition, be hostile to the suitability of a capitalist media setup.

Beyond this lack of an agency organized to fundamentally challenge the prerogatives of capital, the inability to criticize capitalism has translated into two specific ideological problems for those inclined to bring the legitimacy of the corporate media structure into the political arena. First, capitalism's being off-limits means, almost by definition, that the propriety of private control for selfish purposes of society's productive resources, in general, is unassailable. In the debate over broadcasting in the 1930s, for example, the opposition movement was willing to challenge the private control of radio but not the private control of society; the reformers were willing to accept the marketplace as a satisfactory social arbiter elsewhere but not in the realm of broadcasting. Although their distinction was quite logical, it put them in a bind when they encountered the arguments of the commercial broadcasters. If the private marketplace was essentially good and democratic elsewhere, why not in radio? To all but some committed reformers this may have seemed an arbitrary distinction. The same dilemma has haunted the efforts of would-be reformers ever since.

Second, to the extent that capitalism has been removed from critical public evaluation, it has been characterized in the dominant culture in a highly sanitized fashion. The legitimate vision of capitalism is not that of an economic system that rests on a highly skewed class basis and that, in fact, re-creates a class system by its very operations. Rather, the sanitized and accepted version of capitalism is one of free and equal individuals voluntarily entering into exchange in the marketplace. This is not an entirely inaccurate description of capitalism; rather it is merely incomplete and therefore misleading when presented as the whole picture. Conspicuously absent is an acknowledgment of the class basis of production, which is the heart of the system, as even neoclassical economic theory acknowledges in the form of presupposition.[5]

It was a sanitized vision of capitalism that was emphasized by the commercial broadcasters in their ideological campaign in the 1930s. They were able to successfully attach commercial broadcasting to the ideological wagon that equated capitalism with the free and equal marketplace, the free and equal marketplace with democracy, and democracy with "Americanism." Hence the status quo easily became the "American Plan," where the public interest was assured, as it always was, by the machinations of the marketplace. Challengers to the efficacy of the marketplace in broadcasting drew the raised eyebrows of the dominant culture as malcontent "special interests," incapable of meeting the public's needs in the marketplace and therefore dispensers of essentially worthless "propaganda."

This was the powerful logic staring at the opposition movement in the 1930s. As Rosen concluded: "Any attempt to challenge or criticize the arrangement [commercial broadcasting] represented a direct assault on the larger society as well as a rejection of the nation's past."[6] Thus the inability, if not unwillingness to present an alternative vision of capitalism and U.S. society left the opposition movement in a tenuous position. This is not to say a "radical" approach to the debate would have been successful; rather, that a "mainstream" approach by definition was in the contradictory position of having to accept dominant ideological mores that seriously handicapped any reform efforts. In particular, an argument that private commercial radio undermined democracy necessitated an understanding of U.S. capitalism as a class system to be effective. This contradiction has plagued all subsequent efforts to politicize the issue of media control in the United States.

The second hypothesis for the lack of debate over the control and structure of the media is that the corporate media have actively cultivated, with considerable success, the ideology that the status quo is the only rational media structure for a democratic and freedom-loving society. The corporate media have encouraged the belief that even the consideration of alternatives was tantamount to a call for totalitarianism. In the 1930s, the proponents of commercial broadcasting spared no expense or effort to popularize this position, and with the demise of the opposition movement it quickly became unchallenged (and unchallengeable) in the dominant discourse. As David Sarnoff, president of the Radio Corporation of American, commented in 1936:

> I believe that a free radio and a free democracy are inseparable; that we cannot have a controlled radio and retain a democracy; that when a free radio goes, so also goes free speech, free press, freedom of worship, and freedom of education.[7]

The implications of this were not always left unspoken. "He who attacks the American system" of broadcasting, CBS president William Paley informed a meeting of educators in 1937, "attacks democracy itself."[8] A few years earlier a similar statement would have attracted outright derision.

In the 1930s the commercial broadcasters worked incessantly and successfully to grab hold on to the ideological coattails of the newspaper industry, which had built up a largely impenetrable ideological armor to protect its role in U.S. society. The depth of this "laissez-faire" ideology which prevents public discussion of, examination of, and intrusion into the affairs of the newspaper industry is staggering. The fundamental argument used by the commercial broadcasters to demand deregulation—in the late 1930s through today—is that despite the physical scarcity of the ether, broadcasting is more competitive than the largely monopolistic newspaper industry. They argue, therefore, that there is no longer any meaningful justification to single out broadcasters for regulation in the public interest.

Barron and others have taken this acknowledgment that the competitive market is no longer an accurate description for the newspaper industry to what, on the surface, would seem to be a logical conclusion: since the laissez-faire model based on access in a competitive market was no longer appropriate, and the marketplace was therefore an ineffective regulator, the state has a right to intervene as it has in broadcasting to assure that the press acts in the best interests of a democratic polity. Barron's effort to promote this idea was dismissed categorically.[9] Indeed, proponents of the status quo will even acknowledge the legitimacy of Barron's arguments, but simply refuse to countenance any alteration of the "laissez faire" ideology, regardless of the empirical evidence.[10] Even media critic Ben Bagdikian, whose work has been germinal in bringing attention to the antidemocratic implications of the corporate, commercial media system, simply presupposes the superiority of a capitalist media setup, despite all his evidence to the contrary.[11] The laissez-faire media ideology has been internalized to such an extent that it has become an article of faith for anyone committed to democracy.

Furthermore, given the oligopolistic basis of the modern media industries, an additional problem has presented itself to the commercial broadcasters and the major media corporations. They need not merely establish the capitalist media setup as the best possible system, but, moreover, they must establish that, unlike any alternative, the status quo is innately nonpartisan and committed to the truth rather than any sort of ideological axe grinding. This is a critical point that must be established by a highly concentrated media system, capitalist or otherwise; unless it can establish social neutrality, the very legitimacy of the system as a primary dispenser of political information is quickly, and rightfully, suspect. Hence in the early 1930s the commercial broadcasters placed great emphasis on establishing their social neutrality and debunking the opposition movement's charges of "private censorship."[12] The major media corporations have found two invaluable allies as they go about their ideological chores.

The first ally is found in the hundreds of departments and schools of journalism and communications that have sprung up over the past few generations in colleges and universities across the nation. These departments were frequently established at the behest of commercial media and rely upon maintaining close and cordial relationships with the commercial media. Even the most hard-hitting of criticism tends to pull punches when the legitimacy of the corporate media is challenged. As one media educator recently acknowledged in a trade publication:

> We all know, whether we're candid enough to acknowledge it or not, that the advertising, news and public relations industries that provide employment for our students—plus other benefits—expect us to follow the "company line" on issues involving the special interests of mass communication.[13]

These departments of journalism have had little difficulty, until quite recently, and then only in a handful of instances, accepting the corporate line that attacks on a corporate media system are attacks on a free press. Generations of students have been and are being trained that this is the best possible and only conceivable media system available to the U.S. people. The issue is generally not even open to contemplation.

The second ally is found in the ideology of professional journalism, which, regardless of its merits, is indispensable for the legitimation of an oligopolistic media system. It is not entirely coincidental that professional journalism emerged precisely as the newspaper industry was becoming a mature and concentrated industry.[14] Moreover, despite the ostensible claim that the ideology of professional journalism protects the news product from the pressures of advertisers and media owners attempting to cast undue influence over the news, the ideology of professional journalism clearly internalized the commercial dictates of the newspaper enterprise as it developed, in addition to internalizing the class structure and values of the emerging modern capitalist political economy. Professional journalism was far more a complementary than antagonistic development to the emergence of the modern capitalist media setup and modern capitalism itself.

Professional journalism serves as a critical agent for legitimation as it shifts responsibility for media performance from the broader economic context to the specific conduct of reporters and editors following a set of professional standards and operating within a presupposed broader context. Indeed, the logic of the ideology is such that the actual ownership and support mechanisms become incidental to explaining news media performance. Interestingly, not only does the ideology of professional journalism exempt media corporations from public scrutiny, it exempts the journalists themselves.

Paradoxically, as far as any form of media criticism is palatable to professional journalists, it is that from the Right, which receives ample play in the mainstream press.[15] Arguably, this is due to the flattering manner in which right-wing media criticism stresses the autonomy and power of the journalists and editors over the news product. More important, the criticism of the press as being too disrespectful of authority—as the Right routinely charges—is necessary for the legitimation of the profession. The alternative of a press corps being roundly praised by conservatives for their subservience to the powers-that-be would hardly meet even the rudimentary standards for a profession and would cast the legitimacy of the entire media structure into doubt. In this sense, those like Noam Chomsky have a point when they argue that journalists would have to invent right-wing criticism if it did not already exist.

A similar open-mindedness toward criticism does not extend to those questioning the very legitimacy of media institutions. To some extent this may be due to the relative powerlessness left media critics ascribe to individual reporters and editors, seen mostly as hostages to their institutions, sources, and professional ideologies. In any case, professional journalists, despite long-standing and deep-seated conflicts with corporate media management, have accepted the corporate line that attacks on the corporate control of the industry are the equivalent to attacks on free speech and a free press as well as their professional prerogatives. In the 1930s, for example, the Newspaper Guild, unlike many if not most labor unions and newspaper-related industries at the time, showed no interest in the debate over radio policy. However, it did pass a resolution denouncing one clause in the Communications Act of 1934 which permitted the president the right to censor the news during a national emergency. The balance of the debate over broadcasting apparently had nothing to do with free speech issues, at least to the trained professionals in U.S. newsrooms.

The third and final hypothesis for the lack of legitimate debate regarding the ownership, structure, and control of the media in U.S. political life owes to the nature of the corporate media themselves. Here the reference is not to the political and economic muscle that accompanies any powerful industry in the United States; rather the reference is to two additional benefits the media corporations enjoy beyond those generally enjoyed by other wealthy and powerful institutions. Indeed, in the following respects, the corporate media are no doubt the envy of the balance of the corporate community.

First, given the media's control over the flow of information, few politicians have any desire to antagonize the media industry as a whole, with the conceivable repercussions that might entail for their political careers and agendas. "Politicians fear the media," Bagdikian commented, regarding the manner by which media firms were able to circumvent business regulations with greater ease than other firms, "and the bigger the media; the greater the fear."[16] How telling it is that the two U.S. presidents who created the greatest furor attacking the "liberal" bias of the press, Nixon and Reagan, were the same two presidents who encouraged the further consolidation and profitability of the media. Need it be added that these two presidents received overwhelming support from the nation's media at election time?[17] Attacking the liberal bias of journalists is permissible; attacking the corporate, commercial basis of the media is political suicide, at least as politics has been practiced in the U.S. in modern times.

This was an important factor accounting for the demise of the opposition movement in the early 1930s. One reformer estimated that 70 percent of the Senate and 80 percent of the House favored broadcast reform legislation in 1931. "Were it not for a little group of reactionary leaders in both branches of Congress," he states, reform "legislation would have passed by this time."[18] The commercial broadcasters carefully cultivated their relationships with the relevant congressional committee chairmen, such that much of the opposition movement abandoned any hope for congressional action by 1933 and directed its attention to President Franklin D. Roosevelt. Indeed, there was reason for optimism in this regard as many key members of the New Deal, including TVA chairman Arthur Morgan, were outspoken critics of commercial broadcasting and proponents of sweeping reform of the status quo. Nevertheless, Roosevelt was not interested in antagonizing the commercial broadcasters, especially when he had to deal with the largely Republican newspaper industry. He ignored the opposition movement and cooperated in total with the legislative agenda of the commercial broadcasters. NBC and CBS provided Roosevelt with unimpeded access to the ether, which he exercised more than 50 times in his first year in office, far surpassing any previous president.[19]

Second, and related to the first part of this hypothesis, the corporate media are in an ideal position to control the public perception, or lack thereof, of any possible debate regarding the control and structure of the media. The media have shown two basic responses to efforts to challenge their legitimacy. First, they simply ignore the issue or provide it minimal coverage. This is standard operating procedure. Second, the corporate media distort the issues to suit their own purposes. Hence challenges to the corporate media, which are generally predicted upon the desire to open up the channels of communication, are invariably framed not as challenges to corporate rule, but as threats to free speech, democracy, and the "rights of man."

This was a central dilemma for the broadcast reformers of the early 1930s. Facing an entrenched industry that had no incentive to publicize the debate over its existence, the reformers needed to receive ample and, with hope, sympathetic coverage in the print media to generate popular momentum for their cause. As it was, the debate received minimal coverage and what there was was skewed tremendously toward the proponents of the status quo.[20] Indeed, the newspaper industry, which in other nations had forcefully led the fight to decommercialize broadcasting, quickly became defenders of the commercial broadcasters as their corporate brethren and opposed broadcast reform with only a handful of exceptions. One of the leading activists for broadcast reform, the ACLU's Morris Ernst would go so far as to argue that reform of the status quo had been and would continue to be impossible because "the cohesion of business sentiment of the press and radio has never allowed these ideas to filter out to a forum of public discussion or wide consideration."[21]

Given the lack of debate over the media since the 1930s, there have been precious few instances where this thesis could be tested subsequently. However, even related issues, like the titanic mergers of the 1980s have been covered by the press with kid gloves and mostly as business stories.[22] As for the implications for democracy and free expression of this consolidation of the media industry, Bagdikian notes that "the mainstream media, despite pious insistence that they never select their output for self-serving reasons, are close to absolute in their self-censorship on the subject."[23] Perhaps a couple of the most interesting case studies have been C. Anthony Giffard's and Edward S. Herman's respective studies of the U.S. press coverage of the period leading up to the U.S. withdrawal from UNESCO in the early 1980s.[24] The U.S. press criticized UNESCO unmercifully and with near unanimity, largely due to UNESCO's support for a New World Information and Communication Order (NWICO), which the U.S. press regarded as a distinct threat to its modus operandi overseas. The press coverage was totally one-sided; it would have been virtually impossible for a U.S. media consumer to generate any conception of why the United States might wish to remain in UNESCO.

Moreover, the NWICO was blown all out of proportion as an aspect of UNESCO's other activities, of which there was virtually no mention. In addition, no effort was made to present the Third World position on the matter, which, whatever the merits of their case, had little to do with their desire to smash free speech and a great deal to do with their desire to exercise greater control over their media services, which were increasingly controlled by Western corporations and news services. Rather, the U.S. press characterized the NWICO as a callous effort by second-rate hacks to manipulate the news and interfere with a free press. The fundamental questions of who controls the news and the role of large corporations seeking profit, so important to the Third World position on the NWICO, disappeared entirely from the U.S.

press accounts. Rather, it became a classic battle for free speech reminiscent of John Peter Zenger and James Franklin. In sum, the press defended its corporate interests to a T, and the public was woefully misinformed. The corporate media rattled their sabers over what was clearly a less than life-threatening challenge in the case of the NWICO. It should not require great imagination to conceive of the obstacles in store for any potential media reformers in the way of media coverage should they begin to question the very legitimacy of the corporate domination of the media.

Conclusion

Although these hypotheses are intended to explain the lack of debate over the control and structure of the media in U.S. political life, they are not intended as a gloomy forecast that any alteration of existing conditions will be forever impossible. While these are extremely powerful factors that account for the present situation, there may be countervailing forces on the horizon that may eventually signal a shift in the status of the debate over the fundamental contours of the U.S. media system.

First, and more important, the "American Century" is literally and figuratively nearing an end and the halcyon days of a bustling capitalism may well be in the past. Eventually, this may undermine the inability to criticize capitalism in U.S. political culture. This is clearly a decisive factor; any viable campaign to reconstruct the media system must be part of a broad-based movement that is attempting to reform the basic institutions of U.S. society.[25] Without this "radical" or, at the least, "non-mainstream" political foundation, any effort at media reform will quickly be washed up on the same shores that received the opposition movement in the early 1930s. And the centerpiece of any viable alternative political movement in the U.S. must be the shared belief that contemporary capitalism is working effectively for only a minority of the citizenry and, moreover, that its core tendencies are frequently at odds with democratic ideals. This may well be a working definition for any social movement that could possibly revitalize U.S. democracy: it would have to put those central social institutions that have been off-limits back on the political agenda, precisely where they belong. Politics must begin addressing core issues that directly affect the way people's lives are led.

Second, there has been a quantum leap in the quantity and quality of media criticism. The dominant myths, mentioned in the second hypothesis above, have been held up to scrutiny and, for the most part, they have not fared well. The antidemocratic implications of the present media setup are recognized in communications circles, although critical scholarship remains a minority phenomenon. This scholarship is vital if society is to learn to regard its media system in a critical manner, rather than as an unalterable "given."

Moreover, U.S. political culture is awash in a crisis of cynicism, ignorance, and apathy—almost universally recognized—in which the corporate media system is culpably implicated. This is a crisis that shows no sign of disappearing of its own volition. Although there is no reason to anticipate a radical transformation of the status quo in the near future, this is no time for critical scholars to throw in the proverbial towel and abandon any hope of qualitatively transcending the existing situation. The system is far from healthy. Now, as always, scholars must be willing to make a "ruthless criticism of everything existing," which "must not be afraid of its own conclusions, nor of conflict with the powers that be."[26] "The future is still open," Samir Amin reminds those disinterested in viewing the present historically, "It is still to be lived."[27]

16

The Internet and U. S. Communication Policymaking in Historical and Critical Perspective

Two oppositional and epoch-defining trends dominate U.S. and global media and communication. On one hand, there have been rapid corporate concentration and commercialization of media industries. The 1995 mergers of Disney with Capital Cities/ABC and Time Warner with Turner Broadcasting, as well as the sale of CBS to Westinghouse, highlight this trend. Many business analysts expect even more merger and buyout activity, leading to as few as six to ten colossal conglomerates dominating global communication before the market stabilizes.[1] According to some political theorists, this rampant commercialization of communication poses a severe challenge to the social capacity to generate a democratic political culture and public sphere.[2] Virtually all known theories of political democracy would suggest that such a concentration of media and communication in a handful of mostly unaccountable interests is little short of an unmitigated disaster.

On the other hand, newly developed computer and digital communication technologies can undermine the ability to control communication in a traditionally hierarchal manner. The most dramatic development along these lines has been the Internet, which permits inexpensive, global, interactive, and mass computer communication, as well as access to a previously unimaginable range of information. The Internet has been alternately described as a "functioning anarchy" that is virtually impossible to control from a centralized command post and "a grassroots, bottom-up system."[3] Mitchell Kapor notes the historical significance of what is now termed *cyberspace:* "Instead of a small number of groups having privileged positions as speakers—broadcast networks and powerful newspapers—we are entering an era of communication of the many to the many . . . the nature of the technology itself has opened up a space of much greater democratic possibility."[4] The executive director of the Internet Society characterizes the Internet as "a profound turning point in the evolution of human communication—of much greater significance than the creation of the printing press."[5]

The long-term trend toward corporate concentration derives from the core logic of capitalism and is presently the dominant force of the two. My fundamental question, then, is to what extent can the emerging communication technological revolution, particularly the Internet, override the antidemocratic implications of the media marketplace and foster more democratic media and a more democratic political culture? This issue is addressed here as a matter of communication policymaking, concentrating upon the U.S. experience. In the first section I locate communication policy debates in the broad tradition of U.S. political history and discuss how corporate control of communication has been effectively removed from these debates. This was especially true in the 1990s, as Congress, the White House, and the Federal Communications Commission (FCC) addressed how best to develop the information highway. This presupposition of corporate, for-profit control reduces the range of legitimate policy debates to tangential issues. According to this premise, corporate control of communication should be maximized and the technological possibilities for decentralized, citizen communication should remain minimized, except where profitable. I argue for genuine, democratic, public participation in communication policymaking, with the aim of establishing non-market mechanisms to achieve socially determined goals.

In the second section of this chapter I take up the claim that the traditional policy concerns outlined in the first section are irrelevant for the new computer communication technologies. These technologies have such a powerful intrinsic democratic bias that the traditional issue over who should control them is essentially moot. To address this contention, I locate the rise of the new technologies in the emergence of global corporate capitalism and the tensions between democracy and capitalism. I argue that the new communication technologies are the product and a defining feature of a global capitalism that greatly enhances social inequality. For the Internet and the eventual infor-mation highway to approach their full democratic potential will require the types of policy measures now being broached only marginally.

Although I compare Internet and contemporary communication policy-making to the historical case of broadcasting, the differences in the technolo-gies suggest it is highly unlikely that they will develop along similar lines. The Internet has vastly more potential as an engine of democratic communication, and the real issue before us is how much of that potential will be fulfilled. I conclude that the policy issues surrounding the emerging communication revolution must be accompanied by a nearly unprecedented degree of politi-calization in the United States, if we are to approach the democratic potential of these technologies. The communication revolution also presents a special challenge to the discipline of communication in the United States and globally. Just as the global economy and the communication system are in the throes of a turbulent transformation, communication research and education in the United States are at a crossroads. The stance communication scholars assume toward communication policymaking in the coming years may determine the status of the field for generations.

The Internet and U.S. Policymaking

Two sets of fundamental political questions emerge when discussing the development of any major communication technology. The first set asks, who will control the technology and for what purpose? The corollary to this ques-tion is, who will not control the new technology and what purposes will not be privileged? In the case of U.S. television, for example, a few enormous cor-porations were permitted to control the medium for the purpose of maximiz-ing profits, which would be realized by selling advertising time. Thus the United States put the development of television on a very distinct trajectory, a path rather unlike that which was adopted in most parts of Europe.

The second set of questions deals with the social, cultural, economic, and political impact of the new communication technology on the overall society and explores why the new communication technology is important. The insti-tutional structures created to answer the first set of policy questions will gen-erally determine the answers to the second set. In fact, much of communication policymaking at this second level consists of trying to coerce the communication system—its owners and operators—into behavior they ordinarily would not pursue. The classic case in point would be the constant discussion about reducing the level of television violence. At the same time, the second set of policy questions cannot be limited entirely to structural issues, or it would not need to be considered fundamental. Regardless of how a communication technology is owned and operated, it will have consequences that are often unintended and unanticipated, and related only in varying degrees to its structural basis. Thus television dramatically altered the domestic culture of U.S. households in the postwar years and it has arguably had a strong effect upon the nature of journalism and public discourse.[6]

The process by which society answers these questions can be regarded as policymaking. The more a society is genuinely democratic, the more that society's policy debates concerning the application and development of paramount communication technologies will be open, informed, thoughtful, and passionate. Regardless of how democratic the policymaking process may be, however, these questions still emerge and will be answered in one form or another. As a rule of thumb, if certain forces thoroughly dominate a society's political economy, they will thoroughly dominate its communication system, and the first set of policy questions will not even be subject to debate. So it is and so it has been with the Communist Party in various "people's republics," and, for the most part, with big business interests in this country.

The United States is in the midst of a fundamental reconfiguration of communication media, often characterized as the information superhighway, or the era of the interactive telecomputer. This is a truly revolutionary era not because of the awesome and bedazzling developments in technology, but because these new digital and computer technologies are likely to break down the traditional communication media industries and call forth a reconstitution of the communication infrastructure across the board. In short, the first set of policymaking questions have reemerged, and the answers we find to them may well set the course of development for generations.

Moreover, the current communication revolution continues, rather dramatically, the historical process whereby mediated communication has become increasingly central to the political economies and cultures of the world's peoples. Global capitalism, politics, culture, and education, to mention a few examples, are being reconstructed in this new era of the information highway. The entire manner in which individuals interact with the world is in the process of being transformed. Hence, the second set of policy issues concerning the social implications of the new communication technologies are of the utmost importance.

The current communication revolution is not unprecedented. It corresponds most closely to the 1920s, when the emergence of radio broadcasting forced society to address the two sets of political questions mentioned above. As with the Internet in the 1990s, radio broadcasting was a radically new development, and there was great confusion throughout the 1920s concerning who should control this powerful new technology and for what purposes. There was little sense of how radio could be made a profitable enterprise, and there was considerable discussion of how liberating and democratic it could be. Much of the impetus for radio broadcasting in the first decade came first from amateurs and then from nonprofit and noncommercial groups that immediately grasped the public service potential of the new technology.[7] It was only in the late 1920s that capitalists began to sense that through network operation and commercial advertising, radio broadcasting could generate substantial profits. Through their immense power in Washington these commercial broadcasters were able to dominate the Federal Radio Commission such that the scarce number of air channels were effectively turned over to them with no public and little congressional deliberation on the matter.

In the aftermath of this commercialization of the airwaves, elements of U.S. society coalesced into a broadcast reform movement that attempted to establish a dominant role for the nonprofit and noncommercial sector in U.S. broadcasting.[8] They recognized quickly that their task was doubly difficult, as they had squandered their opportunity to establish a nonprofit system in the 1920s, when the commercial interests were still wrestling with the question of how to capitalize on radio. These reformers were explicitly and nonnegotiably radical; they argued that if private interests controlled the medium and their goal was profit, no amount of regulation or self-regulation could overcome the bias built into the system. Commercial broadcasting, the reformers argued, would downplay controversial and provocative public affairs programming and emphasize whatever fare would sell the most products for advertisers. Theirs was a sophisticated critique of the limitations of capitalist communication systems for a democratic society, which foreshadowed much of the best media criticism and scholarship of recent years.

The reform movement disintegrated after the passage of the Communications Act of 1934, which established the. FCC (which would be substantially altered for the first time by the Communications Act of 1995, as explained below). The 1930s reformers did not lose to the commercial interests, however, in any fair debate on a level playing field. The radio lobby dominated because it was able to keep most Americans ignorant or confused about communication policy matters then under discussion in Congress through their control of key elements of the news media and sophisticated public relations aimed at the remainder of the press and the public. In addition, the commercial broadcasters became a force that few politicians wished to antagonize; almost all of the congressional leaders of broadcast reform in 1931–32 were defeated in their reelection attempts. With the defeat of the reformers, the industry claims that commercial broadcasting was inherently democratic and American went without challenge and became internalized in the political culture. Thereafter the only legitimate manner by which to criticize U.S. broadcasting was to assert that it was uncompetitive and, therefore, needed aggressive regulation. The basis for the "liberal" claim for regulation was that the scarce number of channels necessitated regulation, not that the capitalist basis of the industry was fundamentally flawed. This was a far cry from the criticism of the 1930s broadcast reformers, who argued that the problem was not simply one of lack of competition in the marketplace, as much as it was the rule of the marketplace per se. It also means today that, with the vast expansion in the number of channels in the current communication revolution, the scarcity argument has lost its power and liberals are at a loss to withstand the deregulatory juggernaut.[9]

This constricted range of policy debate was the context for the development of subsequent communication technologies, including facsimile, FM radio, and television in the 1940s. That the communication corporations had first claim to these technologies was unchallenged, even to such public-service-minded New Dealers as James Lawrence Fly, Clifford Durr, and Frieda Hennock. In comparison to the public debate over radio in the 1930s, there was almost no public debate concerning alternative ways to develop these technologies. By the 1940s and thereafter, liberals knew the commercial basis of the system was inviolate, and they merely tried to carve out a nonprofit sector on the margins. This was problematic, because whenever these nonprofit niches were seen as blocking profitable expansion, their future was on thin ice. Thus the primary function of the nonprofit sector in U.S. communications has been to pioneer the new technologies when they were not yet seen as profitable—for example, AM radio in the 1920s and FM radio and UHF television in the 1950s—and then to be pushed aside once they have shown the commercial interests the potential of the new media. This has already been the fate of the Internet's computer networks, which, after substantial public subsidy, were turned over to private operators.[10]

Policy and the Profit Motive

The emergence of the Internet and related technologies is forcing a reconsideration of media policy unlike, say, television or FM radio, because the nature of digital communication renders moot the traditional distinctions between various media and communication sectors. It is clear that the broadcasters and newspaper chains that have ruled for generations will not necessarily rule, or even survive, in the coming age, although the companies that own them will fare better if they move strategically into the new digital world. This theme dominates the business pages of the press and the business-oriented media. The key question, then, is to identify which firms and which sectors will dominate and capitalize on the communication revolution, and which firms and which sectors will fall by the wayside. This is the tale being told in our business press, and, by prevailing wisdom, this is the key policy battle concerning the Internet and the information highway.

Consistent with the pattern set in the mid-1930s, the primacy of corporate control and the profit motive is a given. All sectors of the federal government repeatedly emphasize that the information superhighway "will be built, owned, and operated by the private sector."[11] The range of legitimate debate extended from those like Newt Gingrich, who argued that profits were synonymous with public service, to those like then-Vice President Al Gore, who argued that there were public interest concerns that the marketplace cannot resolve, but can only address once the profitability of the dominant corporate sector had been assured.[12] The historical record of communication regulation indicates that although the Gore position can be dressed up, once the needs of corporations are given primacy, the public interest will invariably be pushed to the margins. Nowadays, liberal politicians rarely invoke the rhetoric of public interest regulation that, though mostly hollow, typified the mid-twentieth century. In fact, the debate is so truncated that the preferred (some would argue, the only) means of regulating communication firms is to create incentives for them, that is, pay them to act differently such that their profits do not fall.[13]

This situation exists for many of the same reasons broadcast reformers were demolished in the 1930s. Politicians may favor one sector over another in the battle to cash in on the highway, but they cannot oppose the cashing-in process without placing their political careers in jeopardy. Both the Democratic and Republican parties have strong ties to the large communication firms and industries, and the communication lobbies are perhaps the most feared, respected, and well endowed of all who seek favors on Capitol Hill.[14] The only grounds for political courage in this case would be if there were an informed and mobilized citizenry ready to do battle for alternative policies. Where would citizens get informed, though, if not through the news media, where news coverage is minimal and restricted to the range of legitimate debate, which, in this case, means no debate at all? That is why the information superhighway is covered as a business story, not a public policy story. Perhaps it is only coincidental that the firms that control U.S. journalism are almost all major players in the corporate jockeying for the inside lane on the information highway. This is not a public policy issue to them, and they have no desire for it to become one.[15] It is a stunning conflict of interest that goes without comment.

These factors all crystallized with the passage by the Senate and the House of Representatives of the Communications Act of 1995. Perhaps one of the most corrupt pieces of legislation in U.S. history, the bill was effectively written by and for business. Much is made of the new law's commitment to competitive markets. This is a euphemism for a deregulation that almost certainly will lead to increased concentration, if the historical record provides any insight.[16] As Aufderheide notes, the law "proposes, in essence, to let the big get bigger, and more vertically integrated," placing complete trust in the communication corporations.[17] The limited opposition to the legislation has come primarily from those firms that did not see enough benefits thrown their way, or felt that their competitors got too many. "In all these years of walking the halls of Congress, I have never seen anything like the Telecommunications Bill," one career lobbyist noted. "The silence of public debate is deafening. A bill with such astonishing impact on all of us is not even being discussed."[18] In sum, the debate over communications policy is restricted to elites and those with serious financial stakes in the outcome. It does not reflect well on the caliber of U.S. participatory democracy.

The effect of the Communications Act of 1995 is to assure that the market, and not public policy, will direct the course of both the Internet and the information highway. It is, in effect, a preemptive strike by corporate America to assure that there will be little public intervention in the communication system in coming years, and that government will exclusively serve the needs of the private sector. To answer the question of whither the Internet, one need only determine where the greatest profits are to be found. Indeed the commercialization of the Internet is growing at an exponential rate. More venture capital was invested in Internet companies in the first quarter of 1995 than in all of 1994.[19] "The rush to commercialize . . . the Internet has created an investor frenzy not seen in the technology industry since the early days of the personal computer more than a decade ago," the *New York Times* reports.[20] The revenues will come from Internet software, Internet access fees and online services, Internet-generated hardware sales, and Internet consulting and market research.[21] Online direct selling and advertising are also vaulting into prominence. The A. C. Nielsen Company now prepares a survey of Internet users to expedite Internet commerce and advertising even more.[22]

Much of the commercial involvement with the Internet is still speculative and not generating a profit, much as it was with private radio station owners of the 1920s, who knew they had a potentially hot ticket, but did not yet know how to cash it in. Businesses are frightened of being outflanked in cyberspace, as suggested by the AT&T advertisement promoting the Internet as a business's "secret weapon against the other guys." Corporate media giants, in particular, are aggressively working to dominate the Internet. Levy contends that these corporate media ambitions in cyberspace will be foiled because of the anti-monopolistic bias of the technology.[23] If so, in the current political environment, that may well mean that the Internet will never fulfill its vast potential and will remain on the margins of the media culture. Aufderheide concurs, arguing that the Internet will eventually be regarded as "a demonstration project on the electronic frontier."[24] In any case, the Communications Act of 1995 guarantees that the eventual information highway based on the interactive telecomputer will be a thoroughly commercial enterprise with profit maximization as its founding principle.[25] It is too early to predict where the non-profit and noncommercial sector of cyberspace will fit into that picture, but its survival and growth will be based strictly on technology, not policy.

Those forces that benefit from this situation claim that the market is the only truly democratic policymaking mechanism because it rewards capitalists who "give the people what they want" and penalizes those who do not. When the state or labor unions or any other agency interferes with the workings of the marketplace, this reasoning goes, they produce outcomes hostile to the public interest. These were also the precise claims of the commercial broadcasters as they consolidated their hold over the radio spectrum in the 1930s. This ideology of the infallible marketplace in communication and elsewhere has become a virtual civic religion in the United States and globally in the 1990s.

This argument remains infallible only to the extent that it is a religion based on faith and not a political theory subject to inquiry and examination. Under careful examination, the market is a highly flawed regulatory mechanism. Let me provide three brief criticisms along these lines. First, the market is not predicated upon one-person, one-vote, as in democratic theory, but rather upon one-dollar, one-vote. The prosperous have many votes and the poor have none. Is it any surprise that the leading proponents of the market are predominantly well-to-do, and that markets invariably maintain and strengthen class divisions in society? Second, the market does not "give the people what they want" as much as it "gives the people what they want within the range of what is most profitable to produce." This is often a far narrower range than what people might ordinarily enjoy choosing from. Thus, in the case of broadcasting, many Americans may well have been willing to pay for an advertising-free system, but this was a choice that was not profitable for the dominant commercial Interests, so it was not offered in the marketplace. As Barbara Ehrenreich puts it, "A consumer in a market can never be more than a stunted caricature of a citizen in a genuine democracy."[26] Third, markets are driven solely by profit considerations and downplay long-term concerns or values not readily associated with profit maximization. One need think only of the global ecology to see the disastrous consequences of a blind embrace of the market. Yet, such an embrace is precisely what has occurred.

If not the market, what then would be a truly democratic manner to generate communication policymaking? The historical record points to two basic principles that should be made operational. First, in view of the revolutionary nature of the new communication technologies, citizens should convene to study what the technological possibilities are and to determine what the social goals should be. At this point, several alternative models of ownership and control should be proposed and debated, and the best model selected. In short, the structural basis of the communication system should be decided after the social aims are determined. The key factor is to exercise public participation before an unplanned commercial system becomes entrenched. This runs directly counter to the present U.S. experience, whereby the decisions are essentially made by self-interested parties whose goal is to entrench a commercial system before there is any possibility of public participation. Is such public participation an absurd idea? Hardly. In the late 1920s, Canada, noting the rapid commercialization of the U.S. and Canadian airwaves, convened precisely such a public debate over broadcasting that included public hearings in twenty-five cities in all nine provinces. The final decision to develop a nonprofit system was adopted after three years of active debate.[27] Is this a ridiculous extension of democracy? One hopes not. If the shape of the emerging communication system that stands to alter our lives radically for generations is not fair game for democratic debate, one must wonder just what is.

Second, if such a public debate determines that the communication system needs a significant nonprofit and noncommercial component, the dominant sector of the system, must be nonprofit, noncommercial, and accountable to the public. The historical record in the United States and globally is emphatic in this regard. In addition, it is arguable that commercial interests, too, must always be held to carefully administered public service standards. There are legitimate reservations about government involvement with communication. The purpose of policymaking, in this case, should be to determine how to deploy these technologies to create a pluralistic, decentralized, accountable, nonprofit, and noncommercial sector that can provide a viable service to the entire population. Fortunately, communication technologies seem to be quite amenable to such an approach. One suspects that if our society would devote to this problem only a fraction of the time it has devoted to commercializing communication, we could find some workable public service models.

Perhaps these two principles seem entirely unfeasible for contemporary U.S. political culture, but is the only alternative to turn the entire coordination of and responsibility for the new communication system over to the private sector? The communication corporations "don't have our best interests, they have their best interests at heart," David Bunnell, a former Microsoft executive and trade publication publisher, warns. "They're supposed to create profit for their stockholders . . . this information highway is just too important to be left to the private companies."[28] This sentiment is shared by many of the most creative minds in the communications industries, seemingly to no avail.[29] As this basic question is off-limits in contemporary U.S. political culture, most Americans do not even know that it is their right to entertain thoughts along these lines and act accordingly.

Nonetheless, there are numerous Americans currently working to generate a viable nonprofit and noncommercial sector in the information highway, preparing insightful proposals along these lines.[30] These reformers find themselves ignored by the press and shunted aside by politicians. They face the classic dilemma that has haunted U.S. communication activists since the mid-1930s: to be taken seriously, one must acknowledge the primacy of corporate rule, that is, concede that it is a battle for the margins, not the heart, of the communication system. As gloomy as the situation may be, as long as the identity of the eventual corporate masters of communication is being fought over, there are possibilities for concessions that will not exist once the industry is stabilized. Prior to 1934, for example, commercial broadcasters devoted ample time to noncommercial programming in an attempt to persuade the public that they could be trusted with the control of broadcasting. Once the organized opposition disappeared, however, the commitment to noncommercial broadcasting did as well. So, in this sense, there might be some hope to promote and protect a nonprofit sector, and in the current political culture that may well be the only immediate option. Nonetheless, by historical standards, there is little reason to believe the nonprofit sector could survive a sustained commercial assault, and any concessions gained now need to be written in such a way as to be protected from later attack.

If, indeed, this is to be the course of the Internet and the information highway, what will be the nature of the U.S. policy debates in the coming generation? By the logic of this argument, the legitimate policy issues will be tangential, the province of lobbyists, lawyers, bureaucrats, and academics, and will assume the role of the market as natural. When the contours of the eventual commercial system become clear, so too will the precise nature of the legitimate policy issues. Moreover, the distinct attributes of the Internet and the information highway, for example, interactivity, will create unanticipated policy issues. Clearly the past paradigm of commercial broadcasting policymaking cannot be imposed willy-nilly. At present, the issue of state censorship of the Internet is a reigning concern, and it is crucial to protect free speech, especially since the record suggests that the impetus toward censorship will increase with pronounced Internet deviation from mainstream thought.[31] At the same time, without a principled critique of the market and the types of censorship it systematically imposes, this blanket adoption of the First Amendment can also serve to provide the purely commercial aspirations of corporate America with a constitutional shield from justified public criticism. Such has been the case in commercial broadcasting and with advertising. In these cases, the First Amendment has been used to contract the arena of public debate, and not to expand it.[32]

The New Super-Powerful Democratic Technology?

Even if the market is permitted to determine the course of the information highway and there is minimal public deliberation over fundamental communication policy issues, there is no evidence that the Internet, or the subsequent information highway, can possibly come under the same sort of monopoly corporate control as have broadcasting and traditional media. "The very architecture of the Net," one scholar argues, "will work against the type of content control these folks have over mass media."[33] Others contend that, whereas the large commercial enterprises will develop their "cybermalls," the rest of cyberspace will be "unpaved," thereby opening the door to a genuine cultural and political renaissance.[34] The issue here is not whether a citizen-based, nonprofit sector of cyberspace can survive in the emerging regime. That seems guaranteed. Nor is the issue whether this sector can thrive in the emerging regime, because that, too, seems likely if the wildfire growth of the past few years is any indication of what is to follow. If nothing else, cyberspace may provide a supercharged, information-packed, and psychedelic version of ham radio. Nor is the issue whether the nonprofit sector of cyberspace will be a significant part of a process that transforms our lives dramatically. That may well take place. Rather, the key issue is whether the nonprofit, noncommercial sector of cyberspace will be able to transform our societies radically for the better and to do so without fundamental policy intervention. In short, will this sector be able to create a twenty-first-century, Habermasian "public sphere," where informed interactive debate can flower independent of government or commercial control? This follows the critical strain of democratic theory that argues that the structural basis for genuine democratic communication lies with a media system free from the control of either the dominant political or economic powers of the day.[35]

I have framed the question from a critical perspective, where the market is not assumed ipso facto to be beyond reproach. In my view, the evidence indicates the market is far from a neutral or value-free arbiter of culture and ideas.[36] This is also the perspective of the Internet's most articulate advocates. "The Internet represents the real information revolution," a member of Alternet argues, "the one that removes the governmental and corporate filters that have so long been in place with traditional mass media."[37]

Mainstream observers who exult in the potential of the Internet would disagree with the notion that the market or capitalism is an impediment to the development of a democratic public sphere. Some of these analysts often see the Internet and the information highway as elevating existing capitalism to an even higher level of sheer perfection.[38] In this view, capitalism is synonymous with democracy; therefore the more that social affairs can be turned over to private interests the better. The function of government is to protect private property and not much else. Indeed, some marketphiles take a technological, deterministic stance, asserting that the new communication technologies, since they eliminate the monopolies on knowledge that large corporations have, will lead to a new global economic regime of small entrepreneurs and flexible production. The transnational corporations that presently dominate the global economy will eventually appear like so many clumsy dinosaurs on their way to rapid extinction. Market enthusiasts see this as especially true in communication industries, where size will prove to be a competitive disadvantage. In this perspective, the information highway will be the basis for a new golden age of high-growth, competitive capitalism, and an accompanying renaissance in culture and politics.[39] As appealing as this may be to some at an ideological level, though, there is no empirical evidence to support this view or to suggest it is on the horizon. In fact, the shift to digital technologies has produced convergence, meaning that the traditional distinctions among media types are disappearing. This in turn enhances synergy, meaning corporations can expand their profit-making abilities by building empires, thereby accelerating the momentum toward global corporate concentration.[40] Contrary to the claims of the marketphiles, the empirically verifiable consequence of the digital revolution is that the telecommunication, computer, media, and entertainment industries, which traditionally have been relatively independent of one another, are now merging and coalescing into grand combinations of unprecedented global scope.[41]

Other mainstream observers may not revel to such a degree in capitalism, but they see the market as the natural order of things and pliable enough to permit the technological revolution to work its magic for both business and the public.[42] In either approach, the market is presupposed to be innately wonderful, or at least neutral, so it is not subjected to any further analysis. The markedly dominant role of corporations and the wealthy in the U.S. political economy goes unmentioned. If the information highway fails to deliver the goods, it will not be the fault of the market or of those who profit by the system.

The capitalism one finds described superficially in the literature on the Internet and the communication highway is an intoxicating one. It is composed of venture capitalists, daring entrepreneurs, and enterprising consumers. There are no cheap, exploited laborers; no environmental degradation; no graft or corruption; no ingrained classes; no economic depressions; no instances of social decay; and no consumer rip-offs. There are bold, open-minded winners and hardly any losers. It is capitalism at its best. Even to the extent there is a grain of truth in this sanitized version of capitalism, the notion that the communication system is a consequence of the free market is bogus. For example, many of the communication technologies associated with the communication revolution, particularly the Internet, grew directly out of government, usually military, subsidies. Indeed, at one point fully 85 percent of research and development in the U.S. electronics industry was subsidized by the federal government, although the eventual profits accrued to private firms.[43]

I have spelled out my criticism of the market as a democratic regulator of communication and all else in the first section of this chapter. If we are to accurately evaluate the potential of the Internet and the information highway, we need to replace this mythological portrayal of capitalism with one that is more theoretical, historical, and critical. We also need a more viable notion of

the relationship of democracy to capitalism and the relationship of communication to each of them. Only then can we evaluate the claim that the Internet
is a supremely powerful democratic force.

The relationship of capitalism to democracy is a rocky one. It is true that
historically capitalism has been instrumental in giving birth to modern democratic regimes, but it has also worked to limit the extent or viability of that
democracy. On one hand, capitalism tends to generate a highly skewed class
basis that permits a small section of society, the wealthy, to have inordinate
power over political and economic decision making to the detriment of the balance of society. On the other hand, capitalism encourages a culture that places
a premium on commercial values and downplays communitarian ideals.
Capitalism thereby undermines two prerequisites for genuine democracy.

Political democracy has always been a problem for a capitalist society like
the United States, where a minuscule portion of the population makes fundamental economic decisions based upon its self-interest. This becomes an
acute problem when a mature, corporate-dominated, capitalist society also
grants near universal suffrage. There is the constant threat, inherent to democracy, that the dispossessed might unite, rise up, and demand greater control
over basic economic decisions. In the minds of the powerful, therefore, the
system works best when the crucial political and economic decisions are
made by elites outside of the public eye, and the political culture concentrates
upon superficial and tangential matters. Autonomous labor organizations,
social movements, and political parties that oppose the rule of capital are discouraged through a variety of mechanisms, and, when necessary, are sometimes repressed. Moreover, the tendency of capitalism to commercialize every
nook and cranny of social life renders the development or survival of nonmarket political and cultural organizations far more difficult. It is these independent associations that form the bulwark of democracy, making it possible for
individuals to come together and become informed political actors.[44] In sum,
fundamental political activity is discouraged, and, in this context, political
apathy appears as rational behavior for those outside the inner circles. This
has been, and remains, the reigning characteristic of U.S. politics.[45] As Noam
Chomsky notes, it is considered a "crisis of democracy" in conventional
thinking when the long-dormant masses rise up and begin to pursue their
own interests.[46] Therefore, it is not surprising that a major development in the
twentieth century has been the rise of public relations—or what is often sys-

tematic corporate propaganda—to promote elite interests and to undermine ideas and groups that might oppose corporate rule.[47] The role of the masses is to ratify elite decisions.

Communication is essential to meaningful participatory democracy. Although the record is certainly mixed, on balance U.S. commercial journalism and media have failed to provide the groundwork for an informed citizenry. In Habermasian terms, the media became sources of great profitability in the twentieth century and have been colonized by the corporate sector, thereby losing their capacity to provide the basis for the independent public sphere so necessary for meaningful democracy. The upshot of most critical media research is that the commercial news media tend to serve elite interests and undermine the capacity for the bulk of the population to act as informed citizens. Recent scholarship suggests that increasingly concentrated corporate ownership and commercial support of the media have further destroyed the capacity of the press to fulfill a democratic mission.

Communication is increasingly essential, too, in the market economy. That is why an analysis of global capitalism needs to be at the center of any study of communication systems in the coming years. It is no coincidence that the communication revolution appears at the same historic moment as the current globalization of capitalism. The tremendous desire by corporations and capitalists to expand globally has provided much of the spur to innovation in computers and telecommunications, with striking effect.[48] In the early 1970s, only 10 percent of global trade was financial, with the remaining 90 percent being trade-in goods and services. The percentages flip-flopped in the subsequent two decades and grew at a rate far greater than global economic activity.[49] Communication and information-related industries are now, by near unanimous proclamation, at the very heart of investment and growth in the world economy, occupying a role once played by steel, railroads, and automobiles.[50]

So what are the observable, new, and important tendencies of this global capitalist order? Several related points are accepted by most observers, though how they are framed and their relative importance are subject to debate. First, the ease of trans-border capital flows has lessened the capacity of national governments to determine economic policies that might promote any interests apart from those of transnational business, as capitalists can quickly move to more profitable climes.[51] John Maynard Keynes once noted that democracy would be impossible if capital could move beyond national borders; indeed, the immobility of capital is a core assumption of neoclassical economic theory.[52] Second, the new global capitalism has also had the effect of giving the international business community far greater leverage in its dealings, not only with government regulations and policies, but with labor as well. As a result, the global trend is toward deregulation, in the hope of luring capital and reducing the power of labor and labor unions, since if they are too effective, business will invest elsewhere. Environmental regulation is an immediate casualty of globalization, as are most government services, which must be eliminated in order to reduce taxes on the well-to-do (capital flight) and reduce economic stagnation.

A third effect is that this process of globalization has been accompanied by decreasing economic growth in the United States and globally in each decade since the 1960s. In fact, globalization emphasizes one of capitalism's basic flaws: What is rational conduct for the individual capitalist is utterly irrational and counterproductive for the system as a whole. Rational investors seek out low-wage areas and use the threat to keep domestic wages low even if they do not move abroad.[53] The consequence is that there is a strong downward pressure on buying power, i.e., economic demand, which leads to a decline in profitable investment possibilities, i.e., continued economic stagnation.[54] Moreover, governments are incapable of exercising the traditional Keynesian policies to stimulate economic growth, as these measures run directly counter to those policies necessary to attract and keep investment. Stimulative economic measures are no longer even a legitimate policy option; even if the World Bank and International Monetary Fund do not veto them, the global capital markets will.[55]

In addition, investment in information and communication tends to destroy existing jobs almost as well as it creates new ones. Unlike steel and automobiles, these new paradigm-identifying industries seem to be incapable of resolving the crisis of unemployment that afflicts the global working class. In this sense, the immediate consequence of the information revolution is not liberation from drudgery, but a sentencing to a life of sheer destitution.[56] Finally, because of the wildfire growth of enormous transnational global financial markets that are well beyond the powers of any effective national or international regulation, there is an element of overall instability to the global economy unknown since the 1930s.[57] In sum, the economic thrust of global capitalism is one of deteriorating public sectors, environmental recklessness, stagnation, instability, and widening economic stratification.[58] For those lucky few who sit atop the global pyramid, the future never appeared brighter; for the bulk of humanity, the present is grim and the future is an abyss. Nothing on the horizon suggests any other course.

Salvaging Political Culture

The implications of the global order for political culture are mostly negative. Capitalism's two inherent and negative traits for democracy—class stratification and the demise of civic virtue in the face of commercial values—are enhanced in the new global regime. There is nothing short of a wholesale assault on the very notion of democracy, as the concept of people gathering, debating, and devising policy has been supremely truncated. This is often presented as a crisis of national sovereignty; in fact, it is a crisis of sovereignty writ large. There is nothing really left to debate in the new world order since nations are required either to toe the global capitalist line or to face economic purgatory. Hence, the range of legitimate debate has shrunk considerably, with socialists and conservatives alike effectively pursuing the same policies. The great paradox of our age is that formal democracy extends to a greater percentage of humanity than ever in history; yet, concurrently, there may well be a more general sense of political powerlessness than ever before. Since the democratic system seems incapable of generating ideas that address the political economic crises of our times, the most dynamic political growth in this age is with anti-rationalist, fundamentalist, nationalistic movements that blame democracy for capitalism's flaws and threaten to reduce humanity to untold barbarism.

The communication revolution is implicated in these developments. On one hand, the transnational communication corporations—among the greatest beneficiaries of globalization—have been leading the fight for NAFTA, GATT, and other institutional arrangements advantageous to global capital.[59] These firms have set their sights on dominating world communication, entertainment, and information. Public sector broadcasting and communication across the planet have been dismantled and replaced by capitalist, often transnational, communication systems.[60] In particular, the great public service broadcasting systems of Europe, and their associative journalistic and cultural values, have been either eliminated or required to adopt commercial principles in order to survive in the global marketplace.[61] This new world order of communication tends to be uncritical of capitalism and commercialism and to be preoccupied with satisfying the needs of the relatively affluent, a minority of the world's population. In short, the new world order of global communication, among the most profitable consequences of global capitalism, tends to reinforce the status quo.

In this gloomy scenario, what are the prospects that the Internet and the technological revolution in communication might break down oligarchy and lead to a revitalization of democratic political culture? Proponents emphasize the attributes of the Internet that make it so special: It is relatively cheap, easy to use, difficult to prevent access to, and almost impossible to censor. William Gibson characterizes the Internet as "a last hope for democracy as we know it."[62] The most thoughtful arguments, and the most concerted activity, on behalf of the Internet as a means for revitalizing democracy tend to emphasize how it can empower individuals and groups presently ignored or distorted by the existing media industries. In effect, the Internet, especially the bulletin boards and discussion groups, can provide democracy's much needed public sphere that has been so corrupted by the market. Moreover, given the instantaneous and global nature of the Internet, proponents of the "Internet as public sphere" argue that this permits the creation of a global public sphere, all the more necessary in light of the global political economy. In Mexico, for example, these computer networks may well have permitted the pro-democracy forces to bypass the atrocious media system and to survive and prosper, whereas in earlier times these forces would have been crushed.[63] As evidence to bolster the belief that this is a viable alternative to commercial media, supporters point to a Rand Corporation memorandum indicating considerable dissatisfaction with the existence of these uncontrolled networks of communication and suggesting state surveillance or regulation to keep them in line.[64]

Although it is true that the prospects for computer networks are encouraging for activists, I believe the following qualifications are appropriate before we can extrapolate that the Internet will provide an unambiguous boon for democracy. First, assuring universal access and computer literacy is far from a certainty, and, without it, the democratic potential of the information highway seems supremely compromised. By 1995, only a third of the nation's population owned computers, and many of them could not get access to the Internet.[65] Personal computers are still not affordable for a large number of people, and computer manufacturers favor producing the big ticket PCs with heftier profit margins.[66] Although the extent of diffusion of PCs can only be guessed, there is little reason to believe that it will approach the level of either indoor plumbing or television, if left to the market. Significant portions of the U.S. population do not have cable television, and in poor neighborhoods up to one-third of the population goes without telephone service.[67] Hence the only way to ensure universal access and computer literacy will be to enact public policy to that effect, and in this era of fiscal constraint, that might prove to be a tall order. Schools and libraries are often pointed to as the key agents that will democratize computer usage, yet these institutions are in the throes of long-term cutbacks that seem to render absurd the notion that they could undertake this mission. And without universal access and computer literacy, as *BYTE* magazine contributing editor Nicholas Baran emphasizes, the PC may well "become a tool for further increasing the economic and educational disparity in our society."[68]

Aside from the question of access, bulletin boards and the information highway more generally do not have the power to produce political culture when it does not exist in the society at large. Given the dominant patterns of global capitalism, it is far more likely that the Internet and the new technologies will adapt themselves to the existing political culture rather than create a new one. Thus, it seems a great stretch to think the Internet will politicize people; it may just as well keep them depoliticized. The *New York Times* cites *Wired* magazine approvingly for helping turn "mild-mannered computer nerds into a super-desirable consumer market," not into political activists.[69] In particular, having mass, interactive bulletin boards is a truly magnificent advance, but what if nobody knows what they are talking about? This problem could be partially addressed if scholars and academics shared their work with and tailored their analyses to the general public, thereby engaging in a public dialogue. Unfortunately, such behavior runs directly counter to the priorities, attitudes, and trajectory of academic life.

This is precisely where journalism (broadly construed) and communication policymaking enter the picture. Journalism provides the oxygen for democratic discussion; it provides the research and contextualization necessary to understand politics and to see behind the official proclamations of those in power. Journalism does not constitute the range of debate; rather, it provokes it, informs it, and responds to it. As a rule, it is not something that can be done piecemeal by amateurs. It is best done by people who make a living at it and who have training and experience. Although journalism per quo is justly criticized for its failures, mostly due to commercial constraints, journalism per se is indispensable to any notion of democracy worth the paper it is written on. Quality journalism seems mandatory if the "Internet as public sphere" is to be a viable concept, and current theories along these lines are at a loss to address this problem.

Moreover, journalism is presently in the midst of a deep and profound crisis. The corporate concentration of ownership and the reliance upon advertising have converted much of U.S. journalism into a travesty of entertainment, crime, and natural disaster stories. The professional autonomy of journalists—always an ambiguous notion, especially in a commercial environment—has suffered severe body blows. Journalism, real journalism, is not profitable, and resources dedicated to it have been cut back.[70] Without resources, journalists are unable to do any investigative work and must rely upon the public relations industry (generally corporate) and official sources (mostly politicians, corporate-sponsored think tanks, and government officials) for news stories. Morale for U.S. journalists is arguably at an all-time low. Michael Eisner, former CEO of the Walt Disney Company, said that his firm's prospective growth was based on a "nonpolitical" product that did not threaten political regimes around the world, yet Eisner was the leader of one of the world's largest journalistic organizations.[71] In short, the market has little apparent interest in serious journalism, nor is such interest in the offing.

Some have described how the Internet will dramatically improve journalists' access to information, but none have come forth with ideas for how it will address the crisis noted above. The primary contribution of the Internet to journalism at present is ideological. Some mainstream scholars and industry public relations agents point to the vitality of cyberspace as an explanation for why there is no need for alarm at the concentrated corporate control of global communication or for political action to address the problem.[72] In the new mythology, the Internet joins the now battered notion of the professional autonomy of journalists as the public's protection from the negative consequences for democratic journalism of an oligopolistic, commercial media system. This argument evades the core point that journalism requires resources and institutional support. In this context, the battle for public and community broadcasting is crucial both in the United States and globally. It is not about the survival of Big Bird as much as it is about the survival of a structural basis for journalism and public affairs. In sum, the Internet can reproduce only part of the public sphere, and its part will not necessarily be worth much if there is not the institutional framework for a well-subsidized and independent journalism. Shapiro argues in this fashion that public policy must move aggressively to promote and protect and, by implication, subsidize a public forum in cyberspace.[73]

The third qualification to the "Internet as public sphere" hypothesis is that it often seems to exhibit an unchecked enthusiasm for these technologies, and technology in general; that is unwarranted. At its most extreme, some argue that the quantitative improvement in communication technology is leading to a truly qualitative shift in human consciousness. By this reasoning, the computer networks are liberating humanity from the material chains that have kept human imagination and creativity locked up.[74] Some argue that cyberspace has created genuine communities that offer a glimpse of how we might truly become a global human family.[75] Both of these utopian views recognize that commercial and government forces seek to undermine the transcendental potential of the Internet and the information highway, yet both emphasize the revolutionary power of technologies to liberate humanity. At its best, this perspective emphasizes cyberspace as a spawning ground for counterculture, and often harks back to the 1960s and other eras of communitarian ideals. Yet, as appealing as this line of reasoning may be, it really is a nonsensical notion of how history is going to unfold, and, at its worst, this argument degenerates, as Stallabrass puts it, into "business people and their camp followers (engineers and intellectuals) spinning universalist fantasies out of their desire to ride the next commercial wave."[76]

Indeed, one could characterize the adoption of the Internet as public sphere as not so much a grand victory as it is a case of making the best of a bad situation. The motor force behind the development of these technologies is business and business demand. Hamilton noted sixty years ago that "business succeeds rather better than the state in imposing restraints upon individuals, because its imperatives are disguised as choices."[77] We did not elect to have these technologies, nor did we ever debate their merits. They have been presented either as some sort of product of inexorable natural evolution or as a democratic response to pent-up consumer demand, when in fact they are here because they are profitable and because a market was created for them. Now that they are here, people can ignore them only at the risk of jeopardizing their careers and their ability to participate in society. As Postman notes, "New technologies do not always increase people's options; just as often they do exactly the opposite."[78] I am not advancing a Luddite argument; I merely point out that a central part of democratic communication policymaking is to evaluate the effects of a new technology before adopting it, to look before we leap. That has not been the case with the Internet or the information highway.

Communication technologies have unanticipated and unintended effects, and one function of policymaking is to understand them so that we may avoid or minimize the undesirable ones. The digitalization and computerization of our society are going to transform us radically, yet even those closely associated with these developments express concern about the possibility of a severe deterioration of the human experience as a result of the information revolution. As one observer notes, "Very few of us—only the high priests—really understand the new technologies, and these are surely the people least qualified to make policy decisions about them."[79] For every argument extolling the "virtual community" and the liberatory aspects of cyberspace, it seems every bit as plausible to reach dystopian conclusions. Why not look at the information highway as a process that encourages the isolation, atomization, and marginalization of people in society? Cannot the ability of people to create their own community in cyberspace have the effect of terminating a community in the general sense? In a class-stratified, commercially oriented society like the United States, cannot the information highway have the effect of simply making it possible for the well-to-do to bypass any contact with the balance of society altogether? These are precisely the types of questions that need to be addressed and answered in communication policymaking and precisely the types of questions in which the market has no interest.[80] At any rate, a healthy skepticism toward technology should be the order of the day.

Democracy, Scholarship, and Communication Technology

The nature of contemporary communication policymaking in the United States is only superficially democratic, and, therefore, there is little reason to believe that the results of such a system will do much more than satisfy the interests of those responsible for the decisions. Communication policymaking follows the contours of political debate in general. This is a business-run society, and the communication system is tailored to suit corporate interests. The role of the citizenry is to conform its ambitions and goals to satisfy the needs of business and profit maximization. It is not the responsibility of those directing the economy to make their activities meet the democratically determined aims of the citizenry or to be accountable for the social consequences of those actions, as democratic theory would suggest. In fact, the market is hardly a substitute for democracy. At most it is a tool, like technology, to be thoughtfully employed in a democracy. And the immediate consequence of the market for global communication is one of increasingly private concentration and commercialization, which are hardly the stuff of democracy.

It is also appealing to think that the new communication technologies can solve social problems, but they cannot. Only humans, acting consciously, can address and resolve problems like poverty, environmental degradation, racism, sexism, and militarism. As Singer notes, our task is to overcome "the contradiction between our technological genius and the absurdity of our social organization."[81] We encounter the magnificent potential of the new technologies with the wet blanket of conventional wisdom draped over the fires of our social and political imaginations. Nor is the blanket there by accident: Those who benefit from the status quo have helped place it there and are holding it down. So, can the Internet and communication technologies save democracy from capitalism? No, not unless they are explicitly deployed for public service principles. In the short term, that means struggling for universal access, for computer literacy, and for a well-subsidized and democratic noncommercial and nonprofit media sector. In the long term, that means working for explicit public planning and deliberation in crafting fundamental communications policy. Any hope of success will depend on linking and integrating communication concerns to larger efforts to bring heretofore underrepresented segments of the citizenry into the political arena, thereby reducing the power of business and working toward lessening inequality in our society.

Is that possible? Given my argument about the nature of the global economy and the demise of sovereignty, one might assume the situation to be nearly hopeless, and that the only rational course would be to try to eke out the best possible reforms from the existing regime. And since even minor public interest reforms within the existing corporate communication system have proven nearly impossible, some may therefore regard the overall situation as hopeless for the foreseeable future.

I believe the exact opposite is the case. The current pro-market policies are going to be little short of disastrous for the quality of life for a majority of people both in the United States and globally. In the coming generation there will be a pressing need for alternative policies that place the needs of the bulk of the citizenry ahead of the demands of global capital. The Internet may possibly play crucial role in expediting these developments. We are entering a critical juncture in which no social institutions, including corporations and the market, can remain exempt from public scrutiny. The challenge for those committed to democracy is, as Greider notes, "to refashion the global economy . . . so that it enhances democracy rather than crippling it, so that economic returns are widely distributed among all classes instead of narrowly at the top."[82] The tension between democracy and capitalism is becoming increasingly evident, and communication—so necessary to both—can hardly serve two masters at once. From a critical perspective, where democracy is privileged over profit, this is the context for communication policymaking. Given the centrality of communication to global capitalism, the move to reform communication must be part and parcel of a movement to reform the global political economy, as Greider suggests. It is unthinkable otherwise.

By this reasoning, there is a special role for communication scholars to play in debating and devising democratic communication policies, but the academic context for critical research is in turmoil. The rise of the Internet and the information highway places the future of communication research and education at U.S. universities in jeopardy. It demands a restructuring, or at least a rethinking, of the very field of communication, precisely at a time that many U.S. universities are downsizing as a consequence of the global economic trends outlined above, specifically stagnation and the collapse of the public sector. This is putting considerable pressure on universities to redirect their activities to elicit support from the corporate sector. In effect, there is increased pressure to move away from the traditional standard of intellectual and scholarly autonomy and link education and research explicitly to the needs of business.[83] This has clear implications for the nature of the scholarship that the new "lean and mean" university will produce, which perhaps explains why the promarket political Right is most enthusiastic about the elimination of academic autonomy. The stars on campus are the departments and individuals who attract the most grant money, and departments and scholars who fail to do so face an uncertain future.

Nowhere are these pressures more apparent than in communication. It is a paradox that precisely at the historic moment that communication is roundly deemed as central to global political economy and culture, those academic departments expressly committed to communication research are facing severe cutbacks or even elimination. This can be attributed to the historic weakness of communication on U.S. campuses. When cutbacks need be made, communication is easier to attack than more established disciplines. The pressures are doubly strong, therefore, to link up communication research and education to the masters of the corporate communication order, and to opt for what Paul Lazarsfeld termed the "administrative" rather than the "critical" path for scholarship.[84]

Although cultivating ties to the capitalist communication sector may appear a logical management move, it will probably lead to the demise of communication as a viable discipline. The administrative turn is morally deplorable. It takes communication away from what Innis termed the "university tradition," a source of honest, independent inquiry in service to democratic values.[85] At a practical level, too, business schools are far better suited to conduct research along these lines, especially as communication is now a central business activity. Who needs departments predicated upon public service and professional principles like journalism when the whole idea is to maximize profit? There is no alternative, then, but to do honest independent scholarship and instruction, with a commitment first and foremost to democratic values. Let the chips fall where they may. The field of communication needs to apply the full weight of its intellectual traditions and methodologies to the daunting questions before us. They desperately require scholarly attention. The lesson of the last fifty years on U.S. campuses is clear. If the field of communication does not do it, nobody else will. It will make for a rocky road, but what other choice is there?

17

U.S. Left and Media Politics

Democracy in the United States is in deep trouble. Cynicism and distrust of the political system, fueled at least in part by imposed ignorance, have grown steadily in recent years. There are several reasons for this, but few as important as the condition of our media. Many Americans, especially those on the Left, know that after a generation of rampant consolidation and conglomeration, the U.S. media are dominated by less than twenty firms—and that a half-dozen or so corporate giants hold the commanding positions. These firms use their market power to advance their own and other companies' corporate agendas. And they increasingly commercialize every aspect of our culture. By any known theory of political democracy, this tightly held media system, accountable only to Wall Street and Madison Avenue, is a poisonous proposition.

A healthy democracy depends on an informed and educated public, but the wealthy and powerful few who make the most important media decisions deny that as a possibility. Theirs is a system in which crucial political issues are barely mentioned, or are molded to fit the confines of their elite debate. The public is thus denied the tools it needs to participate as an informed citizenry. Moreover, the media system not only serves the ideological needs of our business-run society, but is itself a major sector of the economy.

One would expect to see an exploration of ways to fight back, among those who see the industry's concentrated power and untrammeled commercialism as roadblocks in the path of democracy. Yet for generations the control and structure of the media industries have been decidedly off-limits as a subject of political debate on the Left.

As long as this holds true, it is hard to imagine any permanent qualitative change for the better in the U.S. media system. Without reform of the industry, prospects for the United States improving the quality of our democracy seem dim indeed. It is mandatory for the U.S. Left to put media reform on its agenda.

Until after the Second World War, concern about media reform was less pressing, because labor and the Left understood the importance of communicating with and educating their own members and supporters. Every labor union and political group had its own publications in the late nineteenth and early twentieth centuries. Some of the more successful and aggressive unions and political parties had extensive media outlets. In the early 1900s, Socialist Party members and supporters published some 325 English and foreign-language daily, weekly, and monthly newspapers and magazines. Most of these were privately owned or were the publications of one or another of the 5,000 Socialist Party locals. Together they had more than two million subscribers.

Similarly, from the late nineteenth century on, just about every labor union had its own newspaper. In the mid-1930s, when the Congress of Industrial Organizations (CIO) was organized, it explained to its members that the labor movement could not thrive if the press remained the exclusive property of capital, and made the creation of labor and public service media a high priority. So did the more conservative American Federation of Labor's central labor council in Chicago, which established a local radio station as a conscious first step in setting up a pro-working-class network. All of this was part of a broader effort during the period to establish a cultural popular front. It was overwhelmed by corporate opposition in the '30s, and was given the final blow with the start of the Cold War in the late '40s.

In sum, labor and the Left's declining interest in developing its own independent media can be traced to postwar labor-corporate accommodation and the disruption and decline of the broader left as a result of Cold War anticommunism. The process was aided, too, by the change in corporate journalism in these years from a more open conservativism to a new, ostensibly nonpartisan or "objective" professionalism, a change designed to broaden the appeal—and the advertising revenue—of newspapers, magazines, and, later, television.

Then, too, labor and the Left, like their corporate opponents, came to see the media largely as a form of public relations. Thus they fell victim to the belief that the media were not important, that the "real action" for social change lay in organizing and militant activity. Attracting media attention became more important than having a means of communication that might educate members and leaders of progressive organizations.

After taking a beating in the media for fifty years, however, organized labor has begun to show some interest in media reform. Labor leaders today are more aware of the huge barrier that the corporate media presents to labor's advance. Yet this sentiment remains largely inchoate. At the 1997 AFL-CIO annual convention, perhaps one of the most political and vibrant meetings in the organization's history, the issue of media was not even mentioned in passing. Under John Sweeney, the AFL-CIO's initial foray into media activity did not go beyond the half-baked idea of spending a small fortune on TV ads and hiring PR firms in an attempt to massage the press. In contrast, the United Auto Workers (UAW) invested heavily in the United Broadcasting Network, a 100-station radio operation that also publishes a biweekly newspaper. The UAW tried something similar in the 1940s, in a failed attempt to combat the antilabor bias of the commercial radio broadcasters of that era. Yet aside from this effort by the UAW, the structural barriers to a democratic or pro-labor media remain unchallenged by labor, at both the national and local levels.

When one sees how labor and progressive social movements have fared in the U.S. media throughout most of the twentieth century, the importance of media reform becomes less abstract. In the '30s and '40s, nearly every daily newspaper with a medium-to-large circulation had at least one full-time labor editor or beat reporter. When the Flint sit-down strikes established the UAW as a major trade union in the late thirties, it was front-page news. True, the coverage was often unsympathetic, but at least the public knew what was happening. In the nineties, fewer than ten labor reporters remained on daily newspapers in the entire nation. Conversely, there are seemingly thousands of business writers who, daily, fill the nation's papers with their stories. Thus, in 1989, when the largest sit-down strike since Flint took place in Pittston, Virginia, it went virtually unreported. When several leading U.S. trade unions formed a new Labor political party in 1996, that, too, was unreported in the commercial media. Labor coverage has been reduced to stories about how strikers are threatening violence or creating a burden for the people in their communities. If one read only the commercial media, it would be difficult to determine what good was served by having labor unions at all. I do not mean to suggest that corporate media hostility to labor is swallowed hook, line, and sinker by the public. The 1997 Teamster strike against UPS elicited the usual right-wing hysteria about labor, but the remarkable public support for the strikers forced some of the media to deal more fairly with the Teamsters, despite the fact that the press was far from sympathetic to the union.

Meanwhile, the idea of organizing for structural media reform is ignored or opposed by the entire democratic Left in the United States. New progressive party groups—such as the Labor Party and the New Party—avoided any mention of media in their core platforms in the '90s. Some chapters of the Green Party made an issue of media ownership and control, perhaps influenced by Ralph Nader's persistent call for stricter control over the publicly owned airwaves, but these are token gestures at best. The Progressive caucus of the U.S. Congress showed only slight interest in the matter. Congressman Bernie Sanders recognized that "this is an issue that is absolutely vital to democracy, and that only the left can address. The New Party, the Green Party, the Labor Party, as well as progressive Democrats, should be all over this issue," though he laments, "for most of the Left, it's not even on the agenda." Sanders, the most successful American socialist politician in half a century, is unequivocal about the importance of media reform: "The challenge of our time is to make media relevant for a vibrant democracy."

To a large extent, the absence of informed media politics reflects the power of U.S. media corporations to control and dominate not only mainstream debate, but also debate on the Left. After all, why pick a fight with these guys when the chances for success seem so slim, and when there seems to be little public recognition of structural media issues or opposition to the status quo? The corporate media may well be the most powerful adversary in the ranks of capital. They control what the general public sees and reads about the political process in the United States. Critical discussion of media structure is the last thing they want the general public to consider. They prefer to leave analysis of media ownership and advertising to the business pages and the trade press, where such questions are covered solely from investors' point of view. In this climate, it is no surprise that even leftist critics of the corporate media rarely discuss organizing to change the system; the very prospect seems implausible.

But the Left's disinterest in media is not merely the product of ignorance or intimidation. Some on the Left dismiss media activism as a waste of time. Their arguments are rarely the result of sustained thought, and range from the idea that the media system is unreformable to the notion that the corporate media system isn't that bad or that influential. The correct path, from this perspective, is simply to develop independent left media on the margins, while devoting organizing efforts elsewhere. Media reform struggles, therefore, are dismissed as the logical province of liberals and single-issue advocates with narrow political vision or platform. Real battles with the ruling class, from this viewpoint, should be fought elsewhere.

This approach is correct on a couple of key points. Firstly, media reform is no substitute for building a democratic Left. But the options are not either/or. Virtually all leading Left media critics incorporate media criticism into a range of broader political activity. Secondly, it is correct to argue that if we ever build a solid Left or labor movement, it will have its own media and we will have less reason to be concerned about how the corporate media system operates. But that begs the question of why we have been incapable of building even a tiny Left in the United States for the past forty years. The corporate media system is not the sole (or even the primary) reason for the lack of a Left or a strong labor movement, but it powerfully reinforces the ideological and political power of business.

The political "free market" Right understands the importance of media far better than the Left. Indeed, the relative success of the right is largely the result of the development of its own media and influence on the corporate media. Right-wing individuals and foundations have devoted considerable resources to campaigns that have pushed the media to support their programs—social as well as economic. Billionaire right-wingers establish political media primarily to propagate pro-business politics and push the range of political debate ever rightward. Since the '70s the Right has worked mightily and with considerable success to establish right-wing journalism.

The political right leads the fight against all forms of noncommercial and nonprofit media. It also battles tirelessly to see that the Public Broadcasting System and National Public Radio stay within the same ideological boundaries as the commercial media. As a result of this pressure, PBS refuses to permit labor to sponsor programs about workers, even while it begs business lavishly to subsidize programs extolling free enterprise. At the same time, progressive and mainstream foundations virtually ignore this right-wing assault. These groups fear being "political." They end up trying to keep people from falling overboard while conceding the privilege of steering the ship to the right.

Making media reform a component of the labor and Left agenda has many potential benefits. Although the issue receives scant public attention, there is evidence of growing public dissatisfaction with the hyper-commercialized media. In few areas are the conflicts between corporate rule and the needs of a democracy more apparent. The Left can use media as an educational tool to explain the flaws in the existing social order and to present its vision of what a more democratic society would look like. Many people from across the political spectrum, as well as entirely depoliticized people, are appalled by the commercial carpet bombing of our culture (especially children's culture), and by the collapse of journalism. The Left can offer coherent explanations and viable, democratic solutions. Nobody else can.

Labor and the Left can also use media reform as an issue that unites its disparate elements, such as environmentalists, feminists, civil rights advocates, and labor activists, along with journalists, artists, educators, librarians, parents, and many others who are discomfited by the commercialization of public life. We should not forget that if the Left ignores media reform, it hands the game to the far Right, whose bogus analysis and frightening solutions do not keep it from being an active player.

The Struggle for Democratic Media

So what should the Left do to address the commercial media system? First and foremost, it has to put media reform on its agenda and work to get its reform proposals before the general public. The core principle is that control over communication has to be taken away from Wall Street and Madison Avenue and put in the hands of citizens, journalists, and others whose concerns are not limited to the defense of corporate profitability.

In nations ranging from New Zealand and Canada to India and Brazil, democratic left electoral parties are increasingly making the breakup of corporate commercial media, and the establishment of a viable nonprofit media sector, a main part of their platforms. This was a striking development in the 1990s. In Sweden, the Left Party—which represents those disenchanted with the Social Democratic Party's move toward the right—made media reform a cornerstone of its platform. In 1998, the Left Party scored 12 percent of the vote in national elections, doubling its previous level. Moreover, in many

nations there are nascent grassroots media organizations struggling to promote noncommercial and nonprofit media.

Here in the United States, there are a few new media reform efforts, but
some are narrowly conceived and suffer from a lack of democratic vision.
There is the drive to establish, for example, a civic or public journalism that
is largely devoted to counteracting the sensationalism of print and television.
Unfortunately, the movement works hand in hand with the very corporate
chieftains who have created and molded the existing media. This version of
public journalism, not surprisingly, is averse to what it calls "ideological"
approaches to the news, opting instead for a supposed objectivity that avoids
lively debate and political conflict. Instead it works toward the sort of boring-
ly balanced and antiseptic newsfare that could put the entire nation into a
deep, uninformed slumber. By claiming that they want to give readers news
that is important to their lives, advocates of public journalism may in fact be
assisting in the process of converting journalism into the type of noncontroversial consumer news that delights the advertising community. Such is the
logic of a commercialized and depoliticized society.

Those who wish to increase the integrity of commercial journalism should
advocate increased power for journalists, which in the commercial media can
only be achieved by establishing strong, progressive unions. Media workers'
unions need to be supported. The assault on journalists' unions in the United
States has been an important factor in the decline of the quality of journalism.
Ideally, journalists' and media workers' unions should negotiate for as much
control as possible of the editorial and creative process. We need to work to
eradicate the control of capital over our journalism and culture, without sub-
stituting deadening bureaucratic control.

Another burgeoning area of interest is the media literacy movement,
whose aim is to educate people to be skeptical and knowledgeable users of
the media. Media literacy has considerable potential as long as it involves
an explanation of how the media system actually works, and leads people
to want to work toward a better system. But the media literacy movement
has a highly visible wing that accepts money from corporate media and
advertisers. This version of media literacy implicitly buys into the line that
the commercial media simply "give the people what they want." So the
media literacy crowd's job is to train people to demand better fare from
their presumably willing and obedient corporate media servants. Like pub-

lic journalism, this attracts foundation support because it is noncontroversial. But this approach may simply help to perpetuate the current situation. "Hey, don't blame us for the lousy stuff we provide," the corporate media giants will say. "We even bankrolled media literacy to train people to demand higher quality fare. The morons simply demanded more of what we are already doing."

Fortunately, some other media groups are more promising. Fairness & Accuracy In Reporting (FAIR), a media watchdog group launched in the 1980s, provides consistent analysis of media trends through published reports and its magazine *Extra!* FAIR's work helps both those who wish to improve the quality of existing journalism and those who seek structural change. Similarly, the Cultural Environment Movement (CEM), founded in the mid-nineties, attempts to draw all sorts of nonprofit and public-interest groups into the campaign for media reform. Like FAIR, it works for improvement within the status quo as well as broader structural reform.

Local media alliances have also been established in numerous North American cities to create alternative media and to watchdog the local commercial media. These local groups have shown some potential to draw the public into media politics by targeting issues like violence-obsessed local TV news, newspaper "redlining" of poor neighborhoods, the proliferation of alcohol and cigarette billboards in poor and working-class neighborhoods, and the commercialization of education.

Likewise, microradio broadcasting—unlicensed, low-power, noncommercial broadcasting conducted on open slots in the radio spectrum—has become a significant enterprise throughout the nation in the past few years. It offers poor, dispossessed, and marginalized voices an opportunity to be heard.

That all of this activity has blossomed in the current political environment suggests that there may be a wellspring for further media reform activity. However, the movement lacks the resources to exploit this opportunity. This should be the province of organized labor and the philanthropic community. Not surprisingly, given the absence of a coherent political left, the movement also lacks an understanding of where media reform fits into a broader movement democracy. To be successful, media reform needs a resurgent left. But, conversely, for the left to succeed it will need to support the existing nonprofit media to a far greater extent (e.g., *Monthly Review, The Progressive, Z, The Nation, In These Times, Counterpunch, Dollars and Sense, Adbusters, Left*

Business Observer, *NACLA Report*, *MERIP*, *Dissent*, Pacifica, Globalvision), create its own media, and fight for media reform.

For these two areas to reinforce each other, labor and the Left will have to use their own resources to support and create better noncommercial media and agitate for better results from commercial media. Some labor unions and federations, for example, have encouraged the production of labor video documentaries. But all of labor needs to support newspapers, magazines, broadcast stations, and Web sites of their own, and give money and resources to existing community and nonprofit media without direct labor affiliation. This is crucial. Labor needs to grant considerable editorial leeway to media it subsidizes. Unless it does so, the media will tend to be timid, overly concerned with pleasing labor's political hierarchy, and unlikely to produce anything vital or interesting to a general public.

Unlike the Right, labor and the Left can never consider funding alternatives or independent media a satisfactory media program in and of itself. The agenda and activities of the Right mesh well with the corporate control of the media, and Right media figures move comfortably at all echelons of the corporate media system. A well-established, independent, Left media can and will influence mainstream media in a positive manner, but marriage is out of the question, given the differences in social status. The upper limit of this approach is to establish a strong Left niche on the margins. This point holds true for the Internet which, for the most part, assimilated into the corporate media. Technology alone cannot undermine the media system.

In addition, labor and the Left need to take another page from the political right, which masterfully manipulates traditional U.S. journalism. Like the Right, labor and the progressive philanthropic community need to support think tanks of experts who can provide labor and Left perspectives on social issues for commercial and noncommercial journalists alike. It can also monitor the massive right-wing campaigns to shape news coverage. The Institute for Public Accuracy, under the direction of Norman Solomon and Sam Husseini, is one example.

Government media policies also must be changed. There is nothing natural about the existing corporate media system; it is the result of laws, regulations, and extensive public subsidies that have been pushed through by the corporate media lobby with almost no public awareness or participation in the legislative process. Our objective is a more diverse and competitive commercial system with a significant nonprofit and noncommercial sector.

There are several legislative proposals to organize around. First, we need to make it easier for people—not just rich people—to make donations to non-profit media. Why not let everyone deduct $150 from their taxes if they donate it to a nonprofit medium? Second, let's establish a bona fide noncommercial public radio and television system, with local and national stations and networks. The expense should come out of the general budget, though we need to establish a governing mechanism to keep the public broadcasters accountable but not suffocated by politicians. Third, let's really make some demands on commercial broadcasters, and finally get something in return for letting them become filthy rich using the scarce public airwaves at no charge. Why not insist on eliminating advertising on children's and news programs, and use 5 percent of the broadcasters' revenues to subsidize three or four hours per day of children's and news shows on every channel? And put the control over these shows in the hands of journalists and creative people, not advertising executives! And why not ban running any political ads as a condition for getting a license to broadcast? Fourth, let's go back to the original spirit and intent of our antitrust statutes and break up the media giants, whose concentrations of power should be unthinkable in a democracy. (When the United States occupied Japan and Germany following the Second World War, it instituted policies discouraging media concentration, as this was seen as antidemocratic and fascist-promoting. What was smart policy in this case in 1945 is smart policy today.)

If we won the reforms above, it would automatically add a strong progressive presence to the Internet, because all of the above media would necessarily have an online component.

There are numerous other policies that would promote democratic media. In the short term, the most important thing is to put the issue on the political agenda, have sympathetic members of Congress draft legislation that we can organize around, and get the discussion moving forward. This will not be an easy area in which to gain victories. Few mainstream politicians wish to tangle with the media giants. But it is an area with unusual promise for labor and the left. There is little evidence that people are captivated by commercial media fare to the extent the media giants' PR declares. And the bottom line, so to speak, remains clear. Unless we can make some headway on the media front, it will be difficult to get very far anywhere else.

18

Global Media and Its Discontents

Broadcasting is too important to the functioning of a democracy for decisions
to be left entirely to the broadcasters.

—British Parliamentarian Tony Benn

Our democracy depends on the free flow of ideas and information. When that
flow is blocked, and our access to information is controlled by the few and the
wealthy, our ability to make informed choices suffers, as does our democracy.
This is exactly what is happening as media conglomerates continue to
increase their share of the communications market unfettered by government
regulation or control. . . . [A] healthy democracy demands an informed electorate. We need policies that limit media concentration and ensure a rich
exchange of ideas. We believe that diversity of expression must be promoted
through tax incentives to assist community groups, cooperatives or entrepreneurs to invest in community media, and that newspaper owners should not
also own broadcasting corporations.

—Platform of Canada's New Democratic Party, 2001

There cannot be a democratic country, democratic society without freedom of
the press.

—Jose Ramos-Horta,
Nobel Laureate, Minister of Foreign Affairs for East Timor

Crippled by the rigidly enforced minutae of a political moment in which the country's leaders and their "major" parties proclaim their commitment to a grotesque bipartisanship that stifles all but the most inconsequential conflict, U.S. public life features little in the way of debate about the role a truly free and diverse media could play in shaping a truly free and diverse democracy.

In other countries, however, media is treated as an issue. In Canada, in 2001, there was an explosion of serious debate over the damage that monopoly ownership of newspapers does to the editorial freedom of individual publications and the quality of the broader public discourse. The debate, which ought to be highly instructive for Americans at a time when ownership in this country's press is being concentrated in fewer and fewer hands, began when a corporation owned by a wealthy family with close ties to then-prime minister Jean Chretien started buying up major daily newspapers across the country. That company, CanWest Global, did not just want to homogenize the look and content of the fourteen metropolitan daily newspapers that came under its control (a standard step by media conglomerates seeking to reduce costs and increase profits), it also wanted to impose a single editorial ideology so that all the newspapers would speak in one voice—that of the powerful and politically connected Asper family. Journalists working on newspapers with distinct political and regional differences resisted the one-size-fits-all approach. But they soon got a reminder of the truth of the old complaint: Freedom of the Press only exists for those who own a press.

When a major scandal within Chretien's administration was exposed in 2002, Canadians looked to the editorial page of the *Ottawa Citizen* newspaper. The dominant daily in the nation's capital city, and historically one of the most outspoken newspapers in North America, did not disappoint. Instead of a canned editorial from its new owners at CanWest, the newspaper published a bold denunciation of Chretien that called for the prime minister to step down. The Aspers, a family that has had a long and mutually beneficial relationship with Chretien and his Liberal Party, were not amused. They fired the local publisher of the paper for "non-compliance" with the corporation's Chretien-is-off-limits line. The publisher, Russell Mills, was not the first CanWest newspaper employee fired for deviating from the company's ideological line. Prior to this, several prominent columnists had also been sacked for criticizing Chretien's Liberal Party government. But the firing of the top man at the premier paper in the nation's capital did not pass unnoted.

"Russell Mills was fired because the prime minister's buddy happened to be his boss," declared Alexa McDonough, parliamentary leader of Canada's opposition New Democratic Party. "That is downright dangerous to democracy. We need a full public inquiry into media concentration, ownership and convergence."

McDonough joined other opposition party members of Canada's House of Commons in forcing a remarkable public debate on media and democracy issues in the summer of 2002. The New Democratic Party, a social democratic party with a long history of condemning corporate excess, was in a position to play a leadership role in that debate because it had gone out of its way to make media an issue. And they quickly pushed the debate beyond a narrow discussion of the firing of one man on one newspaper. "As unsettling as these abuses of journalistic practice are, focusing on the high-handed actions of the Aspers alone ignores the real disease that is eating away at our democratic fabric—the truly alarming scale of media concentration and commercialization in this country," McDonough declared in the days following the firing of Mills. "Last week's events call for a reversal of the past 15–20 years of media and broadcasting policy in this country. The multi-media conglomerates must be broken up. They have been encouraged by federal policymakers in the mistaken belief they would defend the country's cultural sovereignty. They are having the opposite effect."

McDonough's comments could be echoed in most nations these days—including the United States. Yet, McDonough's savvy focus on structural concerns distinguished the Canadian debate, in which the prospect of real reform is at least on the table.

Indeed, if there is a measure of the seriousness with which a nation ponders it potential to address fundamental issues, then that measure may well be found in the depth of its discussion about media and democracy.

Surely, that is the case in East Timor, the Pacific island state that proudly bills itself, "The World's Newest Democracy." In August 2001, East Timor emerged from a quarter-century of brutal repression at the hands of Indonesian military rulers to hold a historic round of free elections for its Constituent Assembly. More than two-dozen political parties jockeyed for position in a competition where there was a powerful sense the winners would not merely govern but would define the scope and character of a freshly minted democracy.

In this election contest, issues of media and democracy were not abstractions. The Indonesian military had limited democratic discourse at every turn, and after the East Timorese voted overwhelmingly for independence in 1999, the offices of the region's only daily newspaper were sacked and burned during a rampage by the Indonesian soldiers and militias allied with them. In East Timor, political leaders and citizens well understood that media was a serious political issue. The different parties developed detailed policy statements and platforms on issues of broadcast diversity, concentration of media ownership, and the role that the new government of East Timor ought to play in fostering the free flow of information and the open debate that is fundamental in a democracy. The party that swept those elections, FRETILIN (The Frente Revolucionaria do Timor Leset Independente) produced a manifesto, "Towards the Restoration of Independence and the Freedom of our People," that touched on issues ranging from health care to housing to the role that the new nation would play in the world. A full section in the manifesto explained that to restore freedom, it would be necessary to "democratise mass media."

"The democratisation of mass media must deserve privileged attention in a national development policy; it must aim at extending freedom of expression and the press," the manifesto declared. "The FRETILIN Administration will stand for an objective and independent media in search of factual truth. The Administration will pursue efforts to extend radio and TV networks nation-wide and guarantee a timely access to information to every citizen. FRETILIN will pursue a national policy favouring the diversification of media operators as a way to fight private or state monopolies and defend the freedom of the press."

Within months of the election, a FRETILIN-led government produced a new Constitution that did, indeed, include a substantial section guaranteeing "freedom of the press and other mass media." Far more detailed than the First Amendment mention in the U.S. Constitution, the document enacted in East Timor declared, "The monopoly of the mass media shall be prohibited." The document also detailed the rights of journalists and declared, "The state shall guarantee the existence of a public radio and television service that is impartial in order to, inter-alia, protect and disseminate the culture and the traditional values of the Democratic Republic of East Timor and guarantee opportunities for the expression of different lines of opinion."

"These rights are fundamental to a true democracy," explained Virgilio da Silva Guterres, the president of the Timor Lorosa'e Journalists Association, in a statement detailing the explosion of new and diverse media in a place where there is little mystery about the necessity of a truly free press in the development of a truly free country.

Virgilio da Silva Guterres was, of course, correct to view East Timor's bar on media monopoly, its guarantees of the rights of journalists, and its promise of a vibrant and diverse public broadcasting service as "fundamental to a true democracy."

Yet, that statement would surely draw debate, perhaps even ridicule, in the United States, where media monopolies are expanding at a breakneck pace and where public broadcasting services are being squeezed to the point of dysfunction by politicians who—with strong encouragement from private broadcast lobbies—have successfully strangled public funding for public broadcasting.

Between the experience of the expanding democracy of East Timor (where the 2001 assembly elections drew a 93 percent turnout) and the rapidly waning democracy of the United States (where less than 40 percent of eligible voters participate in the "off-year" congressional elections), there is a world of difference. But, around the world, wherever there is a real debate about democracy, as was the case in Canada, there is an understanding that media is a political issue of utmost importance.

It should come as no surprise then that, when we look at what is happening to debates about media abroad, we see a growing willingness on the part of democratic forces to organize for media reforms that challenge the patterns of globalization and corporate domination. These calls for media reform are also proving popular with voters, if not with the business class. In this chapter the nature of the emerging global commercial media system and the contours of the democratic resistance to it are outlinned. We believe that there are hopeful and powerfully instructive lessons for Americans in these global developments.

But first, let's look at the developments to which movements for media reform are responding. Since the 1980s, a global commercial media market has developed. As a result of deregulation of national media markets, new communication technologies, and heavy pressure from the U.S. government and the international business community, the face of media has undergone striking change in virtually every country on the planet. Whereas media systems were formerly best understood as a series of national systems, with a varying role played by media imports depending upon the nation, today it is more appropriate to regard media as a global system with national variants.

The global media system is the province of fewer than one hundred firms that provide the vast majority of the world's media fare. There are two distinct tiers to this hierarchy. The first tier is composed of less than ten transnational media conglomerates (including AOL Time Warner, Disney, Bertelsmann, News Corporation, Viacom, Sony, and Vivendi Universal) that all collect between $10 billion and $35 billion per year in annual media-related revenues. These firms tend to be dominant players in numerous media sectors and to do business all across the world. The remaining eighty or ninety firms are smaller, tend to concentrate more upon one or two media sectors, and are more likely to be national or regional powerhouses. A great chasm separates the first-tier media firms and those near the bottom of the second tier. AOL Time Warner or Viacom, for example, has annual sales some fifty times greater than the fiftieth largest media firm in the world.

The transnational media giants, as one leading media analyst notes, "are increasingly setting their sights on global expansion." In 1999, for example, Disney completely reorganized its corporate structure to expand and strengthen its "global presence." Disney's enthusiasm is understandable; experts project that the major Hollywood studios, which earned around one-half of their income outside the United States, will see that portion rise in the coming generation. An examination of the top-ten grossing films in each of the eight largest national markets after the United States in the summer of 1999 reveals that Hollywood films, each produced by a first-tier media giant, accounted for seventy of them.

But the global media system should not be perceived as one where U.S.-based transnational conglomerates dump their standard fare on new audiences. On the contrary, the media giants localize their content whenever feasible, and almost always enter new markets in a partnership with local firms and investors. Sony's Hollywood-based studios have been most aggressive in producing films and localized TV content, doing so across Europe, Latin America, and Asia. Rupert Murdoch's News Corporation, however, is the flagship firm for establishing major joint ventures with local firms across the globe, especially with regard to cable and satellite television. By 1999, even

India's massive domestic film industry had been penetrated by joint ventures with News Corp.'s Fox studios and several other Hollywood giants.

The balance of the largest media firms are meeting the challenge and going global with a vengeance. Liberty Media and Microsoft have both made major investments in global cable systems. Even second-tier global media firms find it necessary to move beyond their national or regional markets in order to grow and to avoid being taken over by more aggressive competitors.

Nor is this pattern of global growth and concentration exclusive to the largest, mostly U.S.-based firms. Deregulation of national media ownership restrictions has both opened up national markets to outsiders and permitted domestic giants to grow ever more powerful. Spanish media and telecommunication firms, for example, "are invading Latin America in search of its corporate treasures." Major national media markets like Mexico, Brazil, and India are each increasingly dominated by just a few massive media firms, and these firms all work closely in joint ventures with the transnational media giants. In no sense can the massive capitalist media firms of the developing world like Mexico's Televisa or Brazil's Globo be characterized as "oppositional" to the global corporate media system; they are integral players in that system.

This is not just a process taking place in what has been called the Third World. In Britain, the television and newspaper industries have undergone a tremendous consolidation, and U.S.-based firms are now prominent players in these oligopolistic markets. Indeed, most nations have vastly more concentrated ownership of media than the United States, if only due to their smaller populations and geographic sizes. And the process is far from over.

The European Union, for example, is working to help European media firms become not only regional, but global, powers. As a result of deregulation, the *New York Times* observed that "Europe's television industry is suddenly in the grip of an American-style consolidation." In addition to first-tier media giants like News Corp. and Bertelsmann, European TV is falling into the hands of a few regional giants like Canal Plus, SBS, and Fininvest. These firms hope to use their European base as the foundation for eventual expansion into the United States, either directly or through joint ventures.

One other development is working hand-in-hand with global media concentration: the rise of a highly concentrated global advertising industry. For the past decade the advertising agency industry has consolidated at a rate even greater than that of the media industry, and it is now dominated by three to six global giants that dwarf the remaining players. These giants tend to have subsidiaries in every major market, and they increasingly represent corporate clients who need global marketing campaigns. These ad agency titans find that the global media giants are best positioned to provide them with the global reach their clients need and demand.

In 2001 and 2002 many of these burgeoning media giants fell on hard times. From Vivendi Universal and Kirch to AOL Time Warner and News Corporation, stock prices plummeted as earnings collapsed. In most cases, however, the underlying media activities were still profitable; the problem was that these firms had vastly overpaid in a number of extravagant deals during the halcyon days of the Internet expansion in the late 1990s. The upshot was a reshuffling of assets among the big boys, but no alteration in the operating logic of the system.

The state of the global media system may not be widely known, and it is hardly controversial. The pages of business and trade publications teem with this information on a daily basis. And were we to leave the discussion at this point, investors might be the only audience with a direct interest in the subject. But we are not discussing the widget market here, or some other incidental commercial undertaking. We are discussing the means of communication and information distribution—the lifeblood of journalism and culture—and, accordingly, the foundation of democracy. The most striking way to conceive of the negative implications of the global commercial media market is quite simple: As the power of the largest firms grows, they use that power to commercialize content to the greatest extent possible and, if necessary, to protect their political interests, and they denigrate any notion of public service that might interfere with either of those aims.

This attack on public service assumes many forms. Deregulation and the rise of the commercial media market have cast the future of public service broadcasting in grave jeopardy. Traditional public service broadcasters, such as the British Broadcasting Corporation (BBC), have begun to look like square pegs in a world of round holes. They are increasingly pressured to adopt the practices of commercial firms in order to establish their efficiency and worth, but as they go commercial they lose their *raison d'être*. They even get chastised for being publicly subsidized competitors to the now dominant commercial media. *The Economist* calls this the "conundrum" of public service broadcasting: "If it goes upmarket, nobody watches it, so it is hard to justify state finance. If it goes downmarket, it ceases to look like public-service broadcasting, so it is hard to justify state finance." There is a crucial change assumed in that formulation, however. At its best, public broadcasters sought to provide high-quality, noncommercial fare to the entire population regardless of what the commercial media were doing. This made it possible for them to develop mass audiences while providing noncommercial standards. In this new era where corporate media giants ride roughshod over governments, public service broadcasters are expected to concede popular programming to commercial interests, and to concentrate upon that for which there is not much of a market. A vicious cycle is created, wherein underfunded public broadcasting outlets are unable to compete for viewers, are told to turn to commercial support, and ultimately are threatened with privatization.

Until public broadcasters are again provided with the resources and mandate to provide noncommercial programming to large audiences, they are on a dead-end street. They may survive as quasi-commercial entities, but they will not survive as genuine public service broadcasters. The defense of public broadcasting—and its reformation along less bureaucratic lines—is one of the cornerstones of media reform movements worldwide. There is a growing sense that we are on the verge of losing a unique and indispensable cultural resource. It is a concern well expressed by an Australian senator during a debate over funding the Australian Broadcasting Corporation (ABC): "Starving the ABC of its funds means that the ABC cannot afford to purchase the rights to a whole spectrum of content, including sport, and especially cannot afford to produce its own content."

As in the United States, a striking and important consequence of the global commercial media market has been the attack on journalism, and the reduction in its capacity to serve as the basis for an informed, participating citizenry. Let us be clear here: we are not blaming the global media system for all the flaws in journalism. Establishing a media system that fosters a free-wheeling, independent, wide-ranging, and vibrant journalism and political culture is no easy matter, though it is something that all democratic societies should aspire to develop. National press systems prior to—and in conjunction with—the global commercial system were and are sometimes adequate at this job, but many were failures. Frequently, the media have been owned by wealthy individuals or firms that have clearly censored journalism to support their usually reactionary politics, as is the case in Turkey today. Both public and commercial broadcasters in many nations have often been handmaidens of the dominant political parties and interests. In places like Mexico, Peru, and Brazil, the dominant commercial broadcasters have tended to be in bed with the dominant pro-business political parties, and to use their media power aggressively and shamelessly to maintain the favored parties in power. Editors and reporters from dissident media who courageously bucked the system and reported on those in power have often found themselves arrested or on the receiving end of a beating or a gunshot. These practices continue today across the world.

Consider the case of Venezuela, where elected president Hugo Chávez's populist advocacy on behalf of programs to aid his country's impoverished masses conflicted with the neoliberal agenda of privately owned newspapers and television stations. The press coverage accorded Chávez by this privately owned "free press" would have earned Josef Goebbels's or Joe Stalin's deepest admiration. When business, corrupt unions, and factions within the military deposed Chávez in a coup in April 2002, the banner headline of one of the nation's largest newspapers announced that it was "A Step in the Right Direction." The columns of the press and broadcast commentary blamed Chávez for the shooting deaths of demonstrators on the day of the coup and quickly relegated the ousted president to the dustbin of history. "They say history elevates or buries men; for you it has reserved a pit beside the Venezuelan leaders infamous for their atrocities," the newspaper *El Nacional* declared. Similar sentiments were expressed in enthusiastic editorials that appeared in the *New York Times* and other U.S. papers. Though popular with press barons, the coup proved less appealing on the streets of Caracas and other Venezuelan cities. Even though reports of Chávez's removal were spun as great news, the streets filled with citizens demanding the restoration of their elected president to office. As the protests grew, the media simply stopped covering the news. Newspapers ceased to publish, the state television station was pulled off the air, and privately owned stations started showing a steady stream of soap operas.

Only when the protesters took over the state television station did Venezuelans begin to receive news of what was happening in their country, as a British academic, Jon Beasley-Murray, reported in an analysis of events in Venezuela penned for the North American Congress on Latin America. "State television had, amazingly, come back onto the airwaves," wrote Beasley-

Murray, who was in Venezuela during and after the coup. "The people who had taken over the state television station were clearly improvising, desperately. The colour balance and contrast of these studio images was all wrong, the cameras held by amateur hands, and only one microphone seemed to be working. Those behind the presenters' desk were nervous, one fiddling compulsively with something on the desk, another shaking while holding the microphone, but there they were: a couple of journalists, a 'liberation theology' priest, and a minister and a congressman from the previous regime. The minister spoke first, and very fast. She gave a version of the violent end to Thursday's march that differed absolutely from the narrative the media had put forward to justify the coup that had followed: the majority of the dead had been supporters of Chávez (not opposition protesters), and the snipers firing upon the crowds were members of police forces not under the regime's control. Moreover, the former president had not resigned; he was being held against his will at a naval base on an island to the north. The current president, Carmona, was illegitimate head of a de facto regime that was the product of a military coup. Thousands of people were on the streets outside the presidential palace demanding Chavez's return. A counter-narrative was emerging.

"The congressman appealed directly to the owners and managers of other television stations to portray what was happening in Caracas," the account continued. "No change (appeared) on those other channels, however, most of which had returned to their regular programming. And then the state channel went off the air."

Beasley-Murray titled his analysis, "The Revolution Will Not Be Televised"—referencing a famous song by Gil Scott-Heron. And, just as the agitating poet and songwriter predicted, the revolution succeeded in spite of the media's blackout. When Chávez returned to power, he did not sanction the media. But the citizens of Venezuela—who had relied on the Internet, cell phones, and other new technologies to spread the word of their protests—had learned a powerful lesson about where the mainstream media stood on the question of democracy. And the cheerleading from U.S. newspapers and television commentators served as a reminder that the sympathies of those who enjoy the freedom of the press in the United States do not lie with those who seek to preserve basic freedoms and democracy in other lands.

In theory, the rise of the global media giants was regarded as a plus to many countries; these organizations, it was thought, would use their money, power, and prestige to bring neutral, professional, nonpartisan journalism to nations desperate for such fare. And, indeed, to the extent "globalization" affects national media regulation to undermine censorship of the news, that is a good thing. The sad truth, however, is that the caliber of the journalism provided by these giants tends to be deplorable. When a journalist actually attempts to maintain a higher standard, she quickly learns that she does not fit into the new media landscape. Award-winning writer Robert Fisk was until 1986 the Middle East correspondent for the *Times* of London. He left, he says, because of the quality of journalism—or is it lack of quality?—demanded by *Times* owner Rupert Murdoch. "I would not accept the Murdoch ethos. Over and over again, I was writing against the paper's presumptions. I was in the odd situation where the *Times* didn't want me to leave but they would find themselves embarrassed at the content of what I wrote. The *Times* is an example of what has happened to much [of] journalism in Britain and Europe, which has become dominated by the micro-journalism of television and radio newscasts of one minute each."

It should come as no surprise, then, that reporters and editors connected to the media giants are only rarely the ones who show up as the arrested and murdered reporters on the annual list published by the Committee to Protect Journalists. The media giants are not interested in pursuing dangerous stories that cost a lot of time and money to pursue, promise little financial payoff, and can antagonize governmental authorities with whom the media barons desperately want to stay on good terms. Most indicative of this trend has been the manner in which four of the five largest media firms in the world have fallen over themselves attempting to please the government of China. Disney's and News Corp.'s campaign to please the Chinese rulers by watering down their journalism and operations has been chronicled elsewhere. Time Warner and Viacom entered the fray in the fall of 1999. What these episodes make clear is that no viable system of journalism can be expected from a system under the thumb of massive self-interested commercial organizations.

The most visible manifestation of the rise of the global commercial media has not been its journalism but its broader popular consumer culture, as its fare is drenched in advertising and commercialism. Report after report chronicles the rapid and stunning shift in culture, especially among middle- and upper-class youth, across the world as the commercial media system subsumes each nation's television system. Although there is considerable debate over whether this is a "U.S. invasion" or a broader corporate invasion, or whether this is good or bad, there is little debate over one point. This is a generation that is under pressure from the media it consumes to be brazenly materialistic, selfish, depoliticized, and non-socially minded. To the extent one finds these values problematic for a democracy, we all should be concerned. The commercial media system is the ideological linchpin of the globalizing market economy. Consider the case of the Czech Republic. Not long ago the young generation led the "Velvet Revolution" against the communist regime under the slogan: "Truth and love must prevail over lies and hatred." Ten years later even the *Wall Street Journal* acknowledged that the Czech Republic had turned into a demoralized morass, where "an unnerving dash to the free market" had created a society awash with greed, selfishness, corruption, and scams.

The type of political culture that accompanies the rise of the corporate media system worldwide looks to be increasingly like that found in the United States: in the place of informed debate or political parties organizing along the full spectrum of opinion, there will be vacuous journalism and elections, dominated by public relations, big money, moronic political advertising, and limited debate on tangible issues. It is a world where the market and commercial values overwhelm notions of democracy and civic culture, a world where depoliticization runs rampant, and a world where the wealthy few face fewer and fewer threats of political challenge.

It is this context that many people around the world are organizing to reform their media systems to better serve the democratic needs of the great mass of citizens. These movements are many and they are varied. They take place at the local, national, regional, and global levels. They remain largely uncoordinated. Yet, all share basic values regarding media. They understand that the corporate media system is in many respects the advancing army of a global economic system that is hell-bent on producing profits regardless of the social and environmental implications. This global "free-market" economic system has produced considerable benefits for some (usually very wealthy) people, and notable benefits for many more (usually the middle and upper middle classes), but it has come at a very high cost. Social inequality is increasing in nearly every nation, as is the divide between rich nations and poor nations. For working-class and poor people, especially women, the results of the global "free market" can be disastrous.

Because of the obvious linkages between the corporate media system and the global economic system, media reform is seen by a growing number of activists around the world as a necessary part of any democratic political platform; rarely is it seen anymore as a "single issue" reform activity. In country after country, media reform is being integrated into the platforms, the campaigns, and the parliamentary initiatives of political parties that refuse any longer to operate in denial of the role that media plays in a democracy. This is absolutely essential for success; although media activism can and must assume many forms, it is when that activism is advanced by political parties and related mass movements that media reform can most effectively be linked to broader issues of social justice. This, of course, is the fundamental step that is required for the development of the broad-based support necessary for success. The importance of political parties as vehicles for pushing media reform issues into the public discourse is arguably the single most vital lesson from abroad for Americans to learn concerning media reform.

It would, of course, be unduly romantic to suggest that the development of the global commercial media market has been paralleled by a political response of equally definitional force. Challenges to monopoly and commercialization have yet to reach critical mass in any nation, let alone on an international scale that might cause the media giants to tremble—as, for instance, the campaign against genetic modification of food caused multinational conglomerates such as Monsanto to quake. Indeed, one of the great tragedies regarding media activism is that, as the processes of globalization, conglomeration, and commercialization sped up in the early 1990s, many traditional parties of the left abandoned the critiques of commercial media that had, historically, been among their core values.

Take as an example the British Labour Party. Throughout much of its history, the Labour Party was an explicitly socialist grouping that nurtured a healthy skepticism regarding media giants within Great Britain and beyond its borders. Targeted for trashing by "the Tory press" from its earliest days, the party displayed little caution in proposing tough controls on media monopoly, and campaigning for a strong, publicly funded broadcasting authority. It also showed a penchant for direct action on the newsstands. On and off during its early history, the Labour Party published its own mass-circulation daily newspaper, the *Daily Herald*, which like the German Social Democrats' *Vorwarts* and the French Socialists' *L'Humanité* competed directly and at times quite successfully with publications owned by the press barons. In the 1970s and 1980s, Labour cabinet ministers such as Tony Benn were in the forefront of a brief flurry of serious discussion about the role that the government might play in guaranteeing ideological diversity in print and broadcast media. Benn recalls sparking an intense national debate in the 1970s by declaring that "broadcasting is too important to the functioning of a democracy for decisions to be left entirely to the broadcasters." Benn's battle cry resonated with Labour Party activists and media watchdogs who developed Britain's innovative Campaign for Press and Broadcast Freedom in 1979. Through the 1980s, the Labour Party maintained an openness to the proposals of the Campaign for Press and Broadcast Freedom, which emphasized the need for strengthening the BBC, diversifying ownership of broadcast and print media, and challenging the supremacy of media conglomerates. As late as 1992, the Labour Party continued to advocate for what by U.S. standards would be considered radical reform of the media landscape. Its 1992 campaign platform contained a lengthy section on "The Media," which stated: "Labour wants a wider choice for listeners and readers in the broadcast and printed media. Promoting greater diversity and tackling concentration of ownership will ensure wider choice." That commitment was followed by specific proposals for full-funding of the BBC, development of monopoly controls to prevent concentration of ownership of newspapers and broadcast outlets, and a host of other plans.

As the 1990s wore on, however, Labour became increasingly comfortable with big media. The political rise of Tony Blair and his "New Labour" allies saw the party that once decried corporate media as little more than a vehicle for recounting "the frivolous doings of the idle rich" move to the right of the Conservative Party of Margaret Thatcher and John Major on media issues. Labour's abandonment of its traditional stance created such a "topsy-turvy affair," according to British journalists Dan Glaister and Andrew Culf, that in 1996, "a Conservative government laid down a 20 percent threshold restricting newspaper groups from diversifying into television, while Labour united with right-wing Tory rebels to scrap the limits altogether." Effectively, Labour became the defender of media conglomeration and monopoly. Around the same time, Blair flew to Australia to meet with Rupert Murdoch, who soon after switched his mass-circulation *Sun* newspaper from an ardently Thatcherite Conservativism to a position of fervent support for Blair's "New

Labour." By 1999, Blair was carrying Murdoch's water, using his role as British prime minister to advance Murdoch's business ambitions in both Italy and China.

With the rise of the Blair-generated "Third Way" ideology—characterized by its advocacy for market "solutions," free trade, and a diminished governmental role in regulation of the economy in general and corporations in particular—the old parties of the left abandoned for the most part their commitment to challenging private media monopolies and to using governmental policies and spending to promote the sort of ideologically diverse media that sustains democracy. Germany's Gerhard Schroeder and a host of other leaders of social democratic parties joined leaders of historically liberal parties—such as the American Democrats and the Canadian Liberals—in embracing a neoliberal, market-driven, corporation-defined, privatizing vision of government. Gregor Gysi, leader of Germany's rapidly growing Party of Democratic Socialism, accurately described this as an "unhistoric" politics in which "social justice and ecological sustainability are strangers."

"The old-line parties have abandoned the playing field. They have stopped fighting for social and economic justice, choosing instead to seek the favor of the corporations the people want them to be battling," said Svend Robinson, a New Democratic Party member of the Canadian parliament. "I don't know if there is anyplace where this is more evident than in battles over media monopoly, corporate conglomeration and foreign control of our media."

As the old parties made their peace with markets, corporate capital, globalization of the economy, and the media that these patterns produce, they have left a void. In country after country, that void is being filled by new political groupings that, as part of a broader critique of neoliberalism, are making noise about the dangers posed to democracy by corporatization of the discourse. Just as Green parties—many of which have embraced media reform proposals—forced nations to look anew at questions of environmental protection and sustainability in the 1980s, so these new-line parties are forcing media issues onto the agenda. "This is an issue that's emerging all over the world. It's a huge concern. People are genuinely alarmed that at the same time we're witnessing growing concentration of ownership of media we're also seeing massive cuts in publicly owned media. It's a double whammy," said Canada's Robinson. "This neoliberal, right-wing takeover of the media is something that people are aware of, and they don't like it. But the old-line parties aren't willing to address the issue. This is what is going to distinguish new-line parties all over the world—a willingness to talk frankly about issues of media control and to propose an alternative to what's happening. It's inevitable. After you've had somebody say to you for the thousandth time, 'How come we never hear about these issues in the media,' you start to realize that the media itself is the issue."

A number of the parties that have taken the most aggressive stances regarding media issues—as part of broader programs that challenge corporate conglomeration and market-driven globalization—refer to themselves as members of "The Third Left." The name is intended to suggest an advancement from the narrowly focused political or economic critiques historically associated with pre-Marxist and orthodox Marxist movements toward an approach that comfortably links feminist, green, and traditional Left values in a new model of politics. Critical to the message of these red-green groupings around the world is a determination to present a clear vision of the more humane, sustainable, and functional society that these parties would use political power to develop. "We work for a society in which all people have equal worth and the same right to a good life," declared the program of Sweden's Left Party, which experienced a steady growth in its electoral strength as opinion polling identified the party as that country's third-most popular political grouping. "We want to live in a world where people solve conflicts by peaceful means and live in harmony with nature. In community and cooperation a living culture is created which strengthens people's identity and self-esteem and provides society valuable inspiration and criticism."

An awareness of the relationship between ideologically diverse media and real democracy is a constant among third-Left parties, as well as the green, non-socialist left, and even non-left-wing groupings that have begun to embrace media issues in countries around the world. "From the point of view of democracy, it is essential that all political decision-making is preceded by a genuine and interactive discussion in which all interested parties and even temporary coalitions are openly and impartially heard. In addition to political decision-making, essential economic decisions should also be as public as possible," argued the platform of Finland's Left Alliance, a party that maintained a Third Left vision as part of that country's governing coalition. "The openness and public nature of decision-making can only be guaranteed with the aid of free, pluralistic and diversified communications. In an open society, communications must go in all directions, which is why we need the possibility of interactive communications in addition to the mass media. In a democratic society the freedom of communication and the diversity of the media represent in principle a positive direction in development, because the fragmentation of the media and the public gives people a wider freedom and choice than before. Advanced information technology offers increasing possibilities for contacts and interaction between people and different NGOs. In a world of diversifying media, society ensures that ownership is not excessively concentrated, and that diversity and variability as well as the accessibility of the media and public communication services are supported by taxes wherever necessary."

Sweden's Left Party has made media reform central to its politics, emphasizing at every turn that "Prerequisites for democracy are freedom of speech and press freedom . . . " and arguing that "in a living democracy it is necessary to have a broad and independent choice of media. Everyone should be able to express their opinions in one form or another. All opinions should be able to reach the public." The Left Party pushes aggressive and innovative media reforms, including abolition of all advertising on radio and television and a program of subsidies for print media designed to guarantee that democracy is enriched by the broad availability of publications expressing distinct and sometimes unpopular views. The party, which in 1998 national elections saw its vote double to 12 percent of the total, does not simply talk about big ideas and grand visions, however. It has joined with labor groups to boycott a television station that refused to honor a Swedish law barring the airing of advertisements aimed directly at children, it has developed sophisticated newspapers, magazines, and Web sites to advance its ideas, and its members have been active players in the creation of radio programming designed to serve Sweden's growing immigrant community, women, and young people.

Sweden's experience with the Left Party and the ban on TV advertising to children points to an important lesson: Once the Left gets media reform in play, the traditional parties can no longer serve the interests of the corporate media with abandon. Moreover, media reform is an issue that has appeal across the political spectrum. Most of Sweden's parties now support the ban on TV advertising to children—it is popular with voters. Greece and Norway have enacted similar bans, and other European nations are contemplating doing so as well.

The coalition building that is at the heart of these evolving parties—like the fall 1999 anti-World Trade Organization protests in Seattle, the spring 2000 anti-IMF and World Bank protests in Washington, the summer 2001 protests at the G8 summit in Genoa, Italy—recalls Popular Front models of the 1930s. In refreshing contrast to traditional liberal parties, "inside-outside" approaches characterize their challenge to global media. No longer do party strategists and "consultants" form policy positions in isolation. Parties of the Left and even of the center are raising media issues because their positions are informed by the groundbreaking work of media unions, watchdog groups, academics, and grassroots activists. These activists, who had a hard time getting a hearing from old-line parties, frequently find that newer, less bureaucratic and more politically open parties are enthusiastic about incorporating media issues into their agenda. Thus, in the new political dynamic of post-apartheid South Africa, the comprehensive stance on broadcasting policy advanced by the Congress of South Africa Trade Unionists (COSATU) had influenced the approach not only of the African National Congress and the South African Communist Party, with which the unions had long maintained close ties, but also of smaller parties of varying ideologies.

In nations like New Zealand and Australia, political organizing around media reform emerged dramatically in the late 1990s. The crisis over journalism in Canada grew to such an extent that it moved to the forefront of political debate. As part of a reshaping of the Canadian New Democratic Party to better respond to the debate over globalization, the party made media reform issues a central focus of its agenda. The party platform attacked media conglomerates by name: "One company, CanWest Global—a major contributor to the Liberal Party—now owns 40 percent of our print media as well as television stations in eight provinces reaching 88 percent of English-speaking Canadians." Furthermore, it placed the struggle for democratic media in the context of broader struggles over globalization. "Our cultural identity has been put in jeopardy by an American media tide, globalizing economic forces and the new communications technologies. The Liberals have done nothing to stem this tide. In fact, their trade deals have turned our culture into a commodity—opening the door to split-run magazines today and other U.S. attacks tomorrow. Severe funding cuts have undermined our public broadcaster, the CBC. And, media barons have been able to buy up our news-papers, television and radio stations, severely limiting the scope of information that reaches the public," the platform declared. "In a global information society, the voices of our artists, writers, creators and citizens need to be strengthened, not undermined. Media ownership must be balanced with strong independent voices to ensure the free flow of ideas and the health of our democracy. And governments must make it clear that our cultural identity is not for sale by ensuring that trade deals include protection for our culture. New Democrats are fighting for investments and policies that protect Canadian culture."

The New Democratic Party updated that message in the debate over the firing of the *Ottawa Citizen* publisher after the newspaper criticized the prime minister. Displaying the confidence of a party that is on top of media issues, McDonough and New Democratic Party Culture and Communications Critic Wendy Lill quickly declared, "Among the steps called for are re-imposition of the ban on common ownership of newspapers and TV stations in the same community and a strict limit on the number of television, radio or specialty licenses that may be held by any one operator. The policy also calls for increased local and regional programming requirements from broadcasters and the promotion of noncommercial media though increased public support for the CBC, community broadcasters and other nonprofit media." Recalling a groundbreaking study of media and democracy issues in Canada, McDonough and Lill argued: "Twenty years ago, the Kent Commission report was eloquent in defining our challenge—'to increase the number and quality of independent voices finding expression, voices undaunted and undiminished by dollar concerns.' We are now witnessing the results of the federal government's failure to meet that challenge. But it is not to late to pick up the torch lit by the Kent Commission."

The most exciting developments in media activism may well be at the global level, though these remain nascent. The global justice movement that has been organizing across national lines against the neoliberal economic deals and organizations like the WTO, the IMF, and the World Bank has made media one of the main targets for change. (It is this spirit that fuels much of the national activism described in this chapter.) At the World Social Forum in Porto Alegre in February 2002, where 70,000 people from across the world gathered to generate an alternative to neoliberal capitalism, media was one of the defining issues. The United Nations convened a World Summit on the Information Society in December 2003, and leading scholars and activists continue to work to make the need for autonomous, well-funded nonprofit, and noncommercial media a major area for discussion. Among global democratic activists there is an emerging consensus that unless the road to democratic renewal includes structural media reform, that road will be a dead-end street.

All of this is important for people in the United States for two reasons. First, it highlights the increasing importance of media reform politics around the world; the United States is, if anything, somewhat of a laggard in this regard. There are useful and necessary lessons to be learned. Second, it points to what is ultimately the global nature of media reform struggles. The issues are similar everywhere, the reform proposals are all variants of a handful of themes. The forces of darkness—large profit-driven media corporations and their spoon- fed politicians and regulators—work their commercial schemes everywhere. This is a global struggle.

This notion that a diverse and independent media is vital to democracy is not new. But it has too rarely been expressed on a regular basis in the corridors of political and governmental power. Once the issue is raised, however, the debate shifts. Suddenly, questions that seem technical, obscure, complex, or inconsequential take on a new meaning. No longer are citizens willing to cede to industry lobbyists and their political pawns control of the debate over ownership of the means by which a democracy discusses fundamental questions.

So says Bharati Ray, a former top administrator of the University of Calcutta, who served in the upper chamber of the Indian Parliament in the early 2000s. Over lunch in her modest quarters near the great governmental buildings of Delhi, she listened with open delight to a review of the evidence of mounting media activism and its embrace by parties of the Left. One of the most articulate advocates for the Indian Left, which has a long history of raising concerns about foreign ownership of media, print, and broadcast monopolies, and commercialization, she was genuinely pleased to learn that issues that concerned her and so many Indians were being raised in other lands.

But then Ray scowled. "Why are we unaware of these developments?" she asked. "Why do we not know more of this activity?" Ray knew the answer, of course. She was well aware that few reports on international media activism are featured on the evening news. Yet, the veteran teacher was not accepting excuses. "We must begin immediately to discuss what is being done around the world. We must come together. We must hear what others are doing so that we may imitate them. We must tell others what we are doing so that they may imitate us," she said. "Once we all begin to realize that we are not working in isolation, that we are a part of a great response to globalization, I think that the potential for the forces of democracy to succeed will be very great indeed."

Indeed.

19

Theses on Media Deregulation

In 2002, Britain considered a new media law that would significantly "deregulate" the media system. Deregulation in practice in media markets is synonymous with increased commercialization. Some of the impetus for the proposed changes came from developments in the United States, the world leader in media and communication markets by a wide margin. The United States has always had a more laissez-faire attitude toward commercial media and with the passage of the Telecommunications Act of 1996, the United States ushered in an era of explicitly replacing what government regulation exists with free markets. According to conventional wisdom, the effect has been rapid commercial development of spectacular new technologies, more competitive markets that "give the people what they want," plus a tremendous spur to economic growth in the information age. This is the spirit that infused Britain's lurch to an ever-greater dependence upon the market to regulate media.

In what follows I will argue that the conventional wisdom about the U.S. media situation is wrong on several crucial points. I do so as an American who has studied the media situation and the U.S. political economy for years. I offer the following to provide a counter to the public relations campaigns that are geared up to promote the joys of deregulated media markets. I believe that Britons were being sold a bill of goods by self-interested commercial media concerns, and that they needed to scrutinize claims about "media deregulation" with utmost skepticism. In my view, a rigorous public examination and debate of media policy issues requires no less.

Coincidentally, the U.S. Federal Communications Commission (FCC) was considering a considerable relaxation of its remaining media ownership laws, with hopes that the matter would be resolved by the beginning of 2003. The following points are just as valid for Americans contemplating the future of the U.S. media system.

The notion that the choice for media policy is government regulation versus deregulation and free markets is inaccurate. All media systems are the result of explicit government policies, subsidies, grants of rights and regulations. Cable, satellite, and terrestrial broadcasting are based upon government-sanctioned monopoly rights to scarce frequencies and franchises. If a private individual attempts to broadcast on a frequency the government has licensed to someone else, that person will be subject to criminal prosecution. This is a serious form of government regulation. Even publishing, music, and films require government regulation to exist as they do. Consider, for example, the role of copyright. Indeed, to have anything close to competitive markets in media requires extensive government regulation in the form of ownership limits and a myriad of other policies.

More broadly, to have a market regulation of anything, including media, requires explicit government laws and policies recognizing and enforcing private ownership, contracts, the sanctity of profit, etc. Markets are not "natural." But the nature of media industries—for example, use of spectrum, need for copyright—makes government regulation doubly foundational.

So the real issue is not regulation versus free markets, but, to the contrary, regulation in the public interest versus regulation to serve purely private interests. The latter is often called deregulation, but that is not the case. Deregulation is better thought of, in most instances and certainly in the case of media, as a misleading term for unabashed and unacknowledged regulation on behalf of powerful self-interested private parties.

This also points to the fundamentally public and social nature of media systems. Public policy comes first, and media systems follow. Private media systems are not exogenous to society, but, rather, they are sanctioned by society. The key issue is: How does a particular society determine to structure its media system? In a democracy, these decisions ought to be the result of informed debate. Specifically, private media systems are sanctioned because a society determines that such systems, on balance, best serve the needs of the citizenry.

The nature and caliber of the public debates over media policies, subsidies, and regulations is therefore of the utmost importance. The more democratic a society, as a general rule, the more likely there will be widespread public participation in these debates. The more widespread the public participation, the more likely the resulting policies will best serve the needs of the people. That is liberal democracy.

Media policymaking debates have varied in quality across democratic nations. One point is certain: once a nation "deregulates" much of its media to private interests, it is very difficult to maintain public involvement in the policymaking process. Private interests are able to use their cultural, economic, and political power to prevent open evaluation of whether they are the proper stewards of the nation's media. Once this "deregulation" process is near completion, it is very difficult to reverse the process, as extremely powerful interests block the democratic path.

The U.S. Example

One look at the United States provides a crystal clear example of the degradation of media policymaking once the system has been "deregulated" to private interests. In the United States important media and communication policy decisions are made regularly by the federal government. Many of these are of the utmost importance for determining the structure and nature of the media system. Yet the vast majority of the population—conservatively, 99 percent—have no clue about this policymaking process. Even members of Congress not on the relevant committees are largely clueless. There is almost no press coverage whatsoever, except in the business pages where media policymaking is covered as a story of importance to investors and managers and advertisers, not of importance to citizens in a democracy. The hegemony of the status quo is the starting point for all debate, so there is no debate. This state of affairs is also a striking commentary on the nature of democratic governance in the United States today.

It is in this context that the notion is spread that media systems are "naturally" the province of private interests in pursuit of profit, and that any public involvement that might "interfere" with their profit making is "onerous" regulation, a genuine threat to a free society. A more self-serving and purely ideological notion would be difficult to imagine. What in truth is happening is that core democratic rights have been terminated, replaced by the rule of far less accountable private interests.

Perhaps the best way to capture the media policymaking process in the United States is to consider the 1974 Oscar-winning film, *The Godfather II*. Roughly halfway through the film a bunch of American gangsters, including Michael Corleone, assemble on a Havana patio to celebrate Hyman Roth's birthday. This is 1958, pre-Castro, when Batista and the mob ruled Cuba. Roth is giving a slice of his birthday cake, which has the outline of Cuba on it, to each of the gangsters. As he does so, Roth outlines how the gangsters are divvying up the island among themselves. And Roth triumphantly states how great it is to be in a country with a government that works with private enterprise.

This is how communication policymaking works in the United States. But do not think it is a conspiracy where the corporate interests peacefully carve up the cake. Powerful corporate lobbies and trade associations fight it out with each other over who gets the largest slice of the U.S. cake that is doled out by the FCC, Congress, and other federal agencies. They flood politicians with campaign donations to gain influence. What they all agree upon is that it is *their* cake and nobody else should be permitted to participate in policy deliberations. The function of the FCC, as one former chair informed William Kennard as he assumed the chair in 1997, "is to referee fights between the wealthy and the super wealthy." When one factors in the enormous campaign contributions made to members of Congress, and the tempting jobs in the private sector awaiting regulators, the stench of corruption becomes thick like that emanating from an overflowed latrine.

Nor is this corruption exclusive to the policymaking process. Almost everywhere that media and communication are "deregulated," there follow waves of corruption in the practices of these firms. Large private firms use the lack of public oversight to fleece shareholders, workers, customers, and taxpayers. This is perfectly rational behavior for private firms seeking maximum profit, though it has deplorable and disastrous consequences for society. It is what logically follows when the media system is made first and foremost the province of private interests, rather than the province of public interest.

This is not exclusive to media, but applies to all industries that have traditionally been heavily regulated or publicly owned. In the United States recent examples of such corruption have been Enron, WorldCom, and Global Crossing. These scandals are a direct result of "deregulation."

In media policymaking debates the claim is often made that relaxing ownership regulations to allow more concentration and capital mobility will lead to increased marketplace competition, with lower prices and higher quality for the general public. Of course, if deregulation were to threaten a ferocious wave of genuine competition, powerful private interests would never let it take place. To the contrary, the pattern under "deregulation" is a follow-up wave of mergers in the affected industries. Corporations claim they love competition, but they only love it for other firms and for their workers. For themselves, sane capitalists want as little competition as possible, and that is what tends to result from deregulation. Firms use relaxed ownership rules to get much larger, and therefore make it much more difficult for newcomers to enter their markets.

Consider what has happened in U.S. radio, the one industry most directly reshaped by the 1996 Telecommunications Act. Whereas the 1996 Act advised the FCC eventually to deregulate ownership in other media sectors in the future, it explicitly wrote the radio deregulation requirements into the law. In keeping with the way media policy is done in the United States, the section pertaining to radio was apparently written by lobbyists; there was no public or congressional debate on the matter, and many members of Congress had little idea it was even in the bill that they had voted for.

So what happened to radio? Prior to 1996 a single company was permitted to own twenty-eight stations nationally, and no more than four in a single community. (Until the 1980s the limits had been much stricter.) The 1996 Act removed the national limit and permitted a single firm to own up to eight stations in the largest communities. Since 1996 well over half of U.S. stations have been sold, and a stunning consolidation has hit the industry. One firm, Clear Channel, now owns nearly 1,200 stations. Every market is dominated by two or three firms that own nearly all the stations between them. The firms have stripped radio of local content, especially journalism, and have substituted generic, inexpensive national programming. The amount of advertising and commercialism has increased. Radio—which is so inexpensive to produce and receive that it is ideal for decentralized, creative, and local uses—has been turned into a cash cow for a few large companies. Everyone else loses. Everywhere one turns in the United States, one hears complaints about the dreadful state of radio. It is blamed on the greed of capitalists rather than deregulation policy.

Related to this, the political commentary on U.S. commercial radio is almost entirely on the far political Right. Commentators unsympathetic to the role of corporations in U.S. political and economic life and sympathetic to the concerns of poor people and the working class, not to mention traditional liberals, are locked out by owners and advertisers. Even communities that vote to the liberal-Left overwhelmingly, like Eugene, Oregon; Detroit, Michigan; and Madison, Wisconsin, are inundated by far-Right radio programming. Were a Martian to visit the United States, they might determine from listening to U.S. commercial radio that the nation was populated almost entirely by militantly hard-line far-rightists.

But the problem lies less with evil owners than with the failure of democratic policymaking. A simple shift in policy—to, say, a limit of just two or three stations per owner—would change the situation almost instantly. There are no economic reasons to justify concentration in the industry, as the physical cost of transmission is very low. Indeed, as in most other media industries, all the benefits of concentrated control in radio have gone directly and exclusively to shareholders. None to the public at large. But the corrupt policymaking process makes reform of radio laws in the public interest impossible. Indeed, the radio station-owning lobby is so powerful that it successfully neutered attempts to launch 1,000 low-power noncommercial radio stations on the dial. The behemoths love to talk about competition, but what they really want is monopoly. It is not their fault; the problem is the failure of policymaking that granted them so much unaccountable power.

Markets and Media

Most of the above is not controversial. But adherents of "deregulation" claim that, regardless of the facts, the turn to private domination is necessary and beneficial for society as a whole. The claim has three parts. First, even if the policymaking is corrupt, the market, even a highly concentrated market, is the best means to rule media as well as everything else. Second, there is no alternative. Every other media system that has been tried, including the system that dominated in Britain for much of the twentieth century, has failed. Third, new technologies, especially the Internet, make traditional justifications for regulation and public involvement in media obsolete.

Regarding the market, whatever its strengths in other areas, it has clear limitations in the area of media. Hence the U.S. style of regulation, which effectively seeks to allow private firms to make as much money as possible, is not only corrupt, it is indefensible. The media system is not simply an economic category; it is responsible for transmitting culture, journalism, and politically relevant information. Fulfilling those needs is mandatory for self-governance. The media system is better understood as a social institution similar to the education system, which few would argue should be turned over to market forces. Even as economic entities, most media are *public goods*. That means traditional notions of supply and demand do not apply because the use of the product is non-rivalrous. In the case of broadcasting, once a program is produced, whether ten people watch the program or 10 million do, does not affect the cost of the program. If I watch a movie or read a book, it does not mean I keep another person from watching the same movie or reading the same book. It is not like buying a car or eating a hamburger. It is this non-rivalrous nature of media that led to the rise of copyright and other policies to deal with their unusual nature. It is a core reason why media systems have long been shaped, their character determined, by public policy decisions.

There is a long literature examining the limitations of the market with regard to media, but I want to make just a few points most pertinent to the policymaking matters at hand. It is said that competition in the market forces media firms to "give the people, what they want." In truth, competition in the market forces firms to "give the people what they want within the range of where they can make the most profits." This tends to be a much smaller range than that from which people might wish to select. Certain crucial desires people have—for less advertising and commercialism, or for exposure to new cultural forms—are very difficult, if not impossible to express in the commercial marketplace. They can only be expressed in public-policy debates.

Indeed, in many media markets the primary audience is not the general public, but advertisers. This changes the nature of the media market considerably. It introduces a layer of commercial vetting of content—and nothing good comes from that—and it gives media tremendous incentive to appeal to those audience members that the advertisers wish to reach. In general, advertisers are interested in people with disposable income, so the reliance upon advertising magnifies the class bias in media content. This has proven to have especially dreadful effects on commercial journalism in the United States, and worldwide. Commercial journalism routinely emphasizes business stories and issues of importance to investors. Material concerning poor and working-class communities is very uncommon, and usually framed in terms of how it affects the more privileged. It is a poison pill for democratic governance.

The problem of the market becomes magnified in highly concentrated oligopolistic markets, which is the nature of most media markets. The higher the degree of concentration the more the power in the market is shifted from the consumer to the producer. This is elementary microeconomic theory. It is a main reason why democratic media policies have had a strong bias toward encouraging competition. Where technology or capital requirements, or other factors, make it impossible to enhance competition, democratic media policy often uses regulation to make sure that dominant media firms do not exploit their market power to take advantage of the public.

But the fact remains that, even where there is considerable competition, markets are a flawed mechanism for regulating media. In addition to being *public goods,* media have what economists call *externalities.* This means that there are costs associated with markets that neither the buyer or seller assumes, but for which society pays. The traditional example is pollution. Neither the manufacturer nor the consumer have to "pay" for the pollution; it is irrelevant to their calculations. But society as a whole has to live with the pollution and deal with it. There are positive externalities, too, as when a firm builds an unusually beautiful building that gives pleasure to all who pass it by. But firms are adept at capitalizing upon their positive externalities as much as possible and avoiding their negative ones.

Media have enormous externalities. If the market generates a lousy journalism that keeps the citizens poorly informed, the entire society suffers—not just the consumers of particular media—because the resulting political governance will be shoddy. If it leads to an unnecessary war or to massive corruption, for example, we all pay. It does not just affect buyer and seller. Conversely, if the market generates a splendid journalism that leads to wise policies, everyone benefits, even those who are not purchasing specific media products. There can be tremendous positive externalities. In another example, routinely carpet-bombing children with advertising and commercialism, or programming featuring sex and violence, may generate profits for media firms, but it will produce self-evident negative externalities for those children and everyone in society down the road. The list goes on and on. In short, media markets make some of their profit by passing the actual social costs of their activities off to others. It is the factoring in of these externalities that lays at the heart of much democratic media policymaking. Adept policymaking attempts to maximize positive externalities and minimize negative ones.

In the case of broadcast media, the historical lesson is clear: private commercial broadcasters must be held by publicly determined, public interest regulations to address the matter of externalities. If they are not, it puts inordinate pressure on the public broadcaster to maintain public service standards, and tends to lead to the entire system unraveling into a commercial morass. One sample of U.S. television or radio is a clear indication of what this "deregulatory" regime offers.

Alternatives?

As for the notion that there is no alternative, that depends upon how one frames it. If, as in the United States, the matter is framed as one of either having the existing commercial system or a system like that found in the old Soviet Union, then indeed there is no alternative. But that is a bogus framing. There is no reason a society cannot maintain a regulated commercial system, a democratically accountable public media system, and also have a large nonprofit and noncommercial media sector. None of this entails any government content censorship, as it has been traditionally understood. It merely means identifying the values that are important in the media system, and attempting to determine policies that will produce a media structure that will be most likely to generate those values, and minimize the negative externalities.

There are several superior policy proposals that would improve the diversity and quality of our media system without opening the door to any form of censorship. We *can* have a pluralistic media system with a significant independent nonprofit and noncommercial sector, as well as media markets that are not under the thumb of a small number of massive private corporations. If leaders in nations—and scholars interested in the subject—devoted a hundredth of the energy to working on such policies as they do on trying to make a personal fortune in media industries, we would have a mother lode of policy options to examine and debate. The problem is that powerful private interests work at many levels to prevent such a democratic debate, and the political class in many countries—especially the United States—lacks the capacity or courage to stand up for the public interest.

The BBC is a striking example of what public policy can accomplish in the area of media. Left to the market, nothing like it would have ever existed.

Some argue that any effort to limit capitalist domination of media is an underhanded backdoor effort to eliminate capitalism. It is true that for those who are socialists or who are critical of capitalism, having a commercial media system is problematic; the track record is that such a system will not have much enthusiasm for hard-edged social criticism, especially from the Left. But even those who believe in the legitimacy of capitalism need not believe that media should be the sole province of capitalists. Indeed, they should not, if they value democracy. Market economies can survive, arguably even prosper, without having U.S.-style commercial media systems. The real question is whether democracy can survive as anything more than a fig leaf covering concentrated private power.

As for the argument that new digital technologies render regulation—meaning regulation that might impede private interests, not regulation that assists them—obsolete, it does not even pass rudimentary analysis. Merely being able to launch a Web site is wonderful and it has opened up the media system, but what is striking is how little effect it has had on the commercial media system so far. Not a single new commercially viable media content concern has been introduced on the Internet. The power of the market trumps the magic of the technology. If we want the Internet to spawn a new generation of viable media content providers, we cannot look to the market to produce that outcome. It will require explicit policies to generate such an outcome.

Moreover, however one might want the Internet to develop, policy decisions will go a long way in pointing it in its ultimate direction. Global trade agreements, intellectual property laws and regulations, traditional media subsidies and regulations, and the like will be decisive in determining the future of the Internet. As with media writ large, the question is not whether we want regulation, but what type of regulation we want.

It is worth noting as an addendum, that the Internet itself is a tremendous testament to public sector policymaking and cooperative economic and social activity. The Internet would never have developed if left to the market. The same is true of many other innovations in communication. In short, the public sector has a cornerstone role in communication, and fundamental interests to protect. This also suggests that the positive economic benefits from developing the media-information sector can, should, and do come from significant public sector involvement.

20

Rich Media, Poor Democracy: Communication Politics in Dubious Times

Our era rests upon a massive paradox. On the one hand, it is an age of daz-zling breakthroughs in communication and information technologies. Communication is so intertwined with the economy and culture that our times have been dubbed the Information Age. Sitting high atop this golden web are a handful of enormous media firms—exceeding by a factor of ten the size of the largest media firms of just fifteen years earlier—that have established global empires and generated massive riches providing news and entertain-ment to the peoples of the world. This commercial media juggernaut provides a bounty of choices unimaginable a generation or two ago. And it is finding a welcome audience. According to one study, the average American consumed a whopping 11.8 hours of media per day in 1998, up over 13 percent in just three years. As the survey director noted, "The sheer amount of media prod-ucts and messages consumed by the average American adult is staggering and growing."[1] The rise of the Internet has only accentuated the trend. Although some research suggests that the Internet is replacing some of the time people have spent with other media, other research suggests its more important effect is simply to expand the role of media in people's lives.

On the other hand, our era is increasingly depoliticized; traditional notions of civic and political involvement have shriveled. Elementary under-standing of social and political affairs has declined. Turnout for U.S. elections—admittedly not a perfect barometer—has plummeted over the past thirty years. The 2000 presidential election had one of the lowest turnouts of eligible voters in national elections in U.S. history, as just one-half of the eligible voters turned out on election day. For poor people—who, as Aristotle noted, are the *raison d'etre* of a democracy, the measure of its strength—electoral democracy has become little more than a charade; exit polls indicate that over one-half of those who voted in November 2000 came from the wealthiest 20 percent of the population. And, to add insult to injury, the candidate who received the most votes from the poor, Al Gore, actually won the election, but had his victory stolen from him in one of the most brazen examples of corruption in U.S. history. The collapse of the democratic system is palpable, except to those who benefit from the status quo. The cynicism and depoliticization will only continue to increase until the invariable social crisis, that many contend is a long way aways. For the time being, we are living, to employ a phrase coined by Robert Entman, in a "democracy without citizens."

By conventional reasoning, this is nonsensical. A flowering commercial marketplace of ideas, unencumbered by government censorship or regulation, should generate the most stimulating democratic political culture possible. The response comes that the problem lies elsewhere, that "the people" obviously are not interested in politics or civic issues, because, if they were, it would be in the interests of the wealthy media giants to provide them with such fare. There is an element of truth to that reply, but it is hardly a satisfactory response. Virtually all defenses of the commercial media system justifying the privileges they receive—defenses typically made by the media owners themselves—are based on the notion that media play an important, perhaps a central, role in providing the institutional basis for having an informed and participating citizenry. If this is, indeed, a democracy without citizens, the media system has much to answer for.

I contend that the media have become a significant *antidemocratic* force in the United States. The wealthier and more powerful the corporate media giants have become, the poorer the prospects for participatory democracy. I am not arguing that *all* media are getting wealthier, of course. Some media firms and sectors are faltering and will falter during this turbulent era. But, on balance, the dominant media firms are larger and more influential than ever before, and the media *writ large* are more important in our social life than ever before. Nor do I believe the media are the sole or primary cause of the decline of democracy, but that they are a part of the problem and closely linked to many of the other factors. Behind the lustrous glow of new technologies and electronic jargon, the media system has become increasingly concentrated and conglomerated into a relative handful of corporate hands. This concentration accentuates the core tendencies of a profit-driven, advertising-supported media system: hyper-commercialism and denigration of journalism and public service. It is a poison pill for democracy.

This chapter, then, is about the corporate media explosion and the corresponding implosion of public life, the rich media/poor democracy paradox. This paradox has two components. First, it is a political crisis. I mean this in two senses. On the one hand, the nature of our corporate commercial media system has dire implications for our politics and broader culture. On the other hand, the very issue of *who* controls the media system and for what purposes is not a part of contemporary political debate. Instead, there is the presupposition that a profit-seeking commercial media system is fundamentally sound, and that most problems can be resolved for the most part through less state interference or regulation, which (theoretically) will produce the magic elixir of competition. In view of the extraordinary importance of media and communication in our society, I believe that the subject of how the media are controlled, structured, and subsidized should be at the center of democratic debate. Instead, this subject is nowhere to be found. This is not an accident; it reflects above all the economic, political, and ideological power of the media corporations and their allies. And it has made the prospect of challenging corporate media power, and of democratizing communication, all the more daunting.

The second component of the media/democracy paradox concerns media ideology, in particular the flawed and self-serving manner in which corporate media officers and their supporters use history. The nature of our corporate media system and the lack of democratic debate over the nature of our media system are often defended on the following grounds: communication markets force media firms to "give the people what they want"; commercial media are the innate democratic and "American" system; professionalism in journalism is democratic and protects the public from nefarious influences on the news; new communications technologies are inherently democratic since they undermine the existing commercial media; and, perhaps most important, that the First Amendment to the U.S. Constitution authorizes that corporations and advertisers rule U.S. media without public interference. These are generally presented as truisms, and nearly always history is invoked to provide evidence for each of these claims. In combination these claims have considerable sway in the United States, even among those who are critical of the social order otherwise. It is because of the overall capacity of these myths, which are either lies or half-truths, to strip citizens of their ability to comprehend their own situation and govern their own lives that I characterize these as "dubious" times in the chapter's subtitle.

In this chapter I will address central trends in U.S. media at the dawn of the twenty-first century: the concentration of media industries; the decline of notions of public service in our media culture and a corresponding denigration of journalism; the commercialization of the Internet; the government's antitrust case against Microsoft; and the prospects for renewed politicization in the new century.

Media Concentration

The United States is in the midst of an almost dizzying transformation of its media system, whose main features are concentration and conglomeration. It may seem ironic that these are the dominant structural features when, to the casual observer, the truth can appear quite the opposite. We seem inundated in different media from magazines and radio stations to cable television channels and now, Web sites. But, to no small extent, the astonishing degree of concentrated corporate control over the media is a response to the rapid increase in channels wrought by cable, satellite TV, and digital media. Media firms press to get larger to deal with the uncertainty of the changing terrain wrought by new media technologies. "If you look at the entire chain of entities—studios, networks, stations, cable channels, cable operations, international distribution—you want to be as strong in as many of those as you can," News Corporation president Peter Chernin stated in 1998. "That way, regardless of where the profits move to, you're in a position to gain."[2] Yet, any explanation of media concentration and conglomeration must go beyond media technologies. They also result from changes in laws and regulations that now permit greater concentration in media ownership. But the bottom line, so to speak, is that concentrated media markets tend to be vastly less risky and more profitable for the firms that dominate them.

The U.S. media industries were operated along noncompetitive oligopolistic lines for much of the twentieth century. In the 1940s, for example, broadcasting, film production, motion picture theaters, book publishing, newspaper publishing, magazine publishing, and recorded music were all distinct national oligopolistic markets, each of them dominated by anywhere from a few to a dozen or more firms. In general, these were *different* firms dominating each of these industries, with only a few exceptions. Throughout the twentieth century there were pressing concerns that these concentrated markets would inhibit the flow and range of ideas necessary for a meaningful democracy.

Concentration proceeded in specific media markets throughout the 1990s, with the proportion of the markets controlled by a small number of firms increasing, sometimes marginally and at other times dramatically. The U.S. film production industry has been a tight-knit club effectively controlled by six or seven studios since the 1930s. That remains the case; the six largest U.S. firms accounted for over 90 percent of U.S. theater revenues in 1997. All but sixteen of Hollywood's 148 widely distributed (in six hundred or more theaters) films in 1997 were produced by these six firms, and many of those sixteen were produced by companies that had distribution deals with one of the six majors. The newspaper industry underwent a spectacular consolidation from the 1960s to the 1980s, leaving a half-dozen major chains ruling the roost.[3] The emerging consolidation trend in the newspaper industry is that of "clustering," whereby metropolitan monopoly daily newspapers purchase or otherwise link up with all the smaller dailies in the suburbs and surrounding region.

There were numerous massive media deals, which included Viacom swallowing up CBS to create the third largest media conglomerate in the world; AOL combining with Time Warner in what at the time was largest media deal in history (valued at around $160 billion); and the Tribune Company buying Times Mirror, so that every major newspaper chain is now part of a larger media conglomerate.

It is also clear that many more mergers will take place in the years to come, especially as the few remaining federal restrictions on media ownership are relaxed. It was the FCC's 1999 decision allowing firms to own more than one TV station in a market, for example, that paved the way for the CBS-Viacom deal. When the federal prohibitions are lifted on owning a daily newspaper and a TV station or a cable system and a TV station in the same market look for a wave of colossal deals, as the first-tier media conglomerates grow even fatter.

Denigration of Journalism

Not only is media ownership becoming concentrated into ever fewer extremely large conglomerates, the denigration of journalism continues unabated. By journalism I mean both the product of the commercial news media as well as the journalism of NPR and PBS. After two decades of conservative criticism and corporate inroads, the public system is now fully within the same ideological confines that come naturally to a profit-driven, advertising-supported system. There were several case studies in 1999 and 2000 on the shortcomings of corporate-controlled journalism for a democratic society.

Some of the problems come from the inherent limitations of journalism as conducted by self-interested, profit-motivated companies. Others are due to faults in the professional practice of journalism, faults that date to the beginning of the twentieth century. In particular, the professional reliance upon official sources and the need for a news peg, or event, to justify coverage of a story plays directly into the hands of those who benefit from the status quo. But many problems result from the enhanced corporate pressure to make journalism a source of huge profits; this leads to easy-to-cover trivial stories and an emphasis on the type of news that will have appeal to the upper and upper-middle classes. The combination of all three of these factors leads to the woeful state of U.S. journalism in the twenty-first century.

A long-term problem of local commercial media—notably daily newspapers and television broadcasters—is their consistent reluctance to provide critical investigations of the most important and powerful local commercial interests. Professional standards notwithstanding, there has been a kind of "Eleventh Commandment" in the commercial news media: Thou Shalt Not Cover Big Local Companies and Billionaires Critically. This makes very good economic sense, as the local powers are often major advertisers. It makes sense politically and socially, too, as the media owners and managers run in the same circles as the major shareholders and executives of the local corporate powerhouses. They are not the sort of people or institutions that smart businesses wish to antagonize—and the media are businesses no less than any other profit- maximizing firms. This is truer than ever in an era when investigative journalism of any sort is generally frowned upon as too expensive and bad for profits.

Along these lines, the *Boston Herald* suspended its consumer affairs columnist, Robin Washington, in the spring of 2000. He had written a series of articles about FleetBoston Financial Corporation, the nation's eighth-largest bank, which not only advertised in the *Herald* but also had outstanding loans to the *Herald*. The bank contacted the *Herald*'s publisher at least twice to complain about the coverage, which emphasized how customers had been getting a higher fee structure since BankBoston and Fleet Financial merged in 1999. The bank did not aim its fire at the accuracy of the findings, only Washington's methods, specifically that he had arranged for a friend to pose as a customer at the bank. Washington's case drew public protest and his suspension was eventually lifted, largely because he was one of only four African-American journalists on an editorial staff of 235.

The lesson to other reporters was one that should have been understood already: the evidentiary and methodological standards for doing critical work on local corporate powerhouses are vastly higher than they are for other institutions. Smart journalists who want successful careers will avoid them, and happy smart journalists will do as others before them: internalize the view that such stories are not really very good journalism anyway.

Another long-term problem of the system is the commercial media's willingness to provide favorable coverage of politicians who provide them with favorable subsidies and regulations. This violates every canon of ethical or professional journalism, too, but its practice is rarely noted. Ben Bagdikian's *The Media Monopoly* used the Freedom of Information Act to uncover how major newspaper chains effectively promised Richard Nixon editorial support in his 1972 reelection campaign if he supported the Newspaper Preservation Act. The deal led to newspaper monopolies in many U.S. cities and made shareholders in newspaper corporations far wealthier than they would have been otherwise. One can only speculate, but perhaps a newspaper industry less involved with the Nixon reelection campaign might have pursued the Watergate story with a modicum of gusto in the five months preceding the 1972 election, possibly sparing the nation a great crisis.

Of course, the tacit quid pro quo of favorable coverage for favorable legislation and regulation rarely draws comment, so it is unusual to find the sort of smoking gun that Bagdikian located. When important legislation affecting media arises on Capitol Hill, for example, the corporations sometimes have the managers of their local stations or the publishers of their local papers call on their representatives in Congress to ask them to support the corporation's position on the bill. No threat or promise about news coverage has to be made; the message is loud and clear.

The corruption of journalistic integrity is always bad, but it becomes obscene under conditions of extreme media concentration, as now exist. This is a primary reason why antitrust needs to be applied to the media industry. In San Francisco a textbook example of the problem arose. Under deposition, it was revealed that a top executive of the Hearst Corporation, owner of the *San Francisco Examiner*, offered favorable editorial coverage to San Francisco mayor Willie Brown—then up for reelection—if Brown would give official blessing to Hearst's purchase of the *San Francisco Chronicle*, the other daily in town. The records show emails and other communications among top Hearst executives approving the offer. Mayor Brown says he made no promises. But in his 1999 re-election campaign against insurgent Tom Ammiano, the *Examiner* portrayed Ammiano harshly, while tending to view Brown with rose-tinted glasses. A Bay Area reporter summed up the situation: "Hearst, like all big media chains these days, sees journalism first and foremost as a business, a way to make money. And when it comes to the bottom line, all ethical rules are off."[4]

Another way to measure the limitations of the contemporary corporate news media is to look at which sorts of stories receive elaborate attention and which receive less coverage or virtually no coverage at all. In the summer of 1999, the deaths of John F. Kennedy Jr., his wife, and her sister were treated by the cable news channels and the media writ large as a story approaching the magnitude of the return of the messiah or the discovery of intelligent life on Mars. Television sets were turned into virtual aquariums for hours as cameras scanned the Atlantic in search of Kennedy's aircraft. The news was the fates of three private citizens made famous by their lineage, wealth, beauty, and media decision making.

Four months later the news media were presented with another story, the World Trade Organization (WTO) meeting in Seattle. Reporters had long claimed that they could not cover the social and political implications of the global economy because there was no news peg to justify coverage. If they pursued the story it would look as if they were pushing an agenda. Then the

WTO meeting and the massive demonstrations that shut it down gave journalists their news peg. But here journalists came into direct conflict with the modern corporate ethos. For one, media corporations are among the largest beneficiaries of the global capitalist economy since they use groups like the WTO and liberalized trade to increase their sales and activities outside the United States. And media's main advertisers tend to be among the largest firms eager to expand their markets across the planet.

Meanwhile, mainstream news and "business news" have effectively morphed in recent decades as the news is increasingly pitched to the richest one-half or one-third of the population. The affairs of Wall Street, the pursuit of profitable investments, and the joys of capitalism are now often taken to be the interests of the general population. The affairs of working-class people have virtually disappeared from the news. Now journalists rely on business or business-oriented think tanks as sources when covering economics stories. These factors place strong pressure on journalists to write favorably about the globalization of capitalism, and to regard the WTO protesters as dubious, if not purely fraudulent.

Compared to reporting on the JFK Jr. plane crash, coverage of the WTO meeting and demonstrations was sparse. There was no week of prime-time special reports on the cable news channels, despite the fact that what was transpiring touched on the most central political and social issues of our age. Indeed, Seattle was not given anywhere near the attention that Elián, Monica, O.J., or JonBenet got. News coverage of the demonstrations tended to emphasize property damage and violence and, even there, it downplayed the activities of the police. There were, to be fair, some outstanding pieces produced by the corporate media, but those were the exceptions to the rule. More of the same took place in April 2000 during the IMF-World Bank meetings and protests in Washington, D.C. The handful of good reports that did appear were lost in the continuous stream of pro-capitalist pieces. The sad truth is that the closer a story gets to corporate power and corporate domination of our society, the less reliable the corporate news media is.

What types of important stories get almost no coverage in the commercial news media? The historical standard is that there is no coverage when the political and economic elites are in agreement. Military spending is a classic example. The United States spends a fortune on the military for no publicly debated or accepted reason. But it serves several important purposes to our economic elite, not the least of which is as a lucrative form of corporate welfare. Since no element of the economic elite is harmed by military spending, and nearly all of them benefit by having an empire to protect profit making worldwide, it rarely gets criticized—unlike federal spending on education or health care or environmental improvements. If a reporter pursued the story of why we are spending some $700 billion on the military and war in 2008, he or she would appear to have an axe to grind and therefore to be unprofessional, since top official sources are not critical of the spending.

In recent years, the increased focus by the commercial news media on the more affluent part of the population has reinforced and extended the class bias in the selection and tenor of material. Stories of great importance to tens of millions of Americans will fall through the cracks because those are not the "right" Americans, according to the standards of the corporate news media. Consider, for example, the widening gulf between the richest and the poorest Americans, throughout the 1980s and 1990s real income declined or was stagnant for the lower 60 percent, while wealth and income for the rich skyrocketed. By 1998, discounting home ownership, the top 10 percent of the population claimed 76 percent of the nation's net worth, and more than half of that is accounted for by the richest 1 percent. The bottom 60 percent has virtually no wealth, aside from some home ownership; by any standard the lowest 60 percent is economically insecure, as it is weighed down by very high levels of personal debt. As Lester Thurow notes, this peacetime rise in class inequality may well be historically unprecedented and is one of the main developments of our age.[5] It has tremendously negative implications for our politics, culture, and social fabric, yet it is barely noted in our journalism except for rare mentions when the occasional economic report points to it. One could say that this can be explained by the lack of a news peg that would justify coverage, but that is hardly tenable when one considers the cacophony of news media reports on any economic boom or blip. In the crescendo of news media praise for the genius of contemporary capitalism, it is almost unthinkable to criticize the economy as deeply flawed. To do so would seemingly reveal one as a candidate for an honorary position in the Flat-Earth Society. The *Washington Post* has gone so far as to describe ours as a nearly "perfect economy." And it does, indeed, appear more and more perfect the higher one goes up the socioeconomic ladder, which points to the exact vantage point of the corporate news media.

The Internet

Moving on from journalism, the most striking media and communication development since January 1999 has been the rapid commercialization and expansion of the Internet. It is ironic that the media giants use the rise of the Internet and the prospect of new competition to justify their mega-mergers because, if anything, the Internet is spurring more concentration in media ownership, as well as other corporate sectors. The Internet will not launch a wave of commercially viable challengers to the existing media giants. Merely being able to launch a Web site is not sufficient to contend with the enormous market advantages of the media giants as they colonize the Internet. Recent evidence has borne that out in spades. Indeed, when AOL announced its deal with Time Warner, that pretty much hammered the nail in the coffin that the Internet would launch a new wave of media competition and drive the traditional media giants into extinction. For what AOL paid for Time Warner, it could have duplicated Time Warner's physical assets many times over. But what it needed was Time Warner's semi-monopolistic market position, which is nearly priceless.

As all communication switches to digital format, what seems most likely is that the corporate media giants will increasingly merge and partner with the few remaining corporate computer and telecommunication giants. We will have a global communication oligopoly of ten to twelve unbelievably huge firms, rather than a media oligopoly of six to eight believably huge ones.

The U.S. media system is not the result of the "free market" or of natural law. On the contrary, it is the result of explicit governmental laws, regulations, and subsidies that have created the giants that rule the roost. But the policies that put the system in place in our name and with our monies have been made in secret, without our informed consent.

The corrupt nature of U.S. communication policymaking continues on course. Vital decisions are made all the time concerning the future of our media system, but they are made behind closed doors to serve powerful special interests, with nonexistent public involvement and minuscule press coverage. Commercial broadcasters have effectively stolen control of digital television from the American people, with the support of their well-paid politicians. The one sop thrown to the public, the Gore Commission, which was to recommend suitable public-interest requirements for commercial broadcasters in return for the free gift of some $50–$100 billion of public property, was a farce.

In 2000 the FCC, under pressure from the broadcasters and their congressional allies, continued with the quiet development of plans for the transition from analog to digital radio broadcasting. This is business as usual. It would be possible to add numerous channels in every community while maintaining the present stations and converting them to digital. It would be an easy and effective way to bring localism and diversity to our homogenized and commercially saturated airwaves. Instead, the FCC adopted a plan that would keep the system as it was, and merely convert the status quo to digital. Hence the FCC generated a policy that protected the market power and massive profits of the semi-monopolists that dominated U.S. radio broadcasting, and did nothing for the majority of the population.

But the bankruptcy of communication policymaking is most apparent where it is the most important: with the rise of the Internet and digital communication systems. The shadowy history of how the Internet went from being a public-sector creation to being the province of Wall Street needs to be written, but this much is known: both political parties are thoroughly in the pay of the firms and sectors that benefited by the expansion of the commercialized Internet. The explicit policy of both parties was to fan the flames of this expansion as much as possible, all with the aim of making the Internet ubiquitous as quickly as possible. If the corporations have their way, soon it will be virtually impossible even to raise the issue of how the Internet should develop because its course will have been set in stone, or at least in code, and will be protected by powerful lobbies. (Fortunately, as I discuss in other chapters of this book, Internet policies, especially Net Neutrality, are becoming central political issues with the emergence of the media reform movement.) Even more important, there will no longer be any option about whether one wishes to participate in the "e-society." It will be all but mandatory, if one is to participate in U.S. life. All along the way we will be told of the great advantages we will enjoy by being online most of the time, of the unimaginable power and control over our lives it will give us. The commercialized Internet will soon appear as natural to us as our system of roads.

The analogy to automobiles is intentional, as the Internet in many ways is coming to play the same role in the twenty-first-century economy and social structure that cars have over the past seventy-five years or so. When automobiles were introduced—and especially after their prices came down—they provided revolutionary mobility for people. Who could not want to have a car? Soon networks of roads were built with public funds and the suburban sprawl that has engulfed so much of our countryside began in earnest. It became impossible to survive in the United States, except in a handful of locations, without having an automobile. Not one car per family either, but one per adult. Cars became as American as apple pie. And then, slowly, by the final third of the twentieth century it became clear that the toll automobiles were taking on human life was enormous. Air pollution, atomized suburban living conditions, the decline of the cities, traffic congestion, and a myriad of other social problems related to the automobile began to draw attention. Yet the problems were difficult to address because the automobile had become such an ingrained part of the society. One could speculate that, had the American people democratically considered all the pros and cons of the automobile back before, say, the 1940s, they might have opted to emphasize mass transit and downplay the usage of cars. But that was a debate that powerful interests made certain we never had.

Could the same be true of the Internet? Is the "Damn the Torpedoes" Internet policy a bit like driving at night on a strange mountain road at a hundred miles an hour with the headlights off? Might there be a dark side to the commercial cyberworld? Already there are concerns about Internet privacy, concerns that the ability to expand commerce necessarily also means the ability of corporations and governments to keep much closer tabs on individuals. Some foresee a panoptic society where traditional notions of personal privacy will be virtually eliminated.[6] There are concerns as well that the new digital system will make it possible for poor people to be entirely written out of the world experienced by the middle and upper classes, making political democracy that much more fragile. Similarly, scholarly research is beginning to show that those who spend the most time online risk becoming more antisocial and increasingly unhappy. In short, there are serious questions that have been pushed aside in the mad dash to commercialize the Internet. They will only get taken up, I suspect, years from now when they will be written as laments.

As with the automobile, the primary justification for this Internet commercialism is economic. As the automobile provided the basis for the expansion of twentieth-century industrial capitalism, so, we are told, the Internet and digital technology will provide the basis for economic growth in twenty-first-century capitalism. This is not debated so much as it is reiterated. Some of the claims about the Internet and the economy are clearly false, such as the popular cry that the Internet would smash up traditional giant corporations and create an economy dominated by small, hungry, lean and mean Internet-based entrepreneurial firms operating in competitive markets. A more important claim is that the Internet will provide the basis for sustained investment and economic growth that will raise living standards and the quality of life for generations, much as the automobile did. It is probably too early to pass judgment on that issue, but one 2000 study finds little evidence that the Internet will stimulate massive investment and economic growth.[7]

Even if one accepts that the Internet is to some extent the foundation of our current and future economic success, the important social questions remain: Who in the economy truly benefits? How much do the benefits spread to the bulk of the population—and at what social cost? So far the benefits are passing to a relatively small sector of the population, and there is little reason at present to anticipate the type of job creation associated with the auto industry with all of its related industries like oil, steel, rubber, glass, and construction. Only in a political and media culture where the affairs of Wall Street investors are presumed to be the same as the interests of the average person can these issues be ignored.

The Microsoft Antitrust Case

News on the policy front has not been all bad. Perhaps the most encouraging development in 1999–2000 was the government's prosecution and victory, for the time being, in its case against Microsoft. The Microsoft case provided a welcome change from the benign neglect that has overtaken antitrust for the past few decades to the delight of Wall Street and wealthy campaign contributors. The question now is whether the case will reinvigorate the notion of antitrust in our political culture and return it to its original populist purpose of breaking up concentrated wealth as a cancer to democratic governance. Among leading academic and scholarly antitrust experts like Eben Moglen and Robert H. Lande there is a growing sense that the media industry has precisely the type of concentrated power that antitrust was meant to address.

Although none of the top seven media conglomerates is a monopoly in any one national market, à la Microsoft or Standard Oil, theirs are closed markets for all intents and purposes. It is not merely the economic power of these firms, nor even their cultural power that causes concern. It is their political power. They have gotten so large that they are close to being untamable by government. The way media corporations treat politicians like playthings is evidence of this power.

It is somewhat ironic that even media executives grasp the situation at hand. Time Warner CEO Gerald Levin stated in January 2000 (on a CNN millennium media special) that the media is "fast becoming the predominant business of the twenty-first century, and we're in a new economic age, and what may happen, assuming that's true, is it's more important than government. It's more important than educational institutions and nonprofits." Levin went on to observe that "we're going to need to have these corporations redefined as instruments of public service."

Regulators in Washington are sticking to the recent orthodoxy that holds antitrust should only be deployed when a firm has close to a monopoly in a specific market. In May 2000 the Justice Department approved Viacom's purchase of CBS, meaning that all the TV networks, all the top film studios, all the major music companies, most cable TV channels, and much, much more are under the control of just seven media conglomerates. "We don't think big is per se bad," said Joel Klein, the assistant U.S. attorney general who spearheaded the case against Microsoft. The *New York Times* noted in May 2000 that "with a few exceptions, regulators during the Clinton years have signed off on big mergers, many of which would have been unthinkable a generation ago." As one law professor put it, "In merger law, the Clinton administration has a great deal in common with the Reagan and Bush years." Indeed, the main force that encourages antitrust action in the current environment is not concern for the public, but, on the contrary, pressure on antitrust regulators from firms asking them to intervene and help them vis-à-vis a competitor. This practice has limits, as these same firms wish to be involved in mergers themselves.[8]

But there is momentum in the application of antitrust to media beyond the writings of antitrust scholars. On Capitol Hill progressive legislators, such as Representative John Conyers (D-MI) and the late Senator Paul Wellstone (D-MN), supported applying antitrust to the existing media system. "There's no question that we have to start talking in a serious way about media, about media mergers and monopolies, about the balance between public and commercial television, about how we can encourage more diversity in ownership and in content," said Wellstone. "There's no question that we ought to be talking about the role that media plays in a democracy where most people don't vote. There's no question of any of this."

Nor is this an issue with appeal only for those on the left. When Time Warner removed Disney's ABC from its cable offerings in New York City (and elsewhere) on May 1, 2000, then-Mayor Rudolph Giuliani told reporters: "This is an example of what happens when you allow monopolies to get too big and they become too predatory and then the consumer is hurt. For the life of me, I can't figure out why the Justice Department has spent so much time on Microsoft and so little on this industry." Similarly, William Safire implored his fellow conservatives to rally to the cause of applying "vigorous antitrust prevention and enforcement" to the giant firms that rule the existing media system. "Concentration of power over what we see in the news," Safire concluded, "is a danger to democracy."[9]

Prospects for Media Reform

Antitrust is just the tip of the iceberg. Across the United States there is growing interest in media reform, ranging from local media literacy campaigns in schools to campaigns for revamping public television and radio at the national level. The objective, in the end, is to reduce the power of Wall Street and Madison Avenue and increase the power of everyone else. Antitrust is crucial, but it is not sufficient. Even more competitive media markets would leave too much power in the hands of owners and advertisers; that is why we need a viable, heterogenous nonprofit and noncommercial sector. Media reform activity continues to grow. Moreover, as the Safire comments indicate, this issue is not just the province of the political Left. Indeed, political conservatives like Phyllis Schlafly have worked with progressive media reform groups like Ralph Nader's Commercial Alert to challenge advertising and commercialism in public schools, an issue closely related to media reform. A May 1999 national survey sponsored by the Project on Media Ownership concluded that a majority of Americans from all backgrounds supported the sort of structural media reform that is off-limits to debate in mainstream political circles.[10] (No wonder the media giants do not want this to become a public issue!)

I would go so far as to say that media reform is not an issue that is best cast along left-right lines. It is better thought of as elementary to democracy. To the extent people not on the left support rudimentary democracy, they can and should support media reform as providing the basic groundwork for a democratic political culture.

Prospects for Political Renewal

There have been indications that we are entering an era of renewed politicization. On college campuses, for example, the 1999–2000 year saw an explosion of student organizing against sweatshops on some two hundred campuses. What has been striking to me is the growth in interest in anti-capitalist political organizing at a rate unprecedented for a quarter of a century. Also apparent, and so very refreshing, is that political organizing, though very serious, is also fun for the first time for students in a very long time. "With a joie de vivre that the American economic left has probably lacked since before WWI," an observer wrote, "college students are increasingly engaged in well-organized, thoughtful and morally outraged resistance to corporate power." This new political culture provides a marked contrast to the wet blanket of the phony corporate world pitched at the "youth market," with commercially sponsored "alternative" music events and contrived MTV hipness, all aimed at turning young people upside down and shaking the money out of their pockets. An alternative political culture is emerging along with a movement, much in evidence at the astonishing demonstrations in Seattle for the WTO meeting in late 1999 and in Washington, D.C., for the IMF-World Bank meetings in April 2000. A big part of this movement is the importance of alternative media, and the explicit critique of the limitations of corporate media. The new movement "appears to have legs," one business writer informed his readers. "The world's financial and corporate elites would do well to listen up."[11]

Nor are campuses the only site of activism. Movements against the death penalty and against police brutality are growing across the nation, especially in communities of color. The labor movement is in the midst of a renaissance of sorts, as more union shops get organized, especially among low-paid minority and women workers. Environmental activism, too, is going on all around the nation. The most exciting moments are when these various concerns—about class exploitation, about the environment, about racism—converge and draw people together. Such is the case with the anti-sweatshop movement, the environmental justice movement, the anti-WTO/IMF-World Bank movement, and the movements to organize low-wage workers. If a new and powerful Left is going to emerge in the United States, this is where the embryo will be found.

Almost all of this is taking place beneath the radar of the corporate news media, with their reliance on official sources and their close ties to those at the top of the social pecking order. Indeed, it is the lack of attention to these issues in the media, or the distorted nature of the coverage when there is attention, that underlines the importance of media activism to the new generation of activists. Similarly, the national electoral system is largely immune to these developments; awash in massive campaign contributions from billionaires and multimillionaires, the Democrats and Republicans spend a fortune on manipulative and insulting advertisements aimed at the dwindling numbers that take them seriously. The corporate media rake in this money for TV ads, highlight only the activities of politicians who support their agenda, and then pretend that this charade has something to do with democracy.

I have asked several political scientists and electoral campaign veterans what percentage of the vote the Democrats and Republicans would get in five or ten years if there were proportional representation for party votes in Congress (as opposed to winner-take-all for each seat) and if there were publicly financed campaigns for all parties. In other words, how much support would the two parties get if their duopoly, protected by the electoral system and massive campaign contributions, did not exist? The answers have ranged from 25 to 40 percent for both parties combined. It is worth noting that that is pretty much the range that the old Communist parties of Eastern Europe have received in the open elections since the collapse of communism. Although there are crucial differences, I think it is fair to say that our parties are about as responsive to the needs of the people as were the old Communist parties of the one-party-state era.

It is with this new progressive movement that the fate of media reform resides. Media reform cannot win without widespread support and such support needs to be organized as part of a broad anti-corporate, pro- democracy movement. If progressive forces can just get media reform on the agenda, merely make it part of legitimate debate, they will find that it has considerable support from outside the ranks of the Left. (It may even encourage people to take a closer and more sympathetic look at the Left.) This has been the pattern abroad: where Left parties have gotten media issues into debate, the mainstream parties could no longer blindly serve the corporate media masters. And this point is well understood by the media giants, which do everything within their considerable power to see that there is not even the beginnings of public discussion of media policy.

We are in precarious times. The corporate media system is consolidating into the hands of fewer and fewer enormous firms at a rapid rate, providing a hypercommercialized fare suited to wealthy shareholders and advertisers, not citizens. At the same time, there is a budding movement for media reform which is part and parcel of a broader anti-corporate movement. At present the smart money says that the big guys will win and the wise move is to accept the inevitable and abandon any hope of social change. But the same smart money once said that communism was going to last forever unless overthrown from without, and that South African apartheid could never be removed peacefully so it was best to work with the status quo white regime. Smart money is often more interested in protecting money than in being smart. Nobody can predict the future, especially in turbulent times like these. All we can do is attempt to understand how the world works so we can try to protect and expand those values we deem important. And if enough people come together to protect and expand democratic values—as it is in their interest to do—anything can happen.

21

The Case for U.S. Public Broadcasting and Implications for Philanthropists

Public service broadcasting is in a crisis at present in the United States. Never lavishly funded or supported, the system struggles to survive in a fairly small niche of the media market. Critics charge that public broadcasting is a dubious institution in principle, and now has become a bureaucratically ossified relic of a bygone era made irrelevant by the plethora of new cable channels and Web sites that offer everything under the sun. Hence there is no longer any justification for public subsidy in broadcasting; the market combined with new technologies can do a superior job of serving the public interest.

Here I respond to this criticism. First, I challenge the notion that public broadcasting must assume the form it presently does in the United States, and that our media system is inherently and rightfully the province of large commercial organizations. I place the present dilemma of U.S. public broadcasting in historic context, looking specifically at the nature of political debates over media policymaking and public broadcasting. Second, I question the proposition that whatever the rationale for public broadcasting in the past, the rise of the Internet and multi-channel television systems eliminates such a rationale. The market is now competitive and will "give the people what they want" far better than any government bureaucrat. Critics of public broadcasting claim that public broadcasting no longer merits significant support, be it public or philanthropic. I will argue to the contrary that the evidence points in the opposite direction, that the need for viable public service broadcasting in the United States is greater than ever before. It is an essential component of a broader media system worthy of being described as democratic; it can only prosper, perhaps even survive, if it is understood in that context.

The Immediate Context

The roots of the crisis can be found in the distinct manner in which public broadcasting was founded in the United States; indeed, it is the only way to comprehend the current situation. In large parts of the world, public service broadcasting refers to a nonprofit, noncommercial broadcasting service directed at the entire population and providing a full range of programming. In theory it should be accountable to the citizenry, have some distance from the dominant forces holding political power, and not rely upon the market to determine its programming. There are problems with managing a viable public broadcasting service in a democracy, but the international experience shows that it can be done, if there is a political commitment to make it happen. Indeed, much political economic media analysis globally addresses how best to construct public broadcasting to see that it accomplish its goals while remaining accountable and efficient. If the United States subsidized a public broadcasting service comparable to Britain's per capita rate for supporting public broadcasting, for example, it would have a budget approaching $20 billion annually. This would make it one of the two or three largest domestic media operations, and provide an enormous, almost incomprehensible, spur to audio-visual production. In Europe, a large amount of work that would never clear the hurdles of a commercial system has been produced as a result of this subsidy.

Why has public service broadcasting been a marginal phenomenon in the United States in comparison to nearly every other developed democracy? The main reason is that public broadcasting took off in other nations because its proponents were able to get it established before commercial broadcasting had emerged, and could use their powerful lobby to make the airwaves commercial. The hegemony of commercial broadcasting in the United States made such a course impossible; by 1934 the airwaves had become dominated by commercial interests, who were hostile to having viable public service broadcasting. The commercial broadcasters argued then that nobody would listen to commercial radio if they could hear quality entertainment programming on stations without advertising—which they conceded people did not wish to hear—so it was unfair to allow public broadcasting to exist. The U.S. government did establish extremely well-funded noncommercial broadcasting services in the 1940s and beyond—but it was to be directed at those outside the United States. Indeed, the quid pro quo with the commercial broadcasting industries was that those services—Voice of America, Armed Forces Radio and Television, Radio Free Europe—would not be accessible in the United States. On one hand the explanation was that explicit government propaganda should be restricted to foreigners, but—and this applies to Armed Forces broadcasting—a clear concern for the commercial broadcasters was that the American public not be exposed to well-funded noncommercial fare. When television came along in the 1940s, the FCC and the federal government adopted the commercial model without a shred of public debate over prospective alternatives.

The commercial broadcasting lobby finally acceded to the establishment of a national public radio and television service in the 1960s, but not to a full-service BBC type operation, where noncommercial public service was the dominant aspect of broadcasting. The plan for what became PBS and NPR did not call for such a system—the commercial dominance of the airwaves was a given—but, rather, for a broadcasting service that concentrated exclusively upon providing the public service programming the commercial stations were constantly lambasted for avoiding. The commercial broadcasters got first claim to do the programming that was popular, and the public broadcasters were to do programming that had little or no profit potential. Or, to put it another way, public broadcasters were left to do the programming for which there was not much of an immediate audience. At its best, as in the famous Carnegie Commission Report, U.S. public broadcasting was seen as doing cutting-edge political and creative programming that commercial broadcasting found unprofitable, and serving poor and marginalized audiences of little interest to the commercial networks. In the minds of the Carnegie Corporation, this would be a well-funded service, with an annual budget that would be in the $2–3 billion range in 2003 dollars.

The Carnegie vision was doomed from the start. As the public broadcasters were consigned to do the programming for which there was little or no audience, legislators soon determined that it would be wrong to give an unused service (with little popular support) such a lavish budget. In response, if a public broadcaster attempted to do popular programming, the commercial broadcasting lobby would complain to Congress that the government was subsidizing competition to commercial broadcasting, so the practice would get shot down. Public broadcasters realized they could only count on the federal government for a fraction of their budgets—in 2003 the figure was $365 million, about the same as what ESPN received in subscriber fees every two months—and did the rational thing. They turned away from anything more than a rhetorical commitment to marginal and poor audiences, or to edgy programming, and began cultivating a sliver of the middle class with business, educational, and high-culture programming. This provided a solid base for periodic "pledge drives" as well as a political constituency that commanded respect in Washington. It also made public broadcasting increasingly attractive to advertisers, or underwriters, as they were euphemistically termed. This logic has built into it a certain clear path. The prospect of government subsidy continues to decline, because as the public broadcaster goes more and more commercial, its justification for a subsidy decreases. Likewise, management of the pubic stations increasingly apes the mores and modus operandi of commercial broadcasting, with its obsession with ratings and target demographics.

To be accurate, and in fairness to U.S. public broadcasters, most of them are principled and dedicated public servants who have done wonders with the hand they have been dealt. They have never been in the institutional position or had the resources to develop the sort of service found in Europe or parts of Asia that generate considerable and widespread popular support. Local PBS and NPR stations often have been jewels in their local media environments. The children's programming on PBS, for example, has been a ray of sunshine on the television dial. But the overriding pressures have been too great; libraries and bookstores are filled with tomes by former public broadcasters and scholars chronicling the limitations of the institution. And, to add insult to injury, politicians in Congress, especially those on the political right, use what moneys Congress does provide as leverage to continually badger public broadcasters to stay within the same ideological range found on the commercial networks. Conservatives are obsessed with public broadcasting because the traditional sources of control in commercial media—owners and advertisers—are not in place, and that means there is a greater possibility that critical work might get produced by the public system. Between the state and the market, U.S. public broadcasting experiences the worst of both worlds.

The Broader Context

Acknowledging that public service broadcasting was put in a precarious position from its outset is the starting point for understanding the ongoing crisis, but it is not sufficient. After all, the argument goes, the media system in the United States is, by constitution, economy, culture, and custom, a commercial enterprise. It was only natural that public broadcasting would be a marginal enterprise, that it would be a foreign square peg in the American round hole. Commercial media and commercial broadcasting are in the American DNA. It is our natural system requiring no special edicts to bring it into place; it merely assumes its role naturally without the need for government regulation.

There is an element of truth to this claim, to the extent that the United States has always been a commercially oriented society and entrepreneurs invariably seek out areas in which to invest and earn profit. But otherwise the notion that U.S. media are naturally or organically commercial, at least in the modern sense of the term, is false. The nature of the marketplace in 1790 or 1840 was radically different from the marketplace in 1910, 1960, or 2008. This is especially true of the media marketplace. The media system in the Republic's first two generations looks almost nothing like the media system of the past half-century. It was highly partisan and was not a central engine for profit making in the economy. It was as much or more about politics than commerce.

Most important, there is nothing natural about the media system, today or in the past. The contemporary system is the direct result of explicit government policies; it would not exist anything as it presently does without such policies. Every large media company today is the beneficiary of government granted and enforced monopoly rights—be they licenses for scarce radio and TV channels, monopoly cable TV and satellite TV systems, and/or copyright—and these firms pay not one penny to the government for these monopoly franchises worth in the tens of billions of dollars on an annual basis. Indeed contemporary debates about "deregulating" media are nothing of the kind. The media system will continue to be regulated; what deregulation means is that the regulation will be done strictly to serve the dominant commercial interests.

Nor are media policies a new development. In fact, conscious media policies are inscribed in the Constitution and in the laws of the early Republic. Those founders who gave the matter the most thought—Madison and Jefferson—were arguably the most brilliant and visionary thinkers of their times. In the early Republic there was no sense whatsoever that media were naturally the province of capitalists seeking to make profits, and the function of government was to stay out of their way, letting the chips fall where they may. Governments established copyright, funded literacy training, provided large printing subsidies to provide for newspapers both through Congress and the State Department, and, most important, provided a huge subsidy for the mailing of newspapers and periodicals. (Indeed, Madison argued that all periodicals should always be mailed at no charge by the government to encourage a vibrant and diverse press.) The result of these explicit policies was a flowering media and political culture in the United States in the first half of the nineteenth century, and a level of political democracy, at least among white males in the Northern states, which were the envy of the world. These policies were often enacted, as in the case of the postal subsidy, after extensive and passionate public debate.

In short, freedom of the press was seen as a crucial social right shared by all citizens in a democracy, and it was the responsibility of enlightened policy-making to create the structures that would generate a free press. It was not seen as a private right for media owners to do as they wished to maximize profits, with the public forced to accept the consequences, for better or for worse. That notion of a free press came much later, when powerful commercial interests aggressively proselytized the notion.

So it has been that though media policies have been every bit as important to constructing the media system in the past century as they were during the first generations of the republic, the caliber of the public and congressional debates surrounding these policies has changed dramatically. As media and communication became a source of tremendous profit making, the debates became less public and more under the domination of powerful commercial interests. When telegraphy developed in the nineteenth century, for example, the Western Union monopoly was able to stymie the considerable public support for establishing a national nonprofit system, along the lines of the post office. Crucial to Western Union's success was its very close relationship to the newspaper industry, which relied upon Western Union for its monopolistic Associated Press wire service. The leading newspapers trivialized, denigrated, and ignored all the efforts to challenge the Western Union monopoly.

This has been a pattern throughout the twentieth century and true to the present day: the large commercial media interests, which have a distinct self-interest in the outcome of media policy debates, use their media power to support their commercial aims. They have become an exceptionally formidable power, and the public has been effectively removed from any participation in these policy deliberations. The nature of the debates, then, has been largely about commercial concerns among competing business lobbies. Concerns about the implications of media policies and resulting structures for democratic governance have fallen by the wayside, except for periodic rhetorical flourish.

Nowhere has this been more apparent or disastrous than in the case of broadcasting. Commercial interests used their immense political power to grab the monopoly licenses to the scarce radio channels, and then were able to push through a law—the Communications Act of 1934—to crystallize the commercial system. A feisty and heterogeneous group of Americans attempted to organize public opinion to support the establishment of a viable nonprofit and noncommercial broadcasting sector prior to 1934, but the movement was crushed, receiving almost no publicity in the news media. The commercial broadcasting lobby worked assiduously then, as it has subsequently, to reduce or eliminate any public role in the media policymaking process. The goal has been and is to make the dominant commercial system appear natural and inviolable. But the truth is that only after 1934 did commercial broadcasting become regarded as the "natural" American system. Indeed, as late at 1926 or 1927, the notion of commercial broadcasting as it would come to be understood barely existed, and to the extent it was understood, it was roundly criticized from nearly all quarters. The right of commercial interests and commercial values to have first claim to the media system became enshrined in the political culture then, though the courts would continue to uphold the fundamental democratic right of the public to determine media policies that might oppose commercial interests in a number of crucial decisions throughout the twenteith century.

The marginalization of public debate and, with that, the denigration of public interest values in media policymaking hurt the entirety of our media system, but it was and is absolutely disastrous for public broadcasting. Policy debates are premised on the assumptions that the market works and is innately democratic, and that noncommercial and nonprofit institutions are highly suspect until proven otherwise. Profitability is taken as a measure of success, not only for the affected commercial enterprise but for society as a whole. The link of media policymaking to core democratic values—so central to Madison and Jefferson and the founding generation—is lost. In this context, public broadcasting has little traction in which to generate significant public support. And there is nothing natural or innately "American" about it. It is pure old-fashioned power politics, and highly corrupt.

In sum, media policymaking is a necessary and unavoidable function of government in a modern society, be it democratic or otherwise. Even a so-called free market or libertarian system is based on explicit policies. The question is not whether there will be policies, but rather in whose interests and toward what values they will be made. And it is here that the caliber of public participation in media policymaking debates is decisive. Even with all the limitations built into U.S.-style public broadcasting, it remains a service that most Americans rank high on the list of government programs they approve funding. Yet far less popular programs receive vastly greater federal funding. The reason is to be found in the secretive and corrupt nature of the policymaking process.

Revisiting the Case Against Public Broadcasting

Even allowing for the flawed mandate provided to U.S. public broadcasting and the dubious and corrupt nature of U.S. media policymaking, some contemporary critics still argue that the rationale for public broadcasting no longer exists. The reasons are twofold: because new technologies eliminate spectrum scarcity and hence the justification for publicly subsidized media; and without scarcity the free market can work its magic, "giving the people what they want." Both explanations contain a kernel of truth, but they are at best half-truths; taken out of context they serve to obscure far more than they reveal.

We have already shown that the premise that publicly subsidized broadcasting is unnatural and an intrusion on a commercial broadcasting system is a recent proposition, and one never formally debated or considered by the broad polity. But even if one accepts this premise for the sake of argument, the case that new technologies have eliminated spectrum scarcity and the justification for public broadcasting is bogus. The justification for public broadcasting need not nor should not be based on spectrum scarcity; it goes to the very roots of democratic media policymaking and the notion of freedom of the press in the founding of the Republic. Moreover, spectrum scarcity in any meaningful sense has not disappeared.

The rise of the Internet is often held up as making preposterous the idea that there are limits to the number of media channels. After all, the cost of launching a Web site is minimal, there are millions and millions of Web sites, and people have access to a range of information and ideas that was simply unfathomable as recently as ten or fifteen years ago. The Internet has radically transformed our media system, and in many respects it has done so for the better. There is much that is true about these statements, but the picture they present is incomplete. The ability to launch Web sites is well and good, but that does not guarantee the ability to launch well-subsidized commercially viable media content Web sites. And that is the crucial issue here, because journalism and entertainment fare require substantial resources and institutional support to be effective. And after more than a decade of the commercialized World Wide Web, and hundreds of millions of dollars in investment, the Internet has yet to produce any viable commercial competition to the existing media firms. The advantages of the market trump the subversive potential of the technology.

What is clear is that how the Internet does develop, and what role it ultimately plays in our media system, ultimately depends upon a range of media policy issues, including copyright, regulation, and public broadcasting. Media ownership regulations are crucial as well. Ironically, large media firms argue they need to be allowed to grow larger and larger to deal with the threat of new competition from the Internet. What they really mean is they need to be permitted to get larger and larger so they can reduce or snuff out the threat of new competition from the Internet. Likewise, when the largest media firms press the government to eliminate ownership caps on radio and TV licenses due to all this new competition from both the Internet and digital television, they argue that the monopoly privileges once conferred by a radio or TV licenses are no longer applicable. The problem with this argument, however, is that it does not square with the facts. If TV (and radio) licenses no longer conferred monopoly power—and immense profitability—in the marketplace, if the value of a TV license was lost in the maze of Web sites and cable channels, one would expect the value of TV and radio stations to begin to stagnate, and eventually plummet. After all, why pay a fortune to purchase the rights to a TV license if, instead of assuring a large audience and profits, it was but a grain of sand on the media beachfront. Instead, the value of TV stations has increased dramatically over the past decade, well in excess of the rate of economic growth or inflation. Monopoly still has its privileges.

It is the rise of multi-channel and digital cable television systems—offering hundreds and hundreds of commercial channels, many of which are profitable—that is most often held up as decisive evidence that a plethora of channels exists that can accommodate every possible interest; hence to have the government subsidize one or two of them is an absurd misuse of resources. Commercial interests have plenty of channels to use to satisfy all of the public's tastes. If there is no commercial market for a channel in this context, it is certainly unwanted by the public and cannot justify a public subsidy.

There are two elements involved in this "give the people what they want" argument that need to be addressed. The first is that whether the commercial media marketplace per quo is an effective regulator of media on behalf of the public interest. The second element is whether the market per se is an effective and appropriate engine to regulate the media system. Often people will accept the latter while highlighting problems with the former. The assumption is that in a best of all possible worlds, the market is the optimum solution. And since the new technologies provide the best of all possible worlds, it is time to unchain the market in all its fury and majesty. I will argue that the market fails on both counts.

The problems with the commercial media market per quo are legion. Even in an age of boundless technologies, it is not a competitive market, but an oligopolistic one. Hence power in the market shifts from the consumer to the producer. Firms give the people what they want, but within a far narrower range than consumers may want, because firms have the market power to offer that which is most profitable. Hence vulgar fare and violent content are proven inexpensive attention getters. The role of advertising as a primary source of revenues distorts the market, as consumers become a means to an end, not an end in themselves. That most people do not want so much advertising or commercial intrusion on the media is dismissed by media owners, as that is the source of their profits. (So much for giving the people what they want.) Then when people consume what they are exposed to, they are told they are getting what they want. And over time, people logically develop a taste for what they are exposed to; the defense of the market becomes tautological. It is also worth noting that in a society like the United States with significant economic inequality, the market, based as it is on one-dollar, one-vote, is far from democratic. The rich have many votes and the poor have few or none.

But it is the problems with the commercial media market per se that are most important, and that provide the basis for the fundamental argument on behalf of public broadcasting, and a viable nonprofit, noncommercial media sector writ large. Even if media markets were competitive and even if income distribution were more egalitarian, the market would be a significantly flawed mechanism for regulating the media system in a free and democratic society. This is not to say that there would not be a role for the commercial marketplace, merely that the commercial media should not be hegemonic. *The basic problem is that markets cannot deal with all sorts of important values people may wish to see in their media, and they understand as being necessary for their media system to generate.* For an analogy, polls show most Americans are strong supporters of subsidizing an extensive national park system even if they do not use national parks personally; such a belief cannot be expressed in the market. So it is with important media values. Another way to put this is that what media owners rationally do to maximize their profits produces very negative outcomes for society as a whole, outcomes most Americans do not desire. These negative outcomes are not just philosophical concerns; they are hard effects that markets cannot address.

Economists call these problems with markets "externalities." These refer to the effects of economic actions that are not factored into the market transaction because neither the buyer nor seller has to pay the costs, but they affect all of society. A manufacturer of an automobile and the consumer of the automobile need not worry about the air pollution the automobile creates in the cost of the product. But the effect on society from lousy air becomes immense and there is a significant cost to be paid by society to address the problem. Externalities can also be positive, where owners are incapable of capturing all of the value of their product. When a company builds an especially beautiful factory or office building, it gives pleasure to all that see it, though the company

sees no market benefit from such satisfaction. It is the role of government policymaking to discourage negative externalities, and encourage positive externalities. Without such government intervention, for example, pollution generated by the marketplace would almost certainly render the human species
extinct—and our failure to regulate carbon dioxide might just do this.

Externalities in the media marketplace are immense and of the utmost
importance. Consider but two areas central to the public broadcasting mandate—children's programming and journalism. In the case of children's television, firms make money by attracting young viewers whose attention they
sell to advertisers. The effects of commercial television upon children, aside
from winning their immediate attention, do not factor into the commercial
equation. Indeed they cannot, because if a firm lets other concerns alter its
judgment, it will lose viewers and advertising revenues to competitors and
eventually be out of business. But what if the programming tends to be inane
and superficial and encourage socially troubling values, like an obsession with
branded products, money, and physical appearance? Obviously the children
lose, and their parents might be concerned and try to regulate their television
consumption. But all of society loses in the long run, even people without
children, if such television programming is widely produced and consumed
because it will lead to long-term antisocial behavior that will affect everyone.
And it will lead to high economic costs to repair the damage in the form of
education, if the damage can even be undone. This is why several industrial
democracies prohibit television advertising to children under the age of
twelve, and it is a growing movement worldwide. Indeed, with healthy policies, the ideal would be for children's television to generate widespread *positive* externalities.

The case is similar with journalism. Here media owners increasingly produce inexpensive "news" that avoids costly in-depth and controversial public
affairs issues, and concentrate upon trivial or inconsequential stories or the
regurgitation of press releases and public comments by those in power. The
owners make money and the consumers consume what they are given and
appear satisfied, so all is well, right? Wrong. There is a massive negative exter-
nality: the dismal journalism effects all in society, including those who are not
consumers of commercial journalism. It leads to an ill-informed electorate
that makes poor decisions, which affects public life and the health of the economy. It makes democracy, the notion of informed self-government, less plau-

sible. As mentioned above, the founders understood that journalism was a social institution of the highest magnitude that could not be left to private commercial interests to do as they pleased. Moreover the entire history of U.S. journalism points to the limitations of regarding it as a commercial enterprise; the purpose of modern professional journalism is to insulate journalism from the negative externalities generated by commercial influence and emphasize those positive characteristics of journalism that there is little commercial incentive to produce.

And here we can return in full to *per quo* from *per se*. The past decade, perhaps generation, has seen a deterioration of the professional protection from commercial imperatives and a consequent drop in the caliber of journalism. Leading journalists, such as the editors of the *Washington Post*, document the decline of their craft. Linda Foley, president of the journalist union, the Newspaper Guild, reports that the commercial encroachment upon journalism is the number one concern of her membership. Journalism has all but ceased to exist on U.S. commercial radio and is in a dubious state on local U.S. television stations. Investigative journalism is barely anywhere to be found. As professional journalism has declined, a vicious know-nothing partisanship has returned to elements of the mainstream news media, exclusively supporting right-wing political views of the media owners. It is often little short of propaganda. This has occurred at the same time that there has been a vast increase in the number of TV channels. The situation is not getting better, it is getting worse. We are in the midst of a severe and prolonged crisis.

Conclusion

The first and most important conclusion is that the United States needs a strong nonprofit and noncommercial media sector. Such a sector is necessary for high-quality children's programming, for providing experimental and high-quality entertainment material frowned upon by the market, and a variety of other important needs. Most important, a nonprofit media sector is mandatory for providing some, perhaps much, of the journalism and public affairs material befitting a democracy. If such a sector is well funded and well managed, it can have repercussions across the entire media system. It can reverberate across the entire social and political culture.

In our times the flagship of the nonprofit media sector is public broadcasting. The United States already has a substantial public television system, with hundreds of valuable channels providing a well-recognized and established national network. Philanthropic funding that went toward journalism and public affairs programming would be assured a potential audience of massive dimensions. PBS management is committed to seizing the initiative and providing airtime for such programming; it is mandatory to fulfill the PBS mission to establish the core link between public broadcasting and the communication requirements of a self-governing people. But what such journalism and public affairs programming also requires are significant resources, light years beyond what PBS is capable of providing at present. In the current political environment, it is imperative that the philanthropic community provides the lion's share of money to subsidize this journalism and pubic affairs programming. Otherwise it will not get done. What was stated by a prominent 1930s media activist struggling for public service broadcasting applies in spades today: "The market has failed; the state has failed; philanthropy must enter the field."

This is not the end to our story, however. Whereas a major influx of foundation funding is mandatory, without sounding too loud of an alarm, for the survival of democracy, it is not the long-run solution to the problem. It is not even the medium-run solution to the problem. As wealthy as foundations are, they cannot bankroll viable public broadcasting for generations, and even if they were that wealthy, they have other major demands upon their resources. What is ultimately necessary is to have viable public funding for public broadcasting. This will require an aggressive grassroots campaign to generate a significant increase in organized popular support for public broadcasting. And in that campaign, the high-quality journalism and public affairs programming provided by philanthropic funds will be Exhibit A in the case for the tremendous public need for a well-subsidized public broadcasting sector.

This is not a fight that PBS can engage in itself, as that would be political suicide, not to mention inappropriate. Third parties must lead this effort, parties that can also have formal distance from PBS, remaining independent and critical of aspects of PBS while organizing campaigns on its behalf. So foundations that devote large resources to public affairs programming production for PBS should consider devoting a percentage of their funds to a public outreach campaign on behalf of public broadcasting. The good news is that organizing a first-rate grassroots campaign is far less expensive than producing high-quality content. And it has a potentially much greater payoff.

For an independent grassroots campaign for public broadcasting to be successful, it cannot merely advocate for public broadcasting as it is, but it must provide a bold vision of what public broadcasting can be. This will involve rethinking the organization structure of the public broadcasting system, which is almost incomprehensible to the untrained eye. It will involve a vision that draws new communication technologies into the heart of the mission. The term public service broadcasting ultimately must be seen as misleading; it is truly public service media. Along these lines, we need to conceive of public media as including a variety of institutions, e.g., community and low-power radio and television stations and Web sites, with PBS and NPR the flagships. Public broadcasting must see itself in a cooperative, not a competitive, relationship with other nonprofit and noncommercial media.

Finally, advocates and supporters of public broadcasting must avoid the temptation to see the dreadful state of journalism and the mainstream media writ large as being acceptable because it makes such a clear and overwhelming case for the need for PBS to provide an alternative. This is the public broadcasting of fools. It makes a virtue of a (hopefully short-term) necessity. The historical record and the international experience are clear: viable public broadcasting cannot survive if it is to remain an island of virtue in a sea of vulgarity and commercialism. Public broadcasting has been at its best in an environment where there is a healthy commercial sector that produces quality content. Accordingly, it is in the interests of proponents of public broadcasting to see that crucial media policymaking debates be as wide open and public spirited as possible, even on issues such as media ownership rules that do not pertain directly to public broadcasting. The more public involvement there is in media policymaking debates, the more likely the policies will generate a media system that best serves the public interest. This creates a hospitable environment for public broadcasting. Accordingly, a grassroots campaign for public broadcasting must see itself as an integral part of a broader movement for democratic media policymaking. Indeed, in the final analysis, it is only as part of a broader movement that the campaign for renewed and recharged pubic broadcasting stands any hope for success.

22

The Escalating War Against Corporate Media

A recurring issue for the Left historically has been how to address the capitalist media. In recent years the problem has grown ever more severe, and no small amount of attention has been given to examining the problems of the commercial media and how closely they reinforce and accentuate problems within the broader social order. The logic of this criticism has become clear: progressives need to work on challenging the corporate domination of media as part of the broader struggle for social justice. If changing media is left until "after the revolution," there will be no revolution, not to mention fewer chances for social reform. But politicizing control over media has proven to be extraordinarily difficult for activists. That is why the massive and largely unanticipated 2003 campaign in the United States to stop further media concentration, which almost overnight reached a scale not seen in media reform struggles since the 1930s, is so important and instructive. This chapter chronicles that revolt.

The Media Reform Movement Comes to Life

Today we can see that hidden from public view in the 1990s had been a mounting concern over media. The changes wrought by neoliberal measures such as the 1996 Telecommunications Act only fanned the flames of this burgeoning movement. Magazines such as *The Nation*, *The Progressive*, and *In*

These Times began to feature stories not only criticizing mainstream media but also reporting on nascent efforts to change media policies. The progressive media watch group Fairness & Accuracy In Reporting flourished, as did the Media Education Foundation, the premier producer of critical videos on media. Across the nation local media watch groups, reform organizations, and independent media outlets began to sprout. Critical books on media and journalism began selling better than they had in the past. National "media and democracy" conferences were held in San Francisco and New York in 1996 and 1997, respectively, drawing many hundreds of activists.

Media activism was enjoying a distinct dynamism. The emergence of Independent Media Centers in the wake of the Seattle protests against the World Trade Organization in 1999 galvanized opposition to corporate media among a generation of young activists. Already media reform activism had reached a level not seen in many decades, but it still had not reached the levels of the Progressive Era and the 1930s. Despite all the activity and despite evidence that the American people were concerned about this issue, the media reform movement was almost entirely outside the mainstream political culture and invisible within the commercial news media.[1] It did not exist in the minds of the overwhelming majority of the American people.

At the dawn of the twenty-first century, the media reform movement had its first notable skirmish in the battle for low-power FM radio (LPFM). The technology began in the late 1980s when it became possible to transmit radio signals easily and inexpensively, and soon several people began conducting low-power broadcasting on the open FM frequencies in their communities. The pioneer was an African-American activist, Mbanna Kantako, who began broadcasting to his neighborhood in Springfield, Illinois. By the 1990s scores of people were engaging in low-power broadcasting, and they were doing so without licenses from the Federal Communications Commission (FCC). Commercial broadcasters demanded that the FCC stop the "pirates," and the FCC obliged—taking legal action against several micro-broadcasters. But it soon became apparent that the low cost and ease of use of the technology made it virtually impossible to police. That these broadcasters were able easily to locate open slots in the FM band—and therefore not interfere with existing stations—made LPFM seem benign, and it roused no public concern.

FCC chairman William Kennard recognized the difficulty in policing LPFM and decided to implement a widespread but cautious program to legalize LPFM stations across the nation. He was especially concerned with how the lifting of the radio ownership caps in 1996 had led to a sharp decline in the number of African-American station owners. Because most minority station owners generally held only a small number of stations, they found it impossible to compete with emerging giants like Clear Channel and were forced to sell out. Kennard wanted a plan that would get LPFM licenses into the hands of community groups representing people underserved by the commercial radio system.

After months of study the FCC released its plan—generally regarded by LPFM advocates as being more cautious than necessary—for the establishment of more than one thousand LPFM stations in 2000. These noncommercial stations would be licensed to locally-based nonprofit organizations. On the surface this looked like a clear victory for the American people: more stations, more choice, no commercialism, and more local content. Only one very small group of individuals disliked the plan: owners and managers of commercial broadcasting companies. These broadcasters did not want more competition for "their" listeners, especially not of a noncommercial and local variety. Such competition might require them to reduce advertising and increase local content to keep listeners from defecting, and those changes would come directly out of their profit margins.

The National Association of Broadcasters put a full court press on Congress to overturn Kennard's LPFM plan. The lobby could not, for PR purposes, admit to greed as a motive; instead it argued that one thousand new LPFM stations would create interference with the signals transmitted by existing broadcasters. The problem with this claim, as Kennard futilely explained, was that the engineering plans for inserting the new stations into the FM band were drawn largely from recommendations made a few years earlier by engineers who represented commercial broadcasters—when they wanted to make their own changes to the radio dial. Those changes had been implemented without causing signal interference.

The House, led by the commercial broadcasters' chief advocate in that body, Representative Billy Tauzin, voted to overturn Kennard's plan and reduce the number of LPFM stations to around two or three hundred, mostly in small cities and rural areas. The Senate was less willing to oblige corporate broadcasters, significantly because the ranking Republican on the relevant Senate Commerce Committee, Arizona's John McCain, refused to comply with the NAB's wishes. Of considerable importance, too, was the appearance of an organized lobbying effort with a significant grassroots element provided by LPFM advocates, including the Future of Music Coalition and the Prometheus Radio Project. This campaign drew a broad range of support, including organized labor, church groups, and civil rights organizations. This organizing effort was instrumental in mobilizing congressional support for the Kennard LPFM plan.

In the end, the NAB won—and the number of LPFM stations was reduced from one thousand to a few hundred. It was not through a majority vote on the Senate floor, but through a rider put on the budget bill in late December 2000.[2] "There were no hearings. It was done in the appropriations process at a time when all the special interests know that their power is greatly enhanced because it is done in the dark of night," Kennard later explained in an interview. "You know, you wake up the next day and legislation is written. The people who had the most to say about it are completely cut out of the process. If I sound bitter, I am."[3]

Media reform activists learned crucial lessons from the LPFM fight: organizing around tangible reform proposals could actually generate popular support and sustained attention on Capitol Hill. For the first time in memory, organized people were challenging organized money on media policy issues. The industry had been forced to resort to a middle-of-the-night maneuver to get its way. Momentum for media reform continued to grow. In the spring of 2002, then-Representative Bernard Sanders of Vermont convened the first-ever "congressional town meetings" to address the problem of "corporate control of the media." Held on consecutive nights in Montpelier and Burlington, the events drew overflow crowds of several hundred people to everyone's surprise. Sanders, who had held scores of town meetings in Vermont on a wide range of public policy issues since entering Congress in 1991, could not recall ever getting such an enthusiastic response. "I think this shows that the movement for democratic media reform strikes a chord among the citizenry. It is going to be a long-term process but, after these last two days, I really think we can win it."[4]

The issue that finally put the media reform movement on the map was media ownership regulations. The 1996 Telecommunications Act required the five-member FCC to review its media ownership rules every two years to see if they needed to be revised in view of changing circumstances. The FCC held these biennial reviews twice after 1996 as required and ruled each time that conditions had not changed sufficiently to warrant changes in ownership rules. The new FCC chairman Michael Powell, chosen by President George W. Bush to replace Kennard, formed a media ownership working group of FCC staffers to study the matter in October 2001.[5] He was expressly committed to scrapping media ownership rules as rapidly as possible. Instead, the hard work of the Consumers Union and the Consumer Federation of America, intended to keep Congress aware of what the FCC was planning and to slow down Powell, prevented him from moving quickly. As the Consumers Union's Gene Kimmelman recalls, "Industry was extremely angry that Powell 'wasted' six to nine months" in 2001 and 2002 before he got on track.[6]

Not willing to rely simply on the FCC, the corporate media lobbies were simultaneously working the court system in an attempt to have all the ownership rules thrown out. In February and April 2002, in two rulings, the U.S. Court of Appeals for the District of Columbia Circuit, known for its neoliberal bent, sided with industry lawyers. It pronounced that unless the FCC could prove that media ownership rules clearly served the public interest, the intent of Congress in the 1996 Telecommunications Act was that they be abolished.

The FCC announced its next biennial review of media ownership rules in September 2002. As a result of this review, ownership restrictions would have to be defended or else the rules would be tossed and media ownership would be subject only to antitrust enforcement, like other industries. Six rules were under review, including the prohibition against newspaper-broadcast cross-ownership and the rules regulating the number of TV stations a single firm could own locally and nationally. At that point, firms were permitted to own only one TV station in a market, except in the very largest cities, where they could own two. Firms were also prohibited from owning TV stations that, in total, reached more than 35 percent of the population, though both Viacom and News Corporation had been granted waivers by the FCC to exceed that figure. These were the rules that the industry was most eager to see relaxed or eliminated.

Powell and Copps Take the Stage

It was ironic that FCC chairman Michael Powell would be the official responsible for demonstrating to the courts that media ownership rules could be justified as serving the public interest. The son of Colin Powell, Michael Powell was being groomed for a career as a major player in the Republican Party. Long before the autumn of 2002, Powell had emerged as an enthusiastic, almost religious, proponent of neoliberal ideology and called for extending "full First Amendment rights" to commercial broadcasters.[7] In theory that meant unvarnished praise for free markets, in practice it meant giving the corporate media lobbies whatever they wanted. For example, he opposed Kennard's LPFM plan. Even if deregulation led to more concentration, even monopoly, Powell's approach was to damn the torpedoes and plow full-speed ahead: "I don't see why we have to tell companies they have to eat their vegetables before they get their dessert." Powell saw the role of the FCC as facilitating profit making for corporations, pure and simple: "Government policy needs to follow the rule of capital and investment, not always the other way around."[8]

Powell had never been especially concerned about media concentration. "Monopoly is not illegal by itself in the United States," Powell commented in early 2002. "People tend to forget this. There is something healthy about letting innovators try to capture markets."[9] While he acknowledged that a complete monopoly was problematic legally, he characterized the duopoly of satellite television—with two firms controlling the entire market—as "a vibrant competitive market."[10] Powell conceded that he found the very notion of public interest regulation dubious: "The public interest works with letting the market work its magic."[11] In Powell's view, he was "working himself out of a job" at the FCC by having public interest regulation eliminated, and the sooner he did it, the better.[12]

Having this corporate media enthusiast in charge of defending the FCC's right to regulate media ownership in the public interest was like putting Florida's Republican then-secretary of state Katherine Harris in charge of Al Gore's Florida recount team in November 2000. The other two Republican members of the FCC were, if anything, even more devoted to advancing commercial media interests. Kathleen Q. Abernathy had been a corporate lobbyist before joining the FCC and was characterized as a "quiet warrior" for ownership deregulation. She almost never appeared in public and was seen as a "reliable vote" for Chairman Powell.[13] Abernathy was much appreciated among corporate media lobbyists; she lavished praise upon the corporate-controlled plan for digital radio as "a win-win for everyone."[14] The other Republican, Kevin Martin, had worked as a lawyer in the powerhouse Washington law firm of Wiley, Rein & Fielding, whose business was representing corporate communication clients. Richard Wiley, Martin's boss and a former FCC member, was a zealous advocate of eliminating media ownership rules. Wiley spent so much time in FCC headquarters that he was dubbed the "sixth member" of the FCC.[15] Martin also worked full-time on the Bush-Cheney election campaign as a general counsel from 1999 to 2001.[16]

Because the commission had a vacancy for a Democratic member in the fall of 2002, the one dissenting voice to a thorough relaxation of media ownership rules was Michael Copps, a Democrat with a doctoral degree in history, who had been appointed to the commission in 2001. Copps, too, was a patronage appointee, having served as an aide for many years to Senator Ernest "Fritz" Hollings, the ranking Democrat on the Senate Commerce Committee. Perhaps it was because the Democrats were out of power and therefore less deferential to the media lobby—or perhaps it was simply because Copps was cut from a different cloth—but early on it became clear that he was not at all like Kennard and the other Democrats who had recently served on the FCC. A self-described New Dealer, Copps's was the one vote against approving Comcast's takeover of AT&T's cable systems in 2002: "The sheer economic power created by this mega-combination, and the opportunities for abuse that would accompany it, outweigh the very limited public interest benefits that either the Applicants or the majority find here." Copps rejected the Powell-Abernathy-Martin formulation that if a merger generated increased efficiencies (generally measured by profits) it meant the deal would be beneficial to the public: "It strikes me as bedrock that our review of proposed consolidations must venture beyond economic efficiencies if we are to ensure that combinations serve the public interest."[17]

Copps was adamant that the FCC's review of media ownership rules needed to reach out to the public. "We need much wider participation," he argued. "This is not an inside-the-Beltway issue."[18] Copps thought the commission's plan to allow for sixty days of public comment was insufficient in view of the stakes involved. He suggested that the FCC hold a series of hearings around the nation to gauge public opinion on the issue. Powell, supported by the other commissioners, was "unenthusiastic" and formally rejected Copps's recommendation in November.[19] By this time, relations between Powell and Copps had already become frosty. Copps issued a release expressing "alarm" and "disappointment" at Powell's refusal to hold public hearings or to find other ways to generate increased public participation.[20]

At the end of 2002 all indications were that the Republican majority would get their way and ownership limits would be greatly relaxed, if not eliminated. The courts were on board. The FCC majority was on board. Only three votes were required; the deck was stacked against Copps. But in January 2003 the tide slowly but perceptibly began to change. Jonathan Adelstein, an aide to then-Senator Tom Daschle, joined the FCC as the second Democrat and immediately demonstrated that he shared Copps's concerns. "It violates every tenet of a free society to let a handful of powerful companies control our media," he stated.[21] The organizing effort against media consolidation began to get attention in Congress; several letters were sent by members of the House and Senate, by Republicans as well as Democrats, to Powell calling on him to open up the process, slow it down, and take concerns about media consolidation more seriously.

In particular, Powell and the FCC came in for a grilling on Capitol Hill in two January hearings.[22] Here the work of the Consumers Union and other activist organizations to educate members of Congress on media ownership issues paid dividends. As Copps noted, members of Congress expressed considerable concern that Powell was planning to railroad through ownership rule changes without public or congressional input. Recounting a hearing before the Senate Commerce Committee in January that included testimony from FCC members, Copps explained, "This was supposed to be a hearing on telecommunications. We weren't into that hearing two minutes, I'll bet, before one senator after another started asking about media consolidation and what's going on down there at the Commission. Equally interesting, it wasn't just the Democratic side, but it was also the Republican side."[23]

Copps fanned these flames of interest by encouraging a public hearing on media ownership at Columbia University in January. Powell, Adelstein, and Martin attended the informal hearing. Although the panels were evenly balanced with industry and nonindustry participants, the tenor of the audience was decidedly anxious about media consolidation.

Beltway Opposition Stiffens

By the end of January 2003, any hope that Michael Powell and the FCC majority were going to breeze through relaxation of media ownership rules was dashed. Powell's refusal to join Copps and Adelstein in a series of public hearings around the nation to solicit public input was becoming more and more of a PR problem. Finally, "clearly feeling the pressure," as one broadcasting trade publication observed, Powell made an "unusual turnaround" and agreed to hold one official hearing in Richmond, Virginia, in February.[24] It was "a victory of sorts for Copps," and the trade press noted that Powell hoped this would put an end to talk about public hearings.[25] Powell dismissed the idea that additional FCC public hearings on media ownership would be necessary or beneficial. He selected Richmond for its proximity to Washington—it would make it a day trip for FCC officials and lobbyists—and he intimated to the trade publication *Broadcasting & Cable* that he thought the Richmond hearing would be a waste of time.[26] There was too much real work to be done in Washington studying the issue of media ownership, he argued, to gallivant around the country. Anyway, "in the digital age, you don't need a nineteenth-century whistle-stop tour to hear from America." Powell invited Americans to use the Internet to send him and the FCC their thoughts on the relaxation of media ownership rules.[27]

In truth, Powell had a pretty clear idea long before the Richmond hearing of how he wanted to change the rules. But the specifics would remain a closely guarded secret until May, three weeks before a final vote, when the law required Powell to disclose them to the other commissioners.[28] Powell and his staffers discussed the matter with Abernathy, Martin, and their staffers to make sure their votes were safe, but Adelstein and especially Copps were outside the loop.[29] Powell used much of the spring to sell media rule changes to Congress and the public, so the process would look like a legitimate undertaking, not a kowtowing to well-heeled corporate interests. Sure, he knew he was going to get his three votes no matter what, but the bumpier the ride at the FCC the harder the fight might be later in Congress and the more political fallout might hit the White House.

The problem was made much more desperate for Powell because Copps and Adelstein were both so openly contemptuous of how the FCC was proceeding. Copps was planning to hold public hearings in the spring of 2003 across the nation, without Powell if need be, and use them as a "bully pulpit" to bring media ownership "to the public's attention."[30] This was historically unprecedented for the FCC; in the past an FCC chair like Powell would have never had to worry about dissent from other members or public concern about FCC operations. "I don't recall ever seeing before the level of open and very public dispute among the commissioners on these issues," a lobbyist for Clear Channel and News Corporation commented.[31] Powell was in dangerous, uncharted territory.

In a sense, Powell deserves some sympathy. His career had been built upon lavishing praise on the market and unbridled contempt for ownership rules or regulation in the public interest—but, as the response from Congress and the public made clear by January, that tack would be counterproductive in 2003. Powell began to present himself as an earnest pragmatist repelled by extremism and incendiary rhetoric. "I am absolutely a good middle-of-the-road moderate," he told an audience at Harvard in April.[32] His moderation, however, was not based on any moderation of his extreme views on regulation, but, rather, upon his willingness to proceed at a slower pace to get what he wanted.

Powell spent much of the first half of 2003 painting himself as the reluctant deregulator. "These rules, if I do nothing, will be dead soon," Powell remarked to an audience of investors organized by Goldman Sachs. Why? "Because the courts say so—the courts demand that a regulatory agency justify its rules."[33] "Keeping the rules exactly as they are, as some so stridently suggest," is "not a viable option."[34] As Powell's point man Ken Ferree put it, "Courts are saying, 'Hey, don't come here and tell us this rule is necessary because you believe it to be. You've got to come in with empirical evidence and show exactly what harms you're preventing, and how you do the balancing.' "[35]

The court of appeals in Washington had based its 2002 ruling on the belief that Congress's intent in the 1996 Telecommunications Act was to eliminate media ownership rules unless incontrovertible and overwhelming evidence justified their continuation in the public interest. Powell accepted this view and elected not to appeal the court's interpretation. "Congress shifted the burden to the FCC, rather than the industry, to demonstrate the need for a rule," Powell explained. "The congressional bias is for deregulation and the standard for maintaining a rule is an enormous hill to climb."[36] To Copps and Adelstein, Powell's response defied logic, since the law that established the FCC mandated the commission to serve the public interest. As Copps observed, "That phrase, 'serving the public interest, convenience, and necessity,' appears 112 times in the statute. So I think Congress was serious about us serving the public interest."[37]

Had Powell elected to appeal the court's interpretation of the Telecommunications Act, he would have had a powerful legal case. The act merely states that every two years the FCC "shall determine whether any of such rules are necessary in the public interest as the result of competition. The Commission shall repeal or modify any regulation it determines to be no longer in the public interest."[38] Although the spirit of the law pushed toward relaxation of the rules, since competition was presumed to be increasing, Senator John McCain, chairman of the Senate Commerce Committee, argued that the law permitted the FCC to *tighten* media ownership rules if it found market conditions warranted doing so in the public interest.[39] At any rate, conditions had not changed much since 1996 when the law was passed. If Congress had wanted to throw out the ownership rules in 1996, it could have done so itself. Indeed, the evidence from Congress was clear: many who voted for the Telecommunications Act intended ownership rules to remain unless striking, unforeseeable developments occurred. The FCC's job was to monitor these developments.

Few in Congress bought Powell's line that "the courts are making me do this." Literally scores of members of Congress wrote to Powell in 2003 making explicit their conviction that the appeals court interpretation of congressional intent was wrong. Powell and the FCC "could maintain limits if they wanted to," the media activist Jeff Chester maintained. "He doesn't want to."[40]

Powell's Three Arguments

In general, as Powell made his case for relaxing the media ownership rules, he seemed to be channeling Rupert Murdoch or Sumner Redstone as he spoke. This hardly helped his image as a moderate pragmatist determined to salvage what he could of public interest regulation in a hostile world, or at least, in the face of a hostile appeals court. Powell made three points over and over during the course of 2003. First, he argued that with the radical increase in media channels due to cable TV and the Internet, concerns over media concentration were quickly becoming "a moot issue."[41] "Today choices abound," Powell wrote in *USA Today*. "This abundance means more programming, more choice, and more control in the hands of citizens." In addition to hundreds of TV channels, "Americans now have access to a bottomless well of information called the Internet."[42] Powell maintained that this "democratization of technology" undermined traditional concerns about media concentration and any rationale for ownership regulation.[43] Here Powell echoed NBC CEO Robert Wright, who termed media ownership rules "ridiculous."[44] Indeed, Powell proclaimed that the problem with the media system was not too much concentration but "hyper-competitiveness" that led desperate firms to present vulgar fare they might not produce otherwise.[45]

Although Powell was correct about the emergence of new channels, the argument that this undermined the need for ownership regulation was far from convincing. Chris Murray of the Consumers Union pointed out, "Yes, there are 500 channels on cable television, but five companies control the same market share that the three networks did in the 1970s."[46] The degree to which the same large media corporations owned the TV networks, the cable TV channels, and the Hollywood film studios was a subject that Powell, with his purported obsession with quantitative data, never acknowledged. If the FCC relaxed the ownership rules further, those five companies would only increase their hold. Although there were a gazillion Web sites, that hardly qualified as genuine commercial competition.

But there was an even more fundamental problem with Powell's argument that the multitude of new media undermines concerns about media concentration. There *was* and *is* an empirical measure of the truth behind this statement, a way to determine whether conditions had changed sufficiently to justify relaxing media ownership limits on broadcasters. The traditional justification for having media ownership rules was based on the idea that the government was granting firms beachfront property in the media system when they were given monopoly licenses to broadcast channels. Therefore the public had an interest in preventing firms from monopolizing these scarce licenses and dominating the media system. If the existence of so many new media channels through cable TV and the Internet had undermined the market power of the broadcast licenses, then having a TV or radio channel was no longer owning beachfront property but rather holding a mere grain of sand on the digital beach, as Michael Powell suggested.

In that scenario, one would rationally expect the value of radio and TV licenses to stagnate and eventually fall. After all, what rational capitalist would spend hundreds of millions of dollars to purchase a TV station if someone else could effectively compete with him by spending a pittance to produce a hundred Web sites? In fact, the value of radio and TV licenses had increased since 1996, and at a much greater rate than the rate of inflation. These licenses do indeed continue to confer tremendous market power or, as economists would say, monopolistic power. That is why large media companies lobby incessantly to relax the ownership rules: they want to purchase more stations. That is why media ownership rules continue to be necessary. When News Corporation and Viacom and Disney and General Electric are dumping their TV stations and the price of a license is going into the toilet, Powell will have a more convincing case.

Powell's second argument on behalf of relaxing media ownership rules was related to the first; he claimed that unless big media companies could own more and more TV stations they would not be able to make a profit and "free TV" would end.[47] The current media ownership rules were going to drive the major TV networks out of business.[48] In making this argument, Powell presented himself as a populist crusader focused on the needs of those who could not afford cable TV, satellite TV, or pay-per-view channels.[49] (This of course seemed to contradict his first argument about everyone having access to limitless choice on the Internet.) The hardship claim was straight out of the TV networks' playbook. Viacom president Mel Karmazin told the Senate Commerce Committee in May that network television is "not a very good business."[50] Viacom's lobbyists argued that media ownership rules had to be relaxed "to help ensure that free, over-the-air broadcasting continues to be available across America."[51] Rupert Murdoch told Congress that allowing broadcast companies to own more stations was necessary for over-the-air television to survive: "It's about impossible to run an entertainment network at a profit."[52]

There were two problems with this argument. First, even if true, is it rational public policy to protect firms in a dying industry? Shouldn't there be a broader debate about how best to deploy public resources, if the network TV structure had become outdated? Also, even if the networks were struggling, the parent companies were almost all doing very well and also owned most of the cable TV channels. What guarantee was there that these firms would maintain free television in the future? Perhaps these companies would get to own all the stations and then determine that there was a more profitable use of the public airwaves. Was Powell prepared to require these companies to broadcast free television in exchange for receiving more TV channels? In short, Powell's "policy" with regard to saving network TV seemed half-baked.

The second problem with Powell's campaign to "save free TV" was that it was premised on a bogus claim—in fact, an outright lie. Media mogul Barry Diller, who built the Fox TV network, scoffed at Powell's concerns about the networks' financial health: "Anybody who thinks they're in trouble hasn't read the profit statements of these companies. The only way you can lose money in broadcasting is if somebody steals it from you."[53] Ironically, exactly at the moment Powell was pressing this case, in May 2003, the same TV networks that claimed to be on their deathbed recorded the greatest wave of advance advertising sales in U.S. history. The head of Disney's ABC was ecstatic. "It's like being back in college and pulling those all-nighters," he said of their efforts to process all the sales.[54] "Broadcast Nets Hit the Jackpot," one headline read, with the article concluding, "The market was red-hot everywhere this year."[55] "By the time you read this," one trade publication plastered on its front page, "many TV ad sales executives will be on the golf course celebrating the record $21 billion upfront market."[56] Moreover, market research suggested that broadcast advertising was expected to continue to climb at a healthy clip through 2007.[57] Their economic future was bright indeed.

Powell's third argument contradicted the logic of his second argument, in which he suggested that media mergers might save free TV. He now claimed that the relaxation of media ownership rules that the FCC proposed would not amount to a big deal: "I think there will be an increase in mergers, but not to the extent that it would cause public policy concerns."[58] "The United States has the most diverse media marketplace in the world," Powell wrote, adding, "our nation's media landscape will not become significantly more concentrated as a result of changes to the FCC rules."[59] Therefore, Powell suggested, his opponents were making much ado about nothing.

Powell provided no evidence for this argument. Indeed, there was considerable evidence that the largest media firms and Wall Street investment banking houses anticipated a major wave of media mergers once the rules were relaxed. "Everyone is waiting for the new rules; then they'll pounce," one banker predicted.[60] The trade press teemed with articles throughout the first half of 2003 in which industry insiders discussed the impending merger mania. The tone was often giddy.[61] "Major media companies are drawn and cocked," the *Denver Post* publisher and MediaNews Group CEO William Dean Singleton announced. Singleton was especially pleased because the FCC rule changes would make it possible for firms like his to grow so large as to assure their dominance of the Internet: "We are in the news and information business. In fact, we own it."[62]

The greatest wave of mergers was expected at the local level, where the profit potential of owning the daily newspaper, two or three TV stations, and eight radio stations was the stuff of media owner fantasies. After all, look at what Clear Channel had accomplished with radio since 1996. Imagine if you could toss in the daily newspaper and a few TV stations, too. As one investment analyst put it, "The media companies' top priority is more concentrated power in local markets."[63] "The big guys will get bigger," a leading media financial analyst concluded, sounding a bit like Don Corleone, "and the little guys will have to decide whether they want to exist anymore."[64] Or as Senator Ron Wyden of Oregon said, Powell's decision to loosen media ownership rules "rings the dinner bell for big media corporations who are salivating to make a meal out of the nation's many small media outlets."[65]

Of course, no one knew for certain what would happen. Perhaps time would prove Powell's third argument correct and there would not be all that many deals as a result of rules relaxation. But to Copps and Adelstein this was reckless policymaking, when the prudent course was to be cautious. "Some argue that the concern about the threat to American democracy is overblown since it is so strong and resilient," Adelstein said. "While our democracy is strong and not about to crumble, does it mean we can afford to weaken it?"[66] "This is a huge and foolhardy gamble with the future," Copps warned.[67] "Suppose for a moment that the FCC votes to remove or significantly modify the concentration protections. Suppose that turns out to be a mistake," Copps questioned. "How would we ever put the genie back in the bottle? The answer is we could not. That's why we need a national dialogue on the issue and better data and analysis."[68]

Opposition Grows Beyond the Beltway

Michael Powell's campaign to advance the case for loosening media ownership rules in the spring of 2003 was based upon contradictory arguments constructed with dubious evidence. In the battle for public opinion, this put him at a decided disadvantage. His arguments did not appear to convince people who were not invested in the system and did not share his euphoric attitude toward the U.S. commercial media system. In years past, that wouldn't have mattered because Americans would have been clueless about the FCC's proceedings. But in 2003 many things had changed, not the least of which was that FCC member Michael Copps had taken it upon himself to rouse public interest and involvement in the issue.

"This is still, in my mind, very much an inside-the-Beltway issue," Copps explained in February. "It has not become one where the country is really plugged into it and knows what's going on here. That's because the country doesn't really know. If it did know, I think a lot of people would be vitally interested in the outcome." Copps was blunt about his mission: "I am trying to raise as much ruckus as I can about it."[69] In doing so, Copps found the public to be receptive; people had considerable concerns about media, and when they learned these concerns could be attached to a specific policy, their interest grew dramatically. Fairly soon, Copps had many more allies than he could have anticipated, far beyond the stalwart public interest groups in Washington.

The official FCC hearing in Richmond on February 27 was an omen. Four of the five hours were devoted to panelists, and most of the twenty-one experts were from out of town, including a large contingent of industry representatives. The public then had an hour to make statements—and every speaker opposed relaxing the media ownership rules. "What stood out most," Copps commented afterward, "was the level of concern on the issue and the level of dissatisfaction."[70] Powell immediately announced that the Richmond hearing provided "enough" input from the public and that it was imperative to get the process completed as quickly as possible. "This is one of the most extensively developed records in the history of the commission," Powell stated. You can hold hearings until "you're blue in the face but at some point people expect you to take a position."[71] Powell, Abernathy, and Martin would not attend any of the subsequent public hearings on media ownership.

Over the next three months twelve more public hearings were held across the nation, almost all attended by Copps and many by Adelstein, who termed this their "magical mystery tour." The events were always nonpartisan, organized by a local university or civic group, and featured representatives of the broadcasting industry. Numerous activists groups, like Jeff Chester's Center for Digital Democracy and the Benton Foundation helped organize the events. There were also a number of smaller events, sometimes attended by

Copps or Adelstein separately.[72] In most cases, members of Congress from the area participated. Some events were attended by fewer than 200 people, as in Detroit, Chicago, and Phoenix, but most of the rest became standing-room-only affairs with 400–1,000 attendees, as in Seattle, Philadelphia, Burlington, Atlanta, and San Francisco.[73] Even more than the turnout, it was the public's comment that caught the attention of Copps and Adelstein and energized them as they squared off with Powell and the Republicans back at FCC headquarters. "Of the hundreds of citizens I heard from, many extremely articulate, not one of them stood up to say, 'I want to see even more concentration in our media ownership.' Not one," Adelstein observed. "The public knows instinctively what the FCC is supposed to do—protect them from large entities gaining too much control over critical channels of communication."[74]

This attendance was all the more incredible because the local press gave little or no advance coverage and in most cases no follow-up coverage either—especially curious since local media often had executives on hearing panels.[75] "That people even found out about these meetings," Copps acknowledged, "is a miracle."[76] This pointed to a problem that faced the activists throughout 2003: the paucity of mainstream news coverage. As a study conducted for the *American Journalism Review* concluded, in the first five months of 2003, commercial TV and the cable networks offered "virtually no coverage" of the FCC deliberations on media ownership. Even the handful of newspapers that covered the story on occasion throughout the year, like the *Chicago Tribune*, "seemed to lose interest in the consumer and democracy angles, treating the story mainly as a business and investment issue." As the author of the study concluded, "You wouldn't have learned much about the controversy from the many news outlets that were eager to cash in."[77] Instead, the organizers had to rely upon alternative media and the Internet to do much of their outreach; one can only imagine what the response would have been had the conventional news media given this anything close to the attention that a story of such magnitude—but not involving the corporate media—would have merited.

Despite the mainstream news blackout, the movement grew rapidly. What happened to radio following the relaxation of radio ownership rules in the 1996 Telecommunications Act spurred Americans' concern about media policies. Radio was often invoked as the "canary in the coal mine" that would predict what would happen when ownership rules for television, cable, and newspapers were relaxed. And the consensus about radio was almost universally negative.

Local news had disappeared, musical variety had diminished, and commercialism had increased.[78] "So television's going to be more like radio now," the TV critic Tom Shales mused in a column on Powell's media ownership plans. "Gosh, that's swell. Let's have a little dancing in the streets, because this is no small accomplishment—finding a means to make TV worse, I mean."[79]

"If you really like what happened in radio," Copps argued, "you'll love what's barreling down the FCC track toward you."[80] Or, as he told his colleagues, "This experience should *terrify* us."[81] As one reporter put it, "The sorry state of the radio industry is sabotaging FCC chairman Michael Powell's plans to let media conglomerates run wild." Much opposition to ownership relaxation in the African-American and minority communities could be attributed to the bad experience with radio, an industry that saw minority ownership collapse since 1996 and journalism for minority groups shrivel.[82] Indeed, Powell acknowledged that radio was in crisis, but he refused to let its condition influence his evaluation of ownership rules changes for other media.[83]

Another issue that mobilized citizens was the fate of journalism under media concentration. The FCC had ignored or mangled this topic in its study with its twelve reports; indeed, if one looked at who actually wrote or produced news in local markets, the effects of concentrated ownership on journalism would be apparent, as would the likely impact of further relaxation of ownership.[84] A study released by the Project for Excellence in Journalism in February 2003 concluded that larger TV station-owning companies used their market power to reduce their commitment to local journalism.[85] Powell not only defended the status quo but also argued that increased media concentration would improve journalism: "Scale and efficiency are becoming more vital to delivering quality news and public affairs."[86] Not many shared Powell's enthusiasm. Common Cause, the public interest citizens group, received so much concern from its several hundred thousand members about how concentrated media ownership would affect journalism and public life that it made fighting Powell its main organizing issue in 2003. Common Cause's president, Chellie Pingree, remarked that she had never seen so much rank-and-file interest in an issue. Common Cause, which had never worked on media policy before, had suddenly become a media reform organization.

Even more striking was the opposition to the relaxation of media ownership rules that came from working journalists. Their ire certainly undercut

Powell's effort to wrap his media ownership plan in the guise of protecting the First Amendment. Those on the front lines saw what concentration had done to journalism and they did not want to see more of it. From the *Columbia Journalism Review* to avidly pro-deregulation trade publications such as *Broadcasting & Cable*, working journalists criticized relaxation of media ownership rules as bad for journalism.[87] Linda Foley, president of the Newspaper Guild, detailed the pronounced concern over media concentration among her members. The guild and AFTRA, the union representing broadcast journalists, made stopping the relaxation of media ownership rules central to their lobbying work in 2003.[88]

The National Association of Black Journalists and the National Association of Hispanic Journalists both came out against relaxing the rules. Working with the National Association of Black Owned Broadcasters, they were able to generate interest in this issue among members of the Congressional Black Caucus and the Hispanic Caucus, which would prove valuable down the road. For what may have been the first time in its history, the International Federation of Journalists, representing 500,000 journalists in more than 100 countries, weighed in on a U.S. media ownership policy matter, calling Powell's plan "a dangerous shift of power at the expense of democracy."[89]

Journalists were not the only ones closely connected to the media industries who spoke out. All the Hollywood unions worked to oppose Powell and the FCC, in combination with most of the independent producers.[90] "This is really unprecedented," the president of the West Coast branch of the Writers Guild of America noted. "It's remarkable how this one issue seems to have captured the entire community."[91] Driven by the media unions, the AFL-CIO Executive Council formally opposed the relaxation of media ownership rules in March 2003.[92] Even the Public Relations Society of America condemned Powell, and leading advertisers criticized media concentration.[93] Numerous independent media owners such as Frank Blethen, publisher of the *Seattle Times*, stepped forward to fight against rule relaxation. Even the huge conglomerate Sony expressed concerns about concentration in the TV industry.[94] The arguments invariably were that concentration produces lousier media content.

Powell and his supporters could rightly claim that much of this opposition within the media industries came from self-interested parties who had much

to lose. But Powell's entire base of support also came from self-interested parties with much to gain. And it hardly helped Powell's cause that those on the
inside of these industries, such as journalists, stated emphatically that concentration was bad for quality media content.

Left and Right Join the Fight

As impressive as this opposition to Powell looked, two additional developments
generated what would be the lion's share of the more than three million
Americans who would formally oppose the relaxation of media ownership rules
in 2003. First was the U.S. invasion and subsequent occupation of Iraq. During
the buildup to the war, in the first three months of 2003, the burgeoning antiwar movement spent considerable time castigating what it regarded as the
uncritical and propagandistic nature of TV news coverage of the Bush administration's war rationale. Phil Donahue's program was terminated by MSNBC in
February; its cancellation came in the wake of an internal NBC report claiming
that Donahue projected a "difficult public face for NBC in time of war. He
seems to delight in presenting guests who are antiwar, anti-Bush, and skeptical
of the administration's motives." The report worried that Donahue would
become "a home for the liberal antiwar agenda at the same time that our competitors are waving the flag at every opportunity."[95] Cable giant Comcast refused
to air an antiwar ad during Bush's State of the Union address.[96]

The concentrated world of radio was seen as being particularly hostile to
all who did not support the Bush administration.[97] Clear Channel's DJs led
pro-war rallies, fired the South Carolina 2002 "Radio Personality of the Year"
allegedly for her antiwar politics, and, along with fellow radio giant Cumulus,
dropped the Dixie Chicks from its playlists after a member of the band criticized Bush at a concert in England.[98] When activists learned that the same
companies that seemed most aggressively pro-war—e.g., Clear Channel and
Rupert Murdoch's News Corporation—were leading the lobbying fight to
acquire even more media, activists started publicizing the FCC issue. Around
this time, Murdoch announced his intention to purchase DirecTV, the firm
that dominated U.S. satellite television delivery.

When Powell praised the outstanding and "thrilling" TV news coverage of
the Iraq War as justifying his contention that media concentration actually

promotes better journalism, it was like waving a red flag in front of a bull.[99] (Copps, in contrast, observed that TV news coverage of the war lacked "clash and a diversity of ideas.")[100] The liberal, online activist group MoveOn.org was deluged with comments from many of its million plus members demanding that MoveOn organize to oppose Powell and the FCC. With its huge email lists, MoveOn was able to generate hundreds of thousands of supporters for media reform during the course of 2003.

The second striking development was the emergence of conservative opposition to the relaxation of media ownership rules.[101] Some of it grew from public distaste with the vulgarity of radio and television—what conservative media activist Brent Bozell termed "the raw sewage, the ultraviolence, the graphic sex, the raunchy language that is flooding their living rooms day and night."[102] This persistent lewdness was exacerbated by media concentration, because huge firms provided the cheapest fare possible and were unaccountable to local communities. Conservatives also disliked the decline of local ownership and localism in commercial media. "I am a conservative. I believe in free markets and limited government," then-Representative Richard Burr of North Carolina said in explaining his opposition to Powell. "But I also believe in another important conservative ideal—the right of local citizens to influence decisions that impact their communities."[103]

The National Rifle Association shared these concerns—it regarded the big media conglomerates as unsympathetic to gun owners—and, at the urging of its membership, became an aggressive force against the FCC in the spring of 2003. The NRA generated several hundred thousand postcards in opposition to relaxing media ownership rules.[104] People were astounded by the emerging alliance, with Jesse Helms in tandem with Jesse Jackson.[105] "When all of us are united on an issue, then one of two things has happened," Bozell observed. "Either the earth has spun off its axis and we have all lost our minds or there is universal support for a concept."[106]

As popular opposition grew, increased attention turned to what, exactly, the FCC was doing. Although Powell claimed he was too busy to attend any of the public hearings in the spring, he apparently was able to carve out time to attend major conferences of media owners. In his speech before the NAB in Las Vegas in April he dropped the role of the moderate pragmatist and technocrat and urged broadcasters to support "comprehensive deregulation of the broadcast industry."[107] Three weeks later, in Seattle, Powell told the nation's newspaper owners that they were "likely to fare well" under his media ownership rule changes. "I could have written the speech myself," CEO William Dean Singleton of MediaNews announced ecstatically.[108]

Then, in May, a revealing report from the nonpartisan Center for Public Integrity (CPI) disclosed what Powell and FCC staffers had been doing most of the spring. Since the formal review of media rules had been announced in September 2002, FCC officials had held seventy-one closed-door, off-the-record meetings with corporate media CEOs and their lobbyists, but only five such meetings with public interest groups. Rupert Murdoch and Viacom's Mel Karmazin had each had a series of meetings with commissioners and staffers in late January and early February, precisely when the FCC was crafting its new ownership rules.[109] On March 11, a group of Disney executives met with eighteen different FCC officials in six different closed-door meetings. That was probably more contact than most consumer groups had had with the FCC in a decade.

The CPI also reported that corporate interests had lavished $2.8 million on FCC members for junkets over the previous eight years and that much of the data the FCC used to make its determinations of policy was provided by industry.[110] Finally, on June 2, a *Wall Street Journal* investigative report disclosed that Bear Stearns media analyst Victor Miller, whose job is to advise large investors concerning media stocks, played a central role in helping the FCC draft the new ownership regulations. Michael Powell's top aide, Susan Eid, defended Miller's role: "His analysis is rock-solid."[111] (Before the end of 2003, Michael Powell's chief of staff who helped craft the new ownership rules left the FCC to become a top lobbyist for the NAB.)[112] As Charles Lewis, CPI's director, concluded: "The idea that the FCC can render an objective, independent judgment about media ownership is laughable."[113]

In February Powell had encouraged Americans to use the Internet to let the FCC know their thoughts on media ownership. In the past, on its most controversial issues, the FCC had received about 5,000 calls and letters.[114] With interest picking up speed like a hurricane crossing the open sea, the number of email messages, letters, and petition signatures reaching the FCC had climbed to an extraordinary 750,000 by the end of May. There was so much incoming email that the FCC's computers crashed. All examinations of the contents indicated that a good 99.9 percent opposed relaxing the media ownership rules, and many citizens favored tightening them.[115] There was almost no indication that anyone in the country, aside from big media owners, strongly favored relaxing the rules.

When the CNN business program *Moneyline with Lou Dobbs* ran an on-air poll in May asking whether "too few corporations own too many media outlets," fully 98 percent said yes.[116] The city councils in Chicago and Seattle passed resolutions against the relaxation of media ownership rules—Chicago by a unanimous vote.[117] What was most astonishing, as a *Christian Science Monitor* study determined, was that this resistance had developed with very little press coverage, especially for a story of this magnitude.[118] Shamelessly, Powell boasted about the "extraordinary amount of public comment" the FCC had received, enabling it to address the issues "through the eyes and ears of the American public."[119] But no matter how Powell tried to spin it, he had decisively lost the battle for public opinion.

From the FCC to Congress

Throughout the spring as public attention was being drawn to the issue of media ownership, a sense of impending doom hung over the opposition since it was obvious that Powell was determined to ram the changes through. The counsel Powell was getting from the Bush administration fortified his resolve. In April, Commerce Secretary Don Evans informed Powell in no uncertain terms that the White House expected the ownership rules to be relaxed as planned and without delay.[120] The Bush administration's interest in delivering relaxed media ownership rules to the media giants could be explained by its ideological commitment to "deregulation." It was possibly influenced as well by media corporations' large political donations, especially toward Republicans. Certainly the Bush administration's stance did nothing to discourage such donations.[121]

In addition, the Bush administration counted some close political friends in the corporate media community. Some of the media firms most aggressively lobbying against the ownership rules were strong ideological allies. Clear Channel had a close relationship with Bush going back to his stint as Texas governor, and its stations were notorious for their pro-Republican slant. Rupert Murdoch's Fox News Channel was similarly well known as a bastion of Republican support; in October 2003, Charles Reina, who worked as a producer and writer at Fox News Channel from 1997 until he resigned in 2003, revealed that the station's management gave daily directives on issues and angles to cover that tended to correlate with White House spin.[122] Indeed, Roger Ailes, head of Fox News Channel, had offered advice to President Bush about how to react to the 9/11 attacks.

There were even suggestions in the trade press that the administration's FCC stance was payback to the media for its treatment of Bush during the 2000 election and after, with an eye toward encouraging continued favorable coverage in the future.[123] Generally soft media coverage extended beyond news reporting. In September 2003, Viacom's Showtime aired a docudrama, *DC 9/11: Time of Crisis*, which portrayed George W. Bush as a cross between Winston Churchill and Abraham Lincoln. Only two months later, Viacom's CBS canceled a miniseries on Ronald Reagan when Republican critics charged it was unsympathetic; the station then passed a watered-down version to Showtime to fend off critics charging censorship.[124] The *Financial Times* noted that News Corporation's Fox News Channel hammered CBS on this issue and Viacom caved in exactly as the media ownership rules were in jeopardy on Capitol Hill.[125] Even the rabidly anti-regulation trade publication *Broadcasting & Cable* was appalled by CBS's cave-in, paraphrasing Viacom's position as "we'd better do what we're told by the D.C. powers that be—in this case, the Republican National Committee—if we want to be able to buy more stations."[126]

Whereas we may never know the Bush administration's precise motives, it was clear that relaxation of media ownership rules had become a high priority. From its vantage point, supporting the media giants seemed to be a no-lose proposition.

On the opposing side, in the spring of 2003, activists intensified their pressure on Powell to disclose the proposed rules changes so that the public could provide input before the FCC vote.[127] Even the trade publication *Television Week* urged Powell to "bring the public into the process."[128] "We don't know what we're going to be working on," a frustrated Copps said in early May. "It's like a state secret."[129] The new rules were finally turned over to Copps and Adelstein on May 12, exactly three weeks before the planned June 2 vote, the legal minimum notice. As expected, the rules called for eliminating the ban on cross-ownership, permitting companies to purchase two TV stations in most markets and three TV stations in the largest markets, and letting the biggest TV station-owning companies increase their market coverage from 35 percent to 45 percent of the population. Copps and Adelstein immediately asked for a delay of the vote, a "traditional right of commissioners," which had never been denied in anyone's memory.[130] Powell rejected the request, citing counsel by Abernathy and Martin. Over Memorial Day weekend, for yet another first in U.S. media history, demonstrations protesting the FCC's impending relaxation of media ownership rules took place in fourteen cities.[131]

The outcome of the June 2 FCC meeting was a foregone conclusion, but the debate was far from anticlimactic. Copps and Adelstein each delivered long and meticulous dissenting statements that exposed the majority's arguments to be baseless and the FCC's review to be nothing short of fraudulent. As Adelstein put it, the review was a "results-driven process" in which principles were non-existent and evidence was emphasized or ignored depending upon whether it justified the desired end. (When analysts for the Consumers Union and the Consumer Federation of America were finally able to spend weeks inspecting the FCC's 257-page order, the federation's research director concluded, "The FCC cooked the books to come up with the result they wanted—and the books aren't even half baked.")[132] Copps and Adelstein both were clearly moved by the outpouring of popular support during the process. "We'll look back upon this 3–2 vote as a pyrrhic victory," Copps concluded. "The Commission faces a far more informed and involved citizenry. The obscurity of the issue that many have relied upon in the past, where only a few dozen inside-the-Beltway lobbyists understood the issue, is gone forever."[133] Adelstein ended his statement by paraphrasing Winston Churchill: "This is not the end, or even the beginning of the end, but just the end of the beginning."[134]

Adelstein was more accurate than he may have realized. In all the commotion surrounding Powell and the FCC during the first half of 2003, Congress's role had received little attention. In fact, the FCC is not a body like the Supreme Court, established to be independent of the legislative branch. To the contrary, the FCC was created by Congress, funded by Congress, and expected to fulfill the interests of the American people as specified by Congress. The court decision shifting the burden of proof to the FCC to justify the continuation of media ownership rules was predicated on that being the will of Congress. Powell acknowledged at all times that if Congress was dissatisfied with the FCC's actions, all it had to do was pass legislation instructing him to do something else.

Under normal circumstances, Congress would be unlikely to pester the FCC to act against powerful media interests, due to the media industry's massive lobbies, control over the news, and hefty campaign contributions. But these were not normal circumstances. Even if Bush's FCC appointees Powell, Abernathy, and Martin could afford to ignore the input of 750,000 Americans, members of Congress had to pay closer attention to their constituents. And Congress was getting the message. Two days after the FCC vote, the Senate Commerce Committee called all five FCC commissioners to the Hill to explain the vote and spewed unbridled contempt. "We are moving to roll back one of the most complete cave-ins to corporate interests I've ever seen by what is supposed to be a federal regulatory agency," Senator Byron Dorgan of North Dakota declared.[135] Then-Ranking Democrat Ernest Hollings of South Carolina accused Powell of "spin and fraud" and slammed the FCC as an "instrument of corporate greed."[136]

A few days later, Republican committee chairman John McCain remarked that the media ownership issue had "sparked more interest than any issue I've ever seen that wasn't organized by a huge lobby."[137] A handful of conservative Republicans such as Trent Lott and Representative Frank Wolf of Virginia came out strongly against the FCC changes, despite pressure from on high. "I did not get elected to be a potted plant," Wolf asserted, "and I don't care what the White House thinks."[138] "In all the years I've been here," California Senator Barbara Boxer observed, "I've not seen such deeply held feelings across ideologies."[139] "It's an issue that has huge momentum," McCain concurred. "It's a classic populist issue."[140] The politicians with their fingers firmly on the national pulse, the nine candidates campaigning for the Democratic presidential nomination, all came out strongly against Powell and the FCC.[141] By the end of June the Senate Commerce Committee, with significant Republican support, voted to overturn key elements of the FCC rule changes. The vote shocked the political establishment and demonstrated that the issue was in play on the Hill.

Public opinion research confirmed what members of Congress were sensing. A Pew Research Center poll conducted in summer 2003 found that the number of Americans who had heard "a lot" or "a little" about the FCC's review of media ownership rules had doubled to nearly 50 percent since February. Most striking, the figures showed dramatically that the more people knew about what the FCC was doing, the less likely they were to support it.

Of those 12 percent of Americans who had "heard a lot," seven in ten believed that the effects of relaxing media ownership rules would be negative, while only 6 percent thought they would be positive.[142]

By now Powell and the commercial media had quit suggesting that rule relaxation had popular support. To the contrary, they started arguing that most Americans were apathetic and that apathy should be interpreted as support for the status quo.[143] Powell asserted that he represented the "silent majority" of Americans, those who "yawn at the whole thing."[144] His constituency was made up of those who "are in a fraternity watching TV and drinking beer and happy" and oblivious to the debate. Powell presented a contradictory stance: he announced that support for his ownership plan was minuscule only because the public debate had been "lopsided" against him—yet he had done everything possible to avoid public debate because, as surveys showed, the more people knew, the more ground he lost.[145] His strategy, as he tacitly acknowledged, was to keep people ignorant—the FCC's modus operandi—so he could then claim their support for whatever he did.

The poll energized activists, who knew that the more people learned about the issue and the more members of Congress heard from their constituents, the more likely Congress could be persuaded to overturn what the FCC had done. Russ Feingold related that on a trip home to Wisconsin, the popular opposition to the FCC overwhelmed him. "When they heard that these rules came out," Feingold recalled, "They were angry."[146] For the balance of the summer and fall, activist attention went toward generating more public pressure upon members of Congress. On Capitol Hill, a wide range of public interest groups conducted the lobbying effort, led by Consumers Union, Free Press, Common Cause, MoveOn.org, and organized labor. On numerous occasions MoveOn.org used its vast subscriber list to generate petition signatures and telephone calls by constituents to Congress. In one afternoon alone, House members received an estimated 40,000 dissenting telephone calls from constituents. As Democratic Representative David Price of North Carolina put it, his colleagues were saying, "Call off the dogs, my office is being flooded with constituent calls on this issue."[147] By the calculation of FCC commissioner Jonathan Adelstein, over 2.3 million comments registering opposition to media concentration were made to either the FCC or Congress by the end of the summer.

The problem facing opponents of the FCC ownership plan was getting legislation through Congress. Despite having a clear majority of members of Congress opposing the FCC, White House pressure and the Republican leadership were able to keep the measure from coming to the floor of Congress for a vote. For media activists across the nation it seemed like the fix was in. Big money rigged the system to foil the will of the people.

But all was not lost, not at all. The activist group, Media Access Project, filed a petition with the Third Circuit Court of Appeals in Philadelphia, on behalf of the Philadelphia-based Prometheus Radio Project, arguing that the media ownership rule changes violated federal statutes and were generated improperly. To get the case out of the dreaded Washington court of appeals, activists had filed lawsuits in federal courts around the country. When all the cases were consolidated, a lottery was used to pick a federal appeals court to adjudicate. The D.C. court had three-to-one odds stacked against it, and Philadelphia won.[148] Even so, winning the case was regarded as a longshot, but on September 3 the court agreed to hear the case. More important, the court issued an immediate stay so that the rule changes would not be put into effect. "The harm to petitioners absent a stay would be the likely loss of an adequate remedy should the new ownership rules be declared invalid in whole or in part," the court wrote. "In contrast to this irreparable harm, there is little indication that a stay pending appeal will result in substantial harm to the commission or to other interested parties."

Copps was satisfied by the turn of events: "The court has done what the commission should have done in the first place."[149] As the *New York Times* noted, "The court raised tough questions for the commission and its industry supporters" that suggested the future could not be predicted.[150] It constituted an enormous victory for opponents of media concentration; and it bought time to work the halls of Congress to get the FCC's rules overturned before they could go into effect. By the beginning of 2004, the meager mainstream news coverage had disappeared, and there were considerable pressures to have the issue return to back rooms with a billion-dollar ante for admission. But there was no reason to think public opinion had shifted back. In December, CNN's *Lou Dobbs Tonight* ran another informal poll on the question "Do you agree big media companies should be broken up?" Over 96 percent of the 5,000 plus respondents said yes.[151]

The media ownership fight of 2003–4 was a remarkable and unprecedented moment in U.S. media history. For the first time in generations, media policy issues were taken from behind closed doors and made the stuff of democratic discourse and political engagement. The change in climate since 1996—when the corrupt Telecommunications Act had been drafted, debated, and passed in almost total silence—could not have been more dramatic. Most incredible of all, in January 2003 nobody anticipated this transformation.

In June 2004, victory came when the Third Circuit Court of Appeals in Philadelphia ruled for Prometheus and threw out the FCC's media ownership rules changes. In its decision, the court cited the FCC's shoddy procedures and dismissal of the enormous amount of public input on the matter. The organizing paid off, and the movement could grow and develop for when the FCC returned to media ownership rules in 2006 and for a wide range of other media policy issues. In the subsequent four years the media reform movement enjoyed tremendous growth to become one of the great success stories of U.S. grassroots politics of recent decades.

23

The U.S. Media Reform Movement
Going Forward

All social scholarship ultimately is about understanding the world to change it, even if the change we want is to preserve that which we most treasure in the status quo. This is especially and immediately true for political economy of media as a field of study, where research has a direct and important relationship with policies and structures that shape media and communication and influence the course of society. Because of this, too, the political economy of communication has had a direct relationship with policy makers and citizens outside the academy. The work, more than most other areas, cannot survive if it is "academic." That is why the burgeoning media reform movement in the United States is so important for the field. This is a movement, astonishingly, based almost directly upon core political economic research.

In this concluding chapter for this section and the book, I take a closer look at this relationship of political economy of media to the media reform movement. (I will not provide a detailed assessment of the media reform movement and its dramatic recent history, as I do that in the final chapter of *Communication Revolution*.)

The political economy of media is dedicated to understanding the role of media in societies—e.g., whether the media system on balance encourages or discourages social justice, open governance, and effective participatory democracy. The field also examines how market structures, policies and subsidies, and organizational structures shape and determine the nature of the media system and media content. The entire field is based on the explicit understanding that media systems are not natural or inevitable, but they result from crucial political decisions. These political decisions are not made on a blank slate or a level playing field; they are strongly shaped by the historical and political economic context of any given society at any point in time. We make our own media history, to paraphrase Marx, but not exactly as we please. We do not make it under self-selected circumstances, but under circumstances existing already, given and transmitted from the past. "The tradition of all dead generations weighs like a nightmare on the brains of the living."

For much of the past century there has been a decided split in the political economy of media between U.S. scholars and those based in almost every other nation in the world. In the United States it generally has been assumed, even by critical scholars devoted to social change, that a profit-driven, advertising-supported corporate media system was the only possible system. The media system reflected the nature of the U.S. political economy, and any serious effort to reform the media system would have to necessarily be part of a revolutionary program to overthrow the capitalist political economy. Since that was considered unrealistic, even preposterous, the structure of the media system was regarded as inviolable. The circumstances existing and transmitted from the past allowed for no alternative.

Elsewhere in the world, capitalism was seen as having a less solid grasp on any given society, and the political economy was seen as more susceptible to radical reform. Every bit as important, media systems were regarded as the results of policies, and subject to dramatic variation even within a capitalist political economy. In such a context it was more readily grasped that the nature of the media system would influence the broader political decisions about what sort of economy a society might have. In other words, the political economy not only shaped the nature of the media system, the nature of the media system shaped the broader political economy. Scholars and activists were more likely to understand that winning battles to reconstruct the media system were a necessary part of a broader process to create a more just society, even if the exact reforms being fought for were not especially revolutionary in their own right.

The "academic" nature of the political economy of media in the United States was frustrating for many of us, especially when we saw the way scholars played direct roles in media activism and politics in other nations. For many of us it became maddening at times as we conducted historical research on media policymaking in the United States. It became increasingly clear that the idea that the corporate commercial system was accepted as "natural" and benevolent was erroneous. At key moments in U.S. history, there had been considerable debate over how to structure the media system, and it was never a foregone conclusion that the system should be turned over to powerful commercial interests to do with as they please. Indeed, my research found that there was considerable opposition to the commercial media status quo, especially in the Progressive Era (1900–1915), and the 1930s and 1940s.

A more accurate way to understand the relationship of media to political economy in the United States in the decades since the 1940s was that because the system seemed entrenched, because it seemed to have no discernible opposition, it was assumed that it was simply a "given." Our research on the United States tended to demonstrate how closely linked the media system was to the needs of those atop the status quo; the point of the research was seen as providing intellectual self-defense, with no notion of playing offense. For political struggles over media, those of us who studied the political economy of media tended to concentrate upon struggles in other nations for a more equitable media system, because that was where the issues were in play. We often looked at the role the U.S. government played to undermine legitimate democratic aspirations via the media (and much else) in other nations.

This is not to say that there was not a certain amount of activism over media policy issues in the generations connecting the Second World War to the new century. But the policymaking process was corrupt and dominated by commercial interests. Politicians were in the pocket of industry, and there was no press coverage so nearly all of the public was in the dark. Media was a non-issue. So the television system was gift-wrapped and hand-delivered to Wall Street and Madison Avenue without a shred of public awareness and participation. The same thing happened with FM radio and cable and satellite television. There was very little public participation during these years, except for moments during the 1970s when popular organizing around black power and women's rights spilled over slightly to the media realm. Even then the most radical reform proposals barely threatened corporate dominance of the media system.

We hit rock bottom with the Reagan years and the advent of full-throttle neoliberalism in the 1980s. Communication was an area Wall Street and the political Right had zeroed in on as being exhibit A in their campaign to have corporate interests flower and the notion of the public interest become eviscerated. Soon all that remained to conduct public interest organizing on media issues were a handful of very small shops in Washington, with almost no staff, no budget, and no popular awareness or support. These groups battled their best, but the range of outcomes was narrow. The overwhelming bipartisan support for the passage of the 1996 Telecommunications Act, regarded as the Magna Carta for communication corporations at the time, was the logical culmination of this process.

Not surprisingly, in such a hostile political climate, political economists of media in the United States began to lose their muster by the 1990s. If the system was unchangeable and reflected the will of the people, what was the point of studying its flaws, except to torture one's self. The field began to decline. From being among the most dynamic areas in media research in the 1970s and early 1980s, it gravitated toward obscurity.

At the same time, though, beneath the radar of academia, mainstream media, and the official political culture, something was happening. Driven by research by the likes of Ben Bagdikian, Noam Chomsky, and Edward Herman, and journalism by Alexander Cockburn, Jeff Cohen, and Norman Solomon, a burgeoning and sophisticated popular critique of the limitations of the media system for self-government began to spill past academic classrooms into the broader community. The linkages between the needs of the wealthy and powerful and the nature of what was covered and how it was covered in the mainstream media—the contours of legitimate debate—became more apparent. For citizens, and activists, the critique was like setting a match to a gas canister: if the media system was inhospitable to democracy and social justice and we were serious about democracy and social justice, we had to change the media system.

So it was during the late 1980s and especially in the 1990s a grassroots media reform movement was born. It was signified by groups like Fairness & Accuracy In Reporting and the two Media & Democracy conferences organized by Don Hazen in 1996 and 1997. It was demonstrated by the increased interest in media critique and issues in progressive publications like *The Nation*, *In These Times*, *Monthly Review*, and *The Progressive*. But in the dispirited political times there was still little sense that we could do very much to change the situation. For a while, though, there was a certain momentum built upon the fact that people understood they were not alone in their concerns about media, that they were not insane.

And it was not simply people on the political left who were alarmed by developments in the media. If radical critics had zeroed in on the weaknesses and biases of mainstream journalism in the best of times, by the 1990s it was obvious that we were heading toward the worst of times. With the concentration of ownership and the weakening of labor, the informal commitment by commercial media organizations to canons of professional journalism—as flawed as they were in some respects—experienced commercial and at times political stress. Editorial staffs were downsized, bureaus closed, and there was a softening of news standards to include more salacious and trivial material. Working journalists themselves made a fairly rapid transition from being the most stalwart defenders of the status quo to among its leading critics. More broadly, the spread of commercialism (and, with it, vulgarity) throughout the media culture was disturbing to many not on the left. In short popular acceptance of the media system was weakening.

Looking back to that ancient history from today's vantage point, we can now see that during these years the current media reform movement was enjoying a necessary "pre-history," much like the civil rights movement in the 1940s and early 1950s, of the environmental movement in the 1960s. The tipping point came early in the new decade when the connection was made between the nature of the media system and a variety of policies and subsidies that created it. The anti-globalization movement triggered by the 1999 Seattle WTO protests organically pushed people to media activism, as the expansion of commercial media and its "rah-rah business" journalism was so central to the process. The Big Lies protecting the corporate media system—that the United States had a free market media system, and that this was the system ordained as the only possible democratic one by the Founders in the Constitution—began to crumble. Certainly the United States had a profit-driven media system, but it was not the result of free markets. It was the result of policies made corruptly to the benefit of corporate interests behind closed doors. The Founders themselves had implemented enormous printing and postal subsidies to spawn a vibrant press; they were under no illusions that a free press could be generated by letting rich people try to make as money as possible in publishing and hoping you lucked out.

The specific issue that vaulted media reform to movement status came with the media ownership fight of 2003. The Federal Communications Commission was required by the 1996 Telecommunications Act to review the existing media ownership rules every two years, and it had fallen behind schedule. These rules limited the number of government-granted monopoly broadcast licenses a single firm could own, locally and nationally. They also put limits on how much other media, specifically newspapers, a company receiving the gift of a monopoly broadcast license to the public-owned airwaves could own. The spirit behind these rules was to have as much ownership diversity as possible. The long-standing rules were popular with everyone, except the big media conglomerates that were salivating at the thought of expanding and lessening competitive pressures.

These ownership rules were so popular that even in the Reagan era they could only be loosened by the FCC. But with George W. Bush at the helm, the big media firms went in for the kill. Many of them, like Murdoch's News Corporation, Clear Channel, and Belo Corp., had been ardent supporters of Bush in his quest for the presidency in 2000, and they were leading the fight to eliminate the ownership rules. The three Bush appointments to the five-member FCC all made clear their support for the relaxation of the media ownership rules even before any research had been done, and they had the votes to pass the reforms they wanted. With Congress also under Republican control the matter looked all but lost in the spring of 2003.

This was when the opposition to the proposed relaxation of the media ownership rules exploded, seemingly out of thin air. Within a year at least two million people, maybe more, had contacted the FCC and Congress to protest the relaxation of the rules. The protests came from across the political spectrum and for a variety of reasons; anger against the media coverage of the buildup to the invasion of Iraq in March 2003 was certainly a large factor. Years of bottled up frustration with media came bursting forth when people gained the recognition that our media system was not natural, but the result of policies and subsidies, that had been made in their name but without their informed consent. The contemporary U.S. media reform movement was born.

In the five-plus years since the ownership battle the movement has grown dramatically. It is no longer the province of a handful of activists operating in near total obscurity in Washington, with little public awareness or conscious support. It is uniting the grassroots with the policymaking process. I cofounded a group, Free Press, in December 2002 with John Nichols and Josh Silver. Free Press had only a few staffers in 2003. In the spring of 2008 Free Press had a staff of thirty-five, and a membership approaching 400,000. Although Free Press is the largest media reform group in the United States, there are numerous others, and many of them emerged since 2003. A full listing along with descriptions of the 165 U.S. organizations working on media reform can be located at www.freepress.net. Some two dozen of these media reform groups came together to establish the Media & Democracy Coalition in 2005. A significant element of the media reform movement also characterizes itself as the media justice movement, because it links issues of media specifically with questions of social justice, in particular as they apply to women and communities of color. Locally based media reform groups are forming all the time.

There are several distinguishing characteristics between the emerging media reform movement and the media activism conducted prior to 2003 in the United States. First, although media ownership and battling media concentration is the issue that galvanized the movement, several other issues have come into play subsequently. Free Press has led a coalition fight under the Save the Internet banner to preserve Network Neutrality on the Internet; that is, to stop the cable and telephone companies from effectively privatizing the Internet by deciding which Web sites travel at the fastest speeds. Likewise coalitions have fought the efforts of the Bush administration to generate fake news and otherwise subvert freedom of the press. And similar coalitions battled to protect public and community broadcasting from sharp cutbacks in 2005. Looking forward there are numerous important policy issues in play or on the horizon. Each of these issues brings different constituencies into the movement; our job is to get them to see that they have a stake in all the other media reform issues that exist as well. It is not too much to say that the course of the digital communication system will be determined to a large extent by the outcome of these fights.

Second, the goal of the media reform movement is simply to make media policy a political issue. Once the matter is debated in the light of day, there will be progressive outcomes. The strength of the corporate status quo was not that it was so popular or democratic, but, rather, that it cultivated the notion that there was no alternative to the status quo; it had been mandated by the Founding Fathers, Adam Smith, or God, or some combination thereof. Once it became clear that that was purely propagandistic, and the media system was subjected to a clear-eyed analysis, the debate shifted radically. This is the moment we are in now, where millions of Americans understand that there is nothing natural about the media system and they have a right and a responsibility to participate in policy deliberations. This, too, has been the source of major victories for the media reform movement. As a result of its work, Congress required the FCC to hold six public hearings around the nation in 2006 and 2007 before it make any changes in the media ownership rules. The FCC has also agreed to hold public hearings in 2008 on the future of the Internet, due to activist pressure. In 2008, too, Representative Edward Markey (D-Mass.) and Chip Pickering (R-Miss.) co-sponsored the Internet Freedom Act, legislation that not only calls for Network Neutrality but requires the FCC to hold a minimum of eight major public "broadband summits" across the nation on the future of the Internet. This is all revolutionary, the democratization of media policymaking, and it may be the one great contribution of the movement to activists working in other areas of public life.

Third, although the media reform movement concentrates upon policy activism, it is closely linked to groups creating independent media, which has exploded on the Internet, and to those who provide criticism of the mainstream media. Those doing independent media need success in the policy realm to assure they have a possibility to be effective while those doing criticism and educational work do so with the ultimate aim of changing the system. The three branches of media activism rise and fall together. And all of them are dependent upon strong relations with media workers in the corporate sector, who increasingly find themselves estranged from the needs and values of their owners. Hence the struggle for free trade unions representing media workers is a core demand of the media reform movement. As we are discovering today in the United States in the struggle to keep newspaper journalism alive, it is the newspaper unions alone within the system that have a clear stake in seeing that viable journalism exist. The conglomerate owners could not care less.

Fourth, the United States, which was the global laggard in media activism for decades, has become something of a leader. Activists from other nations now attend the periodic media reform conference sponsored by Free Press to get up to speed on developments in the United States. By 2007 Canadians were beginning to work on establishing an organization similar in scope to Free Press. In the coming years it will be crucial that activists not only develop their movements in their own nations, but that they continue to coordinate their labors, as so many of the issues are global and revolve around trade and economic regulatory policies.

How far the U.S. media reform movement can go as a global leader is uncertain. Although the movement is nonpartisan and attracts support from elements of the political right, in the final analysis its success depends upon the growth and rise in power of popular political forces; i.e., the political Left. This is the point I made to conclude chapter 5. These forces are weak and largely inchoate in the United States. Ultimately, the battle over media is about whether people or corporations, public interest or private profit, should rule the realm of communication. And in view of the centrality of communication to the political economy that increasingly leads to the question of who should direct all of society. This means at some point a direct confrontation with capital. An emergent Left supporting progressive media reform is much easier to see in places like Latin America, Africa, or even Europe where capitalism is less stable or where a stronger Left has traditionally existed. Some of the appeal of media reform movement in the United States is that by blasting open the media it will make it possible for progressive media to have a chance to succeed and contribute to generating a stronger and more vibrant political culture, which likely will mean a rejuvenated Left.

No one thinks any longer that media reform is an issue to solve "after the revolution." Everyone understands that without media reform, there will be no revolution. In that sense it is similar to the labor movement, where the demand for free trade unions, hardly revolutionary in its own right, is a necessary precondition to building a viable organized left that can contest for power. Even if we do not get the revolution in the United States, media reform much like organized labor can make the nation a more just and humane place, for its own inhabitants and the peoples of the world.

What should be evident is that the emergence of the U.S. media reform movement has been of incalculable value for political economists of media. In each of the areas mentioned above political economy has played a constructive role and before it lay myriad opportunities for research and public engagement. As a subfield, political economy of media was an area on respirators in the 1990s when the thrall of neoliberalism deemed the market the natural ruler of all things existing and made critical research appear scholastic and irrelevant. The Internet had magically "solved" the problem of the media, so we could all shutter our windows and track down new professions. In the span of a mere decade those propositions were turned on their heads. Today we understand that media systems are the result of complex political economic factors and crucial policy decisions. The need for engaged scholarship has never been more pronounced, in the United States and worldwide. This is our moment in the sun, our golden opportunity, and as political economists of the media we must seize it.

Notes

Introduction

1   For a superb discussion of this point, see Dean Baker, *The Conservative Nanny State* (Washington, DC: Center for Economic and Policy Research, 2006).

SECTION I. Journalism
1. The Problem of Journalism

This chapter first appeared in a slightly different form as Robert W. McChesney, "The Problem of Journalism: A Political Economic Contribution to an Explanation of the Crisis in Contemporary US Journalism," Journalism Studies 4/3 (2003): 299–29. Some of this material was also used in chapters 2 and 3 of Robert W. McChesney, The Problem of the Media.

1   For critics of the political economic approach, see: Daniel C. Hallin, *We Keep America on Top of the World* (New York: Routledge, 1994), 11–13; Michael Schudson, *The Power of News* (Cambridge, MA: Harvard University Press, 1995), 4. For different approaches that draw in valuable material, see Richard L. Kaplan, *Politics and the American Press: The Rise of Objectivity, 1865–1920* (Cambridge: Cambridge University Press, 2002); and David T. Z. Mindich, *Just the Facts: How "Objectivity" Came to Define American Journalism* (New York: New York University Press, 1998).

2   Jeffrey L. Pasley, *"The Tyranny of Printers": Newspaper Politics in the Early American Republic* (Charlottesville: University Press of Virginia, 2001).

3   Harry J. Maihafer, *War of Words: Abraham Lincoln and the Civil War Press* (Washington, DC: Brassey's, 2001).

4   Gerald J. Baldasty, *The Commercialization of News in the Nineteenth Century* (Urbana: University of Illinois Press, 1992); Gerald J. Baldasty, *E. W. Scripps and the Business of Newspapers* (Urbana: University of Illinois Press, 1999).

5   Rodger Streitmatter, *Voices of Revolution: The Dissident Press in America* (New York: Columbia University Press, 2001).

6   John Graham, ed., *"Yours for the Revolution": The Appeal to Reason, 1895–1922* (Lincoln: University of Nebraska Press, 1990).

7   Tom Goldstein, ed., *Killing the Messenger: 100 Years of Media Criticism* (New York: Columbia University Press, 1989), ix.

8   Upton Sinclair, *The Brass Check* (Urbana: University of Illinois Press, 2003).

9   For the classic statement on professional journalism, see Joseph Pulitzer, "Selection from the College of Journalism," in *Killing the Messenger*, ed. Tom Goldstein (New York: Columbia University Press, 1989), 190–99. (Originally published in *North America Review*, May 1904).

10   Horst J. P. Bergmeier and Rainer E. Lotz, *Hitler's Airwaves: The Inside Story of Nazi Radio Broadcasting and Propaganda Swing* (New Haven: Yale University Press, 1997), 70–73.

11   The classic treatments of this topic include: Gaye Tuchman, *Making News: A Study in the Construction of Reality* (New York: Free Press, 1978); Herbert J. Gans, *Deciding What's News* (New York: Pantheon Books, 1979); Mark Fishman, *Manufacturing the News* (Austin: University of Texas Press, 1980). For a more recent critique from a Canadian perspective, see Robert A. Hackett and Yuezhi Zhao, *Sustaining Democracy? Journalism and the Politics of Objectivity* (Toronto: Garamond Press, 1998).

12   I am indebted to Ben Bagdikian for much of what follows. See Ben H. Bagdikian, *The Media Monopoly* (Boston: Beacon Press, 2000).

13   Stephen Ponder, *Managing the Press: Origins of the Media Presidency, 1897–1933* (New York: Palgrave, 1998).

14   Ina Howard, "Power Sources," *Extra!* June 2002.

15   Commission on Civil Disorders, "The Role of the Mass Media in Reporting of News About Minorities," in Goldstein, *Killing the Messenger,* 200–27.

16   Stuart Ewen, *PR! A Social History of Spin* (New York: Basic Books, 1996); Sheldon Rampton and John Stauber, *Trust Us, We're Experts: How Industry Manipulates Science and Gambles with Your Future* (New York: Putnam, 2001); Alicia Mundy, *Dispensing with Truth: The Victims, the Drug Companies, and the Dramatic Story Behind the Battle Over Fen-Phen* (New York: St. Martin's Press, 2001).

17   Suzanne Vranica, "Publicist Group Bolsters its PR Holdings," *Wall Street Journal*, May 30, 2001.

18   For a brilliant discussion of this and its implications for democracy, see Christopher Lasch, *The Revolt of the Elites and the Betrayal of Democracy* (New York: W. W. Norton, 1995), chapter 9.

19   Joseph N. Cappella and Kathleen Hall Jamieson, *Spiral of Cynicism: The Press and the Public Good* (New York: Oxford University Press, 1997).

20   James Fallows, *Breaking the News: How the Media Undermine American Democracy* (New York: Vintage, 1996).

21   Bagdikian, *Media Monopoly.*

22   Edwin C. Baker, *Media, Markets and Democracy* (New York: Cambridge University Press, 2002), 106.

23   George Farah and Justin Elga, "What's *Not* Talked About on Sunday Morning? Issue of Corporate Power Not on the Agenda," *Extra!* September/October 2001, 14–17.

24   Interview with Charles Lewis, in *Orwell Rolls Over in his Grave*, documentary by Robert Pappas.

25   For examples of the CPI's work, go to http://www.publicintegrity.org.

26   See, for example, Edward Jay Epstein, *News from Nowhere: Television and the News* (New York: Vintage Books, 1973); Bill Kovach and Tom Rosenstiel, *Warp Speed: America in the Age of Mixed Media Culture* (Century Foundation Press, 1999); W. Lance Bennett, *News,*

the Politics of Illusion (New York: Longman, 2001); Jeffrey Scheuer, *The Sound Bite Society: Television and the American Mind* (New York: Four Walls Eight Windows, 1999).

27   Harold Meyerson, "If I Had a Hammer: Whatever Happened to America's Working Class?" *Los Angeles Times*, September 2, 2001.

28   Jon Fine, "California Dreaming, Scheming," *Advertising Age*, April 30, 2001, S1.

29   See, for example, Judith Serrin and William Serrin, eds., *Muckraking! The Journalism that Changed America* (New York: New Press, 2002); Nancy J. Woodhull and Robert W. Snyder, eds., *Defining Moments in Journalism* (New Brunswick, NJ: Transaction Publishers, 1998).

30   For a collection of their reports collected into a book, see Donald L. Bartlett and James B. Steele, *America: What Went Wrong* (Kansas City, MO: Andrews McMeel, 1992).

31   Kovach and Rosenstiel, *Warp Speed*.

32   See, for example, George W. Pring and Penelope Canan, *First Amendment and Libel: The Experts Look at Print, Broadcast & Cable* (New York: Harcourt Brace Jovanovich, 1983) and *SLAPPs: Getting Sued for Speaking Out* (Philadelphia: Temple University Press, 1996).

33   Much of this has been written by prominent journalists like Bagdikian. See also, James D. Squires, *Read All About It! The Corporate Takeover of America's Newspapers* (New York: Times Books, 1993); Doug Underwood, *When MBAs Rule the Newsroom* (New York: Columbia University Press, 1993); John H. McManus, *Market-Driven Journalism: Let the Citizen Beware?* (Thousand Oaks, CA: Sage, 1994).

34   Michele Greppi, "All's Not Well at ABC News," *Electronic Media*, May 28, 2001, 3. The definitive work on this issue is Penn Kimball, *Downsizing the News: Network Cutbacks in the Nation's Capital* (Baltimore: Johns Hopkins University Press, 1994).

35   Dan Trigoboff, "No Good News for Local News," *Broadcasting & Cable*, November 18, 2002, 12.

36   Paul Tharp, "Kann Gives Angry WSJ-ers a New Lesson in Capitalism," December 5, 2002, http://www.nypost.com.

37   Felicity Barringer, "Publisher Who Resigned Urges Editors to Put Readers First," *New York Times*, April 7, 2001; David Laventhol, "Profit Pressures," *Columbia Journalism Review* May/June (2001), 18–22.

38   Wayne Walley, "Fox News Sweeps to TV Marketer of Year," *Advertising Age*, November 4, 2002, 1, 22.

39   Robert W. McChesney interview of Rick Kaplan, former president of CNN, March 2001.

40   *Economist*, "It Pays to Be Right," December 7, 2002, 60.

41   Jill Goldsmith and Pamela McClintock, "Extra! TV Mavens Eye Paper Route," *Variety*, March 12–18, 2001, 1, 58.

42   Meg Campbell, "Newsplex Puts the New in Newsroom," *Editor & Publisher*, December 12, 2002.

43   Christina Hoag, "CBS 4 and Herald Form Media Alliance," *Miami Herald*, November 23, 2002.

44   Dan Trigoboff and Steve McClellan, "Watchdogs Howl Over ABC/CNN," *Broadcasting & Cable*, November 25, 2002, 1.

45   Tom Lowry, "Online Extra: The Case Against an ABC/CNN Merger," December 2, 2002, http://www.businessweek.online.

46   Av Westin, "'Minutes' Master Misses Mark," *Variety*, April 16–22, 2001, 35.

47   Felicity Barringer, "Wire Service Says Reporter It Fired Invented his Sources," October 22, 2002, http://www.nytimes.com; "Editor Is Dismissed Over Truth of Article," *New York Times*, November 19, 2002.

48   Trudy Lieberman, "You Can't Report What You Don't Pursue," *Columbia Journalism Review* May/June 2000.

49   Nolan Reeds and Freda Colbourne, "Fewer Gatekeepers, More Open Gates," *Strategy Magazine*, November 6, 2000, 25.

50   Marion Just, Rosalind Levine, and Kathleen Regan, "Investigative Journalism Despite the Odds," *Columbia Journalism Review*, November/December 2002, 103.

51   Interview with Charles Lewis, in *Orwell Rolls Over in his Grave*, documentary by Robert Pappas.

52   Brett Schaeffer, "Minority Reporter," *In These Times*, August 19, 2002, 8.

53   Rampton and Stauber, *Trust Us, We're Experts*.

54   Elisabeth Bumiller, "Bush Criticized by Lawmakers on Corporate Governance," *New York Times*, August 1, 2002.

55   See, for example, Richard W. Stevenson and Elisabeth Bumiller, "Parties Jousting over Wrongdoing by U.S. Businesses," *New York Times*, July 8, 2002; Alison Mitchell, "Democrats See Scandals as Chance to Attack Privatizing Social Security," *New York Times*, July 13, 2002.

56   See, for example, Patricia Moy and Michael Pfau, *With Malice Toward All? The Media and Public Confidence in Public Institutions* (Westport, CT: Praeger, 2000).

57   Av Westin, *Best Practices for Television Journalists* (Arlington, VA: The Freedom Forum, 2000), 5.

58   Louis Chunovic, "News Departments Boost Bottom Line," *Electronic Media*, January 7, 2002, 6.

59   Pew Research Center, "Self Censorship: How Often and Why," April 30, 2000, http://people-press.org/reports/display.php3?ReportID_39.

60   See, for example, Janine Jackson and Peter Hart, "Fear & Favor 2000: How Power Shapes the News," *Extra!*, May/June 2001, 15–22.

61   Erin White, "P&G to Use Plugs in TV News Stories to Send Viewers to its Web Sites," *Wall Street Journal*, March 7, 2001.

62   Felicity Barringer, "Concerns on Space and Revenue Spur Growth of Paid Obituaries," *New York Times*, January 14, 2002; Bruce Orwall, "Dinosaur Ad Crosses a Line at Newspapers," *Wall Street Journal*, July 18, 2001; *Wall Street Journal*, "Gannett Allows Front-Page Ads at Local Papers," May 25, 2000; "CNN Headline News to Display Ad Logos," August 1, 2000, http://www.accessatlanta.com.

63   Robert Feder, "Is Medical Magazine Healthy for Journalism?" *Chicago Sun-Times*, October 23, 2002; Paul Raeburn, "The Corruption of TV Health News," *Business Week*, February 28, 2000, 66, 68; Karissa S. Wang, "WCBS in Ethics Firestorm over Ad," *Electronic Media*, April 17, 2000, 3, 44; Diana Zuckerman, "Hype in Health Reporting," November 25, 2002, , http://www.alternet.org.

64   *O'Dwyer's PR Daily*, "Releases Go into the Garbage," November 13, 2002.

65   Mark Jurkowitz, "When Journalists Become Pitchmen," *Boston Globe*, February 10, 2000.

66   Lloyd Grove, "For CBS Correspondent Rose, Things Go Better with Coke," *Washington Post*, April 23, 2002.

67   Sally Beatty, "As Hard News Get Even Harder, CNN Segues to Glossier Format," *Wall Street Journal Online*, July 5, 2002; Paula Bernstein, "CNN to Revamp Format, Highlight Personalities," *Variety*, December 11–17, 2000; Kim Campbell, "TV News Moves Toward Hollywood Star System," *Christian Science Monitor*, January 25, 2002.

68   Richard Huff, "Singles to See If Fox's Price Is Right," New York *Daily News*, November 21, 2002.

69   Richard Huff, "Doc Quits ABC for Tylenol," December 10, 2002, http://www.nydailynews.com.

70   David Folkenflik, "Medical Show Packages Stories and Sponsors," *Baltimore Sun*, May 8, 2002.

71   See J. D. Lasica, "Synergy and the Day of Infamy," *Online Journalism Review*, May 31, 2001; Lisa de Moraes, "Exclusive Perks: CNN's Red-Carpet 'Get' in the Blake Story," *Washington Post*, April 23, 2002. For a longer discussion of the corporate influence over ABC News, see Jane Meyer, "Bad News: What's Behind the Recent Gaffes at ABC?" *The New Yorker*, August, 14, 2000, 30–36.

72   Edward Helmore, "News Going Nowhere?" *The Observer*, August 20, 2000, 7.

73   Norman Solomon, "Announcing the P.U.-litzer Prizes for 2002," January 3, 2003, http://www.commondreams.org.

74   Bill Carter, "At CBS, the Lines Between News and Entertainment Grow Fuzzier," *New York Times*, June 26, 2000.

75   Elizabeth Jensen, "Headline News Faces Criticism for Channeling Viewers," *Los Angeles Times*, August 20, 2001.

76   "Ken Auletta: 'The Drive to Achieve Synergy Is Often Journalism's Poison,'" December 19, 2000, http://www.iwantmedia.com.

77   See, for example, Alex Kuczynski, "Newsweeklies Turn a Cold Shoulder to Hard News," *New York Times*, May 14, 2001.

78   Dan Trigoboff, "It Depends on What 'Hard' Is," *Broadcasting & Cable*, May 27, 2002, 18.

79   Tom Shales, "When Serious News Goes Pop," *Electronic Media*, November 18, 2002, 23.

80   De Moraes, "Exclusive Perks."

81   Michele Greppi, "Newsmags Hold Key to ABC's Sweeps Bump," *Electronic Media*, November 18, 2002, 2.

82   Karissa S. Wang, "Study: TV News Big on Violence," *Electronic Media*, December 10, 2001, 16.

83   Brian Lowry, "Newscasts Too Often Employ Scare Tactics," *Los Angeles Times*, October 16, 2002.

84   See, for example, Lee Hall, "20th Anniversary: CNN Headline News; Q&A: Larry Goodman, President, Sales and Marketing," *ElectronicMedia*, December 16, 2002, 26, 32.

85   Patricia Callahan and Kevin Helliker, "Knight Ridder Loses Readers but Charges More to Reach Them," *Wall Street Journal*, June 18, 2001.

86   See, for example, William J. Puette, *Through Jaundiced Eyes: How the Media View Organized Labor* (Ithaca, NY: ILR Press, 1992).

87   Peter Johnson, "Few TV News Stories Focus on Hispanics," *USA Today*, December 16, 2002.

88   Ben H. Bagdikian, "A Secret in the News: The Country's Permanent Poor," April 2, 2001, http://www.znet.org.

89   U.S. Newswire, "Public Misconception About Poverty Continues," January 7, 2003, http://www.usnewswire.com.

90   Joan Oleck, "Training Scribes for the Biz Beat," *Business Week*, May 28, 2001, 16.

91   "Sunday Morning Talk Shows Ignore Corporate Power Issues," 2000, http://www.essentialaction.org.

92   Norman Solomon, "Bloomberg's Victory and the Triumph of Business News," *Creators Syndicate*, November 8, 2001.

93   Dan Fost, "Strained Relations: Business Magazines Struggle to Maintain Objectivity Under Pressure from Their Biggest Tech Advertisers," *San Francisco Chronicle*, January 16, 2002; Dan Fost, "When Scoops Are Product Placements, Press 'Leaks' Can Serve a Corporate Agenda," *San Francisco Chronicle*, September 1, 2002.

94   Vincent Boland, "Media Face Clash with Regulators Over Analysts," *Financial Times*, November 23–24, 2002, 1.

95   Howard Kurtz, "On CNBC, Boosters for the Boom," *Washington Post*, November 12, 2002; Phillip J. Longman, "Bad Press: How Business Journalism Helped Inflate the Bubble," *The Washington Monthly*, October 2002.

96   Norman Solomon, "The Old Spin on the 'New Economy,'" July 18, 2002, http://www.alternet.org.

97   Simon Romero and Riva D. Atlas, "WorldCom Files for Bankruptcy; Largest U.S. Case," *New York Times*, July 22, 2002.

98   William Greider, "The Enron Nine," *The Nation*, May 13, 2002, 18–22.

99   Robert Weissman and V. Mokhiber, "Cracking Down on Corporate Crime, Really," July 23, 2002, http://www.zmag.org.

100 Bob Herbert, "Joined at the Hip," *New York Times*, January 10, 2002.

101 Joshua Chaffin, "Enron in California: A Titanic Error," *Financial Times*, November 22, 2002, 20; Andrew Wheat, "System Failure: Deregulation, Political Corruption, Corporate Fraud and the Enron Debacle," *Multinational Monitor*, January/February (2002), 34–42.

102 Matt Bliven, "Enron's Washington," January 24, 2002, http://www.thenation.com; Charles Lewis, "Enron Scandal Goes Deep," *Wilmington Sunday News Journal*, February 24, 2002; *Multinational Monitor*, "Andersen, Politics and Money: By the Numbers," January/February (2002), 44.

103 Amy Borrus, "Global Crossing Tossed More Cash Around Town than Enron," *BusinessWeek*, February 11, 2002, 49.

104 Orville Schell, "How Big Media Missed the Big Story," July 19, 2002, http://www.msbnc.com.

105 *CounterPunch*, "From Enron to Black Hawk Down," January 1–15, 2002, 1, 2.

106 Kurt Eichenwald, "For WorldCom, Acquisitions Were Behind its Rise and Fall," *New York Times*, August 8, 2002; for what the media missed at the time, see Bernie Ebbers, "Character and Business Methods Sowed the Seeds of Disaster," *Financial Times*, December 19, 2002, 11.

107 Ben Schiller, "Where Did All the Reporters Go?" February 13, 2002, http://www.alternet.org.

108 James Ledbetter, "The Boys in the Bubble," *New York Times*, January 2, 2003.

109 Richard Blow, "Money, Power and Influence: Muckrakers Become Buckrakers," January 31, 2002, http://www.tompaine.com; Howard Kurtz, "Enron-N.Y. Times Co. Deal

Highlights Media's Dilemma," *Washington Post*, July 18, 2002; Rebecca Smith, "Blockbuster, Enron Agree to Movie Deal," *Wall Street Journal*, July 20, 2000.

110 FAIR Media Advisory, "PBS's 'Commanding' Conflict of Interest: Enron and Other Corporate Giants Sponsored New Globalization Series," April 3, 2002, http://www.fair.org.

111 John Dunbar, Robert Moore, and MaryJo Sylwester, "Enron Executives Who Dumped Stock Were Heavy Donors to Bush," *The Public I*, February (2002), 1, 2, 6; Herbert, "Joined."

112 The party was videotaped and released in December 2002. See Associated Press, "Enron Video from 1997 Reportedly Parallels Future Scandal," December 16, 2002.

113 Jason Leopold, "Secrets and Lies: Bush, Cheney and the Great Rip-Off of California Ratepayers," November 21, 2002, http://www.counterpunch.org.

114 See, for example, Richard A. Oppel Jr. "Senator Releases Documents on Gore Aide's Enron Ties," *New York Times*, November 13, 2002.

115 Richard A. Oppel Jr., "Senate Report Clears Rubin of Illegality in Enron Matter," *New York Times*, January 3, 2003.

116 Russ Lewis, "The Press's Business," *The Washington Post*, January 30, 2002.

117 Tom Shales, "Too Entertained to Be Outraged," *Electronic Media*, July 22, 2002.

118 Adolph Reed, "The Road to Corporate Perdition," *The Progressive*, September 2002, 31.

119 Jill Goldsmith, "H'Wood's High-priced Suits," *Variety*, April 23–29, 2001, 1, 48; Paul Krugman, "The Outrage Constraint," *New York Times*, August 23, 2002.

120 Mark Gimein, "You Bought, They Sold," *Fortune*, September 2, 2002, 64–74; Peter Thal Larsen, Adrian Michaels, Ien Cheng, and Christopher Grimes, "SEC to Probe Forecasts Made as AOL Chiefs Sold Shares," *Financial Times*, August 23, 2002, 1; Diane Mermigas, "Investigation Dampening News of Deal," *Electronic Media*, August 26, 2002, 20.

121 Nanette Byrnes and Tom Lowry, "A Different Yardstick for Cable," *Business Week*, September 2, 2002, 56; Tamara Conniff, "Labels Upbraided at State Hearings on Accounting," September 25, 2002, http://www.hollywoodreporter.com.

122 *Economist*, "Messier's Mess," June 8, 2002, 55–7; Sallie Hofmeister, "Charter to Slash Jobs in Wake of U.S. Probe," December 11, 2002, http://www.latimes.com; Jo Johnson and Peter Thal Larsen, "Vicendi Prepares to Face Legal Scrutiny," *Financial Times*, January 10, 2003, 20; Victor Mallet and Peter Thal Larsen, "Criminal Problem Deals Fresh Blow to Vivendi," *Financial Times*, November 5, 2002, 1; Reuters dispatch "Eisner's Participation in IPO Under Review," December 18, 2002, http://www.latimes.com; David Streitfeld, "Feds Subpoena Firm Controlled by News Corp.," October 3, 2002, http://www.latimes.com; *Wall Street Journal Online*, "Gemstar Announces Transition of SEC Probe to Formal Status," October 21, 2002.

123 Peter Thal Larsen, Tally Goldstein, Jonathan Moules, and Peter Spiegel, "Former Adelphia Chiefs Arrested," *Financial Times*, July 25, 2002, 1.

124 Julia Angwin and Martin Peers, "Investment in Advertisers Was Key to AOL Income," *The Wall Street Journal Online*, August 26, 2002; *Economist*, "A Steal?" October 26, 2002; Christopher Grimes, "AOL Inflated Advertising Revenues by Nearly $200m," *Financial Times*, October 24, 2002, 1; David R. Kirkpatrick, "New Charges Made in Suit on Homestore," *New York Times*, November 16, 2002; David D. Kirkpatrick and Saul Hansell, "U.S. Initiates Investigation of Accounting at AOL Unit," *New York Times*, August 1, 2002; Peter Thal Larsen, "AOL Time Warner Sued over Homestead Deals," *Financial Times*, November 18, 2002, 19; Martin Peers and Laurie P. Cohen, "SEC

Probes AOL-Oxygen Pact for Double-Booking of Revenue," *Wall Street Journal Online*, October 7, 2002.

125 David D. Kirkpatrick and Simon Romero, "AOL's Swap Deals with 2 Others Said to Be a Focus of the S.E.C.," *New York Times*, August 23, 2002.

126 Miles Maguire, "Business as Usual," *American Journalism Review*, October (2002).

127 "The Corporate Crime Wave: The Response," *Multinational Monitor*, December 2002, 5.

128 Evelyn Nieves and Elisabeth Bumiller, "In Twin Speeches, Bush and Cheney Vow to Fight Fraud," *New York Times*, August 8, 2002.

129 Richard S. Dunham, Amy Borrus, and Mike McNamee, with Lorraine Woellert, "Reform Lite," *Business Week*, April 1, 2002, 30–32; Robert Kuttner, "So Much for Cracking Down on the Accountants," *Business Week*, November 18, 2002, 24.

130 Molly Ivins, "Surprise! Real Corporate Reform Isn't Happening," *Boulder Daily Camera*, October 9, 2002.

131 Mark Weisbrot, "Making Accountants Liable for Corporate Fraud," January 2, 2003, http://www.counterpunch.org.

132 Jennifer Loven, "Newspapers Warned About Bottom Line," Associated Press dispatch, April 10, 2002.

133 Paula Bernstein, "Serious Newscast Puffed Out," *Variety*, November 6–12, 2000, 13, 17; *The Economist*, "Come Back, Ed Murrow," October 7, 2002, 42.

134 Susan J. Douglas, "Navel-Gazing the News," *In These Times*, January 20, 2003, 9.

135 Felicity Barringer, "An Old-times Newspaper War for Young Loyalists," *New York Times*, October 31, 2002; Oliver Burkman, "US Press Move to Youth Groove," *The Guardian* (UK), November 14, 2002.

136 Bruce A. Williams, and Michael X. Delli Carpini, "Heeeeeeeeeeeeere's Democracy!" *The Chronicle of Higher Education*, April 19, 2002, B14.

137 Michael Schneider, "Local Newscasts Fall Victim to Cost Cuts," *Variety*, January 25–February 3, 2002, 22; Dan Trigoboff, "Live at 11? Maybe Not for Long," *Broadcasting & Cable*, February 11, 2002, 29.

138 David Halberstam, "The Powers that Were," *Brill's Content*, September (2000), 23–26; Michael Margolis, "PBS President Speaks on U.S., World Media," *Cornell Daily Sun*, November 14, 2002; Jaime McLeod, "Media Icon Walter Cronkite Remains as Sharp as Ever," October 30, 2002, http://www.moonrecordstar.com; Cris Ramon, "'Dateline' Reporter: Remain Critical of Media," November 13, 2002, http://www.dailynorthwestern.com.

139 See, for example, William Serrin, ed., *The Business of Journalism* (New York: New Press, 2000); Kristina Borjesson, ed., *Into the Buzzsaw: Leading Journalists Expose the Myth of a Free Press* (Amherst, NY: Prometheus Books, 2002).

140 Leonard Downie Jr. and Robert G. Kaiser, *The News About the News: American Journalism in Peril* (New York: Alfred A. Knopf, 2002).

141 Howard Gardner, Mihaly Csikszentmihalyi, and William Damon, *Good Work: When Excellence and Ethics Meet* (New York: Basic Books, 2001), chapter 7.

142 Deborah Potter, "Pessimism Rules in TV Newsrooms," *Columbia Journalism Review*, November/December (2002), 90.

143 Robert W. McChesney, interview with Linda Foley, Washington, DC, July 2002.

144 Rich Opel, "The Anticorporate Crowd's Foolish Self-Destruction," *Austin American-Statesman*, December 8, 2002; Danielle M. Parker, "Study Asks Whether TV News Is Slipping," *Electronic Media*, October 9, 2000, 20.

145 Jay T. Harris, "News and Profits," *The Nation*, May 28, 2001, 6.

146 James Carey, "American Journalism On, Before, and After September 11," in *Journalism After September 11*, ed. Barber Zelizer and Stuart Allan (London and New York: Routledge, 2002), 89.

147 Ann Coulter, *Slander: Liberal Lies About the American Right* (New York: Crown, 2002); Bernard Goldberg, *Bias: A CBS Insider Exposes How Media Distort the News* (Washington, DC: Regnery, 2001); Sean Hannity, *Let Freedom Ring: Winning the War of Liberty Over Liberalism* (New York: Regan Books, 2002).

148 Coulter, *Slander*; Goldberg, *Bias*; Hannity, *Let Freedom Ring*.

149 Robert Parry, "Price of the 'Liberal Media' Myth," January 1, 2003, http://www.consortiumnews.com.

150 See, for a recent example, Kathleen Hall Jamieson and Paul Waldman, *The Press Effect* (New York: Oxford University Press, 2003).

151 See L. Brent Bozell III and Brent H. Baker, eds., *And That's the Way It Isn't: A Reference Guide to Media Bias* (Alexandria, VA: Media Research Center, 1990). To establish that even media corporations like General Electric have a "liberal" bias, the authors point to how GE's philanthropic arm gives a few hundred thousand dollars annually to numerous mainstream groups (e.g., the NAACP, the Council on Foreign Relations, the Audubon Society). GE's enormous contributions to politicians and multimillion-dollar lobbying armada do not rate any mention whatsoever.

152 Robert W. McChesney, *Rich Media, Poor Democracy* (Urbana: University of Illinois Press, 1999), 245.

153 Lawrence Jarvik, *PBS: Behind the Screen* (Rocklin, CA: Forum, 1997).

154 Another question to be asked, is what, exactly, is a conservative? The "business-can-do-no-wrong" neoliberal of the early twenty-first century is a very different animal from the classical conservative of earlier times.

155 Tom Adkins, "They're Just a Bunch of Unregenerate Socialists," December 8, 2002, http://www.philly.com.

156 Alexander Stille, "Thinkers on the Left Get a Hearing Everywhere but at Home," *New York Times*, November 11, 2000; Antonia Zerbisias, "American Media Keep the Liberals Invisible," *Toronto Star*, October 1, 2002.

157 David Shaw, "Journalists Losing Touch with the Man on the Street," December 8, 2002, http://www.latimes.com.

158 Telephone interview with Jeff Cohen, producer, *Donahue*, MSNBC, December 2002.

159 Robert Parry, "Media-Homeless Liberals," November 13, 2002, http://www.consortiumnews.com.

160 John Leo, "Newsroom Monoculture Inhibits Objective Reporting," *Wisconsin State Journal*, July 17, 2001.

161 Quoted in *Washington Post*, August 20, 1992.

162 Comment of Joseph Farah, in Mark O'Keefe, "Right Wing's Strength in Talk Radio, New Media Frustrates Democrats," *Newhouse News Service*, November 24, 2002.

163 Geoffrey Nunberg demolished bias in a series of articles in 2002. See, for example, Geoffrey Nunberg, "Sill Unbiased: Closing the Case on Media Labeling," May 15, 2002, http://www.prospect.org.

164 Mark Jurkowitz, "Leaning on the Media," January 17, 2002, http://www.boston.com.

165 People for the American Way, *Buying a Movement: Right-Wing Foundations and American Politics*, 1995, available at http://www.pfaw.org.

166 Kim Campbell, "A Call to the Right," *Christian Science Monitor*, July 25, 2002; Kimberley Conniff, "All the Views Fit to Print," *Brill's Content*, March 2001; Michael Dolny, "The Rich Get Richer," *Extra!*, May/June 2000, 23; Blaine Harden, "In Virginia, Young Conservatives Learn How to Develop and Use Their Political Voices," *New York Times*, June 11, 2001; Sam Husseini, "Checkbook Analysis: Corporations Support Think Tanks—And the Favor Is Returned," *Extra!*, May/June (2000), 23.

167 Robert Kuttner, "Comment: Philanthropy and Movements," *American Prospect*, July 15, 2002.

168 John F. Harris, "Mr. Bush Catches a Washington Break," *Washington Post*, May 6, 2001, B1.

169 Geoffrey Nunberg, "Label Whores," *The American Prospect*, May 6, 2002.

170 See, for example, Parry, "Price of the 'Liberal Media' Myth"; Bill Carter and Jim Rutenberg, "Fox News Head Sent a Policy Note to Bush," *New York Times*, November 19, 2002; Steve Rendall, "Fox's Slanted Sources," *Extra!*, July/August 2001, 13.

171 Kimberley Pohlman, "Solid Ratings Don't Protect Progressive Radio Voices," *Extra!*, July/August 2000, 22.

172 E. J. Dionne Jr. "The Rightward Press," *Washington Post*, December 6, 2002.

173 Michael Kelly, *Washington Post*, "Media Now More Like the Public: Democratic," *The News-Gazette* (Champaign, IL), December 20, 2002.

174 Paul Fahri, "Talk Radio, Top Volume on the Right," *Washington Post*, May 8, 2002.

175 Steve Carney, "22% of Americans Get News From Talk Jocks," January 10, 2003, http://www.latimes.com.

176 Statistic in Paul Begala, "UAW CAP Conference Delegates Engage in Lively Discussion with Media Panel," February 6, 2001, http://www.uaw.org.

177 Robert W. McChesney interview.

178 Harold Evans, "The Watchdog Didn't Bark," July 16, 2002, http://www.salon.com; Paul Krugman, "The Insider Game," *New York Times*, 12 July 2002; David Teather, "Memo Emerges to Haunt President," *Guardian* (UK), November 2, 2002.

179 Robert Kuttner, "Bush Making it a Rocky New Year," *Boston Globe*, January 1, 2003.

2. A Century of Radical Media Criticism in the United States

This chapter first appeared in a slightly different form as Ben Scott and Robert W. McChesney, "A Century of Radical Media Criticism in the USA," in Radical Mass Media Criticism: A Cultural Genealogy, *ed. David Berry and John Theobald (New York: Black Rose Books, 2006), 177–91.*

1   Robert McChesney and Ben Scott, eds., *Our Unfree Press: 100 Years of Radical Media Criticism* (New York: New Press, 2004).

2   Ben H. Bagdikian, *The Media Monopoly* (New York: Beacon Press, 1983); Ben H. Bagdikian, *The New Media Monopoly* (Boston: Beacon Press, 2004); Edwin C. Baker, *Media, Markets and Democracy* (New York: Cambridge University Press, 2002); Edward Herman and Noam Chomsky, *Manufacturing Consent* (London: Vintage, 1988); Robert W. McChesney, *Rich Media, Poor Democracy: Communication Politics in Dubious Times* (New York: New Press, 1999).

3   Communication Workers of America, *Media Unions, Members of Congress Call on FCC Chairman Powel to Hold Full Public Hearings on Media Ownership,* press release, July 20, 2004.

4   Leonard Downie Jr. and Robert Kaiser, *The News About the News: American Journalism in Peril* (New York: Alfred A. Knopf, 2002).

5   James Carey, "The Press, Public Opinion, and Public Discourse. On the Edge of the Postmodern," in *James Carey: A Critical Reader*, ed. Eve Stryker Munson and Catherine A. Warren (Minneapolis: University of Minnesota Press, 1997).

6   Will Irwin, *The American Newspaper* (Ames: Iowa State University Press, 1969), 8.

7   Upton Sinclair, *The Brass Check* (Urbana: University of Illinois Press, 2003), 241.

8   Ibid., 248; Oswald Garrison Villard, "Some Weaknesses in Modern Journalism," in *The Coming Newspaper*, ed. Merle Harrold Thorpe, (New York: Holt, 1915), 77.

9   P. Greer, "The Confession of a Reporter," *Nonpartisan Leader*, May 13, 1918, 5.

10   W. White, "Don't Indulge in Name-Calling with Press Critics," *Editor & Publisher*, April 22, 1939, 14.

11   Joseph Pulitzer Jr., ed., Frontispiece," *St Louis Post-Dispatch Symposium on Freedom of the Press* (St. Louis: *St. Louis-Post Dispatch*, 1938).

12   Alfred McClung Lee, *The Daily Newspaper In America* (New York: Macmillan, 1937), 678–79.

13   Isabelle Keating, "Reporters Become of Age," *Harper's*, November 1935, 601.

14   Herbert Harris, *American Labor* (New Haven: Yale University Press, 1938), 173, 185.

15   Morris Leopold Ernst, *The First Freedom* (New York: Macmillan, 1946), 63, 69, 74, 77–79.

16   Morris Leopold Ernst, *The Best Is Yet . . .* (New York: Harper & Brothers, 1945), 90.

17   Todd Gitlin, *The Whole World Is Watching: Mass Media in the Making and Unmaking of the New Left* (Berkeley: University of California Press, 1980).

18   Brent Cunningham, "Rethinking Objective Journalism," *Columbia Journalism Review*, July/August 2003.

19   Robert W. McChesney, *The Problem of the Media* (New York: Monthly Review Press, 2004), chapter 7.

20   Michael J. Copps, *Biennial Regulatory Review—Review of the Commission's Broadcast Ownership Rules and Other Rules Adopted Pursuant to Section 202 of the Telecommunications Act of 1996.*

3. Upton Sinclair and the Contradictions of Capitalist Journalism

This chapter first appeared in a slightly different form as Robert W. McChesney and Ben Scott, "Upton Sinclair and the Contradictions of Capitalist Journalism," Monthly Review 54/1 (2002): 1–14.

1   Upton Sinclair, *The Brass Check*, 9th rev. ed. (Long Beach, CA: The Author, 1928), 147. All page number references are to this edition of Sinclair's book.

2   Ibid., 153.

3   Ibid., 429.

4   John Ahouse, *Upton Sinclair: A Descriptive, Annotated Bibliography* (Los Angeles: Mercer & Aitchison, 1994), 42.

5   Leon Harris, *Upton Sinclair: American Rebel* (New York: Thomas Y. Crowell, 1975), 177–78.

6   Sinclair, *Brass Check*, 294, 376.

7   All of these quotations are taken from Greg Mitchell, *The Campaign of the Century: Upton Sinclair's Race for Governor of California and the Birth of Modern Media Politics* (New York: Random House, 1992), x–xvi.

8   See Mitchell, *Campaign of the Century*, for his detailed analysis of the 1934 race, as well as the material in this paragraph. See also, Upton Sinclair, *I, Candidate for Governor: And How I Got Licked*, with an introduction by James Gregory (Berkeley: University of California Press, 1994). Originally published in 1934 and 1935.

9   See Frank Luther Mott, *American Journalism*, rev. ed. (New York: Macmillan, 1950), 519; Marion Marzolf, *Civilizing Voices: American Press Criticism, 1880–1950* (New York: Longman, 1991).

10   Hugo Munsterberg, "The Case of the Reporter," *McClure's*, February 1911, 435–39; Will Irwin, *The American Newspaper: A Series First Appearing in Collier's, January–July 1911* (Ames: Iowa State University Press, 1969), 8; Charles Edward Russell, "The Press and the Public," *La Follette's Magazine*, June 4, 1910, 7–8.

11   Max Sherover, *Fakes in American Journalism*, 3rd ed. (Brooklyn: Free Press League, 1916), 7; Hamilton Holt, *Commercialism in Journalism* (Boston: Houghton Mifflin, 1909), 3–4; Robert La Follette, *La Follette's Autobiography* (Madison: University of Wisconsin Press, 1960), 258–59.

12   S.E., "The 'Free Speech' Fallacy," *The Socialist Review*, April 1920, 273; Livy S. Richard quoted in "Our Problem of the Press," *La Follette's Magazine*, July 20, 1912, 15; Edward Alsworth Ross, "The Suppression of Important News," *Atlantic Monthly*, March 1910, 310.

13   Ross, "Suppression," 304; Robert La Follette, *La Follette's Autobiography*, 259; William Salisbury, *The Career of a Journalist* (New York: B. W. Dodge, 1908), 523.

14   Sinclair, *Brass Check*, 285.

15   Ibid., 294.

16   Ibid., 222.

17   Ibid., 262.

18   Ibid., 404.

19   Ibid., 353.

20   Ibid., 221.

21   Ibid., 234.

22   Ibid., 421.

23   Ibid., 440.

24   Ibid., 201.

25   Ibid., 325–26.

26   One of those exceptions was the movement to establish a significant nonprofit and non-commercial component to U.S. radio broadcasting in the early 1930s. See Robert W. McChesney, *Telecommunications, Mass Media, and Democracy: The Battle for the Control of U.S. Broadcasting, 1928–1935* (New York: Oxford University Press, 1993).

27   Sinclair, *Brass Check*, 276.

28   Ibid., 248. A striking example of this is television journalist Ted Koppel's response to Disney's plan to replace Koppel's highly successful news-interview show *Nightline* on ABC (owned by Disney) with the David Letterman comedy-entertainment show, if Disney could lure the comedian from CBS. According to Koppel, "It is perfectly understandable that Disney would jump at the opportunity to increase earnings." Koppel quoted in William Safire, *New York Times*, Op-Ed, March 7, 2002.

29   Irwin, *American*, 71.

30   James Squires, *Read All About It!* (New York: Times Books, 1993).

4. Telling the Truth at a Moment of Truth: U.S. News Media and the Invasion and Occupation of Iraq

This chapter first appeared in a slightly different form as Robert W. McChesney, "Telling the Truth at a Moment of Truth: US News Media and the Invasion and Occupations of Iraq," in Socialist Register 2006: Telling the Truth, *ed. Leo Panitch and Colin Leys (New York: Monthly Review Press, 2005), 116–33. Portions of this chapter later appreared in* Tragedy & Farce, *the book I authored with John Nichols in 2005.*

1   Letter to W. T. Barry, August 4, 1822, in *Letters and Other Writings of James Madison*, vol. 3, ed. Philip R. Fendall (Philadelphia: Lippincott, 1865), 276.

2   See Karl Marx, *On Freedom of the Press and Censorship*, ed. and trans. Saul K. Padover (New York: McGraw-Hill, 1974).

3   See Robert W. McChesney, *The Problem of the Media* (New York: Monthly Review Press, 2004), chapter 2.

4   Edward S. Herman and Noam Chomsky, *Manufacturing Consent: The Political Economy of the News Media* (New York: Pantheon, 1988).

5   Howard Friel and Richard A. Falk, *The Paper of Record: How the New York Times Misreports U.S. Foreign Policy* (New York: Verso, 2004).

6   Jonathan Mermin, "The Media's Independence Problem," *World Policy Journal* 21/3 (2004): 69.

7   Steve Rendall and Tara Broughel, "Amplifying Officials, Squelching Dissent: FAIR Study Finds Democracy Poorly Served by War Coverage," *Extra!* May/June, 2003, http://www.fair.org/extra/0305/warstudy.html.

8   "Watchdogs of War," *Editor & Publisher*, September 8, 2003; Greg Mitchell, "Why We Are in Iraq," *Editor & Publisher*, September 8, 2003.

9   Cited in Eric Alterman, "'Case Closed.'" *The Nation*, April 25, 2005.

10   Glen Rangwala, "Claims in Secretary of State Colin Powell's UN Presentation Concerning Iraq, 5th Feb 2003," http://middleeastreference.org.uk/powell030205.html.

11   See, for example, Scott Ritter, "Is Iraq a True Threat to the US?" *Boston Globe*, July 20, 2002, http://www.commondreams.org/views02/072102.htm.

12   Antonia Zerbisias, "The Press Self-Muzzled Its Coverage of Iraq War," *Toronto Star*, September 16, 2003.

13   Mermin, "The Media's Independence Problem," 67.

14   Ibid.

15   Seymour Hersh, "The Unknown Unknowns of the Abu Ghraib Scandal," *Guardian*, May 21, 2005.

16   Michael Massing, "Iraq, the Press and the Election," *New York Review of Books*, December 16, 2004.

17   L. Roberts et al., "Mortality Before and After the 2003 Invasion of Iraq: Cluster Sample Survey," *The Lancet* 364 (9448), 1857-64. It should be noted that the figure of 100,000 deaths was a controversial one, arrived at by extrapolating from a comparison of prewar and wartime mortality rates in a sample of Iraqi neighborhoods. For a critique see Fred Kaplan, "100,000 Dead—or 8,000. How Many Iraqi Civilians have Died as a Result of the War?," October 29, 2004, http://slate.msn.com/id12108887. The effort to produce an accurate casualty estimate continues today. British and American researchers in the Iraq Body Count project maintain a database (http://www.countthecasualties.org.uk/) of media-reported civilian deaths in Iraq resulting from the military invasion and occupation. It estimates the casualties, in the period of January 1, 2003–June 15, 2005, to be between 22,248 and 25,229.

18   Howard Kurtz, "Paint by Numbers: How Repeated Reportage Colors Perceptions" (Media Notes), *Washington Post*, July 12, 2004.

19   Danny Schechter, "Is Our Media Covering Its Errors or Covering Them Up?," *CommonDreams.org*, August 16, 2004, http://www.commondreams.org/views04/0816-04.htm.

20   Mermin, "The Media's Independence Problem," 67–68.

21   Statements quoted in Massing, "Iraq, the Press and the Election." See also Michael Massing, "Now They Tell Us," *New York Review of Books*, February 26, 2004.

22   Massing, "Iraq, the Press and the Election."

23   Edward Wasserman, "Cowardice in the Newsrooms," *Miami Herald*, September 6, 2004.

24   Andrew Ackerman, "War Reporters at ASNE Say Iraq Remains Frightening," *Editor & Publisher*, April 15, 2005.

5. How to Think About Journalism: Looking Backward, Going Forward

Some of the material in this chapter appeared in Communication Revolution. *After publication herein, a revised version of this chapter appeared in* Explorations in Communication and History, *Barbie Zelizer, ed. (New York: Routledge, 2008).*

1   William Powers, "Hamlet's BlackBerry: Why Paper Is Eternal," Discussion Paper Series, Joan Shorenstein Center on the Press, Politics and Public Policy, Harvard University, 2007, 1.

2   See Naomi Wolf, *The End of America: Letter of Warning to a Young Patriot* (White River Junction, VT: Chelsea Green, 2007); Joe Conason, *It Can Happen Here: The Authoritarian Peril in the Age of Bush* (New York: St. Martin's Press, 2007). For a recent analysis of the importance of journalism for democracy, with an eye to the current crisis, see Jeffrey Scheuer, *The Big Picture: Why Democracies Need Journalistic Excellence* (New York: Routledge, 2008).

3   Leonard Downie Jr. and Robert G. Kaiser, *The News About the News: American Journalism in Peril* (New York: Alfred A. Knopf, 2002). See also Eugene Roberts, Thomas Kinkel, and Charles Layton, eds., *Leaving Readers Behind: The Age of Corporate Newspapering* (Fayetteville: University of Arkansas Press, 2001).

4   The report details the hard decline in the number of reporters actually covering communities over the past two decades as well as the domination of commercial values of the public interest in the determination of news. See Project for Excellence in Journalism, "State of the Media 2006: An Annual Report on American Journalism," http://www.stateofthenewsmedia.org/2006/index.asp.

5   Paula Constable, "Demise of the Foreign Correspondent," *Washington Post*, February 18, 2007; http://www.washingtonpost.com/wp-dyn/content/article/2007/02/16/AR2007021601713_pf.html.

6   Go to http://www.savejournalism.org/.

7   Michael Schudson, "Owning Up: A New Book Stops Short of Deepening the Discourse on Media Concentration," *Columbia Journalism Review*, January–February 2007, 58. See also Michael Schudson, *The Sociology of News* (New York: W. W. Norton, 2003), 38, 40.

8   Several authors have assessed the news coverage of the Iraq invasion and occupation. My analysis can be found in John Nichols and Robert W. McChesney, *Tragedy and Farce: How American Media Sell Wars, Spin Elections and Destroy Democracy* (New York: New Press, 2005). See also Jeff Cohen, *Cable News Confidential: My Misadventures in Corporate Media* (Sausalito, CA: PoliPoint Press, 2006); Robin Andersen, *A Century of Media, A Century of War* (New York: Peter Lang, 2006); Norman Solomon, *War Made Easy* (Hoboken, NJ: John Wiley & Sons, 2005); Frank Rich, *The Greatest Story Ever Sold: The Decline and Fall of Truth from 9/11 to Katrina* (New York: Penguin Press, 2006); Sheldon Rampton and John Stauber, *The Best War Ever: Lies, Damned Lies, and the Mess in Iraq* (New York: Penguin Books, 2006); Michael Isikoff and David Corn, *Hubris: The Inside Story of Spin, Scandal, and the Selling of the Iraq War* (New York: Crown, 2006); Bill Katovsky and Timothy Carlson, *Embedded: The Media At War in Iraq* (Guilford, CT: Lyons Press, 2003); Norman Solomon et al., *Target Iraq: What the News Media Didn't Tell You* (New York: Context Books, 2003); Philip M. Seib, *Beyond the Front Lines: How the News Media Cover a World Shaped by War* (New York: Palgrave Macmillan, 2004); Ralph D. Berenger, ed., *Global Media Go to War: Role of News and Entertainment Media During the 2003 Iraq War* (Spokane, WA: Marquette Books, 2004); Ralph D. Berrenger, ed., *Cybermedia Go to War: Role of Converging Media During and After the 2003 Iraq War* (Spokane, WA: Marquette Books, 2006); Michael Massing, *Now They Tell Us: The American Press and Iraq* (New York: New York Review Books, 2004); Howard Tumber, *Media at War: The Iraq Crisis* (London: Sage, 2004); Alexander G. Nikolaev and Ernest A. Hakanen, *Leading to the 2003 Iraq War: The Global Media Debate* (New York: Palgrave Macmillan, 2006); David Miller, *Tell Me Lies: Propaganda and Media Distortion in the Attack on Iraq* (London: Pluto Press, 2004); David Dadge, *The War in Iraq and Why the Media Failed Us* (Westport, CT: Praeger Publishers, 2006); Danny Schechter, *When News Lies: Media Complicity and the Iraq War* (New York: Select Books, 2006).

9   Gilbert Cranberg, "Cranberg wants a serious probe of why the press failed in its prewar reporting," *Nieman Watchdog*, February 7, 2007, http://www.niemanwatchdog.org/index.cfm?fuseaction=ask_this.view&as kthisid=00261.

10   Neil Henry, *American Carnival: Journalism Under Siege in an Age of New Media* (Berkeley: University of California Press, 2007).

11   This argument in defense of allowing greater media concentration has a loud proponent in FCC Chair Kevin Martin. See Kevin J. Martin, "The Daily Show," *New York Times*, November 13, 2007.

12   See Thomas E. Patterson, preparer, *Creative Destruction: An Exploratory Look at News on the Internet* (Cambridge, MA: Joan Shorenstein Center on the Press, Politics and Public Policy, Harvard University, August 2007), 13.

13   See Jennifer Saba, "The New Math: Putting Numbers to Work for You," *Editor & Publisher*, January 2008, 22–24.

14   See: John H. McManus, *Market-Driven Journalism: Let the Citizen Beware?* (Thousand Oaks, CA: Sage, 1994); Penn Kimball, *Downsizing the News: Network Cutbacks in the Nation's Capital* (Washington, DC: Woodrow Wilson Center, 1994); James D. Squires, *Read All About It! The Corporate Takeover of America's Newspapers* (New York: Random House, 1995); Doug Underwood, *When MBAs Rule the Newsroom: How Marketers and Managers are Reshaping Today's Media* (New York: Columbia University Press, 1993).

15   For a recent discussion of this issue by an ex-journalist, see David Simon, "Does the News Matter to Anyone Anymore?" *Washington Post*, January 22, 2008.

16   This is research that Ben Scott has been doing at the University of Illinois and is the basis of his Ph.D. dissertation, "Labor's New Deal for Journalism: The Newspaper Guild in the 1930s" (University of Illinois, 2007).

17   See Al Gore, *An Inconvenient Truth: The Crisis of Global Warming* (New York: Viking, 2006), 160–65. Gore pursues this issue again in *The Assault on Reason* (New York: Penguin Press, 2007), chapter 7.

18   See Theodore Hamm, *Gloves Off: How the New Blue Media Is Reshaping Progressive Politics* (New York: New Press, 2008).

19   See Benjamin R. Barber, *Consumed* (New York: W. W. Norton, 2007).

20   Go to http://www.publicintegrity.org. See also: John H. Cushman Jr., "Web Site Assembles U.S. Prewar Claims," *New York Times*, January 23, 2008.

21   See also Danny Schechter, "New Study Claims Mistruths Shaped Rush to War," Common Dreams Web site, January 24, 2008.

22   See Carlin Romano, "Big Fish and Small Fry," *Columbia Journalism Review*, January–February 2008, 50.

23   Although two of the books were published in 1980, they were all written in the 1970s. Herbert Gans, *Deciding What's News: A Study of CBS Evening News, NBC Nightly News, Newsweek and Time* (New York: Random House, 1979); Mark Fishman, *Manufacturing the News* (Austin: University of Texas Press, 1980); Gaye Tuchman, *Making News: A Study in the Construction of Reality* (New York: Free Press, 1978); Todd Gitlin, *The Whole World Is Watching: Mass Media in the Making and Unmaking of the Left* (Berkeley: University of California Press, 1980). One other excellent book on journalism produced in the 1970s was journalist Edward Jay Epstein's *News from Nowhere: Television and the News* (New York: Vintage Books, 1973). Another sociologist who wrote an influential book on journalism in this period was Michael Schudson, *Discovering the News: A Social History of American Newspapers* (New York: Basic Books, 1978).

24   The critical work in Britain in the 1970s produced a good deal of work on journalism, some of it was influential on this side of the Atlantic. But it never provided the basis for a critique that would generate fruitful studies of U.S. journalism that would have significant staying power in the United States. One of the classic works that I read in graduate school

and found eye-opening was: Glasgow University Media Group, *Bad News* (London: Routledge and Kegan Paul, 1976). There were several other volumes published by this research group. See also Stuart Hall, Chas Critcher, Tony Jefferson, and Brian Roberts, *Policing the Crisis* (London: Macmillan, 1978).

25   Herman and Chomsky had clear differences from Bagdikian in tone and emphasis, and much was made of their being radicals whereas Bagdikian was a liberal. Bagdikian was certainly accorded more respect by working journalists. There are important differences between them and they are worth pursuing, but they are in my opinion much less important than the common ground the three authors share. I have read their works closely and have had the privilege of getting to know all three of them quite well. The more I studied them and spoke with them, the more I found their critiques of journalism to be highly complementary.

26   "Wordplay," *Time*, June 6, 1983.

27   John F. Burns, "Moscow Broadcaster Who Altered Scripts Is Returned to Work," *New York Times*, December 15, 1983.

28   Noam Chomsky is responsible for shining a light on the Danchev affair, and pondering its implications for Western news media. See Noam Chomsky, *Necessary Illusions: Thought Control in Democratic Societies* (Boston: South End Press, 1989), 144; see, in particular, Noam Chomsky, "Afghanistan and Vietnam," in *The Chomsky Reader,* James Peck, ed. (New York: Pantheon Books, 1987), 223–26.

29   For a fascinating set of essays on the role of propaganda in the United States today, several of which are written by prominent journalists, see Andras Szanto, ed., *What Orwell Didn't Know: Propaganda and the New Face of American Politics* (New York: Public Affairs, 2007).

30   See, in particular, *Corporate Media and the Threat to Democracy* (New York: Seven Stories Press, 1997).

31   There is another story, better known, of a group of Soviets, not journalists, touring the United States. After reading the newspapers and watching TV, they were amazed to find that, on the big issues, all the opinions were the same. "In our country," they said, "to get that result we have a dictatorship, we imprison people, we tear out their fingernails. Here you have none of that. So what's your secret? How do you do it?" See John Pilger, *Tell Me No Lies* (New York: Random House, 2004), 9.

32   This is the text of the First Amendment: "Congress shall make no law respecting an establishment of religion, or prohibiting the free exercise thereof; or abridging the freedom of speech, or of the press; or the right of the people peaceably to assemble, and to petition the government for a redress of grievances."

33   C. Edwin Baker, "The Independent Significance of the Press Clause Under Existing Law," Presentation to the Reclaiming the First Amendment: Constitutional Theories of Media Reform Conference, Hofstra University, Hempstead, New York, January 19, 2007.

34   A classic example is Potter Stewart, "Or of the Press," *Hastings Law Journal* 26/631 (1975). See also: Gerald Gunther and Kathleen M. Sullivan, "Freedom of the Press," in *Constitutional Law*, 13th ed. (Westbury, NY: Foundation Press, 1997), 1420–60; Geoffrey R. Stone et al., "Freedom of the Press," in *Constitutional Law*, 5th ed. (New York: Aspen Publishers, 2005), 1442–83.

35   Whenever I write about freedom of the press issues and the Constitution I find myself invoking the name Ed Baker, because his work provides the foundation on which I stand. It is ironic that a law professor is doing so much cutting-edge communication research. His lat-

est book is another example of his enormous talent: C. Edwin Baker, *Media Concentration and Democracy: Why Ownership Matters* (New York: Cambridge University Press, 2006).

36   In what follows do not mistake my position on the Founders and Madison and Jefferson. They are not deities. Although I find their writings on freedom of the press enlightened and extraordinary, they were complex figures and far from perfect, even if viewed from the vantage point of their own historical period. I discuss the antidemocratic aspects of Madison's thought in *Rich Media, Poor Democracy*. A recent talk by my colleague Pedro Cabán delved into the racism and white supremacy of the Founders. Pedro Cabán, comments for the forum, "Disempowering Racial Oppression, Discontinuing Chief Illiniwek and Other Forms of Racial 'Entertainment,'" University of Illinois at Urbana-Champaign, February 9, 2007.

37   I discuss this at some length in Robert W. McChesney, *The Problem of the Media* (New York: Monthly Review Press), chapter 1.

38   As Mark Lloyd makes clear in *Prologue to a Farce*, the nature of capitalism in the United States in the founding period through much of the nineteenth century was quite unlike what we think of as capitalism today. For starters, the majority of people were neither employers nor employees. They were self-employed farmers, tradespeople, mechanics, etc. And corporations barely existed. In this environment, the idea that private media were regarded as large profit-generating corporate entities was nonexistent and would be for a good century. U.S. history from this period is filled with ringing denunciations of the emerging corporate sector from leading figures, both on economic and political grounds. As Lloyd demonstrates, Lincoln made a series of criticisms of corporations, and even capitalism, which were not entirely dissimilar to what Karl Marx was writing at the same time in England. See Mark Lloyd, *Prologue to a Farce: Democracy and Communication in America* (Urbana: University of Illinois Press, 2007), 60–61, 294.

39   See, for example, Eric Burns, *Infamous Scribblers: The Founding Fathers and the Rowdy Beginnings of American Journalism* (New York: Public Affairs, 2006).

40   For some sense of the crucial role of the press in the development of participatory democracy in the United States, see Sean Wilentz, *The Rise of American Democracy: Jefferson to Lincoln* (New York: W. W. Norton, 2005).

41   My point in this discussion is not to reify the Constitution. It is not a flawless document. See Sanford Levinson, *Our Undemocratic Constitution: Where the Constitution Goes Wrong (And How We the People Can Correct It)* (New York: Oxford University Press, 2006); Bruce Ackerman, *The Failure of the Founding Fathers: Jefferson, Madison, and the Rise of Presidential Democracy* (Cambridge: Belknap Press of Harvard University Press, 2005). Even if I thought the Founders explicitly conceived of the First Amendment as requiring a corporate-run, commercial media system regardless of the consequences for self-government, my argument in this book would remain the same. Fortunately, I believe there is powerful evidence to suggest that the Constitution can and should be interpreted in the manner I suggest. One of the great strengths of the Founders, especially Madison and Jefferson, was their bedrock understanding of the role of a free press in self-government, and their understanding of what this entailed in an institutional sense. It is one of the great contributions of U.S. politics to the world.

42   *Associated Press v. United States*, 326 U.S. 1 (1945), http://caselaw.lp.findlaw.com/scripts/getcase.pl?court=US&vol=326&invol=1.

43   *New York Times Co. v. United States*, 403 U.S. 713 (1971), http://www.law.cornell.edu/supct/html/historics/USSC_CR_0403_0713_ZC.html.

44   *New York Times Co. v. United States*, 403 U.S. 713 (1971), http://www.law.cornell.edu/ supct/html/historics/USSC_CR_0403_0713_ZC3.html.

45   This figure is derived by the staff of FCC commissioner Michael Copps in consultation with various experts and based upon evaluating the amounts raised during recent spectrum auctions. See "Remarks of Commissioner Michael J. Copps," National Conference on Media Reform, Memphis, Tennessee, January 12, 2007.

46   For a detailed investigation of this "irony" of deregulation, see Robert Britt Horwitz, *The Irony of Regulatory Reform: The Deregulation of American Telecommunications* (New York: Oxford University Press, 1989).

47   See, for a recent example, "Net Discrimination," *Wall Street Journal*, January 2, 2007.

48   Sandra Braman has extended this argument, contending that the nature of the modern state has been transformed in the past few decades from a bureaucratic welfare state to an "information state," with information policymaking at its heart. Her argument will be a subject of debate and study in the field in the coming years. See Sandra Braman, *Change of State: Information, Policy, Power* (Cambridge: MIT Press, 2006).

49   Amy Schatz, "Industry Braces for Net-Neutrality Fallout," *Wall Street Journal*, January 2, 2007.

50   Comments of Edward Markey, National Conference on Media Reform, Memphis, Tennessee, January 13, 2007.

51   Kate Ackley, "AT&T Takes Shape as Lobbying Giant," *Roll Call*, February 20, 2007.

52   See Common Cause, *Wolves in Sheep's Clothing: Telecom Industry Front Groups and Astroturf* (Washington, DC: Common Cause, 2006), available at http://www.common-cause.org/site/pp.asp?c=dkLNK1MQIwG&b=1499059.

The classic text on this practice is Sheldon Rampton and John Stauber, *Toxic Sludge Is Good for You: Lies, Damn Lies and the Public Relations Industry* (Monroe, ME: Common Courage Press, 1995). For two recent examples of this practice by communication firms, see the Web site for Verizon's Consumers for Tech Choice, which organizes popular support for Verizon's positions in Massachusetts: http://www.consumersfortechchoice.org/. Note that the name Verizon cannot even be located on the Web site. In Illinois AT&T created TV4US to do its bidding surreptitiously. See Anna Marie Kukec, "'Astroturf' groups represent industries, not members," *Daily Herald*, February 11, 2007; http://www.daily-herald.com/business/story.asp?id=280048.

More broadly, in view of what is at stake in terms of government subsidies and licenses, the industry lobbying effort is no surprise. They spend this amount because they are fighting with each other for the biggest slice of the pie.

53   See Jeff Chester, *Digital Destiny: New Media and the Future of Democracy* (New York: New Press, 2007).

54   Robert W. McChesney, "Free Speech and Democracy: Louis G. Caldwell, the American Bar Association, and the Debate Over the Free Speech Implications of Broadcast Regulation, 1928–1938," *American Journal of Legal History* 35 (October 1991): 351–92.

55   Viewed this way the framing of debates around media looking exclusively or primarily at "media concentration" is wide of the mark, at times even a red herring. Even if concentration in a media sector is not increasing, or may even be in decline, that does not mean all is well in the world. Media concentration tends to be a bad thing, but it is far from the only thing that matters in media. To the "immaculate conception" crowd, once it is shown that concentration is not growing at dramatic rates, the conclusion is invariably that the system works just fine, thank you, and critics should shut up and shop. The real issue is why

do we create and subsidize media systems built around profit-maximization and advertising in the manner that we do? I am reminded of the Chinese student dissidents in the late 1980s when they protested the meetings of Chinese government leaders with elected heads of state. "Who elected you?" they would chant. That is the question to be asked about the WGNs and AT&Ts in our world: "Who elected you?"

56   I approached the top telecommunication or media researchers at each of the four "free-market" think tanks in 2007 asking if they could help me determine the size of the subsidy in a number of specific areas. I thought this might be an area of interest because these think tanks tended to be so adamantly opposed to government subsidies and welfare that they might be interested in determining the extent of such practices. I received gracious and thoughtful replies in three cases; in each response, I was informed that this was an area they knew nothing about and they knew no one who was working on the subject. The other think tank did not respond, and on none of the Web sites did I find any research remotely close to this topic. It is worth noting that some economists raised concerns about the "rents" AT&T received as a result of its monopoly status back in the 1960s and 1970s. The point then was more to open up the telecommunications market to other firms than to consider what the public might rightfully demand in exchange for those rents.

57   See chapter 4 in this volume, and McChesney, *The Problem of the Media.*

58   The Knight Foundation produced research along these lines in 2006. Go to http://firstamendmentfuture.org/.

59   See Joe Strupp, "Another Chip in the Wall," *Editor & Publisher*, January 2008, 30–36.

60   Due to government polices, the Internet in China is very different from the Internet elsewhere. See "Alternative Reality," *The Economist*, February 2, 2008, 69–70.

61   "Spies, Lies and FISA," *New York Times*, October 14, 2007.

62   James Rorty, *Our Master's Voice: Advertising* (New York: John Day, 1934).

63   And not just Americans. Digital technology has converted China into a nation filled with video screens pummeling people with advertising. See Frederik Balfour, "Catching the Eye of China's Elite," *Business Week*, February 11, 2008, 55–56.

64   Richard Hoffman, "When It Comes to Broadband, U.S. Plays Follow the Leader," *Information Week*, February 15, 2007, http://www.informationweek.com/story/showArticle.jhtml?articleID=197006038. This piece draws from: S. Derek Turner, *Broadband Reality Check II: The Truth Behind Americas Digital Decline* (Free Press, September 2006). Available at www.freepress.net/docs/bbrc2-final.pdf.

65   Comments of Markey, National Conference on Media Reform.

66   For a discussion of how AT&T came to dominate the South through dubious political influence, not by providing good service in the market, see Kenneth Lipartito, *The Bell System and Regional Business: The Telephone in the South, 1877–1920* (Baltimore: Johns Hopkins University Press, 1989).

67   Kent Gibbons, "Five Questions for Jeff Chester," *MultiChannel News*, February 5, 2007, available at http://www.multichannel.com/article/CA6413144.html?display=Opinion.

68   Comments of Markey, National Conference on Media Reform.

69   Quoted in a PBS Bill Moyers special, *The Net at Risk*, broadcast in October 2006, http://www.pbs.org/moyers/moyersonamerica/print/netatrisk_transcript_print.html.

70   Even a former top executive in the telecommunication and cable industries has spoken up on the crucial need to preserve Net Neutrality. See Leo Hindery, "Let Cable Companies Compete in Battle for Broadband," *Financial Times*, January 18, 2008, 9.

71   Michael Calabrese, email to the author, February 9, 2007.

72   Tim Wu, "Wireless Network Neutrality," Social Science Research Network working paper, January 2007, http://papers.ssrn.com/sol3/papers.cfm?abstract_id=962027; for Milton Mueller's work, go to http://blog.internetgovernance.org/blog.

73   Because this chapter addresses journalism specifically, I will stop the discussion here, recognizing that digital communication is radically overturning most media industries. Music is already on the chopping block; terrestrial broadcasting, daily newspapers, and film are in the on-deck circle. All the other media industries are in line behind them, waiting their turn. We need to rethink copyright and intellectual property laws so that creative workers can receive just compensation for their labor without letting corporations put up barbed wire all over cyberspace, destroying the public domain and handcuffing creativity. In many respects, the commercial media system as it has developed is a very bad fit for digital technology. Copyright has become, to some extent, a policy to protect out-of-date industries from change that would benefit everyone else, rather than a progressive policy and subsidy to promote creativity and culture.

74   Phil Rosenthal, "Cap Times Puts Cap on Print Editions," *Chicago Tribune*, February 10, 2008.

75   See Scott Gant, *We're All Journalists Now: The Transformation of the Press and Reshaping of the Law in the Internet Age* (New York: Free Press, 2007).

76   See, for example, Cass R. Sunstein, *Infotopia: How Many Minds Produce Knowledge* (New York: Oxford University Press, 2006).

77   A recent study by the Government Accountability Office puts the present and future of public television in bleak terms barring major policy intervention. See: United States Government Accounting Office, *Telecommunications: Issues Related to the Structure and Funding of Public Television* (Washington: United States Government Accounting Office, January 2007), available at http://www.gao.gov/new.items/d07150.pdf.

78   Cass Sunstein, "How the Rise of the Daily Me Threatens Democracy," *Financial Times*, January 11, 2008, 9.

79   See the September–October 2007 edition of *Extra!*, the publication of Fairness & Accuracy In Reporting, for a special issue on how the news media ignore the issues of concern to the poor and working class.

80   Overholser is working on developing a variety of structural policy measures. See Geneva Overholser, "On Behalf of Journalism: A Manifesto for Change," paper published by the Annenberg Public Policy Center, University of Pennsylvania, 2006, available at: http://www.annenbergpublicpolicycenter.org/Overholser/20061011_JournStudy.pdf. For background, see Geneva Overholser and Kathleen Hall Jamieson, eds., *The Press* (New York: Oxford University Press, 2005).

81   Charles Lewis, "The Nonprofit Road," *Columbia Journalism Review*, September–October 2007, 32–36.

82   Bree Nordenson, "The Uncle Sam Solution," *Columbia Journalism Review*, September–October 2007, 37–41.

83   "I used to feel that there was hope in addressing corporate governance. I was part of a group of former editors pressing for such measures as more retired journalists on boards, committees to audit journalism and the like. I think it's too late for that now, the crisis is too advanced. We need more sweeping reform proposals that might provide dramatic change to address the magnitude of this crisis." Geneva Overholser, email to the author, February 26, 2007.

84   James Rainey, "Scion Offers Ideas for Times: In an opinion piece to run Sunday, Harry
      Chandler proposes community ownership," *Los Angeles Times*, November 11, 2006;
      Harry B. Chandler, "A Chandler's Advice for the L.A. Times: The newspaper can only
      thrive if its owners and editors make drastic changes," *Los Angeles Times*, November 12,
      2006.

85   See, for example, C. Wright Mills, *The Power Elite* (New York: Oxford University Press,
      1956); C. B. Macpherson, *The Life and Times of Liberal Democracy* (New York: Oxford
      University Press, 1977).

86   This is why collective action—e.g., independent labor unions—is the foundation of mass
      democratic political action, and why it is despised by those who benefit by the existing
      division of power.

87   In November 1864, for example, as the postwar era was on the horizon, Lincoln wrote: "I
      see in the near future a crisis approaching that unnerves me and causes me to tremble for
      the safety of my country. As a result of the war, corporations have been enthroned and an
      era of corruption in high places will follow, and the money power of the country will
      endeavor to prolong its reign by working upon the prejudices of the people until all wealth
      is aggregated into a few hands and the Republic is destroyed." See Lloyd, *Prologue to a
      Farce: Democracy and Communication in America,* 60–61, 294.

6. The Battle for the U.S. Airwaves, 1928–1935

*This chapter first appeared in a slightly different form as Robert W. McChesney, "The
Battle for the U.S. Airwaves, l928–l935,"* Journal of Communication 40/4 *(1990): 29–57.*

1   For work by scholars who have been willing to examine the political and economic foun-
     dations of mass communication see Noam Chomsky, *Necessary Illusions: Thought Control
     in Democratic Societies* (Boston: South End Press, 1989); Edward S. Herman and Noam
     Chomsky, *Manufacturing Consent: The Political Economy of the Mass Media* (New York:
     Pantheon Books, 1988); Herbert I. Schiller, *Culture. Inc.: The Corporate Takeover of
     Public Expression* (New York: Oxford University Press, 1989).

2   The best treatment probably has been Philip T. Rosen, *The Modern Stentors: Radio
     Broadcasters and the Federal Government, 1920–1934* (Westport, CT: Greenwood Press,
     1980), 161–78. Since the Communications Act of 1934 largely restated the Radio Act of
     1927 verbatim, the preponderance of the scholarship concludes the "real debate" over
     broadcasting must have taken place prior to 1927. If one concentrates upon that period,
     one would be perfectly justified in arguing that the status quo emerged without significant
     opposition. For excellent scholarship that addresses this earlier period see Mary S.
     Mander, "The Public Debate About Broadcasting in the Twenties: An Interpretive
     History," *Journal of Broadcasting* 25 (Spring 1984): 167–85; see also Susan J. Douglas,
     Inventing American Broadcasting, 1899–1922 (Baltimore: Johns Hopkins University
     Press, 1987); Elaine J. Prostak, "'Up In the Air': The Debate Over Radio Use In the
     1920s," Ph.D. dissertation (University of Kansas at Lawrence, 1983); Susan Renee
     Smulyan, "'And Now a Word From Our Sponsors': Commercialization of American
     Broadcast Radio, 1920–1934," Ph.D. dissertation (Yale University, 1985).

3   Federal Communications Commission, *Digest of Hearings, Federal Communications
     Commission Broadcast Division, under Sec. 307(c) of "The Communications Act of 1934"
     October 1–20, November 7–12, 1934* (Washington, DC: FCC. 1935), 180–249; S. E.
     Frost, *Educations Own Stations* (Chicago: University of Chicago Press, 1937), 4.

4   C. M. Jansky Jr., "The Problem of the Institutionally Owned Station" in *Radio and Education: Proceedings of the Second Annual Assembly of the National Advisory Council on Radio in Education. Inc. 1932*, ed. Levering Tyson (Chicago: University of Chicago Press, 1932), 213–23; Werner J. Severin, "Commercial vs. Noncommercial Radio During Broadcasting's Early Years,"*Journal of Broadcasting* 20 (Fall 1978): 491–504.

5   Henry A. Bellows, "The Right to Use Radio," *Public Utilities Fortnightly*, June 27, 1929, 770–74; Jansky Jr., "The Problem," 215.

6   Martin Codel, "Who Pays for Your Radio Program?" *Nation's Business* 17 (August 1929): 39; "Federal Control of Radio Broadcasting" *Yale Law Journal* 32 (1929): 250; U.S. Congress, House of Representatives. 70th Cong., 1st Sess. *Hearings Before the Committee on the Merchant Marine and Fisheries* on *H. R. 8825* (Washington, DC: U.S. Government Printing Office, 1928), 129.

7   Merlin H. Aylesworth, "Radio's Accomplishment," *Century* 118 (1929): 214–21; David Sarnoff, "Address to Chicago Chamber of Commerce, April 1924" in *Broadcasting Its New Day*, ed. Samuel L. Rothafel and Raymond Francis Yates (New York: Arno Press, 1971), 171–84.

8   John W. Spalding, "1928: Radio Becomes a Mass Advertising Medium," *Journal of Broadcasting* 8 (1963–1964): 31–44.

9   Carl J. Friedrich and Jeanette Sayre, *The Development of the Control of Advertising on the Air* (New York: Radio Broadcasting Research Project, 1940); Edward F. Sarno, "The National Radio Conferences," *Journal of Broadcasting* 13 (1969): 189–202.

10   *Education by Radio,* February 12,1931; Jansky Jr., "The Problem," 214–17.

11   Marvin R. Bensman, "The Zenith-WJAZ Case and the Chaos of 1926–27," *Journal of Broadcasting* 14 (Fall 1970): 423–40; Stephen B. Davis, "The Law or the Air," in *The Radio Industry: The Story of Its Development*, ed. Anton de Haas (Chicago: A. W. Shaw, 1928), 150–88; Daniel E. Garvey, "Secretary Hoover and the Quest for Broadcast Regulation," *Journalism History* 3 (Autumn 1976): 66–70, 85; "Pending Litigation Marks Beginning of Radio Jurisprudence," *American Bar Association Journal* 15 (March 1929): 173–78.

12   Erik Barnouw, *A Tower in Babel* (New York: Oxford University Press, 1966), 281; Carl J. Friedrich and Evelyn Sternberg, "Congress and the Control of Radio Broadcasting," *American Political Science Review* 37 (October 1943): 797–818; Donald G. Godfrey, "The 1927 Radio Act: People and Politics," *Journalism History* 4 (Autumn 1977): 74–78; National University Extension Association, Committee on Radio Broadcasting, "Report of the Committee on Radio Broadcasting," in *Proceedings of the Twelfth Annual Convention of the National University Extension Association 1927*, vol. 10, (Boston: Wright & Potter, 1927), 182–88.

13   Louis G. Caldwell, "The Standard of Public Interest, Convenience or Necessity as Used in the Radio Act of 1927," *Air Law Review* 1 (July 1930): 295–330; Clarence C. Dill, "Safe-Guarding the Ether—The American Way," *Congressional Digest* (August–September 1933): 194–196.

14   James M. Herring, "Public Interest, Convenience or Necessity in Radio Broadcasting," *Harvard Business Review* 10 (April 1932): 280–91.

15   American Bar Association, Standing Committee on Radio Law, "Report of the Standing Committee on Radio Law," in *Report of the Fifty-second Annual Meeting of the American Bar Association, 1929* (Baltimore: Lord Baltimore Press, 1929), 404–506; Laurence F. Schmeckebier, *The Federal Radio Commission* (Washington, DC: Brookings Institution,

1932), 22–23.

16   U.S. Congress, Senate, 70th Cong., 2d Sess., *Hearings Before the Committee* on *Interstate Commerce on S. 4937* (Washington, DC: U.S. Government Printing Office, 1929), 24.

17   U.S. Congress, House of Representatives. 70th Cong., 1st Sess. *Hearings Before the Committee on the Merchant Marine and Fisheries* on *H. R. 8825* (Washington, DC: U.S. Government Printing Office, 1928), 68, 74, 108–9; U.S. Congress, Senate. 70th Cong., 1st Sess., *Hearings Before Committee on Interstate Commerce on the Confirmation of Federal Radio Commissioners* (Washington, DC: U.S. Government Printing Office, 1928), pt. 2, 192.

18   American Bar Association, "Report of the Standing Committee on Radio Law," 57. Murray Edelman, *The Licensing of Radio Services in the United States, 1927 to 1947* (Urbana: University of Illinois Press, 1950), 38–39.

19   Harold A. LaFount, "Educational Programs in Radio Broadcasting," *School and Society* 34 (December 5 1931): 758–60.

20   U.S. Congress, *Hearings Before Committee on Interstate Commerce*, 1928, pt. 1, 151, 191; U.S. Congress, *Hearings Before the Committee on Interstate Commerce on S. 4937*, 142.

21   Bethuel M. Webster Jr., "Notes on the Policy of the Administration with Reference to the Control of Communications," *Air Law Review* 5 (April 1934): 107–31.

22   American Bar Association, "Report of the Standing Committee on Radio Law," 459.

23   Lucas A. Powe Jr., *American Broadcasting and the First Amendment* (Berkeley: University of California Press, 1987), 65.

24   U.S. Congress. House of Representatives. 70th Cong., 2d Sess., *Hearings Before the Committee on the Merchant Marine and Fisheries on H.R. 15430* (Washington, DC: U.S. Government Printing Office, 1929), pt. 1, 75.

25   "The Menace of Radio Monopoly," *Education by Radio*, March 26, 1931, 27; "The Power Trust and the Public Schools," *Education by Radio*, December 10, 1931, 150; Thomas Porter Robinson, *Radio Networks and the Federal Government* (New York: Columbia University Press, 1943), 26–27; Christopher H. Sterling, *Electronic Media: A Guide to Trends in Broadcasting and Newer Technologies, 1920–1983* (New York: Praeger, 1984), 12.

26   Cited in "Radio Censorship and the Federal Communications Commission," *Columbia Law Review 39* (March 1939): 447–59.

27   "Chain Income from Time Sales," *Variety*, January 8, 1935, 40; Herman S. Hettinger, "Some Fundamental Aspects of Radio Broadcasting," *Harvard Business Review* 13 (1935): 14–28.

28   Henry Volkening, "Abuses of Radio Broadcasting," *Current History 33* (December 1930): 396–400.

29   Barnouw, *A Tower in Babel*, 270; Rosen, *The Modern Stentors*, 12.

30   W. S. Gregson. letter to B. B. Brackett, February 25, 1932, National Association of Educational Broadcasters Manuscripts, Wisconsin Historical Society, Madison, Wisconsin, Box 1a, General Correspondence, 1932.

31   *Congressional Record 78*, May 15, 1934, 8830–34; Federal Communications Commission, *Digest of Hearings, Federal Communications Commission Broadcast Division, under Sec. 307(c) of "The Communications Act of 1934"* October 1–20, November 7–12, 1934, 180–249; "Superpower," *Education by Radio*, May 7, 1931, 50.

32 Federal Radio Commission, *Third Annual Report of the Federal Radio Commission to the Congress of the United States* (Washington, DC: U.S. Government Printing Office, 1929), 31–36.

33 *Education by Radio,* May 7, 1931, 49.

34 Harold A. LaFount, "Contributions of the Federal Radio Commission," in *Education on the Air: Second Yearbook of the Institute of Education by Radio,* ed. Josephine H. MacLatchy (Columbus: Ohio State University, 1931), 14–20.

35 Joy Elmer Morgan (statement), "On Behalf of the National Committee on Education by Radio and the National Education Association," in *Official Report of Proceedings Before the Federal Communications Commission . . . Hearings in Re: Before the Broadcast Division of the Federal Communications Commission* on *Section 307(c) of the Communications Act of 1934,* vol. 1, Smith & Hulse, Official Reporters (Washington, DC: FCC, 1935), 19–29, 43–48.

36 Advisory Committee on Education by Radio (Wilbur Committee), *Report of the Advisory Committee on Education by Radio Appointed by the Secretary of the Interior* (Columbus, OH: F. J. Heer, 1930).

37 W. J. Cooper, Letter of Transmittal, Office of Education Manuscripts, National Archives, Washington, DC, RG 12, Box 31; *Proceedings, Conference* on *Radio Education Problems, October 13, 1990* (Washington, DC, 1930), 7.

38 The nine organizers were the NEA, the National University Extension Association, the American Council on Education, the National Council of State Superintendents, the Association of College and University Broadcasting Stations, the Jesuit Educational Association, the National Catholic Educational Association, the Association of the Land Grant Colleges and Universities, and the National Association of State Universities.

39 Joy Elmer Morgan, "The National Committee on Education by Radio," in MacLatchy, *Education on the Air: Second Yearbook of the Institute of Education by Radio,* 3–14.

40 "Education Demands Freedom of the Air," *Education by Radio,* April 28, 1932, 64; Joy Elmer Morgan, "Education's Rights on the Air," in *Radio and Education: Proceedings of the First Assembly of the National Advisory Council on Radio in Education, 1931,* ed. Levering Tyson (Chicago: University of Chicago Press, 1931), 120–136.

41 Morgan, "Education's Rights on the Air," 123, 128; Joy Elmer Morgan and E. D. Bullock, *Selected Articles on Municipal Ownership* (Minneapolis, MN: Wilson, 1911).

42 Morgan, "Education's Rights on the Air," 120–21.

43 Joy Elmer Morgan, "The Radio in Education," in *Proceedings of the 17th Annual Convention of the National University Extension Association 1932,* vol. 15 (Bloomington: Indiana University Press, 1932), 74–87.

44 Nathan Godfried, "The Origins of Labor Radio: WCFT, the 'Voice of Labor,' 1925–1928," *Historical Journal of Film, Radio and Television* 7 (1987): 143–59; Robert W. McChesney, "Crusade Against Mammon: Father Harney, WLWL and the Debate over Radio in the 1930s," *Journalism History* 14 (Winter 1987): 118–30.

45 Godfried, "The Origins," 149.

46 American Federation of Labor, "Resolution No. 171.200," in *Report of the Fifty-Fourth Annual Convention of the American Federation of Labor Held at San Francisco, California October 1 to 12, Inclusive 1934* (Washington, DC: Judd & DetWeiler, 1934), 611–12; "Massachusetts Urges Government Radio," *Education by Radio,* September 19, 1935, 47.

47   Edward N. Nockels, *Public Interest, Convenience, and Necessity, and the Last of the Public Domain* (Washington, DC: 1936), 13.

48   Edward N. Nockels, "The Voice of Labor," *American Federationist* 37 (April 1930): 414–19.

49   William Leiss, Stephen Kline, and Sut Jhally, *Social Communication in Advertising: Persons, Products, and Images of Well Being* (New York: Methuen, 1986), 78; Frank W. Peers, *The Politics of Canadian Broadcasting, 1920–1951* (Toronto: University of Toronto Press, 1969), 77.

50   "Government Operation Proposed," *Education by Radio*, October 17, 1935, 51.

51   "A.N.PA Fails to Renew Radio Attack, California Body Urges European System," *Broadcasting*, December 1, 1931, 8; "Broadcasting Doesn't Belong in Advertising Account," *Printer's Ink*, August 6, 1925, 125–128; Robert S. Mann, "After All, Why Radio Advertising?" *Editor & Publisher*, June 6, 1931, 12; "A Mistake to Broadcast Advertising by Radio," *Printer's Ink*, February 22, 1923, 157.

52   H. O. Davis, *Empire of the Air* (Ventura, CA: Ventura Free Press, 1932); Ventura Free Press, *American Broadcasting: An Analytic Study of One Day's Output of 206 Commercial Radio Stations Including Program Contents and Advertising Interruptions* (Ventura, CA: Ventura Free Press, 1933).

53   "Radio Threat Concerns Press, Says Don Gilman," *Broadcasting*, February 15, 1932, 8.

54   "Radio and the Press," *Broadcasting*, November 15, 1931, 18.

55   Caleb Johnson, "Newspapers Share Radio's Revenue," *Broadcasting*, May 15, 1932, 17.

56   "Elzy Roberts Quits Press Radio Post," *Broadcasting*, May 15, 1932, 17.

57   "Radio and the Press."

58   Roger Baldwin, "Memorandum on Radio in Relation to Free Speech," May 19, 1933, American Civil Liberties Union Manuscripts, 1933, vol. 599, Princeton University, Princeton, NJ.

59   Roger Baldwin, letter to Harris K. Randall, April 4, 1933, American Civil Liberties Union Manuscripts, 1931–1933, vol. 513, Princeton University; Harry F. Ward, letter to Federal Communications Commission, August 24, 1934, American Civil Liberties Union Manuscripts, 1934, vol. 694, Princeton University.

60   Roger Baldwin, letter to Harris K. Randall, October 30, 1933, American Civil Liberties Union Manuscripts, 1933, vol. 510, Princeton University.

61   Joy Elmer Morgan, "The New American Plan for Radio," in *A Debate Handbook on Radio Control and Operation*, Bower Aly and Gerald T. Shively, eds. (Columbia, MO: Staples, 1933), 81–111.

62   See John Dewey, "Radio—For Propaganda or Public Interest," *Education by Radio*, February 28, 1935, 11; John Dewey, "Our Un-Free Press." *Common Sense*, November (1935): 6–7; E. Pendleton Herring, "Politics and Radio Regulation," *Harvard Business Review* 13 (1935): 167–178; E. Pendleton Herring, *Public Administration and the Public Interest* (New York: McGraw Hill, 1936); Alexander Meiklejohn, *Political Freedom* (New York: Harper & Brothers, 1948), 86–87. For Hamilton's influence see Richard Joyce Smith, "The Ultimate Control of Radio in the United States," in *Radio and Education: Proceedings of the Second Annual Assembly of the National Advisory Council on Radio in Education, Inc., 1932*, ed. Levering Tyson (Chicago: University of Chicago Press, 1932), 181–94. For Sinclair's position see *Education by Radio*, December 24, 1931, 156; Frederick Lewis Allen, "Radio City: Cultural Center?" *Education by Radio*, May 12,

1932, 65–68; Bruce Bliven, "Shall the Government Own, Operate, and Control Radio Broadcasting In the United Slates?" in *Radio and Education: Proceedings of the Fourth Annual Assembly of the National Advisory Council on Radio in Education, Inc., 1934*, Levering Tyson, ed. (Chicago: University of Chicago Press, 1934), 76–83, 106–15; "H. L. Mencken," *Education by Radio*, August 27, 1931, 101–2.

63   Jerome Davis, *Capitalism and Its Culture* (New York: Farrar & Rinehart, 1935); William Aylott Orton, *America in Search of Culture* (Boston: Little, Brown, 1933); James Rony, *Order on the Air!* (New York: John Day, 1934); James Rorty, *Our Master's Voice: Advertising* (New York: John Day, 1934).

64   Much of this criticism, which has been largely overlooked by subsequent media critics, ages rather well and anticipates much of the best modern media criticism, from Herbert J. Gans, *Deciding What's News* (New York: Pantheon Books, 1979); Gaye Tuchman, *Making News* (New York: Basic Books, 1978); Ben H. Bagdikian, *The Media Monopoly* 3rd ed. (Boston: Beacon Press, 1990); Edward S. Herman and Noam Chomsky, *Manufacturing Consent*.

65   Morgan, "Education's Rights on the Air," 122.

66   S. C. Hooper, "Comments on Report of Majority Members of Committee and Discussion of Position of Minority Member," Franklin Delano Roosevelt Manuscripts, Franklin Delano Roosevelt Presidential Library, Hyde Park, NY, OF 859a, 1933–1945.

67   "The Ideals of a Great Citizen," *Education by Radio*, April 7, 1932, 56.

68   Cited in "Radio's Legal Racket," *Education by Radio*, May l0, 1934, 19.

69   "Canadian Radio Proposal Is Challenge to U.S. Broadcasters, Dill Tells Senate," *Broadcasting*, May 15, 1932, 8; Martin Codel, "Canadian Broadcasting to Be Nationalized," *Broadcasting*, May 15, 1932, 7–8; "Nationally Owned Radio System for Canada," *Education by Radio*, July 7, 1932, 81–82.

70   U.S. Congress, House of Representatives. 73rd Cong., 2d Sess., *Federal Communications Commission Hearings Before the Committee on Interstate and Foreign Commerce on H.B. 8301* (Washington, DC: U.S. Government Printing Office, 1934), 284.

71   "Listener's Utopia," *Education by Radio*, November 7, 1935, 55.

72   See James M. Herring, "The Radio Regulation Challenge," *Public Utilities Fortnightly* 16, September 12, 1935, 303–11. He concluded that any competition would be "unequal" and favor the government because its stations would not have to carry advertising, "which in most cases detracts from the appeal of the program."

73   Morgan, "The Radio in Education," 83.

74   Joy Elmer Morgan, "Radio and Education," in *Radio and Its Future*. ed. Martin Codel (New York: Harper Brothers, 1930), 76–77; "Should the U.S. Adopt the British System of Radio Control," *Congressional Digest*, August–September 1933, 202–6; "Education's Rights on the Air," 124.

75   Vita Lauter and Joseph H. Friend, "Radio and the Censors," *Forum*, December 1931, 359–65.

76   "Advertising Is Basis of Radio Existence," *Federation News*, August 5, 1933, 6; U.S. Congress, Senate, 73rd Cong., 2d Sess., *Hearings Before the Committee* on *Interstate Commerce on S. 2910, 1934* (Washington, DC: U.S. Government Printing Office, 1934), 186.

77   David R. Mackey, "The National Association of Broadcasters—Its First Twenty Years," Ph.D. dissertation (Northwestern University, Evanston, IL, 19560, 1; Eddie Dowling,

"Radio Needs a Revolution," *Forum* 91 (February 1934): 67–70; Orrin E. Dunlap Jr., "Council Reviews Meet of Radio on American Life," *New York Times*, April 29, 1934; Tracy Tyler, letter to Roger Baldwin, October 26, 1933, American Civil Liberties Union Manuscripts, 1933, vol. 599, Princeton University: Bethuel M. Webster Jr., Second General Counsel, Federal Radio Commission (1929), telephone interview, February 18, 1987.

78   Morgan, "Should the U.S. Adopt the British System of Radio Control," 204; Sol Taishoff, "Session of Radio-Minded Congress Nears," *Broadcasting*, December 1, 1931, 5–6.

79   National Association of Broadcasters, *Broadcasting In the United States* (Washington, DC: NAB, 1933); National Broadcasting Company, *Broadcasting*, vols. 1–4 (New York: NBC, 1935).

80   Morgan, "The New American Plan for Radio."

81   Barnouw, *A Tower in Babel*, 204–6; Dunlap, "Council Reviews"; Francis D. Farrell, *Brief History of the Advisory Council of the National Broadcasting Company* (New York: National Broadcasting Company, 1939), 2; Louise M. Benjamin, "Birth of a Network's 'Conscience': The NBC Advisory Council, 1927," *Journalism Quarterly* 66 (Autumn 1989): 587–90; Levering Tyson, confidential memorandum to Dr. Roben Hutchins, January 14, 1933, R. M. Hutchins Papers Addenda, vol. 99, University of Chicago.

82   William Panerson, memorandum to Merlin H. Aylesworth, 1933. R. M. Hutchins Papers Addenda, vol. 99, University of Chicago.

83   See James E. Pollard, "Newspaper Publicity for Radio Programs," in *Education on the Air: Fifth Yearbook of the Institute for Education by Radio*, Josephine H. MacLatchy, ed. (Columbus: Ohio State University, 1934), 216–27.

84   See "Can America Get the Truth About Radio?" *Education by Radio*, March 15, 1934, 9.

85   See Robert W. McChesney, "Free Speech and Democracy! Louis G. Caldwell, the American Bar Association and the Debate Over the Free Speech Implications of Broadcast Regulation, 1928–1938," *American Journal of Legal History* 35/4 (1991): 351–92.

86   "Discussion Following Friday Morning Session, May 21, 1931," in *Radio and Education: Proceedings of the First Assembly of the National Advisory Council on Radio in Education, 1931*, ed. Levering Tyson (Chicago: University of Chicago Press, 1931), 144–47.

87   "Assails Chicago Station," *New York Times*, April 19, 1932, 34; "Caldwell Off to Madrid," *Broadcasters' News Bulletin*, July 30, 1932; "Four Stations Appeal Radio Orders," *New York Times*, November 12, 1929, 42, 70.

88   "Legal Racketeering?" *Education by Radio*, August 27, 1931, 101; "Radio From the Citizen's Point of View," *Education by Radio*, October 8, 1931, 112.

89   Louis G. Caldwell, "Radio and the Law," in *Radio and its Future*, ed. Martin Codel (New York: Harper, 1930), 226–31.

90   American Bar Association, Standing Committee on Radio Law, "Report of the Standing Committee on Radio Law," 459.

91   Taishoff, "Session of Radio-Minded Congress Nears," 6.

92   Chomsky, *Necessary Illusions*.

93   Taishoff, "Session of Radio-Minded Congress Nears," 5.

94   "President Shaw Warns," *Broadcasters' News Bulletin*, January 11, 1932.

95   Edward N. Nockels, "Labor's Rights on the Air," *Federation News*, February 7, 1931, 2.

96   "Labor Bill Headed for Congress," *Broadcasters' News Bulletin*, February 21, 1931; "Labor's Big Fight for Freedom of the Air," *Federation News*, March 21, 1931, 9.

97   Marlin Codel, "Dill and Davis Seen Powers in Radio Rule Under Roosevelt," *Broadcasting*, November 15, 1932, 8.

98   Morris Ernst, letter to Gordon W. Moss, November 19, 1931. American Civil Liberties Union Manuscripts, 1931–1933, vol. 513, Princeton University.

99   *Congressional Record* 75, January 4, 1932, 1194–95; *Congressional Record* 75, January 7, 1932, 1412–13; Sol Taishoff, "Commission Opens Sweeping Radio Inquiry," *Broadcasting*, February 1, 1932, 5, 28.

100 Federal Radio Commission, *Commercial Radio Advertising* (Washington, DC: U.S. Government Printing Office, 1932).

101 "Indisputable Facts," *Broadcasting*, June 15, 1932, 20; "A Congressional Investigation of Radio," *Education by Radio*, December 8, 1932, 105.

102 Tracy Tyler, letter to Roger Baldwin, October 26, 1933.

103 Most prominent was Eddie Dowling; Dr. Arthur Morgan, chairman of the Tennessee Valley Authority; and economist Adolph A. Berle. See Dowling, "Radio Needs a Revolution"; Arthur E. Morgan, "Radio as a Cultural Agency in Sparsely Settled Regions and Remote Areas," in *Radio as a Cultural Agency: Proceedings of a National Conference on the Use of Radio as a Cultural Agency in a Democracy*, Tracy F. Tyler, ed. (Washington, DC: National Committee on Education by Radio, 1934), 77–83.

104 Josephus Daniels, Letter to Franklin D. Roosevelt, January 15, 1935. Franklin Delano Roosevelt Manuscripts, Franklin Delano Roosevelt Presidential Library, Hyde Park, NY, PPF 86, 1935.

105 Josephus Daniels, letter to Franklin D. Roosevelt, January 15, 1935. For a more complete analysis of the Roosevelt administration and broadcast policy, see Robert W. McChesney, "Franklin Roosevelt, His Administration, and the Communications Act of 1934," *American Journalism* 5 (1988): 204–30; Rosen, *The Modern Stentors*, 170–80.

106 Sol Taishoff, "'War Plans' Laid to Protect Broadcasting," *Broadcasting*, March 1, 1933, 5; See also, American Bar Association, Standing Committee on Communications, "Report of the Standing Committee on Communications," *Report on Fifty-fifth Annual Meeting of the American Bar Association, 1932* (Baltimore: Lord Baltimore Press, 1932), 423–87.

107 See U.S. Congress, Senate, 73rd Cong., 2d Sess., *Hearings Before the Committee on Interstate Commerce on S. 2910. 1934*, 53–55; Henry A. Bellows, letter to Stephen E. Early, February 28. 1934. Franklin Delano Roosevelt Manuscripts, Franklin Delano Roosevelt Presidential Library, Hyde Park, NY, OF 859a. 1933–1945.

108 See Rosen, *The Modern Stentors*, 173–74.

109 Interdepartmental Committee (Roper Committee), *Study of Communications by an Interdepartmental Committee, Letter from the President of the United States to the Chairman of the Committee on Interstate Commerce Transmitting a Memorandum from the Secretary of Commerce Relative to a Study of Communications by an Interdepartmental Committee* (Washington, DC: U.S. Government Printing Office, 1934).

110 Ibid.; "Control Board Planned for All Communications," *New York Times*, December 14, 1933, 2.

111 James Couzens, "The Channels of Information," *Public Utilities Fortnightly* 4 (August 22, 1929): 216–20; Rosen, *The Modern Stentors*, 178.

112 S. C. Hooper, "Comments."

113 "President Orders Broadcast Survey," *NAB Reports*, February 3, 1934, 287; Sol Taishoff, "Roosevelt Demands Communications Bill," *Broadcasting*, February 15, 1934, 5–6.

114 "Broadcasting Survey Postponed," *NAB Reports*, February 24, 1934, 309; "Broadcast 'Study' Shelved as Futile: Roper-Proposed Investigation Discouraged by Congress," *Broadcasting*, March 1, 1934, 15; "Dill Will Push Communications Bill," *NAB Reports*, February 10, 1934, 299.

115 Daniel C. Roper, letter to Hohenstein. March 6, 1934. Department of Commerce Manuscripts, National Archives, Washington, DC, NARG 40, General Correspondence, File 80553/13-G.

116 "Communications Bill Speeded," *NAB Reports*, March 10, 1934, 323.

117 "Roosevelt Approves Communications Board to Rule Radio Telephone, Telegraph, Cable," *New York Times*, February 10, 1934.

118 Taishoff, "Roosevelt Demands," 5.

119 *New York Times*, February 10, 1934; U.S. Congress, Senate, 73rd Cong., 2d Sess., *Hearings Before the Committee* on *Interstate Commerce on S. 2910, 1934*, 106.

120 "Labor Aids Bill for Free Radio," *Federation News*, April 7, 1934, 6; "Labor Toils for Radio Freedom," *Federation News*, May 26, 1934, 1, 3; James McVann, *The Paulists, 1858–1970* (New York: Society of St. Paul the Apostle, 1983), 896; U.S. Congress, Senate, Senate Interstate Commerce Committee Manuscripts, National Archives, Washington, DC, Sen 73A-J28, tray 155.

121 "Air Enemies Unite Forces," *Variety*, May 8, 1934, 37, 45.

122 Henry A. Bellows, "Report of the Legislative Committee," *NAB Reports*, November 15, 1934, 617–22.

123 Francis T. Maloney, correspondence with Eugene Sykes, April 25, 1934, April 28, 1934, Federal Communications Commission Manuscripts, National Archives, Suitland, Maryland, NARG 173, Legislation, Acts Radio, FCC General Correspondence, Box 38; Sol Taishoff, "Powerful Lobby Threatens Radio Structure," *Broadcasting*, May 15, 1934, 6; Rosen, *The Modern Stentors*, 179.

124 Rosen, *The Modern Stentors*, 179.

125 Bellows, "Report of the Legislative Committee," 618.

126 Orrin E. Dunlap Jr., "New Deal in Radio Law to Regulate All Broadcasting," *New York Times*, June 24, 1934; "New Communications Bill 15 Aimed at Curbing Monopoly in Radio," *New York Times*, May 20, 1934. For an immediate response by a liberal FCC member to the asininity of this interpretation, see George Henry Payne, *The Fourth Estate and Other Addresses* (Boston: Microphone Press, 1936), 42. Some broadcasting historians assert this argument despite that the Communications Act of 1934 restated the Radio Act of 1927 virtually verbatim and had been the conscious result of keeping the public and Congress as far removed as possible from any debate over broadcasting issues. See Waller B. Emery, "Broadcasting Rights and Responsibilities in Democratic Society," *Centennial Review* 8 (1964): 306–22.

127 "Government Interference Fear Groundless, Say Commissioners," *Broadcasting*, October 1, 1934, 18; Clifton Read, Letter to Hadley Cantril, October 25, 1934, American Civil Liberties Union Manuscripts, 1934, vol. 699. Princeton University.

128 "Federal Communications Commission Reports to Congress," *Education by Radio*, January 31, 1935, 5.

129 Arthur G. Crane, "Safeguarding Educational Radio," in *Education on the Air . . . and Radio and Education, 1935*, Levering Tyson and Josephine MacLatchy, eds. (Chicago: University of Chicago Press, 1935), 117–25.

130 Robert W. McChesney, "Constant Retreat: The American Civil Liberties Union and the Debate Over the Meaning of Free Speech for Radio Broadcasting in the 1930s," in *Free Speech Yearbook, 1987*, vol. 26, Stephen A. Smith, ed. (Carbondale: Southern Illinois University Press, 1988).

131 Cited in "In Their Own Behalf," *Education by Radio*, June–July 1938, 21.

132 William S. Paley, "The Viewpoint of the Radio Industry," in *Educational Broadcasting 1937*, C. S. Marsh, ed. (Chicago: University of Chicago Press, 1937), 6–12.

133 Louis G. Caldwell, "Freedom of Speech and Radio Broadcasting," in *Radio: The Fifth Estate*, ed. Herman S. Hellinger, Supplement of Annals of the American Academy of Political and Social Science, Volume 117 (January 1935): 179–81; Louis G. Caldwell, "Comment on the Current Problems of the Law of Communications," *American Bar Association Journal* 22 (December 1936): 848–52.

134 Rosen, *The Modern Stentors*, 180.

135 Paul F. Lazarsfeld, *The People Look at Radio* (Chapel Hill: University of North Carolina Press, 1946), 89. For a more theoretical discussion of why fundamental media issues have remained "off-limits" in U.S. public culture, see Robert W. McChesney, "Off Limits: An Inquiry into the lack of Debate Concerning the Ownership, Structure, and Control of the Mass Media in U.S. Political Life," chapter 15 in this book.

136 Ben H. Bagdikian, "The Lords of the Global Village," *The Nation*, June 12, 1989, 805–20; Bagdikian, *The Media Monopoly*.

137 Cited page 1 in *New York Times*, October 3, 1989.

138 See Robert M. Entman, *Democracy Without Citizens: Media and the Decay of American Politics* (New York: Oxford University Press. 1989).

7. The Payne Fund and Radio Broadcasting, 1928–1935

This chapter first appeared in a slightly different form as Robert W. McChesney, "The Payne Fund and Radio Broadcasting, 1928–1935," in Children and the Movies: Media Influence and the Payne Fund Controversy, *Garth S. Jowett, Ian C. Jarvie, Kathryn H. Fuller, eds. (New York: Cambridge Press, 1996), 303–35.*

1 Summary of the Payne Fund's Activities in Radio, undated memorandum, ca. June 1933, PFP, C40 f768.

2 Ibid.; Charters to Morgan, January 31, 1931, PFP, C68 ,1343; Agenda, Meeting of the Board of Directors of the Payne Fund, April 18–20, 1930, PFP, C56 f1066.

3 Perry to Clymer, 7 January 1931, PFP, C68 f1343.

4 See, for classic statements, Ben H. Bagdikian, *The Media Monopoly* (Boston: Beacon Press, 1992); Edward S. Herman and Noam Chomsky, *Manufacturing Consent: The Political Economy of the Mass Media* (New York: Pantheon, 1988). For an extended treatment of this theme, see Robert W. McChesney, "An Almost Incredible Absurdity for a Democracy," *Journal of Communication Inquiry* 15/1 (1991): 89–114.

5 I review this aspect of U.S. broadcasting history in greater detail in McChesney, *Telecommunications, Mass Media, and Democracy* (New York: Oxford University Press, 1993), chapter 2.

6 "The Menace of Radio Monopoly," *Education by Radio*, March 26, 1931, 27; "The

Power Trust and the Public Schools," *Education by Radio*, December 10, 1931, 150; "Radio Censorship and the Federal Communications Commission," *Columbia Law Review* 39 (March 1939): 447. The 97 percent figure cited in William Boddy, *Fifties Television* (Urbana: University of Illinois Press, 1990), 36.

7   Martin Codel, "Networks Reveal Impressive Gains," undated, sometime in January 1931, entry in scrapbook for North American Newspaper Alliance, news service that covered radio, among other topics, for approximately sixty U.S. daily newspapers in the early 1930s. In Martin Codel papers, State Historical Society of Wisconsin, Madison, vol. 61 (hereafter cited as NANA); Michele Hilmes, *Hollywood and Broadcasting: From Radio to Cable* (Urbana: University of Illinois, 1990), 52.

8   Henry Volkening, "Absues of Radio Broadcasting," *Current History* 33 (1930): 396–400; Philip T. Rosen, *The Modern Stentors: Radio Broadcasters and the Federal Government, 1920–1934* (Westport, CT: Greenwood Press, 1980), 12; Erik Barnouw, *A Tower in Babel* (New York: Oxford University Press, 1966), 270.

9   Armstrong Perry, "The Ohio School of the Air and Other Experiments in the Use of Radio in Education," May 29, 1929, PFP, C69 fl353.

10   Perry to Clymer, April 6, 1929, PFP, C56 fl067.

11   Ibid.; Clymer to Executive Committee, Department of Superintendence, National Education Association, April 6, 1929, PFP, C56 fl067.

12   Perry to Clifton, August 21, 1929, PFP, C56 fl068.

13   *Official Report of Proceedings Before the Federal Communications Commission on Section (307)s of the Communications Act of 1934*, Smith & Hulse, Official Reporters (Washington, DC: Federal Communications Commission, 1935), 180–249.

14   Advisory Committee on Education by Radio, *Report of the Advisory Committee on Education by Radio Appointed by the Secretary of the Interior* (Columbus: F. J. Heer, 1930), 35–37.

15   Ibid., 76.

16   Cooper to Shipherd, March 31, 1930, Office of Education papers, RG 12, National Archives, Washington, DC, Box 31 (hereafter cited as OEP); Perry to Crandall, March 17, 1930, PFP, C56 fl069.

17   Cooper to Presidents of Land Grant Institutions Having Broadcasting Stations, undated, Summer 1930, OEP Box 32; Armstrong Perry, "The Status of Education by Radio in the United States," in *Education on the Air*, ed. Josephine MacKatchy (Columbus: Ohio State University Press, 1930), 80–81.

18   Crandall to Perry, July 9, 1930, PFP, C56 fl070.

19   Crandall to Perry, July 17, 1930, PFP, C56 fl070; Crandall, "Memorandum of Conference with Mr. Perry," July 23, 1930, PFP, C69 fl352.

20   Much of this correspondence is in the Herbert Hoover papers, Herbert Hoover Presidential Library, West Branch, Iowa, Commerce series, Box 148. See, in particular, Cooper to Wilbur, December 8, 1930; for RCA's attempt to influence Bolton see memorandum of meeting between Mrs. Bolton and Mr. Dunham, October 29, 1930, PFP, C69 fl352.

21   Perry to Crandall, October 14, 1930, PFP, C56 fl070; "Proposed Plan of Action," October 2, 1930, PFP, C69 fl352.

22   Minutes of the Conference on Educational Radio Problems, Stevens Hotel, Chicago, October 13, 1930, at the Invitation of the U.S. Commissioner of Education, OEP Box 31.

23   The nine groups included the NEA, the National Association of State Universities, the National University Extension Association, the Association of College and University Broadcasting Stations, the Association of Land Grant Colleges and Universities, the National Council of State Superintendents, the Jesuit Education Association, the National Catholic Education Association, and the American Council on Education.

24   Minutes, October 13, 1930, OEP Box 31; Morgan to Davis, March 8, 1932, PFP, C47 f901.

25   Crandall to Perry, December 2, 1930, PFP, C56 f1071.

26   Bolton to Morgan, June 17, 1932, PFP, C42 f812.

27   Darrow to Clymer, February 3, 1931, PFP, C68 f1343.

28   Perry to Klauber, March 9, 1931, PFP, C55 f1052.

29   Joy Elmer Morgan, "Education's Rights on the Air," in *Radio and Education*, Levering Tyson, ed. (Chicago: University of Chicago Press, 1931), 10.

30   Wright to Reid, May 26, 1930, PFP, C41 f796.

31   Armstrong Perry, "Weak Spots in the American System of Broadcasting," in *Radio—The Fifth Estate*, vol. 117 of the *Annals of the American Academy of Political and Social Science*, ed. Herman S. Hettinger (1935), 26; Perry, "Report of the Service Bureau," March 1931, PFP, C38 f743; Lohnes to Tyler, January 10, 1933, PFP, C44 f854.

32   See Joy Elmer Morgan and E. D. Bullock, *Selected Articles on Municipal Ownership* (Minneapolis, Wilson, 1911); for an example of Morgan's anticorporate beliefs see Joy Elmer Morgan, "The Corporation in America," *Journal of the National Education Association* 23 (1934): 227–29.

33   Joy Elmer Morgan, "The National Committee on Education by Radio," in *Education on the Air*, Josephine H. MacLatchy, ed. (Columbus: Ohio State University Press, 1931), 128.

34   Ibid., 123, 128.

35   Ibid., 120–21.

36   Joy Elmer Morgan, "The Radio in Education," in *Proceedings of the Seventeenth Annual Convention of the National University Extension Association 1932*, vol. 15 (Bloomington: Indiana University Press, 1932), 79; Morgan to McAndrew, September 20, 1932, Joy Elmer Morgan papers, National Education Association, Washington, DC, 1932 correspondence, FCB 2, Drawer 3.

37   Tyler to Cunningham, November 2, 1933, PFP, C47 f916.

38   "The Fittest Survive," *Broadcasting*, January 15, 1933, 16; " 'Listeners Society,'" *Broadcasting*, April 1, 1933, 14; "When Educators Differ," *Broadcasting*, June 1, 1933, 20; "Exit Mr. Morgan," *Broadcasting*, September 15, 1935, 30.

39   Coltrane, "A Brief Statement in Support of Representative Fulmer's Resolution for a Study of Radio Broadcasting," March 2, 1933, PFP, C54 f1034.

40   Brackett to Beaird, December 15, 1931, National Association of Educational Broadcasters papers, State Historical Society of Wisconsin, Madison, Box 1a, General Correspondence 1932 (hereafter cited as NAEBP).

41   Perry, "Institutes for Education by Radio," December 1935, PFP, C52 f986.

42   Brackett to Charters, August 27, 1931, NAEBP, Box 1a, General Correspondence, 1929–1931.

43   Summary of Miss Crandall's Discussions with Dr. Charters, March 14, 1931, PFP, C69 f1352.

44 Radio Research Work at Ohio State University, December 6, 1933, PFP, C69 f1352.

45 Morgan to Coltrane, November 22, 1932, PFP, C41 f783.

46 Evans to Woehlke, October 18, 1932, PFP, C60 f1167; Memorandum re Conference, Dr. Joy Elmer Morgan and Miss Crandall, October 1, 1932, PFP, C42 f812; Perry, "National Education Association," December 1935, PFP, Cp f986.

47 Levering Tyson, "Where Is American Radio Heading?" in *Education on the Air*, Josephine H. MacLatchy, ed. (Columbus: Ohio State University Press, 1934), 15.

48 Perry, "National Broadcasting Company," December 1935, PFP, C52 f986; Merlin H. Aylesworth, "Broadcasting Today," *Dun's Review* 5 (1932), 3.

49 Tyson to Keppel, January 2, 1934, Carnegie Corporation of New York papers, Columbia University, New York, NACRE Box 1, NACRE 1934 (hereafter cited as CCP).

50 Tyson to Keppel, December 4, 1929, CCP, NACRE Box 1, NACRE 1929.

51 Tyson to Patterson, November 29, 1932, National Broadcasting Company papers, State Historical Society of Wisconsin, Madison, B12 f15 (hereafter cited as NBCP).

52 Evans to Harris, October 8, 1934, PFP, C69 f1350

53 Crandall, "Memorandum to Mr. Perry re General Situation of Radio in Education," December 29, 1930, PFP, C69 f1352.

54 Tyson to Keppel, October 28, 1930, CCP, NACRE Box 1, NACRE 1930; Tyson to Keppel, January 2, 1934, CCP, NACRE Box 1, NACRE 1934.

55 Crandall to Bolton, June 23, 1932, PFP, C52 f983.

56 *Proceedings of the Nineteenth Annual Convention of the National University Extension Association*, vol. 17 (Bloomington: Indiana University Press, 1934), 86.

57 Barnouw, *A Tower in Babel*, 261; Robert K. Avery and Robert Pepper, "An Institutional History of Public Broadcasting," *Journal of Communication* 30/3 (1980): 126–38.

58 Crandall to Davis, April 15, 1931, PFP, C59 f1142.

59 Ibid.

60 Davis to Maxfield, June 12, 1931, PFP, C59 f1142; Evans to Bernays, March 3, 1932, PFP, C69 f1350; Crandall to Davis, October 13, 1931, PFP, C59 f1143.

61 Evans to Williams, December 9, 1932, PFP, C60 f1174; Davis to Evans, July 30, 1931, PFP, C59 f1142.

62 Walter Woehlke Memorandum, undated, Summer 1931, PFP, C49 f945.

63 H.O. Davis to H.L. Williamson, September 25, 1931, NBCP, B5 f65.

64 Woehlke to Evans, September 1, 1931, PFP, C60 f1163; Evans to Davis, September 5, 1931, PFP, C59 f1143.

65 Davis to Bolton, September 9, 1931, PFP, C40 f764; Evans, "Memorandum re Payne Fund Relationship with Davis Radio Campaign," September 18, 1931, PFP, C49 f945.

66 For Davis's final proposal as such, see H. O. Davis, *Empire of the Air* (Ventura, CA: Ventura Free Press, 1932), 99.

67 McChesney, *Telecommunications, Mass Media, and Democracy*, chapter 7.

68 Summary of Expenditures of Ventura Free Press Radio Project, June 1932, PFP, C59 f1145; "Free Press Most Widely Quoted Newspaper West of the Rockies," *Ventura Free Press*, July 28, 1932, 1, 3.

69 "A Vicious Fight Against Broadcasting," *Broadcasting*, December 1, 1931, 10.

70   Randall to Mason, July 3, 1934, NBCP, B25 f58.

71   "Editors Favor American Plan," *Broadcasters' News Bulletin*, June 13, 1931.

72   Davis to Bolton, September 9, 1931, PFP, C40 f764.

73   Crandall to Perry, June 3, 1931, PFP, C56 f1072.

74   Woehlke to Evans, November 25, 1931, PFP, C60 f1164.

75   Bolton to Davis, September 1, 1931, PFP, C59 f1143.

76   Crandall to Davis, October 1, 1931, PFP, C59 f1143; Memorandum re Discussion at Board Meeting Held October 30, 1931 Regarding the Ventura Free Press Campaign Against Radio Monopoly, October 30, 1931, PFP, C61 f1178.

77   All of these groups are profiled in McChesney, *Telecommunications, Mass Media, and Democracy*, chapter 4. For a discussion specifically of the role played by organized labor, see Robert W. McChesney, "Labor and the Marketplace of Ideas," *Journalism Monographs* (1992).

78   Morgan, from the NCER, observed, it was impossible to find *any* intellectual in favor of commercial broadcasting unless that person was receiving money or airtime from a commercial station or network. See Joy Elmer Morgan, "The New American Plan for Radio," in *A Debate Handbook on Radio Control and Operation*, ed. Bower Aly and Gerald D. Shively (Columbus: Staples, 1933), 82.

79   Woehlke to Evans, December 22, 1932, PFP, C60 f1147.

80   "Neither Sponsors nor Stations Heed Listeners' Grumbling," *Business Week*, February 10, 1932, 18–19; cited in "From the Newspapers," *Education by Radio*, March 5, 1931, 14.

81   Joy Elmer Morgan, "A National Culture," in *Radio as a Cultural Agency*, ed. Tracy F. Tyler (Washington, DC: National Committee on Education by Radio, 1934), 26, 28.

82   Davis to Lighter, December 1, 1931, PFP, C59 f1143.

83   "Report of the Committee on Radio Broadcasting," in *Transactions and Proceedings of the National Association of State Universities in the United States of America 1931*, vol. 29, ed. A. H. Upham (National Association of State Universities, 1931), 150; Morgan, "Education's Rights on the Air," 130; Morgan, "The New American Plan for Radio," 93.

84   Armstrong Perry, "Comments following talk by C.M. Jansky Jr.," in *Radio and Education*, ed. Levering Tyson (Chicago: University of Chicago Press, 1932), 223.85 Eugene J. Coltrane, "A System of Radio Broadcasting Suited to American Purposes," in *Radio Control and Operation*, ed. E.R. Rankin (Chapel Hill; University of North Carolina Extension Bulletin, 1933), 36.

86   See, for example, Joy Elmer Morgan, "The Radio in Education," 83.

87   Perry to British Broadcasting Corporation, December 17, 1935, PFP, C58 f1110.

88   Perry to Charters, undated, early summer 1930, PFP C56 f1069.

89   Woehlke to Evans, December 22, 1932, PFP, C60 f1167.

90   Perry to Crandall, March 8, 1932, PFP, C59 f1144.

91   Evans to Woehlke, February 15, 1932, PFP, C60 f1165.

92   Bruce Bliven, "For Better Broadcasting," *New Republic 3* (1934): 201; "I'm Signing Off," *Forum*, February 1932, 114. For a particularly acute example of blaming the audience for the alleged asininity of commercial programming, see "The Dominant Moron," *Catholic World*, May 1934, 135–37.

93   This topic is addressed in Robert W. McChesney, "Press-Radio Relations and the Emergence of Network, Commercial Broadcasting in the United States, 1930–1935, *Historical Journal of Film, Radio and Television* 11/1 (1991): 41–57.

94   Tyler to Baldwin, October 26, 1933, American Civil Liberties Union papers, Princeton University, Princeton, NJ, 1933, vol. 599.

95   For two classic statements along these lines, see National Association of Broadcasters, *Broadcasting in the United States* (Washington, DC: National Association of Broadcasters, 1933); National Broadcasting Company, *Broadcasting*, vol. 1–4 (New York: National Broadcasting Company, 1935).

96   Paul F. Peter, NBC Chief Statistician, "Appearances by U.S. Federal Officials over National Broadcasting Company Networks, 1931–1933," November 1933, NBCP, B16 f26.

97   Morgan to McCracken, August 2, 1932, PFP, C42 f801.

98   Amlie to Tyler, May 24, 1932, PFP, C43 f825.

99   Perry, "Columbia Broadcasting System," December 1935, PFP, C52 f986.

100 "Better Business," *Broadcasting*, December 15, 1931, 18.

101 Sol Taishoff, "Session of Radio-Minded Congress Nears," *Broadcasting*, December 1, 1931, 5.

102 Edward N. Nockels, "Labor's Rights on the Air," *Federation News*, February 7, 1931, 2.

103 Bolton to MacCracken, October 9, 1931, PFP, C40 f768.

104 Evans to Woehlke, December 22, 1931, PFP, C60 f1164.

105 Evans to Woehlke, February 29, 1932, PFP, C69 f1358.

106 FRC, "In re: The use of radio broadcasting stations for advertising purposes," December 21, 1931, PFP, C60 f1159.

107 Davis to Crandall, February 23, 1932, PFP, C59 f1144.

108 Davis to Crandall, March 8, 1932, PFP, C59 f1144.

109 Tyler to Marsh, April 7, 1932, PFP, C39 f744; Morgan to Bolton, PFP, C42 f812.

110 Crandall, "Review of the Program of the National Committee on Education by Radio," August 11, 1932, PFP, C56 f1075.

111 Davis to Brooks, October 5, 1932, PFP, C59 f1145. For a copy of the FRC report, see Federal Radio Commission, *Commerical Radio Advertising* (Washington, DC: U.S. Government Printing Office, 1932).

112 Davis to Woehlke, undated, Summer 1932, PFP, C60 f1167.

113 Spry to Morgan, May 2, 1932, PFP, C42 f822.

114 Evans to Davis, November 18, 1932, PFP, C59 f1145.

115 Evans to Woehlke, October 7, 1932, PFP, C60 f1167.

116 Evans to Woehlke, December 19, 1932, PFP, C69 f1358.

117 Evans to Coltrane, January 25, 1933, PFP, C41 f783.

118 Memorandum Concerning Payne Fund Cooperation with Commercial Radio Stations, November 15, 1932, PFP, C69 f1352.

119 Davis to Crandall, September 20, 1934, PFP, C59 f1148.

120 Crandall to Cooper, February 19, 1933, PFP, C68 f1337.

121 Aylesworth to Sarnoff, August 20, 1934, NBCP, B32 f7.

122 Crane to Tyler, March 19, 1934, PFP, C41 f785.

123 Arthur E. Morgan, "Radio as a Cultural Agency in Sparsely Settled Regions and Remote Areas," in *Radio as a Cultural Agency*, ed. Tracy F. Tyler (Washington, DC: National Committee on Education by Radio, 1934), 81.

124 See McChesney, *Telecommunications, Mass Media, and Democracy*, chapter 7.

125 Martin Codel, "President Aided by Radio Chains," undated, March 1933, NANA, v. 61; "F.D.R.'s Radio Record," *Broadcasting*, March 15, 1934, 8.

126 See Thomas Ferguson, "Industrial Structure and Party Competition in the New Deal," *Sociological Perspectives* 34 (1991): 493–526; Thomas Ferguson, "Industrial Conflict and the Coming of the New Deal," in *The Rise and Fall of the New Deal Order*, ed. Steve Fraser and Gary Gerstle (Princeton, NJ: Princeton University Press, 1989), 3–31; Michael Patrick Allen, "Capitalist Response to State Intervention," *American Sociological Review* 56 (1991): 679–689; William Domhoff, *The Power Elite and the State* (New York: Aldine–DeGruyter, 1990).

127 Sol Taishoff, "'War Plans' Laid to Protect Broadcasting," *Broadcasting*, March 1, 1933, 5.

128 Rosen, *Modern Stentors*, 177.

129 Petitions and letters found in Robert F. Wagner papers, Georgetown University, Washington, DC, Legislative Files, Box 223; United States Interstate Commerce Committee Papers, National Archives, Washington, DC, Sen. 73A–J28, Tray 155.

130 "Air Enemies United Forces," *Variety*, May 8, 1934, pp. 37, 4S; "Wagner Amendment Up Next Week," *NAB Reports*, May 5, 1934, 375.

131 Tyler to Harney, March 30, 1934, PFP, C44 f850.

132 Harney to Tyler, April 3, 1934, PFP, ibid.

133 Harney to Perry, April 4, 1934, PFP, CS9 f1132.

134 Perry to Crandall, June 15, 1934, PFP, C56 f1079.

135 Henry A. Bellows, "Report of the Legislative Committee," *NAB Reports*, November 15, 1934, 618.

136 Ibid., 618.

137 "Commercial Control of the Air," *Christian Century*, September 26, 1934, 1196–97.

138 "Government Interference Fears Groundless, Say Commissioners," *Broadcasting*, October 1, 1934, 18.

139 Tyler to Dill, June 5, 1934, PFP, C43 f824.

140 Russell to Hard, October 23, 1934, NBCP, B26 f28.

141 Early memo, McIntyre memo, October 20, 1934, October 22, 1934, Franklin D. Roosevelt papers, Franklin D. Roosevelt Presidential Library, Hyde Park, NY, OF 136,1934; "More About TVA Proposal," *Education by Radio*, November 22, 1934, 53.

142 Futrall to Tyler, December 15, 1934, PFP, C49 f941; Crandall memorandum to Bolton, Maxfield, November 5, 1934, PFP, C69 f1352.

143 Perry to Evans, November 28, 1934, PFP, C56 f1080.

144 See Arthur G. Crane, "Safeguarding Educational Radio," in *Education on the Air . . . and Radio and Education 1935*, ed. Levering Tyson and Josephine H. MacLatchy (Chicago: University of Chicago Press, 1935).

145 Cited in "In Their Own Behalf," *Education by Radio*, June–July 1938, 21.

146 William S. Paley, "The Viewpoint of the Radio Industry," in *Educational Broadcasting 1937*, ed. C. S. Marsh (Chicago: University of Chicago Press, 1937), 6–12.

147 Perry to Evans, March 18, 1934, PFP, C56 f1379; Patterson Jr., to Norton, September 5, 1935, NBCP, B36 f38; Memorandum to Bolton from Evans, September 16, 1935, PFP, C69 f1351.

148 Excerpt from Minutes of Executive Committee Meeting on National Committee on Education by Radio, January 18–19, 1936, PFP, C69 f1147; Evans to Crane, June 19, 1936, PFP, C69 f1147.

149 Perry, "National Advisory Council on Radio in Education," December 1935, PFP, C52 f986.

150 Committee on Civic Education by Radio of the National Advisory Council on Radio in Education and the American Political Science Association, *Four Years of Network Broadcasting* (Chicago: University of Chicago Press, 1937).

151 Bagdikian, *The Media Monopoly*; Herman and Chomsky, *Manufacturing Consent*; see also chapter 15, "Off Limits," in this book.

8. Media Made Sport:
A History of Sports Coverage in the United States

This chapter first appeared in a slightly different form as Robert W. McChesney, "Media Made Sport: A History of Sports Coverage in the United States," in Media, Sports, & Society, *ed. Lawrence A. Wenner (Newbury Park, CA: Sage Publishers, 1989), 49–69.*

1   John Stevens, "The Rise of the Sports Page," *Gannett Center Journal* 1 (1987): 1–11.

2   Jack W. Berryman, "The tenuous attempts of Americans to 'catch up with John Bull': Specialty magazines and sporting journalism, 1800–1835," *Canadian Journal of History and Physical Education* 10 (1979): 33–61.

3   William Henry Nugent, "The Sports Section," *American Mercury Magazine* (March 1929): 329–38.

4   John Rickard Betts, "Sporting Journalism in Nineteenth Century America," *American Quarterly* 5 (1953): 39–46; Stevens, "The Rise."

5   Dan Schiller, *Objectivity and the News: The Public and the Rise of Commercial Journalism* (Philadelphia: University of Pennsylvania Press, 1981).

6   John Rickard Betts, *America's Sporting Heritage: 1850–1950* (Reading, MA: Addison-Wesley, 1974).

7   Stevens, "The rise."

8   David Q. Voigt, *American Baseball* (Norman: University of Oklahoma Press, 1966), 94.

9   Melvin L. Adelman, *A Sporting Time: New York City and the Rise of Modern Athletics, 1820–70* (Urbana: University of Illinois Press, 1986).

10   Donald J. Mrozek, *Sport and American Mentality, 1880–1910* (Knoxville: University of Tennessee Press, 1983).

11   Betts, *America's Sporting Heritage*, 377.

12   Betts, "Sporting Journalism," 51.

13   Ibid.

14   Voigt, *American Baseball*, 93.

15   Bill James, *The Bill James Baseball Abstract 1985* (New York: Ballantine, 1985).

16   Harold Seymour, *Baseball, the Early Years* (New York: Oxford University Press, 1960), 351.

17   Guy Lewis, "World War I and the Emergence of Sport for the Masses," *Maryland Historian* 4 (1973): 109–22.

18   John Rickard Betts, "Organized Sport in Industrialized America," Ph.D. dissertation (Columbia University, 1952), 422–23.

19   Warren Susman, "Piety, Profits and Play: The 1920s," in *Men, Women and Issues in American History*, H. H. Quint and M. Cantor, eds. (Homewood, IL: Dorsey, 1975) 191–92.

20   Richard Lipsky, *How We Play the Game* (Boston: Beacon, 1981).

21   Robert Lipsyte, *SportsWorld* (New York: Quadrangle, 1975), 170.

22   Alfred D. Chandler Jr., *The Visible Hand* (Cambridge, MA: Belknap, 1977), 345.

23   Catherine L. Covert, "A View of the Press in the Twenties," *Journalism History* 2 (1975): 66–67, 92–96.

24   Alfred McClung Lee, *The Daily Newspaper in America* (New York: Macmillan, 1937), 173.

25   William Weinfeld, "The Growth of Newspaper Chains in the United States: 1923, 1926–35," *Journalism Quarterly* 13 (1936): 357–80.

26   Paul A. Baren and Paul M. Sweezy, *Monopoly Capital* (New York: Monthly Review Press, 1966); Daniel Pope, *The Making of Modern Advertising* (New York: Basic Books, 1983).

27   Lee, *The Daily Newspaper in America*, 749.

28   Oswald G. Villard, *The Disappearing Daily* (New York: Alfred A. Knopf, 1944).

29   James Harold Slusser, "The Sports Page in American Life in the Nineteen-Twenties," master's thesis (University of California at Berkeley, 1954), 4.

30   Stanley Woodward, *Sports Page* (New York: Simon & Schuster, 1949), 35.

31   Villard, *The Disappearing Daily*, 6.

32   Lee, *The Daily Newspaper in America*, 526.

33   Michael Schudson, *Discovering the News: A Social History of American Newspapers* (New York: Basic Books, 1979), 144.

34   Nugent, "The Sports Section," 338.

35   David Q. Voigt, *American Baseball*, vol. 2 (Norman: University of Oklahoma Press, 1970); David Q. Voigt, *America Through Baseball* (Chicago: Nelson-Hall, 1976).

36   Lipsyte, *SportsWorld*; Leonard Schecter, *The Jocks* (New York: Warner, 1969); John R. Tunis, *Sport, Heroics, and Hysterics* (New York: John Day, 1928).

37   Arthur Stanley Link and William B. Catton, *American Epoch* (New York: Alfred A. Knopf, 1967), 296.

38   Silas Bent, *Ballyhoo* (New York: Boni & Liveright, 1927), 264.

39   John Tebbel, *The Compact History of the American Newspaper* (New York: Hawthorn, 1963), 228.

40   Arthur M. Schlesinger, *The Rise of the City* (New York: Macmillan, 1933), 199.

41   Benjamin Rader, *American Sports* (Englewood Cliffs, NJ: Prentice-Hall, 1983), 199.

42   Benjamin Rader, *In Its Own Image: How Television Has Transformed Sports* (New York: Free Press, 1984), 21; Stevens, "The Rise," 7–8.

43   Tunis, *Sport*.

44   Rader, *In Its Own Image*, 20.

45   Randy Roberts, *Jack Dempsey: The Manassa Mauler* (Baton Rouge: Louisiana State University Press, 1979), 195.

46   Schecter, *The Jocks*, 21–22.

47   Chris Lasch, *The Culture of Narcissism* (New York: W. W. Norton, 1978), 118–20; Jesse Frederick Steiner, *Americans at Play* (New York: McGraw-Hill, 1933), 88–89.

48   Paul Gallico, *Farewell to Sports* (New York: Alfred A. Knopf, 1938).

49   Howard J. Savage, *American College Athletics* (New York: Carnegie Foundation for the Advancement of Teaching, 1929), chapter 2.

50   John Louis Engdahl, Commentary, *The Daily Worker* (1925).

51   John W. Spalding, "Radio Becomes a Mass Advertising Medium," *Journal of Broadcasting* 8 (1963–64): 31–44.

52   Sut Jhally, "The Spectacle of Accumulation: Material and Cultural Factors in the Evolution of the Sport/Media Complex," *Insurgent Sociologist* 3 (1984): 41–57.

53   Betts, *Organized Sport in Industrialized America*, 471.

54   Rader, *In Its Own Image*, 25.

55   Donald Edwin Parente, "A History of Television and Sports," Ph.D. dissertation (University of Illinois, Urbana, 1974), 38.

56   Rader, *In Its Own Image*, 25.

57   Parente, "A History of Television and Sports," 38.

58   Rader, *In Its Own Image*, 27–28.

59   Ron Powers, *Supertube: The Rise of Television Sports* (New York: Coward-McCann, 1984), 48–49; Rader, *In Its Own Image*, 37–39.

60   Rader, *In Its Own Image*, 41.

61   Ibid., 40–46.

62   Ibid., 67–75.

63   Powers, *Supertube*, 52–53.

64   Ibid., 84.

65   Rader, *In Its Own Image*, 89-92.

66   Bert Randolph Sugar, *"The Thrill of Victory": The Inside of ABC Sports* (New York: Hawthorn, 1978), 54–60.

67   Phil Patton, *Razzle Dazzle: The Curious Marriage of Television and Professional Football* (Garden City, NY: Dial, 1984), 59–75.

68   Ron Powers, *Supertube*, 11–22; Rader, *In Its Own Image*, 118–37.

69   Rader, *In Its Own Image*, 117–38.

70   Ibid., 136.

71   Theodore Peterson, *Magazines in the Twentieth Century* (Urbana: University of Illinois Press, 1956).

72   Robert W. McChesney, "Sport, Mass Media and Monopoly Capital: Toward a Reinterpretation of the 1920s and Beyond," master's thesis (University of Washington, 1986).

73   Stevens, "The Rise."

74   Lipsky, *How We Play the Game*; James A. Michener, *Sports in America* (New York: Random House, 1976).

75   Lipsyte, *SportsWorld*.

9. Public Broadcasting in the Age of Communication Revolution

This chapter first appeared in a slightly different form as Robert W. McChesney, "Public Broadcasting in the Age of Communication Revolution," Monthly Review 47/7 (1995): 1–19.

10. The New Theology of the First Amendment: Class Privilege Over Democracy

This chapter first appeared in a slightly different form as Robert W. McChesney, "The New Theology of the First Amendment: Class Privilege Over Democracy," Monthly Review 49/10 (1998): 17–34.

1   See C. Edwin Baker, "Giving the Audience What It Wants," *Ohio State Law Journal* 58/2 (1997): 311–417.

2   For an elaboration of the ACLU position, see Laura W. Murphy, "We Refuse to Sacrifice the First Amendment in a Desperate Attempt to Adopt Reform Legislation," *The Progressive* 61/12 (1997): 20–22.

3   Alexander Meiklejohn, *Political Freedom: The Constitutional Powers of the People* (New York: Harper & Brothers, 1960).

4   See Thomas I. Emerson, *Toward a General Theory of the First Amendment* (New York: Random House, 1963).

5   See Richard N. Rosenfeld, *American Aurora* (New York: St. Martin's Press, 1997); Stanley E. Flink, *Sentinel Under Siege* (Boulder, CO: Westview Press, 1997).

6   See Dan Schiller, *Theorizing Communication: A History* (New York: Oxford University Press, 1996).

7   See Herbert J. Gans, *Deciding What's News* (New York: Pantheon, 1979).

8   See Jerome A. Barron, "Access to the Press—A New First Amendment Right," *Harvard Law Review* 80 (1967): 1641–78.

9   *Miami Herald Publishing Company v. Tornillo*, 94 S. Ct. 2831 (1974), 2840, 2841.

10   I cover this entire episode and the ACLU's transformation in Robert W. McChesney, *Telecommunications, Mass Media, and Democracy: The Battle for the Control of U.S. Broadcasting, 1928–1935* (New York: Oxford University Press, 1993).

11   See David Kairys, "Freedom of Speech," *The Politics of Law: A Progressive Critique*, David Kairys, ed. (New York: Pantheon, 1982), 140–71.

12   See Ben H. Bagdikian, *The Media Monopoly*, 5th ed. (Boston: Beacon Press, 1997).

13   Angus Mackenzie, *Secrets: The CIA's War at Home* (Berkeley: University of California Press, 1997).

14   A strong vocal opposition to the ACLU position has emerged within the ACLU itself; this is the most divisive question in the organization, and is a healthy development.

11. The Commercial Tidal Wave

This chapter first appeared in a slightly different form as Robert W. McChesney and John Bellamy Foster, "The Commercial Tidal Wave," Monthly Review 54/10 (2003): 1–16. Much of this material would later appear in chapter 4 of McChesney, The Problem of the Media.

1   Rance Crain, "Take Me Out to the Ballgame, If Only to Escape Fox Promos," *Advertising Age*, November 4, 2002, p. 20.

2   Charles Pappas, "Ad Nauseum," *Advertising Age*, July 10, 2000, p. 16.

3   J. Max Robins, "Increasingly, TV's a Mess of Messages," www.tvguide.com, February 3, 2002.

4   Vanessa O'Connell, "Amount of Ad "Clutter' on Prime-Time TV Drops," *The Wall Street Journal*, March 1, 2001, p. B16; Chuck Ross, "Peacock Clutters Up Airwaves," *Electronic Media*, August 7, 2000, pp. 1, 39; Louis Chunovic, "ABC Again No. 1 on Clutter List," *Electronic Media*, September 2, 2002, pp. 1, 39; Joe Flint, "Commercial Clutter On TV Networks Rises to Record," *The Wall Street Journal*, March 2, 2000, p. B18.

5   Paul Taylor, "Too Little Time," *The Washington Monthly*, September 2000.

6   Louis Chunovic, "TV Clutter Reaches All-Time High," *Electronic Media*, March 11, 2002, pp. 1, 29.

7   J. Max Robins, "Increasingly, TV's a Mess of Messages," www.tvguide.com, February 3, 2002.

8   Dan Trigoboff, "Spot Squeeze Play in Nashville," *Broadcasting & Cable*, October 21, 2002, pp. 6-7; Michelle Greppi, "Squeezed Shoes Upset Agencies," *Electronic Media*, November 19, 2001, pp. 1, 20; Michelle Greppi, "CBS Time Squeeze Scandal Widens," *Electronic Media*, November 12, 2001, pp. 1, 43; Dan Trigoboff, "Squeeze Play in Pittsburgh?" *Broadcasting & Cable*, November 5, 2001, p. 14.

9   Michael McCarthy, "Digitally Inserted Ads Pop Up in World Series," www.usatoday.com, October 18, 2002.

10   Adam Bruckman, "Time to Cut Clueless Clutter," www.nypost.com, Augsut 21, 2001.

11   Kate MacArthur, "Turner CEO Lambasts Ad-Avoiding Technologies," www.adage.com, October 11, 2002.

12   Richard Tomkins, "As Television Audiences Tire of Commercials, Advertisers Move Into Making Programmes," *Financial Times*, November 5, 2002, p. 15

13   "A Coke and a Smile," *Variety*, July 17-23, 2000, p. 5.

14   Anna Wilde Mathews, "Ford Motor Gets Starring Role On WB Network," *The Wall Street Journal*, March 21, 2001, pp. B1, B4.

15   Richard Tomkins, "As Television Audiences Tire of Commercials, Advertisers Move Into Making Programmes," *Financial Times*, November 5, 2002, p. 15

16. Bill Carter, "Survival of the Pushiest," *The New York Times Sunday Magazine*, January 28, 2001, p. 25.

17. Wayne Friedman, "Magna Sells NBC on Reality Series," *Advertising Age*, November 18, 2003, p. 3.

18   David Goetzl, "TBS Tries Virtual Advertising," *Advertising Age*, May 21, 2001, p. 8; Stuart Elliott, "Advertising: Reruns May Become Testing Ground for Digital Insertion," www.nytimes.com, May 23, 2001.

19   Louis Chunovic, "Placing Value on Placement," *Electronic Media*, December 2, 2002, p. 6.

20   Wayne Friedman, "Goss Ties It All Together at Universal's Brand Group," *Advertising Age*, December 9, 2002, p. 38.

21   See David Desser and Garth S. Jowett, editors, *Hollywood Goes Shopping* (Minneapolis: University of Minnesota Press, 2000).

22   Wayne Friedman, "'Minority Report' Stars Lexus, Nokia," *Advertising Age*, June 17, 2002, p. 41.

23   Bruce Orwall, "Miramax-Coors Deal Married Entertainment and Advertising," *The Wall Street Journal Online*, August 8, 2002.

24   Wayne Friedman, "Pepsi, Coke to Compete at Box Office," *Advertising Age*, March 12, 2001, pp. 3, 41.

25   Lee Pfeiffer, "License to Shill," *Variety*, November 11-17, 2002, "James Bond at 40" special section, p. A13.

26.   Marc Graser, "007's Bid Ad-Venture," *Variety*, October 7-13, 2002, pp. 1, 105; Tim Burt, "His Name's Bond, James Bond and He's Been Licensed to Sell," *Financial Times*, October 5-6, 2002, p. 22.

27   Nicholas Foulkes, "James Bond," *Financial Times*, November 16-17, 2002, Weekend FT section, p. X.

28.   "How Hollywood Brings Brands Into Your Home," *Financial Times*, November 5, 2002, p. 15.

29   Wayne Friedman, "Coming to a Theater Near You: Targeted, Digital Ad Buying," *Advertising Age*, October 21, 2002, pp. 4, 57.

30   Matt Richtel, "Product Placements Go Interactive in Video Games," *The New York Times*, September 17, 2002, p. C1.

31   David D. Kirkpatrick, "Words from Our Sponsor: A Jeweler Commissions a Novel," www.nytimes.com, September 3, 2001; Tim Rutten, "Read Between the Lines and You Might See Commercials," www.latimes.com, June 19, 2002.

32   Matthew Rose and Suzanne Vranica, "Prolonged Ad Slump Puts Media In the Mood to Pander to Buyers," *The Wall Street Journal Online*, May 9, 2002.

33   Chuck Ross, "USA Cozies Up to Advertisers," *Electronic Media*, December 18, 2000, pp. 1, 35.

34   Corie Brown, "Advertisers Seek a Bigger Role in TV Programming," www.latimes.com, January 15, 2002.

35   Laurie Freeman, "If the Product Fits a Series, TNT Wants It," *Electronic Media*, November 27, 2000, pp. 12, 59.

36   Debra Aho Williamson, "G4 Widens Playing Field for Advertisers," *Advertising Age*, June 10, 2002, p. S-14.

37   Joe Flint and Emily Nelson, "TV 'Plot Placement' Yields ABC a Big Advertising Buy," *The Wall Street Journal Online*, March 15, 2002.

38   Andrew Wallenstein, "ESPN Looks Into Longer, Hybrid Ads," www.hollywoodreporter.com, September 24, 2002.

39   Alice Z. Cuneo, "Ace Ads on 'MNF' Starring Madden Blur Content Line," *Advertising Age*, September 2, 2002, p. 3.

40   Nat Ives, "Still More Brand Names to Get Star Roles in a Fox Sports Show," *The New York Times*, January 3, 2003, p. C3.

41   Chris Pursell, "Added Value for Stations in 'Ebay-TV'," *Electronic Media*, November 4, 2002, pp. 1, 21.

42   Brian Lowry, "Going Far Beyond Product Placement," www.latimes.com, July 10, 2002.

43   Michael Schneider, "'Wild' Infomercial Struts Its Stuff," *Variety*, December 9-15, 2002, p. 32.

44   Hank Kim, "Madison Ave. Melds Pitches and Content," *Advertising Age*, October 7, 2002, p. 16.

45   Tobi Elkin, "Getting Viewers to Opt In, Not Tune Out," *Advertising Age*, November 4, 2002, p. 10.

46   Vanessa O'Connell, "Omnicom, NBC Discuss Unusual TV Deal," *The Wall Street Journal*, July 5, 2001, p. B9; Richard Linnett, "McCann Creates Sponsor-Friendly TV Program Unit," *Advertising Age*, August 21, 2000, p. 4; Richard Linett, "Content Contenders," *Advertising Age*, October 9, 2000, pp. 20, 22.

47   Bill Carter, "Skipping Ads? TV Gets Ready to Fight Back," *The New York Times*, January 10, 2003, pp. C1, C4.

48   David Carr, "Magazine Imitates a Catalog And Has a Charmed Life, So Far," *The New York Times*, September 16, 2002, pp. C1, C2.

49   Nat Ives, "Advertising," The New York Times, November 4, 2002, p. C10.

50   Erin White, "Movie-Trailer Ads Blur the Lines of Entertainment and Advertising," *The Wall Street Journal Online*, July 22, 2002; Sheila Muto, "Theaters Showcase Product Pitches," *The Wall Street Journal*, August 29, 2001, p. B8.

51   Mark Gimien, "Program-Free Commercials," www.fortune.com, April 1, 2002.

52   David Goetzl, "BMW Rolls Out DirecTV Channel," *Advertising Age*, September 23, 2002, p. 55.

53   Richard Tomkins, "As Television Audiences Tire of Commercials, Advertisers Move Into Making Programmes," *Financial Times*, November 5, 2002, p. 15.

54   Jane Weaver, "That's Advertainment," www.msnbc.com, October 9, 2002.

55   Stephanie Thompson, "General Mills Adds Disney Characters to Fruit Snack Line," *Advertising Age*, May 8, 2000, p. 22; Stephanie Thompson, "Nestle Product Extends Shelf Life of Disney Tie-ins," *Advertising Age*, February 7, 2000, p. 20; Stephanie Thompson, "Frito, Disney Plane One-Two Punch Promos," *Advertising Age*, March 13, 2000, p. 8; Wayne Friedman, "McDonald's Joins ABC's 'Happy Hour'," *Electronic Media*, September 9, 2002, p. 5.

56   Sherri Day, "Advertising," *The New York Times*, November 12, 2002, p. C8.

57   Jean Halliday, "Toyota Links with Phil Collins," *Advertising Age*, October 14, 2002, p. 8.

58   Jean Halliday, "Automakers Turn to Music," *Advertising Age*, August 19, 2002, p. 6.

59   "Chevrolet is 'Religiously' Supporting 'Rolling Stone,' Too," www.minonline.com, November 2002.

60   Nat Ives, "Advertising," *The New York Times*, November 6, 2002, p. C3.

61   Wayne Friedman, "Music Labels Court Brands," Advertising Age, September 16, 2002, p. 19.

62   Lynette Holloway, "Hip-Hop Sales Pop: Pass the Courvoisier and Count the Cash," *The New York Times*, September 2, 2002, p. C6.

63   Hank Kim, "Def Jam, H-P Explore Branded Music Alliance," *Advertising Age*, September 9, 2002, pp. 4, 28.

64   Rich Thomaselli and Cara B. DiPasquale, "Keeper of the Flame," *Advertising Age*, September 23, 2002, p. 16.

65   Erik Parker, "Hip-Hop Goes Commercial," *The Village Voice*, September 11-17, 2002. Online at www.villagevoice.com.

66   Wayne Friedman, "MasterCard, Universal Eye $100 Mil Deal," *Advertising Age*, December 2, 2002, pp. 1, 56.

67   See David Bollier, *Silent Theft: The Private Plunder of our Common Wealth* (New York: Routledge, 2002).

68   See, for example, Stephanie Thompson, "Pepsi Hits High Note with Schools," *Advertising Age*, October 9, 2002, p. 30; Karen W. Arenson, "Columbia Leads Academic Pack in Turning Profit form Research," *The New York Times*, August 2, 2000, pp. A1, A25; Joan Obra, Stacy Schwandt and Peter Woodall, "Corporate Donors' Influence Spilling into UC Classrooms," *San Francisco Chronicle*, June 26, 2002; Eyal Press and Jennifer Washburn, "The Kept University," *The Atlantic Monthly*, March 2000; Henry Giroux and Kostas Myrsiades, editors, *Beyond the Corporate University: Culture and Pedagogy in the New Millenium* (Lanham, Md.: Rowman & Littlefield, 2001); Chin-tao Wu, *Privatising Culture: Corporate Art Intervention Since the 1980s* (London: Verso, 2002).

69   Sharon J. Kahn, "Corporate America Discovers Key Demos in Indie Scene," *Variety*, August 26-September 1, 2002, Film Fest Guide, p. 5.

70   Thomas Frank and Matt Weiland, editors, *Commodify Your Dissent: Salvos from The Baffler* (New York: W. W. Norton, 1997).

71   Inger L. Stole, "The Gift That Keeps on Giving: Cause Related Marketing in the 1990s," paper presented to the Association for Consumer Research annual convention, Atlanta, Georgia, October 2002.

72   See Al Ries and Lauar Ries, *The Fall of Advertising and the Rise of PR* (New York: HarperCollins, 2002); Sergio Zyman with Armin Brott, *The End of Advertising as We Know It* (Hoboken, N.J.: John Wiley & Sons, 2002).

73   See Todd Gitlin, *Media Unlimited* (New York: Metropolitan Books, 2001); Anna McCarthy, *Ambient Television* (Durham: Duke University Press, 2001).

74   R.J. Smith, "Among the Mooks," *The New York Times Sunday Magazine*, August 6, 2000, pp. 34-41; John De Graaf, David Wann, Thomas H. Naylor, *Affluenza: The All-Consuming Epidemic* (San Francisco: Berrett-Koehler Publishers, 2001).

75   David Shaw, "A Nation Under Siege … By Product Placement," www.latimes.com, November 3, 2002; David W. Dunlap, "New York Tells Microsoft to Get Its Butterfly Decals Out of Town," *The New York Times*, October 25, 2002, p. A30.

76   Sheila Muto, "Signage-it is: More Buildings Sport Billboards," *The Wall Street Journal*, January 10, 2001, p. B10.

77   Randy Kennedy, "Hail a Cab, Read a Commercial," *The New York Times*, August 26, 2001, p. 26; Motoko Rich, "Firms Pitch New Place to Park Ads," *The Wall Street Journal*, July 11, 2001, p. B10; Anna Wilde Mathews, "Clear Channel Readies Plan for Video Ads in Subways," *The Wall Street Journal Online*, December 23, 2002; Gerard O'Dwyer and Bill Britt, "The New Billboards: Buggies," *Advertising Age*, August 19, 2002, p. 11.

78   Robert Johnson, "Ad-packed TVs May Soon Be Boarding City Buses," *The Wall Street Journal*, February 21, 2001, p. B1; Jack Neff, "Vendors Seek to Become Checkstand Media Moguls," *Advertising Age*, March 6, 2000, p. 36; Louis Chunovic, "These TV Channels Can't Be Turned Off," *Electronic Media*, June 25-July 2, 2001, p. 16; Geraldine baum, "Taking News Overload to the next Level," www.calendarlive.com, October 14, 2002.

79   Louis Chunovic, "GE Goes to Hospitals with Patient Channel," *Electronic Media*, September 16, 2002, p. 8.

80   Greg Johnson, "Nowhere to Run, Nowhere to Hide from Ad Barrage," www.latimes.com, July 24, 2001.

81   Michael McCarthy, "Ad Tattoos Get Under Some People's Skin; Boxers Get Paid to Plaster Messages on Their Backs," www.usatoday.com, April 4, 2002.

82   Information available at www.governmentacquisitions.com. Criticism of the practice is available at www.commercialalert.org.

83   "Consumers in the Mist," *Business Week*, February 26, 2001, p. 92.

84   Gerry Khermouch and Jeff Green, "Buzz Marketing," *Business Week*, July 30, 2001, pp. 50-56.

85   Alissa Quart, *Branded: The Buying and Selling of Teenagers* (Cambridge, Mass.: Perseus Publishing, 2003).

86   Stephanie Thompson, "Targeting Teens Means Building Buzz," *Advertising Age*, March 27, 2000, p. 26-27.

87   Gerry Khermouch and Jeff Green, "Buzz Marketing," *Business Week*, July 30, 2001, p. 53.

88   Daniel Eisenberg, "It's an Ad, Ad, Ad World," *Time*, September 2, 2002. Available at www.time.com.

89   Kate MacArthur and Hillary Chura, "Urban Warfare," *Advertising Age*, September 4, 2000, p. 16.

90   "The Spider's Bite," *The Economist*, May 11, 2002, p. 57.

91   Wayne Friedman, "Nicj Signs Up Embassy Suites for $20 Mil Deal," *Advertising Age*, November 20, 2000, p. 53.

92   Brooke Shelby Biggs, "Sesame Street Meets Madison Avenue," www.motherjones.com, March 30, 2001; Daniel Golden, "Channel One Aims to Involve Teachers in Marketing Push," *The Wall Street Journal*, August 28, 2001, p. B7; Geov Parrish, "Ads Creep in the Classroom," www.workingforchange.com, February 6, 2002. See United States General Accounting Office, *Public Education: Commercial Activities in Schools* (Washington, D.C.: General Accounting Office, September 2000).

93   See, for example, James P. Steyer, *The Other Parent: The Inside Story of the Media's Effect on Our Children* (New York: Atria Books, 2002).

94   Suzanne Vranica, "CDC Launches Ads Pushing Children to Be More Active," *The Wall Street Journal Online*, July 18, 2002.

95   Claire Atkinson, "Ad Intrusion Up, Say Consumers," *Advertising Age*, January 6, 2003, pp. 1, 19.

96   Brian Lowry, "Shows Reach Out and Pitch Someone, 24/7," www.latimes.com, January 8, 2003.

97   Alexander Meiklejohn, *Free Speech and Its Relation to Self-Government* (New York: Harper and Brothers, 1948).

98   Paul A. Baran and Paul M. Sweezy, "These on Advertising," *Science & Society*, Winter 1964. In Paul A. Baran, *The Longer View* (New York: Monthly Review Press, 1969), p. 232.

99   James Rorty, *Advertising: Our Master's Voice* (New York: John Day & Company, 1934).

12. Noam Chomsky and the Struggle Against Neoliberalism

This chapter first appeared in a slightly different form as Robert W. McChesney, "Noam Chomsky and the Struggle Against Neoliberalism," Monthly Review 50/11 (1999): 40–47.

13. The New Economy: Myth and Reality

This chapter first appeared in a slightly different form as John Bellamy Foster, Robert W. McChesney, Harry Magdoff, and Paul M. Sweezy, "The New Economy: Myth and Reality," Monthly Review 52/11 (2001): 1–15.

1   For Greenspan's speeches see the Federal Reserve Board Web site at http://www.federal-reserve.gov.

2   Estimates on the contribution of the New Economy to economic growth are those of the Bureau of Economic Analysis. See J. Steven Landefeld and Barbara M. Fraumeni, *Measuring the New Economy*, Bureau of Economic Analysis Advisory Committee Meeting, May 5, 2000, table 2, http://www.bea.doc.gov/papers.htm. U.S. government statistics use what is called a "hedonic price index" to make adjustments for quality improvements, in accounting for real computer spending. This tends to overstate information technology spending in the United States and its contribution to GDP compared to the majority of countries (exceptions being Canada, France, and Japan) that do not use such hedonic indices. See *Economic Report of the President, 2001*, 164–65.

3   It should be noted that there have been major advances in the use of automatic machinery within industrial production as a result of the new technology. This includes not only computers but cybernetics, which has a lot to do with the whole computer technology. To get more automatic, workerless production equipment, various devices of automatic controls and feedback, which use computers or computer-like instruments, are introduced. Hence, data on the utilization of pure information technology within durable manufacturing, such as referred to here, may be somewhat misleading, understating the role that the new technology plays in that sector.

4   On the problems of the application of productivity statistics to the service sector, see Harry Magdoff and Paul M. Sweezy, "The Uses and Abuses of Measuring Productivity," *Monthly Review*, June 1980.

5   Robert J. Gordon, "Not Much of a New Economy," *Financial Times*, July 26, 2000; and "Does the 'New Economy' Measure Up to the Great Inventions of the Past?," *Journal of Economic Perspectives* 14/4 (2000): 49–74.

6   John Cassidy, "The Productivity Mirage," *The New Yorker*, November 27, 2000, 116.

7   Paul Baran and Paul Sweezy, *Monopoly Capital* (New York: Monthly Review Press, 1968), 219–20.

8   Robert Schiller, *Irrational Exuberance* (Princeton, NJ: Princeton University Press, 2000), 4.

9   Quoted in Ibid., 106.

10 See The Editors, "Working-Class Households and the Burden of Debt," *Monthly Review* 52/1 (2000): 1–11.

14. The Political Economy of International Communications

This chapter first appeared in a slightly different form as Robert W. McChesney and Dan Schiller, "The Political Economy of International Communications: Foundations for the Emerging Global Debate about Media Ownership and Regulation," Technology, Business and Society, Program Paper Number 11, October 2003.

1   Jeffrey L. Pasley, *The Tyranny of Printers: Newspaper Politics in the Early American Republic* (Charlottesville, VA: University Press of Virginia, 2001); Dan Schiller,

Objectivity and the News: The Public and the Rise of Commercial Journalism (Philadelpia: University of Pennsylvania Press, 1981); Robert W. T. Martin, *The Free and Open Press: The Founding of American Democratic Press Liberty* (New York: New York University Press, 2001).

2   Richard John, *Spreading the News* (Cambridge, MA: Harvard University Press, 1995).

3   Culver H. Smith, *The Press, Politics, and Patronage: The American Government's Use of Newspapers 1789–1875* (Athens, GA: University of Georgia Press, 1977).

4   William J. Gilmore, *Reading Becomes a Necessity of Life* (Knoxville: University of Tennessee Press, 1989).

5   Siva Vaidhyanathan, *Copyrights and Copywrongs: The Rise of Intellectual Property and How It Threatens Creativity* (New York: New York University Press, 2001).

6   Richard B. DuBoff, "The Rise of Communications Regulation: The Telegraph Industry, 1844–1880," *Journal of Communication* (1984): 52–66.

7   Thomas Streeter, *Selling the Air: A Critique of the Policy of Commercial Broadcasting in the United States* (Chicago: University of Chicago Press, 1996).

8   Robert W. McChesney, *Telecommunications, Mass Media and Democracy: The Battle for the Control of U.S. Broadcasting, 1928–1935* (Oxford: Oxford University Press, 1993).

9   Center for Public Integrity, "Off the Record: What Media Corporations Don't Tell You About Their Legislative Agendas," Center for Public Integrity, 2001, http://www.publicintegrity.org/dtaweb/index.asp?L1=20&L2=L3=0&L4=0&L5=0.

10   Alfred McClung Lee, *The Daily Newspaper in America: Evolution of a Social Instrument* (New York: McGraw-Hill, 1937).

11   James G. Smart, "Information control, thought control: Whitelaw Reid and the nation's news services," *Public Historian* 3/2 (1981): 23–42.

12   Dan Schiller, *Theorizing Communication: A History* (New York: Oxford University Press, 1996).

13   Richard L. Kaplan, *Politics and the American Press: The Rise of Objectivity, 1865–1920* (Cambridge: Cambridge University Press, 2002); Robert W. McChesney and Ben Scott, "Introduction," in *The Brass Check*, by Upton Sinclair (Urbana: University of Illinois Press, 2002).

14   C. B. Macpherson, *The Life and Times of Liberal Democracy* (Oxford: Oxford University Press, 1977).

15   Daniel Headrick, *The Invisible Weapon* (New York: Oxford University Press, 1995).

16   Kaarle Nordenstreng and Lauri Hannikainen, *The Mass Media Declaration of UNESCO* (Norwood, NJ: Ablex Publishing, 1984).

17   Herbert I. Schiller, *Mass Communications and American Empire*, 2nd ed. (Boulder, CO: Westview Press, 1992).

18   See Table 1.1 in United States Conference on Trade and Development (UNCTAD), *World Investment Report 2001: Promoting Linkages* (New York: United Nations, 2001).

19   United States Conference on Trade and Development (UNCTAD), *World Investment Report 2000* (New York: United Nations, 2000), xx.

20   Dan Schiller, *Digital Capitalism: Networking the Global Market System* (Cambridge, MA: MIT Press, 1999).

21   Robert W. McChesney, *Rich Media, Poor Democracy: Communication Politics in Dubious Times* (New York: New Press, 2002), chapter 2; Dan Schiller and Vincent Mosco,

"Introduction: Integrating a continent for a transnational world," in *Continental Order? Integrating North America for Cyber-Capitalism*, Vincent Mosco and Dan Schiller, eds. (Lanham, MD: Rowman and Littlefield, 2001).

22 Vincent Mosco and Dan Schiller, eds., *Continental Order? Integrating North America for Cyber-Capitalism*.

23 David Molony, "Utsumi's Think-Tank to Shake Up ITU," *Communications Week International*, October 4, 1999, 1, 74.

24 Andy Stern, "Microsoft/Telewest deal faces high EC hurdles," *Variety*, April 3–9, 2000, 79.

25 Andy Stern, "EU Questions Pubcaster Aid," *Variety*, May 22–28, 2000, 67; Andy Stern, "EU to Change Pubcaster Financial Rules," *Variety*, January 10–16, 2000, 105.

26 Charles Goldsmith, "BBC forms commercial Internet unit; US firms to take stake in subsidiary," *Wall Street Journal*, August 23, 2000; Peter Thal Larsen "Little Time for Commercial Break," *Financial Times*, August 25, 2000, 15.

27 David D. Kirkpatrick, "Not Quite All-American, Bertelsman Is Big on U.S.," *New York Times*, September 3, 2000.

28 Danny Schecter, "Long Live Chairman Levin!," Mediachannel.org, July 5, 2000.

29 "Scardino's way," *The Economist*, August 5, 2000, 62.

30 "Talk Show," *Business Week*, October 2, 2000, 12.

31 "The World's 100 Largest Public Companies," *Wall Street Journal*, September 25, 2000, R24.

32 Anthony Bianco, "Deal Time At Seagram," *Business Week*, June 26, 2000, 60.

33 Ibid.

34 Saul Hansell, "Murdoch Sees Satellites As Way To Keep News Corp. Current," *New York Times*, June 16, 2000.

35 Diane Mermigas, "Morgan Stanley Banks On Media," *Electronic Media*, May 15, 2000, 17, 20.

36 Jill Goldsmith and Adam Dawtrey, "Murdoch: The Sky's the Limit," *Variety*, August 28–September 3, 2000, 1, 130.

37 Rahul Jacob, "Star Is Shooting Towards Interactive TV," *Financial Times*, June 10–11, 2000, 11.

38 Don Groves, "Star Connects Dot-Coms," *Variety*, May 29–June 4, 2000, 30, 106.

39 *The Economist*, "Star Turn," March 11, 2000, 67, 68.

40 Richard Tomkins, "Zenith Spotlights Advertising Surge," *Financial Times*, July 18, 2000, 21.

41 Stuart Elliot, "Publicist Plans To Buy Saatchi For At Least $1.5 Billion," *New York Times*, June 20, 2000.

42 Ira Teinowitz and Richard Linnett, "Eye on Mergers: Media Behemoths Up Agency Ante," *Advertising Age*, May 8, 2000, 3, 105.

43 David D. Kirkpatrick, "Harper-Collins Plans to Buy a Small British Publisher" *New York Times*, July 11, 2000.

44 Cecilie Rohwedder, "Kirch Tightens Control Over German Broadcast Assets," *Wall Street Journal*, June 29, 2000.

45 Stanley Reed, "A Media Star Is Born," *Business Week*, April 24, 2000, 136, 137.

46   James Brooke, "Canadian TV Makes A Move Into Papers," *New York Times*, August 1, 2000.

47   Elena Cherney, "CanWest Tightens Its Media Grip," *Wall Street Journal*, August 2, 2000.

48   Christopher Brown-Humes, "Bonnier Scotland," *Financial Times*, September 20, 2000, 9.

49   Mary Sutter, "Hicks, Muse Invests $1 Billion in Latin American Drive," *Variety*, January 17–23, 2000, 70.

50   Ron Grover and Richard Siklos, "Where Old Foes Need Each Other," *Business Week*, October 25, 1999, 114, 118.

51   Christina Hoag, "Empire Building: The Slow Track," *Business Week*, September 11, 2000, 126E3–126E4.

52   Mermigas, "Morgan Stanley."

53   Elizabeth Guider, "AFMA Exports Up 22% As Global TV Booms," *Variety*, June 19–25, 2000, 14, 75.

54   Tobias Grey, "Promo Effort Key in France," *Variety*, February 21–27, 2000, 30, 106.

55   Rick Lyman, "No Trace of Anti-Hollywood Bias in French Purchase of Universal," *New York Times*, June 20, 2000.

56   David Rooney, "Ciao Time for Italy," *Variety*, June 19–25, 2000, 72.

57   Liza Foreman, "Teuton Tongues Untied," *Variety*, August 14–20, 2000, 39, 40.

58   "U.S. Cable Channels Tighten Their Grip On Latin American Cable Viewers," *TV International*, June 12, 2000, 6.

59   Claude Brodesser, "Sony's Global Gaze Pays," *Variety*, April 3–9, 2000, 13, 62; Paul F. Duke, "Robinson Explores Asia Films for Sony," *Variety*, August 28–September 3, 2000, 7, 128.

60   "Growing Up," *The Economist*, August 12, 2000, 57–58.

61   Pankaj Mishra, "Yearning to Be Great, India Loses Its Way," *New York Times*, September 16, 2000.

62   Andrew Wheat, "Mexico's Privatization Piñata," *Multinational Monitor* 17/10 (1996).

63   James Perry, "Shades of 1960 Are Superficial Amid Changes In Electorate," *Wall Street Journal*, September 14, 2000.

64   Diane Mermigas, "International Plays Take Media Firms To Next Level," *Electronic Media*, July 31, 2000, 22.

65   Bruce Orwall, "ESPN Adds Entertainment Shows to Its Playbook," *Wall Street Journal*, March 6, 2002.

66   Richard Waters and Christopher Grimes, "A media giant finds the future less rosy," *Financial Times*, March 28, 2002, 15.

67   Carol J. Loomis, "AOL Time Warner's New Math," *Fortune*, February 4, 2002, 98, 102.

68   John Carreyrou, "Vivendi Might Preannounce Big Write-Down," *Wall Street Journal*, March 5, 2002; John Lippman, "News Corp. to Take $2 Billion Charge on Gemstar Stake," *Wall Street Journal*, March 28, 2002; Richard Waters, "Liberty Books $4.1bn Of Write-Downs," *Financial Times*, April 3, 2002, 22.

69   Ashling O'Connor, James Harding, and Matthew Garrahan, "Turmoil Hits UK Digital Television Group," *Financial Times*, March 28, 2002, 17; Juliana Ratner and James Harding, "NTL Expected To Default On $96m Interest Payments," *Financial Times*, April 1, 2002, 13.

70   "Switched Off," *Financial Times*, March 28, 2002, 14.

71   Jamal Henni and Nathalie Silbert, "France's Biggest Cable TV Groups Up For Sale," *Financial Times*, April 3, 2002, 21.

72   James Harding and Bertrand Benoit, "Bankruptcy Deadline Looms Over Ailing Kirch," *Financial Times*, April 3, 2002, 21.

73   Bertrand Benoit, "Axel Springer Offered Stake in Kirch Media," *Financial Times*, March 28, 2002, 17; Edmund L. Andrews, "Kirch Nears Bankruptcy As Loan Deal Falls Apart," *New York Times*, April 4, 2002; "Two German leaders Shun a Berlusconi Role in Kirch," *Wall Street Journal*, March 29, 2002.

74   Matthew Karnitschnig, "Germany Braces For Post-Kirch TV Industry," *Wall Street Journal*, April 3, 2002.

75   Bertrand Benoit and James Harding, "Kirch Leaves Crumbling Empire," *Financial Times*, March 27, 2002, 13.

76   Pamela Druckerman, "Telecom Argentina Plans to Suspend Debt Payments," *Wall Street Journal*, April 3, 2002.

77   Michael J. Wolf, "Here Comes Another Wave Of Media Mergers," *Wall Street Journal*, February 21, 2002.

78   Dan Schiller, *Telematics and Government* (Norwood: Ablex, 1982).

79   Susan G. Esserman, "Telecommunications and the International Trade System," Center for Strategic and International Studies, Washington, DC, February 29, 2000.

80   Richard W. Fisher, "Trade in Telecommunications Services, Testimony Before the House of Representatives Committee on Commerce, Subcommitee on Telecommunications, Trade and Consumer Protection," September, 7, 2000, 3, 5, 11.

81   Charlene Barshefsky, "Electronic Commerce: Trade Policy In a Borderless World," The Woodrow Wilson Center, Washington, DC, (1999): 6; Chantal Bouin, "The WTO Agreement on Basic Telecommunications: A Reevaluation," *Telecommunications Policy* 24/2 (2000): 135, 142.

82   One report claimed that "more than $1 trillion" in state assets were sold to private investors through the late 1990s. See Yochi Dreazen and Andrew Caffrey, "Now, Public Works Seem too Precious for the Free Market," *Wall Street Journal*, November 19, 2001.

83   United States Federal Communications Commission (USFCC), International Bureau, *Report on International Telecommunications markets 1999 Update*, prepared for Senator Ernest F. Hollings, Committee on Commerce, Science and Transportation, U.S. Senate, January 14, 2000.

84   For example, through the Office of the United States Trade Representative, which publishes an annual report on the subject. See United States Trade Representative (USTR), *Results of the 2002 "Section 1377" Review of Telecommunications Trade Agreements*, 2002, available at http://www.ustr.gov/sectors/industry/Telecom1377/2002review.pdf.

85   Rebecca Blumentstein, "Who's On First?," *Wall Street Journal*, September 18, 2000.

86   United States Federal Communications Commission (USFCC), *International Bureau Report*, 2000, sec. 43,82, Circuit Status Data, June 2001, available at http://www.fcc. gove/ib/td/pf/csmanual.html.

87   Almar Latour, "How Europe Tripped Over a Wireless Phone Made for the Internet," *Wall Street Journal*, June 5, 2001.

88   S.D. Oliner and D.E. Sichel, "The Resurgence of Growth in the Late 1990s: Is Information Technology the Story?," Working Paper, May 2000. Available at

http://www.federalreserve.gove/pubs/feds/2000; Bjorn Wellenius, Carlos Alberto, Primo Braga, and Christine Zhen-Wei Qiang, "Investment and Growth of the Information Infrastructure: Summary Results of a Global Survey," *Telecommunications Policy* 24/8–9 (2000): 639, 642.

89   Holman Jenkins Jr., "How a Telecom Meltdown Will Cause the Next Recession," *Wall Street Journal*, September 27, 2000.

90   Dan Roberts, "Glorious Hopes On A Trillion-Dollar Scrapheap," *Financial Times*, September 5, 2001, 10; Michael R. Sesit, "Will Europe's Banks Flounder On The Rocks Of Telecom Debt?" *Wall Street Journal*, January 30, 2001.

91   Rebecca Blumenstein, "How the Fiber Barons Plunged The Nation Into A Telecom Glut," *Wall Street Journal*, June 18, 2001; Evan Ramstad and Kortney Stringer, "In Race To Lay Fiber, Telecom Firms Wreak Havoc On City Streets," *Wall Street Journal*, February 27, 2001.

92   Telegeography Inc., *International Bandwidth 2001*, Washington, DC, 2001.

93   Dan Schiller, "Deep Impact: The Web and the Changing Media Economy," *Info* 1/1 (1999): 39.

94   Wellenius et al "Investment and Growth of the Information Infrastructure."

95   Richard W. Fisher, *Trade in Telecommunications Services*, Testimony before the House of Representatives Committee on Commerce, Subcommittee on Telecommunications, Trade and Consumer Protection, September 7, 2000, 5.

96   Telegeography Inc., *International Bandwidth 2001*, Washington, DC, 2001, 98, 124.

97   Terry Priston, "Phone Service Improves, But Many Are Still Without Power In Lower Manhattan," *New York Times*, September 14, 2001; Shawn Young and Dennis K. Berman, "Trade Center Attack Shows Vulnerability Of Telecom Network," *Wall Street Journal*, October 19, 2001; Shawn Young and Deborah Solomon, "Verizon Effectively Rebuilds Network for NYSE," *Wall Street Journal*, September 18, 2001.

98   Ricardo Alsonso-Zaldivar, "Nation's Infrastructure Crumbling, Report Says," *Los Angeles Times*, March 8, 2001.

99   Claire Milne, "Affordability of Basic Telephone Service: An Income Distribution Approach," *Telecommunications Policy* 24/10–11 (2000): 907, 927; Commission of the European Communities, *Sixth Report on the Implementation of the Telecommunications Regulatory Package*, Communication from the Commission to the Council, European Parliament, Economic and Social Committee and the Committee of the Regions, COM, Brussels, 2000, EU document no. 814.

100 Harry C. Katz, *Telecommunications: Restructuring Work and Employment Relations Worldwide* (Ithaca, NY: Cornell University Press, 1997).

101 Trevor R. Roycroft and Martha Garcia-Murrilo, "Trouble Reports As An Indicator Of Service Quality: The Influence Of Competition, Technology, And Regulation," *Telecommunications Policy* 24/10–11 (2000): 947, 967; Commision of the European Communities, *Sixth Report*.

102 Seth Schiesel, "For Some Who Use Calling Cards, the Number Is 1-800-BEWARE," *New York Times*, February 15, 2001.

103 Richard Cookson, "A $250 Billion Gamble," *The Economist*, January 27, 2001, 10.

104 Om Malik, "Wrong Number," *Red Herring*, January 16, 2001, 66, 68.

105 Steve Rosebush, "Armstrong's last stand," *Business Week*, February 5, 2001, 88; Steve Rosebush, Ron Grover, and Charles Haddad, "AT&T Hits A $5 Billion Wall," *Business Week*, October 15, 2001, 52.

106 Peter Curwen, "Buddy, Can You Spare A Billion?," *Info* 3/1 (February 2001); Gary Silverman, "Review Features Telecoms Loans," *Financial Times*, October 8, 2001, 25; "Moody's Says It May Downgrade Ratings of Telecom Firms," *Wall Street Journal*, October 5, 2001.

107 Jeffrey H. Keefe and Rosemary Batt, "United States," in *Telecommunications: Restructuring Work and Employment Relations Worldwide*, ed. Harry C. Katz (Ithaca, NY: Cornell University Press, 1997); Dan Schiller, *Digital Capitalism*, 68, 69; Douglas A. Galbi, "Growth in the 'New Economy' U.S. Bandwidth use and pricing across the 1990s," *Telecommunications Policy* 25/ 1–2 (2001): table 1, 2, 4; Logica Consulting n.v., *Assessment of the Leased Line Market in the European Union*, study prepared for the European Commission, Brussels, January 19, 2000, available at http://europa.eu.int/ISPO/infosoc/telecompolicy/en/Study–en.htm.

108 Telegeography Inc., 2001.

109 Blumenstein, "How the Fiber Barons."

110 Dan Roberts, "Glorious Hopes on a Trillion-Dollar Scrapheap," *Financial Times*, September 5, 2001.

111 George Gilder, *Telecosm: How Infinite Bandwidth will Revolutionize Our World* (New York: Simon and Schuster, 2000).

112 Roberts, "Glorious Hopes," 10.

113 Barnaby J. Feder, "A Suit Says Worldcom Deals Obscured Millions in Bad Debt," *Wall Street Journal*, March 27, 2002; Barnaby J. Feder, "Metromedia Fiber Slides Toward a Bankruptcy Filing," *Wall Street Journal*, April 2, 2002; Simon Romero and Jennifer L. Rich, "BellSouth in Big Brazilian Debt Dispute," *New York Times*, April 2, 2002; Deborah Solomon, "How Qwest's Merger With A Baby Bell Left Both In Trouble," *Wall Street Journal*, April 2, 2002.

114 Michiyo Nakamoto, "NTT Hit By $16bn Charge To Meet Write Downs," *Financial Times*, April 5, 2002, 17.

115 Seth Schiesel, "Will Ma Bell Be Taken Over By Offspring?," *New York Times*, April 1, 2002.

116 Jonathan Stempel, "Falling Telecom Issues Lead New Slump In Junk Bonds," *Los Angeles Times*, April 5, 2001.

117 Alex Pham, Nortel Forecasts $19.2-Billion Loss, Sets More Job Cuts," *Los Angeles Times*, June 16, 2001.

118 Ken Auletta, "Leviathan," *New Yorker*, October 29, 2000, 50, 54.

119 Blumenstein, "How the Fiber Barons"; Walter Hamilton, "Corporate Tech Spending Helped Set Stage For Slump," *Los Angeles Times*, March 14, 2001.

120 Dan Roberts, "The Tangled Legacy of a Derailed Revolution," *Financial Times*, September 7, 2001, 9.

121 Ken Brown, "Creative Accounting: How To Buff A Company," *Wall Street Journal*, February 21, 2002; Henry Sender, "Telecoms Draw Focus For Moves In Accounting," *Wall Street Journal*, March 26, 2002.

122 Almar Latour, "Sweden's Telia Agrees to Buy Finnish Sonera," *Wall Street Journal*, March 27, 2002.

123 McChesney, *Rich Media, Poor Democracy*, 118.

124 Alan Cullison, "Russia Arrests President Of Big Private Media Company," *Wall Street Journal*, June 14, 2000; Rachel L. Swarns, "Tightening Control On Media Worries

Journalists in Angola," *New York Times*, September 20, 2000; Robert Wright, "Hungary Packs Broadcasters With Party Names," *Financial Times*, March 2, 2000; Michael R. Gordon, "A Russian Press Beholden to Many," *New York Times*, March 17, 2000; "Free to Be Bad," *The Economist*, March 11, 2000, 44: Patrick E. Tyler, "Russian Media Magnate Reports Kremlin Is Trying To Silence Him," *New York Times*, September 5, 2000; Julia Preston, "Mexican TV, Unshackled by Reform, Fights for Viewers," *New York Times*, June 7, 2000.

125   Monroe E. Price, Beata Rozumilowicz, and Stefaan G. Verhulst, *Media Reform: Democratizing the Media* (New York: Routledge, 2002).

15. Off-limits: An Inquiry Into the Lack of Debate Over the Ownership, Structure, and Control of the Media in U.S. Political Life

This chapter first appeared in a slightly different form as Robert W. McChesney, "Off-Limits: An Inquiry Into the Lack of Debate over the Ownership, Structure and Control of the Mass Media in U.S. Political Life," Communication 13 (1992): 1–19.

1   See Ben H. Bagdikian, *The Media Monopoly* (Boston: Beacon Press, 1990).

2   See Edward S. Herman and Noam Chomsky, *Manufacturing Consent: The Political Economy of the Mass Media* (New York: Pantheon, 1988), 22.

3   Comment of the late Professor William E. Ames, University of Washington, Seattle.

4   See István Mészáros, *The Power of Ideology* (New York: New York University Press, 1989), 399–400.

5   See Stuart Hall, "Culture, Media and the Ideological Effect" in *Mass Communications and Society*, ed. J. Curran (Beverly Hills: Sage, 1979), 323.

6   Philip T. Rosen, *The Modern Stentors: Radio Broadcasting and the Federal Government, 1920-1934* (Westport, CT: Greenwood Press, 1980), 181.

7   David Sarnoff, "Broadcasting in the American Democracy" in *Educational Broadcasting*, ed. C. S. Marsh (Chicago: University of Chicago Press, 1937), 154.

8   William S. Paley, "The Viewpoint of the Radio Industry" in *Educational Broadcasting*, ed. Marsh, 6.

9   Jerome A. Barron, "Access to the Press—A New First Amendment Right." See also Stephen L. Carter, "Technology, Democracy, and the Manipulation of Consent," *Yale Law Journal* 93 (1984): 561–607.

10   Lucas A. Powe Jr., *American Broadcasting and the First Amendment* (Berkeley: University of California Press, 1987), 248–56.

11   Bagdikian, *The Media Monopoly*, 223.

12   National Broadcasting Company, *Broadcasting*, vols. 1–4 (New York: National Broadcasting Company, 1935).

13   John DeMott, "'Company Line' Raises Ethical Dilemma," *Media Law Notes* (Spring 1990): 9.

14   See Michael Schudson, "The Profession of Journalism in the United States" in *Professions in American History*, ed. N. O. Hatch (Notre Dame: Notre Dame University Press, 1988), 145–61.

15   Herman and Chomsky, *Manufacturing Consent*, 23.

16   Bagdikian, "American Mass Media and the Future," paper presented to the Annual Convention of the Association for Education in Journalism and Mass Communication Minneapolis, MN, 1990.

17   See Bagdikian, *The Media Monopoly*, 90–101.

18   Edward N. Nockels, "Labor's Rights on the Air," *Federation News*, February 7 (1931): 2.

19   See Robert W. McChesney, "Crusade Against Mammon: Father Harney, WLWL and the Debate Over Radio in the 1930s," *Journalism History* 14 (Winter 1987): 118–30. See also Robert W. McChesney, "Franklin Roosevelt, His Administration, and the Communications Act of 1934," *American Journalism* 5 (1988): 204–30.

20   Robert W. McChesney, "Press-Radio Relations and the Emergence of Network, Commercial Broadcasting in the United States, 1930–1935," *Historical Journal of Film, Radio and Television* 11/1 (1991): 41–57.

21   Morris Ernst, *The First Freedom* (New York: Macmillan, 1946), 126–41.

22   See Edward S. Herman, "Information Flow Threatened by Giant Merger," *Guardian*, September 13, 1989.

23   Bagdikian, *The Media Monopoly*, ix.

24   Anthony C. Giffard, *UNESCO and the Media* (New York: Longman, 1988); Edward S. Herman, "U.S. Mass Media Coverage of the U.S. Withdrawal from UNESCO," in *Hope and Folly: The United States and UNESCO, 1945–1985*, Edwards S. Herman, William Preston Jr. and Herbert I. Schiller, eds. (Minneapolis: University of Minnesota Press, 1989), 203–84.

25   See Herbert I. Schiller, *Culture Inc.* (New York: Oxford University Press, 1989), 157–74. See also Noam Chomsky, *Necessary Illusions; Thought Control in Democratic Societies* (Boston: South End Press, 1989), 136.

26   Karl Marx, "For a Ruthless Criticism of Everything Existing," in *The Marx-Engels Reader*, Robert C. Tucker, ed. (New York: W. W. Norton, 1972), 8.

27   Samir Amin, *Eurocentrism* (New York: Monthly Review Press, 1989), 152.

16. The Internet and U. S. Communication Policymaking in Historical and Critical Perspective

This chapter first appeared in a slightly different form as Robert W. McChesney, "The Internet and U.S. Communication Policy-Making in Historical and Critical Perspective," Journal of Communication 46/1 (1996): 98–124.

1   See A. Stille, "Media Moguls United," *New York Times*, August 28, 1995.

2   For example, see Jürgen Habermas, *The Structural Transformation of the Public Sector* (Cambridge: MIT Press, 1989).

3   M. Lipson, *The Organizational Politics of a Functioning Anarchy: Government of the Internet,* presentation to the Midwest Political Science Association, Chicago, 1995; Joe Flower, "Idiot's Guide to the Net," *New Scientist*, July 1, 1995.

4   Mitchell Kapor, "Mitchell Kapor on Dharma, Democracy, and the Information Superhighway," *Tricycle: Buddhist Review*, Summer 1994.

5   Cited in Flower, "Idiot's Guide to the Net," 26.

6   On the impact of television on domestic culture, see L. Spigel, *Make Room for TV* (Chicago: University of Chicago Press, 1992). On the impact of television on journalism and public discourse, see Neil Postman, *Amusing Ourselves to Death* (New York: Penguin Books, 1985).

7   On the influence of amateurs, see S. Douglas, *Inventing American Broadcasting, 1899–1922* (Baltimore: Johns Hopkins University Press, 1987). On nonprofit groups, see S. Frost Jr., *Education's Own Stations* (Chicago: University of Chicago Press, 1937); and N. Godfried, *The Rise and Fall of Labor Radio: WCFL, Chicago's Labor Station, 1926–1978* (Urbana: University of Illinois Press, 1996).

8   See Robert W. McChesney, *Telecommunications, Mass Media, and Democracy: The Battle for the Control of U.S. Broadcasting, 1928–1935* (New York: Oxford University Press, 1993).

9   See R. Avery, ed., *Public Service Broadcasting in a Multichannel Environment* (New York: Longman, 1993).

10   See R. Kanaley, "Internet Passes Quietly into Private Hands," *Philadelphia Inquirer,* November 4, 1994.

11   "FCC Commissioner Susan Ness: Regulating the Infobahn," *Newslink* 5/2 (1995).

12   Too Fast on Communications Reform," *New York Times,* April 12, 1995.

13   National Telecommunications and Information Administration, *Telecommunications in the Age of Information* (Washington, DC: U.S. Department of Commerce, 1991).

14   On the ties of both parties to large communications firms, see Ken Auletta, "Pay Per Views," *The New Yorker,* June 5, 1995. On the communications lobbies see E. Andrews, "On $700 Billion Data Highway, Persuasion has a Polite Frenzy," *New York Times,* June 14, 1995.

15   See N. Hickey, "Revolution in Cyberia," *Columbia Journalism Review* (July/August 1995): 40–47.

16   See R. Du Boff, "The Rise of Communications Regulation: The Telegraph Industry, 1844–1880," *Journal of Communication* 34/3 (1984): 52–66. See also Stille, "Media Moguls United."

17   P. Aufderheide, *Media Wars in Cyberspace,* presentation to the Conference on Technology and Democracy, Case Western Reserve University, Ohio, April 1995.

18   C. Bien, correspondence with author, July 6, 1995.

19   W. Treese, "The Internet Index #8," *Internet Post,* June 29, 1995.

20   L. Zuckerman, "With Internet Cachet, Not Profit, A New Stock Amazes Wall Street," *New York Times,* August 10, 1995.

21   See P. Taylor, "Revenues of $10bn Forecast," *Financial Times,* June 15, 1995.

22   See D. Caruso, "Digital Commerce," *New York Times,* August 21, 1995.

23   S. Levy, "How the Propeller Heads Stole the Electronic Future," *The New York Times Magazine,* September 24, 1995.

24   Aufderheide, *Media Wars in Cyberspace.*

25   See N. Baran, "Computers and Capitalism: A Tragic Misuse of Technology," *Monthly Review* 47/4 (1995): 40–46. See also H. Besser, "From Internet to Information Superhighway in *Resisting the Virtual Life: The Culture and Politics of Information,* J. Brook and I. Boal, eds. (San Francisco: City Lights, 1995), 59–70.

26　Barbara Ehrenreich, "Global Arches," *New York Times Book Review*, August 20, 1995.

27　See M. Vipond, *Listening In: The First Decade of Canadian broadcasting, 1922–1932* (Montreal: McGill-Queen's University Press, 1992).

28　Cited in M. Flores, "Show Offers Inside Look at Microsoft, Gates," *Seattle Times*, May 25, 1995.

29　See Kapor, "Dharma, Democracy, and the Information Superhighway."

30　See D. Bollier, *The Information Superhighway and the Reinvention of Television* (Washington, DC: Center for Media Education, 1993). See also N. Kranich, *Internet Access & Democracy: Ensuring Public Places on the Info Highway* (Wesfield, NJ: Open Magazine Pamphlet Series, 1994).

31　On censorship see P. Lewis, "On the Net," *New York Times*, July 17, 1995. See also H. Plotkin, "Cleansing the Net," *Isthmus* 20/ 29 (July 27, 1995): 10–12.

32　See H. Schiller, *Culture, Inc.* (New York: Oxford University Press, 1989).

33　J. Newhagen, correspondence with author, July 10, 1995.

34　Flower, "Idiot's Guide to the Net."

35　See Habermas, *The Structural Transformation of the Public Sector.*

36　See Edward S. Herman, "The Externalities Effects of Commercial and Public Broadcasting," in *Beyond National Sovereignty: International Communication in the 1990s*, ed. K. Nordenstreng and H. Schiller (Norwood, NJ: Ablex, 1993), 85–115. See also Herman, *Triumph of the Market: Essays on Economics, Politics, and the Media* (Boston: South End Press, 1995).

37　Cited in F. Beacham, "Questioning Technology: Tools for the Revolution," *Media Culture Review* 4/2 (1995): 18.

38　For example, George Gilder, *Life After Television*, (New York: W.W. Norton, 1994); and Newt Gingrich, *To Renew America*, (New York: HarperCollins, 1995).

39　See D. Broder, "Democrats in Tug-of-War over View of Americans," *Wisconsin State Journal*, June 27, 1995.

40　See G. Murdock, "The New Media Empires: Media Concentration and Control in the Age of Convergence," *Media Development* 41/4 (1994): 3–6.

41　See T. King, "What's Intertainment?," *Wall Street Journal*, September 15, 1995.

42　Among others, see N. Negroponte, *Being Digital* (New York: Alfred A. Knopf, 1995); and C. Scheer, "The Pursuit of Techno-Happiness," *The Nation* 260/18 (1995): 632–34.

43　Noam Chomsky, *World Orders Old and New* (New York: Columbia University Press, 1994).

44　See C. Mills, *The Power Elite* (New York: Oxford University Press, 1956).

45　See C. Macpherson, *The Life and Times of Liberal Democracy* (New York: Oxford University Press, 1977).

46　Noam Chomsky, *On Power and Ideology: The Managua Lectures* (Boston: South End Press, 1987).

47　See Alex Carey, *Taking the Risk Out of Democracy* (Sydney: University of New South Wales Press, 1995).

48　See M. Sullivan-Trainor, *Detour: The Truth About the Information Superhighway* (San Mateo, CA: 100 Books Worldwide, 1994).

49　See Robert W. McChesney, "On Media, Politics, and the Left, Part 1: An Interview with Noam Chomsky," *Against the Current* 10/1 (1995): 27–32.

50   V. Mosco, *Transforming Telecommunications: Political Economy and Public Policy*, presentation to the Conference on Canadian Political Economy in the Era of Free Trade, Carleton University, Ottawa, Canada, 1990.

51   S. Picciotto, "The Internationalization of the State," *Capital & Class* 43 (Spring 1991): 43–63.

52   Cited in Michael A. Bernstein, *The Great Depression: Delayed Recovery and Economic Change in America* (New York: Cambridge University Press, 1987).

53   See Gregory Albo, "Competitive Austerity and the Impasse of Capitalist Employment Policy," in *Socialist Register 1994*, ed. Ralph Miliband and Leo Panitch (London: Merlin Press, 1994), 144–70.

54   See A. MacEwan, "Globalization and Stagnation, *Monthly Review* 45/11 (1994): 1–16.

55   See M. Tanzer, "Globalizing the Economy: The Influence of the International Monetary Fund and the World Bank," *Monthly Review* 47/4 (1995): 1–15.

56   See D. Noble, "The Truth about the Information Highway," *Monthly Review* 47/2 (1995): 47–52.

57   See Paul Sweezy, "The Triumph of Financial Capital, *Monthly Review* 46/2 (1994): 1–9.

58   See K. Cowling and R. Sugden, *Beyond Capitalism: Towards a New World Economic Order* (New York: St. Martin's Press, 1994).

59   W. Glaberson, "Press: A Dispute Over Gatt Highlights The Complex Links Between Newspapers And Their Corporate Parents," *New York Times*, December 5, 1994.

60   See National Telecommunications and Information Administration, *Globalization of the Mass Media*, (Washington, DC: U.S. Department of Commerce, 1993). See also M. Pendakur and J. Kapur, *Think Globally, Program Locally*, paper presented to the Democratizing Communication conference, January 1995.

61   See J. Blumler, ed., *Television and the Public Interest: Vulnerable Values in West European Broadcasting* (London: Sage, 1992).

62   Quoted in B. Harris, "The Geopolitics of Cyberspace," *Infobahn* 1 (1995): 49.

63   See H. Frederick, *North American NGO Computer Networking: Computer Communications in Cross-Border Coalition Building*, (research report for the Rand Corporation/Ford Foundation, Program for Research on Immigration Policy, January, 1995.

64   See J. Simon, "Netwar could make Mexico Ungovernable," *Pacific News Service*, March, 1995. See also J. Wehling, "Netwars," *Z Magazine* 1/7–8 (1995): 63–66.

65   Aufderheide, *Media Wars in Cyberspace.*

66   Baran, "Computers and Capitalism: A Tragic Misuse of Technology."

67   Aufderheide, *Media Wars in Cyberspace.*

68   Baran, "Computers and Capitalism: A Tragic Misuse of Technology," 40.

69   P. Keegan, "The Digerati!," *The New York Times Magazine*, May 21, 1995.

70   See P. Kimball, *Downsizing the News: Network Cutbacks in the Nation's Capital* (Washington, DC: Woodrow Wilson Center Press, 1994).

71   Cited in Ken Auletta, "Awesome," *The New Yorker*, August 14, 1995.

72   See C. Farrell, "Media Control is Narrowing, Should We Worry?" *Business Week*, August 14, 1995. See also Levy, "How the Propeller Heads Stole the Electronic Future."

73   A. Shapiro, "Street Corners in Cyberspace," *The Nation* 261/1 (1995).

74   See D. Rushkoff, *Cyberlaw: Life In the Trenches of Cyberspace* (New York: HarperCollins, 1994).

75 For example, see Howard Rheingold, *The Virtual Community: Homesteading on the Electronic Frontier,* (Reading, MA: Addison-Wesley, 1993).

76 J. Stallabrass, "Empowering Technology: The Exploration of Cyberspace," *New Left Review* 211 (1995): 32.

77 Cited in J. Rofty, *Order on the Air!* (New York: John Day, 1934), 10.

78 Neil Postman, Russell Lecture, Presbyterian College, Clinton, SC, February 1995.

79 T. Charbeneau, "Dangerous Assumptions," *Toward Freedom* 43/7 (1994): 28–29.

80 See G. Chapman, "Virtual Communities," *Texas Observer,* June 2, 1995.

81 Daniel Singer, "The Sound and the Furet," *The Nation* 260/15 (1995): 531–34.

82 William Greider, *Who Will Tell the People? The Betrayal of American Democracy* (New York: Simon &: Schuster, 1992), 403.

83 See L. Soley, *Leasing the Ivory Tower: The Corporate Takeover of Academia* (Boston: South End Press, 1995).

84 Paul Lazarsfeld, "Remarks on Administrative and Critical Communications Research," *Studies in Philosophy and Social Science* 9/1 (1941): 2–16.

85 Cited in J. Carey, "A Plea for the University Tradition," *Journalism Quarterly* 55 (1978): 846–55.

17. U.S. Left and Media Politics

This chapter first appeared in a slightly different form as Robert W. McChesney, "The U.S. Left and Media Politics," Monthly Review *50/9 (1999): 32–41.*

18. Global Media and Its Discontents

This chapter first appeared in a slightly different form as chapter 2 in Robert W. McChesney and John Nichols, Our Media, Not Theirs: The Democratic Struggle Against Corporate Media *(New York: Seven Stories Press, 2002), 81–113.*

19. Theses on Media Deregulation

This chapter first appeared in a slightly different form as Robert W. McChesney, "Theses on Media Deregulation," Media, Culture & Society *25 (2003): 125–33.*

20. Rich Media, Poor Democracy: Communication Politics in Dubious Times

This chapter first appeared in a slightly different form as Robert W. McChesney, "Rich Media, Poor Democracy: Communication Politics in Dubious Times," The Long Term View *5/2 (2001): 46–58.*

1 John Consoli, "The 11.8-Hour Daily Diet," *Mediaweek,* April 20, 1998, 8, 12.

2   Marc Gunther, "The Rules According to Rupert," *Fortune*, Oct. 26, 1998, 104.

3   Ben Bagdikian, *The Media Monopoly*, 5th ed. (Boston: Beacon Press, 1997).

4   Tim Redmond, "Tim White Takes the Fall," http://www.sfbg.com, May 3, 2000.

5   Doug Henwood, "Wealth News," *Left Business Observer*, no. 94 (May 2000), 3; The Editors, "Working-Class Households and the Burden of Debt," *Monthly Review* (2000): 1–11; Lester Thurow, "Falling Wages, Failing Policy," *Dollars & Sense*, September-October 1996.

6   See Reg Whitaker, *The End of Privacy: How Total Surveillance Is Becoming a Reality* (New York: New Press, 1999).

7   Robert J. Gordon, "Does the 'New Economy' Measure Up to the Great Inventions of the Past?" May 1, 2000, draft of a paper for the *Journal of Economic Perspectives*.

8   Stephen Labaton, "Federal Regulators Give Approval to Viacom's Buyout of CBS," *New York Times*, May 4, 2000; Allen R. Myerson, "Divided Against Each Other; United Against the Government," *New York Times*, May 15, 2000.

9   John Nichols and Robert W. McChesney, *It's the Media, Stupid!* (New York: Seven Stories Press, 2000); David Bauder, "FCC Reviews ABC-Time Warner Dispute," Associated Press, May 2, 2000; William Safire, "'Th-Th-That's All, Folks,'" *New York Times*, May 4, 2000.

10   "Findings from a National Survey," sponsored by the Project on Media Ownership and People for Better TV and conducted by Lake Snell Perry & Associates, May 1999.

11   Liza Featherstone, "The New Student Movement," *The Nation*, May 15, 2000; Jerry Useem, "There's Something Happening Here," *Fortune*, May 15, 2000, 234.

21. The Case for U.S. Public Broadcasting and Implications for Philanthropists

This chapter was commissioned by then-PBS president Pat Mitchell in 2003 to be shared with top administrators in the public broadcasting community.

22. The Escalating War Against Corporate Media

This chapter first appeared in a slightly different form as Robert W. McChesney, "The Escalating War Against Corporate Media," Monthly Review 55/10 (2004): 1–29, which is an abridged and revised version of chapter 7 from Robert W. McChesney, The Problem of the Media: U.S. Communication Politics in the Twenty-First Century (Monthly Review Press, 2004).

1   For an overview of media criticism and activism in the United States over the past century, see Robert W. McChesney and Ben Scott, eds., *Our Unfree Press: 100 Years of Radical Media Criticism* (New York: New Press, 2004).

2   Part of the deal to include the reduction of LPFM stations from 1,000 to a few hundred in the budget bill was to call for a study of whether, as the NAB claimed, Kennard's plan would have actually led to interference with the existing radio broadcasters. This study was completed in 2003 and it appears to have exonerated Kennard.

3   Robert W. McChesney, "Kennard, the Public, and the FCC," *The Nation*, May 14, 2001.

4   John Nichols and Robert W. McChesney, "On the Verge in Vermont: Media Reform Movement Nears Critical Mass," *Extra!*, July/August 2002, 26.

5   "FCC Chairman Michael Powell Announces Creation of Media Ownership Working Group," FCC news release, October 29, 2001.

6   Personal communication to author, October 30, 2003.

7   Cherly Arvidson, "FCC's Powell: Time to Give Broadcasters Full First Amendment Rights," http://www.freedomforum.org, April 27, 1998.

8   Jill Goldsmith and Pamela McClintock, "Powell Eyes Update: Chairman Urges Ownership Rules Changes," *Variety* online, October 2, 2002.

9   Frank Rose, "Big Media or Bust," *Wired*, March 2002.

10 "The Antithesis of What the Public Interest Demands,'" *Broadcasting & Cable*, October 14, 2002, 16.

11 Rose, "Big Media or Bust."

12 Dan Roberts, "FCC Chief 'Working Himself Out of a Job,'" *Financial Times*, May 25, 2001, 3.

13 Bill McConnell, "A Quiet Warrior for Ownership Deregulation," *Broadcasting & Cable*, October 13, 2003, 36.

14 "FCC Approves Digital Radio," http://online.wsj.com, October 10, 2002.

15 Jube Shiver Jr., "Citizens Knocking on FCC's Door," *Los Angeles Times*, January 26, 2003.

16 Bill McConnell, "Martin Likes the FCC's Measured Pace," *Broadcasting & Cable*, December 9, 2002, 26.

17 Dissenting Statement of Commissioner Michael J. Copps, *Re: In the Matter of Applications for Consent to the Transfer of Control of Licenses from Comcast Corporation and AT&T Cor, Transferors, to AT&T Comcast Corporation, Transferee MB Docket No. 02-70*, November 2002.

18 Bill McConnell, "Media Face Grilling From Copps," *Broadcasting & Cable*, November 25, 2002, 10.

19 Doug Halonen, "Copps Will Hold Field Hearings on Ownership," *Electronic Media*, November 25, 2002, 3.

20 "Commissioner Michael J. Copps Expresses 'Alarm' and 'Disappointment' with FCC's Media Concentration Decision," FCC news release, November 5, 2002.

21 "Statement of Commissioner Jonathan S. Adelstein, Dissenting," FCC release, June 2, 2003, 5.

22 Doug Halonen, "FCC's Deregulation Proposals Hit Hurdle," *Electronic Media*, January 20, 2003, 4.

23 Robert W. McChesney and John Nichols, "Holding the Line at the FCC," *The Progressive*, April 2003.

24 Pamela McClintock, "FCC to Tackle Ownership Rules," *Variety*, January 20–26, 2003, A11.

25 Bill McConnell, "Powell Grants Dereg Hearing in Richmond," *Broadcasting & Cable*, December 9, 2002, 8.

26 "Onward to Richmond," *Broadcasting & Cable*, December 9, 2002, 40.

27 Catherine Yang, "The FCC's Loner Is No Longer So Lonely," *Business Week*, March 24, 2003, 78; "Ownership Hearings Added," *Electronic Media*, February 10, 2003, 6.

28 Peter Thal Larsen, "Viacom to Seek More U.S. Acquisitions," *Financial Times*, February 12, 2003.

29 Edmund Sanders, "Reflecting on Media Ownership Debate," www.newsday.com, June 2, 2003.

30 Doug Halonen, "Michael Copps," *Electronic Media*, January 20, 2003, 52.

31 Andrew Ratner, "FCC Is Assailed on Plan Aiding Big Media Firms," *Baltimore Sun*, May 25, 2003.

32 Mark Jurkowitz, "FCC Chairman: Consolidation Hasn't Inhibited Variety, Fairness," *Boston Globe*, April 17, 2003.

33 Goldsmith and McClintock, "Powell Eyes Update," October 2, 2002.

34 Demetri Sevastopulo, "Vote to Relax Media Rules Sparks Protest," *Financial Times*, June 3, 2003, 1.

35 Dan Fost, "FCC Media Rules Up for Revision," *San Francisco Chronicle*, February 13, 2003.

36 "Remarks of Michael J. Powell, Chairman, Federal Communications Commission," Media Institute, March 27, 2003.

37 Robert W. McChesney and John Nichols, "Holding the Line at the FCC," *The Progressive*, April 2003.

38 Patricia Aufderheide, *Communications in the Public Interest* (New York: Guilford Press, 1999), 168.

39 Stephen Labaton, "Senators Move to Restore F.C.C. Limits on the Media," *New York Times*, June 5, 2003.

40 Fost, "FCC Media Rules Up for Revision."

41 Staci D. Kramer, "FCC Chairman Michael Powell Sees Bright Future for Online Media," *Online Journalism Review*, http://www.ojr.org, September 4, 2003.

42 Michael K. Powell, "Should Limits on Broadcast Ownership Change?" *USA Today*, January 21, 2003.

43 Todd Bishop, "FCC May Drop Rules Limiting Media Ownership in a Single Market," *Seattle Post-Intelligencer*, April 29, 2003.

44 "Dialogue with NBC Chairman Bob Wright," *Hollywood Reporter*, February 18, 2003.

45 Michael Powell, comments to National Association of Broadcasters Convention, Las Vegas, Nevada, April 2003.

46 Joanna Glasner, "Media More Diverse? Not Really," http://www.wired.com/news, May 30, 2003.

47 Peter Thal Larsen and Demetri Sevastopulo, "Free-to-Air TV Is Under Threat, Warns FCC Chief," *Financial Times*, April 30, 2003, 1.

48 Associated Press, "FCC Chief Wants Ownership Rules Eased," May 27, 2003.

49 Comments of Michael K. Powell, John McLaughlin's *One on One* television program, taped September 4, 2003.

50 Joe Flint, "Loosening Media Regulations Risks Thwarting Innovation," *Wall Street Journal Online*, http://online.wsj.com, June 2, 2003.

51 Edmund Sanders and Jube Shiver Jr., "FCC Relaxes Limits on Media Ownership," *Los Angeles Times*, June 3, 2003.

52 Brooks Boliek, "FCC Majority Set on Rules Rewrite," *Hollywood Reporter*, May 9, 2003.

53   Tom Shales, "Michael Powell and the FCC: Giving Away the Marketplace of Ideas," *Washington Post*, June 2, 2003.

54   Stuart Elliott, "Early Ad Sales for the 2003–4 TV Season Turn Into a 'Runaway Sellers' Market,'" *New York Times*, May 23, 2003.

55   Steve McClellan, "Broadcast Nets Hit the Jackpot," *Broadcasting & Cable*, June 2, 2003, 24.

56   "It's Way Upfront," *Broadcasting & Cable*, June 2, 2003, 1.

57   Jay Sherman, "Study: Broadcast Ad Cash on the Rise," *Television Week*, August 11, 2003, 6; Diane Mermigas, "Broadcast Growth Projected," *Television Week*, June 16, 2003, 3.

58   Jube Shiver Jr., "Senate Committee to Take On FCC Rules," *Los Angeles Times*, June 5, 2003.

59   Michael K. Powell, "New Rules, Old Rhetoric," *New York Times*, July 28, 2003.

60   Catherine Yang and Joseph Weber, "Where Media Merger Mania Could Strike First," *Business Week*, June 9, 2003, 96.

61   For a very small sampling, see Ira Teinowitz and Jon Fine, "Media Giants Gird for Merger Mania," *Advertising Age*, May 19, 2003, 3, 142; Jay Sherman, "Station Deals Wait in the Wings," *Television Week*, May 19, 2003, 1, 62; Mark Fitzgerald and Todd Shields, "After June 2, Papers May Make Broadcast News," *Editor & Publisher*, May 26, 2003, 3–4; Lucia Moses, "On the Road to Freedom," *Editor & Publisher*, March 24, 2003, 14–19, 29.

62   Louis Aguilar, "Post Publisher: FCC to Lift Bans," *Denver Post*, February 23, 2003.

63   Catherine Yang and Joseph Weber, "Media Merger Mania: The First Wave," http://www.businessweek.com, May 30, 2003.

64   Alec Klein and David A. Vise, "Media Giants Hint They Might Be Expanding," *Washington Post*, June 3, 2003.

65   Dominic Timms, "US Media Bill Faces Further Revolt," http://media.guardian.co.uk, July 16, 2003.

66   "Statement of Commissioner Jonathan S. Adelstein, Dissenting," FCC news release, June 2, 2003.

67   "Statement of Commissioner Michael J. Copps, Dissenting," FCC news release, June 2, 2003.

68   Michael Copps, "Crunch Time at the FCC," *The Nation*, February 3, 2003, 5.

69   McChesney, "Holding the Line at the FCC."

70   Edmund Sanders, "FCC Takes Debate on the Road," *Los Angeles Times*, February 28, 2003.

71   David Ho, "Media Ownership Review to Finish in May," Associated Press dispatch, February 26, 2003.

72   Keri Brenner, "FCC Member Warns About Consolidation," *Marin Independent Journal*, April 26, 2003.

73   "The Arizona Forum on Media Ownership," http://www.Benton.org, April 7, 2003, Alwyn Scott, "Move to Ease Media-Ownership Rules Given a Cool Reception in Seattle," *Seattle Times*, March 8, 2003; Hunter Lewis, "FCC Gets an Earful at Hearing," *Herald-Sun*, March 31, 2003, Suzanne Bohan, "Huge Turnout at FCC Meeting," *Argus*, http://www.theargusonline.com, April 3, 2003.

74   Jonathan S. Adelstein, "Big Macs and Big Media: The Decision to Supersize," Remarks at Media Institute, May 20, 2003.

75   Steven T. Jones, "The Democracy Disaster," http://www.sfbg.com, May 6, 2003, Karen Young, "The Midwest Public Forum on Media Ownership," *CMW Report*, Spring 2003, 6–7.

76   John Sugg, "You Say You Wanna Bigger Cox?" http://Atlanta.creativeloafing.com, May 29, 2003.

77   Charles Layton, "News Blackout," *American Journalism Review*, December/January 2004. Available online at http://www.ajr.org.

78   See, for example, Jennifer Lee, " On Minot, N.D., Radio, A Single Corporate Voice," *New York Times*, March 31, 2003; Joanne Ostrow, "Musicians Blast FCC Plan," *Denver Post*, May 23, 2003.

79   Tom Shales, "Dialing In a Bland TV Landscape," *Television Week*, June 2, 2003, 53.

80   Craig Linder, "FCC Dems Hear From Deregulation Opponents," *Hollywood Reporter*, May 28, 2003.

81   "Time for Congress to Save the Media," *Seattle Times*, June 3, 2003.

82   George E. Curry, "FCC Decision Curbs Dissent," *Final Call.com News*, June 22, 2003; "Who Killed Black Radio News?" *The Black Commentator*, issue no. 44, http://www.blackcommentator.com, May 2003.

83   Eric Boehlert, "Clear Channel's Big, Stinking Deregulation Mess," http://www.salon.com, February 19, 2003.

84   Mark Cooper, "Mass Deregulation of Media Threatens to Undermine Democracy," news release of Consumer Federation of America, June 3, 2003; "Key Facts About Media Markets in America," report of Consumers Union and the Consumer Federation of America, Washington, DC, May 2003.

85   Catherine Yang, "The News Biz: Is Bigger Better?" *Business Week*, March 3, 2003, 97.

86   "Powell Remarks," Media Institute.

87   "The Silence of the Lambs: Who Speaks for Journalists Before the FCC?" *Columbia Journalism Review*, January/February 2003; J. Bednarski, "Losing Our Voices," *Broadcasting & Cable*, June 9, 2003, 67.

88   "Pushing Back at the FCC," *The Guild Reporter*, January 24, 2003, 1–2.

89   "IFJ Criticises Proposed Changes in Media Ownership Rules," IFJ news release, May 2003.

90   John Eggerton, "Unions Fight Urge to Merge," *Broadcasting & Cable*, December 30, 2002, 12.

91   Edmund Sanders, "Hollywood Guilds Band Together to Defend Media Ownership," *Los Angeles Times*, January 13, 2003.

92   "Union Movement Says Media Monopolies Threaten Democracy," AFL-CIO news release, March 5, 2003.

93   "PR Society Seeks More Transparency in FCC Broadcast Ownership review," http://www.businesswire.com, May 27, 2003, Ira Teinowitz, "4A's to Dispute FCC Findings on Media Industry Mergers," *Advertising Age*, October 21, 2002, 8; David Verklin, "Go Slow on FCC Rule Change," *Advertising Age*, May 19, 2003, 22.

94   Pamela McClintock, "Sony, Ad Firm Say Consolidation leads to Bland TV," *Variety* news dispatch, February 2, 2003.

95   Rick Ellis, "Commentary: The Surrender of MSNBC," http://www.allyourtv.com, February 25, 2003.

96   Ira Teinowitz, "FCC Chairman Ho-Hums Anti-War Ad Controversy," http://www.adage.com, January 29, 2003.

97   Brent Staples, "The Trouble With Corporate Radio: The Day the Protest Music Died," *New York Times*, February 20, 2003.

98   Andy Paras, "Morning Radio Co-Host Sues Station That Fired Her," http://greenvilleonline.com, July 7, 2003; Paul Schmelzer, "The Death of Loxal News," http://AlterNet.com, April 22, 2003; Tom Shales, "Michael Powell and the FCC: Giving Away the Marketplace of Ideas," *Washington Post*, June 2, 2003.

99   "Powell Remarks," Media Institute; Andrew Ratner, "War Coverage Could Alter U.S. Media Policy," *Baltimore Sun*, March 30, 2003.

100 Ted Hearn, "Commish: Media Copping Out on Coverage," *Multichannel News*, April 29, 2003.

101 See Gal Beckerman, "Tripping Up Big Media," *Columbia Journalism Review*, November/December 2003, 15–20.

102 Marc Fisher, "FCC Tests Reception for Lifting Ownership Limits," *Washington Post*, February 28, 2003.

103 Statement of Richard Burr, Hearing on Media Ownership, Duke University, Durham, NC, March 31, 2003.

104 Wayne LaPierre, "Speak Out Vs. FCC While You Can," New York *Daily News*, July 18, 2003.

105 Richard Burr and Jesse Helms, "Keep Control of TV Local," *Charlotte Observer*, October 19, 2003.

106 "Statement of Michael Copps," June 2, 2003.

107 Mark Wigfield, "FCC's Powell Urges Divided Media Industry to Back Dereg," Dow Jones Business News dispatch, April 7, 2003.

108 Lucia Moses, "Powell to NAA: Expect Ownership Reform," *Editor and Publisher Online*, April 28, 2003.

109 John Nichols, "The FCC Rejects Public Interest," http://www.thenation.com, June 2, 2003; Bob Williams, "Behind Closed Doors," Center for Public Integrity, May 29, 2003.

110 Bob Williams and Morgan Jindrich, "On the Road Again-and Again," *The Public I*, July 2003, 1, 4.

111 Mark Wigfield, "Bear Stearns Analyst Helps FCC Reshape Ownership Rules," Dow Jones Newswires, June 2, 2003.

112 Mark Wigfield, "Top FCC Aide to Become Lobbyist for Broadcasters' Assoc.," Dow Jones Newswires, December 8, 2003.

113 Nichols, "The FCC Rejects Public Interest."

114 Thane Peterson, "Why the FCC Needs a New Chief," *BusinessWeek Online*, September 9, 2003.

115 "Statement of Michael Copps," June 2, 2003.

116 "Adelstein remarks," Media Institute.

117 "Chicago Says No to Dereg," *Broadcasting & Cable*, May 19, 2003, 12.

118 Dante Chinni, "Media Drop Ball on FCC Rules Changes," *Christian Science Monitor*, June 10, 2003.

119 "FCC Chairman Defends Position Ahead of Media Rules Vote," http://www.cnn.com, May 28, 2003; "Powell remarks," Media Institute.

120 David Ho, "U.S. Pushes FCC on Media Ownership Review," Associated Press, April 24, 2003.

121 Annie Lawson, "US Media Dig Deep for Politicians," *The Guardian*, April 7, 2003.

122 Tim Grieve, "Fox News: The Inside Story," http://www.salon.com, October 31, 2003.

123 Alex Ben Block, "FCC: The Fix Was In," *Television Week*, June 9, 2003, 8.

124 Bernard Weinraub, "CBS Is Reconsidering Mini-Series on Reagan," *New York Times*, November 4, 2003.

125 James Harding, "CBS Pulls Reagan Biopic After Lobbying," *Financial Times*, November 5, 2003, 1.

126 "The New Fairness Doctrine," *Broadcasting & Cable*, November 3, 2003, 40.

127 Ron Orol, "FCC to Vote on Media Rules," http://www.thedeal.com, April 15, 2003.

128 "FCC, Powell Must Bring the Public into the Process," *Television Week*, April 21, 2003, 8.

129 David Ho, "FCC Democrats Frustrated on Media Review," Associated Press dispatch, May 10, 2003.

130 Stephen Labaton, "F.C.C. Vote on Media Ownership Unlikely to Be Delayed," *New York Times*, May 14, 2003.

131 "Ownership Protestors March in 14 Cities," *Hollywood Reporter*, May 30, 2003.

132 "Consumer Groups Charge FCC Analysis Supporting Media Ownership Rules Is Fundamentally Flawed," news release of Consumers Union and Consumer Federation of America, July 21, 2003. The full report is Mark Cooper, "Abracadabra! Hocus-Pocus! Making Media Market Power Disappear with the FCC's Diversity Index," issued by Consumer Federation of America and Consumers Union, July 2003.

133 "Statement of Michael Copps," June 2, 2003.

134 "Adelstein Statement," June 2, 2003.

135 Demetri Sevastopulo, "Senators Deploy Veto to Attack Media Rules," *Financial Times*, July 16, 2003, 3.

136 Dominic Timms, "US Media Bill Faces Further Revolt," http://media.guardian.co.uk, July 16, 2003.

137 William Safire, "Regulate the Media," *New York Times*, June 16, 2003, 23.

138 Brooks Boliek, "House Panel Votes to Roll Back Ownership Cap," *Hollywood Reporter*, July 16, 2003. See also http://www.cbc–raleigh.com/capcom/news/2003/corporate_03/fcc_congress/fcc_c ongress.htm.

139 Jube Shiver Jr., Richard Simon, and Edmund Sanders, "FCC Ruling Puts Rivals on the Same Wavelength," *Los Angeles Times*, June 9, 2003.

140 Richard Simon and Janet Hook, "FCC Rule May Bring a Veto Standoff," *Los Angeles Times*, July 25, 2003.

141 Yochi J. Dreazen, "Democrats Seize on FCC Role," http://online.wsj.com, June 4, 2003.

142 Pew Research Center for the People and the Press, "Strong Opposition to Media Cross-Ownership Emerges," A Survey Conducted in Association with the Project for Excellence in Journalism, July 13, 2003; see also Dan Trigoboff, "New FCC Rules Get Thumbs Down," *Broadcasing & Cable*, July 21, 2003, 22.

143 "[Industry-Sponsored] Survey Finds Public Tuning Out FCC Debate," *Hollywood Reporter*, September 3, 2003.

144 Peter J. Howe, "FCC Chief Defends Changes in Media Ownership Rules," *Boston Globe*, June 11, 2003; Mark Jurkowitz, "FCC Chairman: Consolidation Hasn't Inhibited Variety, Fairness," *Boston Globe*, April 17, 2003.

145 Stephen Labaton, "F.C.C. Chief Talks of Frustration and Surprise," *New York Times*, September 22, 2003.

146 Craig Rimlinger, "Feingold Leads Charge Against New FCC Rules," *Capital Times* (Madison, WI), July 16, 2003.

147 Author conversation with Representative David Price, Washington, DC. September 25, 2003.

148 Bill McConnell, "Ownership Reg Faces Murky Outcome," *Broadcasting & Cable*, September 22, 2003, 3.

149 Mark Wigfield, "FCC Suffers Court Setback on Media Ownership Rules," *Wall Street Journal*, September 4, 2003.

150 Stephen Labaton, "U.S. Court Blocks Plan to Ease Rule on Media Owners," *New York Times*, September 4, 2003.

151 *Lou Dobb's Tonight*, December 2, 2003, http://www.cnn.com/CNN/Programs/lou.dobbs.tonight/.

23. The U.S. Media Reform Movement Going Forward

This chapter was written expressly for this volume.

Index